"This is the book on Luke that teachers of (longer is it necessary to wade through comme manuscript discussions to find syntactical and .... It is all here, conveniently and immediately available for busy pastors, along with homiletical suggestions at the end of each section. I look forward to the publication of other texts in this series. Congratulations to Alan Thompson for his diligence, scholarship, and patience in producing this very helpful resource."

—**Paul Barnett,** *retired Bishop of North Sydney; honorary associate in ancient history, Macquarie University, Sydney; teaching fellow, Regent College, Vancouver; and emeritus lecturer, Moore Theological College, Sydney*

"Luke is the longest gospel in Scripture and getting good grammatical help for his inspired work can be hard. That is no longer the case. Luke's Gospel in the *Exegetical Guide to the Greek New Testament* (EGGNT) series by Alan Thompson provides a series of careful observations about the Greek that can help you negotiate the terrain. A wonderful tool."

—**Darrell L. Bock,** *executive director of cultural engagement, Howard G. Hendricks Center for Christian Leadership and Cultural Engagement and senior research professor of New Testament studies, Dallas Theological Seminary*

"In line with the vision of Murray J. Harris, who originated the EGGNT series, Alan Thompson's fine volume on Luke succinctly provides judicious explanation of the Greek syntax, structure, grammatical options, the flow of the argument, and more. This volume will be a gold mine for students and pastors alike who are keeping up their Greek while studying this Gospel closely. Highly recommended."

—**D. A. Carson,** *research professor of New Testament, Trinity Evangelical Divinity School and president, The Gospel Coalition*

"Exegesis of biblical texts must ultimately be rooted in the original languages. But often the phrasing and syntax, along with the content itself, can be perplexing. Alan Thompson has provided a wealth of helpful material for those wanting to think carefully about the Greek text of Luke. One part grammatical guide, one part commentary, this is a valuable resource for anyone—and I hope there are many—striving to understand, teach, or preach the Gospel of Luke based on the Greek text."

—**Brandon D. Crowe,** *associate professor of New Testament, Westminster Theological Seminary, Philadelphia, Pennsylvania*

The Exegetical Guide to the Greek New Testament

Volumes Available

Luke	Alan J. Thompson
John	Murray J. Harris
Ephesians	Benjamin L. Merkle
Philippians	Joseph H. Hellerman
Colossians, Philemon	Murray J. Harris
James	Chris A. Vlachos
1 Peter	Greg W. Forbes

Forthcoming Volumes

Matthew	Charles L. Quarles
Mark	Joel F. Williams
Acts	L. Scott Kellum
Romans	John D. Harvey
1 Corinthians	Jay E. Smith
2 Corinthians	Colin G. Kruse
Galatians	David A. Croteau
1–2 Thessalonians	David W. Chapman
1–2 Timothy, Titus	Ray Van Neste
Hebrews	Dana M. Harris
2 Peter, Jude	Terry L. Wilder
1–3 John	Robert L. Plummer
Revelation	Bruce N. Fisk

EXEGETICAL
GUIDE TO THE
GREEK
NEW
TESTAMENT

LUKE

Alan J. Thompson

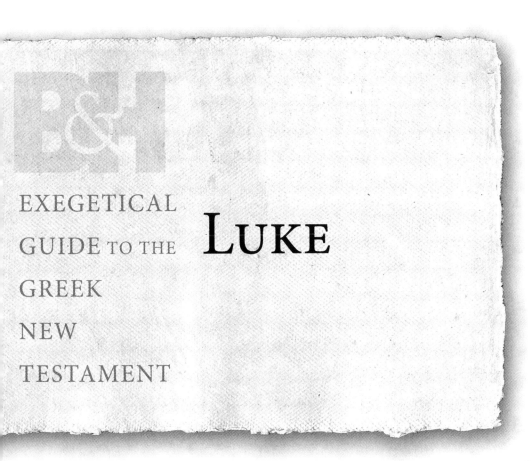

EXEGETICAL
GUIDE TO THE LUKE
GREEK
NEW
TESTAMENT

Andreas J. Köstenberger
Robert W. Yarbrough
GENERAL EDITORS

ACADEMIC

Nashville, Tennessee

Exegetical Guide to the Greek New Testament: Luke

Published by B&H Academic

Nashville, Tennessee

ISBN: 978-1-4336-7617-8

Dewey Decimal Classification: 226.4

Subject Heading: BIBLE. N.T. LUKE—STUDY \ BIBLE. N.T. LUKE—CRITICISM

The Greek text of Luke is from *The Greek New Testament*, Fifth Revised Edition, edited by Barbara Aland, Kurt Aland, Johannes Karavidopoulos, Carlo M. Martini, and Bruce M. Metzger in cooperation with the Institute for New Testament Textual Research, Münster/Westphalia, © 2014 Deutsche Bibelgesellschaft, Stuttgart. Used by permission.

Printed in the United States of America

1 2 3 4 5 6 7 8 9 10 • 22 21 20 19 18 17

VP

*With much gratitude
to Fred, Don, Doug, and Bob,
who first taught me Greek,
and from whom I continue to learn.*

Contents

Acknowledgments

It is a great privilege to be able to spend many hours pouring over the details of God's Word. I would like to thank Murray Harris for inviting me to contribute to this series and for his kind and generous encouragement along the way, the editors of this series, Robert Yarbrough and Andreas Köstenberger, and the team at B&H Academic, for their excellent guidance, the board of Sydney Missionary and Bible College (an affiliated college of the Australian College of Theology) for granting me a sabbatical which, by God's grace, was productive and helped bring this work to completion, Erik Urbach, Agustina Fasano, and Joshua Reeve for their research assistance at various stages, and my wife, Alayne, and our two girls, Deborah and Rebekah, for their loving support.

The richness of God's word and the size of Luke's Gospel mean that there is always more that could be said (see the "Introduction" for the particular focus of this Guide). Nevertheless, it is my prayer that, in keeping with the aims of this series, this Guide will, by God's grace, assist those who, through patient study and reverent reflection on the Greek text of Luke's Gospel, desire to proclaim faithfully and joyfully the good news that the Lord Jesus came "to seek and to save the lost" (Luke 19:10 HCSB). Κύριον τὸν θεόν σου προσκυνήσεις καὶ αὐτῷ μόνῳ λατρεύσεις (Luke 4:8).

Publisher's Preface

It is with great excitement that we publish this volume of the Exegetical Guide to the Greek New Testament series. When the founding editor, Dr. Murray J. Harris, came to us seeking a new publishing partner, we gratefully accepted the offer. With the help of the coeditor, Andreas J. Köstenberger, we spent several years working together to acquire all of the authors we needed to complete the series. By God's grace we succeeded and contracted the last author in 2011. Originally working with another publishing house, Murray's efforts spanned more than twenty years. As God would have it, shortly after the final author was contracted, Murray decided God wanted him to withdraw as coeditor of the series. God made clear to him that he must devote his full attention to taking care of his wife, who faces the daily challenges caused by multiple sclerosis.

Over the course of many years, God has used Murray to teach his students how to properly exegete the Scriptures. He is an exceptional scholar and professor. But even more importantly, Murray is a man dedicated to serving Christ. His greatest joy is to respond in faithful obedience when his master calls. "There can be no higher and more ennobling privilege than to have the Lord of the universe as one's Owner and Master and to be his accredited representative on earth."[1] Murray has once again heeded the call of his master.

It is our privilege to dedicate the Exegetical Guide to the Greek New Testament series to Dr. Murray J. Harris. We pray that our readers will continue the work he started.

B&H Academic

---

1. Murray J. Harris, *Slave of Christ: A New Testament Metaphor for Total Devotion to Christ* (Downers Grove: InterVarsity, 1999), 155.

General Introduction to the EGGNT Series

Studying the New Testament in the original Greek has become easier in recent years. Beginning students will work their way through an introductory grammar or other text, but then what? Grappling with difficult verb forms, rare vocabulary, and grammatical irregularities remains a formidable task for those who would advance beyond the initial stages of learning Greek to master the interpretive process. Intermediate grammars and grammatical analyses can help, but such tools, for all their value, still often operate at a distance from the Greek text itself, and analyses are often too brief to be genuinely helpful.

The Exegetical Guide to the Greek New Testament (EGGNT) aims to close the gap between the Greek text and the available tools. Each EGGNT volume aims to provide all the necessary information for understanding of the Greek text and, in addition, includes homiletical helps and suggestions for further study. The EGGNT is not a full-scale commentary. Nevertheless these guides will make interpreting a given New Testament book easier, in particular for those who are hard-pressed for time and yet want to preach or teach with accuracy and authority.

In terms of layout, each volume begins with a brief introduction to the particular book (including such matters as authorship, date, etc.), a basic outline, and a list of recommended commentaries. At the end of each volume, you will find a comprehensive exegetical outline of the book. The body of each volume is devoted to paragraph-by-paragraph exegesis of the text. The treatment of each paragraph includes:

1. The Greek text of the passage, phrase by phrase, from the fifth edition of the United Bible Societies' *Greek New Testament* (UBS^5).
2. A structural analysis of the passage. Typically, verbal discussion of the structure of a given unit is followed by a diagram, whereby the verbal discussion serves to explain the diagram and the diagram serves to provide a visual aid illumining the structural discussion. While there is no one correct or standard way to diagram Greek sentences, the following format is typically followed in EGGNT volumes:
   a. The original Greek word order is maintained.
   b. When Greek words are omitted, this is indicated by ellipses (. . .).

    c.   The diagramming method, moving from left to right, is predicated upon the following. In clauses with a finite verb, the default order is typically verb-subject-object. In verbless clauses or clauses with nonfinite verb forms, the default order is typically subject-(verb)-object. Departures from these default orders are understood to be pragmatically motivated (e.g., contrast, emphasis, etc.).

    d.   Indents are used to indicate subordination (e.g., in the case of dependent clauses).

    e.   Retaining original word order, modifiers are centered above or below the word they modify (e.g., a prepositional phrase in relation to the verb).

    f.   Where a given sentence or clause spans multiple lines of text, drawn lines are used, such as where a relative pronoun introduces a relative clause (often shifting emphasis).

    g.   Underline is used to indicate imperatives; dotted underline is used to indicate repetition (the same word or cognate used multiple times in a given unit); the symbol ⋮ may be used where an article is separated from a noun or participle by interjected material (such as a prepositional phrase).

    h.   In shorter letters diagrams are normally provided for every unit; in longer letters and Revelation, ellipses may be used to show less detail in diagramming (keeping larger blocks together on the same line) in order to focus primarily on the larger structure of a given unit; in the Gospels and Acts, detailed diagrams will usually not be provided, though less detailed diagrams may be used to illustrate important or more complex structural aspects of a given passage.

3. A discussion of each phrase of the passage with discussion of relevant vocabulary, significant textual variants, and detailed grammatical analysis, including parsing. When more than one solution is given for a particular exegetical issue, the author's own preference, reflected in the translation and expanded paraphrase, is indicated by an asterisk (*). When no preference is expressed, the options are judged to be evenly balanced, or it is assumed that the text is intentionally ambiguous. When a particular verb form may be parsed in more than one way, only the parsing appropriate in the specific context is supplied; but where there is difference of opinion among grammarians or commentators, both possibilities are given and the matter is discussed.

      Verbal forms traditionally labeled deponent (having their lexical form in the middle voice rather than active) are tagged with 'dep.' before the lexical form is given. This is not to overlook that some today argue that 'deponent' is a label that needs to be dropped. It is simply to alert the user of this EGGNT volume to how verbs are still described in many grammars, reference works, and perhaps even their language-learning programs.

4. Various translations of significant words or phrases.

5. A list of suggested topics for further study with bibliography for each topic. An asterisk (*) in one of the "For Further Study" bibliographies draws attention to a discussion of the particular topic that is recommended as a useful introduction to the issues involved.

6. Homiletical suggestions designed to help the preacher or teacher move from the Greek text to a sermon outline that reflects careful exegesis. The first suggestion for a particular paragraph of the text is always more exegetical than homiletical and consists of an outline of the entire paragraph. These detailed outlines of each paragraph build on the general outline proposed for the whole book and, if placed side by side, form a comprehensive exegetical outline of the book. All outlines are intended to serve as a basis for sermon preparation and should be adapted to the needs of a particular audience.[2]

The EGGNT volumes will serve a variety of readers. Those reading the Greek text for the first time may be content with the assistance with vocabulary, parsing, and translation. Readers with some experience in Greek may want to skip or skim these sections and focus attention on the discussions of grammar. More advanced students may choose to pursue the topics and references to technical works under "For Further Study," while pastors may be more interested in the movement from grammatical analysis to sermon outline. Teachers may appreciate having a resource that frees them to focus on exegetical details and theological matters.

The editors are pleased to present you with the individual installments of the EGGNT. We are grateful for each of the contributors who has labored long and hard over each phrase in the Greek New Testament. Together we share the conviction that "all Scripture is inspired by God and is profitable for teaching, for rebuking, for correcting, for training in righteousness" (2 Tim 3:16 HCSB) and echo Paul's words to Timothy: "Be diligent to present yourself approved to God, a worker who doesn't need to be ashamed, correctly teaching the word of truth" (2 Tim 2:15 HCSB).

Thanks to David Croteau, who served as assistant editor for this volume.

Andreas J. Köstenberger
Robert W. Yarbrough

---

2. As a Bible publisher, B&H Publishing follows the "Colorado Springs Guidelines for Translation of Gender-Related Language in Scripture." As an academic book publisher, B&H Academic asks that authors conform their manuscripts (including EGGNT exegetical outlines in English) to the B&H Academic style guide, which affirms the use of singular "he/his/him" as generic examples encompassing both genders. However, in their discussion of the Greek text, EGGNT authors have the freedom to analyze the text and reach their own conclusions regarding whether specific Greek words are gender-specific or gender-inclusive.

Abbreviations

For abbreviations used in discussion of text critical matters, the reader should refer to the abbreviations listed in the Introduction to the United Bible Societies' *Greek New Testament*.

*	indicates the reading of the original hand of a manuscript as opposed to subsequent correctors of the manuscript, *or*
	indicates the writer's own preference when more than one solution is given for a particular exegetical problem, *or*
	in the "For Further Study" bibliographies, indicates a discussion of the particular topic that is recommended as a useful introduction to the issues involved
§, §§	paragraph, paragraphs

Books of the Old Testament

Gen	Genesis	Song	Song of Songs (Canticles)
Exod	Exodus	Isa	Isaiah
Lev	Leviticus	Jer	Jeremiah
Num	Numbers	Lam	Lamentations
Deut	Deuteronomy	Ezek	Ezekiel
Josh	Joshua	Dan	Daniel
Judg	Judges	Hos	Hosea
Ruth	Ruth	Joel	Joel
1–2 Sam	1–2 Samuel	Amos	Amos
1–2 Kgs	1–2 Kings	Obad	Obadiah
1–2 Chr	1–2 Chronicles	Jonah	Jonah
Ezra	Ezra	Mic	Micah
Neh	Nehemiah	Nah	Nahum
Esth	Esther	Hab	Habakkuk

Job	Job	Zeph	Zephaniah
Ps(s)	Psalm(s)	Hag	Haggai
Prov	Proverbs	Zech	Zechariah
Eccl	Ecclesiastes	Mal	Malachi

Books of the New Testament

Matt	Matthew	1–2 Thess	1–2 Thessalonians
Mark	Mark	1–2 Tim	1–2 Timothy
Luke	Luke	Titus	Titus
John	John	Phlm	Philemon
Acts	Acts	Heb	Hebrews
Rom	Romans	Jas	James
1–2 Cor	1–2 Corinthians	1–2 Pet	1–2 Peter
Gal	Galatians	1–3 John	1–3 John
Eph	Ephesians	Jude	Jude
Phil	Philippians	Rev	Revelation
Col	Colossians		

Dead Sea Scrolls

1QM	War Scroll
1QS	Rule of the Community
CD	Damascus Document

General Abbreviations

ABD	D. N. Freedman, ed., *The Anchor Bible Dictionary*, 6 vols. (New York: Doubleday, 1992).
abs.	absolute(ly)
acc.	accusative
act.	active (voice)
adj.	adjective, adjectival(ly)
adv.	adverb, adverbial(ly)
anar.	anarthrous
aor.	aorist
apod.	apodosis
appos.	apposition, appositional
Aram.	Aramaic
art.	(definite) article, articular

attrib.	attributive, attributive(ly)
AUSS	*Andrews University Seminary Studies*
BBR	*Bulletin for Biblical Research*
BDAG	*A Greek-English Lexicon of the New Testament and Other Early Christian Literature*, rev. and ed. F. W. Danker, 3rd ed. (Chicago: University of Chicago, 2000), based on W. Bauer, *Griechisch-deutsches Wörterbuch* (Berlin: Topelmann, 1958). (6th ed.) References to BDAG are by page number and quadrant on the page, *a* indicating the upper half and *b* the lower half of the left-hand column, and *c* and *d* the upper and lower halves of the right-hand column. With the use of dark type, biblical references are now clearly visible within each subsection.
BDF	F. Blass and A. Debrunner, *A Greek Grammar of the New Testament and Other Early Christian Literature*, ed. and rev. by R. W. Funk (Chicago: University of Chicago, 1961).
BGk.	Biblical Greek (i.e., LXX and NT Greek)
BHGNT	M. M. Culy, M. C. Parsons, and J. J. Stigall, *Luke: A Handbook on the Greek Text*, BHGNT (Waco: Baylor University Press, 2010).
Bib	*Biblica*
BibInt	*Biblical Interpretation*
BibRev	*Bible Review*
BJRL	*Bulletin of the John Rylands University Library of Manchester*
Bock	D. L. Bock, *Luke 1:1–9:50*, and *Luke 9:51–24:53*, 2 vols., BECNT (Grand Rapids: Baker, 1994, 1996).
Bock, *Theology*	D. L. Bock, *A Theology of Luke and Acts* (Grand Rapids: Zondervan, 2012).
Bovon	F. Bovon, *Luke 1: A Commentary on the Gospel of Luke 1:1–9:50*, trans. C. M. Thomas, *Luke 2: A Commentary on the Gospel of Luke 9:51–19:27*, trans. D. S. Deer, *Luke 3: A Commentary on the Gospel of Luke 19:28–24:53*, trans. J. Crouch, Hermeneia (Minneapolis: Fortress, 2002, 2013, 2012).
BR	*Biblical Research*
BSac	*Bibliotheca Sacra*

BT	*The Bible Translator*
BTB	*Biblical Theology Bulletin*
Burton	E. de W. Burton, *Syntax of the Moods and Tenses in New Testament Greek*, 3rd ed. (Edinburgh: Clark, 1898).
Campbell, 2007	C. R. Campbell, *Verbal Aspect, the Indicative Mood, and Narrative: Soundings in the Greek of the New Testament*, Studies in Biblical Greek 13 (New York: Peter Lang, 2007).
Campbell, 2008	C. R. Campbell, *Verbal Aspect and Non-Indicative Verbs: Further Soundings in the Greek of the New Testament*, Studies in Biblical Greek 15 (New York: Peter Lang, 2008).
Carroll	J. T. Carroll, *Luke*, NTL (Louisville: Westminster John Knox Press, 2012).
Cassirer	H. W. Cassirer, *God's New Covenant: A New Testament Translation* (Grand Rapids: Eerdmans, 1989).
CBQ	*Catholic Biblical Quarterly*
cf.	*confer* (Lat.), compare
comp.	comparative, comparison
cond.	condition(al)
conj.	conjunctive, conjunction
cstr.	construction, construe(d)
CTJ	*Calvin Theological Journal*
CTR	*Criswell Theological Review*
CurTM	*Currents in Theology and Mission*
dat.	dative
def.	definite
DJG[1]	J. B. Green, S. McKnight, and I. H. Marshall, eds., *Dictionary of Jesus and the Gospels* (Downers Grove: InterVarsity, 1992).
DJG[2]	J. B. Green, J. K. Brown, and N. Perrin, eds., *Dictionary of Jesus and the Gospels*, 2nd ed. (Downers Grove: InterVarsity, 2013)
DNTB	C. A. Evans and S. E. Porter, eds., *Dictionary of New Testament Background* (Leicester / Downers Grove: InterVarsity, 2000).

dir.	direct
EDNT	H. Balz and G. Schneider, eds., *Exegetical Dictionary of the New Testament*, 3 vols. (Grand Rapids: Eerdmans, 1990–93).
ed(s).	edited by, edition(s), editor(s)
Edwards	J. R. Edwards, *The Gospel According to Luke*, Pillar New Testament Commentary (Grand Rapids: Eerdmans; Nottingham: Apollos, 2015).
e.g.	*exempli gratia* (Lat.), for example
Ellis	E. E. Ellis, *The Gospel of Luke*, NCB (Eugene, OR: Wipf and Stock, 2003).
Eng.	English
epex.	epexegetic, epexegetical(ly)
ERT	*Evangelical Review of Theology*
esp.	especially
ESV	English Standard Version (2011)
et al.	*et alii* (Lat.), and others
EvQ	*Evangelical Quarterly*
EVV	English versions of the Bible
ExpTim	*Expository Times*
Fanning	B. Fanning, *Verbal Aspect in New Testament Greek* (Oxford: Oxford University Press, 1991).
Fantin	J. D. Fantin, *The Greek Imperative Mood in the New Testament: A Cognitive and Communicative Approach*, Studies in Biblical Greek 12 (New York: Peter Lang, 2010).
fem.	feminine
fig.	figurative(ly)
Fitzmyer	J. A. Fitzmyer, *The Gospel According to Luke I–IX: A New Translation with Introduction and Commentary*, and *Luke X–XXIV*, 2 vols., AB (Garden City: Doubleday, 1981, 1985).
fut.	future
Garland	D. E. Garland, *Luke*, ZECNT (Grand Rapids: Zondervan, 2011).
Gathercole	S.J. Gathercole, *The Preexistent Son: Recovering the Christologies of Matthew, Mark, and Luke* (Grand Rapids: Eerdmans, 2006)

Geldenhuys	N. Geldenhuys, *Commentary on the Gospel of Luke*, NICNT (Grand Rapids: Eerdmans, 1950).
gen.	genitive
Gk.	Greek
Green	J. B. Green, *The Gospel of Luke*, NICNT (Grand Rapids: Eerdmans, 1997).
GTJ	*Grace Theological Journal*
Harris	M. J. Harris, *Prepositions and Theology in the Greek New Testament* (Grand Rapids: Zondervan, 2012).
HCSB	Holman Christian Standard Bible (2009)
Heb.	Hebrew, Hebraism
HTR	*Harvard Theological Review*
Huffman	D. S. Huffman, *Verbal Aspect Theory and the Prohibitions in the Greek New Testament*, Studies in Biblical Greek 16 (New York: Peter Lang, 2014).
HUT	Hermeneutische Untersuchungen zur Theologie
IBS	*Irish Biblical Studies*
IDBSup	*Interpreter's Dictionary of the Bible (Supplement Volume)*
i.e.	*id est* (Lat.), that is
impers.	impersonal
impf.	imperfect (tense)
impv.	imperative (mood), imperatival(ly)
incl.	including
indef.	indefinite
indic.	indicative (mood)
indir.	indirect
inf.	infinitive
instr.	instrument, instrumental(ly)
Int	*Interpretation*
interr.	interrogative
ISBE	G. W. Bromiley et al, eds., *The International Standard Bible Encyclopedia*, 4 vols. (Grand Rapids: Eerdmans, 1979–88).
iter.	iterative

JBL	*Journal of Biblical Literature*
JETS	*Journal of the Evangelical Theological Society*
Johnson	L. T. Johnson, *The Gospel of Luke*, Sacra Pagina (Collegeville: Liturgical Press, 1991).
JSHJ	*Journal for the Study of the Historical Jesus*
JSNT	*Journal for the Study of the New Testament*
JTS	*Journal of Theological Studies*
Just	A. A. Just Jr., *Luke 1:1–9:50*, and *Luke 9:51–24:53*, 2 vols., Concordia Commentary (St. Louis: Concordia, 1996, 1997).
KJV	King James Version (= "Authorized Version") (1611)
lit.	literal(ly)
LN	*Greek-English Lexicon of the New Testament Based on Semantic Domains,* eds. J. P. Louw and E. A. Nida, vol. 1, *Introduction and Domains.* (New York: United Bible Societies, 1988).
locat.	locative
LTJ	*Lutheran Theological Journal*
LXX	Septuagint (= Greek Old Testament)
Macc	Maccabees
Marshall	I. H. Marshall, *The Gospel of Luke*, NIGTC (Grand Rapids: Eerdmans, 1978).
masc.	masculine
McKay	K. L. McKay, *A New Syntax of the Verb in New Testament Greek: An Aspectual Approach* (New York: Peter Lang, 1994).
Metzger	B. M. Metzger, *A Textual Commentary on the Greek New Testament* (1971; Stuttgart: Deutsche Bibelgesellschaft / New York: United Bible Societies, 1994).
MM	J. H. Moulton and G. Milligan, *The Vocabulary of the Greek Testament Illustrated from the Papyri and Other Non-Literary Sources* (Grand Rapids: Eerdmans, 1972, reprint of 1930 ed.)
mid.	middle
mng.	meaning
Moule	C. F. D. Moule, *An Idiom Book of New Testament Greek*, 2nd ed. (Cambridge: CUP, 1960).

Moulton	*A Grammar of New Testament Greek*, ed. J. H. Moulton, vol. 1 *Prolegomena*, 3rd ed. (Edinburgh: Clark, 1908).
ms(s).	manuscript(s)
MT	Masoretic Text
n.	note
NASB	New American Standard Bible (1995)
NDBT	*New Dictionary of Biblical Theology*, ed. T. D. Alexander and B. S. Rosner (Downers Grove: InterVarsity, 2000).
NEB	New English Bible (1970)
neg.	negative, negation
Neot	*Neotestamentica*
NET	New English Translation Bible (2005)
NETS	New English Translations of the Septuagint (2007)
neut.	neuter
NIDNTT	C. Brown, ed. *The New International Dictionary of New Testament Theology*, 3 vols., (Grand Rapids: Zondervan, 1975–78).
NIDNTTE	M. Silva, ed. *New International Dictionary of New Testament Theology and Exegesis*, 5 vols., (Grand Rapids: Zondervan, 2014).
NIV	New International Version (2011)
NJB	New Jerusalem Bible (1985)
NKJV	New King James Version
NLT	New Living Translation of the Bible (1996)
Nolland	J. Nolland, *Luke 1:1–9:20*, *Luke 9:21–18:34*, and *Luke 18:35–24:53*, 3 vols., WBC (Dallas: Word, 1989, 1993, 1993).
nom.	nominative
NovT	*Novum Testamentum*
NovTSup	Novum Testamentum Supplements
NRSV	New Revised Standard Version (1990)
NSBT	New Studies in Biblical Theology
NT	New Testament
NTS	*New Testament Studies*
obj.	object(ive)

orig.	origin, original(ly)
OT	Old Testament
p(p).	page(s)
pace	(from Lat. *pax*, peace; in stating a contrary opinion) with all due respect to the person named
Pao and Schnabel	D. W. Pao and E. J. Schnabel, "Luke," *Commentary on the New Testament Use of the Old Testament.* eds., G. K. Beale and D. A. Carson (Grand Rapids: Baker, Nottingham: Apollos, 2007).
pass.	passive
periph.	periphrastic
pers.	person(al)
pf.	perfect
pl.	plural
Plummer	A. Plummer, *A Critical and Exegetical Commentary on the Gospel According to St. Luke*, ICC (Edinburgh: T&T Clark, 1909).
Porter	S. E. Porter, *Verbal Aspect in the Greek of the New Testament, with Reference to Tense and Mood*, Studies in Biblical Greek 1 (New York: Peter Lang, 1989).
Porter, *Idioms*	S. E. Porter, *Idioms of the Greek New Testament* (Sheffield: JSOT, 1992).
poss.	possessive, possession
pred.	predicate, predicative
pref.	prefix
prep.	preposition(al)
pres.	present
pron.	pronoun
prot.	protasis
ptc.	participle, participial(ly)
R	A. T. Robertson, *A Grammar of the Greek New Testament in the Light of Historical Research*, 4th ed. (Nashville: Broadman, 1934).
Robertson, *Pictures*	A. T. Robertson, *Word Pictures in the New Testament*, rev. W. J. Perschbacher, vol. 2, *The Gospel According to Luke* (Grand Rapids: Kregel, 2005).

rdg(s).	(textual) reading(s)
RivBib	*Revista Biblica*
ref.	reference
refl.	reflexive
rel.	relative
rev.	revised
RevExp	*Review and Expositor*
ResQ	*Restoration Quarterly*
Rowe	C. K. Rowe, *Early Narrative Christology: The Lord in the Gospel of Luke* (Grand Rapids: Baker, 2009).
RSV	Revised Standard Version (1952)
RTR	*Reformed Theological Review*
Runge	S. E. Runge, *Discourse Grammar of the Greek New Testament: A Practical Introduction for Teaching and Exegesis* (Peabody, MA: Hendrickson, 2010).
RV	Revised Version (NT 1881)
SBJT	*Southern Baptist Journal of Theology*
SBLMS	*Society of Biblical Literature Monograph Series*
SBT	*Studies in Biblical Theology*
SE	*Studia Evangelica*
Sem.	Semitic, Semitism
sg.	singular
sim.	similar(ly)
Sir	Sirach/Ecclesiasticus
SJT	*Scottish Journal of Theology*
SNTSMS	Society for New Testament Studies Monograph Series
Stein	R. H. Stein, *Luke*, NAC (Nashville: B&H, 1992).
ST	*Studia theologica*
subj.	subject(ive)
subjunc.	subjunctive
subord.	subordinate, subordination
subst.	substantive, substantival(ly)
superl.	superlative
SwJT	*Southwestern Journal of Theology*

T	*A Grammar of New Testament Greek* ed. J. H. Moulton, vol. 3, N. Turner *Syntax,* (Edinburgh: Clark, 1963)
TDNT	G. Kittel and G. Friedrich, eds. *Theological Dictionary of the New Testament*, ed. G. W. Bromiley, 9 vols. (Grand Rapids: Eerdmans, 1964–74).
temp.	temporal(ly)
TJ	*Trinity Journal*
Thompson	A. J. Thompson, *The Acts of the Risen Lord Jesus: Luke's Account of God's Unfolding Plan.* Downers Grove: InterVarsity, 2011.
tr.	translate(d), translation(s)
Turner, *Style*	*A Grammar of New Testament Greek*, ed. J. H. Moulton, vol. 4, *Style*, N. Turner (Edinburgh: T&T Clark, 1976).
TynBul	*Tyndale Bulletin*
UBS/UBS[5]	*The Greek New Testament*, ed. B. Aland, K. Aland, J. Karavidopoulos, C. M. Martini and B. M. Metzger, 5th rev. ed. (Stuttgart: Deutsche Bibelgesellschaft/New York: United Bible Societies, 2014); 1st ed. 1966 (= UBS[1]); 2nd ed. 1968 (= UBS[2]); 3rd ed. 1975 (=UBS[3]); 4th ed. 1993 (=UBS[4])
v(v).	verse(s)
var.	variant (form or reading)
vbs.	verb
VE	*Vox evangelica*
voc.	vocative
vol(s).	volume(s)
Wallace	Daniel B. Wallace, *Greek Grammar Beyond the Basics: An Exegetical Syntax of the New Testament* (Grand Rapids: Zondervan, 1996).
Wis	Wisdom of Solomon
WTJ	*Westminster Theological Journal*
WUNT	Wissenschaftliche Untersuchungen zum Neuen Testament

Z	M. Zerwick, *Biblical Greek Illustrated by Examples*, J. Smith (Rome: Pontifical Biblical Institute, 1963).
ZG	M. Zerwick and M. Grosvenor, *A Grammatical Analysis of the Greek New Testament*, 5th rev. ed. (Rome: Pontifical Biblical Institute, 1996).
ZNW	*Zeitschrift für die neutestamentliche Wissenschaft und die Kunde der älteren Kirche*

LUKE

Introduction

AUTHORSHIP

The unanimous testimony of the manuscripts of this Gospel, early church tradition, and church history until the mid-nineteenth century is that the author was Luke, a traveling companion of Paul's. The fact that no other names were attached to this work is all the more remarkable since, as the author himself (the ptc. παρηκολουθηκότι is masc., 1:3) states in his prologue, he was not an apostle or original eyewitness of Jesus' ministry (1:2–3). The following is a brief summary of some of the evidence for Lukan authorship (more may be conveniently found in Bock, *Theology*, 32–41; the introductions to the commentaries mentioned below; and in a comprehensive recent discussion of these introductory matters by C. Keener, *Acts: An Exegetical Commentary* vol. 1, *Introduction and 1:1–2:47* (Grand Rapids: Baker, 2012), 383–434.

1. The earliest ms., a papyrus from c. AD 200 ($\mathfrak{P}$75), states at the end of the Gospel that it is the "Gospel according to Luke." This is the title that is consistently found either at the beginning or end of Luke in nearly all uncial mss. (even at the top of each codex page in abbreviated form in Vaticanus and Sinaiticus, Edwards 4). Thus, it is unlikely to have been an anonymous text (M. Hengel, *The Four Gospels and the One Gospel of Jesus Christ* and J. Bowden Harrisburg: [Trinity Press International, 2000], 37).

2. The widespread testimony of the early church is that the author was "Luke" and that this Luke was a traveling companion of Paul's. Some of this external evidence includes references to Luke as author and companion of Paul in the *Muratorian Canon*, Irenaeus (*Against Heresies* 3.1.1; 3.14.1–4), the "anti–Marcionite prologue" to Luke's Gospel, Clement of Alexandria (*Stromata* 5.12), Tertullian (*Against Marcion* 4.2.2), Origen (*On First Principles* 2.6.7), and Eusebius (*Ecclesiastical History* 3.4.6; 3.24.15). Justin Martyr (*Dialogue* 103; c. AD 160) cites the text of Luke 22:44 as written by one of those who followed the apostles.

3. This connection between the author as "Luke" and a companion of Paul finds confirmation (a) within Luke and Acts, and (b) in three allusions in Paul's letters. First, on the basis of the prologue to Acts (referring to his πρῶτον

λόγον and repeating the addressee as "Theophilus"), it is likely that Acts is written by the same author as Luke's Gospel (this is confirmed with a number of parallels and repeated patterns across Luke-Acts). Within Acts, the "we" passages (where the author uses the first person plural: 16:10–17 [Troas to Philippi]; 20:5–21:18 [Philippi–Troas–Miletus to Jerusalem]; 27:1–28:16 [Caesarea to Rome]) imply that the author of these two works joins the journeys of Paul at these points (noted by Irenaeus, *Against Heresies* 3.14.1). Second, an individual called Luke is also identified in the Pauline literature as a companion of Paul's (Col 4:14; Phlm 24; 2 Tim 4:11). When one considers all the companions of Paul mentioned in the letters, these few refs. to someone named Luke who is with Paul (in Rome) do not make Luke an obvious choice if late-second-century writers were looking for a name to attach to this Gospel and that would result in unanimity across the mss. and early church tradition (*pace* Bovon 1.10).

DATE

Estimating a precise date for Luke's Gospel is more difficult given the fact that (unlike the name) a date is not given in the title. The previous discussion of authorship does, however, have a bearing on this. If the author is a companion of Paul's, as the internal and external evidence indicates, then the date cannot extend too much later than toward the end of the first century (the citation from Justin Martyr [above] means the latest possible date is c. AD 160). The prologue itself indicates that any date in the second half of the first century would be possible (i.e., based on the reports of original eyewitnesses). The decision about a more precise date, however, depends on how one evaluates the following:

1. Given the likelihood that Acts was written after Luke's Gospel (Acts 1:1), the date of Luke's Gospel depends in part on when one dates Acts. This in turn depends on whether the end of Acts indicates the time when Acts was written (i.e., soon after the "two whole years" of Paul's imprisonment [Acts 28:30; thus, soon after approx. AD 62]; internally, the narrative of Acts does not show an interest in later debates such as Gnosticism, etc.). Although Acts is not primarily about Paul so that Luke must tell of all the events that transpired in Paul's life (i.e., the outcome of his trial and his [later] execution), nevertheless, it is the arrival of *Paul* (and companions) in Rome that Luke describes rather than the arrival of the *gospel* in Rome (note Acts 28:14–15).

2. Given the similarities among the Synoptic Gospels, the date of Luke's Gospel also depends in part on whether one thinks there is literary dependence among these Gospels and, if so, whether that literary dependence requires Markan priority. Obviously if Luke used Mark, then the date of Luke depends on the date of Mark. Even so, 30–40 years after the death and resurrection of Jesus is plenty of time for Gospels to be written and circulated. There does not appear to be a consensus on the answer to this complex question, and

     it seems unwise to base too much on proposed reconstructions of literary dependence. The prologue does not require Luke's Gospel to depend on late written Gospels (see the comments on 1:1–2).

3. The date of Luke's Gospel may also depend on whether one requires Jesus' descriptions of the destruction of Jerusalem to have been written after that destruction (i.e., after AD 70). This may relate to how one views Jesus' other predictions in Luke's Gospel, but, as many have noted, the language is sim. to OT prophetic judgments (see comments on 19:43–44; 21:20–24) and need not require a post–AD 70 date. Other opportunities for pointing out the destruction of the temple do not seem to be taken up by Luke (e.g., 24:53; Acts 3–7).

As indicated above, although not essential for the purposes of this guide, my own preference is for a date somewhere between the mid-50s and early-60s (in addition to the introductions to the commentaries and the sources cited there, see also the often overlooked discussion [for an early date] in J. Wenham, *Redating Matthew, Mark and Luke* [London: Hodder and Stoughton, 1991], 223–38; Keener [392–93] argues for a date soon after AD 70 for Luke's Gospel).

AUDIENCE

The name of the addressee, Theophilus, mentioned in the prefaces of Luke and Acts, does not provide any decisive evidence for the audience of these books (the following brief discussion summarizes Thompson, 23–25; see the exegetical comments on 1:1–4 for more details). A common Greek name, it was used by both Jews and Greeks. Theophilus may well have been an official (κράτιστε) and patron of Luke's writing project. Even so, a wider audience is assumed even when a patron is named. Luke's repeated use of the plural pronoun "us" in his preface to the Gospel indicates that he identifies with the readership of his work. As Marguerat notes, "The narrative which follows (the Gospel and Acts) takes place within a readership composed of a common faith in the saving events (the 'events . . . fulfilled among us') and a common adherence to a tradition ('handed on to us by those who from the beginning were eyewitnesses')" (D. Marguerat, *The First Christian Historian* [Cambridge: Cambridge University Press, 2002], 23–24). Thus, a Christian readership is most likely implied by the preface to Luke's Gospel (see the exegetical comments on 1:1–4; e.g., on κατηχήθης).

Other clues in the narrative of Luke-Acts, however, have been the basis for conflicting claims for the readership. Many have focused on whether this Christian readership is primarily Gentile or Jewish. Those in favor of a Gentile-Christian readership point to (1) the emphasis on the Gentile mission in Acts, (2) the absence of primarily Jewish preoccupations (e.g., Matt 5:21–48; 15:1–20), (3) the use of the LXX and the absence of Hebrew and Aramaic terms, and (4) Luke's Greco-Roman preface (e.g., Fitzmyer 57–59). Those in favor of a Jewish-Christian readership (cf. D. Ravens, *Luke and the Restoration of Israel* [Sheffield: Sheffield Academic Press, 1995], 14–16), however, respond by pointing out (1) that the emphasis on Gentile mission needs to be understood in the context of Israel's restoration and does not necessarily entail a complete rejection of the Jews, (2) Luke's many references to primarily Jewish concerns (e.g. the temple in Luke, clean/unclean in Acts 10), (3) the fact that a Greek-speaking Jewish readership could explain Luke's use of the LXX and the absence of Hebrew and Aramaic terms (Edwards [15–16] notes the pervasive presence of Hebraisms), and (4) that many of the Gentile converts in Acts are God-fearers who had already attached themselves to Judaism (without undergoing circumcision). It seems, therefore, that in light of such seemingly conflicting claims for the audience of Luke and Acts, it would be wise to follow the course proposed by Marguerat, that "the Lucan work implies a diversified readership" (Marguerat 83). That is, the intended audience may include both Jewish and Gentile Christian readers. A Jewish or Gentile Christian audience familiar with the language and promises of the Old Testament appears to be the primary target.

PURPOSE(S)

Luke likely had more than one purpose for writing his works. Emphases on fulfillment, witnesses, evidence, and proclamation of the gospel indicate that evangelistic and didactic purposes would be included among the possibilities. Luke's stated purpose in the preface to his gospel, however, indicates that Luke is primarily writing for a Christian audience familiar with the promises and language of the Old Testament in order to provide assurance concerning the continued outworking of God's saving purposes. The following provides a brief summary of the details developed in the exegetical comments of the prologue (summarizing Thompson, 19–20).

In 1:1 Luke tells us that he is joining others in compiling a narrative concerning "the things that have been fulfilled among us." The passive voice of the verb "fulfilled/accomplished" indicates that the events have been fulfilled/accomplished *by God*, and this is in keeping with Luke's emphasis throughout his Gospel and Acts on the fulfillment of God's plan. In 1:4 Luke explicitly states the purpose of his writing project: he is writing in order that (ἵνα) "you may know the certainty of the things you have been taught." The indication here is that readers such as Theophilus had been taught or instructed about the faith. What Luke's audience needed, however, was "certainty" or "assurance" about what they had been taught (Bock 65). When Luke's Gospel and the book of Acts are read in light of this preface, Luke appears to be writing to provide reassurance to believers about the nature of the events surrounding Jesus' life, death, and resurrection; the spread of the message about Jesus; and the nature of God's people following Jesus' ascension. He is providing assurance that these events really are the work of God, that God really has been accomplishing his purposes, that Jesus really is who he said he was, and that believers in Jesus really are the true people of God. All of this is especially important in light of the rejection and persecution faced by these believers, not the least of which came from some of those who also claimed to belong to the heritage of God's people and who read the same Bible.

OUTLINE

I. Prologue: The Context and Purpose of Luke's Writing Project (1:1–4)
II. The Arrival of the Royal Lord of Salvation (1:5–2:52)
III. The Inauguration of Jesus' Public Ministry (3:1–4:13)
IV. Actions that Demonstrate Who Jesus Is and the Salvation He Brings (4:14–9:50)
V. Teaching that Explains the Saving Rule of the Lord (9:51–19:44)
VI. The Lord Accomplishes the Salvation of the Kingdom (19:45–24:53)

For more details see the Exegetical Outline at the end of the book and the explanations given in the introductions to sections in the exegetical comments. Some brief comments here about some practical matters will help orient readers to my focus in this *Guide*. Since one of the aims is to help expositors, I have provided headings that reflect what I think might be the major themes of each section rather than more general headings such as "Ministry in Galilee" or "Journey to Jerusalem." In this regard, and for reasons of space, the Homiletical Suggestions are only of the more "homiletical" type rather than the additional "exegetical" outline type. Although each section of Luke is included in a homiletical suggestion, occasionally this is done by grouping two or three sections together under a broader homiletical suggestion. I hope this will encourage attention to the flow of thought in broader literary units and help facilitate progress in preaching through Luke's Gospel. Homiletical ideas may also be drawn from the section headings. My focus is on the exegesis of the Greek text of Luke's Gospel. For this reason (and because of space limitations), comments on synoptic variations, Old Testament allusions, text-critical matters, and accent rules are kept to a minimum. I have, however, frequently provided references to word usage elsewhere in Luke and Acts. In order to navigate various kinds of cross-references in this *Guide*, I have used "see" to direct readers to earlier full parsing information (see also the list of common verbs in the appendix that are not parsed throughout the *Guide*) and more information about a construction or common term or feature of Luke's Gospel. I have used "cf." for all other general references.

RECOMMENDED COMMENTARIES

Throughout this *Guide* references are made to five commentaries that are written in English or translated into English and based directly on the Greek text of Luke. They are:

Bock, D. L. *Luke 1:1–9:50. Luke 9:51–24:53*. 2 vols. BECNT. Grand Rapids: Baker, 1994, 1996.
Bovon, F. *Luke 1: A Commentary on the Gospel of Luke 1:1–9:50*. Tr. by C. M. Thomas. *Luke 2: A Commentary on the Gospel of Luke 9:51–19:27*. Tr. by D. S. Deer. *Luke 3: A Commentary on the Gospel of Luke 19:28–24:53*. Tr. by J. Crouch. Hermeneia. Minneapolis: Fortress, 2002, 2013, 2012.
Fitzmyer, J. A. *The Gospel According to Luke I–IX: A New Translation with Introduction and Commentary. Luke X–XXIV*. 2 vols. AB. Garden City: Doubleday, 1981, 1985.

Marshall, I. H. *The Gospel of Luke*. NIGTC. Grand Rapids: Eerdmans, 1978.
Nolland, J. *Luke 1:1–9:20. Luke 9:21–18:34. Luke 18:35–24:53*. 3 vols. WBC. Dallas:
    Word, 1989, 1993, 1993.

Frequent use is also made of M. M. Culy, M. C. Parsons, and J. J. Stigall, *Luke: A Handbook on the Greek Text*, BHGNT (Waco: Baylor University Press, 2010). Apart from Marshall, each of the other four commentators listed above provides his own translation. The translation by Nolland (and BHGNT) more clearly reflects his exegetical decisions. I found Bock the least speculative on synoptic comparisons and most helpful on historicity and comments on textual variants. Nolland is especially helpful for succinct explanations of the overall message and theological significance of each section (the exegetical comments often focus on variations in the wording of the Synoptic Gospels). Marshall is an especially succinct combination of the strengths of Bock and Nolland (note the size of the other [2-3 vol.] commentaries). Fitzmyer's introductory summary of "Lucan Language and Style" (107–27) is especially helpful (though this should now be read in consultation with Edwards's references to Hebraisms in Luke [noted above]). Bovon provides extensive information on the history of interpretation of each section. Bovon, Fitzmyer, and Nolland also provide lengthy bibliographies on each section.

The older commentary on the Greek text by A. Plummer (*A Critical and Exegetical Commentary on the Gospel According to St. Luke*, ICC [Edinburgh: T&T Clark, 1909]) is also occasionally cited. Of the many slightly less technical commentaries available, reference is occasionally made to Carroll, Edwards, Garland, Geldenhuys, Green, Johnson, Just (two vols.), and Stein. Space prevents too much interaction with these excellent commentaries (and the smaller vols. by Ellis and Morris). My recommendation for a pastor would be Bock and Edwards.

I. Prologue: The Context and Purpose of Luke's Writing Project (1:1–4)

The opening verses of Luke's Gospel resemble the style of classical Greek found in ancient historians. There is likely a parallel between 1:1–2 and 1:3–4 as follows:

¹ ἐπειδήπερ <u>πολλοὶ</u>
    ἐπεχείρησαν <u>ἀνατάξασθαι διήγησιν</u> περὶ τῶν πεπληροφορημένων ἐν ἡμῖν
      πραγμάτων,
      ² <u>καθὼς παρέδοσαν ἡμῖν</u> οἱ ἀπ᾽ ἀρχῆς αὐτόπται καὶ ὑπηρέται γενόμενοι τοῦ
        λόγου,
³ ἔδοξε <u>κἀμοὶ</u>
    παρηκολουθηκότι ἄνωθεν πᾶσιν ἀκριβῶς <u>καθεξῆς σοι γράψαι</u>, κράτιστε
      Θεόφιλε,
      ⁴ <u>ἵνα ἐπιγνῷς περὶ</u> ὧν κατηχήθης λόγων τὴν ἀσφάλειαν.

The context or precursors for Luke's writing are given in 1:1–2 and the explanation and purpose of Luke's writing in 1:3–4. The underlined words show the parallels between the three lines of 1:1–2 and their corresponding lines in 1:3–4 (see BDF §464; Bock 51; Fitzmyer 288; Marshall 40). Luke is writing about the outworking of past hopes, based on good evidence, so as to provide assurance to his readers.

1:1 The conj. ἐπειδήπερ ("since" NRSV; "inasmuch as" NASB, ESV), though not found anywhere else in the NT or LXX, was a common introduction to a causal clause in classical Greek (usually postpositive; T 318; Bovon 1.16; Fitzmyer 290). Here it introduces the reason (causal rather than concessive, Marshall 41; Nolland 6; completed in 1:3) for Luke's project; he is joining with "many" others (πολλοί; cf. Acts 1:3; Heb 1:1). Questions about who the "many" may be are impossible to answer, but it is unlikely to be limited to only one or two written sources (Robertson, *Pictures* 3). The following three terms describe the work of the many others. Ἐπεχείρησαν 3rd pl. aor. act. indic. of ἐπιχειρέω, "to endeavor," "set one's hand to," "undertake" (most EVV). The term may be viewed:

1. negatively as a criticism of Luke's predecessors due to the use of the term elsewhere by Luke in contexts of failed attempts (Acts 9:29; 19:13) and his emphasis in this context on the comprehensiveness of his own work ("all things," "from the beginning," "accurately," Bovon 1.19; Fitzmyer 291–92); or

*2. in a neutral sense without any implication of criticism due to Luke's associa-tion of himself with these others in the same task (κἀμοί, "to me also"). The term is preceded here with "because," not a concessive "although," and is used outside the NT for undertaking a (difficult) project without any indication of failure in the task (LN 68.59; MM 250d–51a; Marshall 41; Nolland 12).

The aor. mid. inf. ἀνατάξασθαι of dep. ἀνατάσσομαι, "to arrange in order," "compile" (HCSB, ESV), "draw up" (NIV) is complementary (and may refer to oral or written compilations, Bock 56). The acc. sg. fem. noun διήγησιν (διήγησις, -εως, ἡ) is better "account" (NRSV, NASB, NIV) rather than "narrative" (RSV, HCSB, ESV) as the term may be used of both written and oral accounts (F. Büchsel, *TDNT* 2.909; Bock 53). Elsewhere in Luke the cognate vb. διηγέομαι is used for oral accounts (cf. Luke 8:39; 9:10; Acts 8:33; 9:27; 12:17; cf. also Mark 5:16; 9:9; Heb 11:32; e.g., Acts 10:36–43, esp. 10:39, 41). Luke's ref. to his own work (ἔδοξε κἀμοί . . . γράψαι, 1:3) need not limit these prior accounts to written ones (*pace* Fitzmyer 291; Nolland 6). These accounts have been about (περί) πραγμάτων (gen. pl. neut. of πρᾶγμα, -ατος, τό) "things" (NASB, ESV, NIV), "events" (NRSV, HCSB) which have been fulfilled. Πεπληροφορημένων (gen. pl. neut. of pf. pass. ptc. of πληροφορέω, "fulfilled"; NRSV, HCSB, NIV; Bock 57; Bovon 1.20; Fitzmyer 293; rather than "accomplished" NASB, ESV; Nolland 7) is attrib. modifying πραγμάτων. The pf. perhaps highlights the state resulting from the completed events, and the pass. is a divine pass. (i.e., fulfilled by God, as promised; cf. Lukan refs. to fulfillment in Bock 57; Bovon 1.20; Fitzmyer 293; Marshall 41). Ἐν ἡμῖν ("among us") includes Luke with readers such as Theophilus.

1:2 The conj. καθώς places the many compilers of accounts in 1:1 in harmony with the activity of the eyewitnesses in this verse (Robertson, *Pictures* 4). Παρέδοσαν 3rd pl. 2nd aor. act. indic. from παραδίδωμι, "hand over," has been understood to refer to:

1. a general transmission of history (Nolland 8); or
*2. a technical term for the transmission of tradition often by a rabbi to a disciple (Fitzmyer 296; Marshall 41–42).

The context here of "eyewitnesses and servants" (with apostles likely in view) and the use of the term elsewhere in contexts of transmitting tradition lends support to the sec-ond view (cf. 1 Cor 11:2, 23; 15:3; Mark 7:13; Jude 3; cf. the cognate noun παράδοσις in 2 Thess 2:15). The dat. ἡμῖν, "to us," shows that Luke is distinguished from the original eyewitnesses but is nevertheless dependent on them. On "beginnings" (ἀρχή) in Luke-Acts, see Luke 3:23; Acts 1:21–22; 10:37 (cf. John 15:27; 16:4). Ἀπ' ἀρχῆς is perhaps placed forward for emphasis together with the noun (i.e., they were the "from-the-beginning witnesses"). Αὐτόπται καί ὑπηρέται ("eyewitnesses and ser-vants" most EVV) are probably one group as indicated by the placement of "from the beginning" (ἀπ' ἀρχῆς) before and the (subst.) ptc. οἱ . . . γενόμενοι after the two nouns (Bovon 1.21; Fitzmyer 294; Marshall 42; Nolland 7; though *pace* Nolland the art. οἱ modifies the ptc. and is not an example of the "Granville Sharp Rule," cf. BHGNT 3). Οἱ . . . γενόμενοι (nom. pl. masc. of 2nd aor. mid. ptc. of dep. γίνομαι, "those who were") is the subj. of παρέδοσαν. Αὐτόπται (nom. pl. masc. of αὐτόπτης, -ου, ὁ, "eye-witness") highlights the basis for the reliability c.f. the information (Marshall 41; i.e., from those who had firsthand observance) and ὑπηρέται (nom. pl. masc. of ὑπηρέτης, -ου, ὁ, "servant," "assistant," cf. Acts 26:16) clarifies that this role is not one of mere observance but one of service for "the word" (τοῦ λόγου is an obj. gen. and may be inclusive of both Jesus and the "message" about him; cf. Acts 10:36–39; 13:26–31; cf. also 1 John 1:1; Gathercole, 221–27).

1:3 Ἔδοξεν (3rd sg. aor. act. indic. of δοκέω, "think," "seem") together with the dat. κἀμοί (crasis, καί and ἐγώ; "also to me"; idiomatic for "I too decided" NRSV, NIV; BHGNT 4) indicates that Luke does not criticize the efforts of his predecessors but joins his efforts with theirs (Plummer 4). Παρηκολουθηκότι dat. sg. masc. of pf. act. ptc. of παρακολουθέω, "to follow closely" (ESV), i.e., "follow" in a figurative sense mentally ("pay careful attention to" BDAG 767a; in the context of the surrounding modifiers, "investigate" NRSV, HCSB, NIV; Robertson, *Pictures* 6; Bock 60; Bovon 1.21; Fitzmyer 297; Marshall 42). The ptc. is attrib. modifying the dat. κἀμοί (i.e., "also to me, who has investigated" BHGNT 4; ZG 168 suggests that the ptc. is either appos. to ἐμοί or it represents the unexpressed subj. of the inf. γράψαι, cf. Z §394). The adv. ἄνωθεν is temp. and modifies the ptc. (i.e., "investigated everything from the beginning" NIV). It has been understood as referring to:

1. The length of time taken by Luke (e.g., "followed . . . for some time past" RSV, ESV; Marshall 42); or
*2. The earliest events that he has researched (NIV; Robertson, *Pictures* 6; Bovon 1.22).

The second option is preferable as the term is likely synonymous with ἀπ' ἀρχῆς (Luke then begins with the birth narratives after the prologue; Nolland 9; cf. e.g., Acts 26:4 [ἀπ' ἀρχῆς] and 26:5 [ἄνωθεν]). The dat. πᾶσιν is also a complement of the ptc. and is likely neuter here ("all things" ESV; Fitzmyer 297; on the form cf. T 199). The adv. ἀκριβῶς ("carefully") is a third modifier of the ptc. (i.e., "carefully investigated" HCSB, NIV; cf. Fitzmyer 297–98; Marshall 43; Bovon 1.22 and Nolland 9 suggest it should also be linked to γράψαι). The adv. καθεξῆς ("successively," "consecutive order" NASB; "orderly sequence" HCSB) is used only by Luke in the NT (cf. Luke 8:1; Acts 3:24; 11:4; 18:23). It probably includes a broad chronological and historical order as well as a geographical and salvation-historical order, though allowing for topical ordering of narrative sequences too (BDAG 490c; Bock 62–63; Bovon 1.22; Fitzmyer 298–99; Marshall 43). The aor. act. inf. γράψαι is complementary with ἔδοξεν ("it seemed good . . . to write"). The voc. superl. (for elative, T 31; Wallace 303) adj. κράτιστε (of κράτιστος) could be:

*1. a term of honor in addressing officials (elsewhere in the NT only at Acts 23:26; 24:3; 26:25; so Theophilus may be an official of some high rank, Robertson, *Pictures* 6; Wallace 303); or
2. a polite form of address that is common in dedications (BDAG 565b; BDF §60[2]; Marshall 43).

Although the term does not reappear with Theophilus's name in Acts 1:1 (indicating that #2 is possible), the use of the term elsewhere in Acts suggests that #1 is more likely (on the voc. in Luke-Acts cf. T 33; Wallace 69; possibly, though not necessarily, indicating that Theophilus might be a patron or financial supporter of Luke's work, Fitzmyer 299–300). The name "Theophilus" by itself does not indicate whether a Jew or Gentile is being addressed. There is evidence in the next verse that this "most excellent Theophilus" is a Christian. As with other dedications (e.g., Josephus, *Against Apion* 1.1), the dedication to an individual does not exclude a wider audience that shares his perspective (Nolland 10).

1:4 The use of ἵνα with the subjunc. ἐπιγνῷς signals the purpose of this writing project. Ἐπιγνῷς 2nd sg. 2nd aor. act. subjunc. of ἐπιγινώσκω, "to know." Ἀσφάλειαν (at the end of the sentence for emphasis, Bock 64; Bovon 1.23; Fitzmyer 300; Nolland 10) acc. sg. fem. of ἀσφάλεια, -ας, ἡ, "certainty" (HCSB, ESV, NIV), "truth" (NRSV), "exact truth" (NASB). The noun is used in Acts 5:23 for the safety or security of the locked jail, and related terms are used elsewhere in Acts (adv. ἀσφαλῶς 2:36; adj. ἀσφαλής, -ές 21:34; 22:30; 25:26) to refer to assurance or knowledge of facts with certainty. The combination with a vb. of knowing here indicates that a secure knowledge or "assurance" is meant here (Bock 65; Fitzmyer 300). This assurance or certainty is "concerning" (περί) "the things which [ὧν . . . λόγων] you have been taught." The rel. pron. ὧν is gen. by attraction to λόγων (BDF §294[5]; Z §16; ZG 168). Κατηχήθης 2nd sg. aor. pass. indic. of κατηχέω ("teach"), is "taught" (NASB, ESV, NIV), or "instructed" (NRSV, HCSB; Bock 66; Fitzmyer 301; Marshall 43–44 [though allowing for an evangelistic purpose as well]; cf. Acts 18:25), rather than "report information" in the sense of merely "told" ("informed" RSV; Nolland 11; cf. Acts 21:24). The context here of 2nd person personal prons. (1:2 "fulfilled among us," "handed down to us") together with the reference to "certainty/assurance," indicates that Theophilus is a Christian who has received instruction or teaching already, and is in need of assurance (perhaps in the face of persecution) concerning what he has been taught about Jesus and the fulfilment of God's promises.

FOR FURTHER STUDY

1. The Prologue to Luke's Gospel (1:1–4)

Alexander, L. C. A. "Luke's Preface in the Context of Greek Preface Writing." Pages 90–116 in *The Composition of Luke's Gospel: Selected Studies from Novum Testamentum*. Edited by D. E. Orton. Leiden: Brill, 1999.

_____. *The Preface to Luke's Gospel: Literary Convention and Social Context in Luke 1.1–4 and Acts 1.1*. Cambridge: Cambridge University Press, 1993.

Barnett, P. *Finding the Historical Christ*. Grand Rapids: Eerdmans, 2009. See p. 109–20.

Bauckham, R. J. *Jesus and the Eyewitnesses: The Gospels as Eyewitness Testimony*. Grand Rapids: Eerdmans, 2006.

HOMILETICAL SUGGESTIONS[1]

The Truthfulness of the Gospel (1:1–4)

1. Based on multiple sources (1:1)
2. Based on eyewitness testimony (1:2)
3. Based on careful investigation (1:3)
4. Leads to confidence in the faith (1:4)

---

1. Although each section of Luke is included in a homiletical suggestion, occasionally this is done by grouping two or three sections together under a broader homiletical suggestion. It is hoped that this will encourage attention to the flow of thought in broader literary units and help facilitate progress in preaching through Luke's Gospel. Homiletical ideas may also be drawn from the section headings.

II. The Arrival of the Royal Lord of Salvation (1:5–2:52)

After the preface, the opening two chapters of Luke's Gospel introduce Jesus as the Lord who brings the long-awaited salvation. His greatness is accentuated through contrasts made with John (their parents, births, and future roles), who is himself great, and through songs of praise that resound with joy. Broadly speaking, the births of John and Jesus highlight divine promises (1:5–56) being fulfilled (1:57–2:40; Marshall 49).

A. ANGELIC VISITATION TO ZECHARIAH: JOHN'S BIRTH ANNOUNCED (1:5–25)

1. Angelic Visitation to Zechariah (1:5–17)

The account of the angelic visitation first focuses on the heritage, character, and occupation of Zechariah and the heritage, character, and condition of Elizabeth. Then the setting and announcement are described with a focus on the role of their son, John, as a forerunner for the Lord.

1:5 Ἐγένετο (as well as καὶ ἐγένετο and ἐγένετο δέ, cf. 1:8, 23) followed by a temporal phrase is common in Luke (and the LXX, BDAG 198b, BDF §472[3], R 107, Z §389, Fitzmyer 119; ἐγένετο occurs sixty-nine times in Luke and fifty-four in Acts; ἐγένετο δέ is found only in Luke and Acts in the NT). Ἐν ταῖς ἡμέραις is "In the days of" (HCSB, ESV), "During the reign of" (NET), "In the time of" (NIV). The gen. sg. masc. βασιλέως (of βασιλεύς, -έως, ὁ) is in appos. to Ἡρῴδου. The gen. τῆς Ἰουδαίας is subord. (BHGNT 7) and incorporates the wider political territory of Judea, Galilee, and a large part of Perea and Syria (Bock 75; Fitzmyer 322; Marshall 51). It is also possible that Luke focuses attention on the narrower sense of Judea here and throughout the infancy narratives (Nolland 25). The nom. sg. masc. ἱερεύς τις (of ἱερεύς, -έως, ὁ, "a priest") is the subj. of ἐγένετο. Ὀνόματι, dat. of ref. (Z §53; ZG 168). The nom. Ζαχαρίας is in appos. to ἱερεύς. Ἐφημερίας (gen. sg. fem. of ἐφημερία, -ας, ἡ), "division," "class" (of temple priests), is only found here and 1:8 in the NT (seventeen times in 1–2 Chron., twenty-three in LXX; on their "daily" activity for one week [twice a year] see BDAG 419c). The prep. phrase ἐξ ἐφημερίας indicates source. Ἀβιά, indecl., gen. Καί introduces a new clause with γυνή the subj. of an implied equative vb. (BHGNT 8). Αὐτῷ, dat. of poss. The phrase ἐκ τῶν θυγατέρων also indicates source ("from the daughters of" HCSB, ESV; "a descendant of" NRSV, NIV). Again, καί introduces a new clause. The nom. τὸ ὄνομα is the subj. of an implied equative vb. Ἐλισάβετ, is a pred. nom. Elizabeth, as a "daughter of Aaron" was also of priestly descent (K. G. Kuhn *TDNT* 1.4). The priestly references highlight the heritage of Zechariah and Elizabeth and their interest in the affairs of the temple.

1:6 Ἦσαν 3rd pl. impf. act. indic. of εἰμί. Δίκαιοι nom. pl. masc. of δίκαιος, adj. "righteous." Ἀμφότεροι nom. pl. masc. adj. of ἀμφότεροι, -αι, -α, "both," the subj. of ἦσαν. Ἐναντίον, "before" (ESV), "in the sight of" (NIV; sim. HCSB; LN 90.20; ZG 168; common in the LXX, only used by Luke in the NT, cf. 20:26; 24:19; Acts 7:10; 8:32). Πορευόμενοι (nom. pl. masc. of pres. mid. ptc. of dep. πορεύομαι) in this context focuses on their lifestyle (LN 41.11; BHGNT 9; ZG 168–69); "observing," (NIV), "walking" (NASB, ESV), "living" (NRSV, HCSB), and further explains the previous statement about the couple's righteousness (either periph. with ἦσαν, Bock 77, or attendant circumstance, BHGNT 8). Δικαιώμασιν, dat. pl. neut. of δικαίωμα, -ατος, τό, "requirements" (NASB, HCSB), "regulations" (NRSV), "statutes" (ESV), "decrees" (NIV). The one art. ταῖς with ἐντολαῖς καὶ δικαιώμασιν closely associates the two nouns (T 181; Z §184; ZG 169; and possibly indicates that the first entity is a sub-set of the second, Wallace 287). The pred. adj. ἄμεμπτοι (nom. pl. masc. of ἄμεμπτος, -ον), "blameless," could be used with an implied ἦσαν (BHGNT 9), or as an adv. (BDF §243; Marshall 53). The term does not mean "sinless" but living in accordance with the law.

1:7 Καί may be adversative (Marshall 53; *pace* BHGNT 9). In light of the previous verses, their lack of children is not because of sin or blame on the couple. Αὐτοῖς, dat. of poss. (the phrase is a Sem., ZG 169). The causal conj. καθότι gives the reason for their childlessness (a conj. only used by Luke in the NT; cf. 19:9; Acts 2:24, 45; 4:35; 17:31). Στεῖρα pred. nom. sg. fem. of στεῖρα, -ας, ἡ, "barren" (NASB, ESV), "could not conceive" (HCSB, sim. NIV). Προβεβηκότες (nom. pl. masc. of pf. act. ptc. of προβαίνω, "go forward," "advance") with ἦσαν is a pluperfect periph. cstr. The ptc. with the dat. (ref., T 220) ἐν ταῖς ἡμέραις αὐτῶν is idiomatic for old age ("advanced in years," ESV; BDF §197; ZG 169 [a Heb.]). The circumstances here prepare the reader for the surprising work of God's grace to come.

1:8 On ἐγένετο see 1:5. Ἐν τῷ ἱερατεύειν is a temp. inf. cstr. (pres. act. inf. of ἱερατεύω, "serve as priest." This term occurs twenty-seven times in the LXX but only here in the NT; on this temp. cstr. cf. Wallace 595; Z §§387, 389–90). The acc. αὐτόν is the subj. of the inf. (Zechariah in this context). Ἐν τῇ τάξει [dat. sg. fem. of τάξις, -εως, ἡ, "order"] τῆς ἐφημερίας ["division," see 1:5] αὐτοῦ provides the temp. setting ("when his divi-sion was on duty" HCSB, ESV; BHGNT 10). The time has come for Zechariah's week of service in the temple. The prep. ἔναντι (only here and Acts 8:21 in the NT; frequently ἔναντι κυρίου in LXX) is locat. ("before God" most EVV; "serving God in the Temple" NLT).

1:9 Κατὰ τὸ ἔθος τῆς ἱερατείας (ἔθος acc. sg. neut. of ἔθος, -ους, τό, "custom" [10 out of twelve NT occurrences are in Luke-Acts]; ἱερατείας gen. sg. fem. of ἱερατεία, -ας, ἡ, "priestly office," "priesthood" most EVV) modifies the following phrase (ἔλαχεν; HCSB, NIV; BHGNT 11; Marshall 54; rather than the preceding, or both, *pace* Bovon 1.34). Ἔλαχεν 3rd sg. 2nd aor. act. indic. of λαγχάνω, "to choose by lot" (cf. also Acts 1:17; LN 30.106). The aor. act. art. inf. τοῦ θυμιᾶσαι indicates that the choosing of the lot was to "make an incense offering" (on θυμιάω cf. BDAG 461c; LN 53.25; "burn incense" most EVV) in the temple (εἰς τὸν ναόν, acc. sg. masc. of ναός, -οῦ, ὁ, i.e., "Holy Place" NET; elsewhere in Luke, only 1:21, 22; 23:45). The aor. ptc. εἰσελθών (nom. sg. masc. of 2nd aor. act. ptc. of dep. εἰσέρχομαι) modifies the inf. θυμιᾶσαι (Z §393; ZG 169; rather than ἔλαχεν) and could be:

1. temp. with the offering of incense (i.e., to offer incense after entering the temple [Bock 100]; on the nom. cf. Z §393; as pendent cf. Marshall 54); or
2. a ptc. of result ("thus entering the sanctuary" BHGNT 12, arguing that if temp. the ptc. would be acc.).

The large number of priests meant that this was a once-in-a-lifetime event for Zechariah (Marshall 54; Nolland 23, 27).

1:10 Πᾶν τὸ πλῆθος ("multitude" ESV; "assembled worshippers" NIV) is the nom. subj. of the periph. ptc. cstr. ἦν . . . προσευχόμενον (nom. sg. neut. of pres. mid. ptc. of dep. προσεύχομαι). The impf. periph. cstr. is frequent in Luke (Z §361; ZG 169; Nolland 28). Τοῦ λαοῦ, partitive gen. Τῇ ὥρᾳ, temp. dat. Τοῦ θυμιάματος, gen. sg. neut. of θυμίαμα, -ατος, τό, "[at the hour] of the incense offering" (NET), "[at the hour] of incense" (HCSB, ESV); "[the time for] the burning of incense" (NIV). Thus, the parallel is made between Zechariah's offering of sacrifices (incl. burning incense) inside the temple and the gathered crowd praying outside the temple.

1:11 Ὤφθη 3rd sg. aor. pass. indic. of ὁράω, "appear" (often followed by the dat. in the NT; cf. Wallace 165 n. 72). Ἄγγελος κυρίου is the subj. of ὤφθη and, esp. in light of 1:19, is indefinite ("an angel of the Lord," BHGNT 13, Bovon 1.35; Nolland 28). Κυρίου is probably a gen. of source. The (intrans.) ptc. ἑστώς (nom. sg. masc. of 2nd pf. act. ptc. of ἵστημι) is attrib. (agreeing with ἄγγελος). Ἐκ is often used with the pl. δεξιῶν as a locat. "at the right side" (BHGNT 13; cf. Harris 106–7; 20:42; 22:69; 23:33; Acts 2:25). Τοῦ θυσιαστηρίου, gen. sg. neut. of θυσιαστήριον, -ου, τό, "altar" (θυμιάματος, see 1:10). The emphasis here is on a real appearance rather than a dream (Marshall 55).

1:12 Ἐταράχθη 3rd sg. aor. pass. indic. of ταράσσω, "troubled" ("terrified" NRSV; Marshall 55). Ἰδών nom. sg. masc. of 2nd aor. act. (temp.) ptc. of ὁράω. The nom. φόβος is the subj. of ἐπέπεσεν (3rd sg. 2nd aor. act. indic. of ἐπιπίπτω, "fall upon"); "fear fell upon him" (ESV), "overcome with fear" (HCSB). For ἐπ' αὐτόν cf. BDAG 366d (with ref. to a condition which comes upon someone).

1:13 Luke often uses πρός followed by the acc. after verbs of speaking (for the simple dat., Z §80; ZG 169; Fitzmyer 116). The impv. φοβοῦ (2nd sg. pres. mid. impv. of dep. φοβέομαι) is a prohibition with the neg. μή. Although this implies the prohibition of an action already in progress, it is the context of 1:12 rather than the pres. tense of the impv. itself that indicates this (cf. Huffman 138; though cf. BDF §336[3]; Wallace 724; Z §246; ZG 169). The nom. sg. fem. δέησίς (of δέησις, -εως, ἡ, "entreaty," "prayer," though perhaps a more specific petition, Marshall 57; the second accent is from the enclitic σου, BHGNT 15) is the subj. of εἰσηκούσθη (3rd sg. aor. pass. indic. of εἰσακούω, "hear," "with the implication of heeding and responding to what is heard," LN 24.60). The pass. here is "heard by God" (cf. NLT). Thus, the reason Zechariah is not to fear is "because" (διότι, causal, cf. BDF §456) his prayer (for a child and for Israel, Fitzmyer 325; Marshall 56) has been heard. Γεννήσει, 3rd sg. fut. act. indic. of γεννάω, "beget," "give birth to." The dat. σοι could be advantage (BHGNT 15) or indir. obj. (Wallace 142). The fut. καλέσεις (2nd sg. fut. act. indic. of καλέω) functions as an impv. ("you shall call" ESV; T 86; Wallace 570; Z §280; ZG 169; cf. also 1:31; on the double acc. [τὸ ὄνομα αὐτοῦ Ἰωάννην] see BDF §157[2]). God, rather than Zechariah, is naming the child, foreshadowing the special God-given role that will be explained in the following verses.

1:14 Ἔσται 3rd sg. fut. mid. indic. of εἰμί. Χαρά . . . ἀγαλλίασις ("joy and gladness," nom. sg. fem. of ἀγαλλίασις, -εως, ἡ) could be a compound subj. of ἔσται ("Joy and gladness will come to you" NET, sim. NASB, ESV; Bovon 1.35) or the pred. nom. with the implied subj. being John ("He will be a joy and delight to you" NIV; BHGNT 16; cf. 1:15). There is little difference in mng. The dat. σοι is poss. (Wallace 150). Πολλοί (nom. pl. masc. of πολύς, πολλή, πολύ) is the subj. of χαρήσονται (3rd pl. 2nd fut. pass. indic. of χαίρω). Ἐπί with τῇ γενέσει (dat. sg. fem. of γένεσις, -εως, ἡ, "birth") is causal (Z §126; ZG 170; though a broader ref. to John's coming is likely included, Marshall 57; Nolland 30). Rejoicing will come to both Zechariah and many others due to the significance of John's birth (as explained in the following verse).

1:15 Ἔσται, see 1:14. Here the implied subj. is John. The reason (γάρ) for this joy is that he will be "great" (μέγας) "before the Lord" (cf. Mal 3:1; Luke 7:27–28; in contrast to Jesus, who will be "great" without qualification, cf. 1:32). The preposition ἐνώπιον ("before," "in the sight of" NASB, HCSB, NIV; it takes the gen.) is used twenty-two times in Luke and thirteen in Acts (though only once in John and none in Matthew and Mark). Οἶνον καὶ σίκερα ("wine or strong drink") is the obj. of πίῃ (3rd sg. 2nd aor. act. subjunc. of πίνω, "drink"). This is the only occurrence of σίκερα (acc. sg. neut. of σίκερα, τό [indecl.], "strong drink") in the NT (cf. Num 6:3). Οὐ μή with the subjunc. is an emphatic neg. (BDF §365[3]; Robertson, *Pictures* 10; T 96; Z §444; ZG 170). Πλησθήσεται 3rd sg. fut. pass. indic. of πίμπλημι. The gen. πνεύματος ἁγίου is content (Wallace 94; perhaps anar. due to being monadic, Wallace 249). The combination of ἔτι ἐκ is an emphatic temp. ref. (κοιλίας, gen. sg. fem. of κοιλία, -ας, ἡ, "womb"; "before he is born" NIV; BDAG 400a; cf. 1:41, 44; a Heb. Robertson, *Pictures* 10; T 180; Bock 86; Bovon 1.37; Fitzmyer 326; Marshall 58; Nolland 31). The use of πίμπλημι for being "filled with the Holy Spirit" is common in these early chapters (1:41, 67; cf. also 2:25–27) and throughout Luke-Acts (cf. Acts 1:8; 4:8, 31) for empowerment to proclaim the good news about Jesus. The following verses will highlight John's unique role in this.

1:16 Πολλούς (acc. pl. masc., see 1:14) is the obj. of ἐπιστρέψει (3rd sg. fut. act. indic. of ἐπιστρέφω, "turn" [trans.], with John as still the subj.). The gen. τῶν υἱῶν is partitive. Ἐπί is locat. The acc. τὸν θεόν is in appos. to κύριον. Together with the previous verse, John's prophetic role is highlighted as he will "turn" (NASB) many in Israel to the Lord their God. The identification of this "Lord" awaits further clarification in the narrative.

1:17 Αὐτός is nom. subj. (referring again to John), though without special emphasis (Z §199; ZG 170; αὐτός or καὶ αὐτός is often used like this in Luke [καὶ αὐτός occurs forty-one times in Luke, three times in Acts], and in the LXX, Fitzmyer 120). Αὐτός is frequently used in Luke to refer to an existing subject (Marshall 58). Προελεύσεται 3rd sg. fut. mid. indic. of dep. προέρχομαι, "go forward." In the context of 1:16 αὐτοῦ refers to κύριον τὸν θεόν (Bock 88; Fitzmyer 326). The following narrative, however, will identify this Lord as the Lord Jesus (cf. Rowe 56–77). The dat. phrase ἐν πνεύματι καὶ δυνάμει could indicate manner (BHGNT 18; cf. NLT; Bock 88), means (BDAG 328d; cf. NRSV), or association (Z §116; ZG 170). The gen. Ἠλίου is association (BHGNT 18). Two inf. phrases (ἐπιστρέψαι . . . ἑτοιμάσαι) give the purpose of John's task, with the second inf. being loosely attached to the first (Marshall 59). The purpose of this forerunner is "to turn" (ἐπιστρέψαι, aor. act. inf. of ἐπιστρέφω) the hearts of the fathers (πατέρων, "fathers" most EVV; "parents" NRSV, NIV; on the pl. cf. T 23) to (ἐπί, locat.) the children (Z §282; ZG 170; cf. Mal 3:24). The acc. pl. ἀπειθεῖς ("disobedient") is a subst. adj. and dir. obj. of an implied ἐπιστρέψαι. Ἐν is locat. ("to" BDAG 327d; for εἰς BDF §218; T 257; though cf. ZG 170) and parallels ἐπί. Φρονήσει, dat. sg. fem. of φρόνησις, -εως, ἡ, "way of thinking," "attitude" (NASB), "understanding" (HCSB), "wisdom" (NRSV, ESV, NIV). The gen. δικαίων is likely subj. (e.g., "understanding of the righteous" HCSB). The two lines "fathers to children" and "disobedient to . . . righteous" reflect horizontal (familial) and vertical (Godward) reconciliation in calling all to return to God (Bock 90; Marshall 60; though cf. 12:53, Nolland 31). The purpose (inf., ZG 170) of John's ministry is then further defined as "to prepare" (ἑτοιμάσαι aor. act. inf. of ἑτοιμάζω) "for the Lord" (κυρίῳ, dat. of advantage) a people (λαόν, acc. dir. obj.) "prepared" (κατεσκευασμένον acc. sg. masc. of pf. pass. ptc. of κατασκευάζω, "prepare," an attrib. ptc. "a prepared people" HCSB; "a people prepared" most EVV). In light of 1:16–17, 76; 3:4; 7:27; the "Lord" Jesus (2:11) will be identified with the "Lord" of Mal 3.

2. Zechariah's Response (1:18–25)

1:18 The interr. κατὰ τί ("how?") occurs only here in the NT (cf. Gen 15:8; BHGNT 19; Wallace 658). The question here is stronger than Mary's (see 1:34). Γνώσομαι, 1st sg. fut. mid. indic. of γινώσκω. The antecedent of the demonstrative pron. τοῦτο is the angelic announcement of 1:13–17 (BHGNT 19), though the following reason indicates that Zechariah's doubt concerns the specific prospect of having a child (Bock 91;

cf. Wallace 334). The reason (γάρ) for Zechariah's skeptical response here is that he is an "old man" (πρεσβύτης, nom. sg. masc. of πρεσβύτης, -ου, ὁ) and his wife is likewise advanced in years (προβεβηκυῖα nom. sg. fem. of pf. act. ptc. of προβαίνω, "advance," "well along" HCSB, NIV). Προβεβηκυῖα could be periph. (with ἐστίν implied, BHGNT 19) or a pred. ptc. (Wallace 618). "Advanced in her days" is idiomatic for old age.

1:19 Ἀποκριθείς (nom. sg. masc. of aor. pass. ptc. of dep. ἀποκρίνομαι, "answer") is a pleonastic attendant circumstance ptc. (with εἶπεν; cf. T 155–56; Wallace 625, 649; Z §366; Fitzmyer 114). The (intrans.) ptc. παρεστηκώς (nom. sg. masc. of pf. act. ptc. of παρίστημι, "stand") is attrib. modifying Γαβριήλ (NASB, HCSB). Ἐνώπιον τοῦ θεοῦ is locat. ("in the presence of God" all EVV). Ἀπεστάλην 1st sg. 2nd aor. pass. indic. of ἀποστέλλω (the pass. implies, sent "by God," Z §236; Fitzmyer 328). The aor. act. inf. λαλῆσαι (of λαλέω) and the aor. mid. inf. εὐαγγελίσασθαί (of εὐαγγελίζω) indicate the purpose of sending Gabriel. The demonstrative acc. pl. neut. pron. ταῦτα is the dir. obj. of εὐαγγελίσασθαι ("this good news" most EVV) and refers to all of 1:13–17 including John's role as the forerunner to the Lord.

1:20 The particle ἰδού (though 2nd sg. aor. mid. impv. of ὁράω) is used regularly in narrative (with καί, twenty-six times in Luke) to emphasize what is about to follow (BDAG 468a; a Septuagintalism; BDF §4[2]; LN 91.13; Fitzmyer 121). The fut. ἔσῃ (2nd sg. fut. mid. indic. of εἰμί) with σιωπῶν (nom. sg. masc. of pres. act. ptc. of σιωπάω, "silent") is a fut. periph. ptc. cstr. (see 21:17; along with the neg. and ptc. δυνάμενος, nom. sg. masc. of pres. mid. ptc. of dep. δύναμαι). On Zechariah being unable to speak cf. 1:61–63. Zechariah's "silence" is emphasized with the negative repetition that he will not be able "to speak" (the aor. act. inf. λαλῆσαι is complementary). Ἄχρι ἧς ἡμέρας is temp. Γένηται 3rd sg. 2nd aor. mid. subjunc. of dep. γίνομαι (ingressive in this context, Bock 93). The nom. pl. neut. demonstrative pron. ταῦτα is the subj. of γένηται. Zechariah's discipline, though serious, is not permanent. Ἀντί with the gen. pl. rel. pron. ὧν is causal (T 258; Z §92; cf. Wallace 343). The reason for the onset of this silence is because Zechariah (surprisingly, despite his credentials; see 1:45) did not believe these words (ἐπίστευσας 2nd sg. aor. act. indic. of πιστεύω). The nom. pl. masc. rel. pron. οἵτινες (of ὅστις, ἥτις, ὅτι; on οἵτινες for the rel. οἵ cf. BDF §293[3]; T 47–48; Wallace 344–45; Z §§215–19; ZG 170–71; here τοῖς λόγοις is the antecedent) is the subj. of πληρωθήσονται (3rd pl. fut. pass. indic. of πληρόω). Εἰς τὸν καιρὸν αὐτῶν ("in their time") is locat. (equivalent to ἐν, BDF §206[1]). The prediction emphasizes God's sovereignty in the fulfillment of his promises at the appointed time (cf. 4:21; 9:31; 24:44).

1:21 Προσδοκῶν (nom. sg. masc. of pres. act. ptc. of προσδοκάω, "wait for") with ἦν is an impf. periph. cstr. The impf. ἐθαύμαζον (3rd pl. impf. act. indic. of θαυμάζω, "wonder," "marvel at") may be:

*1. parallel with the impf. periph. ("the people were waiting . . . and wondering " NIV; BHGNT 22); or
 2. ingressive ("the people were waiting . . ., and they began to wonder" NET).

The two impf. cstrs. highlight the duration of the wait and therefore the corresponding concern. The pl. ἐθαύμαζον agrees with the collective sg. λαός (according to sense). Ἐν with the pres. act. art. inf. χρονίζειν (of χρονίζω, "to take a long time," "delay") could be:

1. temp., expressing contemporaneous time ("amazed that he stayed so long" HCSB; Wallace 595; Plummer 18); or
2. causal ("because he delayed," T 146; cf. NET).

Ἐν τῷ ναῷ is locat. (see 1:9). The acc. αὐτόν is the subject of χρονίζειν.

1:22 Ἐξελθών (nom. sg. masc. of 2nd aor. act. ptc. of dep. ἐξέρχομαι, "come/go out") is temp. The impf. of ἐδύνατο (3rd sg. impf. mid. indic. of dep. δύναμαι, "be able") is perhaps conative ("trying to speak but not being able to" BHGNT 23). The inf. λαλῆσαι is complementary (see 1:20; Wallace 599). Thus the words of the angel are immediately fulfilled. Ἐπέγνωσαν 3rd pl. 2nd aor. act. indic. of ἐπιγινώσω, "come to know," "realized" (most EVV; cf. Marshall 61). Ὅτι introduces the content in indir. discourse of what the people realized. Ὀπτασίαν, acc. sg. fem. of ὀπτασία, -ας, ἡ, "vision." Ἑώρακεν 3rd sg. pf. act. indic. of ὁράω, "see." On ἐν τῷ ναῷ see 1:9. Καί is causal or explanatory, explaining how they knew he had seen a vision ("because" NET; "for" NIV; cf. NLT). Διανεύων (nom. sg. masc. of pres. act. ptc. of διανεύω, "make a sign") with ἦν is an impf. periph. ptc. cstr. and is parallel with the impf. διέμενεν (3rd sg. impf. act. indic. of διαμένω, "remain"). Κωφός nom. sg. masc. of κωφός, -ή, -όν, "dumb," "unable to speak" (NRSV, NIV; pace BDAG 580d; LSJ 1019d–20a; and Schneider, *EDNT* 2.334d, note that the term may also be used to refer to someone who is deaf; cf. 1:62; Fitzmyer 329; Marshall 61; Nolland 33; see 7:22; 11:14).

1:23 Ἐγένετο, see 1:5. With ὡς, the phrase is a temp. cstr. (common in the LXX, though only by Luke in the NT; cf. 1:41; 2:15; 19:29; cf. also 11:1). Ἐπλήσθησαν 3rd pl. aor. pass. indic. of πίμπλημι, "fill," "completed" (HCSB, NIV), "ended" (NRSV, NASB, ESV; refers to the completion of a set number of days; BDAG 813d; cf. 1:57; 2:6, 22). Λειτουργίας gen. sg. fem. of λειτουργία, -ας, ἡ, "service." Ἀπῆλθεν 3rd sg. 2nd aor. act. indic. of dep. ἀπέρχομαι, "depart," "went back" (HCSB), "returned" (NIV). Upon Zechariah's completion of his daily tasks of temple service, he returned to his home in the hill country (cf. 1:39).

1:24 Μετά with the acc. ταύτας τὰς ἡμέρας is temp. ("After some time" NET). Συνέλαβεν 3rd sg. 2nd aor. act. indic. of συλλαμβάνω, "take," in this context "conceived" (HCSB, ESV), "became pregnant" (NASB, NIV). Although a common word in the LXX, Luke uses συλλαμβάνω eleven times out of a total of sixteen in the NT, and he is the only one to use it for the conceiving of a child (cf. 1:24, 31, 36; 2:21; Robertson, *Pictures* 12). The art. ἡ γυνή is in appos. to the proper name Ἐλισάβετ (cf. Wallace 49). The impf. περιέκρυβεν (3rd sg. impf. act. indic. of περικρύβω, "hide," "kept herself in seclusion," NASB, HCSB, with the refl. pron.) highlights the ongoing action over the course of the following five months (μῆνας acc. pl. masc. of μήν, μηνός, ὁ). The pres. ptc. λέγουσα (nom. sg. fem. of pres. act. ptc. of λέγω, "say") is attendant circumstance (BHGNT 25; with περίεχρυβεν). Thus, as the following verse will show, there is no indication here that Elizabeth's seclusion is due to shame or grief (*pace* Marshall 62). Luke does not say why she did this, but in the narrative context, her seclusion serves to focus on God's grace to Elizabeth (1:25), the announcement to Mary (1:26–37), and Mary's visit to Elizabeth (1:39–45).

1:25 Ὅτι, recitative (following λέγουσα, all EVV; Bovon 1.40; Fitzmyer 329; Marshall [62] suggests the possibility of "because" here). Οὕτως, "thus," "This is what" (NRSV). Μοι, dat. of advantage. Πεποίηχεν 3rd sg. pf. act. indic. of ποιέω, "do." The dat. rel. pron. αἷς agrees with the temp. phrase ἐν ἡμέραις ("in the days when" NASB, ESV; "in these days" HCSB, NIV). Ἐπεῖδεν (3rd sg. 2nd aor. act. indic. of ἐφοράω, "gaze upon," "looked" ESV) is idiomatic for showing favor (NIV, sim. HCSB; "gracious" NET; LN 30.45; Fitzmyer 329; cf. Acts 4:29). The inf. ἀφελεῖν (2nd aor. act. inf. of ἀφαιρέω, "take away") could be purpose or result here (BHGNT 26; Wallace 592; Bock 99; Fitzmyer 330). Ὄνειδός acc. sg. neut. of ὄνειδος, -ους, τό, "disgrace" (most EVV), "reproach" (ESV), a term found only here in the NT but common in the LXX (cf. Gen 30:23; in this context cf. Luke 1:7).

HOMILETICAL SUGGESTIONS

God's Surprising Grace (1:5–25)
1. God's providence in surprising circumstances (1:5–10)
2. God's surprising promises anticipate joy to come (1:11–17)
3. Surprising responses to God's promises (1:18–25)

B. ANGELIC VISITATION TO MARY:
JESUS' BIRTH ANNOUNCED (1:26–38)

1. Angelic Visitation to Mary (1:26–33)

1:26 Ἐν . . . τῷ μηνὶ τῷ ἕκτῳ is temp. ("In the sixth month" [see 1:24; ἕκτῳ dat. sg. masc. of ἕκτος, -η, -ον]; i.e., "of Elizabeth's pregnancy" NIV). This temp. ref., along with the same heavenly messenger, links the announcement about Jesus to John's conception (Marshall 64). Ἀπεστάλη 3rd sg. 2nd aor. pass. indic. of ἀποστέλλω, "send." Γαβριήλ is nom. in appos. to ὁ ἄγγελος. Ἀπό could be "from" (NASB, ESV; Z §90; ZG 171; i.e., source or origin, from God's presence, Bock 106; Nolland 39–40, 49) or "by" (NRSV, HCSB; sim. NIV; indicating ultimate agency, Wallace 433; Fitzmyer 343; the var. ὑπό is likely a scribal correction). The dat. rel. pron. ᾗ is poss. (i.e., "to which," ZG 171). The nom. Ναζαρέθ is a pred. nom. (with an implied ἦν; BDF §128[3]). On the form of Ναζαρέθ (2:4, 39, 51) see BDF §39[2] (cf. Ναζαρά, 4:16).

1:27 Πρὸς παρθένον (acc. sg. fem. of παρθένος, -ου, ἡ; modifying ἀπεστάλη), "to a virgin" (BDAG 777a; LN 9.39; Bovon 1.49; cf. 2:36). Ἐμνηστευμένην (acc. sg. fem. of pf. pass. ptc. of dep. μνηστεύομαι, "engaged" NRSV, HCSB; "betrothed" ESV; "pledged to be married" NIV) is attrib. in agreement with the fem. παρθένον. The dat. rel. pron. ᾧ is poss. Ἐξ οἴκου, "source," referring to the Davidic descent of Joseph (NASB, NIV; on Jesus' Davidic descent in Luke cf. 1:32, 69; 2:4; 18:38–39; 20:41–44; Acts 2:25–34; 13:22–37; 15:16). The nom. Μαριάμ (on the form see BDF §53[3]) is a pred. nom. (with an implied ἦν; BDF §128[3]). Thus, the verse emphasizes (a) that Mary is a virgin, and (b) that Mary is legally pledged to someone of Davidic descent so that any child of hers will belong to this Davidic line too (Bock 108; Marshall 64).

1:28 The 2nd aor. ptc. εἰσελθών (see 1:9) is attendant circumstance (either "coming in, he said" NASB, implying an indoor setting, Bock 109; Marshall 65; or simply "came to her" HCSB, ESV). Χαῖρε 2nd sg. pres. act. impv. of χαίρω, "rejoice" (NKJV, NJB, HCSB; cf. e.g., Zeph 3:14; Zech 9:9; ZG 171), "greetings" (most EVV; an exclamation rather than an imperative, Wallace 493; therefore a greeting, BDAG 1075b, Bock 109, Fitzmyer 344–45). Κεχαριτωμένη (voc. sg. fem. of pf. pass. ptc. of χαριτόω, "bestow favor upon," "favor highly") is subst. ("O favored one" ESV) and refers to Mary as one who has received divine favor (BDAG 1081a; Bovon 1.50; Fitzmyer 345; Marshall 65; Nolland 50). The combination of χαῖρε with κεχαριτωμένη may be an intentional use of similar sounding words (BHGNT 28; "Rejoice, you who enjoy God's favor" NJB). Ὁ κύριος μετὰ σοῦ (a verbless clause with an implied ἐστίν) is an assurance that God will be with her through the following events (Bock 110; common in the OT; cf. Acts 18:10).

1:29 The nom. fem. art. ἡ is the subj. of διεταράχθη (agreeing in gender with Μαριάμ; cf. Wallace 211–13). Διεταράχθη 3rd sg. aor. pass. indic. of dep. διαταράσσομαι, "very perplexed" (NASB, sim. NRSV), "deeply troubled" (HCSB, sim. ESV, NIV; an intense concern, "greatly perplexed" BDAG 237d; cf. Zechariah's response in 1:12). Ἐπὶ τῷ λόγῳ is causal (HCSB; Bock 110). The impf. διελογίζετο (3rd sg. impf. mid. indic. of dep. διαλογίζομαι, "reason," "pondered" NRSV, "wonder" NET) may be:

1. iter. ("kept pondering" NASB);
2. conative ("tried to discern" ESV); or
*3. ingressive ("began to wonder" NET; Marshall 66).

The nom. sg. masc. interr. adj. ποταπός (of ποταπός, -ή, -όν, "what sort of") is here a pred. (BHGNT 29; R 741, 1045) of the optative εἴη (3rd sg. pres. act. opt. of εἰμί; the opt. form of εἰμί is used predominantly [eleven out of twelve] by Luke in the NT). The opt. introduces an indir. question (i.e., "what kind of greeting this could be" HCSB; BDF §386[1]; R 1031; T 131; Wallace 483 [the opt. is often used in "indirect questions after a secondary tense"]; Z §§346, 339; ZG 172; "about the meaning of this greeting" NET; cf. 1:62). Ἀσπασμός nom. sg. masc. of ἀσπασμός, -οῦ, ὁ, "greeting."

1:30 The fem. dat. αὐτῇ is the indir. obj. of εἶπεν. On the prohibition μὴ φοβοῦ see 1:13. Μαριάμ, voc. The reason for the reassurance is because (γάρ) Mary has found (εὗρες 2nd sg. 2nd aor. act. indic. of εὑρίσκω) "favor with God" (in the sense of "before God" or "in God's sight," a Sem., Bock 111; Marshall 66). In the context of 1:28, this is an expression of God's gracious initiative (Bovon 1.50; "won God's favor" NJB is potentially confusing). Χάρις is not used by Matt or Mark but is common in Luke-Acts with reference to God's gracious help (Conzelmann, *TDNT* 9.392–93; Bock 111).

1:31 Ἰδού see 1:20. Συλλήμψη 2nd sg. fut. mid. indic. of συλλαμβάνω, "conceive," see 1:24. Γαστρί dat. sg. fem. of γαστήρ, -τρός, ἡ, "womb." Τέξη 2nd sg. fut. mid. indic. of τίκτω, "give birth to." On the fut. καλέσεις see 1:13 (note the sim. idiom in Isa 7:14, Robertson, *Pictures* 13–14; Marshall 66; Pao and Schnabel 259c–d also note other Davidic links; *pace* Bock 112; Nolland 51). The acc. Ἰησοῦν is the complement in a double acc. cstr.

1:32 The following verses outline the significance of Jesus. The nom. demonstrative pron. οὗτος is the subj. of ἔσται (1:14) and refers to υἱόν in 1:31. Although John will be "great before the Lord" (1:15), Jesus will be "great" (μέγας) without any qualifiers. The nom. υἱός is the complement in a double nom. cstr. with the pass. κληθήσεται (3rd sg. fut. pass. indic. of καλέω, "call," see BHGNT 30; here essentially "will be" ZG 172). The gen. sg. masc. superl. adj. ὑψίστου (of ὕψιστος, -η, -ον, "highest") is subst. ("the Most High"; used by Luke nine times out of thirteen in the NT; cf. 1:35, 76; 2:14; 6:35; 8:28; 19:38; Acts 7:48; 16:17). The designation here as "Son of the Most High" is to be compared with John who will be called a "prophet of the Most High" (1:76; cf. also 6:35; Acts 16:17). Δώσει 3rd sg. fut. act. indic. of δίδωμι, "give." On τὸν θρόνον Δαυίδ cf. Acts 2:30. Τοῦ πατρὸς αὐτοῦ, "his father" (RSV, NASB, ESV, NIV), "his ancestor" (NJB, NRSV, NLT). On Jesus as "Son" and Jesus' "father" in Luke cf. 1:35; 2:48–49; 3:23; 10:21–22; 20:13; 22:29; 24:49. On Jesus' Davidic descent see 1:27. Although Jesus' Davidic kingship is emphasized in 1:32–33, his "greatness" and unique sonship with God are also hinted at here.

1:33 Βασιλεύσει 3rd sg. fut. act. indic. of βασιλεύω, "reign." Ἐπί is used here with reference to power or control over (BDAG 365d; T 272; instead of an obj. gen. BDF §233[2]; Z §124; ZG 172; Marshall 68). Τὸν οἶκον Ἰακώβ, "the house of Jacob" (NRSV, HCSB, ESV), "Jacob's descendants" (NIV), "Israel" (NLT, NET; cf. Amos 9:8; Isa 14:1; Marshall 68). With εἰς τοὺς αἰῶνας (the pl. is Sem., T 25) and οὐκ ἔσται τέλος the emphasis here is on the everlasting kingdom (βασιλείας) of Jesus. Luke-Acts will show the establishment of this rule through the death, resurrection, and ascension of the Lord Jesus (Acts 2:30–31).

2. Mary's Response (1:34–38)

1:34 Mary's question ("How will this be" ESV, NIV) may relate more to how (πῶς) this will come about. Zechariah's question (1:18), in asking how he can know this (by implication, asking for a sign), seems to doubt the reliability of the announcement and thus whether the event will come about at all (cf. 1:20; BHGNT 32; Bock 118). The conj. ἐπεί ("since") is causal (Wallace 674; Marshall 69; used only here in Luke-Acts). The expression ἄνδρα οὐ γινώσκω (1st sg. pres. act. indic. of γινώσκω, "know") is a euphemism for not "knowing" someone sexually ("I am a virgin" NRSV, NASB, ESV, NIV; cf. NET, HCSB; the NJB, "I have no knowledge of man," is potentially misleading; the RSV, "I have no husband," is too general). The pres. of γινώσκω could be a "perfective present" (Wallace 533) highlighting her current (and previous) state, or it may portray her "current practice of celibacy" (BHGNT 32). The pres. indicates that Mary's question is related to an imminent birth or pregnancy while she does not know a man (cf. also the pf. in 1:28 and the aor. in 1:30; Bock 120; Geldenhuys 80; Nolland 59; Plummer 24), rather than a birth in the future after getting married.

1:35 Ἀποκριθείς, see 1:19. In answer to Mary's question, the angel replies that the Holy Spirit will "come upon" her (ἐπελεύσεται 3rd sg. fut. mid. indic. of dep. ἐπέρχομαι, cf. Isa 32:15; Acts 1:8; Pao and Schnabel 260b–c) and the "power of the Most High" (δύναμις ὑψίστου, see 1:32) will "overshadow" her (ἐπισκιάσει 3rd sg. fut. act. indic. of ἐπισκιάζω). In other words, the child will be conceived "without human agency" (Marshall 70). The term indicates God's presence (cf. Exod 40:35; σοι, dat. complement). The conj. διό highlights the inference which follows the previous promise (result, Marshall 71; consequences, Nolland 55; causal, Fitzmyer 351). The neut. ptc. τὸ γεννώμενον (nom. sg. neut. of pres. pass. ptc. of γεννάω) is likely due to an implied τὸ τέκνον (BDF §138[1]; T 21; Fitzmyer 351; Marshall 71; Nolland 55). The pres. ptc. is fut. referring (BDF §339[2b]; T 87; Z §283; cf. 2:34; 22:19). The combination of τὸ γεννώμενον ἅγιον could be:

  1. γεννώμενον as subst. and the adj. ἅγιον as pred. ("the one [or "child"] to be born will be holy, he will be called . . ." NRSV, NLT, NET; ZG 172; Fitzmyer 351 [though arguing for an implied form of εἰμί], thus, following the conj., Jesus is God's Son because of the Spirit's activity [*pace* Fitzmyer, if the virginal conception is the reason Jesus is called the Son of God, this does not rule out preexistence]);

2. γεννώμενον as attrib. and the adj. ἅγιον as subst. with both as the subj. of the sentence ("the holy one to be born will be called," HCSB, NIV; sim. KJV, NASB; BHGNT 33); or

*3. the adj. ἅγιον as well as υἱὸς θεοῦ are predicates of κληθήσεται ("the child to be born will be called holy—the Son of God," RSV, ESV; Bock 131; Bovon 1.52; Marshall 71; Nolland 55; Plummer 25; Stein 85–86; thus Jesus is holy or set apart because of the Spirit's activity; cf. the sim. cstr. in 2:23).

Κληθήσεται, see 1:32. The use of υἱὸς θεοῦ here goes beyond Davidic kingship (*pace* Bock 124–25) and refers to the unique relationship this holy one has with God (see refs. to Jesus as "Son" in 1:32). Thus the anar. expression υἱὸς θεοῦ is monadic (Wallace 249). Here, and in 1:32, Jesus' divine sonship is the precursor to the granting of Davidic kingship. On the nom. υἱός with the pass. vb., see 1:32.

1:36 The angel assures Mary that God is at work by telling her about Elizabeth (καὶ ἰδού, see 1:20; "And consider" HCSB). Ἐλισάβετ is a pendent nom. (Wallace 51–52). Συγγενίς ([appos.] nom. sg. fem. of συγγενίς, -ίδος, ἡ, "kinswoman" (RSV), "relative" (NRSV, and most EVV). The fem. pron. αὐτή is the subj. of συνείληφεν (3rd sg. pf. act. indic. of συλλαμβάνω, "conceive," see 1:24). Γήρει dat. sg. neut. of γῆρας, -ους, τό, "old age." The demonstrative pron. οὗτος is the subj. of ἐστίν. Μὴν ἕκτος, "sixth month" (see 1:24, 26; the art. is often omitted with ordinal numbers, T 192). The dat. αὐτῇ is a dat. of ref. ("with her" RSV, ESV; "for her" NRSV, HCSB). Elizabeth's prior condition is again noted with the attrib. ptc. καλουμένη (dat. sg. fem. of pres. pass. ptc. of καλέω, "call," "for her who was called" HCSB). Στείρᾳ (dat. sg. fem., see 1:7) is the complement in a double dat. cstr. in agreement with αὐτῇ (BHGNT 35).

1:37 Mary can be assured of these promises because (ὅτι) God's word is powerful. The double neg. οὐκ ἀδυνατήσει (3rd sg. fut. act. indic. of ἀδυνατέω, "impossible") with the subj. is emphatic. The comprehensive ref. to πᾶν ῥῆμα (nom. sg. neut. of ῥῆμα, -ατος, τό) could refer more generally to all that God says and does ("nothing will be impossible" most EVV; BDF §302[1]; Bock 126; Bovon 1.53; Fitzmyer 352; cf. Acts 10:37; on ῥήματα as events, cf. 1:65; 2:15, 19, 51). The use of ῥῆμα in Mary's response in the following verse, however, indicates that it is a reference to the promises spoken in this context ("no word . . . will ever fail" NIV; sim. RV; Robertson, *Pictures* 15). Παρά with the gen. τοῦ θεοῦ highlights "ultimate agency" (Wallace 433; "source" ZG 172; on this use of the prep. cf. BDAG 756b; cf. μὴ ἀδυνατεῖ παρὰ τῷ θεῷ ῥῆμα in LXX Gen 18:14; Marshall 72; Pao and Schnabel 260c).

1:38 In response to this announcement, Mary declares (ἰδού, see 1:20) that she is (with ἐστίν implied, T 305) the Lord's "slave" (δούλη nom. sg. fem. of δούλη, -ης, ἡ, "female slave," BDAG 259d; elsewhere only 1:48 and Acts 2:18 in the NT; here it is the subj. of a nom. clause, BHGNT 36; "You see before you the Lord's servant" NJB; "bond-slave" NASB). Κυρίου is used without the art. as a proper name (Marshall 72). Mary expresses her glad submission as the Lord's slave that these events would happen (γένοιτο 3rd sg. 2nd aor. mid. optative of dep. γίνομαι, on the optative cf. BDF §384;

Wallace 483; expressing acceptance, Bock 131) according to the word of the angel (κατὰ τὸ ῥῆμά σου). Ἀπῆλθεν (see 1:23, here "departed" NASB, ESV).

HOMILETICAL SUGGESTIONS

God's Surprising Power (1:26–38)
1. An unexpected recipient (1:26–30)
2. An unending reign (1:31–33)
3. A supernatural beginning (1:34–38)

C. ELIZABETH'S EXCLAMATION AND MARY'S PRAISE (1:39–56)

Elizabeth's exclamation of blessing and Mary's praise combine the two previous announcement stories and form a fitting conclusion to this section.

1:39 The aor. ptc. Ἀναστᾶσα (nom. sg. fem. of 2nd aor. act. ptc. of ἀνίστημι, "arise," intrans.) is attendant circumstance (with ἐπορεύθη 3rd sg. aor. pass. indic. of dep. πορεύομαι, "go") and is pleonastic (BDF §419[2]; Z §363; ZG 172; Fitzmyer 362; these two vbs. are regularly combined in the LXX and Luke-Acts with ref. to setting out on a journey; cf. 15:18; 17:19; Acts 8:26–27; 9:11; 10:20; 22:10). The temp. ἐν ταῖς ἡμέραις ταύταις is general but links the following events closely with the preceding ("at this time" NASB, cf. BHGNT 38). The three prep. phrases with εἰς (1:39–40) indicate Mary's destination with increasing specificity (Nolland 65). Ὀρεινήν acc. sg. fem. of ὀρεινός, -ή, -όν, "hill country" is a common term in the LXX but only occurs here and 1:65 in the NT (BDAG 721d). Μετὰ σπουδῆς (gen. sg. fem. of σπουδή, -ῆς, ἡ) "with haste" (ESV), "hurried" (HCSB, NIV) reflects Mary's immediate response (Bock 134; Bovon 1.58; Marshall 80). The gen. Ἰούδα is locat. (BHGNT 38; Marshall 80).

1:40 Εἰσῆλθεν 3rd sg. 2nd aor. act. indic. of dep. εἰσέρχομαι, "enter." Ἠσπάσατο 3rd sg. aor. mid. indic. of dep. ἀσπάζομαι, "greet."

1:41 Ἐγένετο, see 1:5 (with ὡς see 1:23). Ἤκουσεν 3rd sg. aor. act. indic. of ἀκούω, "hear" (with ἡ Ἐλισάβετ as the subj.). Ἀσπασμόν, "greeting" (see 1:29; on the acc. with ἀκούω cf. BDF §173). Τῆς Μαρίας, subj. gen. Ἐσκίρτησεν 3rd sg. aor. act. indic. of σκιρτάω, "leap" (only here, 1:44; 6:23 in the NT). Βρέφος nom. sg. neut. of βρέφος, -ους, τό, "baby" (here and in 1:44 for an unborn child; in 2:12, 16, a newly born child; κοιλίᾳ, dat. sg. fem., see 1:15) is the subj. of ἐσκίρτησεν. Ἐπλήσθη 3rd sg. aor. pass. indic. of πίμπλημι, "fill." Πνεύματος ἁγίου is gen. of content (Wallace 94; see 1:15).

1:42 Filled with the Spirit, Elizabeth then cries out (ἀνεφώνησεν 3rd sg. aor. act. indic. of ἀναφωνέω, "cry out," "exclaimed" NIV, "call aloud" LSJ 126c) with a "loud voice" (κραυγῇ dat. sg. fem. of κραυγή, -ῆς, ἡ; μεγάλη, dat. sg. fem. of μέγας, μεγάλη, μέγα) a declaration of the privileged position Mary is in. Εὐλογημένη (nom. sg. fem. of pf. pass. ptc. of εὐλογέω, "bless") is a pred. nom. (Wallace 618; with an implied form of εἰμί). The ptc. is used here as a positive adj. for the superl. (i.e., "most blessed" T 31; Wallace 298; Z §146; ZG 173; though cf. BDF §245[3] for comparative, i.e., "more blessed"). This evaluation is dependent upon her Son as the following declaration of blessing shows (Marshall 81). The nom. ptc. εὐλογημένος (masc. in agreement with ὁ καρπός) is also pred. "The fruit of your womb" is a Heb. (Bock 137; κοιλίας, see 1:15). The notes of blessing in these opening scenes of Luke 1 (vv. 28, 42) recur again at the conclusion of Luke 24 (vv. 50–51; Bovon 1.59).

1:43 The adv. πόθεν ("from where") introduces a question of cause or reason (BDAG 838d; LN 89.38; "How could this happen to me . . .?" HCSB) with ἐστίν (T 240) or γίνομαι (Bock 140; Marshall 81) implied. Ἵνα introduces an epex. clause which explains what "this" (τοῦτο) is (T 45, 139; Z §410; ZG 173; Wallace 476 lists this as possible; BDF §394 notes that an inf. is usual when an epex. phrase refers to a fact; Fitzmyer 364; Marshall 81). Ἔλθη 3rd sg. 2nd aor. act. subjunc. of dep. ἔρχομαι, "come." Although τοῦ κυρίου μου may simply indicate respect in recognition that the child will be superior to her (Bock 137; a messianic ref. Marshall 81; Plummer 29), the use of κύριος by Elizabeth in a few verses (1:45) and earlier by the angel in the announcement to her husband, Zechariah (1:17; cf. 1:76; 2:11; 3:4), indicates a more exalted view of the child early in Luke's narrative (cf. Rowe 40–49).

1:44 Ἰδού see 1:20 (apart from 2 Cor 7:11, the emphatic ἰδοὺ γάρ is only used by Luke in the NT). Ὡς, "temp." Ἀσπασμοῦ, see 1:29 (epex. gen. or gen. of source, BHGNT 40). Ἐγένετο . . . εἰς τὰ ὦτά μου, "reached my ears" (NASB, HCSB, NIV; a Sem. T 254). Ἐσκίρτησεν, see 1:41. Ἐν ἀγαλλιάσει expresses manner (dat. sg. fem., see 1:14–15; or causal, Z §119; ZG 173). Βρέφος (see 1:41; κοιλία, see 1:15, 41) is the subj. of ἐσκίρτησεν.

1:45 Mary is described as "blessed" (μακαρία, a pred. adj.) because she has "believed" (πιστεύσασα nom. sg. fem. of aor. act. ptc. of πιστεύω, a subst. ptc. Wallace 620; not voc. as suggested by Z §34; ZG 173; cf. T 35). Ὅτι expresses the content of what Mary believed ("believed that," NASB, ESV, NIV; ZG 173; Bock 139; Bovon 1.59; Marshall 82; Nolland 68) rather than the cause of Mary's blessing ("blessed because" HCSB; sim. KJV; Z §416; Fitzmyer 365). In the following phrase, τελείωσις (nom. sg. fem. of τελείωσις, -εως, ἡ, "fulfillment") is the subj. (i.e., "the fulfillment will be," BHGNT 41; "that there would be a fulfillment," NRSV, NASB, ESV; ἔσται, see 1:14). The subst. ptc. λελαλημένοις (dat. pl. neut. of pf. pass. ptc. of λαλέω, "speak") is a dat. of ref. The fem. pron. αὐτῇ is a dat. of indir. obj. Παρά indicates the ultimate source (i.e., by the angel but at the Lord's command; BDAG 756b; Wallace 433; Z §90; Bovon 1.59; Marshall 82; not "from the side of" as in T 273). Thus (1) Mary, who has faith, is contrasted with Zechariah (1:20), and (2) the trustworthiness of the Lord's word is highlighted (1:37).

1:46 Mary's response of praise begins with two lines that are parallel (1:46–47). Μεγαλύνει 3rd sg. pres. act. indic. of μεγαλύνω, "make or declare great" ("magnifies" NRSV, ESV; "exalts" NASB; "proclaims the greatness of" HCSB; "glorifies" NIV). In 1:46–49 Mary's praise relates to her unique experience (μου, μου, τῆς δούλης αὐτοῦ, με, μοι) before she turns to praise God for his mercy to his people (Nolland 69). Thus, the uniqueness of Mary's experience is linked to God's saving action for his people.

1:47 In keeping with the parallelism of 1:46–47, Mary's soul is synonymous with her spirit (Bock 148–49; Fitzmyer 366; Marshall 82; a Heb. for "I"). Similarly, to "exalt" the Lord is to rejoice or "exult" in God. The aor. of ἠγαλλίασεν (3rd sg. aor. act. indic. of ἀγαλλιάω, "exult, rejoice") could be (cf. BHGNT 42):

 *1. "timeless" or "comprehensive" and parallel with the pres. tense of 1:46 ("rejoices" NRSV, ESV, NIV; BDF §333[2]; Z §260; Fitzmyer 366; Marshall 82);

 2. "ingressive" ("has begun to rejoice" NET; Bock 150; Bovon 1.64 tentatively; Nolland 69); or

3. as a perfect ("has rejoiced" NASB, HCSB; Wallace 565; Plummer 31–33; cf. Campbell, 2007 125, "perfective contrast" with the "imperfective" pres. tense).

Ἐπὶ τῷ θεῷ is causal (BHGNT 42). The dat. sg. masc. τῷ σωτῆρι (of σωτήρ, -ῆρος, ὁ) is appos. to "God" (Wallace 153). For σωτήρ in Luke-Acts cf. also 2:11; Acts 5:31; 13:23. The use of σωτηρία in 1:69, 71, 77; 19:9 suggests that, as with the language of "redemption" in Luke 1–2, the nature of God's "salvation" will be clarified in Luke-Acts as the "already–not yet" saving rule of the Lord Jesus.

1:48 Two reasons for Mary's praise are given in 1:48 and 49. The first reason is because (ὅτι) God, her Savior, has been gracious toward her. He has "looked upon" (ἐπέβλεψεν 3rd sg. aor. act. indic. of ἐπιβλέπω "looked with favor on" NRSV, HCSB; BDAG 368c; MM 236a; ZG 173; "had regard for" NASB; cf. 9:38) the "humble state" (ταπείνωσιν acc. sg. fem. of ταπείνωσις, -εως, ἡ; BDAG 990d; Fitzmyer 367; Marshall 82; Nolland 69; rather than "humiliation") of Mary, his "slave" (τῆς δούλης αὐτοῦ, see 1:38). The aor. may look back (to the conception, Bock 150) or, as with 1:47, may be "comprehensive" (as indicated by the following explanation which anticipates future "blessing"). Γάρ introduces a clause which strengthens the point being made and reiterates Mary's sense of her blessedness in 1:46–47 (BHGNT 43; Nolland 70; on ἰδού, see 1:20). Ἀπὸ τοῦ νῦν is temp. The art. τοῦ (gen. following ἀπό) turns the adv. νῦν into a subst. (BHGNT 43; cf. the cstr. in 5:10; 12:52; 22:18, 69). Πᾶσαι αἱ γενεαί is the subj. of μακαριοῦσίν (3rd pl. fut. act. indic. of μακαρίζω, "call or consider blessed," cf. LN 25.120).

1:49 Ὅτι introduces a parallel with 1:48a and a second reason for Mary's praise (Bock 151; Fitzmyer 367) rather than a reason for why generations will call her blessed (1:48b; Marshall 83).

Μεγαλύνει ἡ ψυχή μου . . .
καὶ ἠγαλλίασεν τὸ πνεῦμά μου . . .
    ὅτι ἐπέβλεψεν . . .
      [ἰδοὺ γὰρ ἀπὸ τοῦ νῦν μακαριοῦσίν με πᾶσαι αἱ γενεαί]
    ὅτι ἐποίησέν . . .

The subj. of ἐποίησεν (3rd sg. aor. act. indic. of ποιέω) is ὁ δυνατός "the Mighty One" (NRSV, NASB, HCSB, NIV), "he who is mighty" (RSV, ESV, sim. KJV); a designation that recalls 1:35 (δύναμις), 37 (οὐκ ἀδυνατήσει), and anticipates 1:52 (δυνάστας). The subst. adj. μεγάλα (acc. pl. neut.) is the dir. obj. of ἐποίησεν. The dat. μοι (enclitic) is a dat. of advantage. The adj. ἅγιον is pred. in a verbless clause ("His name is holy" HCSB; ἐστίν is implied, T 296), which should perhaps be linked with 1:50 (the parallel καί, the ref. to "fearing," Nolland 70).

1:50 In 1:50 (and perhaps 1:49b) Mary transitions from praise specifically related to her, to praise for God's faithfulness to all who fear him (a theme that will be extended to "God-fearers" in Acts, cf. e.g., Acts 10:35; 13:26). God's mighty power is expressed in his mercy to his people. God's mercy to his people will be a recurring theme in praise (cf. 1:54, 58, 72, 78). Τὸ ἔλεος αὐτοῦ is the subj. with ἐστίν implied. Εἰς γενεὰς καὶ γενεάς is idiomatic for "all generations" and is likely temp. ("from generation to generation" most EVV, sim. NASB; on this "distributive doubling" cf. BDF §493[2]; a Heb. Marshall 83). The subst. ptc. φοβουμένοις (dat. pl. masc. of pres. mid. ptc. of dep. φοβέομαι, "fear") is a dat. of advantage ("for those who fear him" NRSV, ESV). In this context, the fear is not that which is removed by the assurance of the angel, but that reverence which is appropriate before a holy and sovereign God (Nolland 71).

1:51 Ἐποίησεν (see 1:49) with κράτος (acc. sg. neut. of κράτος, -ους, τό, "strength," "power") expresses powerful action ("he has performed mighty deeds" NIV, sim. NASB, HCSB; "he has shown strength" ESV). Likewise, the instr. ἐν βραχίονι αὐτοῦ ("with his arm"; dat. sg. masc. of βραχίων, -ονος, ὁ) is an anthropomorphic expression, common in the LXX, for God's power (T 253). The similarity with 1:49 suggests that Mary's experience is linked to God's saving actions for his people (in a new exodus, Nolland 71). Just as God saves his people, so also he judges ("scatters") his enemies. Διεσκόρπισεν 3rd sg. aor. act. indic. of διασκορπίζω, "scatter." The subst. acc. adj. ὑπερηφάνους ("arrogant," "proud") is the obj. of διεσκόρπισεν (cf. 10:29; 16:15; 18:9–14). The dat. sg. fem. διανοίᾳ (of διάνοια, -ας, ἡ, "thought," "understanding"; καρδίας is sg. for a group, a Sem., T 23) could be:

1. a dat. of sphere ("in the thoughts of their hearts" NRSV, ESV; sim. NASB, NIV);
2. causal ("because of the thoughts of their hearts" HCSB); or
3. a dat. of ref. ("whose pride wells up from the sheer arrogance of their hearts" NET; BHGNT 45; ZG 173; Bock 156; Fitzmyer 368; Marshall 84).

The aor. vbs. in 1:51–54 have been understood as:

*1. prophetic of the future as already present (Z §259; Bock 155; Marshall 84);
2. gnomic (BDF §333[2]; T 74; Z §256); or
3. later Lukan refs. to past events (Fitzmyer 361).

The future hope expressed in 1:48 together with the anticipated fulfilment of the promises to Abraham (1:55) point to an ultimate fulfilment of all that the promised child will accomplish. Judgment on the proud as the enemies of Israel (1:51b) and helping Israel (1:54a) provide the framework for the reversal (in chiasm) of 1:52–53 (Nolland 72).

διεσκόρπισεν ὑπερηφάνους . . .
52   καθεῖλεν δυνάστας ἀπὸ θρόνων
              καὶ ὕψωσεν ταπεινούς,
53   πεινῶντας ἐνέπλησεν ἀγαθῶν
           καὶ πλουτοῦντας ἐξαπέστειλεν κενούς.
54 ἀντελάβετο Ἰσραήλ . . .

1:52 Καθεῖλεν 3rd sg. 2nd aor. act. indic. of καθαιρέω, "take down" ("toppled" HCSB). Δυνάστας (acc. pl. masc. of δυνάστης, -ου, ὁ) could be "the powerful" NRSV, or "the mighty" RSV, HCSB, ESV; in light of the contrast with ταπεινούς (a subst. adj.; acc. pl. masc. of ταπεινός, -ή, -όν, "the lowly" NRSV, HCSB; "the humble" ESV). The addition of ἀπὸ θρόνων ("from their thrones"), however, indicates that δυνάστας is likely "rulers" NASB, NIV. Ὕψωσεν 3rd sg. aor. act. indic. of ὑψόω, "lift up" NRSV, NIV; "exalt" NASB, HCSB, ESV. The people of God are often described in the OT as the humble who depend upon God (cf. Isa 2:11; 66:2; Luke 14:11; 18:14) and await his salvation.

1:53 Πεινῶντας acc. pl. masc. of pres. act. (subst.) ptc. of πεινάω, "to hunger." Ἐνέπλησεν 3rd sg. aor. act. indic. of ἐμπίπλημι, "fill," "satisfy." The gen. ἀγαθῶν is a gen. of content ("with good things," ZG 173). Πλουτοῦντας acc. pl. masc. of pres. act. (subst.) ptc. of πλουτέω, "be rich." Ἐξαπέστειλεν 3rd sg. aor. act. indic. of ἐξαποστέλλω, "send away." The acc. pl. masc. κενούς (of κενός, -ή, -όν, "empty") is the complement in a double acc. cstr. (BDAG 346a). This contrast between the "hungry" and the "rich" also introduces a prominent theme in Luke-Acts in which the "rich" focuses on those who are not "rich towards God" (cf. 12:21).

1:54 In 1:54–55 Mary's praise concludes with a specific focus on God's faithfulness to his promises. Ἀντελάβετο 3rd sg. 2nd aor. mid. indic. of dep. ἀντιλαμβάνομαι, "help." Ἰσραήλ is a gen. complement to ἀντελάβετο (BDAG 89a) and the gen. sg. masc. παιδός (of παῖς, παιδός, ὁ and ἡ) is in appos. to Ἰσραήλ ("his servant Israel"; cf. Isa 41:8–9; cf. 1:77; Acts 1:6–8; Pao and Schnabel 262c–d). The aor. pass. inf. μνησθῆναι (of dep. μιμνήσκομαι "remember") could be (cf. BHGNT 46):

   *1. causal ("He has helped . . . because he remembered" NET; Bock 159; Marshall 85; i.e., God acts on the basis of his covenant mercy);
   2. epex. ("He has helped . . . remembering" NIV; Z §391–92; ZG 174; Nolland 73);
   3. result ("with the result that he showed mercy" BDF §391[4]; T 136); or
   4. purpose ("in order to remember mercy" Fitzmyer 368).

As Marshall (85) notes, God's "remembering is effective and leads to action." The gen. ἐλέους (cf. 1:50) is the dir. obj. of μνησθῆναι (BDAG 652b–c).

1:55 Καθώς introduces a comparison; God's mercy is in keeping with his promises. Ἐλάλησεν 3rd sg. aor. act. indic. of λαλέω, "he spoke" (ESV), in this context, "he promised" (NIV; ZG 174). Following the reference to God's promises "to our fathers," the dat. τῷ Ἀβραὰμ καὶ τῷ σπέρματι αὐτοῦ could be:

   *1. a continuation from 1:54 as the modifier to μνησθῆναι ἐλέους (NIV; BHGNT 47; Bock 160; Bovon 1.63; Marshall 85; Nolland 73; with 1:55a as parenthetical);
   2. in appos. to πρὸς τοὺς πατέρας (NRSV, HCSB, ESV; Fitzmyer 369; Green 99); or

3. a dat. of interest (advantage, "in favor of," T 238; Z §55; ZG 174).

The first option is perhaps most likely. As Bock notes, "speaking . . . forever" is awkward here, and it is unusual for a dat. in appos. to follow an acc. The art. τῷ might be used here to show the case of the indecl. noun Ἀβραάμ. Thus, God's mercy to Abraham and "his seed" extends forever.

1:56 Μαριάμ is the subj. of Ἔμεινεν (3rd sg. aor. act. indic. of μένω, "remain") and is mentioned again here after the hymn to show the resumption of the narrative (Marshall 85). The pron. αὐτῇ ("her") refers to Elizabeth (specified in NIV). This three-month stay means Elizabeth's pregnancy is now at nine months (1:26, 36). The acc. μῆνας τρεῖς ("three months"; see 1:24) is extent of time (approximately, ὡς, LN 78.42). Ὑπέστρεψεν 3rd sg. aor. act. indic. of ὑποστρέφω, "return" (intrans.; 32 of 35 uses in the NT occur in Luke-Acts). The ref. to "her home" (εἰς τὸν οἶκον αὐτῆς) indicates Mary is not yet married to Joseph (Marshall 85).

HOMILETICAL SUGGESTIONS

Glorifying God with Joy in Jesus (1:39–56)

1. Joy in anticipation of God keeping his word (1:39–45).
2. Joy in God as the Mighty One who mercifully helps the humble (1:46–49).
3. Joy in God as the Faithful One who mercifully saves his people and judges enemies (1:50–56).

D. JOHN'S BIRTH AND NAMING (1:57–66)

In the second half of these infancy narratives, the promises of the births of John and Jesus reach their fulfillment, bring joy to God's people, and anticipate the fulfillment of what has been said about the roles of John and Jesus. As with the announcements, the birth of John and the resulting praise point forward to the coming of Jesus, the Lord (Marshall 86).

1:57 Χρόνος is the subj. of ἐπλήσθη (see 1:23 for this use of the term and 1:41 for this form; "fulfilled" RV; "had come" NASB, HCSB). The dat. (of ref.) τῇ . . . Ἐλισάβετ is perhaps placed forward to highlight the shift of attention in the narrative back to Elizabeth (BDF §472[2]; BHGNT 48). The art. 2nd aor. act. inf. τοῦ τεκεῖν (of τίκτω, "give birth") is epex. to ὁ χρόνος (the acc. αὐτήν is the subj. of τεκεῖν). Ἐγέννησεν 3rd sg. aor. act. indic. of γεννάω, "give birth to." Following the time notes given in 1:24, 26, 56, the time has now come for the birth. The promise that Elizabeth would "bear" a son (cf. 1:13) is now fulfilled.

1:58 The nom. pl. masc. subst. adjs. περίοικοι (of περίοικος, -ον) and συγγενεῖς (of συγγενής, -ές; "her neighbors and relatives") are the subj. of ἤκουσαν (3rd pl. aor. act. indic. of ἀκούω, "hear"). These neighbors and relatives had heard that "the Lord had magnified (ἐμεγάλυνεν 3rd sg. aor. act. indic. of μεγαλύνω, "make great," "exult") his mercy towards her" (RV, "shown great mercy" most EVV). On ἔλεος with μετά ("mercy to her") see BDAG 636d (BHGNT 49). The impf. συνέχαιρον (3rd pl. impf. act. indic. of συγχαίρω, "rejoice with") could be ingressive ("began to rejoice" NET; BHGNT 50) or continuous ("were rejoicing with" NASB; "rejoiced with" most EVV; Robertson, *Pictures* 17). See the promise in 1:14.

1:59 Ἐγένετο, see 1:5. Ὀγδόῃ dat. sg. fem. of ὄγδοος, -η, -ον, "eighth." Ἦλθον 3rd pl. 2nd aor. act. indic. of dep. ἔρχομαι, "come." The inf. περιτεμεῖν (2nd aor. act. of περιτέμνω, "to circumcise") expresses purpose (the acc. τὸ παιδίον is the dir. obj.; ZG 174). The impf. ἐκάλουν (3rd pl. impf. act. indic. of καλέω, "call") could be:

    *1. conative ("were going to name him" HCSB, NIV; "would have called him" ESV; BDF §326; Robertson, *Pictures* 17; T 65; Wallace 551; Z §273; ZG 174; Bock 166; Bovon 1.70; Fitzmyer 380; Marshall 88); or

    2. ingressive ("began calling him"; i.e., before Elizabeth corrected them, BHGNT 47, 50).

The neut. αὐτό refers to παιδίον (καλέω normally takes a double acc., Marshall 88). Ἐπὶ τῷ ὀνόματι is idiomatic for naming the child after his father (BDAG 366d; BHGNT 50).

1:60 Ἀποκριθεῖσα nom. sg. fem. of aor. pass. ptc. of dep. ἀποκρίνομαι, "answer" (see 1:19). The neg. οὐχί and ἀλλά introduce a corrective (BHGNT 51). The fut. κληθήσεται (see 1:32) functions as an impv. ("he must be named" NET). Elizabeth is obeying the instructions of 1:13. God, rather than family tradition, has determined the child's name. The special role God has for John, and perhaps the newness signified by John's coming, is accentuated (Nolland 79).

1:61 Ὅτι, recitative. Οὐδείς, "none," is the subj. of ἐστίν. Συγγενείας gen. sg. fem. of συγγένεια, -ας, ἡ, "relatives" (ἐκ τῆς συγγενείας, is partitive). The nom. sg. masc. rel. pron. ὅς is the subj. of καλεῖται (3rd sg. pres. pass. indic. of καλέω, "call"). The dat. τῷ ὀνόματι τούτῳ is instr.

1:62 Ἐνένευον 3rd pl. impf. act. indic. of ἐννεύω, "make signs" (indicating that Zechariah was deaf as well as unable to speak; ZG 174; Bock 168; Marshall 88; see 1:22). The impf. suits the ongoing action involved in making signs (Robertson, *Pictures* 17; Wallace 544). The art. τό serves to nominalize the following interr. clause so that it becomes the dir. obj. of ἐνένευον (BDAG 689a; BDF §267[2]; BHGNT 52; hence it is untranslatable, ZG 174; Luke often uses τό to introduce an indir. question, Fitzmyer 381; Marshall 89). The interr. τί is used in an indir. question (T 130; Wallace 345). The particle ἄν with the optative θέλοι (3rd sg. pres. act. optative of θέλω, "wish," "want") is the apodosis of a fourth-class cond. clause "what he would have called him" RSV; sim. NIV; R 739, 938, 1021, 1044; Robertson, *Pictures* 17; BDF §385[1]; with ἄν see 6:11; 9:46; 15:26; cf. 1:29). The implied protasis could be "if he was able to speak" (BHGNT 52; Wallace 484, 700; Z §346). The inf. καλεῖσθαι (pres. pass. of καλέω) is complementary.

1:63 The aor. ptc. αἰτήσας (nom. sg. masc. of aor. act. ptc. of αἰτέω, "ask," though in this context, "motioned" NLT) is temp. Πινακίδιον acc. sg. neut. of πινακίδιον, -ου, τό, "little tablet," "writing tablet" most EVV. Ἔγραψεν 3rd sg. aor. act. indic. of γράφω, "write." Λέγων is pleonastic (a Heb., BDF §420[2]; Robertson, *Pictures* 18; Wallace 649–50; Z §368; expressing manner, BHGNT 52). On ὄνομα as the subj. (hence "His name is John," all EVV), see T 305; Wallace 43. As with Elizabeth in 1:60, Zechariah obeys the instructions of 1:13. Ἐθαύμασαν 3rd pl. aor. act. indic. of θαυμάζω, "marvel," "astonishment" (NIV, sim. NASB), "amazed" (HCSB); probably at their insistence on this unusual name (Bock 169).

1:64 Ἀνεῴχθη 3rd sg. aor. pass. indic. of ἀνοίγω, "open." Παραχρῆμα, adv. "immediately" (sixteen times in Luke-Acts out of eighteen in the NT [elsewhere only in Matt 21:19–20]); here highlighting the instantaneous change in Zechariah's speech in keeping with the angel's promise in 1:20. Ἡ γλῶσσα is the double subj. (with τὸ στόμα) of the sg. vb. ἀνεῴχθη ("zeugma" with the verb making better sense with the former subject, BHGNT 53; BDF §479[2]; Bock 171; Fitzmyer 381; Marshall 89; Nolland 80; the implied vb. is probably an aor. pass. ἐλύθη, "was loosed," cf. mss. D *f*¹, BHGNT 53; NASB, ESV). The impf. ἐλάλει (3rd sg. impf. act. indic. of λαλέω, "speak") is ingressive ("began to speak" NRSV, NASB, HCSB, NIV). Εὐλογῶν (nom. sg. masc. of pres. act. ptc. of εὐλογέω, "bless," "praising" NRSV, HCSB, NIV) could be *manner or attendant circumstance (BHGNT 53).

1:65 Ἐγένετο, see 1:5 (though here it is with φόβος as the subj.; the word order may be emphatic, BDF §472[2]; Bock 170; Marshall 89). Περιοικοῦντας acc. pl. masc. of pres. act. (subst.) ptc. of περιοικέω, "those who lived around them" HCSB; "neighbors" NRSV, ESV, NIV (cf. περίοικοι in 1:58). Ἐν ὅλῃ τῇ ὀρεινῇ ("in all the hill country"; see 1:39) is locat. Πάντα τὰ ῥήματα ταῦτα ("all these things" most EVV) is the subj.

of διελαλεῖτο (3rd sg. impf. pass. indic. of διαλαλέω, "discussed"). The impf. implies continued discussion (NASB, HCSB; Marshall 89). On ῥήματα as "events," see 1:37.

1:66 The combination of ἔθεντο (3rd pl. 2nd aor. mid. indic. of τίθημι) with ἐν τῇ καρδίᾳ αὐτῶν is idiomatic for thinking about something carefully (LN 30.76; 29.2; "pondered them" NRSV; "took it to heart" HCSB; see 1:51). Ἀκούσαντες nom. pl. masc. of aor. act. (subst.) ptc. of ἀκούω (cf. BDF §413[2]; BHGNT 54; R 772–73; Wallace 620–21) is the subj. of ἔθεντο. Λέγοντες (nom. pl. masc. of pres. act. ptc. of λέγω) expresses manner (BHGNT 55; this ptc. is often pleonastic after vbs. of saying [or thinking] in Luke as a subset of the ptc. of means or manner, cf. Wallace 649–50; Z §368). On the use of the interr. τί for a person see BDF §298[2]. Thus, the question focuses on what will become of John in terms of what kind of role he will have (Bock 170; Marshall 89). The reason (γάρ) for the speculation concerning John's future is the evidence of the Lord's "hand" with him (χεὶρ κυρίου, i.e., the Lord's presence and power; cf. Acts 4:28; 7:25; 11:21). The use of ἦν indicates that this rationale for the question is provided by Luke and not part of the dir. speech (most EVV, Marshall 90; Nolland 80).

For Homiletical Suggestions see the end of the next section.

E. ZECHARIAH'S PRAISE (1:67–80)

Zechariah's praise follows as inspired commentary on the significance of these events and thus is the culmination of the account of John's birth (Marshall 86). Zechariah's praise is in two parts: first, praise for God's salvation in keeping with his promises (1:67–75); second, praise for John's role in going before the Lord to make known his salvation (1:76–79).

1:67 The opening of Zechariah's mouth leads inevitably to praise (1:64, a common theme in these chapters) as the question raised in 1:66 is now addressed (*pace* BHGNT 55; Nolland 82–83). The nom. sg. masc. πατήρ (of πατήρ, πατρός, ὁ) is in appos. to Ζαχαρίας which is perhaps placed forward for emphasis (BDF §472[2]; Bock 177; cf. 1:57). Ἐπλήσθη, see 1:41. Ἐπροφήτευσεν 3rd sg. aor. act. indic. of προφητεύω, "prophesy" (cf. Acts 2:17–18; λέγων, see 1:63).

1:68 Zechariah's praise begins with one long sentence that runs through to the end of 1:75. This outline of the main developments will be explained below:

Εὐλογητὸς . . .
    ὅτι ἐπεσκέψατο
    καὶ ἐποίησεν λύτρωσιν . . .
    ⁶⁹ καὶ ἤγειρεν κέρας σωτηρίας . . .
    ⁷⁰ . . .
            ⁷¹ σωτηρίαν ἐξ . . .
                    ⌐⁷² ποιῆσαι ἔλεος . . .
                    ⌊καὶ μνησθῆναι διαθήκης . . .
                                ⁷³ ὅρκον ὃν ὤμοσεν . . .
                              → τοῦ δοῦναι ἡμῖν ⁷⁴ . . .
                                λατρεύειν αὐτῷ . . .

Εὐλογητός nom. sg. masc. of εὐλογητός, -ή, -όν, "blessed," is a pred. adj. and κύριος is the nom. subj. of this verbless clause (with ὁ θεός in appos.). The function of the art. τοῦ is to identify the case of the indecl. noun Ἰσραήλ (Wallace 241). The reason for praise is because (ὅτι) God has "visited" (ἐπεσκέψατο 3rd sg. aor. mid. indic. of dep. ἐπισκέπτομαι, "visit") in the sense of "come to help" (NET; BDAG 378d; LN 85.11; cf. also 1:78; 7:16; Acts 15:14; see ἐπισκοπῆς, 19:44). This "visitation" is further described with the periph. cstr. ἐποίησεν λύτρωσιν (acc. sg. fem. of λύτρωσις, -εως, ἡ; "provided redemption" HCSB; ἐποίησεν, see 1:49; here BDAG 839d; for "redemption" cf. also λύτρωσις 2:38; ἀπολύτρωσις 21:28; λυτρόομαι 24:21). On the aor. see 1:51 (cf. also the fut. in 1:78). The dat. τῷ λαῷ is advantage. The nature of this redemption still requires clarification in light of Jesus' death and resurrection (24:21, 25–27, 44–49) and awaits the final consummation (e.g., 18:7–8). In this context it includes the final saving rule of God (1:74) and forgiveness of sins (1:77).

1:69 Ἤγειρεν 3rd sg. aor. act. indic. of ἐγείρω, "raise up" (i.e., "brought onto the stage of history" Marshall 91). The phrase κέρας σωτηρίας (acc. sg. neut. of κέρας, -ατος, τό; gen. sg. fem. of σωτηρία, -ας, ἡ [see 1:47]; "horn of salvation") is a metaphor for strength and could refer to the general idea of "salvation/deliverance" (BHGNT 57) or, in light of the following reference to ἐν οἴκῳ Δαυίδ, to the Messiah as powerful ("a mighty Savior" NLT, sim. NRSV; LN 76.16; ZG 175; Bock 180; Marshall 91; i.e., already looking ahead to the One John will go before). Παιδός, "servant" (see 1:54), is in appos. to Δαυίδ.

1:70 As is often the case in Luke-Acts, this action of God is in keeping with (καθώς) what he has already promised in Scripture (cf. 1:55; "his holy prophets," on the gen. sg. neut. στόματος cf. T 25). Ἐλάλησεν, see 1:55. Ἀπ' αἰῶνος is idiomatic for "long ago" (NIV, sim. most EVV; LN 67.25; Bovon 1.73; Marshall 91).

1:71 The acc. sg. fem. σωτηρίαν is in appos. to κέρας σωτηρίας (see 1:69) after the parenthetical remark in 1:70 (ZG 175; Bock 182; Fitzmyer 384; Marshall 91). Μισούντων gen. pl. masc. of pres. act. (subst.) ptc. of μισέω. Deliverance from enemies implies also a reversal of the judgment which led to this condition (hence 1:72 [mercy]; and 1:77 [forgiveness]). As the narrative unfolds, the enemies of God's people are those who hate the Lord Jesus and his people (for "hate" cf. 6:22; 19:14; 21:17 [here incl.

those who hand Jesus' followers over to synagogues]; for "enemies" cf. 10:19; 19:27, 43 [here incl. those who bring judgment on Jerusalem for rejecting Christ]; 20:43).

1:72 The inf. ποιῆσαι (aor. act. of ποιέω, "perform" RSV, "dealt" HCSB, "show" NASB, ESV, NIV) and the inf. μνησθῆναι (see 1:54) could be (cf. BHGNT 58):

*1. result (BDF §391[4]; BHGNT 58; T 136; what salvation shows, Bock 183);
2. purpose (ZG 175; of God's action, Marshall 92 [suggests either purpose or result]; Plummer 41); or
3. epex. to σωτηρίαν in 1:71 ("Thus . . ." NRSV; Fitzmyer 384).

On μετά ("to") with ποιῆσαι ἔλεος see BDAG 636d; BDF §206[3] (cf. 1:58). As 1:55 and 1:73 show, πατέρων ἡμῶν includes Abraham. The gen. sg. fem. διαθήκης ἁγίας is the obj. of μνησθῆναι (BDAG 652b–c). God's action of mercy is paralleled with his action of "remembering" (i.e., carrying out) his covenant promises (e.g., Exod 2:24).

1:73 Ὅρκον (acc. sg. masc. of ὅρκος, -ου, ὁ, "oath") is in appos. to διαθήκης ("covenant") from 1:72. The acc. case of ὅρκον is due to assimilation to the following acc. rel. pron. ὅν ("inverse attraction," BDF §295; T 324; Wallace 339; Z §19; ZG 175) which is the dir. obj. (Wallace 190) of ὤμοσεν (3rd sg. aor. act. indic. of ὀμνύω, "swear," "take an oath," cf. Acts 2:30). The acc. τὸν πατέρα is in appos. to Ἀβραάμ. The inf. τοῦ δοῦναι (2nd aor. act. of δίδωμι, "give," "grant" most EVV, "enable" NIV) will be completed with the inf. λατρεύειν in 1:74 ("This oath grants that we . . . may serve him" NET). The art. inf. τοῦ δοῦναι could:

*1. give the purpose of the oath (T 141 [though "weak"]; Z §385; Bock 184; Plummer 41–42). Thus God acts in mercy, remembering his covenant promises, so that his people may be free to serve him (cf. Exod 3:12); or
2. give the content of the oath (epex., BHGNT 59; Z §392; Bovon 1.74; Fitzmyer 385; Marshall 92; Nolland 87).

1:74 The adv. ἀφόβως ("without fear") modifies λατρεύειν (pres. act. inf. of λατρεύω, "serve," LN 53.14), and (as noted above) λατρεύειν is the dir. obj. of τοῦ δοῦναι in 1:73 (T 149; perhaps ἀφόβως is placed forward for emphasis, Bock 185; Fitzmyer 385; cf. Marshall 92). Ῥυσθέντας acc. pl. masc. of aor. pass. (temp.) ptc. of dep. ῥύομαι, "rescue" ("being delivered" most EVV) picks up on the salvation mentioned in 1:71 (Nolland 88). The acc. case of the ptc. agrees with the implied subj. of the inf. (BHGNT 60; Robertson, *Pictures* 19; ZG 175). Deliverance from enemies and reversal of judgment are not ends in themselves; they are to free God's people to serve and worship him.

1:75 Ἐν ὁσιότητι καὶ δικαιοσύνῃ (dat. sg. fem. of ὁσιότης, -ητος, ἡ; "in holiness and righteousness") expresses the manner of this service (pointing to the transformation anticipated in the new covenant). The dat. πάσαις ταῖς ἡμέραις expresses extent of time (i.e., overlapping with the acc. of time, BDF §201; T 243; Wallace 156).

1:76 With καὶ σὺ δέ and the voc. παιδίον, Zechariah focuses on John and his role in this climactic arrival of God's salvation. The pron. σύ is the subj. of κληθήσῃ (2nd sg. fut.

pass. indic. of καλέω, "call," cf. 1:13, 59–63; with the sense "be," see 1:32). The nom. sg. masc. προφήτης is the complement in a double nom. cstr. (BDAG 502d–503a). Although Jesus is the υἱὸς ὑψίστου (see 1:32; 8:28), John is the προφήτης ὑψίστου. Furthermore, John will go (προπορεύσῃ 2nd sg. fut. mid. indic. of dep. προπορεύομαι, "go on before") "before the Lord" (ἐνώπιον κυρίου, cf. 1:16–17; 7:26–27). In the narrative context of Luke 1–2, Jesus is identified as "Lord," Yahweh incarnate (see 1:17, 43; Nolland 89; Rowe 70; though Father and Son are distinguished, 1:32). The purpose of this advance is to prepare (ἑτοιμάσαι, see 1:17) "his ways" (although the pl. ὁδούς may allude to people [BHGNT 61], the sg. and pl. may be used without any significant change in meaning [e.g., LXX Ps 15:11; Bock 197]).

1:77 The inf. δοῦναι (see 1:73) modifies the previous inf. ἑτοιμάσαι either as (cf. BHGNT 61):

1. means ("by giving knowledge"); or
*2. epex. ("that is, to give the knowledge of salvation" BHGNT 48, 61; *pace* BHGNT, the art. τοῦ could be added for clarity and therefore continues the purpose expression of ἑτοιμάσαι, BDF §400[6]; T 142; Z §385; ZG 175; Bock 189; Marshall 93).

Thus, since ἑτοιμάσαι (1:76) expresses the purpose of John's ministry, the art. inf. δοῦναι, in explaining how John carries out this preparation, also clarifies the purpose of John's ministry of going before the Lord—i.e., so that salvation would come to the people of God. Σωτηρίας (obj. gen.) develops the refs. to "salvation" by Zechariah in 1:69, 71 so that the following prep. phrase ἐν ἀφέσει (dat. sg. fem. of ἄφεσις, -εως, ἡ) should now be seen as adding to the picture of Zechariah's hope (see 1:71). "Knowledge" (γνῶσιν acc. sg. fem. of γνῶσις, -εως, ἡ) of salvation here is the "inward appropriation" or "experience" of salvation (Bovon 1.75; Marshall 93). Ἐν ἀφέσει modifies σωτηρίας and could be instr. ("through" HCSB, NIV; "by" NRSV, NASB; ZG 175) or ref. ("in" RSV, ESV; cf. BHGNT 61; Fitzmyer 386; Marshall 93). Knowledge of God and forgiveness of sins are the new covenant hope and will become a major theme in Luke-Acts (cf. Jer 31:34; Luke 22:20; 24:47).

1:78 The reason for this salvation is "because of" (διά) God's own (a poss. gen.) "merciful compassion" (HCSB; σπλάγχνα acc. pl. neut. of σπλάγχνον, -ου, τό, with ἐλέους, "tender mercy" most EVV; "merciful heart" BDAG 316c). Ἐλέους, is an attrib. gen. (cf. 1:50, 54, 72; Z §40; ZG 175). The prep. and neut. rel. pron. ἐν οἷς (with the antecedent σπλάγχνα) introduces the circumstances in which "God's merciful compassion" is seen (Marshall 94). Ἀνατολή (nom. sg. fem. of ἀνατολή, -ῆς, ἡ), the subj. of ἐπισκέψεται (3rd sg. fut. mid. indic. of dep. ἐπισκέπτομαι, "visit" see 1:68), is "that which rises." The term may be used to refer to a shoot/branch (Fitzmyer 387), star, or sun. Because of the context in which the ἀνατολή comes from above and shines in the darkness, most EVV ref. to the sun: "Sunrise" (NASB), "the Dawn" (HCSB, cf. NRSV), "rising sun" (NIV). It is likely a Messianic reference (Bock 191–92; Bovon 1.76; Marshall 94–95). The fact that this ἀνατολή will "visit" us "from on high" (most EVV), i.e., "from heaven" (NIV, ἐξ ὕψους, gen. sg. neut. of ὕψος, -ους, τό; cf. 24:49) indicates that a pre-existent divine figure is in view (Gathercole 238–42; cf. Nolland 90).

1:79 The inf. ἐπιφᾶναι (aor. act. of ἐπιφαίνω, "shine") expresses the purpose of this visitation (ZG 176). Τοῖς . . . καθημένοις (dat. pl. masc. of pres. mid. ptc. of dep. κάθημαι, "sit" NASB, ESV; "live" HCSB, sim. NIV) is a subst. ptc. Σκότει, dat. sg. neut. of σκότος, -ους, τό, "darkness." Σκιᾷ θανάτου, "shadow of death" (dat. sg. fem. of σκιά, -ᾶς, ἡ). The art. inf. τοῦ κατευθῦναι (aor. act. of τοῦ κατευθύνω, "guide") is epex. to ἐπιφᾶναι, and thus also expresses purpose (Robertson, *Pictures* 20; T 142; Z §385; see above on 1:77). "Peace" (εἰρήνης) is also a recurring theme in the prophetic hope of the new covenant (e.g., Isa 59:8–9) and in Luke's description of the arrival of this salvation (e.g., 2:14; 7:50; 8:48; 19:42; Acts 10:36) which restores harmony between people and God as well as among the people who belong to God (cf. 2:14).

1:80 This summary statement provides background information about John until the account of his ministry in chapter 3. Τὸ . . . παιδίον is the subj. of ηὔξανεν (3rd sg. impf. act. indic. of αὐξάνω, "grow," cf. 2:40; Acts 6:7; 12:24; 19:20; intrans.). The impf. ηὔξανεν and ἐκραταιοῦτο (3rd sg. impf. pass. of dep. κραταιόομαι, "strengthen," pass. "become strong") express ongoing activity (NASB; Robertson, *Pictures* 20). Πνεύματι, dat. of ref. ("strong in spirit" most EVV; "his spirit grew strong" NJB; "spiritually strong" HCSB; ZG 176). The pl. ταῖς ἐρήμοις is an abstract pl. that refers to a general area (BDF §263; Bock 194; Marshall 95). The public ministry of John is then described as the "day of his public appearance to Israel" (NASB, ESV; ἀναδείξεως, gen. sg. fem. of ἀνάδειξις, -εως, ἡ [only here in the NT], "showing forth," "revealed" NET; ["day of . . ."] a Heb. BDF §165; LN 28.54; ZG 176; "commissioning, installation" BDAG 62b; H. Schlier *TDNT* 2.31; Fitzmyer 389; Marshall 96; or nontechnical "manifestation" Nolland 91).

FOR FURTHER STUDY

2. The Hymns and Infancy Narratives

Brown, R. E. *The Birth of the Messiah: A Commentary on the Infancy Narratives in the Gospels of Matthew and Luke.* 2nd ed. New York: Doubleday, 1993.

De Long, K. P. *Surprised by God: Praise Responses in the Narrative of Luke-Acts.* Berlin: de Gruyter, 2009.

Farris, S. *The Hymns of Luke's Infancy Narratives: Their Origin, Meaning and Significance.* Sheffield: JSOT Press, 1985.

————. *DJG*[1] 895–96.

Gathercole, S. J. "The Heavenly ἀνατολή (Lk. 1.78–79)." *JTS* 56 (2005): 471–88.

Koperski, V. *DJG*[2] 566–69.

Martin, C. J. *DJG*[1] 525–26.

See also For Further Study §3.

HOMILETICAL SUGGESTIONS

The Saving Mercy of God (1:57–80)
1. God, in his mercy, brings joy (1:57–66).
2. God, in his mercy, saves us so we can serve him (1:67–75).
3. God, in his mercy, brings forgiveness through the Lord Jesus (1:76–80).

F. JESUS' BIRTH AND ANGELIC VISITATION TO SHEPHERDS (2:1–21)

This section runs through to 2:21 to complete the parallel with the birth, naming, and circumcision of John (1:57–66). The events surrounding Jesus' birth are emphasized (with angelic announcements), while his naming and circumcision are passed over briefly.

1. Jesus' Birth (2:1–7)

2:1 Ἐγένετο, see 1:5. "In those days" links the following account of Jesus' birth with the preceding events surrounding John's birth (though before 1:80). Δόγμα (nom. sg. neut. of δόγμα, -ατος, τό, an imperial "decree," BDAG 254b) is the subj. of ἐξῆλθεν (3rd sg. 2nd aor. act. indic. of dep. ἐξέρχομαι). The source (παρά) of this decree is Καίσαρος Αὐγούστου ("Caesar Augustus"), i.e., Octavian, Roman emperor from 31 BC–AD 14 (given the title Augustus in 27 BC). The inf. ἀπογράφεσθαι (pres. *pass. of ἀπογράφω, "be registered" ESV; BDAG 108c; or mid., BDF §317; Marshall 98; see 2:5) is *epex. (or subj., T 139, or expresses purpose). The registration here is for tax purposes. Οἰκουμένην (acc. sg. fem. noun of οἰκουμένη, -ης, ἡ, or *acc. sg. fem. of pres. pass. ptc. of οἰκέω, BDAG 699d; BHGNT 64), "the inhabited world" (cf. NRSV, NASB, ESV), in this context, the Roman Empire (cf. HCSB, NIV; BDAG 699d; LN 1.83). This does not rule out a local census in Israel, which would be, with all regional censuses, an expression of the emperor's policy for his whole empire (Nolland 103).

2:2 The "census" (ἀπογραφή, nom. sg. fem. of ἀπογραφή, -ῆς, ἡ; cf. the inf. of ἀπογράφω in 2:1) is now described in relation to the administration (ἡγεμονεύοντος gen. sg. masc. of pres. act. ptc. of ἡγεμονεύω, "be governor/administrator," a temp. gen. abs. ptc.) of Quirinius (Κυρηνίου, gen. subj. of the ptc.) in Syria (some interpret this as a ref. to an administrative role of Quirinius in this census as representative rather than as a governor, NET n.; Fitzmyer 402). Bock (903–9) summarizes a range of interpretive options for the historicity of this census (noting also possible translations of πρώτη as "before" Quirinius became governor or "earlier" than the later census of AD 6 [cf. T 32; Nolland 101]; also, a census that began earlier could become associated with Quirinius). The ref. to "first" indicates Luke's awareness of other censuses (i.e., including a census in AD 6; Acts 5:37; Bock 909). The opening clause (αὕτη ἀπογραφὴ πρώτη) may be understood in the following ways (BHGNT 64–65; Wallace 304–05 [noting that the adj. πρώτη (of πρῶτος) is not superl.]):

*1. αὕτη as the subj. of ἐγένετο with ἀπογραφὴ πρώτη as a pred. nom. ("This was the first census," NASB, NIV, sim. NRSV, ESV; BDAG 741d; BDF §292; R 789–90 states that ἀπογραφὴ πρώτη is anar. because it is the pred. [though see 1:36, T 192]; Wallace 304–05; ZG 176; Bovon 1.84; Marshall 98);

2. αὕτη ἀπογραφή as the subj. and πρώτη as the pred. adj. ("This census was the first while Quirinius . . ." BHGNT 63; cf. KJV, NJB). However, "when a demonstrative functions attributively to a noun, the noun is almost always articular" (Wallace 304–05); or

3. αὕτη ἀπογραφὴ πρώτη is the subj. ("This first registration took place" HCSB)

2:3 Ἐπορεύοντο 3rd pl. impf. mid. indic. of dep. πορεύομαι. The inf. ἀπογράφεσθαι (see 2:1) indicates the purpose for "each person" (ἕκαστος is nom. in appos. to πάντες) returning to his own town (with the refl. ἑαυτοῦ differing little from αὐτοῦ, T 191). In light of 2:4, the town here refers to the ancestral town (cf. 2:39).

2:4 Joseph also (δὲ καί, a common cstr. in Luke for emphasis, Plummer 90; ZG 176) went up (ἀνέβη, 3rd sg. 2nd aor. act. indic. of ἀναβαίνω) from his town. Ἀπό may refer to travel away from Galilee whereas ἐκ may refer to the origin of the journey (i.e., Nazareth; BHGNT 66). Plummer (51–52) notes that there is no special distinction here (BHGNT 66; cf. Harris 57–58; R 578); ἀπό is often used for towns (Luke 10:30; Acts 8:26; 13:14; 20:17) and ἐκ for districts (Luke 23:55; Acts 7:4). Εἰς τὴν Ἰουδαίαν and εἰς πόλιν Δαυίδ is locat. The nom. sg. fem. indef. rel. pron. ἥτις (antecedent πόλιν) is the subj. of καλεῖται (see 1:61; on ἥτις for ἥ see 1:20, Z §216). The nom. Βηθλέεμ is the complement in a double nom. cstr. (BHGNT 66). On Bethlehem as "the city of David" cf. 1 Sam 17:12, 58 (Bock 204; Nolland 104). The reason he traveled to "the city of David" is because (διά with the art. pres. act. inf. εἶναι, of εἰμί, cf. Wallace 597) Joseph (αὐτόν, subj. of the inf.) was of the "house" (cf. 2 Sam 7:16) and "family line" (HCSB; πατριᾶς, gen. sg. fem. of πατριά, -ᾶς, ἡ; "lineage" ESV) of David (probably synonymous terms for ancestry, Bock 210; Marshall 105; Nolland 104; cf. 1:27).

2:5 The purpose for this journey is "to register" (ἀπογράψασθαι aor. mid. inf. of ἀπογράφω, see 2:1, 3). Σὺν Μαριάμ may modify:

* *1. ἀνέβη in 2:4 (indicating only that they traveled together, not registered together; Bock 205; Fitzmyer 406–7; Marshall 105); or
* 2. ἀπογράψασθαι in 2:5 (indicating that Mary, too, had to be registered in Bethlehem; Robertson, *Pictures* 22; Nolland 104).

The mid. ἀπογράψασθαι may be a "permissive middle" ("allowed himself to be enrolled," Wallace 426) or "enroll himself" (RV; cf. BDAG 108c). The subst. ptc. ἐμνηστευμένη (dat. sg. fem. of pf. pass. ptc. of dep. μνηστεύομαι, see 1:27) and οὔσῃ (dat. sg. fem. of pres. act. ptc. of εἰμί) further describe Mary's relationship with Joseph as "pledged to be married" (NIV) and "pregnant" (ἐγκύῳ, dat. sg. fem. adj. of ἔγκυος, -ον). The term ἐμνηστευμένη here may not mean that the couple have not married yet, only that the marriage has not yet been consummated (Bock 205–6; Marshall 105; Nolland 104).

2:6 Ἐγένετο, see 1:5. The art. inf. εἶναι (see 2:4; the acc. αὐτούς is the subj.) with ἐν is temp. ("While they were there"). On ἐπλήσθησαν see 1:23. The acc. αὐτήν is the subj. of the inf. τεκεῖν (see 1:57; here epex. to αἱ ἡμέραι).

2:7 Ἔτεκεν 3rd sg. 2nd aor. act. indic. of τίκτω. Αὐτῆς, gen. of relationship ("her son"). Πρωτότοκον acc. sg. masc. adj. of πρωτότοκος, -ον, "firstborn" (in anticipation of 2:22–24; cf. 8:19–20). Ἐσπαργάνωσεν (3rd sg. aor. act. indic. of σπαργανόω, "wrap in cloths") refers to wrapping strips of linen cloth (σπάργανα) around an infant to protect the arms and legs (BHGNT 68; ZG 177; Marshall 106). Ἀνέκλινεν 3rd sg.

*aor. (or impf. ZG 177) act. indic. of ἀνακλίνω, "lay down." Jesus is wrapped and placed in a φάτνῃ (dat. sg. fem. of φάτνη, -ης, ἡ), "manger" (most EVV), i.e., "feeding trough" (HCSB; cf. BDAG 1050c; LN 6.137; MM 665a; Marshall 106; Nolland 105; only 2:7, 12, 16; 13:15 in the NT). The location of the "feeding trough" is not given except for the negation given in the following clause (cf. Bock 208). The reason for this placement is because (διότι) there was no place (τόπος nom. sg. masc., "room" NASB, HCSB; "place" NRSV, ESV) for them (αὐτοῖς) in the "place of lodging" (καταλύματι dat. sg. neut. of κατάλυμα, -ατος, τό, "inn" NRSV, NASB, ESV; "lodging place" HCSB; "guest room" NIV). Although this lodging place could refer to public accommodations in the town (ZG 177; Nolland 105), a different term, πανδοχεῖον, is used for this in 10:34. Since κατάλυμα is found elsewhere in the NT only in 22:11 (and parallel in Mark 14:14) for a guest room within a private house, "guest room" is more likely here (cf. καταλύω, 19:7, BDAG 521d; Bovon 1.86; Marshall 107; Witherington *DJG*[1] 69–70). Thus, the location of a "feeding trough" and "guest room" within a first-century house is probable.

FOR FURTHER STUDY

3. Jesus' Birth (2:1–7)

Bailey, K. E. "The Manger and the Inn: The Cultural Background of Luke 2:7." *ERT* 4 (1980): 201–17.

Bock 1.903–10.

Carlson, S. C. "The Accommodations of Joseph and Mary in Bethlehem: κατάλυμα in Luke 2.7." *NTS* 56 (2010): 326–42.

Hengel, M. *TDNT* 9.49–55.

Köstenberger, A. J., and A. E. Stewart. *The First Days of Jesus.* Wheaton: Crossway, 2015.

Machen, J. G. *The Virgin Birth of Christ.* 2nd ed. New York: Harper and Row, 1932.

Witherington, B., III. *DJG*[1] 60–74.

Young, S. *DJG*[2] 72–84.

See For Further Study §2.

2. Angelic Visitation to Shepherds (2:8–21)

2:8 Ποιμένες, "shepherds" (nom. pl. masc. of ποιμήν, -ένος, ὁ; subj. of ἦσαν; with no indication that they are despised; cf. 15:4). Ἐν τῇ χώρᾳ τῇ αὐτῇ is locat. (the "identical" use of αὐτός, "in the same region" NASB, HCSB, ESV). The ptcs. ἀγραυλοῦντες (nom. pl. masc. of pres. act. ptc. of ἀγραυλέω, "live outdoors," "staying out in the fields" HCSB; cf. BDAG 15b; LN 85.64) and φυλάσσοντες (nom. pl. masc. of pres. act. ptc. of φυλάσσω, "guard," "keep") could be:

> *1. periph. with ἦσαν ("shepherds were staying out . . . and keeping watch" HCSB)
> 2. attrib. with ποιμένες (with the prep. phrase modifying ἦσαν, "in . . . there were some shepherds staying out . . . and watching" NASB, most EVV).

The acc. pl. cognate noun φυλακάς (of φυλακή) with the ptc. is "keeping watch" in which the cognate acc. is the dir. obj. (BDF §153[3]; Wallace 189–90). Some (Robertson, *Pictures* 23; Fitzmyer 409; Nolland 106) suggest that the pl. indicates shepherds guarding in shifts (BHGNT 70). The gen. τῆς νυκτός could be a gen. of time (Wallace 124; ZG 177) or attrib. (Marshall 108; see Bock [226–27] for possible time of year). Ποίμνην, "flock" (acc. sg. fem. of ποίμνη, -ης, ἡ).

2:9 On ἄγγελος κυρίου see 1:11. Ἐπέστη 3rd sg. 2nd aor. act. indic. of ἐφίστημι (intrans.), "stand over," "stood before" (NRSV, HCSB; "appeared" ESV, NIV; the vb. often implies suddenness, NLT, NASB; BDAG 418d; BHGNT 71; eighteen out of twenty-one NT occurrences are in Luke-Acts). In this night setting the brightness of the glory of the Lord "shines around them" (περιέλαμψεν 3rd sg. aor. act. indic. of περιλάμπω, "shine around"). Ἐφοβήθησαν (3rd pl. aor. pass. indic. of dep. φοβέομαι) and the cognate noun φόβον (with the acc. sg. masc. adj. μέγαν), "they feared a great fear" ("filled with great fear" ESV) is a Sem. idiom that intensifies the idea (cognate acc., Wallace 189-90; an acc. of content, BDF §153[1]; Z §62; pass. as intrans. BDF §313; "terrified" NRSV, HCSB, NIV). For similar responses see 1:12–13, 29–30.

2:10 Φοβεῖσθε 2nd pl. pres. mid. impv. of dep. φοβέομαι (a prohibition with the neg. μή, see 1:13). The shepherds should not fear because (γάρ) the angel is announcing good news (εὐαγγελίζομαι 1st sg. pres. mid. indic. of dep. εὐαγγελίζομαι; apart from Matt 11:5, the vb. is only used by Luke among the Gospels [ten times in Luke, with an additional fifteen in Acts]). In contrast to the shepherds' "great fear," the angel announces news of "great joy" (χαρὰν μεγάλην, acc. sg. fem.). This joy is (the rel. pron. ἥτις [see 2:4] is the subj. of ἔσται) for all the people (dat. of advantage). The definition of "all the people" (λαός) will be clarified as the narrative proceeds (cf. 2:14, 32; 24:47). Notes of joy resound throughout the infancy narratives and frame Luke's Gospel (χαρά 1:14; 2:10; χαρᾶς μεγάλης 24:52; χαίρω 1:14, 28; ἀγαλλίασις 1:14, 44; ἀγαλλιάω 1:47; συγχαίρω 1:58).

2:11 Ὅτι could be:

*1. epex. to χαρὰν μεγάλην (ὅτι is untranslated in HCSB, NIV; Z §416), explaining the joyful news (i.e., the content of the good news, Marshall 109, as well as #3).
2. introduction to indir. discourse.
3. causal ("for" NASB, ESV; cf. Marshall 109; Nolland 107), giving the reason for joy.

The complement χαρὰν μεγάλην to εὐαγγελίζομαι in 2:10 makes #2 (i.e., as another clausal complement) unlikely and the causal clause already in 2:10 makes #3 less likely (BHGNT 71–72). Ἐτέχθη 3rd sg. aor. pass. indic. of τίκτω, "give birth to." As with παντὶ τῷ λαῷ in 2:10, ὑμῖν is a dat. of advantage. This is the first occurrence of σήμερον ("today") in Luke's Gospel (eleven times in Luke and nine in Acts). On σωτήρ see 1:47. Χριστός, is the pred. nom. of ἐστίν with κύριος in nom. appos. to χριστός (Fitzmyer 409; Marshall 110). See comments at 1:17, 43, 76 for the significance of κύριος in the narrative context of Luke 1–2.

2:12 The nom. sg. neut. demonstrative pron. τοῦτο is the subj. of a verbless clause (with ἔσται implied), and σημεῖον is the pred. nom. (to which the neut. τοῦτο is attracted, Wallace 334). Εὑρήσετε 2nd. pl. fut. act. indic. of εὑρίσκω. The ptcs. ἐσπαργανωμένον (acc. sg. neut. of pf. pass. ptc. of σπαργανόω, "wrap in cloths," see 2:7) and κείμενον (acc. sg. neut. of pres. pass. ptc. of dep. κεῖμαι, "laid") could be attrib. with the acc. sg. neut. βρέφος ("baby," see 1:41) or the complement in a double acc. cstr. (BHGNT 72). Φάτνη, see 2:7.

2:13 Ἐξαίφνης, adv., "suddenly" (most EVV), "unexpectedly" (BDAG 344b; LN 67.113). Πλῆθος (nom. sg. neut.) is the subj. of ἐγένετο. The gen. (sg. fem.) στρατιᾶς (of στρατιά, -ᾶς, ἡ, "host," "army") is partitive (ZG 177). The gen. (sg. fem.) οὐρανίου could be either source or attrib. (BDAG 737c; LSJ 1272d). The gen. pl. masc. of pres. act. ptcs. αἰνούντων (of αἰνέω, "praise"; in Luke-Acts six times out of eight in the NT; cf. 2:20; 19:37; Acts 2:47; 3:8, 9) and λεγόντων (of λέγω) are attrib. modifying στρατιᾶς (BHGNT 73). The two ptcs. are pl. (though πλῆθος στρατιᾶς is sg.) in accordance with the sense (BDF §134[1b]; Robertson, *Pictures* 24; ZG 177).

2:14 Δόξα ("glory," in this context, honor to God in acknowledging his glory) is the subj. of a verbless clause (ἐστίν is implied) that declares the results of Jesus' birth (Marshall 111; Nolland 108; Fitzmyer [410] describes it as jussive or volitive). The locat. prep. phrase ἐν ὑψίστοις (see 1:32; anar. though def. as the obj. of the prep., Wallace 247) is contrasted with ἐπὶ γῆς and therefore refers to "highest heaven" (BDAG 1045a; Marshall 111). Εἰρήνη see 1:79. The gen. (sg. fem.) εὐδοκίας (of εὐδοκία, -ας, ἡ) in the phrase ἀνθρώποις εὐδοκίας ("people of favor/pleasure," i.e., "to people He favors" HCSB) has better external ms. support with both Alexandrian and Western mss. (ℵ* A B* D W) than the nom. (sg. fem.) εὐδοκία ("goodwill among or toward people," cf. KJV). A smaller raised sigma at the end of the line may have been omitted by a scribe unintentionally (cf. Metzger 111 for Sem. expressions for the elect similar to the gen. rdg.; Bock 220; Bovon 1.91; Fitzmyer 411–12; Marshall 112; Nolland 109). The phrase emphasizes God's initiative and purpose in salvation rather than human merit (Marshall 112; Nolland 109).

2:15 Ἐγένετο (see 1:5) with ὡς see 1:23 (temp.). Οἱ ἄγγελοι is the subj. of ἀπῆλθον (3rd pl. 2nd aor. act. indic. of dep. ἀπέρχομαι, "depart," "go away"). Οἱ ποιμένες (see 2:8) is the subj. of the impf. ἐλάλουν (3rd pl. impf. act. indic. of λαλέω; ingressive NASB; Robertson, *Pictures* 25; Nolland 109). The 1st pl. 2nd aor. act. subjuncs. διέλθωμεν (of dep. διέρχομαι) and ἴδωμεν (of ὁράω) are hortatory. The particle δή ("now," "then," "indeed") could be used to give greater urgency ("Let us go now" NRSV; BDAG 222a; Robertson, *Pictures* 25; Bock 221; Marshall 113) or simply a marker of "relatively weak emphasis" that is "frequently not translated" (LN 91.6; cf. ESV, NIV). Τὸ ῥῆμα τοῦτο is the obj. of ἴδωμεν (ῥῆμα [see 1:37] here refers to "an event that can be spoken about," i.e., "thing," "event," "matter," a Heb., BDAG 905b; MM 563d; Nolland 109). Γεγονός (acc. sg. neut. of 2nd pf. act. [attrib.] ptc. of dep. γίνομαι ("this thing that has happened" ESV). Κύριος is the subj. of ἐγνώρισεν (3rd sg. aor. act. indic. of γνωρίζω, "make known") and indicates that the ultimate source of the angel's message (2:9) is God.

2:16 For ἦλθαν see 1:59 (where the more common form ἦλθον is used; ἦλθαν is used only here in Luke). Σπεύσαντες (nom. pl. masc. of aor. act. ptc. of σπεύδω, "hasten," "hurry") expresses manner ("went with haste" ESV; BDF §418[5]; Robertson, *Pictures* 25; Z §262; ZG 177–78). Ἀνεῦραν 3rd pl. 2nd aor. act. indic. of ἀνευρίσκω, "find out," "look for" ("find by searching" LN 27.28). Τε (enclitic; used for καί, Z §466; ZG 178), though untranslated, serves to connect the family members as a group (BDF §443[3]; T 339). Βρέφος κείμενον, see 2:12. Φάτνῃ, see 2:7.

2:17 Ἰδόντες is temp. (nom. pl. masc. of 2nd aor. act. ptc. of ὁράω; a common cstr. in Luke, cf. 8:34, 47; 22:49; 23:47; the obj. "him" ["them" HCSB] is implied). The obj. of ἐγνώρισαν (3rd pl. aor. act. indic. of γνωρίζω, "make known," cf. 2:15) is also not stated but probably includes Mary and Joseph (cf. 2:19) as well as a larger number of people who are told of these events (NLT; e.g., cf. 2:18 BHGNT 75; Bock 222; Marshall 113; ῥῆμα here is "message" HCSB, "saying" ESV; Nolland 109; see 1:37). Λαληθέντος gen. sg. neut. of aor. pass. (attrib.) ptc. of λαλέω ("the message they were told" HCSB).

2:18 Ἀκούσαντες, see 1:66. Ἐθαύμασαν, see 1:63. Λαληθέντων gen. pl. neut. of aor. pass. (subst.) ptc. of λαλέω. Ὑπὸ τῶν ποιμένων expresses agency (gen. pl. masc., see 2:8; "what the shepherds said" HCSB, NIV).

2:19 Μαριάμ is the subj. of συνετήρει (3rd sg. impf. act. indic. of συντηρέω, "hold," "treasure" most EVV; the impf. may highlight continuing activity, "was treasuring" HCSB; Robertson, *Pictures* 25). Δέ and the impf. συνετήρει indicate a contrast between Mary and the crowds in 2:18–19. Whereas the crowds marveled at the news, Mary's personal response is one of ongoing reflection (Bock 222; though this obviously does not necessitate complete understanding at this point). The acc. pl. neut. adj. πάντα (of πᾶς, πᾶσα, πᾶν) modifies τὰ ῥήματα ταῦτα and is the obj. of συνετήρει ("all these things"; BDAG 905b; cf. 1:37, 65). The contrast in 1:18–19 and the use of τῶν λαληθέντων in 1:18 may indicate that "words" are in view here too ("all these words" NRSV, NET; sim. RV). Συμβάλλουσα nom. sg. fem. of pres. act. (attendant circumstance) ptc. of συμβάλλω, "consider," "ponder" most EVV; "meditating" HCSB (cf. BDAG 956c; perhaps, with the impf., a conative force, Fitzmyer 413; Nolland 110; the dir. obj. "them" is implied).

2:20 Οἱ ποιμένες (see 2:8) is the subj. of ὑπέστρεψαν (3rd pl. aor. act. indic. of ὑποστρέφω). The nom. pl. masc. of pres. act. ptcs. δοξάζοντες (of δοξάζω) and αἰνοῦντες (of αἰνέω, "praise"; see 2:13) express manner (on δόξα see 2:14). To give glory to God is a regular response in Luke (often with ref. to Jesus; cf. 5:25–26; 7:16; 13:13; 17:15; 18:43; 23:47). Ἐπὶ πᾶσιν is causal (Z §126; ZG 178). The dat. pl. neut. rel. pron. οἷς (of ὅς, ἥ, ὅ) is syntactically the dir. obj. of ἤκουσαν (see 1:58) καὶ εἶδον (3rd pl. aor. act. indic. of ὁράω) but is dat. in attraction to πᾶσιν (BHGNT 77; ZG 178). Again (e.g., 1:38, 45), what the shepherds have heard and seen has taken place just as (καθώς) it had been told (ἐλαλήθη 3rd sg. aor. pass. indic. of λαλέω) to them. Praise fittingly concludes this account. The following circumcision and naming of Jesus highlights the (uneven) parallel with the account of John's birth.

2:21 Ἡμέραι ὀκτώ ("eight"; indecl.) is the nom. pl. fem. subj. of ἐπλήσθησαν (see 1:23). The art. inf. τοῦ περιτεμεῖν (see 1:59) could be epex. to ἡμέραι ("at the end of eight days, when he was circumcised" ESV; see similar cstr. in 1:57; 2:6), or an inf. of result (BDF §400[2]; Marshall 115). Τὸ ὄνομα is the subj. of ἐκλήθη (3rd sg. aor. pass. indic. of καλέω). Κληθέν nom. sg. neut. of aor. pass. (subst.) ptc. of καλέω, is in appos. to ὄνομα ("the name given by" most EVV). The art. inf. συλλημφθῆναι (aor. pass. inf. of συλλαμβάνω, "conceive," see 1:24; κοιλία, see 1:15, 41) with πρό is temp. (the action of the inf. is subsequent to the controlling vb.; i.e., "[named] before he was conceived"; Burton §106; R 621; Wallace 596; cf. 22:15). The naming of Jesus obeys God's instructions (1:31). The parallel with John has been made (1:59), so the next section shifts in emphasis with a move to Jerusalem.

FOR FURTHER STUDY

4. Christology in Luke's Gospel (2:11)

Bauckham, R. J. *DJG*[2] 125–33.

Bird, M. F. *DJG*[2] 115–25.

Buckwalter, H. D. *The Character and Purpose of Luke's Christology*. Cambridge: Cambridge University Press, 1996.

Bullard, C. B. *Jesus and the Thoughts of Many Hearts: Implicit Christology and Jesus' Knowledge in the Gospel of Luke*. London: Bloomsbury T&T Clark, 2015.

*Gathercole, S. J. *The Preexistent Son: Recovering the Christologies of Matthew, Mark, and Luke*. Grand Rapids: Eerdmans, 2006.

Porter, S. E. "The Messiah in Luke and Acts: Forgiveness for the Captives." Pages 144–64 in *The Messiah in the Old and New Testaments*. Edited by S. E. Porter. Grand Rapids: Eerdmans, 2007.

*Rowe, C. K. *Early Narrative Christology: The Lord in the Gospel of Luke*. Grand Rapids: Baker, 2009.

Strauss, M. L. *The Davidic Messiah in Luke-Acts: The Promise and Fulfilment in Luke's Christology*. Sheffield: Sheffield Academic Press, 1995.

Thompson, A. J. "The Trinity and Luke-Acts." Pages 62–82 in *The Essential Trinity: New Testament and Practical Relevance*. Edited by B. D. Crowe and C. R. Trueman. London: Inter-Varsity, [Apollos] 2016.

HOMILETICAL SUGGESTIONS

The Birth that Changed the World (2:1–21)

1. Jesus is the center of God's plans for the world (2:1–7).
2. Jesus is the true Savior of the world (2:8–12).
3. Jesus leads us to praise God (2:13–21).

G. SIMEON AND ANNA'S PRAISE IN THE TEMPLE (2:22–40)

Simeon and Anna's praise, after Jesus' birth, corresponds to Zechariah's praise after John's birth. The focus here turns to eschatological fulfilment in Jesus of the long-awaited hopes of the godly in Israel. The location is again in the temple, where the infancy narratives began (1:9) and where the Gospel narrative will conclude (24:53).

2:22 Ἐπλήσθησαν, see 1:23. The gen. (sg. masc.) τοῦ καθαρισμοῦ (of καθαρισμός, -οῦ, ὁ, "purification") is epex. (cf. Lev 12:3–4) and could refer to:

1. the time period (NASB, HCSB); or
*2. the offering at the end of the time period (NRSV, ESV, NIV; "purification offering" NLT)

The gen. pl. masc. pron. αὐτῶν is obj. (although LXX Lev 12:4 has the fem. sg. αὐτῆς, Luke's pl. probably includes Joseph with Mary in the process [rather than Mary and the child], possibly as Joseph would participate in the sacrifice for the dedication of a first born as 2:23 indicates; cf. Exod 13:2; ZG 178; Bock 236; so as to connect "purification" and "presentation" Bovon 1.99; Marshall 116; Nolland 117). Joseph and Mary brought (ἀνήγαγον 3rd pl. 2nd aor. act. indic. of ἀνάγω, "lead/bring up") Jesus up to Jerusalem. Ἱεροσόλυμα is the Greek form of the name, which is used four times in Luke (cf. also 13:22; 19:28; 23:7) and twenty-two times in Acts. Ἱερουσαλήμ is the Sem. form and is used approx. (depending on variants) twenty-seven times in Luke (cf. 2:25, 38, 41, 43, 45) and thirty-six times in Acts. There is no significance to the different spelling in Luke (as also with other authors, e.g., Josephus; BDAG 470d; Bock 255–56). The (aor. act.) inf. παραστῆσαι (of παρίστημι [trans.], "present") expresses the purpose of this trip. Mary and Joseph obey the law of the Lord and dedicate Jesus to the service of the Lord. The following verses specify this obedience.

2:23 Γέγραπται 3rd sg. pf. pass. indic. of γράφω (the pf. perhaps emphasizes the current authority of Scripture, "it is written" most EVV; Wallace 576). The gen. κυρίου is a gen. of source. Ὅτι, recitative (epex. to the subj. of γέγραπται, BHGNT 80; ZG 178; cf. Exod 13:2, 12). Πᾶν ἄρσεν (nom. sg. neut. of ἄρσην, -εν, gen. –ενος, "every male") is the subj. of διανοῖγον (nom. sg. neut. of pres. act. ptc. of διανοίγω, "open up"). Διανοῖγον μήτραν ("opens the womb" NASB, ESV) is an idiom for "firstborn" (elsewhere Luke uses κοιλία; μήτραν [acc. sg. fem. of μήτρα, -ας, ἡ], however, is usually the term used with διανοίγω or ἀνοίγω [BHGNT 80] in the LXX [only here, Rom 4:19 in the NT]). The nom. sg. neut. adj. ἅγιον ("holy," NASB, ESV; "dedicated" HCSB; "consecrated" NIV) is the complement in a double nom. cstr. (κληθήσεται, see 1:32, 35).

2:24 In continuation from 2:22, the purpose (art. inf., BDF §400[6]; ZG 178) of the trip is to offer (δοῦναι, see 1:73) a sacrifice (θυσίαν, acc. sg. fem. of θυσία, -ας, ἡ). As with 2:22–23, the actions of Mary and Joseph are "according to" (κατά) "what was said" (εἰρημένον acc. sg. neut. of pf. pass. [subst.] ptc. of λέγω, "stated" HCSB; cf. γέγραπται 2:23) in the law ("of the Lord," see 2:23; "of Moses" 2:22). The following phrase in appos. to θυσίαν specifies the sacrifice as either a "pair of turtledoves" (ζεῦγος [acc. sg. neut.] τρυγόνων [gen. pl. fem.]) or "two young pigeons" (δύο νοσσοὺς [acc. pl. masc.]

περιστερῶν [gen. pl. fem.]; a common combination in the LXX; for here, see Lev 5:11; 12:8 [for a woman who can not afford a lamb]; Num 6:10 [1 Sam 1–2; dedication of the firstborn, Pao and Schnabel 270d–71b).

2:25 Καὶ ἰδού, see 1:20 (here, transitional, Marshall 118). On Ἰερουσαλήμ see 2:22. The dat. (sg. masc.) rel. pron. ᾧ is a dat. of poss. Συμεών is a pred. nom. (in a verbless clause, R 395). "This man" (ὁ ἄνθρωπος οὗτος, nom. subj. in a verbless clause, BDF §290[1]), Simeon, was "righteous" (cf. 1:6) and "devout" (εὐλαβής, nom. sg. masc. adj. of εὐλαβής, -ές, gen. οὖς, used only by Luke in the NT, cf. Acts 2:5; 8:2; 22:12). Προσδεχόμενος (nom. sg. masc. of pres. mid. ptc. of dep. προσδέχομαι, "wait for," "looking forward to" NRSV, HCSB) is probably in appos. to the pred. nom. δίκαιος καὶ εὐλαβής (BHGNT 82). Παράκλησιν, acc. sg. fem. of παράκλησις, -εως, ἡ, "consolation" (most EVV), "restoration" (NJB, NET). Note sim. hopes in Luke 23–24: here the "righteous" "waits for" the "consolation of Israel" (2:25), and some "wait for" the "redemption of Jerusalem" (2:38); likewise, there the "righteous" "waits for" (προσεδέχετο) "the kingdom of God" (23:50–51), and some hope that Jesus would "redeem Israel" (24:21). The sim. statements of Simeon (1:25) and Anna (1:38) tie this section together. The unusual order of πνεῦμα ἦν ἅγιον is perhaps for emphasis (Marshall 118; here, anticipating the following activity).

2:26 Simeon's hope for Israel receives specific focus. Κεχρηματισμένον nom. sg. neut. of pf. pass. ptc. of χρηματίζω, "reveal," "instruct" (used in the LXX for revelation from God, e.g., LXX Jer 37:2; BDAG 1089b). The ptc. is a pluperfect periph. cstr. (Wallace 583, 649; on the pass. cf. BDF §312[1]). The 2nd aor. act. inf. ἰδεῖν (of ὁράω) is indir. discourse ("that he would not see"). Πρίν ("before"), usually with an inf., is temp. here with the particle ἄν and subjunc. ἴδῃ (3rd sg. 2nd aor. act. subjunc. of ὁράω, cf. BDF §§383[3]; 395; Marshall 118–19; Nolland 119). The gen. κυρίου could be source ("the Messiah from the Lord") or subj. ("the one anointed by the Lord," BHGNT 82; cf. e.g., LXX 1 Sam 24:7; 26:9, 11, 16, 23).

2:27 Simeon came (ἦλθεν 3rd sg. 2nd aor. act. indic. of dep. ἔρχομαι) into the temple courts (ἱερόν, "temple complex" HCSB; with Mary here the ref. could be to the court of the Gentiles or the court of women, Bock 240; Fitzmyer 427). Ἐν τῷ πνεύματι indicates the Spirit's direction ("Guided by the Spirit" NRSV, HCSB; "cause" ZG 179; Bock 240; Marshall 119). Regarding the two acc. that follow the 2nd aor. act. inf. εἰσαγαγεῖν (of εἰσάγω, "lead in," "brought," temp. with ἐν τῷ, BDF §404[2]), τοὺς γονεῖς (acc. pl. masc. of γονεύς, -έως, ὁ, "the parents") is obviously the subj. and τὸ παιδίον Ἰησοῦν the dir. obj. (Wallace 196; on "parents" see Marshall 119; the virgin birth of Luke 1 need not be explained every time Joseph and Mary are mentioned). The art. aor. act. inf. ποιῆσαι (of ποιέω) expresses purpose (with αὐτούς as the acc. subj. of the inf.) following the previous inf. Εἰθισμένον acc. sg. neut. of pf. pass. (subst.) ptc. of ἐθίζω, "custom," "what was customary" (NRSV, HCSB; cf. BDAG 276b; Robertson, *Pictures* 28; ZG 179). The gen. τοῦ νόμου could be source or epex. (BHGNT 83). Περὶ αὐτοῦ is connected to the inf. ποιῆσαι (Nolland 119).

2:28 Αὐτός (i.e., Simeon) signifies a change in subj. (of ἐδέξατο, 3rd sg. aor. mid. indic. of dep. δέχομαι) back to Simeon and completes the temp. phrase introduced in 2:27 (i.e., nonemphatic, Wallace 323; see 1:17). Thus, αὐτό (i.e., ref. to παιδίον, the child, Jesus) is the (acc.) dir. obj. Ἀγκάλας acc. pl. fem. of ἀγκάλη, -ης, ἡ, "arm." Εὐλόγησεν 3rd sg. aor. act. indic. of εὐλογέω.

2:29 The use and position of the adv. νῦν emphasizes this as the climactic moment of Simeon's life (Fitzmyer 427). Ἀπολύεις (2nd sg. pres. act. indic. of ἀπολύω, "release," "dismiss") could be euphemistic for death in this context (BHGNT 84; with ἐν εἰρήνῃ, expressing manner), or a "dismissal" from his duty as a watchman (Nolland 119). The pres. indic. may be descriptive ("now you are dismissing," NRSV, sim. NASB, ESV) or expressing the readiness of Simeon to depart given that he has lived to see his ulti-mate hope ("you may now dismiss," NIV, sim. HCSB; Bock 241; Marshall 119–20). Again, this is κατὰ τὸ ῥῆμά σου (cf. 2:26). As δοῦλος ("slave"), Simeon's request is made as one who recognizes God as his δέσποτα (voc. sg. masc. of δεσπότης, -ου, ὁ, "Master" HCSB, "Sovereign Lord" NIV). Peace is associated with the restoration Jesus brings (see 1:79).

2:30 Simeon's praise and readiness to depart now is because (ὅτι, causal, Wallace 461) he has seen (εἶδον, see 2:20; the nom. οἱ ὀφθαλμοί, is synecdoche for "I," cf. NLT; BHGNT 85) the Lord's "salvation" (acc. sg. neut. of σωτήριος, -ον; see 1:47; 3:6; cf. παράκλησιν τοῦ Ἰσραήλ, 2:25; τὸν χριστὸν κυρίου, 2:26; and τὸ παιδίον Ἰησοῦν, 2:27).

2:31 The acc. sg. neut. rel. pron. ὅ (of ὅς, ἥ, ὅ; antecedent is τὸ σωτήριόν in 2:30) is the obj. of ἡτοίμασας (2nd sg. aor. act. indic. of ἑτοιμάζω). Κατὰ πρόσωπον is idiomatic for "in the presence of" (NRSV, HCSB, ESV), "in the sight of" (NIV; cf. LN 83.34; BDAG 888b; BDF §140). The following verse indicates that "all peoples" (πάντων τῶν λαῶν) includes Gentiles as well as Israel (Bock 243; Fitzmyer 428; Marshall 120–21; Nolland 120).

2:32 The acc. φῶς is in appos. to τὸ σωτήριόν. Εἰς ἀποκάλυψιν (acc. sg. fem. of ἀποκάλυψις, -εως, ἡ) indicates purpose ("a light for revelation" HCSB, ESV, NIV; Marshall 121). The gen. ἐθνῶν is obj. (i.e., revelation to Gentiles, BDF §259[3]; Bock 244). The acc. δόξαν could be:

*1. parallel with φῶς (i.e., "a light for . . ., and the glory of . . ." cf. NLT, NIV; Bovon 1.103; Marshall 121; Nolland 120; Pao and Schnabel 272d–73a [Isa 49:6]); light and glory are distinct for each group.

> φῶς εἰς ἀποκάλυψιν ἐθνῶν
> καὶ δόξαν λαοῦ σου Ἰσραήλ

2. parallel with ἀποκάλυψιν as both developing the significance of φῶς (i.e., "a light for revelation . . . and for glory to," cf. NRSV; NET; BHGNT 85; Bock 244; Fitzmyer 428); light is for both groups, but revelation and glory are distinct.

φῶς
   εἰς ἀποκάλυψιν ἐθνῶν
   καὶ δόξαν λαοῦ σου Ἰσραήλ

2:33 The subj. ὁ πατὴρ αὐτοῦ καὶ ἡ μήτηρ with the sg. ἦν may accentuate one of the subjects in particular (BHGNT 86; McKay 18) or, together with the pl. ptc. (an impf. periph.) θαυμάζοντες (nom. pl. masc. of pres. act. ptc. of θαυμάζω; cf. 1:21, 63; 2:18), the united response of the parents (BDF §135[1d]; Bock 257; Nolland 120). The cause (ἐπί) of their amazement was the things that were being said (λαλουμένοις, dat. pl. neut. of pres. pass. [subst.] ptc. of λαλέω) about Jesus (Z §126). In this context, these things are related to the inclusion of Gentiles in the scope of God's salvation (Marshall 121).

2:34 Εὐλόγησεν, see 2:28. Simeon then turns to declare Joseph and Mary's blessing. The focus, however, is on Mary, and the heart-wrenching times ahead. The demonstrative pron. οὗτος is the subj. of κεῖται (3rd sg. pres. pass. indic. of κεῖμαι, "set," "destined," BDAG 537d; "to exist for" LN 13.73). Εἰς πτῶσιν [acc. sg. fem. of πτῶσις, -εως, ἡ] καὶ ἀνάστασιν ("falling and rising") and εἰς σημεῖον ἀντιλεγόμενον ("a sign that will be opposed" HCSB; "a sign spoken against" NIV) express goal or purpose (BHGNT 87). The "falling and rising" probably refer to the division that will take place in Israel as some accept and some reject Jesus (Bock 247; Fitzmyer 422–23; Nolland 121) rather than to one group who will fall before they can rise (Marshall 122). Ἀντιλεγόμενον acc. sg. neut. of pres. pass. (attrib.) ptc. of ἀντιλέγω, "speak against," "oppose," anticipates opposition to Jesus (a fut. referring ptc. Bock 247; Fitzmyer 429; see refs. at 1:35).

2:35 As the UBS[5] text indicates, 2:35a is likely a parenthetical comment that focuses particularly on Mary's own pain (Bock 248; Bovon 1.105; Fitzmyer 429; Marshall 122; the gen. pron. σοῦ and the intensive gen. pron. αὐτῆς are placed forward for emphasis). A sword (ῥομφαία nom. sg. fem. of ῥομφαία, -ας, ἡ, "a large and broad sword" BDAG 907b) will pierce (διελεύσεται 3rd sg. fut. mid. indic. of dep. διέρχομαι, "pass through") Mary's own soul (fig. for great emotional pain, BDAG 907b, 1099a; Bock 248–50). This could refer to the emotional pain Mary will experience (1) in seeing Jesus' ministry lead to crucifixion (Marshall 123; Nolland 122; cf. 23:49, though Mary is not explicitly mentioned), or (2) as Jesus' ministry downplays the physical ties of his own family and defines his "family" as those who follow him (Bock 250; Fitzmyer 430; cf. 2:41–52). The two are probably not mutually exclusive. The ref. to rejection in the previous verse with the cross ultimately in view there, however, favors the first view. The statements of 2:34 continue with the (purpose) conj. and particle ὅπως ἄν and the subjunc. ἀποκαλυφθῶσιν (3rd pl. aor. pass. subjunc. of ἀποκαλύπτω). The thoughts (διαλογισμοί nom. pl. masc. of διαλογισμός, -οῦ, ὁ, in Luke these are always hostile or questioning, cf. 5:22; 6:8; 9:46–47; cf. the vb. in 20:14) of many hearts (καρδιῶν, as the "center and source of the whole inner life" including thinking, BDAG 508d) will be revealed.

2:36 Although there is a shift in focus with the introduction of Anna, Luke continues the themes of expectation and temple activity. Anna is first described as (1) a prophetess (προφῆτις nom. sg. fem. of προφῆτις, -ιδος, ἡ), (2) a daughter (θυγάτηρ, nom.

in appos. to Ἄννα) of Phanuel (Φανουήλ, gen. of relationship), and (3) of the tribe of Asher (Ἀσήρ). The demonstrative pron. αὕτη begins a new phrase emphasizing Anna's age (with a Heb.). Προβεβηκυῖα (see 1:18) could be a pluperfect periph. ptc. (with implied ἦν, see 1:7) or a pred. ptc. (Wallace 618). Ζήσασα (nom. sg. fem. of aor. act. ptc. of ζάω) modifies προβεβηκυῖα. Together with 2:37, it begins to explain further the age of Anna: she was married for seven years (παρθενίας gen. sg. fem. of παρθενία, -ας, ἡ, "virginity," lit. "from her virginity").

2:37 Luke continues the emphasis on Anna's old age with reference to the length of her widowhood. The nom. sg. fem. pron. αὐτή is the subject and χήρα (of χήρα, -ας, ἡ) is the pred. nom. of a clause with an implied ἦν. The temp. prep. ἕως introduces a length of time, eighty (ὀγδοήκοντα) four (τεσσάρων) years. This could be:

1. her age to which her widowhood extended (NRSV, ESV, NIV; BDAG 423a; Bovon 1.106; Nolland 122); or
2. the length of her widowhood only, making her approximately 105 years old (NET, HCSB; Bock 251–52, Marshall 123–24).

The nom. sg. fem. rel. pron. ἥ is the subject of ἀφίστατο (3rd sg. impf. mid. indic. [intrans.] of ἀφίστημι, "go away," "depart"). Τοῦ ἱεροῦ is a gen. of separation (Wallace 109). The fem. pl. nouns νηστείαις [of νηστεία, -ας, ἡ] καὶ δεήσεσιν (see 1:13) are instr. dats. ("with fasting and prayers," HCSB, sim. NASB, ESV) modifying λατρεύουσα (nom. sg. fem. of pres. act. ptc. of λατρεύω, "serve" NASB, HCSB; "worship" NRSV, NIV). The acc. νύκτα καὶ ἡμέραν is extent of time (R 495; though probably iter., Wallace 202; i.e., she would not have stayed there, Bock 252; Fitzmyer 431; Marshall 124; Nolland 122; cf. 24:53; Acts 20:31; 26:7; *pace* Bovon 1.106).

2:38 The dat. (of time) sg. fem. pron. αὐτῇ is used as a demonstrative in this cstr. ("at that very hour" ESV; R 686; cf. 10:21; 12:12; 13:31; 20:19; 24:33). Ἐπιστᾶσα nom. sg. fem. of 2nd aor. act. (temp.) ptc. of ἐφίστημι, "come upon." The impf. ἀνθωμολογεῖτο (3rd sg. impf. mid. indic. of dep. ἀνθομολογέομαι, "thank," only here in the NT) and ἐλάλει (see 1:64) could express continued activity (Robertson, *Pictures* 30–31; Fitzmyer 431), but in this context (with αὐτῇ τῇ ὥρᾳ) they are ingressive (NRSV, NASB, HCSB, ESV). Whereas Simeon praised God (2:28) and spoke to the parents (2:34), Anna thanks God and speaks to all the faithful people of God about Jesus. Together with πᾶσιν τοῖς, προσδεχομένοις (dat. pl. masc. of pres. mid. ptc. of dep. προσδέχομαι, "wait for") is subst. (dat. indir. obj. of ἐλάλει). See also 2:25; 23:51. Λύτρωσιν, "redemption" (see 1:68).

2:39 Ὡς is temp. Ἐτέλεσαν 3rd pl. aor. act. indic. of τελέω "completed" (HCSB), "performed" (ESV). The acc. pl. neut. art. τά turns the prep. phrase κατὰ τὸν νόμον into a subst. (BHGNT 91). As has been emphasized throughout, Joseph and Mary have obeyed "the law of the Lord." Ἐπέστρεψαν 3rd pl. aor. act. indic. of ἐπιστρέφω, "return" (intrans.). Ναζαρέθ is indecl. so it could be a gen. of identification or an acc. in appos. to πόλιν (BHGNT 91; on the form cf. 1:26). Thus, they return to their home (1:26).

2:40 On ηὔξανεν and ἐκραταιοῦτο see 1:80. Πληρούμενον (nom. sg. neut. of pres. pass. ptc. of πληρόω, "fill") could express manner or attendant circumstance (BHGNT 91) and further defines Jesus' spiritual growth as one of wisdom (cf. 2:41–52; 7:35; 11:49). Σοφίᾳ (sg. fem.) could be a rare dat. of content (Wallace 374), or a dat. of ref. (ZG 180). This (more difficult) reading may explain the (possible change to) gen. σοφίας found in some mss. (see Wallace 94, 171, 374). Χάρις, "grace" (NASB, HCSB, NIV), "favor" (NRSV, ESV).

HOMILETICAL SUGGESTIONS

Jesus: The One Worth Waiting For (2:22–40)
1. The one who was dedicated to the Lord's will from the beginning (2:22–24, 39).
2. The one who brings peace in the midst of pain (2:25–35).
3. The one who is worth giving our whole lives to (2:36–38).

H. JESUS AS A CHILD IN THE TEMPLE, "HIS FATHER'S HOUSE" (2:41–52)

This section is linked to the infancy narratives by way of the concluding summary statement (2:52) that recalls 2:40; 1:80. However, Jesus is now twelve years old rather than an infant and speaks for the first time in the narrative. This episode prepares for the beginning of Jesus' public ministry by showing Jesus' awareness of his unique relationship with the Father.

2:41 This passage continues the focus on Jerusalem (cf. 2:22) and the dedication of Jesus' parents to the faith of Israel. Ἐπορεύοντο, see 2:3 (οἱ γονεῖς, see 2:27). The impf. may provide background information for what follows (BHGNT 92) or be customary/habitual (Wallace 548; cf. McKay 44; Fitzmyer 439 [iter.]). Although the verse does provide background information, the impf. with κατ' ἔτος (distributive, BDF §305; ZG 180) emphasizes repeated action. Τῇ ἑορτῇ ("Feast" NASB, ESV; "Festival" NRSV, HCSB, NIV) is a dat. of time ("at" NASB, ESV; "for" NRSV, HCSB, NIV). The gen. τοῦ πάσχα is appos. (Wallace 99).

2:42 The temp. conj. ὅτε introduces the first of several temp. cstrs. in 2:42–43 (leading to ὑπέμεινεν). The gen. ἐτῶν is pred. (Robertson, *Pictures* 32; note too παιδίον, "boy" in 2:43). Ἀναβαινόντων (gen. pl. masc. of pres. act. ptc. of ἀναβαίνω) with the gen. pron. αὐτῶν is a temp. gen. abs. cstr. and modifies ὑπέμεινεν in 2:43. The pres. suits the journeying involved in the trip (Z §276; ZG 180; Nolland [129] suggests it marks reiteration, hence "they went up again"). On ἔθος see 1:9. Τῆς ἑορτῆς is a gen. of ref.

2:43 Τελειωσάντων (gen. pl. masc. of aor. act. ptc. of τελειόω "complete," "accomplish") is another temp. gen. abs. cstr. (the aor. suits the completion of the event; in contrast to the previous pres. tenses, Fitzmyer 441). The pres. act. inf. ὑποστρέφειν (of ὑποστρέφω) with ἐν τῷ is also temp. ("as they were returning" HCSB, ESV). The acc. αὐτούς is the subj. of the inf. Ὑπέμεινεν, 3rd sg. aor. act. indic. of ὑπομένω, "remain," is, following the temp. cstr. in 2:42–43, the focus of these verses (Bock 265; Nolland 129). The nom. ὁ παῖς (see 1:54) is in appos. to Ἰησοῦς. Although παῖς was "servant" in 1:54, 69, here it is used in contrast to the diminutive παιδίον, "child" (used for Jesus in 2:17, 27, 40; most EVV have "boy" here; cf. e.g., 9:42). Ἔγνωσαν 3rd pl. 2nd aor. act. indic. of γινώσκω.

2:44 Νομίσαντες nom. pl. masc. of aor. act. (causal) ptc. of νομίζω, "suppose," "consider." The acc. αὐτόν is the subj. of εἶναι (see 2:4). Συνοδίᾳ, dat. sg. fem. of συνοδία, -ας, ἡ, "caravan," i.e., "group of travelers" (NRSV; BDAG 973c; ZG 181; used only here in the NT). Ἦλθον, see 1:59. Ἡμέρας is a gen. of time and ὁδόν is an acc. of measure ("a day's journey" Wallace 202; cf. BHGNT 95). The impf. ἀνεζήτουν (3rd pl. impf. act. indic. of ἀναζητέω, "look," "search") is ingressive rather than implying a prolonged search (Robertson, *Pictures* 33; Nolland 130). The compound vb. ἀναζητέω is perhaps "more emphatic or goal-directed" than ζητέω (LN 27.42; Bovon 1.111). The dat. pl. masc. adjs. συγγενεῦσιν ("relatives," see 1:58) and γνωστοῖς (of γνωστός, -ή, -όν, "known," "acquaintances" NASB, ESV; "friends" NRSV, HCSB, NIV; cf. BDAG 204b; LN 28.30, 34.17) are subst. with the art. τοῖς.

2:45 Εὑρόντες (nom. pl. masc. of 2nd aor. act. ptc. of εὑρίσκω, "find") could be temp. or causal. Ὑπέστρεψαν, see 2:20. Ἀναζητοῦντες (nom. pl. masc. of pres. act. ptc. of ἀναζητέω, "look," "search"; see 2:44) expresses purpose (Wallace 637; Z §284). The shift from the aor. εὑρόντες and ὑπέστρεψαν in a summary sense to the pres. compound vb. ἀναζητοῦντες focuses on the continued searching for Jesus (ZG 181; Bock 266; Bovon 1.111).

2:46 Ἐγένετο, see 1:5. Εὗρον 3rd pl. 2nd aor. act. indic. of εὑρίσκω. The three acc. sg. masc. of pres. ptcs. καθεζόμενον (mid. of dep. καθέζομαι, "sit"), ἀκούοντα (act. of ἀκούω; the gen. αὐτῶν is obj.), and ἐπερωτῶντα (act. of ἐπερωτάω, "ask") all modify αὐτόν either as attrib. ptcs. or as complements in a double acc. cstr. (BHGNT 96). This is the only place Luke uses διδάσκαλος for the Jewish teachers. Jesus' questions may imply that he is learning (Bock 267; Fitzmyer 442). Elsewhere in Luke's Gospel, however, Jesus' questions seek to engage his listeners in order to draw out a lesson for them (cf. e.g., 6:9; 9:18; 18:40). The following verse will confirm that the emphasis here is on Jesus' wisdom. He is not sitting at the feet of these teachers; he is "in the midst" of them, as a teacher (Bovon 1.112).

2:47 Ἀκούοντες (nom. pl. masc. of pres. act. [subst. ptc.] of ἀκούω) is the subject of ἐξίσταντο (3rd pl. impf. mid. indic. of ἐξίστημι, "amaze"). The cause of their amazement (ἐπί, ZG 181) is his "understanding" (dat. sg. fem. of σύνεσις, -εως, ἡ) and his "answers" (dat. pl. fem. of ἀπόκρισις, -εως, ἡ); i.e., "his intelligent answers" (a hendiadys, BDF §442[16]; Fitzmyer 442; Marshall 127).

2:48 Ἰδόντες, see 2:17 (temp.). Ἐξεπλάγησαν 3rd pl. 2nd aor. pass. indic. of dep. ἐκπλήσσομαι, "astonished," "amazed" ("overwhelmed" BDAG 308c; the implied subj. is Jesus' parents, NRSV, HCSB, NIV). This astonishment may be due to seeing him in the temple (Marshall 128) or in the sense of relief at finding him (Bock 268). Τέκνον, voc. Ἐποίησας 2nd sg. aor. act. indic. of ποιέω ("treated" most EVV). Ὀδυνώμενοι (nom. pl. masc. of pres. pass. ptc. of ὀδυνάω, "suffer pain," only here, 16:24, 25; Acts 20:38 in the NT; cf. LN 25.236 "great distress") expresses their manner (Wallace 628) in "searching" (ἐζητοῦμέν 1st pl. impf. act. indic. of ζητέω).

2:49 Jesus' first words in Luke's Gospel indicate an early awareness of his unique relationship with God ("My Father"). In light of 1:35, κύριος (1:43; 2:11) and σωτήρ (1:47; 2:11), and, in this narrative context, the use of πατήρ σου in 2:48, the ref. to πατρός μου appears to offer a specific confirmation concerning his divine sonship (Marshall 129; Nolland 132). The cstr. τί ὅτι ("why," BDF §299[4]; "how is it that" with ὅτι as epex., Wallace 460) is rare in the NT (here, Acts 5:4, 9; common in the LXX). Ἐζητεῖτε 2nd pl. impf. act. indic. of ζητέω (2:48; cf. 2:45). The question οὐκ ᾔδειτε (2nd pl. pluperfect act. indic. of οἶδα) expects an affirmative answer. On ὅτι see 1:22. The neut. pl. art. τοῖς is subst. before the (poss.) gen. τοῦ πατρός (Wallace 236). Ἐν τοῖς τοῦ πατρός μου (ἐν is locat.) could be (Bock 269–70):

 *1. "in my Father's house" (most EVV);
  2. "about my Father's business" (NKJV); or
  3. "among those who belong to my Father."

The first option is most likely given the use of ἐν with the neut. pl. art. is a common cstr. for referring to the house (or temple) of someone (e.g., LXX Esth 7:9 [ἐν τοῖς Αμαν, "in the house of Haman"]; Josephus, *Against Apion* 1.118 [ἐν τοῖς τοῦ Διὸς "in the temple of Zeus"]; cf. BDAG 326d, 689a; BHGNT 98; MM 436a; Bock 270; Fitzmyer 443; Nolland 131–32). Furthermore, the context also indicates an answer related to where Jesus was (Marshall 129). The inf. εἶναί (see 2:4) is complementary with δεῖ (3rd sg. pres. act. indic. of δεῖ, "it is necessary"; eight times in Matt and six times in Mark, but eighteen times in Luke and twenty-two times in Acts). The final position of με could be emphatic (Fitzmyer 443). Jesus' role as the authoritative instructor of God's will is possibly being introduced here (cf. 19:47).

2:50 Although many had marvelled at Jesus' "understanding" (cf. συνέσει 2:47), Jesus' parents (αὐτοί) did not "understand" (συνῆκαν 3rd pl. aor. act. indic. of συνίημι; cf. 18:34) "the saying" (τὸ ῥῆμα, see 1:37) that he said to them (ἐλάλησεν is equivalent to a pluperfect here, BDF §347[2]; Z §290). This is a further indication of the magnitude of what Jesus had just said. It would take some time to put all this together! The acc. sg. neut. rel. pron. ὅ (of ὅς, ἥ, ὅ) is the dir. obj. of ἐλάλησεν (see 1:55).

2:51 Κατέβη 3rd sg. 2nd aor. act. indic. of καταβαίνω (i.e., "from Jerusalem"). For ἦλθεν see 2:27. The impf. vbs. in 2:51–52 provide a summary of actions (BHGNT 99) and indicate ongoing actions (Bovon 1.115; Fitzmyer 445; *pace* BHGNT 99). Ὑποτασσόμενος (nom. sg. masc. of pres. pass. ptc. of ὑποτάσσω, "subject," "was obedient" NRSV, HCSB, NIV) with ἦν is an impf. periph. cstr. (portraying continued submission, NASB; Robertson, *Pictures* 35; Z §360; ZG 181). The previous verse has shown that Jesus' continued obedience to his parents is set in the context of his prior obedience to God, his Father (Marshall 130). Διετήρει 3rd sg. impf. act. indic. of διατηρέω, "kept" (HCSB), "stored" (NJB, NLT), "treasured" (ESV, NIV). The pl. πάντα τὰ ῥήματα summarizes more than just the temple incident (on ῥῆμα see 1:37; 2:15).

2:52 Προέκοπτεν 3rd. sg. impf. act. indic. of προκόπτω, "increase" (most EVV), "grew" (NIV). Ἡλικίᾳ dat. sg. fem. of ἡλικία, -ας, ἡ, "stature" (most EVV) could be physically (Robertson, *Pictures* 35–36; Bock 274; Nolland 133; cf. 19:3) or with ref. to maturity with age ("years" NRSV; BDAG 436a; MM 279a–b; Bovon 1.108; Fitzmyer 446; Marshall 130; cf. 12:25). Παρά here is "in the sight of" (BDAG 757b; LN 90.20). Note the development in terms: βρέφος (2:16), παιδίον (2:40), παῖς (2:43), and now Ἰησοῦς (Bock 274, citing Plummer 78).

FOR FURTHER STUDY

5. The Temple

Fay, R. C. "The Narrative Function of the Temple in Luke-Acts." *TJ* 27 (2006): 255–70.
Gurtner, D. M., and N. Perrin, *DJG*[2] 939–47.

Head, P. "The Temple in Luke's Gospel." Pages 101–19 in *Heaven on Earth: The Temple in Biblical Theology*. Edited by T. D. Alexander and S. Gathercole. Carlisle: Paternoster, 2004.

Weinert, F. D. "The Meaning of the Temple in Luke-Acts." *BTB* 11 (1981): 85–89.

HOMILETICAL SUGGESTIONS

Jesus' Preparation for Ministry (2:41–52)

1. Jesus' personal knowledge of his heritage (2:41–45).
2. Jesus' comprehensive knowledge of the law (2:46–47).
3. Jesus' unique knowledge of the Father (2:48–52).

III. THE INAUGURATION OF JESUS' PUBLIC MINISTRY
(3:1–4:13)

The (step) parallelism of Luke 1–2 culminates here as John the prophet preaches repentance in preparation for the "Lord," the "more powerful one." The voice from heaven identifies Jesus as the beloved Son, and the genealogy and temptation accounts show Jesus to be the obedient Son in anticipation of his public ministry.

A. THE FORERUNNER PREPARES . . . AS PROMISED (3:1–20)

1. Introduction to the Ministry of John the Baptist (3:1–6)

3:1 Ἐν ἔτει . . . πεντεκαιδεκάτῳ (dat. sg. neut. of πεντεκαιδέκατος, -η, -ον, "fifteenth") is the first of many temp. phrases in 3:1–2 that prepare for the arrival of God's word to John. Ἡγεμονίας gen. (of ref.) sg. fem. of ἡγεμονία, -ας, ἡ, "government," "reign" (all EVV). The gen. Τιβερίου Καίσαρος is subj. Ἡγεμονεύοντος (see 2:2) is a temp. gen. abs. cstr. The following gens. are all subord. (τῆς Ἰουδαίας . . . τῆς Γαλιλαίας . . . τῆς . . . χώρας . . . τῆς Ἀβιληνῆς, BDF §177; BHGNT 101). The three gen. ptcs. τετρααρχοῦντος (gen. sg. masc. of pres. act. ptc. of τετρααρχέω, "be tetrarch") are all temp. gen. abs. cstrs.

3:2 Ἐπί with the gen. ἀρχιερέως is temp. ("during"; ZG 181–82; Marshall 134). The sg. ἀρχιερέως acknowledges the continued authority of Annas even though Caiaphas was high priest by this time (cf. Acts 4:6). Ῥῆμα (see 1:37; the nom. subj. of ἐγένετο) occurs nineteen times in Luke (out of twenty-six times in the Synoptic Gospels). Here it signifies John's calling as a prophet (Bock 285; cf. Jer 1:1). The gen. θεοῦ is source (NLT; BHGNT 102). Ἐπί is locat. Τὸν . . . υἱόν is in appos. to the acc. Ἰωάννην. The ref. to Zechariah recalls Luke 1–2. The ref. to the wilderness anticipates 3:4.

3:3 For ἦλθεν see 2:27. Εἰς is locat. The (acc. sg. fem.) adj. περίχωρον (of περίχωρος, -ον, "neighboring") when followed by a gen. of a river, refers to the region around the river (BDAG 808b; BHGNT 102; i.e., referring to wide-ranging ministry rather than entry into a different region to 3:2, Bock 287; Marshall 135). Κηρύσσων (nom.

sg. masc. of pres. act. ptc. of κηρύσσω) expresses manner (BHGNT 102; purpose, Fitzmyer 459; the acc. sg. neut. βάπτισμα [of βάπτισμα, -ατος, τό] is the obj.). The gen. (sg. fem.) μετανοίας (of μετάνοια, -ας, ή; eleven times in Luke-Acts; cf. 3:8; 5:32; 15:7; 24:47; μετανοέω fourteen times in Luke-Acts; see 10:13) is descriptive ("characterized by"). Thus, John proclaims the significance of his baptism (Marshall 135). Εἰς ἄφεσιν (acc. sg. fem., see 1:77; "for forgiveness") indicates purpose or goal (ZG 182; cf. 1:77; i.e., that which will come through the ministry of Jesus, Bock 289; Fitzmyer 459; cf. 3:16). The gen. ἁμαρτιῶν is obj.

3:4 Ὡς introduces Isa 40:2 as the explanation for John's ministry (anticipating Jesus' ministry and the book of Acts, Pao and Schnabel 277c–78c). Γέγραπται, see 2:23. The book (βίβλῳ, dat. sg. fem. of βίβλος, -ου, ἡ, anar. due to prep. phrase and a Heb., Z §182; ZG 182) contains the words (λόγων, gen. of content) that Isaiah (gen. of source, or subj. gen.) the prophet (gen. in appos. to Isaiah, Wallace 99) spoke. The nom. sg. fem. Φωνή could be the subj. in a verbless clause (sim. NLT) or a hanging nom. ("A voice of one . . ." HCSB, NIV; BHGNT 103). Βοῶντος, (poss.) gen. sg. masc. of pres. act. (subst.) ptc. of βοάω, "cry aloud." Ἐν τῇ ἐρήμῳ is locat. (cf. 3:2). Ἑτοιμάσατε 2nd pl. aor. act. impv. of ἑτοιμάζω (a "global" aor., ZG 182). The gen. κυρίου is "for the Lord" (HCSB, NIV). Τὰς τρίβους (acc. pl. fem. of τρίβος, -ου, ἡ, "paths") is the dir. obj. of ποιεῖτε (2nd pl. pres. act. impv. of ποιέω; cf. ποιέω in 3:8, 9, 10, 11, 12, 14) with εὐθείας (of εὐθύς, -εῖα, -ύ, "straight") as the complement in a double acc. cstr. (BDAG 840c). The gen. αὐτοῦ is "for him" (NIV); i.e., "the Lord."

3:5 The nom. πᾶσα φάραγξ ("every valley"; distributive, Wallace 253; ZG 182; φάραγξ, nom. sg. fem. of φάραγξ, -αγγος, ἡ) is the subj. of πληρωθήσεται (3rd sg. fut. pass. indic. of πληρόω, "fill"). The nom. πᾶν ὄρος [nom. sg. neut.] καὶ βουνός (nom. sg. masc. of βουνός, -οῦ, ὁ, "every mountain and hill") is the subj. of ταπεινωθήσεται (3rd sg. fut. pass. indic. of ταπεινόω, "humble," "made low"). The sg. vb. treats the compound subj. as one (BHGNT 104; McKay 18). The nom. pl. neut. τὰ σκολιά (of σκολιός, -ά, -όν, "crooked") is the subj. of the sg. ἔσται (see 1:14; Wallace 399–400; the acc. adj. εὐθείαν [see 3:4], "straight," is the obj.; cf. BDAG 291a; BDF §145[1]; R 458, 595; T 253; Wallace 47, for εἰς with the acc. in place of a pred.). The nom. pl. fem. αἱ τραχεῖαι (of τραχύς, -εῖα, -ύ, "rough [ways]") is the subj. of an implied ἔσται (BHGNT 104; the acc. εἰς ὁδοὺς λείας [acc. pl. fem. of λεῖος, -α, -ον, "smooth ways"] is the obj.).

3:6 The nom. πᾶσα σάρξ is the subj. of ὄψεται (3rd sg. fut. mid. indic. of ὁράω). The acc. τὸ σωτήριον (see 2:30) is the dir. obj. (the gen. τοῦ θεοῦ is subj.). On "salvation" see 1:47.

2. The Preaching of John the Baptist on Repentance (3:7–14)

3:7 The impf. ἔλεγεν could be:

1. ingressive (NASB);
2. iter. or habitual ("he would say" Nolland 147; cf. Robertson, *Pictures* 39; Marshall 138; an example of what John said many times); or

3. a vivid emphasis that presents the action as in progress (Bock 302; Marshall 138).

Οὖν is resumptive (of the ref. to baptism and repentance in 3:3; BHGNT 105). Ἐκπορευομένοις (dat. pl. masc. of pres. mid. ptc. of dep. ἐκπορεύομαι) is attrib. with ὄχλοις. The aor. pass. inf. βαπτισθῆναι refers to the purpose of the crowds going out to John (Robertson, *Pictures* 39). Γεννήματα voc. pl. neut. of γέννημα, -ατος, τό, "brood" (most EVV), "offspring" (NET). Ἐχιδνῶν gen. pl. fem. of ἔχιδνα, -ης, ἡ, "vipers" (most EVV), "snakes" (NLT). The interr. pron. τίς is the subj. of ὑπέδειξεν (3rd sg. aor. act. indic. of ὑποδείκνυμι, "show," in this context "warned" all EVV; BDAG 1037a). The question is addressed to those who think that escape from judgment will come from mere baptism (i.e., without repentance, Bock 304; Marshall 139). The 2nd aor. act. inf. φυγεῖν (φεύγω) is the obj. of ὑπέδειξεν. Μελλούσης (gen. sg. fem. of pres. act. ptc. of μέλλω) is attrib. with ὀργῆς (Wallace 618).

3:8 Ποιήσατε 2nd pl. aor. act. impv. of ποιέω (cf. 3:4; a Sem. here, ZG 182). Οὖν indicates that what follows characterizes true repentance, in contrast to the mere act of baptism, in order to escape the wrath to come (Nolland 148). The acc. pl. masc. καρπούς (perhaps due to the specifics to follow, Fitzmyer 468; Nolland 148) is tr. by the collective sg. "fruit" in some EVV (HCSB, NIV; "fruits" in NRSV, NASB, ESV). Ἄρξησθε 2nd pl. aor. mid. subjunc. of ἄρχω (a prohibitive subjunc. with μή, Wallace 469). The pres. act. inf. λέγειν is complementary. The acc. πατέρα is pred. to τὸν Ἀβραάμ (with the art. perhaps showing the case of the indecl. Ἀβραάμ; or appos., Wallace 199). Ἔχομεν 1st pl. pres. act. indic. of ἔχω. Γάρ, causal (giving the reason why they should not rely on physical descent from Abraham). Ὅτι, recitative. The aor. act. inf. ἐγεῖραι is complementary with δύναται (3rd sg. pres. mid. indic. of dep. δύναμαι). God, rather than family descent, determines membership in his family and produces spiritual life. The dat. τῷ Ἀβραάμ is advantage.

3:9 On δὲ καί see 2:4. The nom. sg. fem. ἀξίνη (of ἀξίνη, -ης, ἡ, "axe") is the subj. of κεῖται ("laid," see 2:34). The pres. κεῖται along with the adv. ἤδη emphasizes the nearness of God's judgment (Bock 306). Πρὸς τὴν ῥίζαν (acc. sg. fem. of ῥίζα, -ης, ἡ, "at the root") is locat. Πᾶν . . . δένδρον is the subj. of ἐκκόπτεται (3rd sg. pres. pass. indic. of ἐκκόπτω, "cut off, cut down") and βάλλεται (3rd sg. pres. pass. indic. of βάλλω). Both vbs. are gnomic pres. (Wallace 524). They are tr. as fut. since the warning concerns future consequences if there is no repentance (BHGNT 107). Since πᾶν is distributive ("every"), the emphasis is on individual responses (Marshall 141; cf. the following specifics). Ποιοῦν (nom. sg. neut. of pres. act. ptc. of ποιέω) is attributive (with nom. sg. neut. δένδρον).

3:10 Οἱ ὄχλοι is the subj. of ἐπηρώτων (3rd pl. impf. act. indic. of ἐπερωτάω, see 2:46). The impf. perhaps refers to repeated action (Robertson, *Pictures* 39; Plummer 90) or a vivid portrayal of an action in progress (Bock 316; Marshall 142). Λέγοντες, see 1:66 (cf. 1:63). The subjunc. ποιήσωμεν (1st pl. aor. act. subjunc. of ποιέω) is deliberative (with the interr. τί).

3:11 Ἀποκριθείς, see 1:19. The impf. ἔλεγεν functions as an aor. with the aor. ἀποκριθείς (Wallace 543). The subst. ptc. ὁ ἔχων (nom. sg. masc. of pres. act. ptc. of ἔχω) is the subj. of μεταδότω (3rd sg. 2nd aor. act. impv. of μεταδίδωμι, "give a share"). The acc. δύο χιτῶνας is the dir. obj. (acc. pl. masc. of χιτών, -ῶνος, ὁ, a garment worn under a cloak; "shirt" HCSB, NIV; "tunic" ESV; "coat" NRSV; BDAG 1085b; LN 6.176). Ἔχοντι dat. sg. masc. of pres. act. (subst.) ptc. of ἔχω. Βρώματα, acc. pl. neut. of βρῶμα, -ατος, τό, "food" (pl. is perhaps a ref. to several items, Marshall 142). Ποιείτω 3rd sg. pres. act. impv. of ποιέω.

3:12 Ἦλθον, see 1:59. Καί, "also" (HCSB, ESV), "even" (NRSV, NIV). Τελῶναι nom. pl. masc. of τελώνης, -ου, ὁ, "tax collector." Βαπτισθῆναι, see 3:7. Διδάσκαλε, voc. Ποιήσωμεν, see 3:10.

3:13 The acc. μηδὲν πλέον (acc. sg. neut. of πολύς, πολλή, πολύ, "no more") is the obj. of πράσσετε (2nd pl. pres. act. impv. of πράσσω, "do," "collect" most EVV). The connotation of "extort" is not in the vb. itself but from the comparison made in the context (BHGNT 109–10; *pace* BDAG 860d; Marshall 143). The subst. ptc. διατεταγμένον (acc. sg. neut. of pf. pass. ptc. of διατάσσω, "command") with παρά is comp. (Wallace 297).

3:14 The subst. ptc. στρατευόμενοι (nom. pl. masc. of pres. mid. ptc. of dep. στρατεύομαι, "to make war," hence "serve as a soldier," "soldiers" all EVV; cf. BDF §413[1]; καί, "also") is the subj. of ἐπηρώτων (see 3:10). Λέγοντες, see 1:63, 66. Ποιήσωμεν, see 3:10. The use of καὶ ἡμεῖς ("we also") may indicate that these are Jewish soldiers assisting the tax collectors (Bock 313; Nolland 150; "even we" Marshall 143). The acc. μηδένα ("no one") is the obj. of διασείσητε (2nd pl. aor. act. subjunc. of διασείω, "shake violently," "take money . . . by force" HCSB; cf. BDAG 236a; LN 57.245; MM 153d). Συκοφαντήσητε, 2nd pl. aor. act. subjunc. of συκοφαντέω, "accuse falsely" (with the intent of personal profit, LN 33.434; LSJ 1671a; Fitzmyer 471; Marshall 144). Ἀρκεῖσθε 2nd pl. pres. pass. impv. of ἀρκέω, "be enough," pass. "be satisfied." Ὀψωνίοις dat. pl. neut. of ὀψώνιον, -ου, τό, "wages" (provisions for a soldier, BDAG 747a).

3. The Preaching of John the Baptist on the More Powerful One to Come (3:15–18)

3:15 The gen. ptcs. προσδοκῶντος (gen. sg. masc. of pres. act. ptc. of προσδοκάω, "wait for"; with the gen. subj. τοῦ λαοῦ) and διαλογιζομένων (gen. pl. masc. of pres. mid. ptc. of dep. διαλογίζομαι, "debating" HCSB, "questioning" ESV; with the gen. subj. πάντων; with ἐν ταῖς καρδίαις is a Sem., Marshall 145) are temp. gen. abs. cstrs. The "questioning" of the people about John concerned whether (μήποτε, indicating uncertainty, BDAG 648d; BDF §§370[3], 386[2]; R 939, 940) John might be (εἴη, on the optative see 1:29) the Messiah.

3:16 Ἀπεκρίνατο 3rd sg. aor. mid. indic. of dep. ἀποκρίνομαι (cf. also 1:19). The μὲν . . . δέ contrast highlights the primary importance of the sentence introduced with δέ and thus contrasts John's baptism of water only with Jesus' power to effect change (BHGNT 112; Marshall 145). The dat. (sg. neut.) ὕδατι (of ὕδωρ, ὕδατος, τό) could be *instr. (Bock 320; Marshall 146) or locat. (of sphere; Wallace [155] suggests both). Βαπτίζω 1st sg. pres. act. indic. of βαπτίζω (the pres. is distributive, each person is baptized once, but the action is repeated, Wallace 521). The subst. comp. adj. ἰσχυρότερος is the subj. of ἔρχεται (3rd sg. pres. mid. indic. of dep. ἔρχομαι; the pres. may stress immediacy or certainty here, Wallace 536). The gen. μου is comp. The gen. sg. masc. rel. pron. οὗ functions like a poss. gen. within the clause (BDF §§284–85; Wallace 81–83; with a redundant αὐτοῦ, Bock 321; a Sem., Marshall 146). The inf. λῦσαι is complementary to ἱκανός ("sufficient," "appropriate," with the connotation "worthy, good enough" BDAG 472d; BHGNT 113). Ἱμάντα, acc. sg. masc. of ἱμάς, -άντος, ὁ, "straps." Ὑποδημάτων gen. pl. neut. of ὑπόδημα, -ατος, τό, "sandals." Βαπτίσει 3rd sg. fut. act. indic. of βαπτίζω. Ἐν πνεύματι ἁγίῳ καὶ πυρί (as with the dat. ὕδατι) could be *instr. (ZG 184), or locat. On the options for this phrase cf. Bock 322–23; Fitzmyer 473–74; Marshall 146–47; Nolland 152–53. It has been understood as, on the one hand, a single baptism of either the Spirit's purification only (seen at Pentecost) or judgment only or, on the other hand, as a ref. to two distinct baptisms. The sg. "baptism" and the one prep. without further distinction, together with the following association of fire with judgment, suggest a ref. to one baptism (the ministry of Christ) which results in a division into those who receive the Spirit and those who receive judgment (cf. 12:49–53; 17:29–30).

3:17 Πτύον nom. sg. neut. of πτύον, -ου, τό, "winnowing fork" (BDAG 895c), is the subj. of a verbless clause (ἐστίν is implied). The gen. rel. pron. οὗ goes with πτύον and the gen. pers. pron. αὐτοῦ with χειρί (Marshall 148). The aor. act. infs. διακαθᾶραι (of διακαθαίρω, "clean out") and (2nd aor.) συναγαγεῖν (of συνάγω, "gather") express purpose. Ἅλωνα (acc. sg. fem. of ἅλων, -ωνος, ἡ, "threshing floor," or "threshed grain" on the threshing floor, BDAG 49a) is the dir. obj. of διακαθᾶραι. Σῖτον (acc. sg. masc. of σῖτος, -ου, ὁ, "wheat") is the obj. of συναγαγεῖν. Εἰς τὴν ἀποθήκην αὐτοῦ (acc. sg. fem. of ἀποθήκη, -ης, ἡ, "into his storehouse" NET) is locat. Ἄχυρον (acc. sg. neut. of ἄχυρον, -ου, τό, "chaff") is the obj. of κατακαύσει (3rd sg. fut. act. indic. of κατακαίω, "burn up"). The dat. (sg. neut.) πυρὶ ἀσβέστῳ (of ἄσβεστος, -ον, "unquenchable") is instr. The stronger One dispenses eternal judgment (Marshall 148).

3:18 Μὲν οὖν summarizes the narrative so far and transitions to a new subject (with δέ in 3:19; cf. BDF §451[1]; BHGNT 114; T 337; ZG 184). The acc. pl. πολλὰ . . . ἕτερα ("many other things," T 197; Z §153) is the dir. obj. of παρακαλῶν (nom. sg. masc. of pres. act. ptc. of παρακαλέω). Παρακαλῶν modifies εὐηγγελίζετο (3rd sg. impf. mid. indic. of εὐαγγελίζω) either as attendant circumstance (cf. NIV) or as means ("with many other exhortations, he proclaimed" most EVV, cf. BHGNT 114). The acc. τὸν λαόν is the dir. obj. of εὐηγγελίζετο (where a dat. is expected, cf. BHGNT 114–15; R 474). The "good news" here will include the forgiveness and the purifying work of the Spirit that Jesus will bring (Bock 325; Marshall 149; cf. 1:77; 3:6, 16; *pace* Fitzmyer [475] who says this is simply a ref. to John as an exhorter [ref. 1:19]).

4. The Preaching of John the Baptist that Led to Imprisonment (3:19–20)

3:19 The nom. sg. masc. τετραάρχης (of τετραάρχης, -ου, ὁ) is in appos. to Ἡρῴδης (Herod Antipas of Galilee, son of Herod the Great, is mentioned in 3:1; 8:3; 9:7–9; 13:31–35; 23:6–15; Acts 13:1) which is the subj. of προσέθηκεν in 3:20. The causal ptc. ἐλεγχόμενος (nom. sg. masc. of pres. pass. ptc. of ἐλέγχω, "convict," "rebuke" HCSB) explains Herod's response in 3:20. The rebuke concerned (περί) two things: (1) Herod's marriage to Herodias, who was the wife (the gen. sg. fem. γυναικός is in appos.) of Herod's brother; and (2) "all of the evil things" which Herod did (ἐποίησεν, see 1:49). The gen. pl. neut. rel. pron. ὧν (of ὅς, ἥ, ὅ) is attracted to the case of πονηρῶν though it refers to πάντων (BDF §294[5]; Z §16; ZG 184).

3:20 Προσέθηκεν (3rd sg. aor. act. indic. of προστίθημι, "add to") continues from 3:19 where Ἡρῴδης was introduced as the subject (specified in e.g., NIV; a Septuagintalism, BDF §419[4]; T 227; Marshall 150; *pace* Nolland 156). The demonstrative pron. τοῦτο points to what follows (Z §213) as the worst of Herod's evil deeds (ἐπὶ πᾶσιν indicates that this is a crowning instance, Fitzmyer 478; Marshall 150; though only to this point as Acts 4:27 shows, Nolland 156). Κατέκλεισεν 3rd sg. aor. act. indic. of κατακλείω, "locked up."

FOR FURTHER STUDY

6. John the Baptist

Cummins, S. A. *DJG*[2] 436–44.
Hollenback, P. W. *ABD* 3.887–99.
Murphy, C. M. *John the Baptist: Prophet of Purity for a New Age.* Collegeville, MN: Liturgical Press, 2003.
Scobie, C. H. H. *John the Baptist.* London: SCM/Philadelphia: Fortress, 1964.
Taylor, J. E. *The Immerser: John the Baptist Within Second Temple Judaism.* Grand Rapids: Eerdmans, 1997.
Wink, W. *John the Baptist in the Gospel Tradition.* Cambridge: Cambridge University Press, 1968.
Witherington, B., III, *DJG*[1] 383–91.

See *For Further Study* §7.

HOMILETICAL SUGGESTIONS

True Repentance (3:1–20)

1. Recognizes the predicament of judgment for sin (3:1–9)
2. Results in concrete life changes (3:10–14)
3. Is realized by the Lord Jesus through the Holy Spirit (3:15–18)
4. May encounter a response of hostility from others (3:19–20)

B. JESUS: THE OBEDIENT SON WHO OVERCOMES EVIL
FOR A NEW HUMANITY (3:21–4:13)

1. The Declaration from Heaven at Jesus' Baptism (3:21–22)

3:21 Ἐγένετο (see 1:5) is completed in 3:21–22 with three infs. ἀνεῳχθῆναι . . . καταβῆναι . . . γενέσθαι (Z §389; ZG 184; focusing on the actions "opened . . . came down . . . came" BDAG 198a; Nolland 159). These actions are then set in the context of the temp. refs. to baptism and Jesus at prayer (see 5:16). All of this prepares for the declaration from heaven in 3:22. The aor. pass. inf. βαπτισθῆναι (see 3:7) with ἐν τῷ is temp. (the acc. ἅπαντα τὸν λαόν is the subj.). The aor. may indicate antecedent action ("when all the people were baptized" HCSB, ESV; BDF §404[2]; Wallace 595; Fitzmyer 483; Marshall 152; Nolland 160), simply mark the general occasion with no temp. significance (Burton §109; Porter, *Idioms* 201; Robertson, *Pictures* 43; Z §390), or emphasize a perfective aspect (BHGNT 117). For other aor. infs. with ἐν τῷ see 2:27; 9:34, 36; 11:37; 14:1; 19:15; 24:30. The gen. sg. masc. ptcs. βαπτισθέντος (aor. pass. of βαπτίζω) and προσευχομένου (pres. mid. of dep. προσεύχομαι) with the gen. subj. Ἰησοῦ are temp. gen. abs. cstrs. In this temp. cstr. Jesus' baptism is subordinated so that prayer is the action contemporaneous with the opening of heaven in preparation for the descent of the Spirit and the voice from heaven (Bock 336; Nolland 160–61). The acc. τὸν οὐρανόν is the subj. of the aor. pass. inf. ἀνεῳχθῆναι (of ἀνοίγω, "open," on the form cf. BDF §66[2]; Robertson, *Pictures* 44).

3:22 The acc. τὸ πνεῦμα τὸ ἅγιον is the subj. of the 2nd aor. act. inf. καταβῆναι (of καταβαίνω). The dat. σωματικῷ εἴδει ("bodily form" most EVV; "a physical appearance" HCSB) is a dat. of manner (ZG 184; dat. sg. neut. of σωματικός, -ή, -όν; of εἶδος, -ους, τό). Ὡς with περιστεράν (acc. sg. fem. of περιστερά, -ᾶς, ἡ, "dove") may liken the descent of the Holy Spirit to the way a dove descends (Bock 338), or it may liken the bodily form to that of a dove (Marshall 153). The acc. φωνήν is the subj. of the 2nd aor. mid. inf. γενέσθαι (of dep. γίνομαι). Σύ is the subj. of εἶ (2nd sg. pres. act. indic. of εἰμί) with ὁ υἱός μου ὁ ἀγαπητός as the pred. nom. (on ἀγαπητός as unique and loved, cf. LN 58.53; BDAG 7b). Ἐν σοί is ref. The aor. εὐδόκησα (1st sg. aor. act. indic. of εὐδοκέω, "well pleased with") is not temp. ("I was pleased"!) or ingressive (Wallace 544; Nolland 164–65) but looks at the action as a whole (BHGNT 119; McKay 27; Z §253; ZG 184). Jesus is the Spirit-anointed messianic king and servant of the Lord who represents God's people (Ps 2:7; Isa 41:8; 42:1), and yet, as Son, he is this and more since he also has a unique relationship with God the Father (Luke 1:35; 2:49; 10:22). This unique filial relationship to God is the foundation for Jesus' messianic role (Nolland 165).

FOR FURTHER STUDY

7. Baptism/Jesus' Baptism
Beasley-Murray, G. R. *Baptism in the New Testament*. Grand Rapids: Eerdmans, 1962.

Ferguson, E. *Baptism in the Early Church: History, Theology, and Liturgy in the First Five Centuries*. Grand Rapids: Eerdmans, 2009.

_____. *DJG*² 66–69.

Köstenberger, A. J. "Baptism in the Gospels." Pages 11–34 in *Believer's Baptism: Sign of the New Covenant in Christ*. Edited by T. R. Schreiner and S. D. Wright. Nashville: B&H, 2006.

Schnabel, E. J. "The Language of Baptism: The Meaning of βαπτίζω in the New Testament." Pages 217–46 in *Understanding the Times: New Testament Studies in the 21st Century. Essays in Honor of D. A. Carson on the Occasion of His 65th Birthday*. Edited by A. J. Köstenberger and R. W. Yarbrough. Wheaton: Crossway, 2011.

Stein, R. H. "Baptism in Luke-Acts." Pages 35–66 in *Believer's Baptism* (see above).

HOMILETICAL SUGGESTIONS

See also at the end of 4:13.

The Father's Beloved Son Is the Representative for His People (3:21–22)
    1. Jesus identifies with his people (3:21).
    2. Jesus is the anointed Servant for his people (3:22a).
    3. Jesus is the anointed King over his people (3:22b).

2. Jesus' Genealogy (3:23–38)

3:23–38 Although detailed analysis of the genealogy is not possible here, the following are some general observations on Luke's genealogy compared with Matthew's, followed by some grammatical comments on 3:23. (1.) Matthew places the genealogy at the start of his account, and it leads to Jesus' birth; Luke links the genealogy explicitly to Jesus' adult life (3:23). (2.) Matthew begins with Abraham and works forward to David and then to Jesus; Luke works back from Jesus beyond Abraham to Adam as the son of God. (3.) Luke places the genealogy between Jesus' baptism and temptation so that the ref. to Adam immediately precedes the temptation account with Satan. Jesus is the obedient Adam who is the head of a new humanity.

The pron. αὐτός with Ἰησοῦς may indicate emphasis ("Jesus himself" NASB, NIV; BDF §277[3]; Robertson, *Pictures* 45; Bock 351) or focus attention on Jesus for what follows (BHGNT 119; Wallace 323; ZG 184; Marshall 162; "unstressed" Fitzmyer 499; "pleonastic" Nolland 170; see 1:17). The vb. ἦν is probably connected to ὡσεὶ ἐτῶν τριάκοντα ("was about thirty years old" most EVV [*pace* KJV]; on ὡσεί with the gen. ἐτῶν cf. BDAG 401c) rather than as part of a periph. cstr. with ἀρχόμενος (BHGNT 120; Nolland 170–71; *pace* ZG 184; Bovon 1.136). Ἀρχόμενος (nom. sg. masc. of pres. mid. ptc. of ἄρχω, "begin") is therefore temp. ("when he began [his ministry]"). The ptc. ὤν (nom. sg. masc. of pres. act. ptc. of εἰμί) is attrib. ("being the son" ESV). Ἐνομίζετο (3rd sg. impf. pass. indic. of νομίζω, "suppose") indicates that, although Joseph was Mary's husband and Jesus grew up with them as his "parents," Jesus was not the biological son of Joseph (cf. 1:35; 2:49; Marshall 162). Thus, the passage assumes that Joseph was the legal father of Jesus. For the relationship of Heli to Joseph see the options in Bock 919; Geldenhuys 154; Nolland 171. The genealogy continues from Joseph with names in the gen. (of relationship; without any vb. or υἱός, BHGNT 120). The gen. art. τοῦ, here and throughout the genealogy, is in appos. to the preceding noun (BDF §162[2]): "Jesus was the son . . . of Joseph (who was) the (son) of Eli (who was) the (son) of . . ." (Marshall 162). The final τοῦ θεοῦ (3:38) highlights Adam's special relationship with God (in this instance, recalling the Genesis account and Adam's creation by God, in God's likeness). In the context of 3:23 and 4:3, 9, this anticipates Jesus' obedience as the true Son of God (Fitzmyer 504; Nolland 173).

FOR FURTHER STUDY

8. Jesus' Genealogy

Bauer, D. R. *DJG*[2] 299–302.

Bock, 1.918–23.

Johnson, M. D. *The Purpose of the Biblical Genealogies: With Special Reference to the Setting of the Genealogies of Jesus.* 2nd ed. Cambridge: Cambridge University Press, 1988.

Overstreet, R. L. "Difficulties of New Testament Genealogies." *GTJ* 2 (1981): 303–26.

HOMILETICAL SUGGESTIONS

See the end of 4:13.

3. Jesus Faces and Overcomes Temptation from Satan (4:1–13)

4:1 Ὑπέστρεψεν, see 1:56 ("withdrew" Bock 369; Fitzmyer 513; "depart" Marshall 169; rather than "returned"). The nom. sg. masc. adj. πλήρης (of πλήρης, -ες, "full") could be subst. in appos. to Ἰησοῦς ("Jesus, the one who was full"), a pred. nom. (with ἦν implied, "Jesus was full"), or modifying an attrib. ptc. such as ὑπάρχων ("Jesus, who was full," BDF §418[6]; BHGNT 122; T 159). Ἐν τῷ πνεύματι with the pass. ἤγετο (3rd sg. impf. pass. indic. of ἄγω) could be instr. (cf. 2:27; Robertson, *Pictures* 48; ZG 185; Fitzmyer 513) or more broadly "in association with" (BHGNT 122; Z §116; ZG 185; Nolland 178; cf. 4:14). Ἐν τῇ ἐρήμῳ (dat. sg. fem. as a subst. adj., BDAG 392a) with the impf. ἤγετο is "led around . . . in the wilderness" (NASB; BHGNT 123; ZG 185; cf. Deut 8:2).

4:2 The acc. (for extent of time) ἡμέρας τεσσεράκοντα ("forty days") could modify ἤγετο along with the prep. phrases ("was led around . . . for forty days" NASB, sim. RSV, ESV; Robertson, *Pictures* 48; Bovon 1.141; Fitzmyer 514), or the following ptc. πειραζόμενος ("where for forty days he was tempted" NRSV, NIV; Bock 370; Marshall 169; Nolland 178). Πειραζόμενος (nom. sg. masc. of pres. pass. ptc. of πειράζω) could be attendant circumstance ("being tempted" ESV; BHGNT 123; Robertson, *Pictures* 49; Fitzmyer 514) or purpose ("to be tempted" HCSB; Wallace 636). Ὑπὸ τοῦ διαβόλου indicates agency (Wallace 433). For διάβολος as "the devil" cf. BDAG 226d (the art. is "monadic" Wallace 223–24). Luke uses διάβολος (4:2, 3, 6, 13; 8:12; Acts 10:38; 13:10) and σατανᾶς (10:18; 11:18; 13:16; 22:3, 31; Acts 5:3; 26:18) seven times each in Luke-Acts. These refs. show that the devil is opposed to God's purposes (cf. 8:12; Acts 10:38; 13:10 [cf. also Acts 5:3; 26:18, σατανᾶς]). Thus, although πειράζω could mean no more than "test" (e.g., LXX Gen 22:1; Deut 13:4), the agency of the devil in this context indicates the more sinister and hostile connotation of "tempt" ("entice to improper behavior" BDAG 793a; LN 88.308; LSJ 1354d; Bovon 1.141 [in contrast to δοκιμάζω]; Fitzmyer 514; e.g., Jas 1:13). Ἔφαγεν 3rd sg. 2nd aor. act. indic. of ἐσθίω ("constative" Robertson, *Pictures* 49). Συντελεσθεισῶν (gen. pl. fem. of aor. pass. ptc. of συντελέω, "complete," "finish") is a temp. gen. abs. cstr. with the subj. αὐτῶν referring back to ἡμέρας τεσσεράκοντα. Note the inclusio in 4:13 with the use of διάβολος, πειρασμός, and συντελέω. Ἐπείνασεν 3rd sg. aor. act. indic. of πεινάω (perhaps ingressive, NASB; Robertson, *Pictures* 50).

4:3 The first and third temptations begin with a first-class cond. (εἰ, "if," plus an indic., and assumes that the protasis is true for the sake of the argument; Wallace 11, 692–93; Z §§303–6; ZG 185; *pace* R 1009) which focuses on Jesus' status as the Son of God (εἶ 2nd sg. pres. act. indic. of εἰμί; the anar. pred. υἱός is not indef., Bovon 1.143; cf. 1:32, 35; 3:22). Εἰπέ 2nd sg. 2nd aor. act. impv. of λέγω. Ἵνα could complement εἰπέ ("say . . . that it should . . ." Wallace 475) or form part of a purpose clause ("say . . . so that it becomes," cf. BHGNT 124; Z §406–7; ZG 185). Γένηται 3rd sg. 2nd aor. mid.

subjunc. of dep. γίνομαι. The temptation is to doubt the Father's provision and use his power independently of his obedient sonship.

4:4 Ἀπεκρίθη 3rd sg. aor. pass. indic. of dep. ἀποκρίνομαι (cf. 1:19). Γέγραπται, see 2:23. Ὅτι introduces the quote from Deut 8:3 (recitative). Ἐπί expresses the "basis for a state of being, action, or result" (BDAG 364d; BHGNT 124; ZG 185). The fut. ζήσεται (3rd sg. fut. mid. indic. of ζάω, on the mid. form cf. Z §226) functions with impv. force ("shall not" RSV, ESV, NIV; "must not" HCSB; Wallace 569; rather than simply "does not" NRSV). The art. ὁ in ὁ ἄνθρωπος is generic (as a class, Wallace 230).

4:5 Ἀναγαγών nom. sg. masc. of 2nd aor. act. (temp.) ptc. of ἀνάγω, "lead up," "bring up." Ἔδειξεν 3rd sg. aor. act. indic. of δείκνυμι, "show" (the subj. is ὁ διάβολος, cf. 4:6). Οἰκουμένης, see 2:1. Ἐν with στιγμῇ χρόνου (dat. sg. fem. of στιγμή, -ῆς, ἡ; "moment of time") is temp.

4:6 Δώσω 1st sg. fut. act. indic. of δίδωμι (σοί is the indir. obj. and is emphatic, Bock 375; Fitzmyer 516). The sg. τὴν ἐξουσίαν ταύτην ἅπασαν could mean (1) "all this power" (NJB), (2) "all this authority" (NRSV, ESV, sim. NIV), or (3) "all this domain" (NASB, sim. NET; "sphere in which power is exercised" BDAG 353d). The pl. τὴν δόξαν αὐτῶν looks back to τὰς βασιλείας as the antecedent. The reason the devil is able to do this is then given (ὅτι, causal; though powerful, the devil is lying; cf. e.g., 4:31–37; 8:26–39). The temptation is to seek from the devil what God has promised (cf. Ps 2:8; Dan 7:14). Παραδέδοται 3rd sg. pf. pass. indic. of παραδίδωμι. The forward placement of the pron. ἐμοί parallels σοί in the previous clause. The dat. sg. masc. rel. pron. ᾧ with ἐὰν θέλω (1st sg. pres. act. subjunc. of θέλω; with an implied inf. δοῦναι) is the indir. obj. of δίδωμι (1st sg. pres. act. indic. of δίδωμι). Thus, "I give it to whomever I want [to give it]" (cf. BHGNT 125).

4:7 The use of ἐάν with the subjunc. προσκυνήσῃς (2nd sg. aor. act. subjunc. of προσκυνέω) is a third-class cond. (indicating something that might take place; Z §320; ZG 185). The condition that the devil makes is to submit to his rule and authority, giving to the devil what belongs to God alone (Marshall 172).

4:8 Ἀποκριθείς, see 1:19. Γέγραπται, see 2:23. Jesus quotes again from Deut (6:13). The acc. κύριον is the obj. (with τὸν θεόν in appos.) of προσκυνήσεις (2nd sg. fut. act. indic. of προσκυνέω. Λατρεύσεις 2nd sg. fut. act. indic. of λατρεύω, "serve," "worship" (cf. 1:74). As with 4:4, the futs. are impv. (Z §280; ZG 185). Note the addition of μόνῳ ("to him *alone*," not in Deut 6:13) and the only other use of προσκυνέω in Luke (24:52).

4:9 Ἤγαγεν 3rd sg. 2nd aor. act. indic. of ἄγω (cf. 4:1). Ἔστησε 3rd sg. aor. indic. of ἵστημι, "cause to stand" (with an implied αὐτόν). Ἐπί is locat. Πτερύγιον acc. sg. neut. of πτερύγιον, -ου, τό, "pinnacle" (cf. BDAG 895a; LN 7.53; MM 558a; on the art. and Apollonius's Canon cf. Wallace 239–40). On the cstr. of the protasis, see 4:3. Βάλε 2nd sg. 2nd aor. act. impv. of βάλλω. Ἐντεῦθεν, adv. "from here." Κάτω, adv. "down." The temptation is to test God's care and demand protection (Bock 381).

4:10 The devil provides a scriptural quotation of his own as his supporting rationale (γάρ). Γέγραπται, see 2:23 (used in 4:4, 8; for ὅτι see 4:4; here citing Ps 91:11). The dat. τοῖς ἀγγέλοις complements ἐντελεῖται (3rd sg. fut. mid. indic. of dep. ἐντέλλομαι, "command"). The aor. act. art. inf. τοῦ διαφυλάξαι (of διαφυλάσσω, "guard," "protect") expresses purpose (though cf. BDAG 339c; T 141; ZG 185).

4:11 The quotation (καὶ ὅτι, recitative) continues from the following verse (Ps 91:12). Ἐπὶ χειρῶν, locat. (gen. pl. fem. of χείρ, χειρός, ἡ; "on their hands" NRSV, NASB, ESV). Ἀροῦσίν 3rd pl. fut. act. indic. of αἴρω, "take up," "lift you up" (NIV). The subjunc. προσκόψῃς (2nd sg. aor. act. subjunc. of προσκόπτω, "strike against"; τὸν πόδα is the obj.) with μήποτε is a neg. purpose clause.

4:12 Ἀποκριθείς, see 1:19. Jesus' response with another quotation from Deut (6:16) shows up the devil's misuse of Scripture ("testing God is not trusting Him," Plummer 114). Εἴρηται 3rd sg. pf. pass. indic. of λέγω ("it is said," a stylistic variation from γέγραπται, Marshall 173; perhaps in distinction from the devil's use of γέγραπται in 4:10, Nolland 181; though with the nuance that Scripture is God's speech). Ἐκπειράσεις 2nd sg. fut. act. indic. of ἐκπειράζω, "test" (BDAG 307b; i.e., not in the sense of entice to do wrong but subject to test). On the fut. see 4:4, 8.

4:13 Συντελέσας nom. sg. masc. of aor. act. (temp.) ptc. of συντελέω (see 4:2, an inclusio). In light of the ref. to forty days in 4:2, the acc. sg. masc. obj. πάντα πειρασμόν, "every temptation" (of πειρασμός, -οῦ, ὁ) may refer to a sample of the range of temptations Jesus faced (BDAG 793c; BHGNT 129; Robertson, *Pictures* 53; cf. Z §188) rather than all the temptations Jesus faced (Fitzmyer 517). These three may have come at the end of many temptations (Bock 382; Nolland 182). Ὁ διάβολος is the subj. of ἀπέστη (3rd sg. 2nd aor. act. indic. of ἀφίστημι, "depart," intrans.). The devil's departure, however, is only temporary (ἄχρι καιροῦ, "for a while," BDAG 160d; cf. Acts 13:11).

FOR FURTHER STUDY

9. The Temptation of Jesus

Garlington, D. B. "Jesus, the Unique Son of God: Tested and Faithful." *BSac* 151 (1994): 284–308.
Gibson, J. B. *The Temptations of Jesus in Early Christianity.* Sheffield: Sheffield Academic, 1995.
McKinley, J. E. *Tempted for Us: Theological Models and the Practical Relevance of Christ's Impeccability and Temptation.* Milton Keynes: Paternoster, 2009.
Twelftree, G. H. *DJG*[1] 821–27.
Wilkins, M. J. *DJG*[2] 952–59.

10. Satan/Demons

*Arnold, C. E. "The Kingdom, Miracles, Satan, and Demons." Pages 153–78 in *The Kingdom of God.* Edited by C. W. Morgan and R. A. Peterson. Wheaton, IL: Crossway, 2012.
*Bell, R. H. *DJG*[2] 193–202.

Garrett, S. *The Demise of the Devil: Magic and the Demonic in Luke's Writings.* Minneapolis: Fortress, 1989.

Gathercole, S. J. "Jesus' Eschatological Vision of the Fall of Satan: Luke 10,18 Reconsidered." *ZNW* 94 (2003): 143–63.

Klutz, T. *The Exorcism Stories in Luke-Acts: A Sociostylistic Reading.* Cambridge: Cambridge University Press, 2004.

HOMILETICAL SUGGESTIONS

The Perfectly Obedient Son Wins the Victory over Satan for His People (3:21–4:13)

1. The Father's beloved Son identifies with us (3:21–22)
2. The obedient Son wins the battle for us (3:23–37 and 4:1–13)
3. The powerful Son protects us from the evil one (4:1–13)

The Son Overcomes Satan's Temptations (4:1–13)

1. Provision: Jesus was dependent on, not independent of, the Father (4:1–4)
2. Power: Jesus was submissive to, not opposed to God (4:5–8)
3. Protection: Jesus was obedient to, not manipulative of, the Father (4:9–13)

IV. Actions that Demonstrate Who Jesus Is and the Salvation He Brings (4:14–9:50)

Following the introductory explanation of Jesus' ministry, this major division focuses on the actions of Jesus (with thirteen miracles) in Galilee. The recurring question "who is this?" (5:21; 7:19–20, 49; 8:25; 9:9, 18–20; cf. 4:22, 36) shows a focus on the identity of Jesus.

A. THE POWER OF JESUS' WORD TO BRING SALVATION (4:14–6:49)

This section is characterized by refs. to the power and authority of Jesus' word (cf. 4:32, 36, 41; 5:11, 12, 24, 28; 6:5, 46). The first part of this section concentrates on ministry in Capernaum and is framed by references to Jesus' teaching and preaching in synagogues (4:14–15, 44). Although some begin a new section at 6:12 or 6:17, the sermon (6:17–49) that concludes with the importance of an obedient response to Jesus' word is a fitting conclusion to 4:14–6:49.

1. The Lord Announces His Mission to Proclaim Good News (4:14–30)

4:14 Ὑπέστρεψεν, see 1:56; 4:1; the prep. phrase expresses manner (though cf. ZG 186). The shift in geographical location to Galilee and the following ref. to preaching in synagogues suggest that the ref. to the Spirit here anticipates Jesus' ref. to the Spirit from Isa 61 (rather than an inclusio with 4:1). The nom. sg. fem. φήμη (of φήμη, -ης, ἡ, "report" NRSV, ESV; "news" most EVV; BDAG 1052d–53a; LN 33.211) is the subj. of ἐξῆλθεν (see 2:1). Κατά followed by the gen. (ὅλης τῆς περιχώρου, see 3:3) is a marker of "extension in various directions within an area" ("throughout" BDAG 511a; ZG 186).

4:15 Καὶ αὐτός, see 1:17 (transitions to the main subj.; cf. 3:23). The impf. ἐδίδασκεν (3rd sg. impf. act. indic. of διδάσκω) could be:

   *1. progressive ("was teaching" HCSB, NIV; Robertson, *Pictures* 54); or
    2. ingressive ("began . . ." NRSV, NASB).

The context here indicates that the impf. is probably a summary statement in preparation for the following events and presents the teaching as a process (BHGNT 130; Bock 392; the impf. indicates it was Jesus' teaching ministry that gave rise to the report, Nolland 184). The pron. αὐτῶν is *ad sensum* and refers back to the people of Galilee (4:14; BDF §282[1]; Marshall 177). Δοξαζόμενος (nom. sg. masc. of pres. pass. ptc. of δοξάζω) is probably a ptc. of result (from ἐδίδασκεν, Wallace 638; Bock 392). Every other occurrence of δοξάζω in Luke-Acts refers to glorifying God (2:20; 5:25–26; 7:16; 13:13; 17:15; 18:43; 23:47; Acts 4:21; 11:18; 13:48; 21:20; though cf. 3:13).

4:16 For ἦλθεν see 2:27. Ναζαρά, see 1:26. The gen. rel. pron. οὗ functions as an adv. (after a noun that denotes a locality, BDAG 732d–733a). The pf. ptc. τεθραμμένος (nom. sg. masc. of pf. pass. ptc. of τρέφω, "grow") with ἦν is a pluperfect periph. cstr. ("had been brought up"; cf. Robertson, *Pictures* 54; Wallace 583, 649). This introduction recalls 2:39–40, 50–51, and prepares for 4:23. Εἰσῆλθεν, see 1:40. Κατά with the subst. ptc. εἰωθός (acc. sg. neut. of 2nd pf. act. ptc. of εἴωθα, "be accustomed") is a marker of a norm or standard ("according to custom" BDAG 512d, 295d). The dat. αὐτῷ is a dat. of ref. or poss. (i.e., "as was his custom" ESV, NIV). The pl. (here; cf. e.g., Acts 13:14; 16:13) and sg. of σάββατον are used interchangeably (BDAG 909d; BHGNT 132; ZG 186; Marshall 181). This is the first of six Sabbath passages in Luke (4:16–30, 31–27; 6:1–5, 6–11; 13:10–17; 14:1–6). Ἀνέστη 3rd sg. 2nd aor. act. indic. of ἀνίστημι, "arise" (intrans.). The 2nd aor. act. inf. ἀναγνῶναι (of ἀναγινώσκω, "read") expresses purpose. Ἀνέστη, ἐπεδόθη, ἀναπτύξας of 4:16–17 and πτύξας, ἀποδούς, ἐκάθισεν of 4:20 frame the quotation from Isaiah.

4:17 The nom. sg. neut. βιβλίον (of βιβλίον, -ου, τό, "scroll" ESV, NIV; from βύβλος, "papyrus" BDAG 176c–d; ZG 186) is the subj. of the pass. ἐπεδόθη (3rd sg. aor. pass. indic. of ἐπιδίδωμι). The acc. βιβλίον is the obj. of the temp. ptc. ἀναπτύξας (nom. sg. masc. of aor. act. ptc. of ἀναπτύσσω, "unroll"). Εὗρεν 3rd sg. 2nd aor. act. indic. of εὑρίσκω (thus, perhaps Jesus chose this reading, Bock 404; Fitzmyer 532; Nolland 196). On οὗ see 4:16. The pf. ptc. γεγραμμένον (nom. sg. neut. of pf. pass. ptc. of γράφω) with ἦν is a pluperfect periph. cstr. (cf. Wallace 584–85).

4:18 The nom. πνεῦμα is the subj. of an implied ἐστίν (see 3:22). The gen. neut. rel. pron. οὗ is the obj. of the causal prep. εἵνεκεν ("because of which" BDAG 334d; BHGNT 133; ZG 186). Ἔχρισέν 3rd sg. aor. act. indic. of χρίω, "anoint." The rest of the verse may be structured as follows:

ἔχρισέν με
    εὐαγγελίσασθαι . . .
ἀπέσταλκέν με,
    κηρύξαι . . . καὶ . . .
    ἀποστεῖλαι . . .
    κηρύξαι . . .

The inf. εὐαγγελίσασθαι (see 1:19; expressing purpose) could modify:

1. ἔχρισέν ("anointed me to preach" sim. all EVV; Bock 401); or
2. ἀπέσταλκέν ("sent me to preach" BHGNT 133; Fitzmyer 532; Marshall 183; Nolland 192; cf. NJB, NRSV of Isa 61:1; cf. also Luke 4:43).

Πτωχοῖς is the indir. obj. "The poor" in Isaiah often include the Lord's people who are oppressed by their own leaders (Isa 3:14–15) and the nations and look forward to the deliverance of Yahweh (Isa 29:19; 41:17; cf. e.g., LXX Pss 33:7; 34:10). In Luke the poor are those who have responded to Jesus' ministry (6:20; 7:22; 14:13, 21; 16:20, 22) and ought to receive mercy from followers of Jesus (12:33; 18:22; 19:8; 21:3). Ἀπέσταλκέν 3rd sg. pf. act. indic. of ἀποστέλλω. The aor. act. inf. κηρύξαι (of κηρύσσω) modifies ἀπέσταλκέν and expresses purpose (the indir. obj. is αἰχμαλώτοις, dat. pl. masc. of αἰχμάλωτος, -ου, ὁ, "captive," only here in the NT). In Isaiah the Lord's people are occasionally described as those taken captive by their enemies because of their sin (LXX Isa 5:13; 52:2). Salvation therefore includes ἄφεσιν "release" (NRSV, NASB), "freedom" (HCSB, NIV) from captivity. In Luke's Gospel, this is "release" from captivity to sin and Satan (see 1:77; cf. 4:1–13, 33–37; 13:16). The acc. sg. fem. ἀνάβλεψιν (of ἀνάβλεψις, -εως, ἡ, "recovery of sight," only here in the NT) is the dir. obj. of an implied κηρύξαι (BDAG 59b; τυφλοῖς is the indir. obj.). In Isaiah sight often refers to the spiritual insight which comes to the restoration of spiritually blind people (cf. Isa 6:10; 29:18; 35:5; 42:7, 16–20; 43:8). In Luke the blind are likewise those who receive Jesus' mercy (7:21–22; 14:13, 21; 18:35) and "see" God's salvation (1:79; 3:6; 10:23; cf. Acts 26:18). The aor. act. inf. ἀποστεῖλαι (of ἀποστέλλω, here with ἐν ἀφέσει [manner] giving the sense of "set free" [though cf. ZG 186, instr.]) also modifies ἀπέσταλκέν and expresses purpose. The subst. ptc. τεθραυσμένους (acc. pl. masc. of pf. pass. ptc. of θραύω, "break," "weaken," "oppress," only here in the NT) describes those who are "set free." This line (from Isa 58:6) clarifies that Jesus himself does the "releasing" (Bock 409; cf. e.g., 5:20–21).

4:19 The inf. κηρύξαι (see 4:18) also modifies ἀπέσταλκεν and expresses purpose. The acc. sg. masc. ἐνιαυτόν (of ἐνιαυτός, -οῦ, ὁ, "year") . . . δεκτόν (adj. of δεκτός, -ή, -όν, "favor") is the obj. of κηρύξαι. The expression refers to God's favorable attitude (BDAG 217a) and returns to the quotation of Isa 61:2.

4:20 The aor. ptcs. πτύξας (nom. sg. masc. of aor. act. ptc. of πτύσσω, "fold up," "roll up," only here in the NT) and ἀποδούς (nom. sg. masc. of 2nd aor. act. ptc. of ἀποδίδωμι, "give back") could be temp. or attendant circumstance (τό is anaphoric). The dat. sg. masc. τῷ ὑπηρέτῃ (of ὑπηρέτης, -ου, ὁ, "to the assistant/attendant") is the indir. obj. of ἀποδούς (τῷ used for "simple identification," Wallace 217). Ἐκάθισεν 3rd sg. aor. act. indic. of καθίζω (intrans.). The pres. ptc. ἀτενίζοντες (nom. pl. masc. of pres. act. ptc. of ἀτενίζω, "look intently"; used twelve out of fourteen times in the NT by Luke [ten in Acts]) with the impf. ἦσαν is an impf. periph. cstr.

4:21 The shift from καί in 4:16–17 to δέ signals a shift in focus (BHGNT 135; R 1184). Ἤρξατο 3rd sg. aor. mid. indic. of ἄρχω (λέγειν [see 3:8] is complementary, indicating that Jesus said more than what is recorded here, Bock 412). Ὅτι, recitative. Πεπλήρωται 3rd sg. pf. pass. indic. of πληρόω. The pf., together with σήμερον (cf.

2:11), emphasizes the present fulfillment of "this Scripture" (BDF §341; Bock 412; Marshall 185). Ἐν τοῖς ὠσὶν ὑμῶν is locat. (an idiom emphasizing their immediate experience of hearing the announcement, perhaps alluding to Isa 6:10).

4:22 Ἐμαρτύρουν 3rd pl. impf. act. indic. of μαρτυρέω, "speak well of" (sim. most EVV; "affirm in a supportive manner" BDAG 618c; ZG 186). Although some see the dat. αὐτῷ as one of "disadvantage" (in view of the skepticism at the end of the verse; cf. Marshall 185–86), it is more likely a dat. of advantage in light of the following ref. to being amazed at his words (Bock 413–14; Bovon 1.155). Ἐθαύμαζον 3rd pl. impf. act. indic. of θαυμάζω. Ἐπί, causal ("by" HCSB; "at" ESV, NIV; with the dat., the ground of an emotion, Z §126; ZG 187). The gen. sg. fem. χάριτος (of χάρις, -ιτος, ἡ) might ref. to Jesus' speech as "gracious" (most EVV; cf. Eccl 10:12; Col 4:6; an attrib. gen. Z §40; ZG 187; Bock 414) to the divine influence in Jesus' words which causes the impact (Nolland 198–99; cf. 2:40) or to Jesus' message as concerning God's saving grace (Bovon 1.155; Marshall 186; cf. Acts 14:3; 20:32). The similar phrase in Acts supports the third option. Ἐκπορευομένοις (see 3:7) is attrib. (modifying λόγοις). Ἔλεγον 3rd pl. impf. act. indic. of λέγω. The form of the crowd's question (with οὐχί; a strengthened form of οὐ, BDAG 742c) expects an affirmative answer (i.e., yes, he is only Joseph's son). Thus, although the crowd was impressed by Jesus' speech and claims, it remained skeptical that he was the one who could bring such salvation (cf. 4:23). The inadequate understanding of Jesus' origin recalls 2:49 (and 1:35).

4:23 The adv. πάντως ("certainly," "no doubt" NASB, HCSB, NIV) is a strong affirmation (BDAG 755d; LN 71.16; MM 478b; BHGNT 136, citing Plummer 125). Ἐρεῖτε 2nd pl. fut. act. indic. of λέγω. In this context παραβολήν refers to a proverbial saying (BDAG 759c; Bovon 1.155). Ἰατρέ, voc. sg. masc. of ἰατρός, -οῦ, ὁ, "physician" (cf. 5:31; 8:43; Col 4:14). Θεράπευσον 2nd sg. aor. act. impv. of θεραπεύω. The proverbial exhortation for Jesus to heal "himself" (σεαυτόν) should not be limited to the following demand to prove his power in his "hometown" (πατρίδι, *pace* Marshall 187). The similarity to 23:35 indicates that the statement scoffs at Jesus' claims since he himself does not appear so grand (cf. 2:7; 9:58; Nolland 199). The acc. pl. neut. rel. pron. ὅσα ("as many [things] as," i.e., "all that") is the dir. obj. of ἠκούσαμεν (1st pl. aor. act. indic. of ἀκούω). Γενόμενα (acc. pl. neut. of 2nd aor. mid. ptc. of dep. γίνομαι) is a complement in a double acc. cstr. (BHGNT 137; though cf. BDF §416[1] and R 1040–42, 1122–24 for the ptc. after a vb. of perception or sensation). Ποίησον 2nd sg. aor. act. impv. of ποιέω. Πατρίδι dat. sg. fem. of πατρίς, -ίδος, ἡ, the areas associated with immediate family (BDAG 788d–89a; "hometown" most EVV).

4:24 Ἀμήν with λέγω ὑμῖν is a strong affirmation ("a solemn declaration" BDAG 53d; ZG 187; cf. 12:37; 18:17, 29; 21:32; 23:43). Ὅτι, recitative. The nom. οὐδεὶς προφήτης is the subj. of ἐστίν. Δεκτός, "acceptable" (see 4:19; the one who proclaims the "acceptable" year of the Lord is not "accepted"; Bovon 1.156; Fitzmyer 537; Nolland 200).

4:25 Ἐπ' ἀληθείας δὲ λέγω ὑμῖν is equivalent to ἀμὴν λέγω ὑμῖν (4:24; here ἐπί is "on the basis of" BDAG 365c). Χῆραι nom. pl. fem., see 2:37. Ἐν ταῖς ἡμέραις Ἠλίου is temp. Ἐν τῷ Ἰσραήλ is locat. Ἐκλείσθη (3rd sg. aor. pass. indic. κλείω, "shut"; οὐρανός [in this context, "sky"] is the subj.) is the first of three divine passives (ἐπέμφθη, 4:26; ἐκαθαρίσθη, 4:27; cf. Z §236). Ἐπί with the acc. ἔτη τρία καὶ μῆνας ἕξ ("three years and six months," see 1:24) is a marker of the extent of time (BDAG 367b; Z §70; ZG 187). Ὡς is temp. ("when"). Λιμός nom. sg. masc. of λιμός, -οῦ, ὁ and ἡ, "famine." In this context (4:26–27), the locat. ἐπὶ πᾶσαν τὴν γῆν probably refers to the land of Israel (BDAG 196b).

4:26 Καί, "yet" (Z §455α). Ἠλίας is the subj. of ἐπέμφθη (3rd sg. aor. pass. indic. of πέμπω). In contrast to "none of them" (οὐδεμίαν αὐτῶν), εἰ μή is adversative (used for ἀλλά "but only," BDF §448[8]; LN 89.131 ["a marker of contrast by designating an exception"]; Z §470; ZG 187). Elijah was only sent to Zarephath in Sidon (locat. εἰς), in particular to a woman who was a widow (locat. πρός with the acc. χήραν [see 2:37] in appos. to γυναῖκα).

4:27 The nom. πολλοὶ λεπροί (nom. pl. masc. of λεπρός, -ά, -όν, cf. 5:12–13; 7:22; 17:12) is the subj. of ἦσαν (see 1:6). Ἐπί is a marker of temporal association (with gen., "in the time of"; BDAG 367a; ZG 187; Robertson, *Pictures* 61). As with 4:26, a contrast is highlighted with οὐδεὶς αὐτῶν . . . εἰ μή ("none of them . . . but only"). This time the contrast is between the many lepers "in Israel," and Naaman, the Syrian (with ὁ Σύρος in appos. to Ναιμάν) who was the only one cleansed (ἐκαθαρίσθη 3rd sg. aor. pass. indic. of καθαρίζω). The repeated οὐδεμίαν (4:26) and οὐδείς (4:27) sounds an ominous note for Israel. The corresponding repeated εἰ μή and references to Sidon and Syria (as well as a woman who was a widow and man who was a leper), however, anticipate the changing picture of God's people with the ministry of Jesus.

4:28 Ἐπλήσθησαν, see 1:23 (πάντες is the subj.). Θυμοῦ gen. sg. masc. of θυμός, -οῦ, ὁ, "rage," is gen. of content. Ἀκούοντες, see 2:47 (temp.; the antecedent of the neut. pl. ταῦτα is the teaching of Jesus, Wallace 333).

4:29 Ἀναστάντες (nom. pl. masc. of 2nd aor. act. ptc. of ἀνίστημι, intrans.) is an attendant circumstance ptc. (cf. Z §363; with ἐξέβαλον 3rd pl. 2nd aor. act. indic. of ἐκβάλλω). Ἤγαγον 3rd pl. 2nd aor. act. indic. of ἄγω. Ἕως with the gen. is used as a marker of limit reached (BDAG 423d; LN 84.19). Ὀφρύος gen. sg. fem. of ὀφρῦς, -ύος, ἡ, "brow" (here of a hill ["edge" HCSB]; the gen. τοῦ ὄρους is partitive, Wallace 86). They led Jesus to the edge of the hill upon which (ἐφ᾽ οὗ) the town of Nazareth was built (ᾠκοδόμητο 3rd sg. pluperfect pass. indic. of οἰκοδομέω, on the pluperfect here cf. Wallace 584). Ὥστε with the aor. act. inf. κατακρημνίσαι (of κατακρημνίζω, "throw down a precipice" BDAG 518d; LSJ 896a) expresses purpose (BDAG 1107c; McKay 128; Wallace 591–92; Z §352 [sim. to ἵνα]; ZG 187; not "intended result" Robertson, *Pictures* 62; cf. BDF §391[3]).

4:30 Αὐτὸς δέ shifts attention back to Jesus in contrast to the crowd's intentions (BHGNT 141). Διελθών (nom. sg. masc. of 2nd aor. act. ptc. of dep. διέρχομαι) could be temp. or express manner (BHGNT 141). Ἐπορεύετο 3rd sg. impf. mid. indic. of dep. πορεύομαι.

FOR FURTHER STUDY

11. The Old Testament in Luke

Bock, D. L. *Proclamation from Prophecy and Pattern: Lucan Old Testament Christology.* Sheffield: JSOT Press, 1987.

Kimball, C. A. *Jesus' Exposition of the Old Testament in Luke's Gospel.* Sheffield: JSOT Press, 1994.

Koet, B. J. "Isaiah in Luke-Acts." Pages 79–100 in *Isaiah in the New Testament.* Edited by S. Moyise and M. J. J. Menken. London: T&T Clark, 2005.

Mallen, P. *The Reading and Transformation of Isaiah in Luke-Acts.* London: T&T Clark, 2008.

Pao, D. W. *DJG²* 631–40.

*Pao and Schnabel 251–414.

12. The Holy Spirit in Luke

Bock, *Theology* 211–26.

Hur, J. *A Dynamic Reading of the Holy Spirit in Luke-Acts.* Sheffield: Sheffield Academic Press, 2001.

Peterson, D. "The Pneumatology of Luke-Acts: The Spirit of Prophecy Unleashed." Pages 195–216 in *Issues in Luke-Acts: Selected Essays.* Edited by S. A. Adams and M. Pahl. Piscataway: Gorgias, 2012.

*Turner, M. *Power from on High: The Spirit in Israel's Restoration and Witness in Luke-Acts.* Sheffield: Sheffield Academic Press, 1996.

Woods, E. J. *The "Finger of God" and Pneumatology in Luke-Acts.* Sheffield: Sheffield Academic Press, 2001.

HOMILETICAL SUGGESTIONS

A Foreshadowing of Jesus' Ministry (4:14–30)

1. The anointed preacher who brings about what he announces (4:14–21).
2. The rejected preacher whose audience faces judgment (4:22–27).
3. The hated preacher whose death is on the horizon (4:28–30).

2. The Authority of Jesus' Teaching Demonstrated in Capernaum (4:31–44)

a. The Authority of Jesus' Word Demonstrated over Demons in the Synagogue (4:31–37)

4:31 Κατῆλθεν 3rd sg. 2nd aor. act. indic. of dep. κατέρχομαι, "go down" (i.e., from Nazareth in the hills, Marshall 191; Nolland 205). The acc. πόλιν ("town") is in appos. to Καφαρναούμ. The ref. to Galilee recalls 4:14. Διδάσκων (nom. sg. masc. of pres. act. ptc. of διδάσκω) with ἦν is an impf. periph. cstr. This impf. cstr. along with the pl. ἐν τοῖς σάββασιν could indicate:

*1. a summary of Jesus' teaching activity on that Sabbath (HCSB, ESV, NIV);
2. a general summary of Jesus' ongoing teaching activity in Capernaum (NLT; Fitzmyer 542, 544); or
3. an ingressive sense (NET).

Since the pl. σάββασιν may be interchangeable with the sg. (see 4:16), and this verse introduces the following episode (cf. also Mark 1:21), the impf. provides a background summary for the following account (Marshall 191; Nolland 205).

4:32 Ἐξεπλήσσοντο 3rd pl. impf. pass. indic. of dep. ἐκπλήσσομαι, "amazed," "astonished" (the impf. is progressive, Wallace 553). Ἐπί, causal (BDAG 365a; Z §126). Likewise ὅτι is causal (giving the reason Jesus' teaching caused amazement). Ὁ λόγος αὐτοῦ ("his word" NKJV, ESV ["words" NIV]; "his message" NASB, HCSB) is the subj. of ἦν. Ἐν ἐξουσίᾳ expresses manner (cf. BDAG 330a; "associative" BDF §198[8]; ZG 187; Marshall 192; sim. to power, Nolland 205). The combination of λόγος and ἐν ἐξουσίᾳ frames this account (4:36).

4:33 The nom. ptc. ἔχων (see 3:11) is attrib. (modifying ἄνθρωπος). The acc. πνεῦμα is the obj. of ἔχων. The gen. δαιμονίου ἀκαθάρτου ("unclean demon") is epex. (ZG 187; Bovon 1.162; Nolland 206). This is the first ref. to a demon in Luke's Gospel, and it is the most descriptive (cf. 8:29; 9:42). Ἀνέκραξεν 3rd sg. aor. act. indic. of ἀνακράζω, "cry out." The dat. φωνῇ μεγάλῃ (syntactically an instr. dat.) expresses "the manner in which they shouted" (BHGNT 144).

4:34 The form ἔα could be:

1. an interjection "ha!" (RSV, ESV; Cassirer; Robertson, *Pictures* 63; Bovon 1.162; an exclamation of anger, Fitzmyer 545; used only here in the NT; cf. LXX Job 15:16; 19:5; 25:6); or
*2. an impv. of ἐάω "Leave us alone!" (sim. NRSV, NASB, HCSB, NIV; BDAG 267b; Nolland 206; perhaps ZG 187 and Bock 431; cf. the impf. form in 4:41).

The expression τί ἡμῖν καὶ σοί ("what to us and to you") is an idiom expressing distance ("what have you to do with us" NRSV, ESV; perhaps a dat. of poss., Wallace 150–51). In this context the idiom expresses hostility (BDAG 275d). The voc. Ναζαρηνέ is in appos. to Ἰησοῦ ("Jesus—Nazarene" HCSB; Wallace 71). Ἦλθες 2nd sg. aor. act.

indic. of dep. ἔρχομαι. The aor. act. inf. ἀπολέσαι (of ἀπόλλυμι) expresses purpose. The antecedent of the pl. ἡμᾶς could be the demonic world in general (Bovon 1.162; Fitzmyer 545–46; Nolland 207) or the man and the demon (Bock 432). Οἶδα 1st sg. pf. act. indic. of οἶδα (cf. Wallace 579–80). The acc. σε in the interr. clause is the obj. of οἶδα and gives prominence to the subj. ὁ ἅγιος τοῦ θεοῦ (nom. in appos. to τίς; BHGNT 145). In contrast to the "unclean" demon, Jesus is the "Holy One of God."

4:35 The sovereignty of Jesus over the demonic realm is further accentuated with his "rebuke" (ἐπετίμησεν 3rd sg. aor. act. indic. of ἐπιτιμάω, repeated in 4:39, 41; cf. also 8:24; 9:42) and commands to "be silent" (φιμώθητι 2nd sg. aor. pass. impv. of φιμόω) and "come out" (ἔξελθε 2nd sg. 2nd aor. act. impv. of dep. ἐξέρχομαι) of the man. Ῥῖψαν nom. sg. neut. of aor. act. (temp.) ptc. of ῥίπτω, "throw" (τὸ δαιμόνιον is the subj.). Εἰς τὸ μέσον, locat. Ἐξῆλθεν, see 2:1. Μηδέν expresses manner ("without"; BDAG 647b, 177d [βλάπτω]). Βλάψαν (nom. sg. neut. of aor. act. ptc. of βλάπτω, "harm") expresses manner.

4:36 Θάμβος, nom. sg. neut. (of θάμβος, -ους, τό) or masc. (of θάμβος, -ου, ὁ), "amazement," "wonder" (only here, 5:9; Acts 3:10 in the NT) is the subj. of ἐγένετο. The impf. συνελάλουν (3rd pl. impf. act. indic. of συλλαλέω, "talk with," "discuss") could be ingressive (NASB) or iter. (NRSV, HCSB). Although the opening phrase of the question (τίς ὁ λόγος οὗτος) may be idiomatic for "what's happening here" (NET; BHGNT 147; understanding λόγος as "matter"), the similar expression in 4:32 together with the following ref. to Jesus' commands indicate that the power and authority of Jesus' word is being emphasized (cf. ESV, NIV; cf. ZG 188; Marshall 193; Fitzmyer 547). Ὅτι may introduce the reason for the question ("for" most EVV; BDF §456[2]; Z §420; ZG 188; Bock 435; Marshall 193; Nolland 208), or it may be epex. to οὗτος (NIV; BHGNT 147). Ἐν ἐξουσίᾳ καὶ δυνάμει expresses manner (cf. 4:32) and is placed forward for emphasis (Bock 435). Τοῖς ἀκαθάρτοις πνεύμασιν is the dat. complement to ἐπιτάσσει (3rd sg. pres. act. indic. of ἐπιτάσσω, "order," "command"). Ἐξέρχονται 3rd pl. pres. mid. indic. of dep. ἐξέρχομαι.

4:37 Ἐξεπορεύετο 3rd sg. impf. mid. indic. of dep. ἐκπορεύομαι, "go out" (the subj. is ἦχος, nom. sg. masc. of ἦχος, -ου, ὁ, "report," "news" BDAG 441c; LN 33.211). Εἰς πάντα τόπον ("to every place") is locat. The surrounding region (περιχώρου, see 3:3; 4:14) in this context refers to Galilee (cf. 4:14, 31).

HOMILETICAL SUGGESTIONS

See at the end of 4:44.

b. The Authority of Jesus over Sickness and Jesus' Continued Preaching (4:38–44)

4:38 Ἀναστάς nom. sg. masc. of 2nd aor. act. ptc. of ἀνίστημι (intrans.; temp. with εἰσῆλθεν [see 1:40]; NRSV, HCSB). Πενθερά nom. sg. fem. of πενθερά, -ᾶς, ἡ, "mother-in-law" is the subj. of the impf. periph. cstr. ἦν συνεχομένη (nom. sg. fem. of pres. pass. ptc. of συνέχω, "oppress," "constrained" with the sense of distress, BDAG 971a; LSJ 1714d; used by Luke nine out of twelve times in the NT). The dat. sg. masc. πυρετῷ ([μεγάλῳ] of πυρετός, -οῦ, ὁ, "fever," cf. BDAG 899b) is the complement of συνεχομένη (BDAG 971a; BHGNT 148). Although the subj. of ἠρώτησαν (3rd pl. aor. act. indic. of ἐρωτάω) is not stated, the request shows widespread concern about her condition.

4:39 Ἐπιστάς (nom. sg. masc. of 2nd aor. act. ptc. of ἐφίστημι, "stand over" [intrans.]; with ἐπάνω αὐτῆς "over her") is an attendant circumstance ptc. (with ἐπετίμησεν see 4:35). The rebuke again highlights Jesus' sovereign authority and powerful word. The instantaneous healing and response further accentuates this power and the totality of the healing. At this the fever "left her" (ἀφῆκεν 3rd sg. aor. act. indic. of ἀφίημι). Παραχρῆμα, see 1:64. Ἀναστᾶσα (see 1:39), temp. ptc. The impf. διηκόνει (3rd sg. impf. act. indic. of διακονέω) is ingressive (NRSV, HCSB, ESV, NIV; Robertson, *Pictures* 65; or iter. Fitzmyer 550).

4:40 The gen. ptc. δύνοντος (gen. sg. masc. of pres. act. ptc. of δύνω, "set") with the gen. subj. ἡλίου ("sun") is a temp. gen. abs. cstr. These events take place at the end of one long day (see 4:31, 42). The nom. ἅπαντες is the subj. of ἤγαγον (see 4:29). The nom. pl. rel. pron. ὅσοι is the subj. of εἶχον (3rd pl. impf. act. indic. of ἔχω). Ἀσθενοῦντας (acc. pl. masc. of pres. act. ptc. of ἀσθενέω) is the obj. of εἶχον (i.e., "any who were sick" ESV). The dat. (pl. fem.) νόσοις ποικίλαις (of νόσος, -ου, ἡ; of ποικίλος, -η, -ον; "with various diseases") is a dat. of ref. (or instr. Robertson, *Pictures* 65). The art. ὁ is the subj. of ἐθεράπευεν (3rd sg. impf. act. indic. of θεραπεύω). The impf. ἐθεράπευεν (cf. the locat. dat. ἑνὶ ἑκάστῳ, "on each one") may be iter. (Robertson, *Pictures* 65; or customary Fitzmyer 552). Ἐπιτιθείς (nom. sg. masc. of pres. act. ptc. of ἐπιτίθημι, "place upon") is an attendant circumstance ptc. (with ἐθεράπευεν; Wallace 644). Jesus' personal care is highlighted as well as his power over every ailment.

4:41 The neut. pl. δαιμόνια is the subj. of ἐξήρχετο (3rd sg. impf. mid. indic. of dep. ἐξέρχομαι, "go out," on neut. pl. subj. cf. BDF §133[1]; Wallace 400). For δὲ καί see 2:4. A distinction is made between those having sicknesses in 4:40 and those having demons in 4:41. Κραυγάζοντα (nom. pl. neut. of pres. act. ptc. of κραυγάζω, "cry out" [the var. κράζοντα . . . ὁ χριστός found in later mss. is a scribal clarification) could express manner or be attrib. with δαιμόνια (BHGNT 150). Ὅτι, recitative. Ἐπιτιμῶν (nom. sg. masc. of pres. act. ptc. of ἐπιτιμάω) is an attendant circumstance ptc. (with εἴα 3rd sg. impf. act. indic. of ἐάω, "allow"; cf. 4:34). The pres. act. inf. λαλεῖν (of λαλέω) is complementary. Ὅτι, causal (giving the reason Jesus would not allow the demons to speak). They knew (ᾔδεισαν 3rd pl. pluperfect act. indic. of οἶδα) that he was the Christ. This causal clause associates the two designations "Son of God" and "Christ." The two could be synonymous (Bock 439; Fitzmyer 554), or "Son of God" could recall 1:35; 2:49 and be broader and foundational for "Christ" (Marshall 197).

The acc. pron. αὐτόν is the subj. of the inf. εἶναι (see 2:4), and τὸν χριστόν is a pred. acc. (T 183; Wallace 191, 196). The inf. εἶναι is in indir. discourse (R 1103; Robertson, *Pictures* 66).

4:42 The gen. ptc. γενομένης (gen. sg. fem. of 2nd aor. mid. ptc. of dep. γίνομαι) with the gen. ἡμέρας is a temp. gen. abs. cstr. Ἐξελθών (see 1:22) is an attendant circumstance ptc. with ἐπορεύθη (see 1:39; "he went out and made his way" HCSB). Εἰς ἔρημον τόπον ("to a deserted place"; see 4:1), locat. Ἐπεζήτουν 3rd pl. impf. act. indic. of ἐπιζητέω, "search for." Ἦλθον, see 1:59. Ἕως functions as a prep. as a marker of limit (BDAG 423d; "to" ZG 189). The impf. κατεῖχον (3rd pl. impf. act. indic. of κατέχω, "hold back") is conative (HCSB, NIV; ZG 189; Marshall 198). The neg. inf. μὴ πορεύεσθαι (pres. mid. inf. of dep. πορεύομαι) indicates the crowd's purpose in trying to hold him back (BDF §400[4]; R 1171; though Wallace [599] lists this as complementary). Although this contrasts with the negative reaction to Jesus' message in Nazareth (4:28–29), it is an attempt to co-opt Jesus for their own purposes. The following verse restates God's purpose in sending Jesus.

4:43 Ὅτι, recitative. Ταῖς ἑτέραις πόλεσιν ("in other towns"), locat. The inf. εὐαγγελίσασθαί (see 1:19) is complementary to δεῖ (see 2:49). The acc. τὴν βασιλείαν is the obj. of εὐαγγελίσασθαί (R 474). This is the first ref. to "the kingdom of God" in Luke (though cf. 1:33). The gen. τοῦ θεοῦ could be poss., subj., or both. Here it summarizes the content of Jesus' preaching (cf. 8:1). In Luke's Gospel the kingdom is: both present (10:9, 11; 11:20; 17:21) and future (13:28–29; 19:11; 21:31); both God's (4:43, passim) and Jesus' (22:30; 23:42); and granted by both the Father (12:32) and the Son (22:29) to Jesus' disciples (8:10) who are "the poor" (6:20) or "humble" who "receive" Jesus (18:16–17) and therefore "enter" the kingdom, God's saving rule (18:24–26). Jesus must continue this preaching because (ὅτι, causal) this is the purpose (ἐπί is used as a marker of purpose, BDAG 366a; Wallace 658) for why he was "sent" (ἀπεστάλην, see 1:19; a divine pass.). This statement of Jesus' preaching is a summary of his quotation from Isaiah in Nazareth (4:18–19).

4:44 Κηρύσσων (see 3:3) with ἦν is an impf. periph. cstr. (for continuous activity, Fitzmyer 557). The locat. Ἰουδαίας ("Judea") may ref. to the broader Roman province of Judea rather than just the southern area of Israel (cf. 23:5; perhaps 1:5; this is both the more difficult reading and supported by better external evidence [𝔓⁷⁵ ℵ B]; the var. "of Galilee" is likely a later correction). Jesus' ministry is to the Jews as a whole (Marshall 199; Nolland 216).

FOR FURTHER STUDY

13. The Kingdom of God in Luke (4:43)

Beasley-Murray, G. R. *Jesus and the Kingdom of God.* Grand Rapids: Eerdmans, 1986.

Green, J. B. *DJG*² 468–81.

Kuhn, K. A. *The Kingdom According to Luke and Acts: A Social, Literary, and Theological Introduction.* Grand Rapids: Baker, 2015. See p. 203–74.

Thompson, A. J. *The Acts of the Risen Lord Jesus: Luke's Account of God's Unfolding Plan*. Downers Grove: InterVarsity, 2011.

*Yarbrough, R. W. "The Kingdom of God in the New Testament: Mark Through the Epistles." Pages 125–51 in *The Kingdom of God*. Edited by C. W. Morgan and R. A. Peterson. Wheaton, IL: Crossway, 2012.

Ziccardi, C. A. *The Relationship of Jesus and the Kingdom of God According to Luke-Acts*. Rome: Editrice Pontificia Università Gregoriana, 2003.

HOMILETICAL SUGGESTIONS

The Authority of Jesus' Teaching Demonstrated (4:31–44)

1. Jesus' powerful word to demons (4:31–37)
2. Jesus' powerful word to sickness (4:38–41)
3. Jesus' powerful word to all (4:42–44)

3. The Lord's Power Provides Promise for Peter's Proclamation (5:1–11)

5:1 Ἐγένετο, see 1:5. The pres. mid. (or pass.) inf. ἐπικεῖσθαι (of dep. ἐπίκειμαι, "press upon") with ἐν τῷ is temp. (contemporaneous, ZG 189; the acc. τὸν ὄχλον is the subj.). Καὶ ἀκούειν (pres. act. inf. of ἀκούω) is likewise temp. with the previous ἐν τῷ and inf. (NASB, NIV; BHGNT 154; Fitzmyer 565) rather than purpose (e.g., NRSV, ESV; Z §455γ; ZG 189). The crowds are pressing upon "him" (αὐτῷ) and listening to "the word of God" (τὸν λόγον τοῦ θεοῦ, a subj. gen. or a gen. of source, the word from God, Bock 453; Fitzmyer 565; cf. 8:11, 21; 11:28; and fourteen times in Acts). Καὶ αὐτός . . . completes the introductory ἐγένετο ("and it came about . . . that," BDAG 494d, BDF §442[5]; cf. Wallace 323; see 1:17). Αὐτός is the subj. of the pluperfect periph. cstr. ἦν ἑστώς (of ἵστημι see 1:11; intrans.; a vb. which is often pluperfect with simple past force, Wallace 586; here it is subord. to the following εἶδεν, Marshall 201; Nolland 221). Παρὰ τὴν λίμνην (acc. sg. fem. of λίμνη, -ης, ἡ, "lake"; used by Luke instead of θάλασσα) is locat. Γεννησαρέτ (i.e., the Sea of Galilee) could be acc. in appos. to λίμνην or an epex. gen. (BHGNT 155).

5:2 Εἶδεν 3rd sg. aor. act. indic. of ὁράω, "see." Ἑστῶτα (acc. pl. neut. of pf. act. ptc. of ἵστημι, "standing"; πλοῖα acc. pl. neut. of πλοῖον, -ου, τό) παρὰ τὴν λίμνην here is "lying at the edge of the lake" (NASB; ZG 189; "by the lake" ESV). The acc. ptc. ἑστῶτα could be attrib. or a double acc. cstr. (BHGNT 155). The two boats were not in use as the fishermen (οἱ . . . ἁλιεῖς nom. pl. masc. of ἁλιεύς, -έως, ὁ; on the form cf. BDF §29[5]) had gotten out (ἀποβάντες nom. pl. masc. of 2nd aor. act. [temp.] ptc. of ἀποβαίνω, "get out") of them and were "washing" (ἔπλυνον 3rd pl. impf. act. indic. of πλύνω) their nets (δίκτυα, acc. pl. neut. of δίκτυον, -ου, τό [here, 5:4, 5, 6], used for fishing in deep water, Bock 454; Marshall 202).

5:3 Ἐμβάς nom. sg. masc. of 2nd aor. act. ptc. of ἐμβαίνω, "embark," "go into" could be temp. or attendant circumstance (with ἠρώτησεν 3rd sg. aor. act. indic. of ἐρωτάω). Jesus chooses Peter's boat in particular (the gen. τῶν πλοίων is partitive, following ἕν, Wallace 85; and the gen. Σίμωνος is poss., "belonged to" T 231). The 2nd aor. act. inf. ἐπαναγαγεῖν (of ἐπανάγω, "put out") is indir. discourse. Although UBS[5] has a comma after ὀλίγον (acc. extent of space), the semicolon in NA[28] better accounts for the break before the following clause (BHGNT 155–56). Καθίσας nom. sg. masc. of aor. act. (temp.) ptc. of καθίζω (intrans.). Ἐκ τοῦ πλοίου expresses the direction from which the action of teaching occurs (BDAG 296a; R 597; qualifying ἐδίδασκεν, ZG 189). The impf. ἐδίδασκεν (see 4:15) is ingressive (NASB; Wallace 545).

5:4 Ὡς is temp. Ἐπαύσατο 3rd sg. aor. mid. indic. of dep. παύομαι, "cease," "finished" (most EVV). Λαλῶν (nom. sg. masc. of pres. act. ptc. of λαλέω) is complementary (Wallace 646). Jesus instructs Simon (1) to put out (ἐπανάγαγε 2nd sg. 2nd aor. act. impv. of ἐπανάγω, see 5:3) into deeper water (βάθος acc. sg. neut. of βάθος, -ους, τό, "depth"), and (2) to "let down" (χαλάσατε 2nd pl. aor. act. impv. of χαλάω) his nets. The pl. impv. χαλάσατε indicates the presence of others as well as Peter. The purpose (εἰς, BDAG 290d; Robertson, *Pictures* 70) of these actions is for a "catch" (ἄγραν acc. sg. fem. of ἄγρα, -ας, ἡ), i.e., of fish (NLT; cf. 5:9).

5:5 Ἀποκριθείς, see 1:19. Ἐπιστάτα voc. sg. masc. of ἐπιστάτης, -ου, ὁ, "Master," used only by Luke (seven times on six occasions) in the NT. It is used in the LXX (twelve times) to refer to those who have been put in charge, officials, overseers, and rulers (cf. BDAG 381a; LN 87.50). Parallel accounts in the Gospels use διδάσκαλε (Mark 4:38; 9:38), κύριε (Matt 8:25; 17:4), and ῥαββί (Mark 9:5). Δι᾽ ὅλης νυκτός is temp. and probably placed forward for emphasis (BHGNT 157). Κοπιάσαντες (nom. pl. masc. of aor. act. ptc. of κοπιάω) "toiled" (ESV), "worked hard" (HCSB, NIV; BDAG 558c) is probably concessive with ἐλάβομεν (1st pl. 2nd aor. act. indic. of λαμβάνω), "took" (ESV), here "caught" (most EVV). The temp. phrase ἐπὶ δὲ τῷ ῥήματί σου is also probably placed forward for emphasis and is the basis for Peter's actions (ἐπί with dat. "at," i.e., "depending on" BDAG 364d; cf. Z §126; ZG 189; Marshall 203). Χαλάσω 1st sg. fut. act. indic. of χαλάω, "let down" (see 5:4).

5:6 Ποιήσαντες nom. pl. masc. of aor. act. (temp.) ptc. of ποιέω (τοῦτο is the obj.; "when they did this" HCSB). Συνέκλεισαν 3rd pl. aor. act. indic. of συγκλείω ("catch by enclosing" BDAG 952b; "enclosed" ESV; "caught" most EVV). Πλῆθος ἰχθύων πολύ "a great number of fish" (HCSB; gen. pl. masc. of ἰχθύς, -ύος, ὁ). The impf. διερρήσσετο (3rd sg. impf. pass. indic. of διερρήγνυμι, "tear," "break") could be *ingressive ("began to tear" HCSB, sim. NRSV, NASB, NIV; Bock 457; Marshall 203) or equivalent to "were about to tear" (BDF §323[4]; BHGNT 157; conative ZG 189; Bovon 1.170; Fitzmyer 567). This could be a miracle of knowledge (Bock 457), power, or both. The emphasis on the size of the catch makes it unlikely that just Jesus' knowledge is highlighted.

5:7 They "signaled" (most EVV; κατένευσαν 3rd pl. aor. act. indic. of κατανεύω, LN 33.485) to their "partners" (μετόχοις dat. pl. masc. of μέτοχος, -ον, "business partner" BDAG 643b; or simply "companions"; see 5:10) in the other boat for help. The 2nd aor. mid. inf. συλλαβέσθαι (of συλλαμβάνω, "to help by taking part with someone in an activity" BDAG 955d–56a) completes "the message to be given by the signal" ("they signaled . . . to come and help"; BDAG 522d; with art. BDF §400[7]; R 1068; or with art. τοῦ is purpose "so that" BHGNT 158; ZG 190; though cf. Z §386). The acc. ptc. ἐλθόντας (acc. pl. masc. of 2nd aor. act. ptc. of dep. ἔρχομαι, "come") is an attendant circumstance ptc. modifying the inf. (BHGNT 158; Fitzmyer 567; subj. of the inf. ZG 190). The pron. αὐτοῖς is the dat. complement to συλλαβέσθαι (BDAG 955d–56a). The others came (ἦλθον, see 1:59) and "they filled" (ἔπλησαν 3rd pl. aor. act. indic. of πίμπλημι "both" (ἀμφότερα acc. pl. neut., see 1:6) boats. The result (ὥστε with the inf.; Wallace 593; ZG 190) of this is that the boats began to sink (βυθίζεσθαι, pres. pass. inf. of βυθίζω, "sink," "plunge"; intrans.; the pres. is conative, "in danger of sinking" BDF §338[1]; Z §274; ZG 190; Bovon 1.170; Fitzmyer 567; or ingressive Robertson, *Pictures* 71; Wallace 593; Bock 457; Marshall 203). The acc. pl. neut. pron. αὐτά (of αὐτός, -ή, -ό) is the subj. of the inf.

5:8 Ἰδών (see 1:12) is temp. The combination Σίμων Πέτρος is only here in Luke (common in John). Προσέπεσεν 3rd sg. 2nd aor. act. indic. of προσπίπτω, "to prostrate oneself before someone" (BDAG 884b; LN 17.22), "fell down" (NASB, NRSV,

ESV). The dat. (pl. neut.) τοῖς γόνασιν (of γόνυ, -ατος, τό, "knee") is the complement of προσέπεσεν (BDAG 884b) and the gen. Ἰησοῦ is poss. ("at Jesus' knees" most EVV; "at Jesus' feet" NASB). Ἔξελθε 2nd sg. 2nd aor. act. impv. of dep. ἐξέρχομαι, "go away" (HCSB, NIV). The reason Peter falls to Jesus' knees and requests separation (ἀπ' ἐμοῦ) from the presence of Jesus is "because" (ὅτι) Peter is a "sinful man" (an attrib. adj., Wallace 312). "Simon's response is appropriate to a theophany" (Nolland 222; cf. Marshall 205; cf. Isa 6:5, 8; Ezek 1:28; 2:3; Rev 1:17). The voc. κύριε (used here for the first time in Luke; cf. BDF §474[6] for the position of the voc.) could simply be a term of high respect in this preresurrection context (though recognizing Jesus as God's agent, Bock 459), or *a declaration that Jesus is the supreme Lord in view of the display of Jesus' knowledge and power together with the confession of Peter's sinfulness (Nolland 222). Peter's understanding is obviously still incomplete and capable of further misunderstanding such that here he speaks better than he knows (Rowe 82–89).

5:9 Γάρ is causal giving the explanation for Peter's response in 5:8. Περιέσχεν 3rd sg. aor. act. indic. of περιέχω, "surround," "seize" (θάμβος [see 4:36] is the subj.; i.e., "amazement had seized him" NASB). The emphasis is again on the size of the catch as the cause (ἐπί, Z §126; ZG 190) of the amazement of Peter and all who were with him ("the catch of fish" ἐπὶ τῇ ἄγρᾳ τῶν ἰχθύων, see 5:4, 6). The gen. pl. masc. rel. pron. ὧν is gen. by attraction to ἰχθύων (Wallace 339; Z §16; ZG 190). Συνέλαβον 3rd pl. 2nd aor. act. indic. of συλλαμβάνω, "capture," "catch" (used differently in 5:7, see BDAG 955d), "taken" (most EVV).

5:10 The ref. to amazement in 5:9 is continued here with ref. also (ὁμοίως) to James and John (acc. to an implied θάμβος [περιέσχεν] from 5:9, BHGNT 160), sons of Zebedee (the acc. υἱούς in appos.; absence of art. is not significant when followed by the gen. ZG 190). James and John are then further identified (οἳ ἦσαν, of εἰμί, see 1:6) as "partners" (κοινωνοί, pred. nom. pl. masc. of κοινωνός, -οῦ, ὁ) with Simon (in the fishing business; BDAG 553d; κοινωνοί may be synonymous with μετόχοις in 5:7, or κοινωνοί may be the less technical term, Fitzmyer 567; Nolland 223). Jesus' reply to Simon includes (1) a prohibition not to fear (φοβοῦ 2nd sg. pres. mid. impv. of dep. φοβέομαι, though not due to the threat of the sea, Nolland 223), and (2) a promise concerning a change of vocation. Ἀνθρώπους is acc. as the dir. obj. of ζωγρῶν and is probably placed forward for emphasis (BHGNT 160). The promise then is that Peter will be (a fut. periph. with ἔσῃ, see 1:20; 21:17) "catching alive" (ζωγρῶν nom. sg. masc. of pres. act. ptc. of ζωγρέω, BDAG 429d; Robertson, *Pictures* 71; Bock 461) people rather than fish from now on (ἀπὸ τοῦ νῦν [see 1:48], denoting a fundamental change, Marshall 205, Nolland 223).

5:11 Καταγαγόντες nom. pl. masc. of 2nd aor. act. (temp.) ptc. of κατάγω, "lead," "bring down" (in nautical contexts bring a boat to shore, BDAG 516b; LN 54.16; BHGNT 160). Ἀφέντες (nom. pl. masc. of 2nd aor. act. ptc. of ἀφίημι, "let go") is an attendant circumstance ptc. with ἠκολούθησαν (3rd pl. aor. act. indic. of ἀκολουθέω, "follow"; with αὐτῷ as the dat. complement; as an attendant circumstance ptc. the focus is on the vb. "followed," Wallace 643). This is the first occurrence of ἀκολουθέω in Luke's Gospel (cf. 5:27–28; 9:23, 57–61; 18:22, 28, 43). The plurals here indicate that the other men follow as well as Peter.

HOMILETICAL SUGGESTIONS

The Power of Jesus Provides Assurance for Ministry (5:1–11)

1. The power of Jesus (5:1–7)
2. The purity of Jesus (5:8–10a)
3. The pardon from Jesus (5:10b)
4. The priority of Jesus (5:11)

4. Jesus Heals a Man with Leprosy by His Powerful Word (5:12–16)

5:12 Ἐγένετο, see 1:5. The acc. αὐτόν (ref. to Jesus) is the subj. of the temp. inf. cstr. ἐν τῷ εἶναι (see 2:4, 6). The use of ἐν μιᾷ τῶν ("in one of the . . .," the gen. τῶν πόλεων is partitive, Wallace 85) in 5:12 and 5:17 links these two healing accounts (Nolland 226). The nom. sg. masc. ἀνήρ (of ἀνήρ, ἀνδρός, ὁ) is the subj. of an implied ἦν with the adj. πλήρης (see 4:1) as pred. (BHGNT 161). Λέπρας gen. sg. fem. of λέπρα, -ας, ἡ, a "serious skin disease" (BDAG 592c; cf. 4:27; Lev 13–14). Ἰδών, see 1:12 (temp.). Πεσών (nom. sg. masc. of 2nd aor. act. ptc. of πίπτω; πρόσωπον is anar. as the obj. of ἐπί) is an attendant circumstance ptc. (with ἐδεήθη 3rd sg. aor. pass. indic. of dep. δέομαι). Αὐτοῦ is an obj. gen. The response of the man with leprosy is similar to Peter's (ἰδών . . . προσέπεσεν τοῖς γόνασιν, 5:8; ἰδών . . . πεσών ἐπὶ πρόσωπον, 5:12). As with 5:8, the voc. κύριε is likely more than a polite "Sir" (see Nolland 227; Rowe 90). Ἐάν with the subjunc. θέλῃς (2nd sg. pres. act. subjunc. of θέλω) introduces a third-class cond. (though not implying doubt, Z §§320, 322; ZG 190; cf. Wallace 696–99). Δύνασαι 2nd sg. pres. mid. indic. of dep. δύναμαι. The aor. act. inf. καθαρίσαι (of καθαρίζω) is complementary. The man assumes Jesus' ability to cure his uncleanness; his request only focuses on Jesus' willingness.

5:13 Ἐκτείνας (nom. sg. masc. of aor. act. ptc. of ἐκτείνω, "stretch out") is an attendant circumstance ptc. with ἥψατο (3rd sg. aor. mid. indic. of ἅπτω, "touch"; a "graphic" ptc. Z §363; ZG 190). Αὐτοῦ, obj. gen. Θέλω 1st sg. pres. act. indic. of θέλω. Jesus' touch shows his compassion (cf. 7:14; 13:13; 18:15; 22:51) and his authority over uncleanness. At Jesus' word, however, the man is cleansed (καθαρίσθητι 2nd sg. aor. pass. impv. of καθαρίζω) and the leprosy instantaneously left (ἀπῆλθεν, see 1:23) him.

5:14 Jesus then (καὶ αὐτός, see 1:17) ordered (παρήγγειλεν 3rd sg. aor. act. indic. of παραγγέλλω, "order," "command") the man to tell (εἰπεῖν 2nd aor. act. inf. of λέγω) no one (μηδενί). With ἀλλά the indir. discourse shifts to dir. discourse (so most EVV; BDF §470[2]; ZG 190; the NIV includes the prohibition in dir. speech). Ἀπελθών (nom. sg. masc. of 2nd aor. act. ptc. of dep. ἀπέρχομαι) is an attendant circumstance ptc. (Wallace 643) with the 2nd sg. aor. act. impvs. δεῖξον (of δείκνυμι; ἱερεῖ dat. sg. masc., see 1:5) and προσένεγκε (of προσφέρω, "bring" with "the offering" implied, NET) so should also be tr. as an impv. ("go"). Καθαρισμοῦ, "cleansing" (see 2:22). Προσέταξεν 3rd sg. aor. act. indic. of προστάσσω, "command" (Μωϋσῆς is the subj.). Εἰς indicates purpose (ZG 191). The dat. pl. αὐτοῖς following μαρτύριον ("evidence" NJB; "proof" ESV; "testimony" NIV; ZG 191) could refer to a negative testimony against the priests, a positive witness to the priests (for official authentication, Bovon 1.176), or (since there was only an earlier ref. to "priest" sg.) evidence to the people (RSV; Marshall 210; Nolland 228). In this context it seems as though positive testimony to the priests (and by extension, the people) of Jesus' power over uncleanness is in view (Bock 477).

5:15 Δέ is contrastive. The impfs. διήρχετο (3rd sg. impf. mid. indic. of dep. διέρχομαι) and συνήρχοντο (3rd pl. impf. mid. indic. of dep. συνέρχομαι, "gather," intrans.) summarize the events that take place subsequent to Jesus' instructions to the man for silence concerning the healing (cf. NLT; BHGNT 163). The more the word spread about Jesus (περὶ αὐτοῦ, Marshall 210), the more the crowds came (Robertson, *Pictures* 72).

The large crowds come (the two infs. express purpose) "to hear" (ἀκούειν, see 5:1) Jesus and "to be healed" (θεραπεύεσθαι pres. pass. inf. of θεραπεύω) of their illnesses (ἀσθενειῶν gen. pl. fem. of ἀσθένεια, -ας, ἡ).

5:16 The nom. αὐτός is the subj. of the impf. periph. cstr. (and is unlikely to be emphatic, see 1:17; though cf. NASB). The impf. periph. cstr. of ἦν with ὑποχωρῶν (nom. sg. masc. of pres. act. ptc. of ὑποχωρέω, "withdraw") and προσευχόμενος (nom. sg. masc. of pres. mid. ptc. of dep. προσεύχομαι) is probably iter. ("often" HCSB, NIV; Fitzmyer 575; Nolland 228; rather than just duration, Marshall 210). The locat. ἐν ταῖς ἐρήμοις could ref. to "the wilderness" (RSV, NASB) or "deserted places" (NRSV, HCSB; "lonely places" NIV; see 1:80; 4:1, 42). Following the impf. of 5:15, the more the crowds came in response to the report of the leper, the more Jesus withdrew and prayed (Robertson, *Pictures* 73). Luke regularly refers to Jesus praying (cf. 3:21; 6:12; 9:18, 28–29; 11:1; 23:46).

FOR FURTHER STUDY

14. Leprosy and Clean/Unclean (5:12)

Browne, S. G. *Leprosy in the Bible*. London: Christian Medical Fellowship, 1970.
DeSilva, D. A. *DJG*² 142–48.
Neusner, J. *The Idea of Purity in Ancient Judaism*. Leiden: Brill, 1973.
*Omiya, T. *DJG*² 517–18.
Sprinkle, J. M. "The Rationale of the Laws of Clean and Unclean in the Old Testament."
    JETS 43 (2000): 637–57.
*Wenham, G. "Christ's Healing Ministry and His Attitude to the Law." Pages 115–26 in
    Christ the Lord: Studies in Christology Presented to Donald Guthrie. Edited by H. H.
    Rowdon. Leicester: InterVarsity, 1982.

HOMILETICAL SUGGESTIONS

Jesus Makes Us Clean (5:12–16)

1. Jesus' willingness to cleanse (5:12–13a)
2. Jesus' powerful word cleanses (5:13b)
3. Jesus' purpose remains resolute (5:14–15)

5. Jesus Forgives Sins and Demonstrates His Authority by Healing a Paralytic with His Powerful Word (5:17–26)

5:17 Ἐγένετο, see 1:5 (for ἐν μιᾷ τῶν see 5:12; the gen. τῶν ἡμερῶν is partitive, Wallace 85). Διδάσκων (see 4:31; on αὐτός see 5:16; 1:17) with ἦν is an impf. periph. cstr. (depicting Jesus' ongoing teaching activity, Fitzmyer 580). Φαρισαῖοι καὶ νομοδιδάσκαλοι ("Pharisees and teachers of the law") are the subj. of ἦσαν (see 1:6) καθήμενοι (nom. pl. masc. of pres. mid. ptc. of κάθημαι; an impf. periph. cstr.). This is Luke's first ref. to the Pharisees and scribes. Summary statements about the Pharisees describe a typically hostile response to Jesus (cf. 5:21, 30; 6:7; 7:30; 11:39–44; 11:53–12:1; 15:2; 16:14; 18:11). The infrequent term νομοδιδάσκαλοι (nom. pl. masc. of νομοδιδάσκαλος, -ου, ὁ, only here, Acts 5:34; 1 Tim 1:7 in the NT) is replaced with οἱ γραμματεῖς in 5:21. The rel. pron. οἵ (the antecedent is Φαρισαῖοι καὶ νομοδιδάσκαλοι) is the subj. of ἦσαν ἐληλυθότες (nom. pl. masc. of 2nd pf. act. ptc. of dep. ἔρχομαι; a pluperfect periph. cstr.). The periph. cstrs. help to provide the background for the following story (Nolland 233). Ἐκ πάσης κώμης ("from every village") is probably modified by τῆς Γαλιλαίας καὶ Ἰουδαίας. The city Ἰερουσαλήμ may modify an implied ἐκ (BHGNT 166; Jerusalem is often distinguished from Judea). Εἰς with the art. inf. ἰᾶσθαι (pres. mid. inf. of dep. ἰάομαι) indicates purpose. The combination of ἦν εἰς ("was present (in order) to") may be "was impelling him to" (ZG 191; cf. Wallace 611). The acc. sg. αὐτόν (on the var. gen. αὐτούς see Metzger 115; Rowe 94) is often thought to be the subj. of the inf. ἰᾶσθαι, and the anar. κυρίου is thought to be a ref. to Yahweh (Bovon 1.179; Fitzmyer 582; Marshall 212; Nolland 230). It is also possible, however, that the anar. κυρίου is a ref. to the Lord Jesus (cf. 2:11; 6:5; Acts 2:36; 10:36; cf. Luke 6:19) and the pron. is a proleptic ref. to the man in 5:18 (with καὶ ἰδού functioning as a marker followed by repeated uses of αὐτόν, Rowe 92–98).

5:18 The nom. pl. ἄνδρες is modified by the attrib. ptc. φέροντες (nom. pl. masc. of pres. act. ptc. of φέρω; ἄνθρωπον is the obj.). Ἐπὶ κλίνης (gen. sg. fem. of κλίνη, -ης, ἡ, "on a mat" HCSB, NIV; "stretcher" NET; cf. LN 6.106) is locat. The pf. ptc. παραλελυμένος (nom. sg. masc. of pf. pass. ptc. of dep. παραλύομαι, "weaken," "disable," pass. "paralyzed") with ἦν is a pluperfect periph. cstr. Ἐζήτουν 3rd pl. impf. act. indic. of ζητέω (with the following inf. has the idea of "tried" [most EVV] with serious effort, BDAG 428c; conative, Marshall 212). The acc. αὐτόν is the obj. of the complementary 2nd aor. act. inf. εἰσενεγκεῖν (of εἰσφέρω, "bring in"). The 2nd aor. act. inf. θεῖναι (of τίθημι, "place") is also complementary.

5:19 Εὑρόντες (see 2:45) could be temp. (NKJV, NIV) or *causal (NJB, HCSB). The (indir.) interr. clause ποίας . . . ὄχλον serves as the obj. of εὑρόντες (BHGNT 167). Ποίας gen. sg. fem. of ποῖος, -α, -ον (with an implied ὁδοῦ, BDAG 844a; Bovon 1.179; a rare gen. of place, BDF §186[1]; ZG 191; Marshall 213). Εἰσενέγκωσιν 3rd pl. 2nd aor. act. (deliberative) subjunc. of εἰσφέρω, "bring in." Ἀναβάντες (nom. pl. masc. of 2nd aor. act. ptc. of ἀναβαίνω) is an attendant circumstance ptc. (with καθῆκαν 3rd pl. aor. act. indic. of καθίημι, "let down," "lower," i.e., the focus is on the act of "lowering"). Δῶμα acc. sg. neut. of δῶμα, -ατος, τό, "roof" ("housetop" BDAG 266b; cf. 12:3; 17:31;

Acts 10:9). The men lowered him "through the tiles" (διὰ τῶν κεράμων gen. pl. masc. of κέραμος, -ου, ὁ, [tiles] made of clay, cf. LN 6.224; LSJ 940d). Κλινιδίῳ (dat. sg. neut. of κλινίδιον, -ου, τό, diminutive of κλίνη, 5:18) is a small and temporary object ("stretcher" NJB, NASB, NET; BDAG 549d; LN 6.107). The locat. εἰς τὸ μέσον, refers to the people in the house (HCSB, NIV; ZG 191; pace NET; cf. BHGNT 168). The dramatic moment, however, is highlighted by the fact that he ends up right in front of Jesus (ἔμπροσθεν τοῦ Ἰησοῦ).

5:20 Ἰδών, see 1:12 (temp.). The gen. αὐτῶν is subj. The voc. ἄνθρωπε ("Man" RSV, ESV) used in address is more like "Friend" (most EVV; BDAG 82c; Marshall 213). The pf. ἀφέωνταί (3rd pl. pf. pass. indic. of ἀφίημι) together with σοι (dat. of advantage) is an emphatic statement of forgiveness ("are forgiven," Wallace 576; cf. Marshall 213).

5:21 Οἱ γραμματεῖς καὶ οἱ Φαρισαῖοι (cf. 5:17) is the subj. of ἤρξαντο (3rd pl. aor. mid. indic. of ἄρχω). The pres. mid. inf. διαλογίζεσθαι (of dep. διαλογίζομαι, "reason" NKJV, NASB; "question" NRSV, ESV; "thinking to themselves" NIV, sim. HCSB) is complementary. The following verse clarifies that these were not verbal objections (Bock 483; Fitzmyer 584; Marshall 214). Λέγοντες (see 1:66) is often used after vbs. of deliberating for unexpressed thoughts (Z §368; ZG 191). The following two questions focus on Jesus' identity ("who is this" and "who is able," cf. 7:49; 8:25; 9:9, 18, 20). Jesus' pronouncement is understood as not simply a declaration that God forgives the man's sins but a declaration that Jesus has forgiven the man's sins. Jesus is described as "speaking blasphemies" (the rel. pron. ὅς is the subj. of λαλεῖ [3rd sg. pres. act. indic. of λαλέω]; for the use of the pl. for one saying cf. BDF §142; Marshall 214). They correctly affirm that no one is "able" (δύναται, see 3:8) to forgive (ἀφεῖναι 2nd aor. act. inf. of ἀφίημι) sins, except (εἰ μή; see 4:26) God "alone" (μόνος).

5:22 Ἐπιγνούς (nom. sg. masc. of 2nd aor. act. ptc. of ἐπιγινώσκω) could be temp. or causal. Διαλογισμούς [acc. pl. masc., see 2:35], in light of the ref. to ἐν ταῖς καρδίαις ὑμῶν, is "thoughts" (HCSB, NIV) or "hostile thoughts" (NET). Jesus is regularly described as knowing the thoughts of people (6:8; 7:39–40; 9:47; 11:17), indicating not merely perceptiveness (Fitzmyer 584) but divine knowledge (cf. 16:15; 2 Chron 6:30). Ἀποκριθείς, see 1:19. Διαλογίζεσθε 2nd pl. pres. mid. indic. of dep. διαλογίζομαι.

5:23 The nom. sg. neut. interr. pron. τί (of τίς, τί, gen. τίνος) is the nom. subj. of ἐστίν, and the nom. sg. neut. comp. adj. εὐκοπώτερον ("easier," of εὔκοπος, -ον) is the pred. nom. The inf. εἰπεῖν (see 5:14) is in appos. to τί (BHGNT 170). On ἀφέωνται see 5:20. The (intrans.) impvs. ἔγειρε (2nd sg. pres. act. impv. of ἐγείρω) and περιπάτει (2nd sg. pres. act. impv. of περιπατέω) are at one level harder commands for Jesus to issue as the evidence is immediately obvious and verifiable (Fitzmyer 485). To forgive sin, however, is ultimately harder as it is something "only" (μόνος) God can do!

5:24 The subjunc. εἰδῆτε (2nd pl. pf. act. subjunc. of οἶδα) with ἵνα indicates purpose (or an impv., Bovon 1.184; Nolland 237). Ὅτι introduces the content in indir. discourse. The Son of Man, as the one with divine authority to judge and rule (Dan 7:13–14), by implication has the authority to announce the eschatological verdict of forgiveness (Marshall 215–16). Jesus will demonstrate that he has the authority to render this eschatological verdict already, before the eschaton (ἐπὶ τῆς γῆς, Nolland 237; cf. 4:21). Ἔχει 3rd sg. pres. act. indic. of ἔχω. The pres. act. inf. ἀφιέναι is epex. (BHGNT 170). Παραλελυμένῳ dat. sg. masc. of pf. pass. (subst.) ptc. of dep. παραλύομαι (see 5:18). Ἔγειρε, see 5:23. Ἄρας (nom. sg. masc. of aor. act. ptc. of αἴρω) could be temp. (BHGNT 171) or attendant circumstance (all EVV) with the impv. πορεύου (2nd sg. pres. mid. impv. of dep. πορεύομαι). Κλινίδιόν acc. sg. neut., see 5:19.

5:25 The exact fulfillment is heightened with the repetition of the commands from 5:24 to "rise," "take," and "go." The man "immediately" (παραχρῆμα, see 1:64) "rose," "took," and "went." Ἀναστάς (see 4:38; cf. ἐγείρω in 5:23–24) is an attendant circumstance ptc. with ἄρας (see 5:24) and ἀπῆλθεν (see 1:23). The acc. sg. neut. rel. pron. ὅ (of ὅς, ἥ, ὅ; i.e., the "stretcher") and κατέκειτο (3rd sg. impf. pass. indic. of dep. κατάκειμαι, "recline," "lie down") serve as the dir. obj. of ἄρας (BHGNT 172). Appropriately, the man did this "glorifying God." Δοξάζων nom. sg. masc. of pres. act. ptc. of δοξάζω, expresses manner. On δοξάζω in Luke, see 2:20.

5:26 The nom. sg. fem. ἔκστασις (of ἔκστασις, -εως, ἡ, "astonishment") is the subj. of ἔλαβεν (3rd sg. 2nd aor. act. indic. of λαμβάνω) and (with the obj. ἅπαντας) means "astonishment seized all of them" (LN 25.217). The impf. ἐδόξαζον (3rd pl. impf. act. indic. of δοξάζω) could be ingressive (NASB; BHGNT 165) or a way of showing the ongoing impact on the people of what they had seen (cf. HCSB; Robertson, *Pictures* 76). Φόβου (a gen. of content following ἐπλήσθησαν [see 1:23]; ZG 192) in this context is "awe" (most EVV; cf. LN 53.59). Λέγοντες (see 1:66) indicates result (BHGNT 172; ὅτι, recitative). Εἴδομεν 1st pl. 2nd aor. act. indic. of ὁράω. Παράδοξα acc. pl. neut. of παράδοξος, -ον, something "exceeding expectation" (BDAG 763b; cf. LN 31.44; 58.56; only here in the NT), "incredible things" (HCSB), "extraordinary things" (ESV), "contrary to our expectation" (Nolland 239).

FOR FURTHER STUDY

15. Sin/Sinner and Forgiveness of Sin

*Adams, D. H. *The Sinner in Luke*. Eugene: Pickwick Publications, 2008.
Bird, M. F. *DJG*² 863–68.
Chatraw, J. "Balancing out (W)right: Jesus' Theology of Individual and Corporate Repentance and Forgiveness in the Gospel of Luke." *JETS* 55 (2012): 299–321.
Günther, W. *NIDNTT* 3.573–87.
Neale, D. A. *None but the Sinners: Religious Categories in the Gospel of Luke*. Sheffield: JSOT Press, 1991.
Rengstorf, K. H. *TDNT* 1.317–35.
Spencer, F. S. *DJG*² 284–87.
Wilkins, M. J. *DJG*¹ 757–60.

16. Pharisees (5:17)

*Carroll, J. T. "Luke's Portrayal of the Pharisees." *CBQ* 50 (1988): 604–21.

Chilton, B., and J. Neusner, eds. *In Quest of the Historical Pharisees*. Waco: Baylor University Press, 2007.

*Cohick, L. *DJG*² 673–79.

Saldarini, A. J. *Pharisees, Scribes and Sadducees in Palestinian Society: A Sociological Approach*. Grand Rapids: Eerdmans, 2001.

Westerholm, S. *Jesus and Scribal Authority*. Lund: CWK Gleerup, 1978.

HOMILETICAL SUGGESTIONS

Jesus Forgives Sin (5:17–26)

1. Jesus is the one with power (5:17–19).
2. Jesus declares total forgiveness of sins (5:20).
3. Jesus knows hearts (5:21–22).
4. Jesus demonstrates his authority to forgive sins (5:23–26).

6. Levi Follows Jesus (5:27–32)

5:27 The initiative of Jesus is highlighted here as he "went out" (ἐξῆλθεν, see 2:1), "saw" (ἐθεάσατο 3rd sg. aor. mid. indic. of dep. θεάομαι) Levi, and commanded that he "follow" (ἀκολούθει 2nd sg. pres. act. impv. of ἀκολουθέω) Jesus. The identification of Levi as a "tax collector" (see 3:12) anticipates the following discussion (5:29–30). Ὀνόματι is a dat. of ref. (Z §53). Καθήμενον (acc. sg. masc. of pres. mid. ptc. of dep. κάθημαι) could be attrib. or the complement in a double acc. cstr. (BDAG 445c–d; BHGNT 173). Τελώνιον acc. sg. neut. of τελώνιον, -ου, τό, "tax booth" (NRSV, NASB, NIV).

5:28 Καταλιπών (nom. sg. masc. of 2nd aor. act. ptc. of καταλείπω, "leave behind") could be an attendant circumstance ptc. with ἀναστάς (see 4:38) and the impf. ἠκολούθει (3rd sg. impf. act. indic. of ἀκολουθέω; with αὐτῷ as the dat. complement; cf. NRSV, NIV). Καταλιπών, however, is better understood as a summary of Levi's actions (NET note), and the impf. ἠκολούθει is probably ingressive (NASB, HCSB; BHGNT 174; Robertson, *Pictures* 77) rather than progressive (Fitzmyer 590; Marshall 219).

5:29 Λευίς (the subj. of ἐποίησεν, see 1:49; with meals and banquets has the mng. "give" BDAG 840b; see 14:12) first expresses his commitment to follow Jesus by holding a great "banquet" (NRSV, HCSB, NIV; "feast" ESV; δοχήν acc. sg. fem. of δοχή, -ῆς, ἡ, "an elaborate meal" LN 23.27) for Jesus (αὐτῷ is a dat. of advantage). At this banquet was a large crowd of "tax collectors and others" (τελωνῶν καὶ ἄλλων) who were "reclining" (κατακείμενοι nom. pl. masc. of pres. pass. ptc. of dep. κατάκειμαι; with ἦσαν [see 1:6] is an impf. periph. cstr.) with Levi and Jesus (μετ᾽ αὐτῶν). The periph. cstr. sets the scene for the action to follow (Nolland 245; cf. 5:17).

5:30 Οἱ Φαρισαῖοι καὶ οἱ γραμματεῖς αὐτῶν (see 5:17) is the subj. of ἐγόγγυζον (3rd pl. impf. act. indic. of γογγύζω, an onomatopoetic word, "murmur," "complain" [only here in Luke; cf. διαγογγύζω only 15:2; 19:7 in the NT; also with ref. to Jesus' association with "sinners"]; λέγοντες see 1:66). The impf. could be ingressive (NASB) or progressive (NRSV, HCSB; and probably takes place after the party, Bock 495; Marshall 220). The gen. αὐτῶν qualifies the "scribes" here as belonging to the sect of the Pharisees (cf. NIV). Πρὸς τοὺς μαθητὰς αὐτοῦ and the 2nd pl. pres. act. indic. verbs ἐσθίετε (of ἐσθίω) and πίνετε (of πίνω) indicate that the complaint is directed to Jesus' disciples and thus indirectly to Jesus at this point (cf. 6:22). This is Luke's first use of μαθητής (though cf. 4:38; 5:11). "Disciples" of Jesus are a larger group than the "apostles," though the apostles are chosen from them (6:17). Disciples of Jesus are granted entrance into the kingdom (6:20) and insight into Jesus' teaching (8:9–10; 9:18; 9:43–44; 10:23; 11:1). They are to be characterized by adherence to Jesus' teaching (6:47–48), and they are to prioritize Jesus above all else (14:26–33; Nolland 246). Τελωνῶν καὶ ἄλλων of 5:29 becomes τῶν τελωνῶν καὶ ἁμαρτωλῶν (the one art. unites the two as a group, Robertson, *Pictures* 77; ZG 192; though the first are likely a subset of the second, Wallace 280) in the complaint which asks what reason (διὰ τί "why") there is for eating and drinking with such people.

5:31 Jesus replies (ἀποκριθείς, see 1:19) with a declaration of the purpose of his mission. The subst. ptc. ὑγιαίνοντες (nom. pl. masc. of pres. act. ptc. of ὑγιαίνω, "be in good health") is the subj. of ἔχουσιν (3rd pl. pres. act. indic. of ἔχω). The gen. ἰατροῦ (see 4:23) is obj. (modifying the acc. χρείαν). The subst. ptc. ἔχοντες (nom. pl. masc. of pres. act. ptc. of ἔχω) with the adv. κακῶς ("badly") is an idiom meaning to "be ill" ("experiencing harm in a physical sense" BDAG 502a; MM 317c–d). The sentence implies . . . χρείαν ἔχουσιν . . . ἰατροῦ.

5:32 Jesus "has not come" (ἐλήλυθα 1st sg. 2nd pf. act. indic. of dep. ἔρχομαι) for the purpose (the aor. act. inf. καλέσαι of καλέω expresses purpose) of calling "the righteous" (the adj. is subst.). Rather, he has come for the purpose of calling (there is an implied ἐλήλυθα καλέσαι) "sinners to repentance" (see 3:3). In this context "sinners" refers to everyone since all need to repent (cf. 3:3, 8; 13:1–5; 24:47; note also what Jesus says about the Pharisees in 11:37–52). "Righteous," like "the healthy" of 5:31, therefore, must refer to those who mistakenly "think they are righteous" (NLT; see 15:7; 18:9). Thus, Jesus' encounter with Levi exemplifies his compassion for and fellowship with sinners, as well as his purpose in turning sinners from their sins to follow him.

FOR FURTHER STUDY

17. Repentance (5:32)

Behm, J., and E. Wurthwein. *TDNT* 4.975–1008.
Mendez–Moratalla, F. *DJG²* 771–74.
_____. *The Paradigm of Conversion in Luke*. London: T&T Clark, 2004.
Nave, G. D. *The Role and Function of Repentance in Luke-Acts*. Leiden: E. J. Brill, 2002.

18. Hospitality and Meal Scenes (5:29)

*Blomberg, C. *Contagious Holiness: Jesus' Meals with Sinners*. Downers Grove: InterVarsity, 2005.
Byrne, B. *The Hospitality of God: A Reading of Luke's Gospel*. Collegeville, MN: Liturgical Press, 2000.
Heil, J. P. *The Meal Scenes in Luke-Acts: An Audience-Oriented Approach*. Atlanta: Society of Biblical Literature, 1999.
Karris, R. J. *Eating Your Way Through Luke's Gospel*. Collegeville, MN: Liturgical Press, 2006.
Perrin, N. *DJG²* 492–501.
Powell, M. A. *DJG²* 925–31.
Smith, D. E. "Table Fellowship as a Literary Motif in the Gospel of Luke." *JBL* 106 (1987): 613–38.

HOMILETICAL SUGGESTIONS

Jesus Changes Sinners (5:27–32)

1. Jesus' initiative toward sinners (5:27–28)
2. Jesus' fellowship with sinners (5:29–30)
3. Jesus' purpose for sinners (5:31–32)

7. The Presence of the Bridegroom and the Newness that Jesus Brings (5:33–39)

5:33 Οἱ (as a pers. pron. "they," Wallace 212) is the subj. of εἶπαν and shows a loose connection with the previous verses (cf. 5:30). This time the objection is directed to Jesus (πρὸς αὐτόν) in the form of a statement which functions as a question (though many mss. read διὰ τί which reflects the question in 5:30; cf. Mark 2:18). Οἱ μαθηταὶ Ἰωάννου is the subj. of νηστεύουσιν (3rd pl. pres. act. indic. of νηστεύω, "fast") and ποιοῦνται (3rd pl. pres. mid. indic. of ποιέω). The acc. pl. neut. πυκνά (of πυκνός, -ή, -όν) is adv. ("frequently"; BDAG 897a; ZG 192). Δεήσεις, "prayers" (acc. pl. fem., see 1:13), with ποιέω is an idiom for "praying" (cf. NASB, ESV "offer prayers"; Z §227; Fitzmyer 598). Καί should be read as parataxis (BDF §442[4]) as the issue is not lack of prayer but fasting in contrast to "eating and drinking" (Nolland 247). The art. οἱ probably modifies an implied μαθηταί following the structure at the beginning of the statement (most EVV; Wallace 235). The change from the gen. (Ἰωάννου, τῶν Φαρισαίων) to the dat. σοί (of poss. or ref.) may serve to emphasize the contrast ("the ones belonging to you" BHGNT 177; οἱ . . . σοί "yours" ZG 192). Ἐσθίουσιν and πίνουσιν are 3rd pl. pres. act. indics.

5:34 Jesus answers them with a question which with μή expects the answer "no" (e.g., "You can't . . . can you?" HCSB; ZG 192). Δύνασθε 2nd pl. pres. mid. indic. of dep. δύναμαι. Τοὺς υἱοὺς τοῦ νυμφῶνος (gen. sg. masc. of νυμφών, -ῶνος, ὁ), "sons of the bride chamber," is an idiom for "wedding guests" (NRSV, HCSB, ESV; i.e., friends of the house celebrating the wedding, Z §43; ZG 192; Marshall 225; or the more specific "friends of the bridegroom" NKJV, NIV; BDAG 681a; cf. LN 11.17). Ἐν with the rel. pron. ᾧ is temp. (perhaps with an implied ὁ χρόνος, Bovon 1.191). Νυμφίος nom. sg. masc. of νυμφίος, -ου, ὁ, "bridegroom" (the subj. of ἐστίν). The inf. ποιῆσαι (see 1:72) is complementary to δύνασθε. The aor. act. inf. νηστεῦσαι (of νηστεύω) is complementary to ποιῆσαι (in a causal cstr. BHGNT 178; in this context ποιῆσαι is "make," all EVV; "force" BDAG 840c).

5:35 Ἐλεύσονται 3rd pl. fut. mid. indic. of dep. ἔρχομαι (ἡμέραι is the subj.). Καί may introduce a new sentence or clause (cf. NASB), or it may introduce an epex. clause (most EVV; cf. BDF §382[3]; BHGNT 178). In the dramatic ref. to the time when the bridegroom is taken (ἀπαρθῇ 3rd sg. aor. pass. subjunc. of ἀπαίρω, "take away") from his wedding guests (ἀπ᾽ αὐτῶν), Jesus alludes to his death. Νηστεύσουσιν 3rd pl. fut. act. indic. of νηστεύω. The focus here is the grief and accompanying fasting that will follow Jesus' death (cf. 24:17; and joy in 24:41, 52).

5:36 The impf. ἔλεγεν indicates the continuity of Jesus' parable with the preceding statements (BHGNT 179; BDF §329; Z §272; "he added" ZG 193). As with 4:23, παραβολήν in this context refers to a proverbial saying (BDAG 759c). Although there is continuity (both the old and new are "garments"), what Jesus brings is not just more of the same. The arrival of God's salvation and decisive forgiveness brings an end to the previous institutions that were temporary in anticipation of God's saving rule. Thus, on the one hand (5:36), the new is not just a patch that can be added to the old. On the other hand (5:37), the old with its constraints is not able to contain the new (Nolland

251). Οὐδείς is the subj. and the acc. ἐπίβλημα (acc. sg. neut. of ἐπίβλημα, -ατος, τό, "patch") is the obj. of σχίσας (nom. sg. masc. of aor. act. [temp.] ptc. of σχίζω, "split," "tear"). Οὐδείς in 5:36, 37, 39 highlights these things as something "no one" does. Ἐπιβάλλει 3rd sg. pres. act. indic. of ἐπιβάλλω, "put on" (here "sew on" NRSV). The contrast is between a patch torn from a "new garment" (ἀπὸ ἱματίου καινοῦ) and sown on an "old garment" (ἐπὶ ἱμάτιον παλαιόν [acc. sg. neut. of παλαιός, -ά, -όν; cf. 5:37, 39]). The combination of εἰ δὲ μή γε is used after a neg. clause to introduce a clause that refers to what would happen if this were to occur (i.e., "if he does" ESV; BDAG 278d; BDF §439; ZG 193). The person who does this "will tear" (σχίσει 3rd sg. fut. act. indic. of σχίζω) "the new" (acc. τὸ καινόν). The nom. ἐπίβλημα (the art. τό makes the following prep. phrase ἀπὸ τοῦ καινοῦ an adj.; i.e., "the piece from the new" ESV) is the subj. of συμφωνήσει (3rd sg. fut. act. indic. of συμφωνέω, "agree with," "match" most EVV). Τῷ παλαιῷ is the dat. (sg. neut.) complement to συμφωνήσει. Καινός is used three times in 5:36 with ref. to garments and again in 5:38 for wineskins. Νέος is used four times in 5:37–39 with ref. to wine.

5:37 Βάλλει 3rd sg. pres. act. indic. of βάλλω ("pours" NIV; νέον acc. sg. masc. of νέος, -α, -ον). Ἀσκοὺς παλαιούς, "old wineskins" (acc. pl. masc. of ἀσκός, -οῦ, ὁ). On εἰ δὲ μή γε see 5:36. Ὁ οἶνος ὁ νέος (i.e., "fresh wine" Bovon 1.193; Marshall 227) is the subj. of ῥήξει (3rd sg. fut. act. indic. of ῥήγνυμι, "break apart," "burst"). The nom. αὐτός (the antecedent is ὁ οἶνος ὁ νέος) is the subj. of ἐκχυθήσεται (3rd sg. fut. pass. indic. of ἐκχέω, "it will be spilled" ESV). Furthermore, the wineskins (οἱ ἀσκοί) will be destroyed (ἀπολοῦνται 3rd pl. fut. mid. indic. of ἀπόλλυμι).

5:38 The acc. οἶνον νέον is the obj. of an implied βάλλω. Βλητέον is a verbal adj. "must be put" (only here in the NT; cf. BDF §§65[3], 127[4]).

5:39 Πιών (nom. sg. masc. of 2nd aor. act. ptc. of πίνω) could be temp. (most EVV) or attrib. (NLT). Those who drink "the old (wine)" do not want (θέλει 3rd sg. pres. act. indic. of θέλω) the new because (γάρ) they say "the old (wine)" is "good" (NRSV; ESV; "good enough" NASB; "suits me fine" BDAG 1090a; rather than "better" HCSB, NIV; Bovon 1.194; on the omission of the whole verse in D and for χρηστός [nom. sg. masc. pred. adj. of χρηστός, -ή, -όν] rather than χρηστότερος [comp.], see Bock 534). Those satisfied with the old forms and institutions do not even see the need for the newness that Jesus brings (cf. 5:31–32).

HOMILETICAL SUGGESTIONS

The Radical Significance of Jesus' Arrival (5:33–39)
1. Jesus brings joy (5:33–35).
2. Jesus brings newness (5:36–38).
3. Jesus brings satisfaction (5:39).

8. Jesus Is Lord of the Sabbath (6:1–11)

Following the previous focus on the newness that Jesus brings and the preference some have for the old, this section highlights the conflict that arises when Jesus demonstrates his authority to determine what is good.

a. Jesus Determines What Is Legitimate to Do on the Sabbath (6:1–5)

6:1 Ἐγένετο, see 1:5. The sg. anar. σαββάτῳ (see 4:16) is indef. (Nolland 255). The acc. αὐτόν (ref. to Jesus) is the subj. of the pres. mid. inf. διαπορεύεσθαι (of dep. διαπορεύομαι, "to go through," modifying ἐγένετο). See Marshall (230) for the scribal addition of δευτεροπρώτῳ ("second-first") in Western and Byzantine mss. (cf. NKJV). The adj. σπορίμων (gen. pl. neut. of σπόριμος, -ον, "sown") is subst. ("grain fields" BDAG 939a). Ἔτιλλον 3rd pl. impf. act. indic. of τίλλω, "pick," "pluck." Ἤσθιον 3rd pl. impf. act. indic. of ἐσθίω. Τοὺς στάχυας acc. pl. masc. of στάχυς, -υος, ὁ, "heads of wheat" (BDAG 941d–42a; LN 3.40; cf. Deut 23:25). The pres. ptc. ψώχοντες (nom. pl. masc. of pres. act. ptc. of ψώχω, "rub") could be temp. or means with the dat. pl. ταῖς χερσίν (of sg. χείρ) as instr. (BHGNT 182).

6:2 The 2nd pl. of ποιεῖτε (see 3:4) indicates that this is a general accusation that includes Jesus' disciples. Ἔξεστιν 3rd sg. pres. act. indic. of ἔξειμι (a form absent from the NT), "lawful," "authorized" (cf. BDAG 348d; repeated in 6:4, 9; the rel. clause ὃ οὐκ ἔξεστιν is the obj. of ποιεῖτε). For the pl. σάββασιν, see 4:16.

6:3 Ἀποκριθείς, see 1:19. The particle οὐδέ introduces a question (completed in 6:4) which expects the answer "yes." The acc. demonstrative pron. τοῦτο (with οὐδέ "not even this") is the obj. of ἀνέγνωτε (2nd pl. 2nd aor. act. indic. of ἀναγινώσκω, "read") and points forward to the following description (6:4). Ἐποίησεν (see 1:49) corresponds to ποιεῖτε (6:2). Αὐτὸς καὶ οἱ μετ' αὐτοῦ (the subst. ptc. ὄντες [nom. pl. masc. of pres. act. ptc. of εἰμί] was added for clarification in some mss.) is the subj. of ἐπείνασεν (see 4:2; the sg. vb. indicates the primary importance of David as the subj., BHGNT 183; McKay 18).

6:4 Ὡς introduces the clause as epex. to τοῦτο (6:3; BHGNT 183; R 1032). Εἰσῆλθεν, see 1:40. Λαβών (nom. sg. masc. of 2nd aor. act. ptc. of λαμβάνω) could be temp. or attendant circumstance with ἔφαγεν (see 4:2) and ἔδωκεν (3rd sg. aor. act. indic. of δίδωμι). The dat. art. τοῖς is a nominalizer and makes τοῖς μετ' αὐτοῦ the indir. obj. of ἔδωκεν (BHGNT 184). The acc. pl. masc. rel. pron. οὕς (of ὅς, ἥ, ὅ; the antecedent is τοὺς ἄρτους; προθέσεως gen. sg. fem. of πρόθεσις, -εως, ἡ, "setting forth," "presentation," "sacred bread" HCSB) is the obj. of the 2nd aor. act. inf. φαγεῖν (of ἐσθίω; the inf. is complementary to ἔξεστιν [see 6:2]). Only (μόνους) the priests are authorized to eat this bread (the acc. pl. masc. μόνους τοὺς ἱερεῖς [see 1:5] is the subj. of an implied φαγεῖν, BDF 409[3]; T 149; ZG 193; for εἰ μή see 4:26). On the comparison, see Bock 525; Marshall 232; Nolland 257; Pao and Schnabel 294b–d (6:5 indicates a "greater than David" argument).

6:5 The impf. ἔλεγεν introduces this saying of Jesus as the culmination of this episode (cf. BHGNT 184). The placement of κύριος is emphatic (BHGNT 185; it is the [anar.] pred., ZG 193). Τοῦ σαββάτου is a gen. of subord. Jesus has "the right to authoritatively represent the divine intention for the sabbath" (Nolland 258).

b. Jesus Demonstrates His Authority as Lord and Does What Is Good on the Sabbath (6:6–11)

6:6 Ἐγένετο, see 1:5. Although another episode is introduced with the temp. ἐν ἑτέρῳ σαββάτῳ, the topic of what is lawful (cf. 6:9) on the Sabbath links this account with the previous one. As with 6:1, the infs. εἰσελθεῖν (2nd aor. act. of dep. εἰσέρχομαι) and διδάσκειν (pres. act. of διδάσκω) modify ἐγένετο (Fitzmyer 610). The pres. διδάσκειν may be ingressive (NJB; BHGNT 185) or ref. to progressive action ("was teaching" NASB, HCSB, ESV, NIV). The pred. nom. sg. fem. ξηρά (of ξηρός, -ά, -όν), "withered," refers to a withering of the man's right hand due to disease so that the hand is immobile (BDAG 685b; hence "paralyzed" HCSB; "shriveled" NIV).

6:7 Οἱ γραμματεῖς καὶ οἱ Φαρισαῖοι is the subj. of παρετηροῦντο (3rd pl. impf. mid. indic. of παρατηρέω, "watch closely"; cf. 14:1; 20:20; Acts 9:24). The pres. θεραπεύει (3rd sg. pres. act. indic. of θεραπεύω) perhaps indicates the assumption of the scribes and Pharisees that Jesus does heal on the Sabbath (cf. 4:31–40; on the var. fut. see Bock 536). The particle εἰ is used with indir. questions ("to see whether" NRSV, ESV; BDAG 278b; BDF §440[3]; R 916; ZG 194). The purpose of their careful attention to Jesus is so they could find (ἵνα with the subjunc. εὕρωσιν 3rd pl. 2nd aor. act. subjunc. of εὑρίσκω) something to accuse him of (κατηγορεῖν pres. act. inf. of κατηγορέω, "bring charges" against; cf. HCSB; BDAG 533c; the obj. of εὕρωσιν, sim. to the cstr. of an inf. after a vb. of knowing, Nolland 260). Εὕρωσιν indicates a fact-finding investigation in order to have a basis for their accusation (Nolland 260; *pace* Fitzmyer [610–11] who sees this as an Aram. "be able"). The gen. αὐτοῦ is the obj. of κατηγορεῖν.

6:8 Αὐτός shifts the focus back to Jesus as the subj. (cf. 1:17). Jesus again (cf. 5:22) knows (ᾔδει 3rd sg. pluperfect act. indic. of οἶδα) the thoughts (διαλογισμούς, see 2:35; 5:22) of his accusers. The dat. ptc. ἔχοντι (see 3:11) is attrib. (modifying τῷ ἀνδρί). Jesus' commands to the man to rise (ἔγειρε, see 5:23) and stand (στῆθι 2nd sg. 2nd aor. act. impv. of ἵστημι; ἔγειρε and στῆθι are intrans.) are matched in the man's response as he rose (ἀναστάς, see 4:38; an attendant circumstance ptc.) and stood (ἔστη 3rd sg. 2nd aor. act. indic. of ἵστημι; intrans.).

6:9 Jesus responds to them (δέ is connective, Wallace 671; Ἰησοῦς clarifies the change in subject from the man in 6:8, Nolland 261) with a question of his own (ἐπερωτῶ 1st sg. pres. act. indic. of ἐπερωτάω; εἰ [cf. 6:7] is probably used here to introduce a dir. question, BDAG 278b; BDF §440[3]; R 916; Z §401; ZG 194; though cf. BHGNT 187–88) concerning what is lawful on the Sabbath (ἔξεστιν, see 6:2). The aor. act. infs. ἀγαθοποιῆσαι (of ἀγαθοποιέω, "do good"), κακοποιῆσαι (of κακοποιέω, "do evil"), σῶσαι (of σώζω), and ἀπολέσαι (of ἀπόλλυμι), are all complementary (note the irony in 6:7, 11).

6:10 The aor. ptc. περιβλεψάμενος (nom. sg. masc. of aor. mid. ptc. of dep. περιβλέπομαι, "look around"; on the form cf. BDAG 799d) could be temp. (most EVV) or attendant circumstance with εἶπεν (cf. RSV). At the command of Jesus to stretch out (ἔκτεινον 2nd sg. aor. act. impv. of ἐκτείνω) his hand, the man does so (ἐποίησεν, see 1:49), and his hand is "restored" (ἀπεκατεστάθη 3rd sg. aor. pass. indic. of ἀποκαθιστάνω; on the form cf. BDAG 111d).

6:11 The nom. pl. pron. αὐτοί highlights the shift in subject back to the scribes and Pharisees (BHGNT 189). They are filled (ἐπλήσθησαν, see 1:23) with "mindless rage" (ἀνοίας gen. sg. fem. of ἄνοια, -ας, ἡ, "without understanding," BDAG 84b; "such extreme anger as to suggest an incapacity to use one's mind" LN 88.183; a gen. of content). The impf. διελάλουν (3rd pl. impf. act. indic. of διαλαλέω, "discuss") could be ingressive (HCSB, NIV) or progressive (Bovon 1.204). The particle ἄν with the optative ποιήσαιεν (3rd pl. aor. act. optative of ποιέω) forms an "indirect potential question" (cf. BDF §386[1]; BHGNT 189; McKay 110; Robertson, *Pictures* 83; see 1:62); they discuss "what they might do to Jesus" (HCSB; ZG 194).

FOR FURTHER STUDY

19. Sabbath and Law

*Blomberg, C. L. "The Law in Luke-Acts" *JSNT* 22 (1984): 53–80.

Bock, *Theology* 359–70.

*Carson, D. A. "Jesus and the Sabbath in the Four Gospels." Pages 57–97 in *From Sabbath to Lord's Day: A Biblical, Historical, and Theological Investigation*. Edited by D. A. Carson. Grand Rapids: Zondervan, 1982.

Dunn, J. D. G. *DJG*² 505–15.

*Hagner, D. A. "Jesus and the Synoptic Sabbath Controversies." *BBR* 19 (2009): 215–48.

Jervell, J. "The Law in Luke-Acts." *HTR* 64 (1971): 21–36.

*Moo, D. J. "Jesus and the Authority of the Mosaic Law." *JSNT* 20 (1984): 3–49.

*Nolland, J. *DJG*² 820–23.

Wilson, S. G. *Luke and the Law*. Cambridge: Cambridge University Press, 1983.

HOMILETICAL SUGGESTIONS

Jesus' Authority Is Exercised for the Good of His People (6:1–11)

1. Example 1: Jesus' Sabbath provision (6:1–5)
2. Example 2: Jesus' Sabbath restoration (6:6–11)

9. Jesus Chooses and Designates Twelve Disciples as Apostles (6:12–16)

6:12 Ἐγένετο, see 1:5. The temp. prep. phrase ἐν ταῖς ἡμέραις ταύταις provides a loose connection between the preceding events and the teaching that follows in 6:20. The 2nd aor. act. inf. ἐξελθεῖν (of dep. ἐξέρχομαι) modifies ἐγένετο. Εἰς τὸ ὄρος could be stereotypical for "the hills" (Z §167; ZG 194). Jesus goes out "to pray" (the aor. mid. inf. προσεύξασθαι of dep. προσεύχομαι expresses purpose, Fitzmyer 616), and he prayed "through the whole night" (διανυκτερεύων nom. sg. masc. of pres. act. ptc. of διανυκτερεύω [only here in the NT], with ἦν is an impf. periph. cstr.). Ἐν τῇ προσευχῇ expresses manner. The gen. θεοῦ is obj. See 5:16 for refs. to Jesus and prayer in Luke's Gospel.

6:13 The temp. phrase ὅτε ἐγένετο ἡμέρα indicates that the following actions are the result of Jesus' night of prayer. Προσεφώνησεν 3rd sg. aor. act. indic. of προσφωνέω, "call to" ("summoned" HCSB; BDAG 887b; by implication, "called . . . to him" NASB, NIV). The aor. ptc. ἐκλεξάμενος (nom. sg. masc. of aor. mid. ptc. of ἐκλέγω, "choose") is temp. (or attendant circumstance with ὠνόμασεν, Bock 541; Marshall 238; Nolland 269). The thought is continued in 6:17 with καὶ καταβὰς μετ' αὐτῶν after the relative clause at the end of this verse leads into the names of 6:14–16. The antecedent of the acc. pl. masc. rel. pron. οὕς is δώδεκα. After a rel. pron. (οὕς) καί may be omitted in tr. (Z §463; ZG 194; e.g., ESV). The name (ὠνόμασεν 3rd sg. aor. act. indic. of ὀνομάζω) "apostles" given to the Twelve only occurs two or three times in Matt and Mark (depending on the var. in Mark 3:14) but six times in Luke (here, 9:10; 11:49; 17:5; 22:14; 24:10; and twenty-eight times in Acts 1–16). Luke's use of the term here shows that an apostle, an authorized representative, was chosen by Jesus and was with Jesus from the beginning of his earthly ministry (cf. Acts 1:21–26).

6:14–16 The following list of twelve names, in common with the other lists (in the Synoptics and Acts), has Simon Peter first and Judas last, the same first four names (though they appear in different orders), and Peter, Philip, and James son of Alphaeus at the head of three groups of four (see E. J. Schnabel, *DJG*² 34–44). The names of the Twelve are acc. in appos. to δώδεκα (and ἀποστόλους, Marshall 239). The acc. sg. masc. rel. pron. ὅν is the obj. of ὠνόμασεν (see 6:13). Πέτρον is the complement in a double acc. cstr. Thus, the Twelve are "named" apostles, and Simon is "named" Peter (indicating an allusion to the significance of Peter's role, Nolland 270). The gen. Ἀλφαίου (6:15) is a gen. of relationship. Καλούμενον in 6:15 (acc. sg. masc. of pres. pass. ptc. of καλέω) is attrib., distinguishing this Simon from the one Jesus named Peter and identifying this Simon as the one who was called "Zealot." Ζηλωτήν (acc. sg. masc. of ζηλωτής, -οῦ, ὁ) may simply identify this Simon as "zealous" in the tradition of Phinehas and Elijah (Nolland 271), or as "patriotic" in the sense of being zealous for Israel's freedom from Rome (cf. BDAG 427d; perhaps an allusion to the nationalist group which later became known as the Zealots; Bock 545–46; Bovon 1.211; Marshall 240). The meaning of Ἰσκαριώθ (6:16; cf. 22:3) is debated (see BDAG 480d; Bock 546; Marshall 240–41). Judas is immediately described as the one who would become a traitor (the pred. nom. sg. masc. προδότης, of προδότης, -ου, ὁ), reminding readers of Jesus' passion already (Marshall 241).

HOMILETICAL SUGGESTIONS

Who Were the Apostles? (6:12–16)
They were . . .
1. The outworking of the Father's plan (6:12)
2. Chosen and authorized representatives of Jesus (6:13)
3. Ordinary men (6:14–16)

10. Jesus the Lord Requires Hearing and Obeying His Words (6:17–49)

This sermon completes a logical progression from a focus on Jesus' authority, to the calling of disciples to follow him, to this address to Jesus' disciples outlining what it means to follow Jesus as Lord (Nolland 273; for relationship to Matt, see Bock 931–44). After the setting in 6:17–19, the sermon may be divided into three broad sections: (1) Jesus gives reassurance of God's favor and promises to his disciples as those who have identified with him in the face of hatred and exclusion, and correspondingly, Jesus announces the judgment of those who are satisfied only with this life and the approval of other people (6:20–26); (2) Jesus elaborates on the way of love that his disciples are to show in the face of such hostility, a love that seeks the good of others and reflects the character of God (6:27–38); (3) Jesus concludes that a genuine response to his teaching comes from the heart and demonstrates a recognition of his lordship with obedience to his words (6:39–49).

a. The Setting (6:17–19)

6:17 This summary (cf. 4:14–15, 31–32, 40–41; 5:15; 7:21) serves as an introduction to the following sermon. Καταβάς nom. sg. masc. of 2nd aor. act. (temp.) ptc. of καταβαίνω, resumes the narrative from προσεφώνησεν . . . καὶ ἐκλεξάμενος (6:13; μετ' αὐτῶν modifies the ptc.). Ἔστη, see 6:8. Πεδινοῦ gen. sg. masc. of πεδινός, -ή, -όν, "level place" (in contrast to steep, uneven, or high, BDAG 790d; LN 79.85; common in the LXX but only here in the NT). The rest of the verse emphasizes the great size of the crowd (πολὺς . . . πολὺ . . . ἀπὸ πάσης). The nom. ὄχλος πολύς ("great crowd [of his disciples]") and πλῆθος πολύ ("great multitude [of people]") is the subj. of an implied ἦν (Marshall 242). The large crowd is also emphasized by the geographical location of not only "from all Judea and Jerusalem" (in this cstr. with one art. the second is a subset of the first, Wallace 287) but also extending to the "coastal region" (παραλίου gen. sg. fem. [subst.] adj. of παράλιος, -ον) of Tyre and Sidon (the gen. Τύρου καὶ Σιδῶνος is epex.). "Judea" here is probably a general ref. to the whole of Israel (Bock 564; Bovon 1.213; Marshall 242; Nolland 276; though if Judea in the narrow sense, Luke is referring to people coming to Galilee from elsewhere, Fitzmyer 624).

6:18 The nom. rel. pron. οἵ is the subj. of ἦλθον (see 1:59) and refers back to ὄχλος πολὺς . . . καὶ πλῆθος πολύ. The two aor. act. infs. ἀκοῦσαι (of ἀκούω) and ἰαθῆναι (of dep. ἰάομαι) express purpose (why the crowd came to Jesus). Νόσων, "diseases" (gen. pl. fem., see 4:40; with ἀπό expressing separation). Ἐνοχλούμενοι (nom. pl. masc. of pres. pass. [subst.] ptc. of ἐνοχλέω, "trouble," only here and Heb 12:15 in the NT) is the subj. of ἐθεραπεύοντο (3rd pl. impf. pass. indic. of θεραπεύω). The (second) prep. ἀπό expresses agency (ἀπό is used for ὑπό here, cf. BDAG 107a; BDF §210[2]; Z §90; ZG 195; for "unclean spirit" cf. 4:33). As in 4:40–41, Luke distinguishes between "diseases" and "unclean spirits" (Bock 565).

6:19 Specifically, the whole crowd was trying (the collective sg. πᾶς ὁ ὄχλος is the subj. of ἐζήτουν [see 5:18] according to sense, Wallace 401). The pres. mid. inf. ἅπτεσθαι (of ἅπτω) is complementary (the gen. αὐτοῦ is obj.). The reason for this is because (ὅτι, causal, commonly followed by a progressive impf., Wallace 553) power (δύναμις is the subj. of the following two verbs, most EVV; Nolland 276; cf. 6:20; NLT has "he healed") was coming out (ἐξήρχετο, see 4:41) from him and healing (ἰᾶτο 3rd sg. impf. mid. indic. of dep. ἰάομαι) everyone (πάντας).

b. Jesus Pronounces Blessing and Woe (6:20–26)

6:20 Καὶ αὐτός shifts attention back to Jesus as the subject (see 1:17; 4:15). Ἐπάρας (nom. sg. masc. of aor. act. [temp.] ptc. of ἐπαίρω) is an idiom indicating Jesus' focus on his disciples in particular (Marshall 247; though aspects of the sermon also apply to the crowds, Bock 571). The impf. ἔλεγεν is probably ingressive (NASB; BHGNT 195; though the impf. is also appropriate at the outset of a speech, BDF §329; Wallace 542 n. 6; Z §272; Marshall 248). Μακάριοι is a pred. adj., and οἱ πτωχοί is the nom. subj. of a verbless clause (with an implied εἰσίν). The reason the poor (i.e., Jesus' disciples) are blessed (i.e., recipients of divine favor, BDAG 611a; Fitzmyer 633) is because (ὅτι, causal, Bovon 1.225) the kingdom of God "is yours" ("belongs to you" NET; cf. 12:32; 18:17; 22:29). The nom. sg. fem. pred. adj. ὑμετέρα (of ὑμέτερος, -α, -ον) is emphatic (Nolland 283). The kingdom of God in this context is a comprehensive designation for the blessings of the eschatological saving rule of God (see 4:43; Marshall 249; Nolland 289).

6:21 Πεινῶντες nom. pl. masc. of pres. act. (subst.) ptc. of πεινάω, "hunger" (cf. 6:20 for the cstr. with μακάριοι). Ὅτι, causal (blessed because of the eschatological hope that belonging to the kingdom brings). Χορτασθήσεσθε 2nd pl. fut. pass. indic. of χορτάζω, "filled" (NRSV, HCSB; "satisfied" NASB, ESV, NIV; in contrast to hunger "now" [νῦν]; a divine pass. Z §236). Κλαίοντες nom. pl. masc. of pres. act. (subst.) ptc. of κλαίω. Ὅτι, causal. Γελάσετε 2nd pl. fut. act. indic. of γελάω, "laugh" (in contrast to weeping "now" [νῦν]). God will turn sorrow into joy (Marshall 251).

6:22 Μακάριοι is the pred. adj. of ἐστέ (2nd pl. pres. act. indic. of εἰμί). This final statement of blessedness receives extended explanation as an emphatic conclusion of the promises to Jesus' disciples (Bock 578; Nolland 284). The disciples of Jesus (ὑμᾶς . . . ὑμᾶς . . . ὑμῶν) are blessed when (ὅταν . . . ὅταν, with the following 3rd pl. aor. act. subjunc. vbs.; sim. to a cond., BDAG 731a; Bovon 1.227) they are hated (μισήσωσιν, of μισέω), excluded (ἀφορίσωσιν, of ἀφορίζω, "separate," "exclude" most EVV, "ostracize" NASB, ZG 195), insulted (ὀνειδίσωσιν, of ὀνειδίζω, "revile" NRSV, ESV; "insult" NIV), and slandered as evil because of Jesus. In the final description the ref. to "your name as evil" indicates that ἐκβάλωσιν (2nd aor. of ἐκβάλλω) with τὸ ὄνομα ὑμῶν is idiomatic for "slander" (HCSB; LN 33.396; cf. BDAG 299c; "scorn" NASB; "defame" NRSV; i.e., "name" = "reputation" [Nolland 285] not "Christian" [*pace* Fitzmyer 635]). Ὡς πονηρόν could be the complement in a double acc. cstr. (Wallace 186) or the obj. of an implied ἐκβάλωσιν (BHGNT 197). The final clause identifies the reason (ἕνεκα) for this hatred and clarifies that the "poor," "hungry," "sorrowful," and "hated" are the disciples of Jesus.

6:23 Ἐν ἐκείνῃ τῇ ἡμέρᾳ, temp. (cf. NLT). Χάρητε 2nd pl. 2nd aor. pass. impv. of χαίρω. Σκιρτήσατε 2nd pl. aor. act. impv. of σκιρτάω, "leap (for joy)" (see 1:41). Γάρ, causal (the reason for the joy is again the eschatological hope; ἰδού see 1:20). Their reward (μισθός, of μισθός, -οῦ, ὁ) is great (πολύς is a pred. adj. in a verbless clause) in heaven. Supporting assurance is given (γάρ) with the reminder (cf. NLT) that "the same things" (κατὰ τὰ αὐτά; acc. pl. neut. of αὐτός, -ή, -ό) were done (ἐποίουν 3rd pl. impf. act. indic. of ποιέω; a customary impf., Wallace 548; Bovon 1.228) to the prophets.

6:24 Πλήν introduces four statements of "woe" which stand in contrast to the four pronouncements of divine favor (i.e., "blessed"). The interjection οὐαί, in the context of these contrasts (cf. Luke 6:24–26; 10:13; 11:42–44, 46–47, 52; 17:1–2), expresses the certainty and severity of divine judgment. The dat. pl. ὑμῖν is modified by the appos. τοῖς πλουσίοις (a common cstr. for the interjection οὐαί, Fitzmyer 636; here "the rich" are in contrast to "the poor" in 6:20). Although the pron. ὑμῖν is used, the description of the addressees in 6:17–18 and the restatement in 6:27 indicate that those to whom the woes are directed are presumed absent (Nolland 287). Ὅτι, causal. There is no eschatological promise; their current "comfort" (παράκλησιν, see 2:25) is all they have (ἀπέχετε 2nd pl. pres. act. indic. of ἀπέχω, "receive"; a term used for receipts that indicate full payment, Marshall 256).

6:25 This verse parallels the contrasts in 6:21 between now (νῦν) and the eschatological reversal to come. Ἐμπεπλησμένοι nom. pl. masc. of pf. pass. (subst.) ptc. of ἐμπίπλημι, "fill," "satisfy." Ὅτι, causal (twice). Πεινάσετε 2nd pl. fut. act. indic. of πεινάω, "hunger" (on the form cf. BDF §70[2]; cf. Isa 65:13). Γελῶντες nom. pl. masc. of pres. act. (subst.) ptc. of γελάω, "laugh." Πενθήσετε 2nd pl. fut. act. indic. of πενθέω, "mourn." Κλαύσετε 2nd pl. fut. act. indic. of κλαίω, "weep." The laughter in this context refers to those who are self-satisfied, and perhaps boastful, over the suffering of believers (Marshall 256).

6:26 In contrast to those who are insulted and slandered for Jesus' sake now (6:22), those who are spoken well of (εἴπωσιν 3rd pl. 2nd aor. act. subjunc. of λέγω; subjunc. with ὅταν as in 6:22) by everyone (πάντες) are under condemnation because (γάρ) that is the same way the *false* prophets were treated. Note the parallel structure with 6:23b:

κατὰ τὰ αὐτὰ γὰρ ἐποίουν τοῖς προφήταις οἱ πατέρες αὐτῶν (6:23b)
κατὰ τὰ αὐτὰ γὰρ ἐποίουν τοῖς ψευδοπροφήταις οἱ πατέρες αὐτῶν (6:26b)

In contrast to the approval of God which the disciples of Jesus are assured of in the face of hatred from others, those who desire only approval from people face judgment from God.

FOR FURTHER STUDY

20. Rich and Poor (6:20–26)

Green, J. B. "Good News to Whom? Jesus and the 'Poor' in the Gospel of Luke." Pages 59–74 in *Jesus of Nazareth: Lord and Christ; Essays on the Historical Jesus and New*

Testament Christology. Edited by J. B. Green and M. Turner. Grand Rapids: Eerdmans, 1994.

*Hays, C. M. *Luke's Wealth Ethics: A Study in Their Coherence and Character*. WUNT 2/275. Tübingen: Mohr Siebeck, 2010.

Johnson, L. T. *The Literary Function of Possessions in Luke-Acts*. Missoula: Scholars Press, 1977.

Moxnes, H. *The Economy of the Kingdom: Social Conflict and Economic Relations in Luke's Gospel*. Philadelphia: Fortress, 1988.

Pilgrim, W. E. *Good News to the Poor: Wealth and Poverty in Luke-Acts*. Minneapolis: Augsburg, 1981.

*Seccombe, D. *Possessions and the Poor in Luke-Acts*. Linz: Fuchs, 1982.

c. Jesus Defines How His Disciples Should Respond in Love to Their Enemies (6:27–38)

6:27–28 Jesus again specifies (ἀλλά) that he is addressing his disciples, that is, those who listen to him (ἀκούουσιν [dat. pl. masc. of pres. act. ptc. of ἀκούω] is attrib. modifying ὑμῖν; cf. 6:17–18). The repetition of a ref. to those who "listen" to Jesus (cf. 6:18, 47), together with the forward placement of the dat. pron., is an emphatic introduction to the next major section of the sermon (Fitzmyer 637). In contrast to the way they are treated in hate (6:22), they are commanded to love their enemies (ἀγαπᾶτε 2nd pl. pres. act. impv. of ἀγαπάω). The following three statements (6:27b, 28) may be understood as subordinate to "love" (the verbal impvs.) and "enemies" (those who hate, curse, abuse).

ἀγαπᾶτε [i.e.:]
   καλῶς ποιεῖτε
   εὐλογεῖτε
   προσεύχεσθε
τοὺς ἐχθροὺς ὑμῶν [i.e.:]
   τοῖς μισοῦσιν ὑμᾶς
   τοὺς καταρωμένους ὑμᾶς
   τῶν ἐπηρεαζόντων ὑμᾶς

The four impvs. are placed together in asyndeton (BDF §462[2]; the pres. is appropriate for general [customary] precepts, BDF §335; Fantin 96–98). Καλῶς ποιεῖτε, see 3:4 (sim. to ἀγαθοποιεῖτε in 6:33, 35). Μισοῦσιν dat. pl. masc. of pres. act. (subst.) ptc. of μισέω. Εὐλογεῖτε 2nd pl. pres. act. impv. of εὐλογέω. Καταρωμένους acc. pl. masc. of pres. mid. (subst.) ptc. of dep. καταράομαι. Προσεύχεσθε 2nd pl. pres. mid. impv. of dep. προσεύχομαι. Ἐπηρεαζόντων gen. pl. masc. of pres. act. (subst.) ptc. of ἐπηρεάζω, "mistreat" (HCSB, NIV; BDAG 362d; LN 88.129; "abuse" NASB, ESV; "mistreat by word or deed" Bovon 1.235; "threaten" Nolland 294).

6:29 This hateful opposition to the disciples because of Jesus (6:22, 27–28) is now illustrated, along with their loving response, in terms of specific physical actions (6:29–30). The subst. ptc. τῷ τύπτοντί (dat. sg. masc. of pres. act. ptc. of τύπτω, "strike"; σιαγόνα acc. sg. fem. of σιαγών, -όνος, ἡ, "cheek" BDAG 922a) is the indir. obj. of πάρεχε (2nd sg. pres. act. impv. of παρέχω, "present," "offer"). This response may focus on continued ministry in the face of persecution (Bock 591; Nolland 296). Ἱμάτιον, "coat" (HCSB, NIV), "cloak" (ESV; "outer clothing" BDAG 475a) is the obj. of the subst. ptc. αἴροντος (gen. sg. masc. of pres. act. ptc. of αἴρω; gen. following ἀπό). Χιτῶνα, "tunic" (acc. sg. masc., see 3:11; καί here may be tr. as "either" HCSB, ESV) is the obj. of κωλύσῃς (2nd sg. aor. act. subjunc. of κωλύω, "prevent," "withhold" most EVV; the aor. subj. prohibition with μή could be specific, or view the action as a whole, Huffman 185; cf. Fantin 162; here the neg. is sim. in mng. to πάρεχε "offer," NLT; Nolland 296).

6:30 The subst. ptc. αἰτοῦντί (dat. sg. masc. of pres. act. ptc. of αἰτέω) is the indir. obj. of δίδου (2nd sg. pres. act. impv. of δίδωμι; the acc. σε is the obj. of αἰτοῦντι). The acc.

pl. neut. τὰ σά (art. and possessive adj., "what is yours" ZG 196) is the obj. of the subst. ptc. αἴροντος (see 6:29). Ἀπαίτει 2nd sg. pres. act. impv. of ἀπαιτέω, "ask," "demand back" (ESV, NIV; BDAG 96a; only here and 12:20 in the NT; the pres. neg. with μή views the prohibition as general [customary], Fantin 98; Huffman 129). In light of the variety of responses to opposition elsewhere in Luke-Acts, these illustrations are meant to convey an overarching desire for the good of opponents that does not preclude, for example, insisting on legal procedures, warning of God's judgment, and continued witness to Jesus (e.g., Acts 4:19–20; 7:51–60; 14:19–21; 16:37; 21:37–39; 22:25; 23:3; 25:11; 26:25–29; cf. Nolland 297).

6:31 Θέλετε 2nd pl. pres. act. indic. of θέλω. Ἵνα introduces the following clause as the complement to θέλετε (cf. T 103; Wallace 476; Z §407 for this use of ἵνα). Οἱ ἄνθρωποι is the subj. of ποιῶσιν (3rd pl. pres. act. subjunc. of ποιέω; cf. ESV). Ποιεῖτε, see 3:4.

6:32 In 6:32–34 Jesus provides three negative examples of the kind of love he is not talking about but which is characteristic of "sinners" (i.e., those oriented toward self [6:32–34] and not reflecting the character of God [6:35–36], Adams 136–39). The examples are structured in a similar (though not identical) way and parallel the examples of 6:27–30. Εἰ introduces a first-class cond. (assumed true for the sake of argument, Wallace 692–94). Ἀγαπᾶτε 2nd pl. pres. act. indic. of ἀγαπάω. The subst. ptc. ἀγαπῶντας (acc. pl. masc. of pres. act. ptc. of ἀγαπάω) is the obj. of ἀγαπᾶτε. The interr. clause (ποία [of ποῖος, -α, -ον] . . . χάρις is the subj. of ἐστίν) is the apodosis of the first-class cond. The following refs. to "sinners" and "reward" (6:35) indicate that χάρις ("credit" most EVV; "benefit" ESV) probably refers to a favorable response from God (BDAG 1079d; ZG 196; Bock 599; Fitzmyer 640; Marshall 262; *pace* BHGNT 202; Bovon 1.237). The reason such "love" is not commendable is because (γάρ) this is the behavior of even (καί) "sinners." Οἱ ἁμαρτωλοί is the subj. of ἀγαπῶσιν (3rd pl. pres. act. indic. of ἀγαπάω). The second subst. ptc. ἀγαπῶντας is the obj. of ἀγαπῶσιν.

6:33 Ἐάν with the subjunc. ἀγαθοποιῆτε (2nd pl. pres. act. subjunc. of ἀγαθοποιέω, "do good" [6:9, 33, 35 in Luke]) introduces a third-class cond. (though it is a parallel cstr. with 6:32, ZG 196). Γάρ may be a scribal addition for clarity (Marshall 263; though Bock [627] favors including γάρ due to the parallel with 6:32). The subst. ptc. ἀγαθοποιοῦντας (acc. pl. masc. of pres. act. ptc. of ἀγαθοποιέω) is the obj. of ἀγαθοποιῆτε. As in 6:21, the interr. clause is the apodosis. Again, the comparison is made with sinners. They do (ποιοῦσιν 3rd pl. pres. act. indic. of ποιέω) "the same" (the adj. use of the pron. αὐτός).

6:34 As in 6:33, ἐάν with the subjunc. δανίσητε (2nd pl. aor. act. subjunc. of δανίζω, "lend money," only 6:34–35 and Matt 5:42 in the NT) introduces a third-class. cond. The prep. and gen. rel. pron (παρ' ὧν) introduce those to whom money is lent as those "from whom" repayment is expected. Ἐλπίζετε 2nd pl. pres. act. indic. of ἐλπίζω. Λαβεῖν 2nd aor. act. (complementary) inf. of λαμβάνω. As in 6:21, 33, the interr. clause is the apodosis. Sinners "lend money" (δανίζουσιν 3rd pl. pres. act. indic. of δανίζω) for the purpose (ἵνα) of receiving back ἀπολάβωσιν (3rd pl. 2nd aor. act. subjunc. of ἀπολαμβάνω; cf. 15:27; 16:25; 18:30; 23:41) an equivalent payment (the acc. pl. neut. art. and adj. τὰ ἴσα [of ἴσος, -η, -ον] refers to something equivalent and not necessarily to the same money in return, BDAG 480d–81a; Marshall 263; cf. Bovon 1.237–38). For the mng. of "lending for the purpose of receiving back" see Bock 601, Marshall 263, and Nolland 299 (perhaps a selfish guarantee that future provision [i.e., future pay back] is assured).

6:35 In a concluding summary of the discussion about love from 6:27 (and esp. 6:32–34), Jesus ties these exhortations to God's promises and character. In contrast (πλήν) to the previous three actions (6:32–34) toward only those favorably disposed to the disciples, Jesus exhorts his disciples to love (ἀγαπᾶτε, see 6:27) and do good (ἀγαθοποιεῖτε 2nd pl. pres. act. impv. of ἀγαθοποιέω) to their enemies and to lend (δανίζετε 2nd pl. pres. act. impv. of δανίζω) without expecting return (ἀπελπίζοντες nom. pl. masc. of pres. act. ptc. of ἀπελπίζω, "expect back," BDAG 101c, a play on ἐλπίζω in 6:34 [though cf. Robertson, *Pictures* 91 and ZG 196–97 for the mng. "despair"; a ptc. of manner]). As with 6:20–23, the promise here is of "great reward" (μισθὸς . . . πολύς, see 6:23) to come (ἔσται, see 1:14). In the immediate context this is another way of referring to God's favorable response (χάρις, 6:32, 33, 34). Those who love like this are evidently (ἔσεσθε, 2nd pl. fut. mid. indic. of εἰμί) "sons of the Most High" (see 1:32) because (ὅτι) this kind of love exhibits likeness to God's character (Marshall 264; Nolland 300). Χρηστός, "kind" (see 5:39). Ἐπί is used as a "marker of feelings directed toward someone" (BDAG 366d). The objects of God's kindness are the "ungrateful" (ἀχαρίστους acc. pl. masc. of ἀχάριστος, -ον) and "evil" (πονηρούς; with one art., the first group is a subset of the second, Wallace 280).

6:36 The exhortation to reflect God's character is now made explicit (thus 6:36 concludes 6:27–35; Nolland 300). Γίνεσθε 2nd pl. pres. mid. impv. of dep. γίνομαι. Οἰκτίρμονες, "merciful" (nom. pl. masc. pred. adj. of οἰκτίρμων, -ον; οἰκτίρμων is nom. sg. masc.).

6:37 The following four exhortations (6:37–38a; two negative and two positive) flow out of God's graciousness to his people and pick up on the earlier ref. to rewards from God (Bock 606). The 2nd pl. pres. act. impv. not to "judge" (κρίνετε, of κρίνω; neg. with μή) is paralleled with the impv. not to "condemn" (καταδικάζετε, of καταδικάζω) and thus refers not to the use of discernment but to a final cutting off from the possibility of God's favor (Bock 605; Marshall 265). The double neg. οὐ μή (καί expresses result, Marshall 266) with the 2nd pl. aor. pass. subjuncs. κριθῆτε (of κρίνω) and καταδικασθῆτε (of καταδικάζω) is emphatic (BDF §365[3]; for the cond. idea cf. Wallace 489). In contrast to these prohibitions, Jesus' disciples are to "forgive" (ἀπολύετε 2nd pl. pres. act. impv. of ἀπολύω, "release/pardon"; i.e., debtors BDAG 117d; cf. 7:41–44; 11:4; 13:4) and thus, be forgiven (ἀπολυθήσεσθε 2nd pl. fut. pass. indic. of ἀπολύω). The three passives are divine passives (Z §236; Fitzmyer 641).

6:38 Δίδοτε 2nd pl. pres. act. impv. of δίδωμι. Δοθήσεται 3rd sg. fut. pass. indic. of δίδωμι. The promise in the last of the four exhortations is illustrated in the rest of 6:38. The acc. sg. neut. μέτρον καλόν ("good measure"; of μέτρον, -ου, τό) is the obj.

of δώσουσιν (3rd pl. fut. act. indic. of δίδωμι, "put" NRSV, ESV; "poured" HCSB, NIV). The pl. ("they will pour") could be a substitution for God (most EVV tr. as a 3rd sg. pass. "will be poured"; Z §2; ZG 197; Marshall 267) or an indef. pl. ref. to the practice of pouring out grain (BHGNT 206; cf. Wallace 403). The three acc. sg. neut. ptcs. πεπιεσμένον (pf. pass. of πιέζω, "press"), σεσαλευμένον (pf. pass. of σαλεύω, "shake"), and ὑπερεκχυννόμενον (pres. pass. of dep. ὑπερεκχύννομαι, "pour over," pass. "overflow"; the shift to the pres. due perhaps to the semantics of the vb., BHGNT 206) are all attrib. modifying the "good measure" (Robertson, *Pictures* 93). Κόλπον acc. sg. masc. of κόλπος, -ου, ὁ, "fold of a garment" used as a pocket (BDAG 557b), "lap" (most EVV). The dat. ᾧ . . . μέτρῳ is instr. (or a dat. of rule, Wallace 158). Μετρεῖτε 2nd pl. pres. act. indic. of μετρέω, "measure." Ἀντιμετρηθήσεται 3rd sg. fut. pass. indic. of ἀντιμετρέω, "measure in return" (a divine pass., Bock 608; Fitzmyer 641). Characteristic withholding of forgiveness or generosity in mercy signals the way we wish to be treated by God (Nolland 301).

d. Responding to Jesus' Teaching (6:39–49)

6:39 Παραβολήν in this context refers to a proverbial saying (BDAG 759c; cf. 4:23; 5:36; δὲ καί, 2:4). The question introduced with μήτι expects the answer "no" ("can he?" NASB; BDF §427[2]). The adj. τυφλός is used abs. as a noun and is the nom. subj. of δύναται (see 3:8). The acc. τυφλόν is the obj. of the (complementary) pres. act. inf. ὁδηγεῖν (of ὁδηγέω, "lead," "guide"). Οὐχί expects the answer "yes." Ἀμφότεροι, "both" (see 1:6). Βόθυνον acc. sg. masc. of βόθυνος, -ου, ὁ, "pit." Ἐμπεσοῦνται 3rd pl. fut. mid. indic. of ἐμπίπτω, "fall into" (a deliberative use of the fut. indic., Wallace 465). These questions may warn against false teachers who, as 6:40 indicates, will leave those they teach in blindness (Fitzmyer 642; Nolland 307) or warn the disciples against their own blindness and therefore self-reliance, before Jesus more explicitly calls them to follow him only (Bock 610; Bovon 1.248; Marshall 267). The following context (6:41–45) seems to favor the latter.

6:40 Ὑπέρ is used as a comp. ("greater than," BDAG 1031c; μαθητής is the subj. of ἐστίν). Κατηρτισμένος, nom. sg. masc. of pf. pass. (subst.) ptc. of καταρτίζω, "put into proper condition," "complete" BDAG 526b; "fully trained" most EVV (the subj. of ἔσται). Following the previous warning, this proverbial saying is a further encouragement to follow and therefore faithfully reflect their teacher, Jesus (Bock 613).

6:41 The interr. τί ("why") introduces a rhetorical question. In the context of 6:39–40, 6:41–42 continues the warning against self-delusion and begins to move more specifically to the concluding exhortation to genuinely, rather than superficially, follow Jesus. βλέπεις 2nd sg. pres. act. indic. of βλέπω. Κάρφος acc. sg. neut. of κάρφος, -ους, τό, "speck" ("small piece of straw, chaff, or wood" BDAG 510d). The art. τό turns the prep. phrase ἐν τῷ ὀφθαλμῷ into an adj. modifying κάρφος (cf. the art. τό in 5:36). Δοκόν acc. sg. fem. of δοκός, -οῦ, ἡ, "beam of wood" (e.g., the main beam of a floor or roof of a house, LSJ 443a) is the obj. of κατανοεῖς (2nd sg. pres. act. indic. of κατανοέω, "observe," "notice" most EVV). Likewise, the art. τήν turns the prep. phrase ἐν τῷ ἰδίῳ ὀφθαλμῷ into an adj. modifying δοκόν (BHGNT 208).

6:42 Πῶς introduces another rhetorical question, added in asyndeton (Marshall 270). Δύνασαι, see 5:12. Λέγειν (complementary), see 3:8. The impv. ἄφες (2nd sg. 2nd aor. act. impv. of ἀφίημι) is used here to introduce the hortatory subjunc. ἐκβάλω (1st sg. 2nd aor. act. subjunc. of ἐκβάλλω; "let me take out . . ." cf. BDAG 157b; BDF 364[1]; Burton §161; Wallace 464; ZG 197). Κάρφος, see 6:41. Αὐτός, intensive subj. of βλέπων (nom. sg. masc. of pres. act. ptc. of βλέπω). The ptc. βλέπων (neg. with οὐ, cf. BDF §430[2]; Burton §485; ZG 197) could be temp. ("when," NRSV, NASB, NIV) or concessive ("even though"). Ὑποκριτά, voc. (cf. 12:56; 13:15; "pretender" LN 88.228; i.e., in this context, pretending to be concerned about sin though one's own sin is ignored, Plummer 191). Ἔκβαλε 2nd sg. 2nd aor. act. impv. of ἐκβάλλω. Διαβλέψεις 2nd sg. fut. act. indic. of διαβλέπω, "see clearly." The 2nd aor. act. inf. ἐκβαλεῖν (of ἐκβάλλω) expresses purpose. On the adj. function of the art. τό (before ἐν τῷ ὀφθαλμῷ), τήν (before ἐν τῷ ὀφθαλμῷ), and τό (before ἐν τῷ ὀφθαλμῷ), see 6:41.

6:43 Γάρ (omitted in NRSV, HCSB, NIV) indicates that 6:43–45 is a further clarification of 6:41–42; the hypocrite (6:42) produces bad fruit. A disciple of Jesus, however, obeys from the heart. The nom. δένδρον καλόν (neg. by οὐ) is the subj. of the periph. ptc. cstr. ἐστιν . . . ποιοῦν (nom. sg. neut. of pres. act. ptc. of ποιέω; "no good tree bears" most EVV). Πάλιν, mng. "on the other hand" (NASB, HCSB; BDAG 754a). Σαπρόν nom. sg. neut. of σαπρός, -ά, -όν, "poor quality" (BDAG 913b), "bad" (most EVV).

6:44 Γάρ shows that 6:44 continues to develop the point made in 6:43. Γινώσκεται 3rd sg. pres. pass. indic. of γινώσκω (ἕκαστον . . . δένδρον is the subj.). Ἐκ indicates source (used for ἀπό, Z §87; ZG 198). The 3rd pl. pres. act. indics. συλλέγουσιν (of συλλέγω, "gather") and τρυγῶσιν (of τρυγάω, "gather/pick") are tr. by most EVV as pass. ("are not gathered/picked") as the pl. is impers. (Z §1; ZG 198). Ἀκανθῶν gen. pl. fem. of ἄκανθα, -ης, ἡ, "thorns." Σῦκα acc. pl. neut. of σῦκον, -ου, τό, "figs." Βάτου gen. sg. fem. of βάτος, -ου, ἡ, "thorn bush" (BDAG 171d; only here, 20:37; Acts 7:30, 35; Mark 12:26 [masc.] in the NT; different from βάτος in 16:6), "bramble bush" (NRSV, HCSB, ESV), "briers" (NIV). Σταφυλήν acc. sg. fem. of σταφυλή, -ῆς, ἡ, "(a bunch of) grapes."

6:45 Jesus now specifically applies the previous analogies to the internal realities of individual hearts (cf. also 8:15; 11:39). The nom. ὁ ἀγαθὸς ἄνθρωπος (an attrib. adj.) is the subj. of προφέρει (3rd sg. pres. act. indic. of προφέρω, "bring forth," "produce" most EVV; a gnomic pres., Bovon 1.252). Θησαυροῦ gen. sg. masc. of θησαυρός, -οῦ, ὁ, "treasure." Θησαυροῦ τῆς καρδίας is implied after ἐκ τοῦ πονηροῦ. Περισσεύματος, "abundance." The nom. τὸ στόμα is the subj. of λαλεῖ (see 5:21).

6:46 With this final question (cf. the questions in 6:39, 41, 42) and subsequent illustration (6:47–49), Jesus clarifies that the previous analogies have been about a genuine, rather than superficial, response to his authority and teaching. Καλεῖτε 2nd pl. pres. act. indic. of καλέω. Ποιεῖτε, see 3:4. The acc. rel. pron. ἅ introduces a clause (with λέγω) which functions as the obj. of ποιεῖτε (cf. BHGNT 212). The double voc. κύριε κύριε is emphatic (BDF §493[1]; Bovon 1.253; Marshall 274; cf. other double vocatives in 8:24; 10:41; 13:34; 17:13; 22:31). Κύριε may ref. to Jesus as a respected teacher (Bock 618) or in this context, his ultimate authority (cf. e.g., 2:11; 5:8; 6:5; Marshall 274). A genuine response to Jesus as Lord is required to avert eschatological judgment (6:47–49).

6:47 The concluding ref. to one who "comes" to Jesus and "listens" to Jesus forms an inclusio with the introductory statements in 6:18 and 6:27 (Bock 620). The three (gnomic pres., Wallace 523) nom. sg. masc. ptcs. ἐρχόμενος (mid. of dep. ἔρχομαι), ἀκούων (act. of ἀκούω), and ποιῶν (act. of ποιέω) all modify πᾶς as an introductory topic cstr. (BHGNT 212; governed by the one art., Wallace 275). Ὑποδείξω 1st sg. fut. act. indic. of ὑποδείκνυμι, "show." Τίνι is an indir. interr. that refers to the three nom. ptcs. (thus, the subj. of ὑποδείξω [Jesus] differs from the nom. subj. at the start of the sentence; "anacoluthon," Bock 620; Fitzmyer 644). Note the comp. adj. ὅμοιος (of ὅμοιος, -α, -ον) also in 6:48, 49.

6:48 Ὅμοιός is a pred. adj. with ἀνθρώπῳ as the dat. complement. The dat. ptc. οἰκοδομοῦντι (dat. sg. masc. of pres. act. ptc. of οἰκοδομέω) is attrib. modifying ἀνθρώπῳ. The man "dug" (ἔσκαψεν 3rd sg. aor. act. indic. of σκάπτω; only here, 13:8; 16:3 in the NT), "dug deep" (ἐβάθυνεν 3rd sg. aor. act. indic. of βαθύνω; only here in the NT), and "placed" (ἔθηκεν 3rd sg. aor. act. indic. of τίθημι) the foundation (θεμέλιον acc. sg. masc. of θεμέλιος, -ου, ὁ) on the rock (πέτραν acc. sg. fem. of πέτρα, -ας, ἡ). The gen. (sg. fem.) πλημμύρης (of πλήμμυρα, -ης, ἡ, "flood"; only here in the NT) is the subj. of the temp. gen. abs. ptc. γενομένης (see 4:42). Ποταμός (nom. sg. masc. of ποταμός, -οῦ, ὁ, "river") is the subj. of προσέρηξεν (3rd sg. aor. act. indic. of προσρήσσω, "burst upon") and ἴσχυσεν (3rd sg. aor. act. indic. of ἰσχύω; neg. with οὐκ, "not able"). Σαλεῦσαι aor. act. (complementary) inf. of σαλεύω, "shake." The pf. pass. inf. οἰκοδομῆσθαι (of οἰκοδομέω) with διὰ τό indicates cause (Wallace 597). For the var. ending (NKJV) see Bock 628 (a harmonization to Matt 7:25).

6:49 The nom. sg. masc. of aor. act. [subst.] ptcs. ἀκούσας (of ἀκούω) and ποιήσας (of ποιέω) introduce the contrasting description of one who hears and does not do Jesus' words. He is like a man who built (οἰκοδομήσαντι, dat. sg. masc. of aor. act. ptc. of οἰκοδομέω; attrib. modifying ἀνθρώπῳ) his house without a foundation (χωρὶς θεμελίου). When the river burst upon (προσέρηξεν, see 6:48) this house, it "immediately" (εὐθύς) "collapsed" (συνέπεσεν 3rd sg. 2nd aor. act. indic. of συνπίπτω; only here in the NT). In fact, the "ruin" or "destruction" (ῥῆγμα, nom. sg. neut. of ῥῆγμα, -ατος, τό; only here in the NT) of that house was great (μέγα, a pred. adj.). The placement of μέγα at the end of the sentence brings the warning of judgment to an emphatic conclusion (Bock 623).

HOMILETICAL SUGGESTIONS

Suffering Followers of a Suffering Lord (6:17–49)
1. Hope in the promises of Jesus (6:17–26)
2. Love with the character of Jesus (6:27–38)
3. Trust and obey (from a transformed heart) the words of Jesus (6:39–49)

B. THE NATURE OF JESUS' SALVATION AND THE RESPONSE OF FAITH
(7:1–8:56)

Although each episode is numbered sequentially below, the broad structure of this section may be outlined as follows:

- A. Two miracles demonstrating Jesus' power over death and compassion (7:1–17)
  - B. Explanation of Jesus' ministry and responses to him (7:18–35)
    - C. Jesus forgives sins and saves; sinners trust Jesus and love him (7:36–50)
  - B.¹ Explanation of Jesus' ministry and responses to him (8:1–21)
- A.¹ Four miracles demonstrating Jesus' power over death and compassion (8:22–56)

In the center of this section (7:36–50) is an episode that brings together a cluster of themes central to the saving rule of God in the ministry of Jesus: (1) Jesus' association with sinners (cf. 7:34); (2) an explanation for why "sinners" love Jesus; (3) Jesus' authority to forgive sins; and (4) the identity of Jesus (the above outline is adapted from W. Taylor; cf. www.st-helens.org.uk/resources/preaching-matters; D. Gooding, *According to Luke* [Grand Rapids: Eerdmans, 1987], 124–52). The first and last miracles in this section relate to officials who ask Jesus to heal someone dear to them (note: παῖς, servant, 7:7; παῖς, child, 8:51, 54; cf. μονογενής 7:12; 8:42) who is near death (7:2–3; 8:41–42). In both accounts a message is sent to Jesus while he is on his way requesting that Jesus not trouble himself (σκύλλω; 7:6–8; 8:49). In both accounts faith in Jesus' authority over death is encouraged (7:9; 8:50). In the first miracle Jesus heals someone near death; in the last he restores the dead child to life (8:55). These two chapters encourage faith in Jesus' power to save (σώζω 7:50; 8:12, 36, 48, 50; πίστις 7:9, 50; 8:25, 48; πιστεύω 8:12, 13, 50).

1. Two Miracles that Demonstrate Jesus' Power (7:1–17)

a. Faith in the Power of Jesus' Word (7:1–10)

7:1 Ἐπειδή is a marker of time ("when," "after," BDAG 360d; causal elsewhere in the NT, BDF §455[1]; Bovon 1.260; perhaps giving rise to ἐπεὶ δέ in some mss.). This temp. conj., together with the summary statement about the completion (ἐπλήρωσεν 3rd sg. aor. act. indic. of πληρόω) of all Jesus' words in the hearing of the people (ἀκοάς acc. pl. fem. of ἀκοή, -ῆς, ἡ, "ears," "hearing" most EVV; a Sem., ZG 198; cf. 6:18, 27, 47; τοῦ λαοῦ, a subj. gen.), and the statement about Jesus' change of location (εἰσῆλθεν, see 1:40), all place this event after the sermon and indicate a movement to a new section in the narrative.

7:2 Ἤμελλεν 3rd sg. impf. act. indic. of μέλλω, "about to"; an irregular augment, ZG 198; δοῦλος is the subj.). Τελευτᾶν pres. act. (complementary) inf. of τελευτάω, "die." This slave who is about to die is described as a slave of a certain centurion (the gen. ἑκατοντάρχου . . . τινος is poss.; gen. sg. masc. of ἑκατοντάρχης, -ου, ὁ) and "sick" (on the idiom ἔχων [see 3:11; an attrib. ptc.] and the adv. κακῶς see 5:31). The antecedent of the rel. pron. ὅς is δοῦλος. The antecedent of the pron. αὐτῷ is ἑκατοντάρχου. The pred. adj. ἔντιμος (nom. sg. masc. of ἔντιμος, -ον) could mean "valuable," "precious" (BDAG 340a mng 2; cf. 1 Pet 2:4, 6) or "highly regarded," "respected" (cf. BDAG 340a [mng. 1b]; NASB; "dear to him" RSV, NKJV; Bock 636; Marshall 279).

7:3 Ἀκούσας, see 6:49 (temp.). Ἀπέστειλεν 3rd sg. aor. act. indic. of ἀποστέλλω (πρεσβυτέρους [cf. 9:22; 20:1; 22:52] is the obj.). Ἐρωτῶν (nom. sg. masc. of pres. act. ptc. of ἐρωτάω) expresses purpose (the sg. reflects the centurion's request through these elders, T 157). Ὅπως (with the subjunc. διασώσῃ) introduces indir. discourse (with verbs of asking ὅπως is equivalent to an inf., BDAG 718c; BDF §392[1]; Z §408; ZG 199). Ἐλθών (nom. sg. masc. of 2nd aor. act. ptc. of dep. ἔρχομαι) is an attendant circumstance ptc. and thus takes on the mood of the subjunc. διασώσῃ (Wallace 644; e.g., "to come and save" HCSB). Διασώσῃ 3rd sg. aor. act. subjunc. of διασῴζω, "heal" ESV, NIV; "save the life of" NASB, HCSB (common in the LXX, only here in Luke, five times in Acts, only Matt 14:36; 1 Pet 3:20 elsewhere in the NT; most commonly with ref. to rescue from danger; though "heal" with ref. to sickness, BDAG 237c; MM 154d).

7:4 Παραγενόμενοι (nom. pl. masc. of 2nd aor. mid. ptc. of dep. παραγίνομαι, "arrive") could be temp. (Marshall 280). However, with the pl. art. οἱ it could be subst. and the subj. of παρεκάλουν (3rd pl. impf. act. indic. of παρακαλέω, "pleaded" ESV, NIV): "Those who came to Jesus urged him" (cf. BHGNT 215). Σπουδαίως, adv. "earnestly" (with the impf. emphasizing urgency, Bovon 1.261; Marshall 280; iter. R 884). Λέγοντες, see 1:66. Ὅτι, recitative (which continues into 7:5). The pred. adj. ἄξιος is placed forward for emphasis. The subj. of ἐστίν is the rel. clause ᾧ παρέξῃ τοῦτο ("worthy is the one to whom you should do this"; Fitzmyer 651; BDF §5[3b] describes this as a Latinism). The form of παρέξῃ could be either 2nd sg. fut. mid. indic. (BDF §379; ZG 199; R 872; expressing result, Marshall 280) or 2nd sg. aor. mid. subjunc. of παρέχω, "offer," "grant." The context of a request might suggest the suitability of a subjunc. (BHGNT 218). Yet the subjunc. and fut. indic. may also be used interchangeably (cf. BDAG 777a; BDF §316[3]; Z §343).

7:5 Γάρ, causal (giving the reason the centurion is worthy). He loves (ἀγαπᾷ 3rd sg. pres. act. indic. of ἀγαπάω) the nation of Israel (perhaps as a "God-fearer" Bock 638; Bovon 1.260), and he has built (ᾠκοδόμησεν 3rd sg. aor. act. indic. of οἰκοδομέω) their synagogue (i.e., perhaps provided funds for it to be built; αὐτός is emphatic, "it was he" ZG 199).

7:6 Ἐπορεύετο, see 4:30 (on the impf. cf. T 66). Ἀπέχοντος gen. sg. masc. of pres. act. ptc. of ἀπέχω, "be distant" (a temp. gen. abs. cstr.; αὐτοῦ is the subj.). With the adv. μακράν ("far away"), the neg. οὐ and ἀπέχω highlight the close proximity (i.e., litotes) of Jesus to the house (cf. 15:20, without the neg.). Ἔπεμψεν 3rd sg. aor. act. indic. of πέμπω. With the voc. address κύριε the centurion may simply greet Jesus (through his delegates) with a respectful "Sir" (Fitzmyer 652; sim. to "Rabbi" Bock 639; Marshall 281). However, the following statements of his own unworthiness (7:6), his confidence in the power of Jesus' word (7:7), and his recognition of Jesus' ultimate authority (7:8) reflect Peter's confession of sinfulness before Jesus as Lord (5:8; also using the voc. κύριε; cf. Nolland 317; Rowe 114–17). Σκύλλου 2nd sg. pres. pass. impv. of σκύλλω, "trouble," "bother" (neg. with μή; the impv. here is a request, Wallace 488; cf. 8:49). Γάρ, causal (the adj. ἱκανός is pred. and takes the gen., Wallace 135; cf. ἄξιος in 7:4). Ἵνα introduces a clause that is epex. to ἱκανός (BHGNT 220; Wallace 476, 678; or for a consec. inf., Z §§406, 407; ZG 199). Εἰσέλθῃς 2nd sg. 2nd aor. act. subjunc. of dep. εἰσέρχομαι. Στέγην acc. sg. fem. of στέγη, -ης, ἡ, "roof." This reason, together with the next verse, indicates that σκύλλω here means Jesus can heal from where he is, not (as in 8:49) because it is too late (Bock 640).

7:7 The centurion then explains that this is why (διό) he did not consider himself worthy (ἠξίωσα 1st sg. aor. act. indic. of ἀξιόω, "consider worthy," neg. with οὐδέ) to come to Jesus (ἐλθεῖν 2nd aor. act. inf. of dep. ἔρχομαι; the inf. is perhaps epex. like the ἵνα clause in 7:6, or complementary, BDF §392[1c]; BHGNT 220). In contrast (ἀλλά) to having Jesus come to his house, the centurion displays his confidence in the power of Jesus' word to heal from wherever Jesus is. All Jesus needs to do is "say the word" (εἰπὲ λόγῳ [see 4:3], a cognate instr. dat., lit. "speak with a word" or "say in a word" KJV; Robertson, *Pictures* 101; Z §62; ZG 199; implied cond., R 1023), and the servant (now using παῖς [see 1:54] as synonymous with δοῦλος in 7:2, 3, 8, 10; Marshall 279; cf. παῖς for "child" in 8:51, 54) would be healed (cf. Ps 107:20). The impv. ἰαθήτω (3rd sg. aor. pass. impv. of ἰάομαι, "heal"; a "permissive passive" request Wallace 441, 488 [i.e., "let my servant be healed"]) is the reading of 𝔓⁷⁵ᵛⁱᵈ B L (UBS⁵; NJB, NRSV, ESV; a Heb., ZG 199). The fut. indic. ἰαθήσεται found in ℵ A C D W 𝔐 (NKJV, NASB, HCSB, NIV) could be a scribal assimilation to Matt 8:8 (Metzger 118), or the impv. could be scribal assimilation to the impv. of the preceding vb. (BHGNT 221).

7:8 The reason the centurion thinks this is the sort of thing Jesus could do is because (γάρ) he understands the power of the word of someone who has authority. The centurion, who is himself under authority, has (ἔχων [see 3:11] is attrib.) soldiers under his command (τασσόμενος nom. sg. masc. of pres. pass. [attrib.] ptc. of τάσσω, "arrange," "order"). All the centurion needs to say (the dat. τούτῳ is the indir. obj. of λέγω; the cstr. is equivalent to a cond. sentence, Marshall 282) is "go" (πορεύθητι 2nd sg. aor. pass. impv. of dep. πορεύομαι), and the soldier "goes" (πορεύεται 3rd sg. pres. mid. indic. of dep. πορεύομαι), or "come" (ἔρχου 2nd sg. pres. mid. impv. of dep. ἔρχομαι; λέγω is implied with the dat. ἄλλῳ), and "he comes" (ἔρχεται 3rd sg. pres. mid. indic. of dep. ἔρχομαι). To his slave (λέγω is implied with the dat. τῷ δούλῳ), all he needs to say is "do this" (ποίησον, see 4:23), and "he does it" (ποιεῖ 3rd sg. pres. act. indic. of ποιέω).

7:9 Ἀκούσας, see 6:49 (temp.; ταῦτα is the obj.). Jesus both "marveled at" the man (ἐθαύμασεν 3rd sg. aor. act. indic. of θαυμάζω; [trans.] with αὐτόν, "admired him" BDAG 445a; Nolland 318) and turned (στραφείς nom. sg. masc. of 2nd aor. pass. ptc. of στρέφω; trans.; attendant circumstance) to address the crowd that was following (ἀκολουθοῦντι dat. sg. masc. of pres. act. [attrib.] ptc. of ἀκολουθέω). The dat. τῷ ἀκολουθοῦντι αὐτῷ ὄχλῳ may be locat. ("turning to the crowd," NRSV, HCSB, NIV; Bovon 1.263) or the indir. obj. of εἶπεν ("he said to the crowd," RSV, NASB; Fitzmyer 653). Στραφείς occurs in 7:44; 10:23; 23:28 with πρός to convey the idea of "turned to" (BHGNT 222; though cf. 9:55; 14:25; 22:61). Either way the dat. ὑμῖν is the indir. obj. of λέγω. Jesus' climactic statement is an emphatic endorsement of the uniqueness ("not even in Israel") and greatness ("such great faith"; cf. τοσαύτην [acc. sg. fem. of τοσοῦτος, -αύτη, -οῦτον], BDAG 1012b) of the centurion's faith (Bovon 1.263). Εὗρον 1st sg. 2nd aor. act. indic. of εὑρίσκω. Thus the man exemplifies the appropriate response of faith: humility before the Lord and recognition of the Lord's authority in the power of his word.

7:10 Ὑποστρέψαντες nom. pl. masc. of aor. act. (temp.) ptc. of ὑποστρέφω (intrans.). Πεμφθέντες nom. pl. masc. of aor. pass. (subst.) ptc. of πέμπω; the subj. of εὗρον, see 2:46). The acc. ptc. ὑγιαίνοντα (acc. sg. masc. of pres. act. ptc. of ὑγιαίνω, "in good health" NRSV, HCSB is the complement in a double acc. cstr. (BDAG 411d).

HOMILETICAL SUGGESTIONS

The Faith that Jesus Commends (7:1–10)
1. Recognize our unworthiness (7:1–7a).
2. Trust in Jesus' word (7:7b).
3. Acknowledge Jesus' authority (7:8–10).

b. Jesus' Mercy for the Grieving and Power over Death (7:11–17)

7:11 The new episode is linked to the preceding episode with ἐγένετο (see 1:5) and the temp. marker ἐν τῷ with the adv. ἑξῆς "next." This adv. is only used by Luke in the NT, though elsewhere it is modified by ἡμέρᾳ (cf. 9:37), or ἡμέρα is implied with the use of τῇ (Acts 21:1; 25:17; 27:18; giving rise to some var. rdgs.). Here χρόνῳ needs to be supplied (with the mng. "soon afterward," BDAG 349d; Robertson, *Pictures* 100; Bock 648; Bovon 1.270; Fitzmyer 658; Marshall 284; cf. καθεξῆς in 1:3; 8:1). Ἐπορεύθη, see 1:39. Καλουμένην acc. sg. fem. of pres. pass. (attrib.) ptc. of καλέω (modifying πόλιν, "city" NASB; though the use here is "town" most EVV, or "village" NLT; the term may be used for any "population center of varying size" BDAG 844d). Συνεπορεύοντο 3rd pl. impf. mid. indic. of dep. συμπορεύομαι, "go along with" (only here, 14:25; 24:15; and Mark 10:1 in the NT).

7:12 Ἤγγισεν 3rd sg. aor. act. indic. of ἐγγίζω (ὡς is temp.). Πύλη dat. sg. fem. of πύλη, -ης, ἡ, "(town) gate" (dat. complement, BDAG 270b–c; or a dat. of destination, Wallace 148). Καὶ ἰδού (see 1:20) introduces the main clause after the secondary one (Robertson, *Pictures* 101; Z §457; ZG 200). The nom. ptc. τεθνηκώς (nom. sg. masc. of pf. act. ptc. of θνήσκω, "die") is probably subst. (Marshall 284) and the nom. subj. of ἐξεκομίζετο (3rd sg. impf. pass. indic. of ἐκκομίζω, "carry out," i.e., for burial, BDAG 305a; LN 15.198; it is anar. in LXX Judg 3:25). If so, the nom. sg. masc. adj. μονογενὴς υἱός (of μονογενής, -ές, "only son"; cf. 8:42; 9:38) would be appos. to τεθνηκώς (all EVV; the dat. τῇ μητρί is poss.; cf. BDF §190[4]). Alternatively, μονογενὴς υἱός, modified by τεθνηκώς (as an attrib. ptc.), could be the subj. of ἐξεκομίζετο (BHGNT 225). The plight of the woman is further highlighted with the additional note that she was a widow (χήρα, see 2:37; there is an emphasis on the well-being of widows in Luke-Acts, cf. 18:2–5; 20:47; 21:2–3; [cf. 4:25–26]; Acts 6:1; 9:39–41).

7:13 Ἰδών, see 1:12 (temp., Bovon 1.271). The emphasis in this verse is on Jesus' compassionate initiative. Ἐσπλαγχνίσθη 3rd sg. aor. pass. indic. of dep. σπλαγχνίζομαι, "have compassion" (cf. 10:33; 15:20; cf. also the description of God's character in 1:78). This is the first abs. use of κύριος for Jesus in the authorial material of the narrative so far (Fitzmyer 659), and it will be a common way that Luke refers to Jesus (cf. 7:19; 10:1, 39, 41; 11:39; 12:42; 13:15; 17:5–6; 18:6; 19:8; 22:31 [possibly], 61; 24:3). As the preceding chapters have shown, it is in keeping with the angelic announcement in 2:11, Peter's confession in 5:8, the climactic conclusion to Jesus' sermon in 6:46, and the immediately preceding statement of the Lord's authority by the centurion in 7:6–8 (Nolland 323; Rowe 118). Κλαῖε 2nd sg. pres. act. impv. of κλαίω, "weep" (prohibition with the neg. μή).

7:14 Προσελθών (nom. sg. masc. of 2nd aor. act. ptc. of dep. προσέρχομαι) is an attendant circumstance ptc. (with ἥψατο see 5:13; to halt the procession, Marshall 286; Nolland 323). Σοροῦ (gen. complement [sg. fem. of σορός, -οῦ, ἡ]; cf. BDAG 126b–c), "bier" (KJV, NRSV, ESV, NIV) which is not so much a "coffin" (NASB) as a "stretcher or plank used for carrying a corpse to a place of burial" (LN 6.109; Bock 652; thus perhaps "open coffin" NKJV, HCSB). Βαστάζοντες nom. pl. masc. of pres. act. (subst.)

ptc. of βαστάζω, "carry," "bear" ("pallbearers" HCSB; the subj. of ἔστησαν 3rd pl. 2nd aor. act. indic. of ἵστημι, intrans.). As surprising as Jesus approaching the plank with a dead man on it to touch it might have been, the action of speaking to a dead body and commanding it far surpasses anything up to this point. Νεανίσκε, "young man" (voc. of simple address, sg. masc. of νεανίσκος, -ου, ὁ). Σοί is the indir. obj. of λέγω (emphasizing Jesus' authority, Marshall 286). Ἐγέρθητι 2nd sg. aor. pass. impv. of ἐγείρω (intrans.).

7:15 Ὁ νεκρός, rather than other designations in the narrative such as "only son" or "young man," highlights the significance of what has happened. Ἀνεκάθισεν 3rd sg. aor. act. indic. of ἀνακαθίζω, "sit up" (only here and Acts 9:40 [of Tabitha]). Ἤρξατο, see 4:21. Λαλεῖν (see 4:41), complementary. Ἔδωκεν, see 6:4 (cf. ἀπέδωκεν in 9:42).

7:16 The nom. φόβος is the subj. of ἔλαβεν (see 5:26) and (with the obj. πάντας) is "fear came over everyone" (HCSB). The impf. ἐδόξαζον (see 5:26) could be ingressive (NASB, NET; Robertson, *Pictures* 102). Λέγοντες, see 1:66. Ὅτι, recitative (twice; cf. BDF §470[1]). The nom. προφήτης μέγας is the subject of ἠγέρθη (3rd sg. aor. pass. indic. of ἐγείρω, "arisen" most EVV; "appeared" NIV; the sense here is "has been brought on the scene" Fitzmyer 660). This statement of the crowd is not entirely mistaken (cf. 4:24). Luke's ref. to Jesus as "the Lord," however, together with the following discussion about even John being "more than a prophet" (7:26–28), indicates that the evaluation of the crowd is still inadequate (as elsewhere, e.g., 9:18–19; Rowe 119; *pace* Fitzmyer 658). Ἐπεσκέψατο, see 1:68 (on ἐπισκέπτομαι as "come to help").

7:17 This report (ὁ λόγος οὗτος) of the people about Jesus (περὶ αὐτοῦ; or about this event, Bovon 1.274) went throughout (ἐξῆλθεν, see 2:1) the whole of Judea. In this context, ἐν ὅλῃ τῇ Ἰουδαίᾳ is a ref. to all Israel (Bovon 1.273; on the use of ἐν cf. BDAG 327c; BDF §218; Marshall 287). Περιχώρῳ (the surrounding region; see 3:3; 4:14, 37), perhaps includes Machaerus, where John the Baptist was imprisoned (Marshall 287).

FOR FURTHER STUDY

21. Miracles
*Achtemeier, P. J. "The Lukan Perspective on the Miracles of Jesus: A Preliminary Sketch." Pages 153–67 in *Perspectives on Luke-Acts*. Edited by C. H. Talbert. Edinburgh: T&T Clark, 1978.
Anderson, K. L. *DJG*² 774–89.
Catchpole, D. *Resurrection People: Studies in the Resurrection Narratives of the Gospels*. Macon: Smyth and Helwys, 2002.
*Keener, C. S. *Miracles: The Credibility of the New Testament Accounts*. 2 vols. Grand Rapids: Baker, 2011.
*Twelftree, G. H. *DJG*² 594–604.
_____. *Jesus the Miracle Worker: A Historical and Theological Study*. Downers Grove, Ill.: InterVarsity, 1999.

HOMILETICAL SUGGESTIONS

Lord over Death (7:11–17)
1. Jesus has compassion for the grieving (7:11–13).
2. Jesus has power over our greatest enemy (7:14–15).
3. Jesus embodies God's care for his people (7:16–17).

2. Jesus' Saving Rule Explained with Reference to John the Baptist (7:18–35)

a. Jesus Is Defined in Response to John's Expectations (7:18–23)

7:18 Ἀπήγγειλαν 3rd pl. aor. act. indic. of ἀπαγγέλλω; Ἰωάννῃ is the indir. obj.). The poss. gen. pron. αὐτοῦ refers to John (i.e., John the Baptist). The verse division of 𝔐 begins 7:19 with καὶ προσκαλεσάμενος (RSV, NKJV, NASB, ESV). The verse division of UBS⁵ is followed by NRSV, HCSB, NIV. The acc. δύο τινάς is the obj. of προσκαλεσάμενος (nom. sg. masc. of aor. mid. ptc. of dep. προσκαλέομαι, "call to," "summon"; attendant circumstance with ἔπεμψεν, 7:19). Ἰωάννης is the subj. of ἔπεμψεν (6:19).

7:19–20 Ἔπεμψεν, see 7:6. Ἰησοῦν is found in א A W Θ Ψ 𝔐 (KJV, NKJV, NET; Bock 687). Κύριον is found in B L Ξ *f*¹³ 33 (UBS⁵, most EVV; Metzger 119; Bovon 2.278; Fitzmyer 665; Marshall 289; Nolland 326). A decision in this instance is difficult. Although τὸν κύριον fits with Lukan style (see 7:13), the external evidence favors Ἰησοῦν. Λέγων perhaps expresses purpose here (BHGNT 228; the subj. is Ἰωάννης [through his two disciples]). Σύ is the subj. of εἶ (see 3:22). The subst. ptc. ἐρχόμενος (see 6:47) is a pred. nom. (Burton §433; R 1108). Προσδοκῶμεν 1st pl. pres. act. subjunc. of προσδοκάω, "wait for," "look for"; (ἄλλον is the obj.; the form could be indic. but the nature of the question indicates a [deliberative] subjunc.). As Luke 3:20 indicates (the last episode involving John the Baptist), John sends them with this question from prison. Παραγενόμενοι, see 7:4 (temp.). Ἰωάννης (with ὁ βαπτιστής in appos.) is the subj. of ἀπέστειλεν (see 7:3). From λέγων the statement is identical to 7:19.

7:21 The temp. introduction to this summary (ἐν ἐκείνῃ τῇ ὥρᾳ, "just then" NRSV; "at that very time" NIV) together with the aor. vb. ἐθεράπευσεν (3rd sg. aor. act. indic. of θεραπεύω) may indicate that this is the first part of Jesus' response (BHGNT 229; Bovon 1.278; "as they arrived" Fitzmyer 667). As a parenthetical comment, Luke provides the setting for the following message so that these disciples both hear from Jesus and see what he is doing (cf. ἃ εἴδετε καὶ ἠκούσατε in 7:22; Marshall 290; Nolland 327). Νόσων ("diseases," gen. pl. fem., see 4:40), μαστίγων (gen. pl. fem. of μάστιξ, -ιγος, ἡ, "afflictions" NASB; "plagues" NRSV, HCSB, ESV; "sicknesses" NIV) and πνευμάτων πονηρῶν ("evil spirits") are all the obj. of ἀπό. Illnesses are distinguished from "evil spirits" (cf. 4:33–34; Bock 667; Nolland 329; *pace* Fitzmyer 667). The dat. τυφλοῖς πολλοῖς is the indir. obj. of ἐχαρίσατο (3rd sg. aor. mid. indic. of dep. χαρίζομαι, "grant"). The pres. act. inf. βλέπειν (of βλέπω) is the obj. of ἐχαρίσατο (BDAG 1078c).

7:22 Ἀποκριθείς, see 1:19. Πορευθέντες (nom. pl. masc. of aor. pass. ptc. of dep. πορεύομαι) is an attendant circumstance ptc. (Wallace 644) with the impv. ἀπαγγείλατε (2nd pl. aor. act. impv. of ἀπαγγέλλω). The acc. pl. neut. rel. pron. ἅ (of ὅς, ἥ, ὅ) is the dir. obj. of εἴδετε (2nd pl. aor. act. indic. of ὁράω) and ἠκούσατε (2nd pl. aor. act. indic. of ἀκούω). The entire rel. clause is the dir. obj. of ἀπαγγείλατε (BHGNT 230). The message has six brief clauses: two groups of three joined by καί (Marshall 291; Nolland 330). Τυφλοί ("blind"; see 4:18; cf. 7:21), subj. of ἀναβλέπουσιν (3rd pl. pres.

act. indic. of ἀναβλέπω; cf. τυφλοῖς . . . βλέπειν in 6:21). Χωλοί (nom. pl. masc. of
χωλός, -ή, -όν, "lame"; cf. 14:13, 21), subj. of περιπατοῦσιν (3rd pl. pres. act. indic.
of περιπατέω). Λεπροί (see 4:27), subj. of καθαρίζονται (3rd pl. pres. pass. indic. of
καθαρίζω). Κωφοί ("deaf"; see 1:22), subj. of ἀκούουσιν (3rd pl. pres. act. indic. of
ἀκούω). Νεκροί, subj. of ἐγείρονται (3rd pl. pres. pass. indic. of ἐγείρω; see 7:11–17).
Πτωχοί, subj. of εὐαγγελίζονται (3rd pl. pres. pass. indic. of εὐαγγελίζω; see 4:18).

7:23 Μακάριός is a pred. adj. (μακάριός is rarely preceded by καί, Fitzmyer 668). The
rel. pron. and particle ὅς ἐάν ("anyone who" HCSB, NIV) is the subj. of σκανδαλισθῇ
(3rd sg. aor. pass. subjunc. of σκανδαλίζω, in pass. intrans. "take offence"; neg. with
μή). The beatitude is thus generic and not only for John (Bock 669; Fitzmyer 668).
The whole rel. clause is the subj. of ἐστίν (BHGNT 231). Ἐν ἐμοί is causal (ZG 201).

b. John Is Defined in Relation to the Arrival of the Kingdom Through Jesus (7:24–28)

7:24 The gen. τῶν ἀγγέλων ("messengers" Bovon 1.282; Ἰωάννου could be a gen.
of source) with the gen. ptc. ἀπελθόντων (gen. pl. masc. of 2nd aor. act. ptc. of dep.
ἀπέρχομαι) is a temp. gen. abs. cstr. Ἤρξατο, see 4:21 (the subj. is Jesus). Λέγειν,
see 3:8 (complementary; for the cstr. with πρός see 1:13). Ἐξήλθατε 2nd pl. aor. act.
indic. of dep. ἐξέρχομαι. The aor. mid. inf. θεάσασθαι (of dep. θεάομαι, "to behold")
expresses purpose (ZG 201; the acc. interr. τί is the dir. obj.). If the question mark is
placed after ἔρημον, the question would be, "Why did you go out to the wilderness?"
If it is placed after θεάσασθαι, the question is, "What did you go out to the wilderness
to see?" (UBS⁵; all EVV; Bock 671; Bovon 1.283; Fitzmyer 673; Marshall 293–94;
Nolland 336). The acc. sg. masc. κάλαμον (of κάλαμος, -ου, ὁ, "reed") is the obj. of
an implied ἐξήλθατε (εἰς τὴν ἔρημον) θεάσασθαι. Ἀνέμου gen. sg. masc. of ἄνεμος, -ου,
ὁ, "wind." Σαλευόμενον acc. sg. masc. of pres. pass. (attrib.) ptc. of σαλεύω, "shake"
(or the complement in a double acc. cstr., BHGNT 232). This may ref. to literal reeds
(Bock 671; Nolland 336) or be a figurative ref. to John as supposedly easily swayed
(Fitzmyer 674; Marshall 294).

7:25 Ἀλλά implies a neg. reply ("if not that, then . . ." ZG 201; NIV). Ἐξήλθατε, see
7:24. The inf. ἰδεῖν (see 2:26) expresses purpose. For the following clause, ἐξήλθατε
ἰδεῖν is implied. Μαλακοῖς dat. pl. neut. of μαλακός, -ή, -όν, "soft" (NRSV, NASB,
HCSB, ESV), "fine" (NIV). Ἠμφιεσμένον acc. sg. masc. of pf. pass. (attrib.) ptc. of
ἀμφιέννυμι, "clothe," "dress" (or the complement in a double acc. cstr., BDF §159[1];
BHGNT 232). The subst. ptc. οἱ . . . ὑπάρχοντες (nom. pl. masc. of pres. act. ptc. of
ὑπάρχω) is modified by ἐν ἱματισμῷ [dat. sg. masc. of ἱματισμός, -οῦ, ὁ] ἐνδόξῳ [dat. sg.
masc. of ἔνδοξος, -ον] καὶ τρυφῇ [dat. sg. fem. of τρυφή, -ῆς, ἡ] ("in splendid clothing
and luxury") and is the subj. of εἰσίν (3rd pl. pres. act. indic. of εἰμί). Ἐν τοῖς βασιλείοις
(dat. pl. neut. of βασίλειος, -ον, subst. "in palaces"), locat.

7:26 For ἐξήλθατε ἰδεῖν see 7:24–25. The acc. προφήτην is the obj. of an implied
ἐξήλθατε ἰδεῖν. The acc. sg. comp. adj. περισσότερον (of περισσός, -ή, -όν; "greater,"
"more"; could be masc. or neut.) is subst. and the obj. of an implied ἐξήλθατε ἰδεῖν.
Προφήτου is a gen. of comp.

7:27 Γέγραπται, see 2:23. Ἀποστέλλω 1st sg. pres. act. indic. of ἀποστέλλω. Πρὸ προσώπου is idiomatic for "before" (LN 83.33; BDAG 888b; cf. κατὰ πρόσωπον in 2:31). The rel. pron. ὅς is the subj. of κατασκευάσει (3rd sg. fut. act. indic. of κατασκευάζω, "prepare"). The pron. σου before whom the messenger goes may ref. to the people (Bock 674; cf. κατασκευάζω in 1:17 and σου in Exod 23:20). The ref. to Mal 3:1 (cf. 1:17, 76; 3:4; Mark 1:2), however, indicates that the messenger (i.e., Elijah = John) goes before Yahweh, and Jesus replaces the coming of Yahweh here (Fitzmyer 674; Marshall 296; Nolland 337; Pao and Schnabel 303a).

7:28 The comp. adj. μείζων is a pred. adj. and is modified by Ἰωάννου (a gen. of comp.). The nom. indef. pron. οὐδείς is the subj. of ἐστίν (cf. R 234). Ἐν γεννητοῖς γυναικῶν ("among those born of women"; dat. pl. masc. of γεννητός, -ή, -όν, subst.) is association. The adj. μικρότερος is comp. in form but in this context is probably superl. ("least" all EVV; BDF §§60, 244; Z §147; Bock 675; Bovon 1.284). The gen. αὐτοῦ after the comp. adj. μείζων is another gen. of comp. The significance of "the least" in comparison to John has to do not with personality or personal achievement but with the arrival of the kingdom of God in Jesus (Nolland 338).

c. John and Jesus Are Both Defined in Relation to Reactions to God's Plan (7:29–35)

7:29 The third-person references in 7:29–30 indicate that these verses are an aside by Luke (cf. NRSV, HCSB, ESV, NIV; Bock 676–77). Jesus' speech resumes in 7:31. Ἀκούσας, see 6:49 (temp.). The obj. is implied and could be "John" (Bock 676; Fitzmyer 676) or *Jesus' words about John (all EVV; Marshall 298; Nolland 342). Πᾶς ὁ λαὸς . . . καὶ ("even") οἱ τελῶναι (see 3:12) is the subj. of ἐδικαίωσαν (3rd pl. aor. act. indic. of δικαιόω, "justify," "declare righteous"). Ἐδικαίωσαν in this context means that this crowd declared or acknowledged that God is righteous ("God's way is right" NIV; cf. 7:35). Βαπτισθέντες (nom. pl. masc. of aor. pass. ptc. of βαπτίζω) could express means (NJB; Bock 663) or *cause (NRSV, HCSB, NIV; Marshall 299; Nolland 340; on the acc. obj. βάπτισμα [see 3:3], see Wallace 197, 439; the gen. Ἰωάννου is subj.).

7:30 Νομικοί (nom. pl. masc. of νομικός, -ή, -όν [subst.], "experts in the law" HCSB) is first used here in Luke's Gospel (cf. 10:25; 11:45, 46, 52; 14:3) but is sim. to the terms used in 5:17, 21. The acc. sg. fem. βουλήν (of βουλή, -ῆς, ἡ) is the obj. of ἠθέτησαν (3rd pl. aor. act. indic. of ἀθετέω, "reject" [cf. 10:16]; the gen. τοῦ θεοῦ is subj., Wallace 114). Εἰς ἑαυτούς is "in regard to themselves" ("for themselves" most EVV; Marshall 299; rather than εἰς for ἐν, ZG 202). Βαπτισθέντες, see 7:29 (causal; neg. with μή).

7:31 The dat. sg. neut. interr. pron. τίνι (of τίς, τί, gen. τίνος) introduces a rhetorical question (and resumes dir. speech). Ὁμοιώσω 1st sg. fut. act. indic. of ὁμοιόω, "compare" (the fut. indic. is replacing a hortatory use of the subjunc. here, BHGNT 237, citing McKay 95). The acc. τοὺς ἀνθρώπους is the obj. of ὁμοιώσω (R 1392). This is the first use of the phrase "this generation" in Luke's Gospel. It will consistently be used to ref. to those opposed to Jesus (cf. 9:41; 11:29–32, 50–51; 17:25; 21:32; cf. 16:8). The question concludes with a similar statement concerning what to liken this generation to (though with the pred. adj. ὅμοιοι; τίνι is complementary, BDAG 706d).

7:32 Ὅμοιοι is a pred. adj. Παιδίοις is the dat. complement to ὅμοιοι (BDAG 706d). Ἐν ἀγορᾷ (dat. sg. fem. of ἀγορά, -ᾶς, ἡ, "in the marketplace," on the anar. cstr. see T 179) is locat. The ptcs. καθημένοις (see 1:79) and προσφωνοῦσιν (dat. pl. neut. of pres. act. ptc. of προσφωνέω, "call to") are attrib. (BDF §270[3]; Wallace 618; Marshall 300). Ἀλλήλοις is the dat. complement to προσφωνοῦσιν. The antecedent of the neut. pl. rel. pron. ἅ (which is the subj. of λέγει) is παιδίοις (Nolland 343; though Fitzmyer [680] links the rel. clause to προσφωνοῦσιν). Ηὐλήσαμεν 1st pl. aor. act. indic. of αὐλέω, "play a flute." Ὠρχήσασθε 2nd pl. aor. mid. indic. of dep. ὀρχέομαι, "dance" (neg. with οὐκ). Ἐθρηνήσαμεν 1st pl. aor. act. indic. of θρηνέω, "sing a funeral song" (LN 33.115; cf. BDAG 458d; "sang a lament" HCSB). Ἐκλαύσατε 2nd pl. aor. act. indic. of κλαίω, "weep."

7:33 The reason Jesus likens "this generation" to children in the marketplace who complain (ἅ λέγει, 7:32) when their demands are not followed (Bock 681; Marshall 301) is because (γάρ) of their responses (λέγετε) to John and Jesus. Ἐλήλυθεν 3rd sg. 2nd pf. act. indic. of dep. ἔρχομαι (Ἰωάννης is the subj.). Ἐσθίων nom. sg. masc. of pres. act. ptc. of ἐσθίω (expressing manner; neg. with μή). Πίνων nom. sg. masc. of pres. act. ptc. of πίνω (expressing manner; neg. with μήτε; the combination of μὴ . . . μήτε is rare, LSJ 1129d; Marshall 310). Λέγετε 2nd pl. pres. act. indic. of λέγω. Ἔχει, see 5:24.

7:34 Jesus is contrasted with John's more ascetic manner. For the verbs ἐλήλυθεν, ἐσθίων, πίνων, and λέγετε, see 7:33. For ἰδού see 1:20 (here ἰδοὺ ἄνθρωπος is like "Look at him!" ESV). Φάγος nom. sg. masc. of φάγος, -ου, ὁ, "glutton." Οἰνοπότης nom. sg. masc. of οἰνοπότης, -ου, ὁ, "drunkard." The nom. φάγος καὶ οἰνοπότης is in appos. to ἄνθρωπος (or a pred. nom. with ἄνθρωπος as the subj. of an implied ἐστίν, BHGNT 238). The nom. φίλος is in appos. to φάγος καὶ οἰνοπότης. Τελωνῶν gen. pl. masc., see 3:12 (5:30).

7:35 Καί is contrastive (Z §455α; ZG 203). The apparent gloom of 7:31–34 is not the whole story (Nolland 347). Σοφία is the subj. of ἐδικαιώθη (3rd sg. aor. pass. indic. of δικαιόω, "vindicated" HCSB; "justified" ESV; "proved right" NIV; a gnomic aor., BDF §333; T 73; Wallace 562; Fitzmyer 681; Marshall 303; cf. 7:29). Ἀπό is used for ὑπό to express agency (see 6:18; Wallace 433; Bovon 1.287; Marshall 303). Πάντων τῶν τέκνων αὐτῆς refers to those who respond to John and Jesus.

HOMILETICAL SUGGESTIONS

Who Do We Think Jesus Is? (7:18–35)
1. Jesus corrects mistaken expectations (7:18–23).
2. Jesus' disciples are greater than the prophets and John the Baptist (7:24–28).
3. Jesus' disciples demonstrate God's way to be right (7:29–35).

3. Jesus' Saving Rule Demonstrated in the Forgiveness of Sins Received by Faith (7:36–50)

7:36 Ἠρώτα 3rd sg. impf. act. indic. of ἐρωτάω, "ask," "invited" HCSB, NIV; Bovon 1.293 (indef. pron. τις is the subj.). The impf. may be used to provide background information and set the scene for what follows (BHGNT 240), though it is often used with vbs. of asking (BDF §328). Ἵνα introduces indir. discourse. Φάγῃ 3rd sg. 2nd aor. act. subjunc. of ἐσθίω (with ἵνα). The aor. ptc. εἰσελθών (see 1:9) is an attendant circumstance ptc. with κατεκλίθη (3rd sg. aor. pass. indic. of κατακλίνω, "cause to sit" [act.], "recline" [pass., intrans., BDAG 518c]; only used by Luke in the NT, 9:14, 15; 14:8; 24:30).

7:37 Ἰδού, see 1:20. The introductory ἰδοὺ γυνὴ ἥτις ἦν ἐν τῇ πόλει ἁμαρτωλός could be understood in one of the following ways (BHGNT 241; though none affects the mng:

1. the nom. adj. ἁμαρτωλός could be in appos. to the nom. γυνή (which is the subj. of ἦν). "Behold a woman, who was in the town, a sinner!"
2. the nom. adj. ἁμαρτωλός could be a pred. nom. with the nom. γυνή (with ἦν implied). "Behold a woman, who was in the town, was a sinner."
*3. the nom. adj. ἁμαρτωλός could be a pred. nom. of the rel. clause. "Behold a woman, who was a sinner in the town."

The nom. rel. pron. ἥτις (with the antecedent γυνή; perhaps "of such a kind that" [Robertson, *Pictures* 105] or in place of ἥ, Z §216; ZG 202) is the subj. of ἦν. Ἐν τῇ πόλει could modify ἁμαρτωλός as a Sem. idiom for "publicly" or "well-known" (Nolland 353; cf. Fitzmyer 688). Ἐπιγνοῦσα nom. sg. fem. of 2nd aor. act. (temp.) ptc. of ἐπιγινώσκω (modifies ἤρξατο in 7:38). Ὅτι introduces indir. discourse (following the vb. of perception, BDAG 732a). Κατάκειται 3rd sg. pres. pass. indic. of dep. κατάκειμαι, "recline" (the pres. is retained in indir. discourse, Robertson, *Pictures* 106). Κομίσασα (nom. sg. fem. of aor. act. ptc. of κομίζω, "bring") is an attendant circumstance ptc. with στᾶσα in 7:38 (and also modifies ἤρξατο in 7:38). The acc. ἀλάβαστρον (acc. sg. neut. of ἀλάβαστρον, -ου, τό, "alabaster jar") is the obj. of κομίσασα. Μύρου (gen. sg. neut. of μύρον, -ου, τό, "[expensive] perfumed oil" LN 6.205; cf. 7:38, 46; 23:56) is a gen. of content.

7:38 Στᾶσα (nom. sg. fem. of 2nd aor. act. ptc. of ἵστημι, intrans.) is an attendant circumstance ptc. (with κομίσασα in 7:37). The description of the woman standing behind Jesus and at his feet pictures a setting in which "reclining" at the table meant lying on your side with your body extending away from the table. Κλαίουσα (nom. sg. fem. of pres. act. ptc. of κλαίω, "weep") expresses manner (modifying στᾶσα; Wallace 628). Τοῖς δάκρυσιν (dat. pl. neut. of δάκρυον, -ου, τό, "with tears") is instr. and modifies the pres. act. inf. βρέχειν (of βρέχω, "to rain, wet"; complementary to ἤρξατο [see 4:21]). The placement of the dat. τοῖς δάκρυσιν before the inf. βρέχειν and the main vb. ἤρξατο is emphatic (BHGNT 242). Ταῖς θριξίν (dat. pl. fem. of θρίξ, τριχός, ἡ, "with the hairs [of her head]") is instr. and modifies ἐξέμασσεν (3rd sg. impf. act. indic. of ἐκμάσσω, "wipe dry"). Κατεφίλει 3rd sg. impf. act. indic. of καταφιλέω, "kiss" (cf. 7:45; 15:20;

Acts 20:37). Ἤλειφεν 3rd sg. impf. act. indic. of ἀλείφω, "anoint." Μύρῳ, see 7:37
(here, a dat. of material, Wallace 170). The three impf. vbs. may be impf. to provide
background information (BHGNT 243) but are more likely progressive (NRSV, NLT,
NASB; Robertson, *Pictures* 107 [though ἐξέμασσεν is ingressive]; ZG 202; Bock 697).
On the chain reaction that probably ensued after the woman's tears fell on Jesus' feet
(which were extending away from the table) see Marshall 308–9; Nolland 354–55.

7:39 Ἰδών, see 1:12 (temp.). Καλέσας nom. sg. masc. of aor. act. (attrib.) ptc. of καλέω,
"invited" most EVV. Ἐν and refl. pron. indicate an inward process (BDAG 327b;
BHGNT 243; see 5:21, on λέγοντες). The demonstrative pron. οὗτος could be placed
forward, before the cond. clause, for emphasis (and be the subj. of ἦν; Marshall 309).
Or the pron. could be outside the cond. clause (as it precedes εἰ) and be the subj. of
ἐγίνωσκεν (BHGNT 243–44). Εἰ introduces a second-class cond. clause (i.e., assuming this is not true from the perspective of the speaker, Burton §241; R 1012; Wallace
663, 694–95; Z §§313–14; ZG 203). Ἐγίνωσκεν 3rd sg. impf. act. indic. of γινώσκω.
The particle ἄν introduces the apodosis of the second-class cond. The nom. sg. fem.
τίς καὶ ποταπή (see 1:29) is a pred. nom. with ἐστίν implied ("who and what kind the
woman is," BHGNT 244; R 741; Bovon 1.295). The rel. pron. ἥτις (see 6:37) is the
subj. of ἅπτεται (3rd sg. pres. mid. indic. of ἅπτω, "touch"). Ὅτι could be "that" (the
obj. of ἐγίνωσκεν, NASB, NIV) or "because" (NKJV, ESV; cf. Z §416). Ἁμαρτωλός is
the pred. nom. of ἐστίν.

7:40 Ἀποκριθείς, see 1:19. Σίμων, voc. (a common name and therefore there is no need
to think that Simon the leper in this account is Simon the Pharisee in Matt 26; Mark 14;
John 12; Bock 689–91; Marshall 310; Nolland 355; *pace* Bovon 1.291–93; Fitzmyer
684–88). Ἔχω 1st sg. pres. act. indic. of ἔχω. The dat. σοί (indir. obj.) and the acc.
indef. pron. τι (the obj. of the 2nd aor. act. inf. εἰπεῖν, of λέγω) are placed forward for
emphasis (BHGNT 245). Διδάσκαλε (voc.,) εἰπέ (see 4:3) is Simon's reply (φησίν 3rd
sg. pres. act. indic. of φημί; a rare historic pres. in Luke; BHGNT 245–46; Marshall
310; Nolland 355). This is the first time Jesus is addressed as teacher in Luke's Gospel.
It is equivalent to rabbi and is used most often by nondisciples of Jesus (cf. 10:25;
11:45; 12:13; 18:18; 19:39; 20:21, 28, 39; though by Jesus 22:11, and by the disciples
in 21:7; cf. 8:49; 9:38). In this context, therefore, it is a polite but inadequate description of Jesus (Marshall 310).

7:41 The nom. δύο χρεοφειλέται (nom. pl. masc. of χρεοφειλέτης, -ου, ὁ; "two debtors")
is the subj. of ἦσαν (see 1:6). The dat. (sg. masc.) δανιστῇ τινι (of δανιστής, -οῦ, ὁ) is
the dat. complement to χρεοφειλέται (BHGNT 246; or a dat. of poss.; i.e., "a certain
moneylender had two debtors" ESV; cf. ZG 203). Ὁ εἷς is the subj. of ὤφειλεν (3rd sg.
impf. act. indic. of ὀφείλω, "owe"). Δηνάρια πεντακόσια, "five hundred denarii" (acc.
pl. neut. of δηνάριον, -ου, τό, a transliteration of the Latin *denarius*; i.e., five hundred
days' wages for a laborer; Matt 20:2; Marshall 310; Nolland 355). Ὁ . . . ἕτερος is the
subj. of an implied ὤφειλεν (for ὁ εἷς . . . ὁ δὲ ἕτερος with ἕτερος for the second of a pair,
see BDF §247[3]; R 748; cf. 18:10). Πεντήκοντα, "fifty." Thus, one has ten times the
amount of debt.

7:42 Ἐχόντων gen. pl. masc. of pres. act. ptc. of ἔχω (a causal gen. abs. cstr. with αὐτῶν as the subj.; neg. with μή; HCSB, NIV; with the inf., "be in a position to" ZG 203). The 2nd aor. act. inf. ἀποδοῦναι (of ἀποδίδωμι) is the dir. obj. ("not having [anything] to repay" BHGNT 246). Ἀμφοτέροις, "both" (dat. pl. masc., see 1:6), is the dat. complement to ἐχαρίσατο (see 7:21; "graciously forgave" NASB, HCSB; "cancelled" NRSV, ESV; BDAG 1078d). Ἀγαπήσει 3rd sg. fut. act. indic. of ἀγαπάω (interr. pron. τίς is the subj.). Πλεῖον, adv., is comp.

7:43 Ἀποκριθείς, see 1:19. Ὑπολαμβάνω 1st sg. pres. act. indic. of ὑπολαμβάνω, "I suppose" (all EVV; cf. LN 31.29; MM 658a; either a cautious [Marshall 311] or half-hearted response [Nolland 356]). Ὅτι introduces indir. discourse (after a vb. of thinking, BDAG 732a). The dat. rel. pron. ᾧ is the dat. complement of ἐχαρίσατο (see 7:21, 42; the acc. πλεῖον is the dir. obj.). Ὀρθῶς, adv., "correctly" (NASB, NIV), "rightly" (NRSV, ESV). Ἔκρινας 2nd sg. aor. act. indic. of κρίνω.

7:44 Στραφείς (see 7:9) is probably an attendant circumstance ptc. (with ἔφη 3rd sg. impf. or aor. act. indic. of φήμι). In turning to the woman and speaking to Simon, Jesus directs Simon's attention to the woman (Bock 701). Βλέπεις, see 6:41. The art. in ταύτην τὴν γυναῖκα is a function marker to indicate the attrib. function of the demonstrative pron. (Wallace 241–42). Εἰσῆλθόν 1st sg. 2nd aor. act. indic. of dep. εἰσέρχομαι. The placement of the pron. σου before εἰς τὴν οἰκίαν is emphatic (ZG 203) and highlights the contrast with the woman (αὕτη δέ). The acc. ὕδωρ is the dir. obj. of ἔδωκας (2nd sg. aor. act. indic. of δίδωμι; with μοι as the indir. obj; neg. by οὐκ). Αὕτη is the subj. of ἔβρεξεν (3rd sg. aor. act. indic. of βρέχω, "wet," see 7:38). Τοῖς δάκρυσιν and ταῖς θριξίν (see 7:38; αὐτῆς is poss.) are instr. Ἐξέμαξεν 3rd sg. aor. act. indic. of ἐκμάσσω, "wipe dry" (see 7:38). The first word in each of the following three contrasts highlights Simon's lack (Robertson, *Pictures* 109): ὕδωρ ("water," 7:44), φίλημά ("kiss," 7:45), ἐλαίῳ ("oil," 7:46).

7:45 The acc. sg. neut. φίλημά (of φίλημα, -ατος, τό, "kiss of greeting" NET; cf. 22:48) is the dir. obj. of ἔδωκας (see 7:44 for this form and for μοι and οὐκ). Αὕτη (again, emphasizing the contrast) is the subj. of διέλιπεν (3rd sg. 2nd aor. act. indic. of διαλείπω, "stop"; though common in the LXX, it is found only here in the NT; neg. with οὐ; a hyperbolic statement in this context, Marshall 312). The prep. and rel. pron. ἀφ' ἧς is a temp. phrase which indicates the "point from which something begins" (BDAG 105c; BDF §241[2]; R 977–78; ZG 203; "since" Nolland 357). Εἰσῆλθόν, see 7:44. Καταφιλοῦσά (nom. sg. fem. of pres. act. ptc. of καταφιλέω, "kiss," cf. 7:38) is complementary (BDAG 232b; Burton §459; Robertson, *Pictures* 109). Μου is poss. (modifying τοὺς πόδας).

7:46 The dat. (sg. neut.) ἐλαίῳ (of ἔλαιον, -ου, τό, "oil" most EVV; "olive oil" HCSB) is a dat. of material (Wallace 170). Ἤλειψας 2nd sg. aor. act. indic. of ἀλείφω, "anoint" (neg. with οὐκ; cf. 7:38). Αὕτη (again, emphasizing the contrast) is the subj. of ἤλειψεν (3rd sg. aor. act. indic. of ἀλείφω, "anoint"). Μύρον (see 7:37; for the dat. μύρῳ see 7:38) is contrasted with the less expensive ἔλαιον (Bock 702; note also the contrast in κεφαλήν . . . πόδας).

7:47 The gen. rel. pron. οὗ (the antecedent is the contrast between Simon and the woman) and the prep. χάριν (cf. BDAG 1078d–1079a; ZG 203) indicate reason (BHGNT 250). The phrase with λέγω σοι may give (1) the reason for what Jesus is about to say to Simon ("Therefore I tell you," HCSB, ESV; Fitzmyer 691; Marshall 313; Nolland 358), or (2) the reason for the woman is forgiven (thus, λέγω σοι is parenthetical, "Therefore, I tell you," NRSV, NIV; though the parenthetical λέγω σοι does not necessarily mean her sins are forgiven because of her conduct; see below on ὅτι). The nom. αἱ ἁμαρτίαι . . . αἱ πολλαί is the subj. of ἀφέωνται (see 5:20, 23). Ὅτι has been understood as introducing a clause ("she loved much," ἠγάπησε 3rd sg. aor. act. indic. of ἀγαπάω) that provides the ground or cause of the woman's forgiveness (cf. Bovon 1.297; Fitzmyer 686). However, since the final clause of this verse refers to "loving little" (ἀγαπᾷ, see 7:5) as evidence of being "forgiven little" (ἀφίεται 3rd sg. pres. pass. indic. of ἀφίημι, lit. "to whom little is forgiven" NRSV), ὅτι is better understood as introducing a clause which gives evidence of forgiveness ("that's why she loved much" HCSB; cf. NIV; Moule 147; Robertson, *Pictures* 109; Z §§420–22; ZG 203; Bock 703–5; Fitzmyer 687, 692; Marshall 306; Nolland 358). The final clause is unlikely to ref. to the Pharisee's experience of "little forgiveness" (Fitzmyer 692). As with 5:31–32, the need is to grasp the significance of sin and therefore the greatness of forgiveness (Marshall 313; Nolland 359).

7:48 The nom. αἱ ἁμαρτίαι is the subj. of ἀφέωνται (see 5:20). The pf. ἀφέωνταί repeats what Jesus has said to Simon about the woman in 7:47. Her forgiveness is now explicitly confirmed on the basis of Jesus' authority (Nolland 359). Furthermore, Jesus' declaration to the woman reassures her in the face of Simon's hostility (Bock 705). These concluding statements by Jesus, and the reaction in 7:49 (cf. 5:21), show again that Jesus surpasses the inadequate category of "prophet" (cf. 7:16).

7:49 Συνανακείμενοι nom. pl. masc. of pres. mid. (subst.) ptc. of dep. συνανάκειμαι, "recline with" (cf. 7:36–38; the subj. of ἤρξαντο, see 5:21). Λέγειν, see 3:8. The pl. ἐν ἑαυτοῖς could be "among themselves" (NRSV, HCSB, NIV; i.e., to one another) or "within themselves" (KJV; i.e., private thoughts; cf. 5:22; 7:39; Bock 706). The nom. sg. masc. rel. pron. ὅς is the subj. of ἀφίησιν (3rd sg. pres. act. indic. of ἀφίημι; καί "even"). This climactic statement clarifies that Jesus' declarations about forgiveness in 8:47–48, are not merely statements about God forgiving the woman; Jesus is the one doing the forgiving.

7:50 Σέσωκεν 3rd sg. pf. act. indic. of σῴζω (ἡ πίστις is the subj.). The identical phrase ἡ πίστις σου σέσωκέν σε is found in 8:48 (also followed by πορεύου εἰς εἰρήνην); 17:19; 18:42. Πορεύου, see 5:24. In this context there is no healing involved. The woman is a "sinner" who has been "forgiven." Thus, "salvation" (see 1:47; linked with forgiveness in 1:77) and "peace" (see 1:79) point to wholeness and harmony between the "sinner" and God because Jesus forgives sin.

FOR FURTHER STUDY

22. Salvation (7:50)

*Blomberg, C. L. "'Your Faith Has Made You Whole': The Evangelical Liberation Theology of Jesus." Pages 75–93 in *Jesus of Nazareth, Lord and Christ*. Edited by J. B. Green and M. Turner. Grand Rapids: Eerdmans, 1994.
*Bock, *Theology* 239–78.
Green, J. B. "The Message of Salvation in Luke-Acts." *Ex Auditu* 5 (1989): 21–34.
*Marshall, I. H. *Luke: Historian and Theologian*. Downers Grove: InterVarsity, 1988. See p. 77–215.
Van der Watt, J. G., and D. S. du Toit. *DJG*[2] 829–30.
Yeung, M. W. *Faith in Jesus and Paul: A Comparison with Special Reference to "Faith That Can Remove Mountains" and "Your Faith Has Healed/Saved You."* WUNT 147. Tübingen: Mohr Siebeck, 2002.
York, J. *The Last Shall Be First: The Rhetoric of Reversal in Luke*. Sheffield: JSOT Press, 1991.

HOMILETICAL SUGGESTIONS

Forgiven Sinners and Jesus (7:36–50)

1. Forgiven sinners show loving gratitude to Jesus (7:36–39).
2. Forgiven sinners have grasped the magnitude of sin forgiven (7:40–47).
3. Forgiven sinners have trusted Jesus to forgive their sin (7:48–50).

4. Jesus' Saving Rule Explained with Reference to the Varying Responses (8:1–21)

After an introductory summary of Jesus' proclamation of the kingdom and the exemplary response of many women (8:1–3), the parable of the sower and the following two brief episodes (8:16–18, 19–21) focus on the importance of "hearing" (cf. ἀκούω in 8:8, 10, 12, 13, 14, 15, 18, 21) Jesus' proclamation (ὁ λόγος τοῦ θεοῦ 8:11, 21; ὁ λόγος 8:12, 13, 15). In this setting it also explains the various responses to the good news of the kingdom that Jesus is announcing (8:1, 10) and complements the corresponding explanation of the kingdom in 7:18–35 ("kingdom" 7:28; "hearing" 7:22, 29; responses 7:23, 29–35; for the structure of 7:1–8:56 see the introduction to 7:1).

a. A Transitional Summary: Jesus Preaches the Kingdom Far and Wide (8:1–3)

8:1 Ἐγένετο, see 1:5. The adv. καθεξῆς (see 1:3) is temp. (see sim. cstr. in 7:11). Although often tr. "soon afterward" (NRSV, NASB, HCSB, ESV; ZG 204; Fitzmyer 697), the temp. expression may be general ("afterward" NKJV; "after this" NIV; BDAG 490c; Robertson, *Pictures* 110; Bock 712). Αὐτός (see 1:17; 3:23) is the subj. of διώδευεν (3rd sg. impf. act. indic. of διοδεύω, "go," "travel through"; only here and Acts 17:1 in the NT). Κατά is distributive ("from one town and village to another" HCSB, NIV; BDAG 512a; BDF §224[3]; ZG 204) and modifies διώδευεν (Bock 712; Bovon 1.300; Fitzmyer 697). The ptcs. κηρύσσων (see 3:3) and εὐαγγελιζόμενος (nom. sg. masc. of pres. mid. ptc. of εὐαγγελίζω) express manner (τὴν βασιλείαν [see 4:43] is the obj.). The nom. οἱ δώδεκα (cf. 6:13) is the subj. of a verbless clause (most EVV; or an implied διώδευεν, NJB; this cstr. at the end of the verse serves to focus attention primarily on Jesus, BHGNT 255). This summary (cf. 4:14–15, 43–44) of Jesus' preaching activity will focus on the responses (anticipating 8:4–21) of a range of women (picking up on 7:36–50) who have been impacted by Jesus' ministry.

8:2 The nom. pl. fem. γυναῖκές τινες (of γυνή, -αικός, ἡ) may be the subj. of another verbless clause or a combined subj. with οἱ δώδεκα (BHGNT 255). The rel. pron. αἵ (the antecedent is γυναῖκές) is the subj. of ἦσαν (1:6). The pf. ptc. τεθεραπευμέναι (nom. pl. fem. of pf. pass. ptc. of θεραπεύω) with the impf. ἦσαν is a pluperfect periph. cstr. (an "extensive pluperfect," Wallace 586; Z §290; ZG 204). "Evil spirits" and "diseases" (NIV; ἀσθενειῶν [see 5:15], "ailments" NJB; "infirmities" NRSV, ESV) are again distinguished (Bock 713; cf. 4:40–41). The nom. Μαρία, together with the nom. Ἰωάννα . . . Σουσάννα καὶ ἕτεραι πολλαί in 8:3, are all in appos. to γυναῖκές τινες (BHGNT 255). Καλουμένη nom. sg. fem. of pres. pass. (attrib.) ptc. of καλέω (modifying Μαρία). This designation (Μαγδαληνή, probably from the village Magdala) and the following description indicates that she is being introduced in the narrative for the first time (and not the woman of the previous episode, Bock 713; Bovon 1.301; Marshall 316; cf. 23:55; 24:10). The antecedent of the rel. pron. ἧς is Μαρία (ἀπό for ἐκ, Z §87; ZG 204). The neut. pl. δαιμόνια (modified by ἑπτά, "seven," highlighting the severity of her condition, Nolland 366; cf. 11:26; though note 8:30) is the subj. of ἐξεληλύθει (3rd sg. 2nd pluperfect act. indic. of dep. ἐξέρχομαι; Wallace 400; perhaps in place of a pass. ἐκβάλλω, T 53, 292; Marshall 316).

8:3 The nom. γυνή is in appos. to Ἰωάννα (see the cstr. in 8:2; cf. Ἰωάννα in 24:10). The gen. sg. masc. ἐπιτρόπου (of ἐπίτροπος, -ου, ὁ, "steward" NKJV, NRSV, NASB, HCSB; "household manager" ESV, sim. NIV; BDAG 385b; LSJ 667d) is in appos. to Χουζᾶ ("Chuza"). "Herod" refers to Herod Antipas (see 3:19). Σουσάννα καὶ ἕτεραι πολλαί see 8:2. Σουσάννα is only mentioned here in the NT. The fem. pl. rel. pron. αἵτινες (for αἵ, Z §§215–16; ZG 204) is the subj. of διηκόνουν (3rd pl. impf. act. indic. of διακονέω, "serve," "provided" NRSV, ESV; "supporting" HCSB, sim. NIV). The rel. clause could modify only ἕτεραι πολλαί (cf. the rel. clause in 8:2a) or all the women in 8:2–3a (Nolland 364). The pl. αὐτοῖς has good Alexandrian and Western mss. support. The sg. αὐτῷ is possibly an assimilation to Matt 27:55/Mark 15:41 (Metzger 120–21; Bock 714; Bovon 1.301; Fitzmyer 698; Nolland 363). Ἐκ τῶν ὑπαρχόντων αὐταῖς gives the source (ὑπαρχόντων gen. pl. neut. of pres. act. ptc. of ὑπάρχω; the subst. neut. pl. is "one's belongings," "possessions"; BDAG 1029d; cf. 12:15; 19:8; Acts 4:32). The dat. pron. αὐταῖς is poss.

FOR FURTHER STUDY

23. Men and Women in Luke

*Bock, *Theology* 343–58.

Forbes, G. W., and S. D. Harrower. *Raised from Obscurity: A Narratival and Theological Study of the Characterization of Women in Luke-Acts*. Eugene: Pickwick, 2015.

Köstenberger, M. E. *Jesus and the Feminists: Who Do They Say That He Is?* Wheaton: Crossway, 2008.

Seim, T. K. *The Double Message: Patterns of Gender in Luke-Acts*. Edinburgh: T&T Clark, 1994.

Spencer, F. S. *Salty Wives, Spirited Mothers, and Savvy Widows: Capable Women of Purpose and Persistence in Luke's Gospel*. Grand Rapids: Eerdmans, 2012.

b. Jesus Explains the Varied Responses to His Proclamation of the Kingdom (8:4–15)

8:4 Συνιόντος gen. sg. masc. of pres. act. ptc. of σύνειμι, "coming together" NASB; "was gathering" most EVV (a temp. gen. abs. cstr.; ὄχλου πολλοῦ is the subj.). Καί could be epex. (ZG 204). The art. τῶν turns the distributive prep. phrase κατὰ πόλιν into a subst. ("people from town after town" ESV; cf. sim. in 8:1) and the gen. subj. of the gen. ptc. ἐπιπορευομένων (gen. pl. masc. of pres. mid. ptc. of ἐπιπορεύομαι, "journey to," "go to") into another temp. gen. abs. cstr. (though it is possible that τῶν κατὰ πόλιν ἐπιπορευομένων may just modify πολλοῦ, Nolland 373). The second gen. abs. cstr. may be epex. (ZG 204; Fitzmyer 702; Marshall 319; Nolland 373). The double gen. abs. cstr. serves to emphasize the gathering crowds as Jesus was teaching and anticipates the following explanation of various responses to Jesus' message (Bock 722; Fitzmyer 702). Διὰ παραβολῆς expresses means ("by way of a parable" NASB; ZG 204; "parabolically" Nolland 373). Whereas earlier uses of παραβολή referred to proverbial sayings or metaphors (4:23; 5:36; 6:39), here (cf. 8:9, 10, 11) and in the second half of Luke's Gospel, the term will refer to stories in Jesus' teaching that have longer narratives or comparisons with symbolic meaning (BDAG 759c; LN 33.15; LSJ 1305c).

8:5 Σπείρων nom. sg. masc. of pres. act. (subst.) ptc. of σπείρω (cf. BDF §252; Z §371; the subj. of ἐξῆλθεν [see 2:1]). The art. aor. act. inf. τοῦ σπεῖραι (of σπείρω) expresses purpose (ZG 204; Bock 723). The alliteration of ὁ σπείρων τοῦ σπεῖραι τὸν σπόρον ("a sower . . . to sow his seed" [of σπόρος, ου, ὁ]) provides a striking start to the story (though lost in the NLT with "farmer . . . plant . . . seed"; Bovon 1.307). Ἐν and art. pres. act. inf. σπείρειν is a temp. cstr. ("while," T 145; Z §§387, 390; ZG 204; the acc. αὐτόν is the subj. of the inf.). The neut. rel. pron. ὅ with the particle μέν functions as a demonstrative pron. (BDAG 727d; R 695; T 36). The cstr. μέν followed by the neut. adj. ἕτερον (for ἄλλον, Z §153) in 8:6 means "some . . . and others" (ZG 204; as a collective sg. throughout; "one portion" of the seed, Marshall 319; Nolland 369). Ἔπεσεν 3rd sg. 2nd aor. act. indic. of πίπτω. Παρά with the acc. τὴν ὁδόν could be *"beside the road" (NASB, sim. RV, NKJV, NJB; BDAG 757d [mng. C1bα]; Bock 724; Marshall 319; see 18:35) or "along the path" (HCSB, ESV, NIV; cf. BDAG 757d [mng. C1d]; Nolland 373). Κατεπατήθη 3rd sg. aor. pass. indic. of καταπατέω, "trample under foot" (intensifying the image of rejecting the word, Bock 724; Marshall 319). The nom. pl. neut. τὰ πετεινά (of πετεινόν, -οῦ, τό subst. of πετεινός, -ή, -όν, "birds") is the subj. of κατέφαγεν (3rd sg. 2nd aor. act. indic. of κατεσθίω, "devour," "eat up"). Τὰ πετεινὰ τοῦ οὐρανοῦ, "birds of the sky" is idiomatic for "wild birds" (NET; BDAG 809a).

8:6 Ἕτερον (see 8:5) is the subj. of κατέπεσεν (3rd sg. 2nd aor. act. indic. of καταπίπτω, "fall"; the third consecutive vb. with κατά prefix, Nolland 373). Πέτραν, "rock" (see 6:48; i.e., "a base of rock" under a thin layer of soil, Bock 724). Φυέν nom. sg. neut. of 2nd aor. pass. (temp.) ptc. of φύω, "grow," come up," (intrans.). Ἐξηράνθη 3rd sg. aor. pass. indic. of ξηραίνω, "dry up," "wither" (trans., thus, "by the sun" is implied, BHGNT 258). Διά with the art. pres. act. inf. ἔχειν (of ἔχω; neg. by μή) is causal (Wallace 597; ZG 204). Ἰκμάδα, acc. sg. fem. of ἰκμάς, -άδος, ἡ, "moisture" (only here in the NT; cf. Jer 17:8).

8:7 Ἕτερον (see 8:5) is the subj. of ἔπεσεν (see 8:5). Ἀκανθῶν, "thorns" (see 6:44; a partitive gen.). Συμφυεῖσαι nom. pl. fem. of 2nd aor. pass. (temp.) ptc. of dep. συμφύομαι, "grow up with," (intrans.). Αἱ ἄκανθαι is the subj. of ἀπέπνιξαν (3rd pl. aor. act. indic. of ἀποπνίγω, "choke"; only here and 8:33 in the NT).

8:8 Καί may be tr. "but" (NET) to indicate the contrast with the earlier examples ("Still other seed" HCSB). As with 8:7, ἕτερον (see 8:5) is the subj. of ἔπεσεν (see 8:5). Εἰς τὴν γῆν τὴν ἀγαθήν (an attrib. adj.), locat. Φυέν, see 8:6 (temp.). Ἐποίησεν, see 1:49 (here "produced" NRSV, HCSB; "yielded" ESV, NIV). Ἑκατονταπλασίονα, "a hundred times" could be an acc. attrib. adj. modifying the acc. καρπόν, or it could be an adv. acc. (BHGNT 258). With the temp. pres. ptc. λέγων (Wallace 627), the impf. ἐφώνει (3rd sg. impf. act. indic. of φωνέω) is probably progressive (though common with vbs. of saying, Z §272). Thus, rather than just a concluding statement (e.g., NKJV, NLT; Nolland 369 views the impf. as ingressive), the following exhortation is perhaps something Jesus repeated as he told the parable ("As he said these things he would call out" NASB; BHGNT 259; Fitzmyer 704). Ἔχων, see 3:11 (subst.). The inf. ἀκούειν (see 5:1) could be epex. (consec. ZG 204; Fitzmyer 704) or express purpose. Ἀκουέτω 3rd sg. pres. act. impv. of ἀκούω, "should listen" (NJB, HCSB), "had better listen" (NET; see Fantin 275 for 3rd-person impvs. aimed at the 2nd-person recipients).

8:9 The impf. ἐπηρώτων (see 3:10) could be ingressive (NASB), iter. (Robertson, *Pictures* 112) or used to provide background information (BHGNT 259). The interr. pron. τίς is the pred. nom. introducing an indir. question (with the optative, R 1043–45; Z §346; Bock 727). The nom. demonstrative pron. αὕτη and ἡ παραβολή is the subj. of the optative εἴη (of εἰμί, on the opt. see 1:29; i.e., "might be" NASB; i.e., "meant" most EVV; BDAG 284a; Wallace 483; ZG 205).

8:10 The dat. ὑμῖν (placed forward for emphasis, in contrast to τοῖς δὲ λοιποῖς; Bock 728; Marshall 322) is the indir. obj. of δέδοται (3rd sg. pf. pass. indic. of δίδωμι; a divine pass., cf. Wallace 437–38; Fitzmyer 707; Marshall 322). The acc. τὰ μυστήρια is the obj. of the 2nd aor. act. inf. γνῶναι (of γινώσκω; i.e., "to know the mysteries of the kingdom of God has been granted to you"). The mng. in this context relates to being given divine insight into the inauguration and outworking of God's saving reign through the explanation provided by Jesus of his parables (Bock 730; Nolland 379). Ἐν παραβολαῖς is instr. and modifies an implied vb. such as λέγω (ZG 205). Ἵνα with the subjunc. (neg. with μή) βλέπωσιν (3rd pl. pres. act. subjunc. of βλέπω) and συνιῶσιν (3rd pl. pres. act. subjunc. of συνίημι, "understand") may indicate result ("stating the inevitable," Moule 100; Marshall 323; [perhaps in place of ὥστε and an inf.] Fitzmyer 709; cf. BDF §391[5]; Z §352; T 102–3 suggests causal) or *purpose (BDAG 477b; BDF §369[2]; Wallace 473–74 ["purpose–result"]; Bock 728–29; Bovon 1.312; Fitzmyer 709). The ptcs. βλέποντες (nom. pl. masc. of pres. act. ptc.) and ἀκούοντες (see 2:47) are concessive ("though seeing . . . though hearing" NIV; ZG 205; Fitzmyer 709). Those who reject Jesus' teaching only hear confusing parables that confirm their blindness and ignorance of God's saving plan.

8:11 Ἡ παραβολή is the subj. of ἔστιν with the demonstrative pron. αὕτη as the pred. ("Now the parable is this" NASB, ESV; i.e., "the parable means this" NET, sim. HCSB, NIV; Wallace 241; ZG 205; Fitzmyer 713; Marshall 324; though Bovon 1.308 suggests that αὕτη refers back to 8:9 and tr. as "This parable is . . ."). Ὁ σπόρος ("the seed," cf. 8:5) is the subj. of ἐστίν. On ὁ λόγος τοῦ θεοῦ see 5:1 (in this context, see the introduction to 8:1; cf. also 8:21).

8:12 The nom. pl. οἱ turns the locat. prep. phrase παρὰ τὴν ὁδόν (see 8:5; or an implied πέσοντες, NLT; BHGNT 261) into the subj. of εἰσίν (the masc. form may refer to those represented by the seeds, Marshall 325). The subst. ptc. ἀκούσαντες (see 1:66; in this context, 8:12, 14, 15; on the aor. as generic, cf. Wallace 615) is the pred. nom. of εἰσίν. The ptc. cstrs. are followed by finite vbs. in 8:13 (Z §375; ZG 205). Εἶτα, temp. adv. "then." The nom. ὁ διάβολος (see 4:2) is the subj. of ἔρχεται (see 3:16) and αἴρει (3rd sg. pres. act. indic. of αἴρω). Ἵνα with the subjunc. σωθῶσιν (3rd pl. aor. pass. subjunc. of σῴζω) expresses (the devil's) purpose (Bock 734; Bovon 1.309). Πιστεύσαντες (nom. pl. masc. of aor. act. ptc. of πιστεύω) is an attendant circumstance ptc. (ingressive, Robertson, *Pictures* 113; ZG 205) with the subjunc. σωθῶσιν (and thus takes on the same mood; both are neg. with μή).

8:13 As with 8:12, οἱ . . . ἐπὶ τῆς πέτρας is the subj. of εἰσίν (this time the vb. is implied, Bock 735; Bovon 1.309; Nolland 385). Ἐπὶ τῆς πέτρας is locat. (see 6:48; 8:6). If the structure of 8:12 is repeated here, the rel. pron. οἵ introduces a clause which is the pred. nom. of an implied εἰσίν (see above). Thus, οἵ is the subj. of ἀκούσωσιν (3rd pl. aor. act. subjunc. of ἀκούω; subjunc. with ὅταν is an indef. temp. clause, Wallace 480) and δέχονται (3rd pl. pres. mid. indic. of dep. δέχομαι). Μετὰ χαρᾶς expresses manner and modifies δέχονται. Καί is probably contrastive. The nom. pl. pron. οὗτοι is the subj. of ἔχουσιν (see 5:31; neg. with οὐκ). Ῥίζαν, "root." The pron. οὗτοι could (BHGNT 263):

*1. further modify the previous rel. clause (NET, NIV; Bovon 1.309; Nolland 385); or

2. introduce the following clause in which the rel. pron. οἵ modifies οὗτοι (NLT, HCSB).

The parallel structure seems to favor the first option. Thus, the second rel. pron. οἵ is the subj. of πιστεύουσιν (3rd pl. pres. act. indic. of πιστεύω; modified by the temp. πρὸς καιρόν) and is in appos. to the previous rel. clause. Likewise, the second καί (ἐν καιρῷ πειρασμοῦ [see 4:13]) is also contrastive (NIV). Ἀφίστανται 3rd pl. pres. mid. indic. of ἀφίστημι, "fall away" (most EVV), "depart" (HCSB).

8:14 Τὸ . . . πεσόν (nom. sg. neut. of 2nd aor. act. [subst.] ptc. of πίπτω) introduces the discussion to follow (a pendent nom., Z §25; ZG 205; the neut. sg. recalls ὅ [8:5] and ἕτερον [8:6] and may again represent a portion of the seed, Marshall 326; the aor. is generic, Wallace 615). Εἰς τὰς ἀκάνθας (acc. pl. fem., see 6:44; "among thorns" most EVV) is locat. The nom. pl. pron. οὗτοι is the subj. of εἰσίν (and picks up on the introductory clause; the shift to pl. is *ad sensum*). The subst. ptc. ἀκούσαντες (see 1:66; cf. 8:12) is a pred. nom. Καί (before ὑπό) is contrastive (ZG 205; Bovon 1.310). Ὑπὸ μεριμνῶν (gen. pl. fem. of μέριμνα, -ης, ἡ, "worries") καὶ πλούτου (gen. sg. masc. of πλοῦτος, -ου, ὁ, "riches") καὶ ἡδονῶν (gen. pl. fem. of ἡδονή, -ῆς, ἡ, "pleasures") indicates agency (and modifies συμπνίγονται). The gen. sg. masc. τοῦ βίου (of βίος, -ου, ὁ, "of life," a gen. of ref.) probably modifies all of the items in the preceding prep. phrase (Bock 737; Marshall 326). Πορευόμενοι, see 1:6 (temp.). Συμπνίγονται 3rd pl. pres. pass. indic. of συμπνίγω, "choke" (i.e., "on the way, they are choked by" Nolland 381; cf. 8:42). Τελεσφοροῦσιν 3rd pl. pres. act. indic. of τελεσφορέω, "produce mature fruit" (LN 23.203; LSJ 1770d; MM 629d; neg. with οὐ).

8:15 The art. τό is likely repeating the (pendent nom.) pattern of the previous verse and thus forms part of a subst. ptc. cstr. with an implied πεσόν (see 8:14) which introduces the discussion to follow. Ἐν τῇ καλῇ γῇ, locat. For οὗτοί εἰσιν see 8:14. The rel. pron. οἵτινες (for οἵ, see 1:20) is a pred. nom. and introduces the following rel. clause as the subj. of the 3rd pl. pres. act. indics. κατέχουσιν (of κατέχω, "hold fast"; "retain" NIV is too weak; cf. BDAG 533a) and καρποφοροῦσιν (of καρποφορέω, "bear fruit"). Note the contrast between οὐ τελεσφοροῦσιν (8:14) and κατέχουσιν καὶ καρποφοροῦσιν ἐν ὑπομονῇ (8:15). Ἐν καρδίᾳ καλῇ καὶ ἀγαθῇ could be instr. The two synonyms for "good" pick up on the ref. to καλῇ γῇ earlier in the verse (though here with the connotation of "praiseworthy" BDAG 504d; LN 88.4). Those with a "good heart" are contrasted with those in 8:12 who have the word taken "from their heart" (cf. 6:45). Ἀκούσαντες, see 1:66; cf. 8:12, 14 (temp., NET). Ἐν ὑπομονῇ (modifying καρποφοροῦσιν) may be instr. ("by" HCSB, NIV; "through" NJB) or express manner ("with" NKJV, NRSV, NASB, ESV).

FOR FURTHER STUDY

24. Parables (8:4, 10)

Bailey, K. E. *Poet and Peasant and Through Peasant Eyes: A Literary-Cultural Approach to the Parables in Luke.* Grand Rapids: Eerdmans, 1983.

*Blomberg, C. *Interpreting the Parables.* 2nd ed. Downers Grove, Ill.: InterVarsity, 2012.

*Forbes, G. *The God of Old: The Role of the Lukan Parables in the Purpose of Luke's Gospel.* Sheffield: Sheffield Academic Press, 2000.

Hultgren, A. J. *The Parables of Jesus: A Commentary.* Grand Rapids: Eerdmans, 2000.

Snodgrass, K. R. *Stories with Intent: A Comprehensive Guide to the Parables of Jesus.* Grand Rapids: Eerdmans, 2008.

c. Jesus Insists on the Importance of Careful Listening to His Teaching (8:16–18)

8:16 Οὐδείς is the subj. of καλύπτει (3rd sg. pres. act. indic. of καλύπτω, "cover"; the acc. αὐτόν is the obj.). The acc. sg. masc. λύχνον (of λύχνος, -ου, ὁ, "lamp") is the obj. of ἅψας (nom. sg. masc. of aor. act. [temp.] ptc. of ἅπτω, "light," "kindle," "cause illumination" BDAG 126a; with the acc., Wallace 132; cf. 11:33; 15:8). The dat. (sg. neut. σκεύει (of σκεῦος, -ους, τό, "vessel") could be locat. ("in a clay jar" NIV, sim. NRSV) or instr. ("with a jar" ESV; Robertson, *Pictures* 115). The adv. ὑποκάτω ("under") functions as a prep. and takes the gen. (BDAG 1038a; for ὑπό BDF §§12[3], 215[2]; Z §83; ZG 206). Κλίνης, "bed" (see 5:18). Τίθησιν 3rd sg. pres. act. indic. of τίθημι. Λυχνίας gen. sg. fem. of λυχνία, -ας, ἡ, "lampstand." Ἵνα with the subjunc. βλέπωσιν (see 8:10) expresses purpose. Εἰσπορευόμενοι nom. pl. masc. of pres. mid. (subst.) ptc. of dep. εἰσπορεύομαι). The art. τό might function here as a poss. pron. ("its light" HCSB; "the light" most EVV). Following 8:15, the light here could ref. to the proclamation of the word (i.e., "fruitfulness") by Jesus' disciples (Fitzmyer 718; Marshall 328; Nolland 391). The emphasis on responding to Jesus' teaching in 8:4–15 and hearing in 8:18, 21, however, indicate that the light here is Jesus' teaching which must be received appropriately rather than rejected (Bock 744–45; see also 11:33).

8:17 Γάρ introduces a further development of the previous verse (perhaps that God's truth is made known through the disciples' proclamation [Fitzmyer 720; Marshall 330]; or, because of the following verse, a warning to respond to the light [i.e., Jesus' teaching; Bock 745–46]). The sg. neut. adj. κρυπτόν (of κρυπτός, -ή, -όν, "hidden") is a pred. nom. ("nothing is hidden" most EVV). The neut. rel. pron. ὅ modifies κρυπτόν and is the subj. of γενήσεται (3rd sg. fut. mid. indic. of dep. γίνομαι). The nom. sg. neut. adj. φανερόν (of φανερός, -ά, -όν, "disclosed" NRSV, NIV; "made manifest" ESV) is pred. The nom. sg. neut. adj. ἀπόκρυφον (of ἀπόκρυφος, -ον, "hidden," "secret") is the pred. nom. of an implied ἐστίν (following the structure of the first half of the verse). The neut. rel. pron. ὅ modifies ἀπόκρυφον and is the subj. of the subjuncs. γνωσθῇ (3rd sg. aor. pass. subjunc. of γινώσκω) and ἔλθῃ (3rd sg. 2nd aor. act. subjunc. of dep. ἔρχομαι; both neg. with the emphatic οὐ μή referring to the fut. Z §444; ZG 206).

8:18 Οὖν introduces a summary that draws the discussion from 8:4 to a conclusion. Βλέπετε 2nd pl. pres. act. impv. of βλέπω ("pay attention" NRSV; "take care" HCSB, ESV). Ἀκούετε (2nd pl. pres. act. indic. of ἀκούω) with πῶς refers to the different ways of hearing that the parable has just illustrated (ZG 206; cf. ἀκούω in 8:8, 10, 12, 13, 14, 15). Γάρ is causal (giving the reason for the exhortation to pay attention to how one listens). The rel. pron. and particle ὅς ἄν with the subjunc. ἔχῃ (3rd sg. pres. act. subjunc. of ἔχω) is indef. (Wallace 479). The subj. of δοθήσεται (see 6:38) is not specified (most EVV have "more"). Καί (before ὅς ἄν μὴ ἔχῃ) is contrastive. Καί (before ὅ) "even" (all EVV). The rel. pron. ὅ introduces a clause (δοκεῖ ἔχειν) which is the subj. of ἀρθήσεται (3rd sg. fut. pass. indic. of αἴρω; BHGNT 266). The rel. clause clarifies that the person is not losing something they had. Rather, it was only something they thought (δοκεῖ 3rd sg. pres. act. indic. of δοκέω) they had (ἔχειν [see 8:6] is an inf. of indir. discourse [after a vb. of cognition] BHGNT 267; Wallace 605).

d. Jesus Defines His Family as Those Who Hear and Obey God's Word (8:19–21)

8:19 Δέ is only a general link with the preceding pericope (Bock 749; i.e., "now" [NIV] rather than "then" [NRSV, ESV]). The subj. of παρεγένετο (3rd sg. 2nd aor. mid. indic. of dep. παραγίνομαι, "come") is ἡ μήτηρ καὶ οἱ ἀδελφοὶ αὐτοῦ (Jesus' mother and his brothers). The sg. vb. agrees with nearer sg. subj. ἡ μήτηρ (BDF §135[1]; T 313; Marshall 331; it may indicate that this is the more prominent subj., McKay 18). This nom. phrase is also the subj. of the pl. ἠδύναντο (3rd pl. impf. mid. indic. of dep. δύναμαι; irregular augment; neg. with οὐκ). Καί is contrastive. The 2nd aor. act. inf. συντυχεῖν (of συντυγχάνω, "meet with" HCSB) is complementary. Διὰ τὸν ὄχλον is causal (the art. perhaps refers back to the crowd of 8:4, Nolland 394). As with 8:4, the emphasis on the size of the crowd anticipates Jesus' exhortation to respond to his teaching genuinely.

8:20 Ἀπηγγέλη (3rd sg. 2nd aor. pass. indic. of ἀπαγγέλλω, "announce," "he was told" HCSB, ESV) introduces the report that was given to Jesus in direct speech. On the subj. ἡ μήτηρ σου καὶ οἱ ἀδελφοί σου with a sg. vb. see 8:19. Ἑστήκασιν 3rd pl. pf. act. indic. of ἵστημι (intrans.). The adv. ἔξω implies that the setting is a house though this is not specified here. The inf. ἰδεῖν (see 2:26) is complementary to θέλοντές (nom. pl. masc. of pres. act. ptc. of θέλω; the ptc. may be causal or express manner, BHGNT 268).

8:21 The art. ὁ is the subj. of εἶπεν (Wallace 212; for ἀποκριθείς, see 1:19; for εἶπεν πρός see 1:13) and together with δέ indicates a transition to Jesus as the speaker. The nom. μήτηρ [μου] καὶ ἀδελφοί [μου] could be:

1. the pred. nom. of εἰσίν ("These are my mother and brothers," BHGNT 268; ZG 206; Nolland 395; Plummer 224, due to μήτηρ μου καὶ ἀδελφοί μου being anar.); or
*2. a pendent nom. and introduce the discussion to follow ("My mother and brothers, these are the ones who," with the pron. οὗτοι as the subj. of εἰσίν; Fitzmyer 725).

The sim. cstr. at 8:14, 15 favors the second option (though Fitzmyer incorrectly thinks this still refers to the physical mother and brothers of 8:19–20). The subst. ptcs. οἱ . . . ἀκούοντες (see 2:47) and ποιοῦντες (nom. pl. masc. of pres. act. ptc. of ποιέω) could be in appos. to οὗτοι (see BHGNT 269), the pred. nom of εἰσίν ("These are the ones who," Fitzmyer 725), or attrib. modifying οὗτοι. None of these options alter the sense. For τὸν λόγον τοῦ θεοῦ see 5:1. In this context the word of God is the teaching of Jesus (see the introduction to 8:1; cf. also 8:11). For "hearing" and "doing" cf. 6:46–47.

HOMILETICAL SUGGESTIONS

What Happens When You Truly Hear God's Word? (8:1–21)
The true hearer of God's word . . .

1. Perseveres in fruitful service for Jesus (8:1–15)
2. Receives God-given insight into God's saving rule through Jesus (8:9–10)
3. Pays serious attention to God's revealed truth in Jesus (8:16–18)
4. Demonstrates family relationship with Jesus by obeying God's word (8:19–21)

5. Four Miracles that Demonstrate Jesus' Power (8:22–56)

a. Jesus' Power over a Life-Threatening Storm (8:22–25)

8:22 Ἐγένετο, see 1:5. The introductory temp. expression ἐν μιᾷ τῶν ἡμερῶν (see 5:12, 17) is general (Marshall 333; εἷς is used for τις, Z §155; ZG 206). Αὐτὸς . . . καὶ οἱ μαθηταὶ αὐτοῦ is the nom. subj. of ἐνέβη (3rd sg. 2nd aor. act. indic. of ἐμβαίνω, "embark," "got into" most EVV). Καὶ αὐτός see 1:17. For this cstr. with the sg. vb. see above on 8:19 (though here the subj. precedes the vb.). Διέλθωμεν, see 2:15 (hortatory subjunc.). The adv. πέραν ("beyond," "across") functions as a prep. and takes the gen. (BDAG 797a; BDF §184; R 646). Λίμνης, "lake" (gen. sg. fem., see 5:1). Ἀνήχθησαν 3rd pl. aor. pass. indic. of ἀνάγω, "set sail" (in mid. or pass., BDAG 62a; this nautical use of the word is only found here and in Acts [thirteen times] in the NT).

8:23 Πλεόντων gen. pl. masc. of pres. act. ptc. of πλέω, "sail" (a temp. gen. abs. cstr.; αὐτῶν is the subj.). Ἀφύπνωσεν 3rd sg. aor. act. indic. of ἀφυπνόω, "fall asleep" (only here in the NT; ingressive, Robertson, *Pictures* 115; Marshall 333). The nom. sg. fem. λαῖλαψ (of λαῖλαψ, -απος, ἡ, "whirlwind," modified by the [pleonastic] gen. adj. ἀνέμου "of wind" [see 7:24], "fierce gust of wind" BDAG 581d) is the subj. of κατέβη (see 2:51). The impf. συνεπληροῦντο (3rd pl. impf. pass. indic. of συμπληρόω, "swamped," intrans.; elsewhere only 9:51; Acts 2:1 in the NT) may be ingressive (NASB). The pl. ref. to the people in the boat being swamped has been tr. as a ref. to the boat being swamped in NRSV, NIV (ZG 206; the pl. personalizes the situation, Bock 761). Ἐκινδύνευον 3rd pl. impf. act. indic. of κινδυνεύω, "be in danger."

8:24 Προσελθόντες (nom. pl. masc. of 2nd aor. act. ptc. of dep. προσέρχομαι) is an attendant circumstance ptc. (with διήγειραν 3rd pl. aor. act. indic. of διεγείρω, "wake up"). Λέγοντες, see 1:66. On the voc. ἐπιστάτα see 5:5 (repeated here due to the urgency; cf. refs. at 6:46). Ἀπολλύμεθα 1st pl. pres. mid. indic. of ἀπόλλυμι. The disciples think they are near death (understandably in light of 8:23). However, Jesus is with them in the boat (ὁ δέ may emphasize the shift to the role of Jesus, Marshall 334; Nolland 400). Διεγερθείς (nom. sg. masc. of aor. pass. ptc. of διεγείρω, "wake up") is an attendant circumstance ptc. (with ἐπετίμησεν see 4:35; there is no ref. to demonic involvement here, Bock 762; *pace* Fitzmyer 730). Jesus rebuked both the wind (ἀνέμῳ, dat., see 7:24) and the "waves of water" (κλύδωνι τοῦ ὕδατος, "raging waves" HCSB, ESV; dat. sg. masc. of κλύδων, -ωνος, ὁ). The 3rd pl. aor. mid. indic. ἐπαύσαντο (of dep. παύομαι, "cease") therefore refers to both the wind and the waves. Furthermore, it became "calm" (γαλήνη nom. sg. fem. of γαλήνη, -ης, ἡ).

8:25 The interr. adv. ποῦ ("where") introduces a question with ἡ πίστις as the subj. of an implied ἐστίν (the obj. of their faith in this context is meant to be Jesus, Fitzmyer 730). Φοβηθέντες (nom. pl. masc. of aor. pass. ptc. of dep. φοβέομαι) is an attendant circumstance ptc. (with ἐθαύμασαν see 1:63; ZG 207 describes φοβηθέντες as ingressive). The combination of fear and amazement indicates both the magnitude of what they are trying to grasp and yet the difficulty they had in coming to terms with who Jesus is (the language indicates "an encounter with the presence and activity of God"

Nolland 400). Λέγοντες, see 1:66. Τίς ἄρα οὗτός ἐστιν, "Who then is this?" Ὅτι could be epex. (HCSB, NIV; Wallace 460; Z §420; ZG 207; "result" Bock 764) or causal (NKJV; cf. Fitzmyer 730; as with 4:36, Marshall 334). The reason for their question is because (ὅτι) Jesus commands (ἐπιτάσσει, see 4:36) even (καί, ZG 207; Bovon 1.321) the winds and the water, and they obey him (ὑπακούουσιν 3rd pl. pres. act. indic. of ὑπακούω; αὐτῷ is a dat. complement, BDAG 1028d–29a)! This power is "the prerogative of God alone" (Nolland 401). The twin concerns of Jesus' identity and the required response of faith in him appeared together in 7:48–49 in the context of Jesus' authority to forgive sin (cf. 5:21). They appear here in the context of Jesus' authority over creation and ability to deliver from near-death.

HOMILETICAL SUGGESTIONS

Why Jesus Is Worthy of Trust (8:22–25)
1. His disciples are under his care (8:22–25).
2. His creation is under his control (8:22–25).

b. *Jesus' Power over Life-Threatening Demons (8:26–39)*

8:26 Κατέπλευσαν 3rd pl. aor. act. indic. of καταπλέω, "sail toward" (with εἰς, BDAG 524d; only here in the NT). Τὴν χώραν τῶν Γερασηνῶν, "the region of the Gerasenes." This region perhaps includes a ref. to a village (8:34, 39) on the eastern shore of Galilee, now identified as Kursi, and may also have been referred to as the region of the Gadarenes (Matt 8:28) after Gadara, a larger Decapolis city further inland which overshadowed this coastal village (for textual vars. and discussion cf. Metzger 18–19, 72, 121; Bock 782–84; Bovon 1.326–27; Marshall 336–37). The nom. sg. fem. rel. pron. ἥτις (of ὅστις, ἥτις, ὅτι; for ἥ, Z §216; see 1:20) is the subj. of ἐστίν. The adv. ἀντιπέρα ("opposite"; only here in the NT) functions as a prep. with the gen. of separa-tion (τῆς Γαλιλαίας). The expression refers to the (Gentile) region on the eastern shore of the Sea of Galilee (BDAG 90c; R 638).

8:27 The dat. αὐτῷ is the complement (MM 650c) to ὑπήντησεν (3rd sg. aor. act. indic. of ὑπαντάω, "meet"; ἀνήρ τις is the subj.; "a certain man met him [i.e., met Jesus]"; an adj. use of the indef. pron., Wallace 347). Ἐξελθόντι dat. sg. masc. of 2nd aor. act. (attrib.) ptc. of dep. ἐξέρχομαι (modifying αὐτῷ; i.e., "a certain man . . . met Jesus who had got out [of the boat] onto the land," concordant, ZG 207). The emphasis seems to be on the meeting taking place as soon as Jesus reached shore (hence the temp. tr. in most EVV). Ἔχων, see 3:11 (attrib. modifying ἀνήρ; δαιμόνια is pl.). The dat. of time χρόνῳ ἱκανῷ (BDF §201; R 527; T 243–44; Wallace 156; Z §54; ZG 207) modifies ἐνεδύσατο (3rd sg. aor. mid. indic. of ἐνδύω, "clothe"; neg. with οὐκ). Ἔμενεν 3rd sg. impf. act. indic. of μένω, "remain," "lived" (most EVV). The locat. prep. phrase ἐν οἰκίᾳ is perhaps placed forward to emphasize the contrast with ἐν τοῖς μνήμασιν (dat. pl. neut. of μνῆμα, -ατος, τό; "in the tombs"; BHGNT 275). The destructive and deadly interests of the demons are already apparent (cf. 8:33).

8:28 Ἰδών, see 1:12 (temp.). Ἀνακράξας (nom. sg. masc. of aor. act. ptc. of ἀνακράζω, "cry out") is an attendant circumstance ptc. (with προσέπεσεν see 5:8; the dat. αὐτῷ is complementary). For the dat. φωνῇ μεγάλῃ see 4:33. For the expression τί ἐμοὶ καὶ σοί see 4:34 (though sg. here). Ἰησοῦ is voc., and υἱέ is voc. in appos. (Wallace 71). For Jesus as "Son of the Most High God" see 1:32 (the demons know Jesus' supernatural identity, Nolland 408; cf. 4:34). Δέομαι 1st sg. pres. mid. indic. of δέομαι (takes the gen.). Βασανίσῃς 2nd sg. aor. act. subjunc. of βασανίζω, "torment" (i.e., in judgment, BDAG 168a; Nolland 408; a prohibition with μή; με is placed forward for emphasis).

8:29 Γάρ, causal (giving the reason the demon begged Jesus). Jesus had commanded (παρήγγειλεν, see 5:14; Z §290) the "unclean spirit" (τῷ πνεύματι τῷ ἀκαθάρτῳ, see 4:33) to come out (ἐξελθεῖν, see 6:12; inf. in indir. discourse) of the man. The aor. παρήγγειλεν is found in 𝔓⁷⁵ B Ξ (UBS⁵; "had commanded" most EVV). The impf. παρήγγελλεν is found in ℵ A C L W (SBLGNT) and could be ingressive (NET; Fitzmyer 738; used with vbs. of commanding, i.e., they await a further action, BDF §§328, 331; T 65; Marshall 338) or progressive (Bock 784). Γάρ, causal (giv-ing the reason Jesus had commanded the demon). The demon had "seized" him (συνηρπάκει 3rd sg. pluperfect act. indic. of συναρπάζω, "seize," only here, Acts 6:12;

19:29; 27:15 in the NT; on the pluperfect cf. Z §290) many times (πολλοῖς . . . χρόνοις, dat. of time; R 527; Wallace 156; possibly duration of time, BDF §201; MM 694a; T 243; Z §54). The man would be "bound" (ἐδεσμεύετο 3rd sg. impf. pass. indic. of δεσμεύω; iter. impf., Wallace 549; Marshall 338; or impf. to provide background information, BHGNT 276) with "chains and shackles" (ἁλύσεσιν dat. pl. fem. of ἅλυσις, -εως, ἡ, "chains"; πέδαις dat. pl. fem. of πέδη, -ης, ἡ, "shackles" i.e., for the feet, LN 6.17). Φυλασσόμενος (nom. sg. masc. of pres. pass. ptc. of φυλάσσω, "guard") could be an attendant circumstance ptc. ("bound . . . and kept under guard" NET; BHGNT 277), express purpose ("to restrain him" NJB), or be concessive ("though he was guarded" HCSB). Καί is contrastive (Z §455β). The acc. pl. neut. τὰ δεσμά (of δεσμός, -οῦ, ὁ, "bonds" NRSV, NASB, ESV; "restraints" HCSB; BDAG 219c) is the obj. of διαρρήσσων (nom. sg. masc. of pres. act. ptc. of διαρρήγνυμι, "break"). Ἠλαύνετο 3rd sg. impf. pass. indic. of ἐλαύνω, "drive" (iter., Bovon 1.328; Ὑπὸ τοῦ δαιμονίου indicates the agency of the pass. vb., Wallace 433; i.e., "driven by the demon"). The description emphasizes the power of the demon.

8:30 Ἐπηρώτησεν 3rd sg. aor. act. indic. of ἐπερωτάω. The dat. σοι is poss. Λεγιών, "legion" (a Latinism, ZG 208; a term used to refer to a group of soldiers numbering in the thousands, BDAG 588a). Ὅτι introduces a parenthetical remark that explains the reason for this name. The neut. pl. δαιμόνια πολλά is the subj. of εἰσῆλθεν (see 1:40). The request for the name was not necessary to gain control (*pace* Fitzmyer 738) as Jesus has already demonstrated power over demons without the need for a name (4:31–37; Bock 774; Marshall 338; Nolland 409). The question may further highlight the extent of the man's plight (Bock 773).

8:31 The subj. of παρεκάλουν (see 7:4; on the impf. cf. Z §272) is still δαιμόνια πολλά from 8:30. The impf. could be iter. (NIV) or ingressive (NET; cf. Z §272). Ἵνα introduces the content of their plea in indir. discourse (for an inf., cf. Z §407; ZG 208). Ἐπιτάξῃ 3rd sg. aor. act. subjunc. of ἐπιτάσσω ("command" ESV; "order" NRSV; subjunc. with ἵνα; neg. with μή, BDF §369). Ἄβυσσον acc. sg. fem. of ἄβυσσος, -ου, ἡ, "abyss" (only here, Rom 10:7, and seven times in Rev, in the NT; cf. BDAG 2d; here it refers to the place of ultimate judgment, Nolland 414). Ἀπελθεῖν 2nd aor. act. inf. of dep. ἀπέρχομαι (inf. of indir. discourse).

8:32 Ἀγέλη (nom. sg. fem. of ἀγέλη, -ης, ἡ, "herd") is the subj. of ἦν (χοίρων ἱκανῶν, "of many pigs," is a gen. of content; gen. pl. masc. of χοῖρος, -ου, ὁ). Βοσκομένη (nom. sg. fem. of pres. pass. ptc. of βόσκω, "feed," intrans.) could be part of a periph. cstr. (with ἦν) or attrib. modifying ἀγέλη (cf. BHGNT 279; T 87–88). Ἐν τῷ ὄρει is locat. ("on the hillside"). Παρεκάλεσαν 3rd pl. aor. act. indic. of παρακαλέω. Ἵνα introduces the content of their plea in indir. discourse. Ἐπιτρέψῃ 3rd sg. aor. act. subjunc. of ἐπιτρέπω, "allow," "permit." Εἰς ἐκείνους ("into those") is locat. (the demonstrative pron. refers to the pigs). Εἰσελθεῖν, see 6:6 (a complementary inf.). Although the rationale for their plea is not given, they seem to recognize anything as better than the place of final judgment. Ἐπέτρεψεν 3rd sg. aor. act. indic. of ἐπιτρέπω.

8:33 Ἐξελθόντα (nom. pl. neut. of 2nd aor. act. ptc. of dep. ἐξέρχομαι) is an attendant circumstance ptc. (with εἰσῆλθον see 7:44; with τὰ δαιμόνια as the subj.; ἀπό for ἐκ, Z §87). Χοίρους acc. pl. masc. "pigs" (see 8:32). Ἡ ἀγέλη ("the herd") is the subj. of ὥρμησεν (3rd sg. aor. act. indic. of ὁρμάω, "rush"). Κρημνοῦ gen. sg. masc. of κρημνός, -οῦ, ὁ, "steep slope." Λίμνην, "lake" (see 5:1). Ἀπεπνίγη 3rd sg. 2nd aor. pass. indic. of ἀποπνίγω, "drown" (cf. 8:7). The destructive and deadly interests of the demons are again demonstrated (Nolland 411).

8:34 Ἰδόντες, see 2:17 (temp.). Βόσκοντες (nom. pl. masc. of pres. act. [subst.] ptc. of βόσκω, "feed," "herdsmen" NASB, ESV; "those tending the pigs" NIV; Z §371) is the subj. of ἔφυγον (3rd pl. 2nd aor. act. indic. of φεύγω). Γεγονός (see 2:15; subst.) is the obj. of ἰδόντες. Ἀπήγγειλαν, see 7:18 (εἰς for ἐν, Z §99; ZG 208). Ἀγρούς acc. pl. masc. "countryside" (HSCB, NIV).

8:35 Ἐξῆλθον 3rd pl. 2nd aor. act. indic. of ἐξέρχομαι (an impers. pl., "people" is the subj., most EVV). The inf. ἰδεῖν (see 2:26) expresses purpose (ZG 208). For γεγονός see 2:17 (and above, 8:34; here it is the obj. of ἰδεῖν). Εὗρον, see 2:46. The following description of the man is in stark contrast to his prior condition (8:27, 29). For καθήμενον (and the cstr.) see 5:27. The antecedent of the rel. pron. οὗ (with ἀπό, "from whom") is ἄνθρωπον. Ἐξῆλθεν, see 2:1. The acc. sg. masc. ptcs. ἱματισμένον (pf. pass. of ἱματίζω, "clothe") and σωφρονοῦντα (pres. act. of σωφρονέω, "of sound mind," "in his right mind" most EVV), like καθήμενον, could be attrib. or complementary accs. (BDAG 411d). The ref. to the man sitting at Jesus' feet (πόδας, pl. of πούς) draws attention to Jesus as the source of his transformation as well as his desire to submit to Jesus' teaching (Bock 778; Fitzmyer 739; Marshall 340). It may also allude to the man's worshipful devotion to Jesus (cf. πόδας in 7:38–46; 8:41; 10:39; 17:16; in contrast to Acts 10:25; though cf. Acts 22:3). Ἐφοβήθησαν, see 2:9.

8:36 Ἰδόντες, see 2:17 (subst.) is the subj. of ἀπήγγειλαν (see 8:34). This is eyewitness testimony (Bock 778). Δαιμονισθείς (nom. sg. masc. of aor. pass. [subst.] ptc. of dep. δαιμονίζομαι, "be demon possessed") is the subj. of ἐσώθη (3rd sg. aor. pass. indic. of σώζω).

8:37 The nom. ἅπαν τὸ πλῆθος is the subj. of ἠρώτησεν (see 5:3; for the aor. cf. T 65). The people are said to be from τῆς περιχώρου [see 3:3; 4:14] τῶν Γερασηνῶν, which could be either "of the surrounding country of the Gerasenes" (NRSV, ESV, sim. HCSB, NIV) or "of the Gerasenes and the surrounding district" (NASB, sim. NET; BDAG 808b; LN 1.80; see 8:26). Ἀπελθεῖν (see 8:31) is an inf. of indir. discourse (ἀπελθεῖν ἀπ' αὐτῶν, alliteration, Bock 779). Ὅτι, causal (Bock 779; giving the reason for their request): they were seized. Συνείχοντο 3rd pl. impf. pass. indic. of συνέχω ("seize," "overcome" BDAG 971a; impf. after a causal ὅτι, Wallace 553). Φόβῳ μεγάλῳ, instr. dat. (Robertson, *Pictures* 121). Ἐμβάς, see 5:3. Ὑπέστρεψεν, see 1:56, "returned" (most EVV), "left" (NIV).

8:38 Ὁ ἀνήρ is the subj. of ἐδεῖτο (3rd sg. impf. mid. indic. of dep. δέομαι; αὐτοῦ is an obj. gen.) and the antecedent of the rel. pron. οὗ (with ἀπό, "from whom"). The impf. could be *iter. (HCSB; Robertson, *Pictures* 121), conative (Marshall 341), or provide background to the following actions of Jesus (BHGNT 282). The neut. pl. τὰ δαιμόνια is the subj. of ἐξεληλύθει (see 8:2). The inf. (of indir. discourse) εἶναι modifies ἐδεῖτο, BDF §392[1c]. The man's request to be with Jesus is meant as a positive response in contrast to that of the crowd (8:37; Bock 780; Fitzmyer 740; Marshall 341). Ἀπέλυσεν 3rd sg. aor. act. indic. of ἀπολύω, "release," "sent him away" (most EVV). Λέγων expresses means.

8:39 Jesus sent the man back with two (2nd sg. pres.) impvs: "return" (ὑπόστρεφε, act. of ὑπόστρεφω; in this context cf. 8:37; cf. Wallace 717) to your house (cf. 8:27); and "declare" (διηγοῦ, mid. of dep. διηγέομαι, "relate," "describe"; cf. the cognate διήγησις in 1:1) "how much God has done for you." Luke then describes the man's response: he "returned" (ἀπῆλθεν, see 1:23; in this context cf. 8:37) "proclaiming" (κηρύσσων, see 3:3; a ptc. of manner) throughout the whole city (καθ᾿ ὅλην τὴν πόλιν) "how much Jesus had done for him." The man's proclamation identifies Ἰησοῦς in place of θεός as the subject of ἐποίησεν (see 1:49; perhaps in an emphatic position at the end of each sentence, Fitzmyer 740; Plummer 233). As with the concluding statements in 7:49 and 8:25, Luke invites his readers to marvel at who Jesus is.

HOMILETICAL SUGGESTIONS

Jesus' Power over Destructive Demons (8:26–39)
1. The desperate plight of the demon-possessed (8:26–29)
2. The destructive designs of the demons (8:30–33)
3. The fear of those who recognize supernatural power but reject Jesus (8:34–37)
4. The obedience of those who have been rescued and restored by Jesus' divine power (8:38–39)

c. Jesus' Power over Debilitating Disease and Death (8:40–56)

8:40 The inf. ὑποστρέφειν (see 2:43; on the pres. here cf. T 145) with ἐν . . . τῷ is temp. (the acc. Ἰησοῦν is the subj. of the inf.). Ἀπεδέξατο 3rd sg. aor. mid. indic. of dep. ἀποδέχομαι, "welcome" (ὁ ὄχλος is the subj.). Γάρ, causal. The pres. ptc. προσδοκῶντες (nom. pl. masc. of pres. act. ptc. of προσδοκάω, "wait for") with ἦσαν (see 1:6) is an impf. periph. cstr. (Robertson, *Pictures* 121; Z §§360–61; on the pl. vb. with the collective sg. subj., cf. Wallace 401).

8:41 Ἰδού, see 1:20. Ἦλθεν, see 2:27. The dat. rel. pron. ᾧ is poss. The nom. ὄνομα is the subj. of a verbless clause, and Ἰάϊρος is a pred. nom. The nom. οὗτος is the subj. of ὑπῆρχεν (3rd sg. impf. act. indic. of ὑπάρχω) with the nom. ἄρχων as pred. The description of Jairus as ἄρχων τῆς συναγωγῆς (a rare combination; cf. ἀρχισυναγώγου in 8:49) indicates he was the main elder at the local synagogue (Bock 791). Πεσών, see 5:12 (temp.). For πόδας see 8:35 (in contrast to Acts 10:25). This "ruler" of the Jews recognizes the authority of Jesus. The impf. παρεκάλει (3rd sg. impf. act. indic. of παρεκαλέω) may be ingressive (NASB) or used to add vividness (NET n.; Z §272). Εἰσελθεῖν, see 6:6 (inf. of indir. discourse).

8:42 Ὅτι, causal (giving the reason for Jairus' request). The nom. θυγάτηρ μονογενής ("only daughter," see 7:12) is the subj. of ἦν. The dat. αὐτῷ is poss. Ὡς with numerals is "approximately" (see 1:56). The impf. ἀπέθνῃσκεν (3rd sg. impf. act. indic. of ἀποθνῄσκω) could be ingressive ("about to die," i.e., "at death's door" HCSB; Bock 792; progressive, R 827). The pres. act. inf. ὑπάγειν (of ὑπάγω) with ἐν . . . τῷ is temp. (with the acc. αὐτόν as the subj. of the inf.). The impf. συνέπνιγον (3rd pl. impf. act. indic. of συνπνίγω, "choke"; cf. 8:14) emphasizes the strength of the crowd's pressure as so much that it was hard to breathe (LN 19.48; "nearly crushing him" HCSB, sim. NIV; BDAG 959c).

8:43 The nom. γυνή is the subj. of ἥψατο (in 8:44). Οὖσα nom. sg. fem. of pres. act. (attrib.) ptc. of εἰμί (introducing a description of the woman's predicament). Ἐν is used here to describe the condition of the woman (concomitant circumstances, Z §116; ZG 209). Ῥύσει αἵματος, "flow of blood" (dat. sg. fem. of ῥύσις, -εως, ἡ; [subj.] gen. sg. neut. of αἷμα, -ατος, τό), here may refer to the "loss of blood through menstrual bleeding" (LN 23.182; ἀπό is "from" or "since" BDAG 105c, though with ref. to the actual length of time, cf. examples for distance in BDF §161[1]; Marshall 344). The nom. sg. fem. rel. pron. ἥτις ("such that" Z §215; ZG 209) is the subj. of ἴσχυσεν (see 6:48; neg. with οὐκ). Θεραπευθῆνα aor. pass. (complementary) inf. of θεραπεύω. Ἀπ᾽ οὐδενός indicates agency (with ἀπό used in place of ὑπό, see 6:18). For the clause in brackets in UBS⁵ (προσαναλώσασα [nom. sg. fem. of aor. act. ptc. of προσαναλίσκω, "spend much"] is concessive; ὅλον τὸν βίον is "all her livelihood"; NKJV, NRSV, HCSB, ESV) see Metzger 121; Bock 807. The omission of the phrase in early Alexandrian and Western mss. 𝔓⁷⁵ B D (RSV, NASB, NIV; Nolland 416) indicates that it may be a later scribal harmonization to Mark 5:26. Marshall (344) and Fitzmyer (746) are undecided.

8:44 Προσελθοῦσα (nom. sg. fem. of 2nd aor. act. ptc. of dep. προσέρχομαι) is an attendant circumstance ptc. (with ἥψατο see 5:13; the subj. is γυνή from 8:43). The gen. (complement) κρασπέδου (sg. neut. of κράσπεδον, -ου, τό) could be "edge" BDAG 564b; NIV ("fringe" NRSV, NASB, ESV; Nolland 419) or "tassle" HCSB (cf. LXX Num 15:38–39; Deut 22:12; Bovon 1.338; Marshall 344). The gen. τοῦ ἱματίου is partitive (Wallace 86). Ὄπισθεν, adv. "from behind." Παραχρῆμα, see 1:64 (in this context, 8:44, 47, 55). Ἡ ῥύσις (see 8:43) is the subj. of ἔστη (see 6:8; here "stopped" most EVV, intrans.). One touch brings an instantaneous end to twelve years of hopelessness.

8:45 The subst. ptc. ἁψάμενος (nom. sg. masc. of aor. mid. ptc. of ἅπτω) is the subj. of a verbless clause (with the interr. τίς as the pred.). Ἀρνουμένων gen. pl. masc. of pres. mid. ptc. of dep. ἀρνέομαι, "deny" (temp. gen. abs. cstr. with πάντων as the subj.). Ἐπιστάτα, see 5:5. The nom. οἱ ὄχλοι is the subj. of the 3rd pl. pres. act. indics. συνέχουσιν (of συνέχω, "surround" ESV; "hemming in" HCSB) and ἀποθλίβουσιν (of ἀποθλίβω, "pressing against" HCSB).

8:46 The nom. sg. masc. indef. pron. τις is the subj. of ἥψατο (see 5:13; followed by the gen. μού). Γάρ (causal) introduces the reason Jesus said that someone touched him. Ἔγνων 1st sg. 2nd aor. act. indic. of γινώσκω (ἐγώ may be emphatic, ZG 210). The acc. ptc. ἐξεληλυθυῖαν (acc. sg. fem. of 2nd pf. act. ptc. of dep. ἐξέρχομαι; "had gone out" [NASB] not "going out" [NKJV], T 160–61; a consummative pf., Bock 796) is the complement in a double acc. cstr. (BHGNT 289; though it could be an acc. ptc. in indir. discourse after a vb. of cognition, Robertson, *Pictures* 123; R 1040–42; Wallace 645; Z §268).

8:47 Ἰδοῦσα nom. sg. fem. of 2nd aor. act. (temp. or causal) ptc. of ὁράω (BHGNT 290). Ὅτι introduces indir. discourse and indicates what the woman "saw" (i.e., "realized" NLT; Wallace 458). Ἔλαθεν 3rd sg. 2nd aor. act. indic. of λανθάνω, "escape notice" (neg. with οὐκ). Τρέμουσα (nom. sg. fem. of pres. act. ptc. of τρέμω, "tremble," with ref. to physical shaking, BDAG 1014c) expresses manner and modifies ἦλθεν (see 2:27; Wallace 628; ἡ γυνή is the subj.). Προσπεσοῦσα (nom. sg. fem. of 2nd aor. act. ptc. of προσπίπτω, "fall down before"; the dat. αὐτῷ is complementary) is an attendant circumstance ptc. (with ἦλθεν). Διά, with the acc. rel. pron. ἥν and αἰτίαν (acc. sg. fem. of αἰτία, -ας, ἡ, "cause"), is causal. Thus, the reason she touched (ἥψατο, see 5:13; in this context, 8:44, 46, 47) Jesus is part of the content of what she declared (ἀπήγγειλεν 3rd sg. aor. act. indic. of ἀπαγγέλλω) to the people (Burton §350; Wallace 539; perhaps placed forward for emphasis, BHGNT 290). She also declared how she was immediately healed (ἰάθη 3rd sg. aor. pass. indic. of dep. ἰάομαι).

8:48 Θυγάτηρ, "daughter" (as voc.; cf. 8:42, 49). For Jesus' statement to the woman see 7:50. Jesus' statement explains what has taken place and identifies faith as the means by which his saving power is received.

8:49 Λαλοῦντος gen. sg. masc. of pres. act. ptc. of λαλέω (a temp. gen. abs. cstr.; αὐτοῦ is the subj.). The indef. pron. τις is the subj. of ἔρχεται (see 3:16; a historical present [rare in Luke], adding vividness to what is about to happen, BHGNT 291; Wallace 530; Marshall 346). Παρά indicates source. The gen. sg. masc. τοῦ ἀρχισυναγώγου (of ἀρχισυνάγωγος, -ου, ὁ; cf. 8:41; this term is found in Luke 13:14; Acts 13:15; 18:8, 17) is understood to be "the synagogue ruler's (i.e., Jairus') house" (all EVV; cf. Nolland 421) given that Jairus has been with Jesus (8:41). Ὅτι, recitative. Τέθνηκεν 3rd sg. pf. act. indic. of θνῄσκω, "die" (the pf. may stress the finality of death, Bock 799; perhaps placed forward for emphasis, Marshall 346). The impv. σκύλλε (2nd sg. pres. act. impv. of σκύλλω, "trouble," "bother"; cf. 7:6) is modified by the adv. μηκέτι ("no longer"). Jesus' power saved a helpless woman, but now all hope appears to be gone.

8:50 Ἀκούσας, see 6:49 (temp.). Ἀπεκρίθη, see 4:4. Jesus' response contrasts fear (φοβοῦ [see 1:13] a prohibition with the neg. μή; Z §246; Huffman 141) with belief (πίστευσον 2nd sg. aor. act. impv. of πιστεύω; T 75; Z §242; the obj. of faith is again Jesus). Σωθήσεται 3rd sg. fut. pass. indic. of σώζω. On faith and Jesus' saving power see the introduction to chapter 7 (in this context cf. 8:48).

8:51 Ἐλθών, see 7:3 (temp.). Ἀφῆκεν, see 4:39 ("allow" NRSV; neg. with οὐκ). The inf. εἰσελθεῖν (see 6:6) is complementary. Εἰ μή, "except" (see 4:26). Παιδός, see 1:54 (fem.; 7:7). For Peter, James, and John, cf. 9:28. For Peter and John, cf. also 22:8; Acts 3:1, 3, 11; 4:13, 19; 8:14.

8:52 The nom. πάντες is the subj. of ἔκλαιον (3rd pl. impf. act. indic. of κλαίω, "weep") and ἐκόπτοντο (3rd pl. impf. mid. indic. of κόπτω, "beat one's breast" as an act of mourning, mid. "mourn" BDAG 559b; LN 52.1). The acc. sg. fem. αὐτήν (of αὐτός, -ή, -ό) is the dir. obj. of ἐκόπτοντο ("mourning for her" HCSB, ESV). The reason Jesus exhorts them not to weep (κλαίετε 2nd pl. pres. act. impv. of κλαίω; neg. with μή; T 76; Z §246; Huffman 141) is because (γάρ) she was not dead (ἀπέθανεν 3rd sg. 2nd aor. act. indic. of ἀποθνῄσκω) but asleep (καθεύδει 3rd sg. pres. act. indic. of καθεύδω). The fig. use of "sleep" here does not mean the girl is not actually dead (cf. 8:53, 55). It is a way of saying that, with Jesus, death is not the end (Bock 802; "it is prognosis not diagnosis" Nolland 421).

8:53 The impf. κατεγέλων (3rd pl. impf. act. indic. of καταγελάω, "laugh" most EVV; "ridicule" NKJV, NJB) is probably ingressive in the context of this response to Jesus' statement (NASB, HCSB; the gen. αὐτοῦ is the complement to κατεγέλων, BDF §181). Εἰδότες (nom. pl. masc. of pf. act. ptc. of οἶδα) is causal (HCSB; Wallace 631). Ὅτι is not causal (*pace* Bock 803; the ptc. is causal) but is complementary and introduces indir. discourse ("that"). Ἀπέθανεν, see 8:52.

8:54 Αὐτός (see 1:17) is the subj. of the (attendant circumstance) ptc. κρατήσας (nom. sg. masc. of aor. act. ptc. of κρατέω, "grasp," "take hold of"; followed by the gen.; ingressive, Z §250; ZG 210) and is used here to indicate a return to Jesus as the subj. of the action to follow. Ἐφώνησεν 3rd sg. aor. act. indic. of φωνέω, "call" ("called out" NRSV, HCSB; cf. NLT). How is a dead girl able to respond? The emphasis here is again on the powerful word of Jesus (Nolland 422). Παῖς, nom. for voc. (with the art., BDF §147[3]; Wallace 58; Z §34; ZG 210; "child," cf. 8:51; see 1:54). Ἔγειρε, see 5:23.

8:55 Three details emphasize her full restoration to life: her spirit returns, she rises up, and she is given something to eat (Bock 804). The nom. τὸ πνεῦμα (with the poss. gen. αὐτῆς) is the subj. of ἐπέστρεψεν (3rd sg. aor. act. indic. of ἐπιστρέφω). Ἀνέστη, see 4:16 (modified by the adv. παραχρῆμα, see 1:64). Διέταξεν 3rd sg. aor. act. indic. of διατάσσω, "command." Αὐτῇ is the indir. obj. of the aor. pass. inf. δοθῆναι (of δίδωμι; inf. of indir. discourse; though cf. BDF §392[4]). Φαγεῖν (see 6:4) is probably the subj. of δοθῆναι (BHGNT 294; or expresses purpose, Robertson, *Pictures* 123).

8:56 The nom. pl. οἱ γονεῖς (see 2:27; modified by the poss. gen. αὐτῆς) is the subj. of ἐξέστησαν (3rd pl. 2nd aor. act. indic. of ἐξίστημι, "be amazed"; intrans.). For παρήγγειλεν αὐτοῖς μηδενὶ εἰπεῖν, see 5:14. The subst. pf. ptc. γεγονός (see 2:15) is the obj. of εἰπεῖν ("to tell no one what had happened," most EVV). The command to silence differs from 8:39, 45–47 and the public resurrection in 7:11–17. Jesus has power over death, but did he not come to raise people from the dead "on a daily basis" (Bock 805). Jesus' disciples will still need to understand that they are following a suffering savior (9:22–27).

HOMILETICAL SUGGESTIONS

What Is Trust in Jesus? (8:40–56)
1. Humbly acknowledging the sovereign rule of Jesus (8:40–42)
2. Desperately reaching out for restoration from Jesus (8:43–48)
3. Patiently relying on the compassionate power of Jesus (8:49–56)

C. THE NATURE OF FOLLOWING A SUFFERING SAVIOR: TRAINING THE TWELVE (9:1–50)

The question of Jesus' identity continues in this section (9:9, 18–20), though now with explicit reference to his suffering (9:22, 44). This chapter transitions to preparing the Twelve for following their suffering Savior. Thus, each section in 9:1–50 focuses on the Twelve specifically (9:1, 12 ["apostles" 9:10]), individuals from the Twelve (9:20, 28, 49), or Jesus' own disciples including the Twelve (9:18, 36, 40, 43, 46). The limited understanding (9:13, 21, 33, 45) or failure (9:40, 46, 50–51) of the disciples in these episodes helps transition toward more concentrated teaching in the next major division of Luke's Gospel (9:51–19:44).

1. The Twelve Are Sent Out to Preach the Kingdom with Nothing for the Journey (9:1–9)

9:1 Συγκαλεσάμενος (nom. sg. masc. of aor. mid. ptc. of συγκαλέω, "call together"; the obj. is τοὺς δώδεκα) could be temp. (NIV) or attendant circumstance (NASB, ESV) with ἔδωκεν (see 6:4). The art. τούς is a substantiver with the adj. δώδεκα (BDF §263; Wallace 233; ἀποστόλους is added in ℵ C* L). The acc. δύναμιν καὶ ἐξουσίαν (a comprehensive hendiadys, Bock 813) is the obj. of ἔδωκεν and is implied for the pres. act. inf. θεραπεύειν (of θεραπεύω; ZG 210). The inf. could be epex. (BHGNT 295) or express purpose (Fitzmyer 753). Following the display of Jesus' power over creation, demons, disease, and death in 8:22–56 (cf. 8:46), the only reason the Twelve are able to have such power over (ἐπί, BDAG 365d) "all the demons" (πάντα τὰ δαιμόνια) and to heal diseases (see 4:40) is because Jesus granted this to them (cf. 9:16).

9:2 The two infs. κηρύσσειν (pres. act. of κηρύσσω) and ἰᾶσθαι (see 5:17) express the purpose for Jesus sending (ἀπέστειλεν, see 7:3; cf. ἀπόστολοι, 9:10 [6:13]) the Twelve. On τὴν βασιλείαν τοῦ θεοῦ see 4:43 (cf. also 8:1).

9:3 Αἴρετε 2nd pl. pres. act. impv. of αἴρω (Z §248; ZG 211; subst. μηδέν is the obj.). Εἰς τὴν ὁδόν is "for the road" (HCSB) or "for your journey" (NRSV, HCSB, ESV; with the art. functioning as a poss. pron., Wallace 215). The acc. cstr. μήτε ῥάβδον . . . δύο χιτῶνας could be:

   *1. in appos. to μηδέν (with δύο χιτῶνας as the obj. of ἔχειν [see 8:6] which functions as an impv.; ESV; BDF §389; Bovon 1.345; Fitzmyer 754; Marshall 353; Nolland 424);
   2. the obj. of ἔχειν (which is epex. to μηδὲν αἴρετε, NIV; BHGNT 296; ZG 211); or
   3. consecutive or purpose (i.e., "take nothing . . . so that you have no" McKay 82; cf. BHGNT 296; Nolland 427).

Either way, the opening general impv. is followed by four specific references (Bock 814). Ῥάβδον acc. sg. fem. of ῥάβδος, -ου, ἡ, "staff" (most EVV), "walking stick" (HCSB). Πήραν acc. sg. fem. of πήρα, -ας, ἡ, "bag" (most EVV), "traveling bag" (HCSB; BDAG 811d; LN 6.145; for "carrying provisions" Marshall 353; Nolland

427; in this context it is unlikely to be a "beggar's bag," *pace* Bock 814). Ἀργύριον acc. sg. neut. of ἀργύριον, -ου, τό, "money" (all EVV; BDAG 128d). Δύο χιτῶνας (see 3:11; "two tunics" ESV; i.e., "an extra tunic" NRSV). The prep. ἀνά is distributive with numbers for "each" or "apiece" and specifies that the ref. is to each disciple (BDAG 58a; BDF §§204, 248[1]; LN 89.91; ZG 211; omitted in ℵ B C*, cf. Metzger 123).

9:4 Εἰς introduces a locat. rel. clause (with the rel. pron. ἥν) which is referred to in the following clause with ἐκεῖ ("there") and ἐκεῖθεν ("from there;" BHGNT 297). Εἰσέλθητε 2nd pl. 2nd aor. act. subjunc. (with ἄν; indef. Z §335; ZG 211) of dep. εἰσέρχομαι. Μένετε 2nd pl. pres. act. impv. of μένω. Ἐξέρχεσθε 2nd pl. pres. mid. impv. of dep. ἐξέρχομαι ("go out," i.e., of the town, cf. NIV; Bock 816; Marshall 353).

9:5 The nom. pl. masc. rel. pron. ὅσοι (of ὅσος, -η, -ον) is the subj. of δέχωνται (3rd pl. pres. mid. subjunc. [with ἄν; indef.] of dep. δέχομαι; neg. with μή) and is referred to at the end of the sentence with ἐπ' αὐτούς (ἐπί used here as a marker of opposition, "against them" BDAG 366d; LN 90.34; Robertson, *Pictures* 124; ZG 211; Bovon [1.346] prefers "about them"). Ἐξερχόμενοι nom. pl. masc. of pres. mid. (temp.) ptc. of dep. ἐξέρχομαι. The acc. sg. masc. κονιορτόν (of κονιορτός, -οῦ, ὁ, "dust," cf. 10:11; Acts 13:51) is the obj. of ἀποτινάσσετε (2nd pl. pres. act. impv. of ἀποτινάσσω, "shake off"). Εἰς μαρτύριον gives the purpose for this action. In a Jewish setting the action is symbolic evidence that, in rejecting the message of the kingdom, they were not part of the people of God (Marshall 354; Nolland 428; a warning about impending judgment, Bock 817).

9:6 Ἐξερχόμενοι (see 9:5) is probably an attendant circumstance ptc. (with διήρχοντο 3rd pl. impf. mid. indic. of dep. διέρχομαι). Κατὰ τὰς κώμας is distributive (see 8:1; ZG 211). The nom. pl. masc. ptcs. εὐαγγελιζόμενοι (pres. mid. of εὐαγγελίζω; cf. κηρύσσειν τὴν βασιλείαν in 9:2; 8:1) and θεραπεύοντες (pres. act. of θεραπεύω) express manner. Πανταχοῦ, adv., "everywhere" (adds to the emphasis on comprehensive ministry in the distributive ref. to villages). This summary of the activity of the Twelve forms an inclusio with 9:1–2 (Bock 818; Bovon 1.347).

9:7–8 The subj. of ἤκουσεν (see 1:41) is Ἡρῴδης (with ὁ τετραάρχης in appos.; i.e., Antipas, see 3:19). The acc. τὰ . . . πάντα is the obj. of ἤκουσεν (with the attrib. ptc. γινόμενα, acc. pl. neut. pres. mid. ptc. of dep. γίνομαι, "all that was happening" ESV). The activity of the Twelve, under the authority of Jesus, forms the backdrop for the reports that lead to Herod's perplexity. Διηπόρει 3rd sg. impf. act. indic. of διαπορέω, "greatly perplexed" (LN 32.10; only in Luke and Acts in the NT; the impf., may be progressive, Bock 822; Bovon 1.349). The art. pres. pass. inf. λέγεσθαι (of λέγω) with διά indicates the cause of Herod's confusion (Wallace 597; on the art. cf. R 1069). The following three uses of ὅτι introduce indir. discourse (Robertson, *Pictures* 125; Z §346; ZG 211). It was said (1) by some that John "had been raised" from the dead (most EVV view ἠγέρθη [see 7:16] as pass.; NKJV, NJB, NASB tr. this as mid., "risen"); (2) by some that Elijah had appeared (ἐφάνη 3rd sg. 2nd aor. pass. indic. of φαίνω; on the tr. cf. Z §290); and (3) by others that a prophet from long ago (ἀρχαίων gen. pl. masc. of ἀρχαῖος, -α, -ον, "from ancient times" LN 67.98; perhaps a partitive gen, Wallace

85) had risen (ἀνέστη, see 4:16; cf. the indef. pron. is adj., Wallace 347). The parallel with John and Elijah, together with τῶν ἀρχαίων, indicate that the third option also refers to someone who had risen "from the dead" (Marshall 356; Nolland 432; not just "come on the scene," Bock 823; Fitzmyer 759). All three options consider Jesus to be a prophet of some kind. All three are inadequate in the context of Jesus' display of power in Luke 8 and the answer that is given in 9:18–27, 28–36 (all three view Jesus as someone who has "returned from the realm of the beyond" Nolland 432).

9:9 The acc. Ἰωάννην is the (emphatic) obj. of ἀπεκεφάλισα (1st sg. aor. act. indic. of ἀποκεφαλίζω, "behead," causative "had John beheaded" NASB). Ἀκούω 1st sg. pres. act. indic. of ἀκούω. For Herod's question concerning the identity of Jesus see 9:18 (cf. 7:49; 8:25). The disciples receive instruction on the question of Jesus' identity, whereas the question remains unanswered for Herod (Nolland 433). Ἐζήτει 3rd sg. impf. act. indic. of ζητέω (iter. NLT; Robertson, *Pictures* 125; durative Bock 823). Ἰδεῖν, see 2:26 (complementary; cf. 23:8).

HOMILETICAL SUGGESTIONS

The Ministry of the Apostles (9:1–9)
1. Empowered and authorized by Jesus (9:1)
2. Embodies the ministry of Jesus (9:2)
3. Exhibits the manner of Jesus (9:3–6)
4. Engenders questions about Jesus (9:7–9)

2. The Twelve Are Taught that Jesus Provides (9:10–17)

9:10 This verse refers back to the sending out of the Twelve in 9:1–6 (now referred to as the apostles, cf. 6:13) and signals a continuing interest in the Twelve in this miracle account. They now return (ὑποστρέψαντες, see 7:10; temp.) and report (διηγήσαντο 3rd pl. aor. mid. indic. of dep. διηγέομαι, "relate," "describe"; cf. the cognate διήγησις in 1:1) to Jesus (αὐτῷ) all the things (ὅσα, acc. pl. neut. rel. pron. of ὅσος, -η, -ον) they had done (ἐποίησαν 3rd pl. aor. act. indic. of ποιέω). Παραλαβών (nom. sg. masc. of 2nd aor. act. ptc. of παραλαμβάνω) is an attendant circumstance ptc. (with ὑπεχώρησεν 3rd sg. aor. act. indic. of ὑποχωρέω, "withdraw"). The idiom κατ᾽ ἰδίαν is "privately" (HCSB; BDAG 467c; ZG 212). Καλουμένην (see 7:11) is attrib. and modifies the locat. εἰς πόλιν (on εἰς for πρός cf. Z §97; for πόλις see 7:11).

9:11 Γνόντες nom. pl. masc. of 2nd aor. act. (temp.) ptc. of γινώσκω. Ἠκολούθησαν, see 5:11. Ἀποδεξάμενος nom. sg. masc. of aor. mid. (temp.) ptc. of dep. ἀποδέχομαι, "welcome." The impf. ἐλάλει (see 1:64; on τῆς βασιλείας τοῦ θεοῦ see 4:43) and ἰᾶτο (see 6:19) could be ingressive (NASB) or progressive (ZG 212; Robertson, *Pictures* 125; Bock 829; Bovon 1.356; Fitzmyer 766; Marshall 359; Nolland 441). The subst. ptc. τοὺς . . . ἔχοντας (acc. pl. masc. of pres. act. ptc. of ἔχω) is the obj. of ἰᾶτο. The acc. χρείαν is the obj. of ἔχοντας. Θεραπείας obj. gen. sg. fem. of θεραπεία, -ας, ἡ, "healing."

9:12 Ἤρξατο, see 4:21 (ἡ . . . ἡμέρα is the subj.). The pres. act. inf. κλίνειν (of κλίνω, "to decline," "draw to a close" NET; intrans. Robertson, *Pictures* 125) is complementary (Wallace 599; with the nom. subj., 192). Προσελθόντες (see 8:24) is an attendant circumstance ptc. (with εἶπαν). Ἀπόλυσον 2nd sg. aor. act. impv. of ἀπολύω, "release," "send away." The Twelve then elaborate on the purpose for sending the crowds away. It is so that (ἵνα with the subjunc., Wallace 472) they could:

1. "go to the surrounding villages and countryside" (πορευθέντες [see 7:22] is attendant circumstance; τάς agrees with the nearest noun but does duty for both κώμας καὶ ἀγρούς, ZG 212; the first noun ["villages"] is possibly a subset of the second ["countryside"], Wallace 287; κύκλῳ functions as an adj. "around" BDAG 574c; BDF §199);
2. "receive lodging" (καταλύσωσιν 3rd pl. aor. act. subjunc. of καταλύω, "to halt, rest, find lodging" BDAG 522a; "to experience hospitality . . . lodging" LN 34.61); and
3. "find provisions" (εὕρωσιν [see 6:7] ἐπισιτισμόν [acc. sg. masc. of ἐπισιτισμός, -οῦ, ὁ], "provisions," NRSV, ESV; i.e., "food" BDAG 378b; HCSB, NIV).

The reason for this is because (ὅτι), according to the Twelve, it is a "deserted place" (NRSV, HCSB; "desolate place" NASB, ESV; "remote place" NIV). The addition of the adv. ὧδε may add emphasis (BHGNT 303).

9:13 The pron. ὑμεῖς with the impv. δότε (2nd pl. 2nd aor. act. impv. of δίδωμι) is emphatic (ZG 212; Bovon 1.356; Fitzmyer 766; Nolland 441) and continues the focus on the Twelve in this pericope as Jesus involves them in the solution to this problem. The inf. φαγεῖν (see 6:4) is the obj. of δότε. The dat. ἡμῖν is poss. The comp. adj.

πλεῖον with ἤ is "more than." The idiom εἰ μήτι is "unless" (the interr. μήτι in questions expects a neg. answer, ZG 212; ἰχθύες, nom. pl. masc.). Πορευθέντες (see 7:22; in this context, 9:12) is an attendant circumstance ptc. (with ἀγοράσωμεν 1st pl. aor. act. subjunc. of ἀγοράζω). The subjunc. with εἰ μήτι could be cond. (most EVV; BDF §376; Bock 830; Marshall 360) or deliberative (NLT; BHGNT 304; Z §332; ZG 212). Βρώματα, see 3:11. The disciples lack resources and solutions.

9:14 Γάρ, causal (a parenthetical remark giving the reason for the disciples' response). Ὡσεί is a marker of approximation (BDAG 1106d). Ἄνδρες (nom. pl. masc. of ἀνήρ, ἀνδρός, ὁ) indicates the number would be larger if women and children were also counted. Κατακλίνατε 2nd pl. aor. act. impv. of κατακλίνω, "recline" (see 7:36), "Have them sit down" (with αὐτούς; HCSB, ESV, NIV; Nolland 442). Κλισίας acc. pl. fem. of κλισία, -ας, ἡ, "groups" ("a group of people eating together" BDAG 550a; LN 11.5; LSJ 961d; a cognate acc. after κατακλίνατε as the complement in a double acc. cstr., Wallace 189; Fitzmyer 767 describes it as in appos. to the dir. obj.; Marshall 361 calls κλισίας an acc. of respect). For ἀνά see 9:3 (distributive, "each" most EVV). Πεντήκοντα, "50" (as simply a division of 5000, Fitzmyer 767).

9:15 Ἐποίησαν, see 9:10 (with οὕτως "they did so"). Κατέκλιναν 3rd pl. aor. act. indic. of κατακλίνω, "recline" (see 7:36; 9:14).

9:16 Λαβών, see 6:4 (temp. or attendant circumstance). The arts. τούς . . . τούς are anaphoric, pointing back to 9:13 (Robertson, *Pictures* 126; ἰχθύας, acc. pl. masc., see 5:6). Ἀναβλέψας (nom. sg. masc. of aor. act. ptc. of ἀναβλέπω) is an attendant circumstance ptc. with εὐλόγησεν (see 2:28). Αὐτούς could be "he blessed them" (NASB; i.e., the bread and the fish, Fitzmyer 768; Nolland 443) or "said a blessing over them" (ESV), "gave thanks" (NIV; with αὐτούς as an acc. of respect, i.e., gave thanks to God with respect to the food, Marshall 362). Κατέκλασεν 3rd sg. aor. act. indic. of κατακλάω, "break in pieces." The impf. ἐδίδου (3rd sg. impf. act. indic. of δίδωμι) could be iter. (NASB, HCSB; Robertson, *Pictures* 126; Z §271; ZG 212; Bovon 1.354; Marshall 363; Nolland 444) or ingressive (BHGNT 300). The 2nd aor. act. inf. παραθεῖναι (of παρατίθημι, "set before") expresses purpose. Thus, Jesus, in intimate relationship with the Father, provides for the people, and the Twelve will mediate Jesus' miraculous provision (cf. 9:1; 10:2, 16).

9:17 Ἔφαγον 3rd pl. 2nd aor. act. indic. of ἐσθίω. Ἐχορτάσθησαν 3rd pl. aor. pass. indic. of χορτάζω, "eat to the full," "satisfy." Περισσεῦσαν (nom. sg. neut. aor. act. [subst.] ptc. of περισσεύω, "abound," "left over" most EVV) is the subj. of ἤρθη (3rd sg. aor. pass. indic. of αἴρω). The nom. κόφινοι δώδεκα ("twelve baskets," on κόφινοι [pl. masc. of κόφινος, -ου, ὁ] cf. MM 357a–b; modified by the gen. [of content] pl. neut. κλασμάτων [of κλάσμα, -ατος, τό] "broken pieces") is in appos. to περισσεῦσαν. The emphasis is on the abundance of Jesus' provision for the people of God through his apostles.

HOMILETICAL SUGGESTIONS

Jesus Trains the Apostles (9:10–17)
1. Jesus models compassion before the apostles (9:10–11).
2. Jesus involves the apostles in impossible ministry (9:12–15).

3. Jesus ministers his sufficiency to God's people through the apostles (9:16–17).

3. Who Is Jesus? (9:18–36)

a. The Suffering Messiah (9:18–27)

    i. Jesus Is the Messiah (9:18–20)

9:18 Ἐγένετο, see 1:5. The inf. εἶναι (see 2:4) with ἐν τῷ is temp. (the acc. αὐτόν is the subj. of the inf.). This temp. inf. cstr. forms a periph. cstr. with προσευχόμενον (acc. sg. masc. of pres. mid. ptc. of dep. προσεύχομαι; BHGNT 306; Robertson, *Pictures* 127; ZG 212). Κατὰ μόνας is idiomatic for "alone" (BDAG 659c; BDF §241[6]; i.e., without the crowds, Bock 840; cf. MM 417b for a ref. to "private party," i.e., with a group apart from others; cf. κατ' ἰδίαν, 9:10). Συνῆσαν (3rd pl. impf. act. indic. of σύνειμι) is only used by Luke in the NT. It could mean "be with someone" ("the disciples were with him" most EVV; cf. Acts 22:11; LN 85.2) or "gather/come together" ("his disciples joined him" NKJV, "came to him" NJB; cf. Luke 8:4; BDAG 968c). Either way the preceding cstr. does not say Jesus was "alone" but "praying alone." See 5:16 for refs. to Jesus and prayer in Luke (see 5:30 for refs. to "disciples" in Luke). Ἐπηρώτησεν, see 8:30. Λέγων, see 1:63. Λέγουσιν 3rd pl. pres. act. indic. of λέγω (with οἱ ὄχλοι as the subj.). Εἶναι (see 2:4) is an inf. of indir. discourse (the acc. με is the subj., ZG 213; lexically the interr. pron. τίνα is the pred. even though grammatically it is expected to be the subj., Wallace 195). The question left hanging in 9:9 will now be addressed.

9:19 Ἀποκριθέντες nom. pl. masc. of aor. pass. ptc. of dep. ἀποκρίνομαι (see 1:19). The acc. Ἰωάννην . . . Ἠλίαν follow an implied σε λέγουσιν οἱ ὄχλοι [or ἄλλοι] εἶναι (from 9:18). For the clause following ὅτι see 9:8. The following verse will show that although this view of Jesus as a prophet (see 9:8) is not necessarily false (cf. 4:24; 13:33), it is inadequate.

9:20 The additional pron. ὑμεῖς is placed forward for emphasis (HCSB, NIV; Robertson, *Pictures* 127; Bock 841; Marshall 366). Λέγετε, see 7:33. Εἶναι (see 2:4; on the interr. pron. as pred. see above, 9:18). Ἀποκριθείς, see 1:19. The acc. τὸν χριστόν could follow an implied σε λέγω [or λέγομεν] εἶναι or σὺ εἶ. The gen. τοῦ θεοῦ could be source (cf. 2:26). Jesus' Davidic heritage and royal status have been made explicit in the infancy narratives (e.g., 1:27, 32–33, 69; 2:4), and explicit statements that Jesus is χριστός have been made in the early chapters of Luke (2:11, 26; 4:41; and by implication in 3:15, 22; 4:18). The title χριστός will not occur again in Luke's narrative until Jesus' climactic question to his accusers in 20:41 and will be prominent in Jesus' trial and crucifixion (22:67; 23:2, 35, 39). A true understanding of Jesus as χριστός will not be gained until after his rejection, crucifixion, and resurrection. Luke's Gospel concludes with Jesus' explanations from Scripture about the suffering Messiah (24:26, 46).

ii. Jesus Is the Messiah Who Will Suffer, Die, and Rise (9:21–22)

9:21 Ἐπιτιμήσας (nom. sg. masc. of aor. act. ptc. of ἐπιτιμάω, often "rebuke" in Luke [see 4:35]; with the following vb. it is more like "warn" here) is an attendant circumstance ptc. (with παρήγγειλεν see 5:14) and forms an emphatic hendiadys ("forcefully commanded" NET; Z §261; ZG 213). Although Peter answered (9:20), Jesus' warning is directed to all the disciples (αὐτοῖς). Λέγειν (see 3:8), an inf. of indir. discourse (Robertson, *Pictures* 128; the acc. τοῦτο is the dir. obj.). Μηδενί is the indir. obj. ("to no one").

9:22 Εἰπών (nom. sg. masc. of 2nd aor. act. ptc. of λέγω) modifies the preceding vb. in 9:21 ("he commanded, saying"), and therefore closely links this statement about suffering to the command for silence which was given in response to Peter's confession that Jesus is χριστός (cf. Z §265; Bovon 1.362; Fitzmyer 777). Ὅτι, recitative. The following four infs. (with τὸν υἱὸν τοῦ ἀνθρώπου as the subj.) are complementary to δεῖ (see 2:49): παθεῖν (2nd aor. act. inf. of πάσχω; cf. 17:25; 22:15; 24:26, 46; Acts 1:3; 3:18; 17:3), ἀποδοκιμασθῆναι (aor. pass. inf. of ἀποδοκιμάζω, "reject"; ἀπό is used for ὑπό, see 6:18; the art. τῶν unites the following three distinct parties of the Sanhedrin, Wallace 279), ἀποκτανθῆναι (aor. pass. inf. of ἀποκτείνω), and ἐγερθῆναι (aor. pass. inf. of ἐγείρω; "be raised"; the last inf. is a theological passive Bock 848; Fitzmyer 781; Marshall 371; Nolland 467; though ZG 213 [Z §231] tr. as "rise" [intrans.]). Τῇ τρίτῃ ἡμέρᾳ is a dat. of time (indicating the point of time "when" the action of the vb. will be accomplished, Wallace 156; cf. 18:33; 24:7, 46). The declaration that Jesus is χριστός must be understood in terms of God's sovereign purposes (δεῖ) for the Messiah's death and resurrection. Explicit references to Jesus' suffering will now become more regular (on the journey to Jerusalem; 9:44; 17:25; 18:31–33).

iii. Because Jesus Is the Suffering Messiah, His Followers Must Also Be Prepared to Suffer to the Point of Death in Order to Gain Life (9:23–27)

9:23 Ἔλεγεν, see 6:20. Εἰ introduces a first-class cond. sentence. Θέλει, see 5:39 (the indef. pron. τις is the subj.). The adv. ὀπίσω functions as a prep. followed by the gen. (BDAG 716b; ZG 213). Ἔρχεσθαι pres. mid. (complementary) inf. of dep. ἔρχομαι. The apodosis of the cond. sentence consists of two 3rd sg. aor. impvs. ("must" NASB, HCSB, better than "let him" ESV):

1. ἀρνησάσθω (aor. mid. of dep. ἀρνέομαι, "deny"; followed by the refl. pron. ἑαυτόν),
2. ἀράτω (aor. act. of αἴρω, "take up"; for the expression with σταυρόν as being prepared for suffering even to the point of death, cf. BDAG 941c; LN 24.83; LSJ 1635a; MM 586d; Nolland 482–83; καθ᾽ ἡμέραν is distributive, "daily"; an attitude which views "life in this world as already finished" Marshall 373), and
3. a 3rd sg. pres. act. impv. ἀκολουθείτω (of ἀκολουθέω).

The distinction between the aor. impvs. and the pres. impv. here may be due to the specificity of the aor. commands related to the general instruction of the pres. command to follow Jesus (BHGNT 310–11; *pace* Z §242 who sees the distinction here in terms of "once for all" [aor.] or ongoing [pres.] and so finds the addition of καθ' ἡμέραν to the aor. impv. ἀράτω a "strange addition"). It is possible that the first two aor. impvs. are understood as a prerequisite for the third pres. impv. (Campbell, 2008 89; Bock 852). This summarizing statement is elaborated upon in 9:24–26 with a series of γάρ clauses (Nolland 483).

9:24 Γάρ, causal (giving the reason for the commands of 9:23). The indef. rel. pron. ὅς introduces a relative clause which functions as the subj. of ἀπολέσει (3rd sg. fut. act. indic. of ἀπόλλυμι, "lose" all EVV; BHGNT 311; ZG 213). The parallel use of the refl. pron. ἑαυτόν in 9:25 indicates that ψυχήν here means "life" (all EVV; Bock 855; Fitzmyer 788). The subjunc. θέλῃ (3rd sg. pres. act. subjunc. of θέλω) with ἄν is indef. (Z §335; ZG 213) and functions like the cond. cstr. of 9:23. Ἀπολέσῃ 3rd sg. aor. act. subjunc. of ἀπόλλυμι). The prep. ἕνεκεν followed by the gen. pron. ἐμοῦ indicates cause. The demonstrative pron. οὗτος ("he is the one who" NASB) is the subj. of σώσει (3rd sg. fut. act. indic. of σῴζω) and refers to the previous rel. clause (R 698).

9:25 Γάρ introduces a further elaboration on the previous statements about "losing" one's life. Ὠφελεῖται 3rd sg. pres. pass. indic. of ὠφελέω, "profit" (ESV), "benefited" (HCSB), "what good is it" (NIV; ZG 213). Κερδήσας (nom. sg. masc. of aor. act. ptc. of κερδαίνω, "gain") could be attrib. ("a person who gains"), a ptc. of means with the following ptcs. ("by gaining"), or *cond. ("if he gains" most EVV; R 1129; Wallace 632; ZG 213; see BHGNT 312). The acc. refl. pron. ἑαυτόν is the obj. of the (cond.) ptc. ἀπολέσας (nom. sg. masc. of aor. act. ptc. of ἀπόλλυμι; cf. 9:24, Bovon 1.367). Ζημιωθείς (nom. sg. masc. of aor. pass. ptc. of ζημιόω, "suffer loss," "forfeit" most EVV; BDAG 428a; often contrasted with κερδαίνω in business transactions, LSJ 756a; MM 273c, 341d; Fitzmyer 788) is probably also cond.

9:26 Γάρ, causal (giving the reason for the previously mentioned loss in 9:24–25). The rel. pron. ὅς is the subj. of ἐπαισχυνθῇ (3rd sg. aor. pass. subjunc. of dep. ἐπαισχύνομαι, "be ashamed"; indef. subjunc. with ἄν, Robertson, *Pictures* 129). The entire acc. phrase με καὶ τοὺς ἐμοὺς λόγους is the obj. of ἐπαισχυνθῇ. There is no distinction between being ashamed of Jesus and being ashamed of his words. The demonstrative pron. τοῦτον is the (emphatic, Bock 857; Marshall 376) obj. of ἐπαισχυνθήσεται (3rd sg. fut. pass. indic. of dep. ἐπαισχύνομαι) and refers back to the previous rel. clause. Ἔλθῃ (see 1:43), temp. subjunc. with ὅταν. On ὁ υἱὸς τοῦ ἀνθρώπου see 5:24. On the (second) coming of "the Son of Man" cf. also 12:40; 17:24, 30; 18:8; 21:27). The Son of Man "comes" as judge (Marshall 376). Ἐν τῇ δόξῃ expresses manner (cf. 21:27; for glory associated with God cf. 2:9). The gen. αὐτοῦ καὶ τοῦ πατρὸς καὶ τῶν ἁγίων ἀγγέλων is subj. (i.e., God and the heavenly realm, Nolland 485).

9:27 The adv. ἀληθῶς ("truly") together with λέγω . . . ὑμῖν adds emphasis to the following statement (sim. to ἀμήν; see 4:24). The indef. nom. pl. masc. pron. τινες, modified by the (partitive) gen. subst. ptc. ἑστηκότων (gen. pl. masc. of pf. act. ptc. of ἵστημι; intrans.; pf. with pres. force, Wallace 580; ZG 213) is the subj. of εἰσίν (see 7:25). The neut. gen. αὐτοῦ functions as a deictic adv. "here" (BDAG 154a; ZG 213).

The rel. pron. οἵ is the subj. of γεύσωνται (3rd pl. aor. mid. subjunc. of dep. γεύομαι, "taste"; i.e., "experience" BDAG 195c) which is negated with the emphatic οὐ μή (future referring, BDF §365; Z §444). Ἕως with ἄν and the subjunc. ἴδωσιν (3rd pl. 2nd aor. act. subjunc. of ὁράω) is an indef. temp. clause. Jesus' exaltation, enthronement, and pouring out of the Spirit (Acts 2:33) indicate that the ascension and Pentecost may be in view here (Marshall 378; cf. Acts 1:3–8; on τὴν βασιλείαν τοῦ θεοῦ see 4:43; with the "already" aspect of the kingdom in view, *pace* Fitzmyer 790). The explicit link in 9:28 implies that the following manifestation of Jesus' glory is a "preview" (Bock 859; Nolland 487; cf. ὁράω here and in 9:31, 32, 36; perhaps of the final kingdom). The promise provides assurance to these disciples about what lies in the immediate future.

FOR FURTHER STUDY

25. Disciples/Discipleship (9:18, 23)

*Agan, C. D. J., III. *The Imitation of Christ in the Gospel of Luke*. Phillipsburg: P&R, 2014.
Dunn, J. D. G. *Jesus' Call to Discipleship*. Cambridge: Cambridge University Press, 1992.
Lunde, J. *Following Jesus, the Servant King: A Biblical Theology of Covenantal Discipleship*. Grand Rapids: Zondervan, 2010.
Segovia, F., ed. *Discipleship in the New Testament*. Philadelphia: Fortress, 1985.
Wilkins, M. J. *DJG*² 202–12.

HOMILETICAL SUGGESTIONS

Who Is Jesus? Part 1: The Suffering Messiah (9:18–27)

1. The suffering and rising Messiah (9:18–22)
    a. The inadequate opinions of others (9:18–19)
    b. The (partially understood) correct understanding of Peter (9:20)
    c. The true interpretation from Jesus (9:21–22)
2. His followers likewise suffer to gain life (9:23–27)
    a. Following the cross-centered path of Jesus (9:23)
    b. The assurance of life when the Son of Man comes in glory (9:24–27)

b. The Glorious Son of the Father (9:28–36)

9:28 Ἐγένετο, see 1:5. On ὡσεί see 9:14 ("about a week later" Fitzmyer 797). The nom. ἡμέραι ὀκτώ ("eight days") could be a pendent nom. (Robertson, *Pictures* 129; ZG 214; perhaps the subj. of ἐγένετο, BHGNT 315), a parenthetic nom. (BDF §144; Bock 865), or a (rare) nom. for time (Wallace 64). Μετὰ τοὺς λόγους τούτους is temp. The temp. note and explicit link to the previous discussion (τοὺς λόγους τούτους) indicate that the previous discussion is meant to be understood in connection with these events (whether as the link between Jesus' sufferings and glory [Marshall 382], or as a fulfillment of the previous promise to see the kingdom [Bock 859]). Παραλαβών (see 9:10) is an attendant circumstance ptc. (with ἀνέβη see 2:4). On Πέτρον καὶ Ἰωάννην καὶ Ἰάκωβον cf. 8:51. For εἰς τὸ ὄρος see 6:12. Προσεύξασθαι expresses purpose (see 6:12; see 5:16 for refs. to Jesus and prayer in Luke).

9:29 Ἐγένετο, see 1:5. The pres. mid. inf. προσεύχεσθαι (of προσεύχομαι; with the acc. αὐτόν as the subj.) is temp. Τὸ εἶδος (nom. sg. neut., see 3:22, "the appearance"; modified by the subj. gen. τοῦ προσώπου and poss. gen. αὐτοῦ) is the subj. of an implied ἐγένετο. The adj. ἕτερον ("different") is a pred. nom. ("became different" NASB; "changed" NIV). The nom. ὁ ἱματισμός ("clothing," see 7:25) is the subj. of another implied ἐγένετο. The nom. sg. masc. adj. λευκός (of λευκός, -ή, -όν, "white," here "shining," "gleaming" BDAG 593b) is also a pred. nom. and is modified by ἐξαστράπτων (nom. sg. masc. of pres. act. [attrib.] ptc. of ἐξαστράπτω, "flash like lightning," BDAG 346d; only here in the NT; together tr. as "dazzling white" HCSB, ESV; "bright as a flash of lightening" NIV; cf. 17:24). With this sight, the three disciples see a glimpse of Jesus' glory.

9:30 Ἰδού, see 1:20. Ἄνδρες δύο (cf. 24:4; Acts 1:10) is the subj. of συνελάλουν ("talking with," see 4:36). The nom. pl. rel. pron. οἵτινες (for οἵ, see 1:20; Wallace 345) is the subj. of ἦσαν (see 1:6) and identifies these two men as Moses and Elijah. Although it is possible that Moses represents the prophetic office (see 9:35 with ref. to Deut 18:15; Bock 868; Fitzmyer 799), explicit refs. to Μωϋσῆς elsewhere in Luke associate Moses with the law (2:22; 5:14; 20:28, 37) and distinguish him from the prophets (16:29, 31; 24:27, 44; cf. Bovon 1.376; Plummer 251). Although the ref. to Ἠλίας in 1:17 may suggest his appearance here points to the arrival of the eschatological age (Bock 868; Nolland 503), other explicit refs. to Ἠλίας in Luke and in the immediate context (4:25–26; 9:8, 19) suggest that he may be a representative of the prophets here.

9:31 The nom. pl. masc. rel. pron. οἵ refers back to these two men and is the subj. of ὀφθέντες (nom. pl. masc. of aor. pass. [temp.] ptc. of ὁράω, "appeared" BDAG 719d; most EVV). Ἐν δόξῃ expresses manner. Ἔλεγον, see 4:22. Τὴν ἔξοδον αὐτοῦ, "his exodus" (acc. sg. fem. of ἔξοδος, -ου, ἡ) could refer to:

1. Jesus' "departure" (most EVV; i.e., Jesus' death, resurrection, and ascension, Bovon 1.376; Fitzmyer 800; and its saving significance, Marshall 384–85; Nolland 500);
2. Jesus' "death" (HCSB; cf. BDAG 350d; LSJ 596c; MM 224c; cf. 2 Pet 1:15); or
3. the entire death-parousia career of Jesus (Bock 870).

The following ref. to fulfillment "in Jerusalem" suggests that either "death" or "departure" is understood here (cf. 9:51). Ἤμελλεν, see 7:2. Πληροῦν pres. act. (complementary) inf. of πληρόω, "accomplish" (HCSB, ESV; Marshall 385; "bring to fulfillment" [NIV]; emphasizes the outworking of God's plan, Fitzmyer 800).

9:32 The pl. art. οἱ turns the prep. phrase σὺν αὐτῷ into a subst. which, together with ὁ . . . Πέτρος, is the subj. of ἦσαν (see 1:6). The pf. ptc. βεβαρημένοι (nom. pl. masc. of pf. pass. ptc. of βαρέω, "weighed down") with ἦσαν is a pluperfect periph. cstr. (ZG 214). Ὕπνῳ, dat. sg. masc. of ὕπνος, -ου, ὁ, "sleep" (instr., Robertson, *Pictures* 131). Διαγρηγορήσαντες (nom. pl. masc. of aor. act. ptc. of διαγρηγορέω, "awake fully"; only here in the NT) could be:

  *1. temp. ingressive aor. (RSV, NASB, HCSB, ESV, NIV; BDAG 227c mng. 2; Robertson, *Pictures* 132; ZG 214; Bock 870);
  2. attendant circumstance (NJB); or
  3. causal (NRSV; BDAG 227c mng. 1 "stayed awake"; Nolland 489; a "possibility" Marshall 385).

Εἶδον, see 2:20. The three disciples see Jesus' glory (τὴν δόξαν αὐτοῦ; perhaps as a preview of the second coming, cf. 9:26; 21:27) and the other two men. Συνεστῶτας (acc. pl. masc. of 2nd pf. act. ptc. of συνίστημι, "stand," intrans.) could be attrib. (modifying the acc. pl. masc. τοὺς δύο ἄνδρας) or the *complement in a double. acc. cstr. (BDAG 279d; BHGNT 318).

9:33 Ἐγένετο, see 1:5. The pres. pass. inf. διαχωρίζεσθαι (of διαχωρίζω, "part," "leave") with ἐν τῷ is temp. Αὐτούς refers to Moses and Elijah as the subj. of the inf. Ἀπ' αὐτοῦ refers to Jesus. Ἐπιστάτα, see 5:5. The adj. καλόν is the pred. nom. of ἐστίν. The adv. ὧδε is the pred. of the inf. εἶναι (see 2:4; ἡμᾶς is the subj.). Peter might be attempting to prevent Moses and Elijah from slipping away (Fitzmyer 801) or to prolong the experience (Marshall 386; Nolland 500). Ποιήσωμεν, see 3:10 (hortatory subjunc., ZG 214). Σκηνάς acc. pl. fem. of σκηνή, -ῆς, ἡ, "tents" (BDAG 928b; ESV), "tabernacles" (NKJV, NASB, HCSB), "shelters" (NIV). The three (tents) are then specified with the appos. accs. μίαν . . . καὶ μίαν . . . καὶ μίαν. The acc. sg. neut. rel. pron. ὅ (of ὅς, ἥ, ὅ) with λέγει (the pres. tense is retained in the rel. clause in indir. discourse, cf. Robertson, *Pictures* 132; Z §348) is the subj. of the causal ptc. εἰδώς (nom. sg. masc. of pf. act. ptc. of οἶδα; Wallace 632; neg. with μή).

9:34 Λέγοντος gen. sg. masc. of pres. act. ptc. of λέγω (a temp. gen. abs. cstr.; αὐτοῦ [Peter] is the subj.; ταῦτα is the dir. obj.). Ἐπεσκίαζεν 3rd sg. impf. act. indic. of ἐπισκιάζω, "overshadow" (ingressive, NASB; Robertson, *Pictures* 133; cf. 1:35, i.e., reflecting the presence of God). Ἐφοβήθησαν, see 2:9 (ingressive, HCSB; Robertson, *Pictures* 133). The inf. εἰσελθεῖν (see 6:6; with αὐτούς as the subj.) with ἐν τῷ is temp. See 3:21 for the temp. cstr. with an aor. inf. (all EVV tr. the inf. cstr. as contemporaneous; cf. Burton §109; Z §390). The first αὐτούς refers to the entire group, whereas the second αὐτούς (as the subj. of the inf.) may only refer to the disciples (as the subj.

of ἐφοβήθησαν; i.e., the disciples are not outside the cloud, Bock 873; Bovon 1.378; Nolland 501; *pace* Marshall 387).

9:35 Λέγουσα, see 1:24 (attrib. modifying φωνή). Ἐκλελεγμένος (nom. sg. masc. of pf. pass. ptc. of ἐκλέγω, "choose"; the var. ἀγαπητός in some mss. [NKJV] is probably an assimilation to Matt 17:5; Mark 9:7) could be attrib. (modifying ὁ υἱός) or subst. (in appos. to ὁ υἱός, BHGNT 320). For the significance of this declaration see 3:22 (here, ἐκλελεγμένος strengthens the allusion to Isa 42:1; αὐτοῦ ἀκούετε adds an allusion to Deut 18:15; Pao and Schnabel 312a). Ἀκούετε 2nd pl. pres. act. impv. of ἀκούω (αὐτοῦ, the obj., could be emphatic, Marshall 388; though it reflects the order of LXX Deut 18:15, Bock 874; Fitzmyer 803). The emphasis is on Jesus' glory and unique relationship with the Father. Previous revelation is a precursor to Jesus and his teaching (cf. 9:22–27).

9:36 The aor. inf. γενέσθαι (see 3:22) with ἐν τῷ is temp. (with the acc. φωνήν as the subj.; "after the voice" HCSB; BDF §404[2]; Z §390; cf. the temp. aor. inf. in 3:21). Εὑρέθη 3rd sg. 2nd aor. pass. indic. of εὑρίσκω (with the nom. μόνος as the complement in a double nom. cstr., BHGNT 321). With the pron. αὐτοί the focus shifts to the response of the disciples. Ἐσίγησαν 3rd pl. aor. act. indic. of σιγάω, "be silent" (ingressive, Robertson, *Pictures* 133). Ἀπήγγειλαν, see 7:18 (οὐδενί is the indir. obj.; the acc. οὐδέν is the dir. obj.; "nothing to no one"!). Οὐδέν is modified by the (partitive) gen. pl. neut. rel. pron. ὧν (of ὅς, ἥ, ὅ; with an unexpressed neut. antecedent demonstrative pron., BDF §294[4]; Robertson, *Pictures* 134; Wallace 340; ZG 214) and ἑώρακαν (3rd pl. pf. act. indic. of ὁράω; the pf. may indicate the lasting effects [BDF §342[2]; Marshall 389] or the "intensive" nature of the action [Burton §§77, 78; R 897], rather than being "aoristic" [BDF §343[3]; T 70]).

FOR FURTHER STUDY

26. The Transfiguration
Bock, D. L. *DJG*[1] 203–6.
Gilbert, M. "Why Moses and Elijah at the Transfiguration?" *RivBib* 57 (2009): 217–22.
*Green, J. B. *DJG*[2] 966–71.
Heil, J. P. *The Transfiguration of Jesus: Narrative Meaning and Function of Mark 9:2–8, Matt 17:1–8 and Luke 9:28–36.* Rome: Pontificio Instituto Biblico, 2000.
Lee, S. S. *Jesus' Transfiguration and the Believers' Transformation: A Study of the Transfiguration and Its Development in Early Christian Writings.* WUNT 2/265. Tübingen: Mohr Siebeck, 2009.
Miller, D. M. "Seeing the Glory, Hearing the Son: The Function of the Wilderness Theophany Narratives in Luke 9:28–36." *CBQ* (2010): 498–517.

HOMILETICAL SUGGESTIONS

Who Is Jesus? Part 2: The Glorious Son (9:28–36)
1. Jesus' glory is glimpsed (9:28–29).
2. Jesus' glory is anticipated (9:30–33).
3. Jesus' glory is unique; he is the Son to be obeyed (9:34–36).

4. Jesus Has the Power of God over Demons, Yet He Is Going to Suffer (9:37–45)

9:37 Ἐγένετο, see 1:5. Τῇ ἑξῆς ἡμέρᾳ is a dat. of time (Wallace 157; for ἑξῆς see 7:11; cf. 8:1). Κατελθόντων gen. pl. masc. of 2nd aor. act. ptc. of dep. κατέρχομαι, "come down" (a temp. gen. abs. cstr.; αὐτῶν is the subj.). Συνήντησεν 3rd sg. aor. act. indic. of συναντάω, "meet" (followed by the dat. complement αὐτῷ).

9:38 Ἰδού, see 1:20. Ἐβόησεν 3rd sg. aor. act. indic. of βοάω, "cry out." Διδάσκαλε, voc. (see 7:40). Δέομαι, see 8:28 ("beg"; the gen. σου is obj.). Ἐπιβλέψαι aor. act. inf. of ἐπιβλέπω (see 1:48; inf. of indir. discourse [Bovon 1.385]; rather than aor. mid. impv. [NKJV]). Ὅτι, causal. Μονογενής ("only child," see 7:12) is a pred. nom.

9:39 Ἰδού, see 1:20. Λαμβάνει 3rd sg. pres. act. indic. of λαμβάνω ("take," "seizes" most EVV). The adv. ἐξαίφνης ("suddenly" see 2:13) modifies κράζει (3rd sg. pres. act. indic. of κράζω). The subj. of κράζει could be the boy (most EVV) or the spirit (NJB; cf. NLT "making him scream"). Σπαράσσει 3rd sg. pres. act. indic. of σπαράσσω, "shake," "convulses" (NRSV, ESV), "throws him into convulsions" (HCSB, NIV). Ἀφροῦ gen. sg. masc. of ἀφρός, -οῦ, ὁ, "foam." The adv. μόγις ("scarcely") modifies ἀποχωρεῖ (3rd sg. pres. act. indic. of ἀποχωρέω, "depart," "leave") and expresses the "reluctance with which the demon gives up its control of the child" (Fitzmyer 808). Συντρῖβον (nom. sg. neut. of pres. act. ptc. of συντρίβω, "beat severely/bruise" BDAG 976c; "mauls" NRSV; "wounding" HCSB; "shatters" ESV; "destroying" NIV) could be attendant circumstance (NRSV, ESV, NIV) or manner (NASB).

9:40 Ἐδεήθην 1st sg. aor. pass. indic. of dep. δέομαι, "beg" (also in 9:38). The gen. τῶν μαθητῶν is obj. (the other nine who were not on the mountain, Bock 882; Fitzmyer 809). Ἵνα is used in place of an inf. (Z §407; ZG 215; it could indicate purpose, BHGNT 323 citing McKay 117). Ἐκβάλωσιν, see 6:22 (subjunc. with ἵνα). Καί, contrastive. Ἠδυνήθησαν 3rd pl. aor. pass. indic. of dep. δύναμαι (neg. with οὐκ; an irregular augment, ZG 215). The emphasis is on the failure of the disciples in striking contrast to 9:1.

9:41 Ἀποκριθείς, see 1:19 (with ὁ Ἰησοῦς specified to signal the change in subj.). Ὦ with (the anar. nom. for voc., Wallace 57–58) γενεὰ ἄπιστος καὶ διεστραμμένη conveys deep emotion (Wallace 68–69; Z §35; ZG 215; though it may function here as a voc. and may be tr. "you" HCSB). Who the voc. refers to, however, is not specified. The "generation" could refer to all those present (the crowd, father, and disciples, Bock 883; Fitzmyer 809; Marshall 391) or the disciples who represent what Jesus says about the generation (Nolland 509; pace Plummer 255 who excludes the disciples from this rebuke; see 7:31 on γενεά). Διεστραμμένη voc. sg. fem. of pf. pass. ptc. of διαστρέφω, "perverse" (NRSV, NIV), "rebellious" (HCSB), "twisted" (ESV; "make crooked" i.e., pervert God's ways, BDAG 237b; cf. 23:2; Acts 13:10; Phil 2:15). Ἕως πότε, "until when" ("how long" most EVV; ZG 215). Ἔσομαι 1st sg. fut. mid. indic. of εἰμί (πρός and a stative vb. has the mng. "with," Wallace 359). Ἀνέξομαι 1st sg. fut. mid. indic. of dep. ἀνέχομαι, "endure," "bear with" (the gen. pl. ὑμῶν is complementary, BDAG 78b). Προσάγαγε 2nd sg. 2nd aor. act. impv. of προσάγω, "bring."

9:42 Προσερχομένου gen. sg. masc. of pres. mid. ptc. of dep. προσέρχομαι (temp. gen. abs. cstr. with αὐτοῦ referring to the boy, HCSB, NIV). Ἔρρηξεν 3rd sg. aor. act. indic. of ῥήσσω, "throw down" (BDAG 905c; most EVV; ZG 215; Bock 884; Fitzmyer 810; not ῥήγνυμι, "tear" RSV, though the aor. form for both is the same; τὸ δαιμόνιον is the subj.; αὐτόν refers to the boy as the obj.). Συνεσπάραξεν 3rd sg. aor. act. indic. of συσπαράσσω, "convulse" (cf. σπαράσσω in 9:39). Ἐπετίμησεν, see 4:35 (τῷ πνεύματι τῷ ἀκαθάρτῳ [cf. 4:33] is the dat. complement). Ἰάσατο 3rd sg. aor. mid. indic. of dep. ἰάομαι. The unusual use of this vb. with an exorcism may be due to the additional physical afflictions that the child had endured due to this demon (Bock 884; παῖδα, acc. sg. masc., see 1:54). Ἀπέδωκεν 3rd sg. aor. act. indic. of ἀποδίδωμι (cf. ἔδωκεν in 7:15).

9:43 Ἐξεπλήσσοντο, see 4:32 (the impf. could be summarizing, BHGNT 325; the parallel pres. gen. abs., however, indicates a progressive sense). Ἐπὶ τῇ μεγαλειότητι is causal (dat. sg. fem. of μεγαλειότης, -ητος, ἡ, "greatness" NASB, HCSB, NIV; "majesty" NKJV, ESV; LSJ 1086c; MM 392b; Bovon 1.387; cf. 2 Pet 1:16; the gen. τοῦ θεοῦ is subj., Wallace 113). Luke's ref. to the crowd's response accentuates the focus on Jesus' power as the power of God (NET; LN 76.2; Marshall 392). The introduction to Jesus' words (of 9:44) parallels the amazement of the crowd at God's majesty (for sim. parallels see 8:39; 17:15–16; 18:43; 24:52–53). Θαυμαζόντων gen. pl. masc. of pres. act. ptc. of θαυμάζω (temp. gen. abs. cstr. with πάντων as the subj.). Ἐπί, causal (ZG 215). The cause of amazement is all the things Jesus was doing (ἐποίει 3rd sg. impf. act. indic. of ποιέω; the rel. pron. οἷς is the obj. [dat. by attraction to πᾶσιν]). Jesus' instruction will be directed to his disciples (εἶπεν πρὸς τοὺς μαθητὰς αὐτοῦ).

9:44 The additional pron. ὑμεῖς could be emphatic (Robertson, *Pictures* 136; ZG 215) or redundant (Wallace 323). Θέσθε (2nd pl. 2nd aor. mid. impv. of τίθημι) with εἰς τὰ ὦτα ὑμῶν is idiomatic for the importance of grasping what Jesus is about to say (cf. 1:44; 7:1; a Heb., Marshall 393). Γάρ could be *epex. (NRSV, HCSB, ESV, NIV; Bock 888; Marshall 393), elliptical ("For [I want you to know]" Nolland 512–13), or causal (see BHGNT 326; possibly NKJV, NASB). There is a contrast between the crowd's amazement and the rejection Jesus will soon experience. The crowd's recognition of Jesus (9:43b) in itself is not criticized. As with 9:22, however, a full grasp of Jesus' identity must understand the significance of the cross (τοὺς λόγους τούτους looks ahead to Jesus' words rather than back to the crowd's response, Bock 888; Bovon 1.393; Fitzmyer 813; Marshall 393; Nolland 513; *pace* BHGNT 327). The pres. pass. inf. παραδίδοσθαι (of παραδίδωμι) is complementary to μέλλει (3rd sg. pres. act. indic. of μέλλω). There is a possible play on words between ὁ . . . υἱὸς τοῦ ἀνθρώπου and ἀνθρώπων (Bock 888; Fitzmyer 814; Marshall 394; Nolland 514).

9:45 Ἠγνόουν 3rd pl. impf. act. indic. of ἀγνοέω, "not know/understand" (with the art. οἱ as the subj., Wallace 212). The impf. could be due to the summary that is provided of the result of Jesus' statements (BHGNT 327), or it could be progressive (being simultaneous with the following periph. cstr., cf. Wallace 543). Καί introduces an epex. statement. The pf. ptc. παρακεκαλυμμένον (nom. sg. neut. pf. pass. ptc. of dep. παρακαλύπτομαι, "hide," "conceal"; agreeing with ῥῆμα) with ἦν is a pluperfect periph.

cstr. (Wallace 649; a Heb. with ἀπό, Marshall 394, citing BDF §155[3]). Ἵνα with the subjunc. αἴσθωνται (3rd pl. 2nd aor. mid. subjunc. of dep. αἰσθάνομαι, "perceive," "understand") could express purpose (Robertson, *Pictures* 136; R 998; Marshall 394) or result (Wallace 473 ["possible"]; Z §353; ZG 215; Bock 889; Fitzmyer 814) and refer to God's purposes (i.e., a divine pass.; Fitzmyer 814; Marshall 394; cf. 18:34; 24:16, 31, 45) rather than the work of the devil (*pace* Nolland 514). Ἐφοβοῦντο 3rd pl. impf. mid. indic. of dep. φοβέομαι. The aor. act. inf. ἐρωτῆσαι (of ἐρωτάω) is complementary (BDAG 1061c; BDF §392[1b]).

5. A Lesson on Greatness (9:46–50)

The contrast between the topic of this argument and the immediately preceding reference to Jesus' suffering illustrates the disciples' lack of understanding concerning the cross. Pride leads to rivalry and antagonism. Prioritizing Jesus leads to death to self and love for others.

9:46 Εἰσῆλθεν, see 1:40 (here, "arose" NRSV, NASB, ESV; "started" HCSB, NIV; with διαλογισμός [mng. "argument" rather than "thoughts" due to the following ἐν αὐτοῖς, Bock 894] as the subj. [nom. sg. masc., see 2:35]). The nom. art. τό introduces an indir. question and turns the following clause into a subst. in appos. to διαλογισμός (on this use of τό see 1:62; Wallace 238). On the optative εἴη see 1:29 (on this "potential optative" with ἄν see also Robertson, *Pictures* 137; Z §356; cf. BDF §385[1]; see 1:62). The comp. adj. μείζων is superl. (BDF §244; Z §§147–48). The pron. αὐτῶν could modify μείζων ("greatest of them" HCSB; BHGNT 328) or τίς ("which of them" most EVV).

9:47 Εἰδώς, see 9:33 (causal). The addition of the gen. (of source) τῆς καρδίας αὐτῶν indicates that διαλογισμόν [acc. sg. masc., see 2:35], although mng. "argument" in 9:46, now has the mng. "thoughts" (NRSV, HCSB) or "reasoning" (ESV; cf. BDAG 232d; for Jesus knowing thoughts see 5:22). Ἐπιλαβόμενος (nom. sg. masc. of 2nd aor. mid. ptc. of dep. ἐπιλαμβάνομαι, "take") is an attendant circumstance ptc. (with ἔστησεν see 4:9; with αὐτό, agreeing with παιδίον [diminutive of παῖς] as the obj.). Παρ' ἑαυτῷ is locat. ("next to him" HCSB; παρά is used as "a marker of nearness in space," BDAG 757a; BDF §238).

9:48 The rel. pron. ὅς and particle ἐάν form the subj. of δέξηται (3rd sg. aor. mid. subjunc. of dep. δέχομαι; indef. subjunc. with ἐάν). The rel. clause ὃς ἐάν . . . ἐπὶ ὀνόματί μου (ἐπί, causal; indicating the basis for the action, Robertson, *Pictures* 137; Z §126; ZG 216; Marshall 396) is the subj. of δέχεται (3rd sg. pres. mid. indic. of dep. δέχομαι). Ἐμέ is emphatic (Bock 896; Fitzmyer 817; Plummer 258). The second rel. clause functions the same way. Ἀποστείλαντά (acc. sg. masc. of aor. act. [subst.] ptc. of ἀποστέλλω) is the obj. of the second δέχεται (cf. also 10:16). Ὑπάρχων (nom. sg. masc. of pres. act. [subst.] ptc. of ὑπάρχω, "be") is modified by the (comp. for superl., Wallace 299; Z §146) adj. μικρότερος ("least"). The pred. adj. μέγας could be "great" (HCSB, ESV; Robertson, *Pictures* 138) or "greatest" (NRSV, NIV; positive for superl., T 31; Wallace 298; Z §146; cf. BDF §245).

9:49 Ἀποκριθείς (see 1:19) shows the close connection between this discussion and the preceding (Ἰωάννης is that of 5:10; 6:14; 8:51; 9:28, 54). Ἐπιστάτα, see 5:5. Εἴδομεν, see 5:26 (the acc. indef. pron. τινα is the obj.). Ἐν τῷ ὀνόματί σου is instr. Ἐκβάλλοντα (acc. sg. masc. of pres. act. ptc. of ἐκβάλλω) is the complement in a double acc. cstr. (BDAG 279d; agreeing with τινα; the acc. δαιμόνια is the obj. of the ptc.). The impf. ἐκωλύομεν (1st pl. impf. act. indic. of κωλύω, "hinder," "prevent" [following 𝔓⁷⁵ᵛⁱᵈ ℵ B L] could be conative (Robertson, *Pictures* 138; Wallace 551; ZG 216; Bock 897; Marshall 399; Nolland 522) or progressive (BHGNT 331). The var. aor. (A D W 𝔐) could be simply "we forbade him" (RSV, NKJV; not specifically a single attempt, *pace* Bock 900). Ὅτι, causal (giving the reason for the disciples' opposition). Ἀκολουθεῖ 3rd sg. pres. act. indic. of ἀκολουθέω (the pres. adds vividness, Bock 898; neg. with οὐκ). Μεθ' ἡμῶν indicates association and is better tr. with ἀκολουθεῖ as "follow with us" (NRSV, ESV; the pron. σοι is implied after ἀκολουθεῖ, BDAG 36d; Marshall 399) rather than "follow us" (HCSB).

9:50 Κωλύετε 2nd pl. pres. act. impv. of κωλύω (neg. with μή; the pres. may indicate a general prohibition, Bock 898). Γάρ, causal (giving the reason such people should not be stopped). The rel. pron. ὅς is the subj. of ἔστιν. The rel. clause ὅς . . . ὑμῶν is the subj. of the second ἐστίν (cf. also 11:23). Κατά followed by the gen. ὑμῶν expresses opposition ("against you").

FOR FURTHER STUDY

27. Children

Balla, P. *The Child-Parent Relationship in the New Testament and Its Environment.* WUNT 155. Tübingen: Mohr Siebeck, 2003.

Francis, J. "Children and Childhood in the New Testament." Pages 65–85 in *The Family in Theological Perspective.* Edited by S. C. Barton. Edinburgh: T&T Clark, 1996.

Gundry-Volf, J. M. "The Least and the Greatest: Children in the New Testament." Pages 29–60 in *The Child in Christian Thought and Practice.* Edited by M. Bunge. Grand Rapids: Eerdmans, 2001.

Oepke, A. *TDNT* 5.639–52.

Reeder, C. *DJG*² 109–12.

HOMILETICAL SUGGESTIONS

What Disciples of Jesus Need (9:37–50)
   1. Faith that recognizes our inability and Jesus' majesty (9:37–43)
   2. Divine illumination that grasps the significance of Jesus' suffering (9:43–45)
   3. Humility that prizes association with Jesus above self-promotion (9:46–48)
   4. Humility that prizes association with Jesus above rivalry (9:49–50)

V. Teaching that Explains the Saving Rule of the Lord (9:51–19:44)

This division in Luke's Gospel begins with an explicit statement of travel to Jerusalem (9:51) and concludes with Jesus' approach to Jerusalem (19:41–44). Along the way numerous travel notes remind the reader of this journey (with refs. to Jerusalem in 9:53; 13:22, 33; 17:11; 18:31; 19:28). This journey is also characterized by predictions of the suffering, death, and resurrection of Jesus ([9:22; 9:44]; 12:50; 13:33; 17:25; 18:31–33 [cf. 24:7]). There is a notable shift in emphasis with fewer miracles (four) and more teaching (seventeen parables). Since it is not a straight-line journey (cf. 10:38–42; 17:11), the refs. to Jerusalem and the emphasis on teaching indicate that all of the material is to be understood in light of the backdrop provided by what Jesus will accomplish in Jerusalem.

A. MINISTRY UNDER THE LORD TO THOSE WHO WELCOME AND THOSE WHO REJECT HIS WORD (9:51–11:54)

A characteristic feature of this section is the varying responses to Jesus' word (e.g., 10:16, 39; 11:1, 23, 28, 32, 54) and Jesus' teaching on how to understand and minister to those who welcome or reject Jesus' word (e.g., 9:55; 10:5–12, 16, 20, 37, 42; 11:2, 23, 52).

1. The Lord Shows How to Respond to Opposition in Samaria on the Way to Jerusalem (9:51–56)

9:51 Ἐγένετο, see 1:5. The pres. pass. inf. συμπληροῦσθαι (of συμπληρόω, "fulfill," "approach," NASB, NIV; "drew near" NRSV, ESV; see 8:23; emphasizing the out-working of God's plan, Fitzmyer 827; Marshall 405) with ἐν τῷ is temp. (the acc. τὰς ἡμέρας is the subj.; cf. the same cstr. in Acts 2:1). The gen. sg. fem. ἀναλήμψεως (of ἀνάλημψις, -εως, ἡ) refers to being "taken up" or "taken away" (LSJ 111b). The ref. to Jerusalem here and the sim. description of Jesus' "exodus" which was about to be fulfilled "in Jerusalem" in 9:31 indicate that the ref. here to Jesus being "taken up" refers not just to the "ascension" (NASB; cf. NIV; Robertson, *Pictures* 139; cf. ἀναλαμβάνω, Acts 1:2, 11, 22), but to the events of Jesus' death, resurrection, and ascension (cf.

Pss. Sol. 4:18; ἀναλαμβάνω in LXX 2 Kings 2:9–11; 1 Macc 2:58; ZG 216; Bock 968; Bovon 2.6; Fitzmyer 828; Marshall 405; Nolland 535). On the Heb. use of καί linking the following vb. with the preceding temp. cstr. cf. Z §456; ZG 216. Αὐτός may indicate emphasis ("he himself," Robertson, *Pictures* 139) or focus on Jesus as the subject of the following action (see 1:17; 3:23; ZG 216; "unstressed" Fitzmyer 827). Ἐστήρισεν 3rd sg. aor. act. indic. of στηρίζω, "establish," "set" (on the form of the aor. cf. BDF §71; with τὸ πρόσωπον is a Sem. idiom for firm purpose, BDAG 945b; ZG 216; Bock 968; Marshall 405). The art. inf. πορεύεσθαι (see 4:42; note πορεύομαι in 9:52, 53, 56, 57) could express purpose (Robertson, *Pictures* 139) or is epex. (BHGNT 333; cf. BDF §400[7]; R 1002, 1068).

9:52 Ἀπέστειλεν, see 7:3. For πρὸ προσώπου see 7:27. Πορευθέντες (see 7:22) could be temp. (NRSV, HCSB) or attendant circumstance (NASB, ESV; BHGNT 332) with εἰσῆλθον (see 7:44). The adv. ὡς with the inf. ἑτοιμάσαι (see 1:17; cf. 1:76) expresses purpose (BDAG 1106a; BDF §391[3]; Robertson, *Pictures* 139; R 1091; Wallace 591; ZG 216). The nature of the "preparation" could refer merely to lodging (Marshall 406) or (in view of the similarities to 1:17, 76; 3:4) to a preaching ministry as well (Bock 969; cf. 9:2; 10:1, 8–11).

9:53 Καί is contrastive ("but") Ἐδέξαντο 3rd pl. aor. mid. indic. of dep. δέχομαι (neg. with οὐκ; here "welcome" LN 34.53; HCSB, NIV). Ὅτι, causal (giving the reason the Samaritan villagers did not welcome Jesus). Πρόσωπον (see 7:27; cf. 9:51, 52), idiomatic for "he," is the subj. of ἦν. It may simply be a way of referring to Jesus as the subj. of the journey to Jerusalem (NASB, NIV; ZG 216). However, the expression here with ref. to "going to Jerusalem" recalls the determination mentioned in 9:51 (HCSB; cf. NRSV, ESV; BHGNT 334). Either way, the destination is the problem (Fitzmyer 830). Πορευόμενον (nom. sg. neut. of pres. mid. ptc. of dep. πορεύομαι) with ἦν is an impf. periph. cstr.

9:54 Ἰδόντες, see 2:17 (temp.; Ἰάκωβος καὶ Ἰωάννης are appos. to the subj. οἱ μαθηταί; for John see refs. at 9:49; James is that of 5:10; 6:14; 8:51; 9:28). Κύριε, voc. (the disciples recognize Jesus has authority as Lord to bring divine judgment, but they misunderstand that this Lord has come to face rejection and go to the cross, Rowe 127). Θέλεις 2nd sg. pres. act. indic. of θέλω. Εἴπωμεν (1st pl. 2nd aor. act. subjunc. of λέγω, here "call" HCSB, NIV; "tell" ESV; "command" NKJV, NRSV, NASB) introduces a clause that is the complement to θέλεις (with ἵνα implied, BDF §366[3]; Burton §171; ZG 216; Marshall 407; though Robertson, *Pictures* 140 suggests the absence of ἵνα indicates two questions here). The aor. act. infs. καταβῆναι (see 3:22) and ἀναλῶσαι (of ἀναλίσκω, "consume" HCSB, ESV; "destroy" NIV) are infs. of indir. discourse.

9:55 Στραφείς (see 7:9) is an attendant circumstance ptc. (with ἐπετίμησεν see 4:35; followed by the dat. complement αὐτοῖς). The additions to 9:55–56 in the NKJV are only found in late mss.

9:56 Ἐπορεύθησαν 3rd pl. aor. pass. indic. of dep. πορεύομαι. Ἕτερος is used for ἄλλος (Z §153).

FOR FURTHER STUDY

28. *Journey to Jerusalem/Central Section*

Blomberg, C. L. "Midrash, Chiasmus, and the Outline of Luke's Central Section." Pages
217–61 in *Gospel Perspectives: Studies in Midrash and Historiography*. Edited by R. T.
France and D. Wenham. Sheffield: JSOT Press, 1983.

*Bock 1.23–25, 957–64.

Farrell, H. K. "The Structure and Theology of Luke's Central Section," *TJ* (1986): 33–54.

Matera, F. J. "Jesus' Journey to Jerusalem (Luke 9.51–19.46): A Conflict with Israel."
JSNT 51 (1993): 57–77.

Moessner, D. P. *Lord of the Banquet: The Literary and Theological Significance of the
Lukan Travel Narrative*. Minneapolis: Fortress, 1989.

*Nolland 2.525–31.

Scobie, C. H. H. "A Canonical Approach to Interpreting Luke: The Journey Motif as
a Hermeneutical Key." Pages 327–49 in *Reading Luke: Interpretation, Reflection,
Formation*. Edited by C. G. Bartholomew, J. B. Green and A. C. Thiselton. Carlisle:
Paternoster, 2005.

29. *Samaritans*

Crown, A. D., ed. *The Samaritans*. Tübingen: Mohr Siebeck, 1989.

Haacker, K. *NIDNTT* 3.449–67.

Kartveit, M. *The Origin of the Samaritans*. Leiden: Brill, 2009.

Pummer, R. *Early Christian Authors on Samaritans and Samaritanism*. Tübingen: Mohr
Siebeck, 2002.

Ravens, D. *Luke and the Restoration of Israel*. Sheffield: Sheffield Academic Press, 1995.

Williamson, H. G. M., and M. Kartveit. *DJG*[2] 832–36.

2. The Lord Must Have Priority in the Kingdom (9:57–62)

9:57 Πορευομένων gen. pl. masc. of pres. mid. ptc. of dep. πορεύομαι (temp. gen. abs. cstr.; αὐτῶν is the subj.). The indef. pron. τις (masc. as evident from αὐτῷ in 9:58, ZG 217) is the subj. of εἶπεν. Ἀκολουθήσω 1st sg. fut. act. indic. of ἀκολουθέω (followed by the dat. complement σοι). Ἀπέρχῃ 2nd sg. pres. mid. subjunc. of dep. ἀπέρχομαι (subjunc. with the indef. ὅπου ἐάν). Κύριε is omitted in early and diverse mss.

9:58 Ἀλώπεκες nom. pl. fem. of ἀλώπηξ, -εκος, ἡ, "fox" (the subj. of ἔχουσιν, see 5:31). Φωλεούς acc. pl. masc. of φωλεός, -οῦ, ὁ, "dens" (HCSB, NIV), "holes" (NASB, ESV). Πετεινά, "birds" (the subj. of an implied ἔχουσιν; for πετεινὰ τοῦ οὐρανοῦ see 8:5). Κατασκηνώσεις acc. pl. fem. of κατασκήνωσις, -εως, ἡ, "nests." Ἔχει, see 5:24. The clause following the interr. ποῦ (a marker of place in an indir. question, BDAG 858a; ZG 217) is the complement of ἔχει. Κλίνῃ 3rd sg. pres. or aor. act. subjunc. of κλίνω, "lay down" (a deliberative subjunc. retained in indir. speech, Robertson, *Pictures* 141; Wallace 478). This is the kind of rejection this man needs to expect.

9:59 Ἀκολούθει, see 5:27 (for ἕτερον see 3:18; 9:56; note ἀκολουθήσω in 9:57, 61). The omission of the voc. κύριε in B* D (NJB) is possibly due to a transcriptional error (Metzger 125; i.e., homoeoteleuton). The strong external evidence favors its inclusion (most EVV; cf. Rowe 128–30). Ἐπίτρεψόν 2nd sg. aor. act. impv. of ἐπιτρέπω, "permit" (NASB), "let" (HCSB, ESV, NIV). Ἀπελθόντι (dat. sg. masc. of 2nd aor. act. ptc. of dep. ἀπέρχομαι) could be attrib. (agreeing with μοι, BHGNT 338; Z §393–95; ZG 217). The aor. act. inf. θάψαι (of θάπτω, "bury") is probably the dir. obj. of ἐπίτρεψόν (BDAG 385a).

9:60 Ἄφες, see 6:42. The acc. τοὺς νεκρούς could be the obj. of ἄφες ("leave the dead to bury") or the subj. of θάψαι ("allow the dead to bury" BHGNT 339). Θάψαι, see 9:59. The gen. ἑαυτῶν is poss. (Z §208; ZG 217). "The dead" who do the burying may be symbolic of the "spiritually dead" (Bock 981; Fitzmyer 836; Marshall 411) or a rhetorical ref. to more important matters (Nolland 543). Ἀπελθών, see 5:14. Διάγγελλε 2nd sg. pres. act. impv. of διαγγέλλω, "make known far and wide" (BDAG 227a; in the NT only here, Acts 21:26; Rom 9:17).

9:61 For ἕτερος see 3:18; 9:56 (R 749). Ἀκολουθήσω, see 9:57. Ἐπίτρεψόν, see 9:59. The aor. mid. inf. ἀποτάξασθαι (of ἀποτάσσομαι, "say farewell to" BDAG 123c) is probably the dir. obj. of ἐπίτρεψόν (BDAG 385a). Εἰς is used for ἐν (Z §§99–100; the pl. masc. τοῖς nominalizes the prep. phrase, Bovon 2.14).

9:62 Ἐπιβαλών nom. sg. masc. of 2nd aor. act. (attrib.) ptc. of ἐπιβάλλω, "put on" (modifying οὐδείς, the subj. of ἐστίν). The art. τήν functions as a poss. pron. (cf. Wallace 215). Ἄροτρον acc. sg. neut. of ἄροτρον, -ου, τό, "a plow." Βλέπων, see 6:42 (attrib.). Εἰς with the neut. pl. art. τά and adv. ὀπίσω ("looking to the things behind") is idiomatic for "looks back" (ZG 217). The nom. sg. masc. adj. εὔθετός (of εὔθετος, -ον, "suitable," "fit"; cf. 14:35) is pred. Τῇ βασιλείᾳ is a dat. of ref. (BHGNT 340).

HOMILETICAL SUGGESTIONS

What Does It Mean to Follow Jesus? (9:51–62)

1. Be prepared for rejection like Jesus (9:51–56, 57–58).
2. Be prepared to prioritize proclaiming the kingdom (9:59–60).
3. Be prepared for single-minded allegiance that does not look back (9:61–62).

3. Ministry Is Initiated by the Lord of the Harvest (10:1–24)

10:1 Μετὰ δὲ ταῦτα (temp.) is general and loosely connects this episode with the preceding events "along the way" (9:57). Ἀνέδειξεν (3rd sg. aor. act. indic. of ἀναδείκνυμι) is used elsewhere in the NT only in Acts 1:24 with the mng. "show." In this context it means "appoint" (all EVV; BDAG 62b; ZG 217). The acc. pl. masc. ἑτέρους (of ἕτερος, -α, -ον; implying a ref. to 9:1–6, ZG 217; Bock 994; Marshall 415; possibly also 9:52, Nolland 550) is the obj. of ἀνέδειξεν and is modified by the adj.

> ἑβδομήκοντα, "70" (א A C L W 𝔐; NKJV, NRSV, NASB, HCSB), or
> ἑβδομήκοντα δύο, "72" (𝔓⁷⁵ B D; NJB, NET, ESV, NIV).

Scribes may have been influenced by the frequent refs. to "seventy" in the OT (e.g., Num 11:16, 24–25; Deut 10:22) and so dropped δύο (note the additional δύο ἄνδρες in Num 11:26). The external evidence for "seventy-two" (early and diverse, with both Alexandrian and Western mss.) is also strong (and δύο may have been accidentally omitted due to its occurrence later in the verse). Thus "seventy-two" may be the best reading here and in 10:17 (cf. Metzger 126–27; Bock 1014–16; Bovon 2.26; Fitzmyer 845–46; Marshall 414–15; Nolland 546). Ἀπέστειλεν, see 7:3. For ἀνά see 9:3 (here, with δύο it is "two each," i.e., "in pairs," HCSB). The additional δύο in some mss. (B K Θ) is possibly an assimilation to Mark 6:7. Πρὸ προσώπου, see 7:27 (cf. also 2:32; in this context, 9:52). The gen. rel. pron. οὗ functions as an adv. "where." The pron. αὐτός is the subj. of ἤμελλεν (see 7:2) and could be intensive ("he himself" most EVV) or unstressed and serve to specify Jesus' own travels (NIV; BHGNT 342). Ἔρχεσθαι, see 9:23 (complementary).

10:2 Ἔλεγεν, see 6:20. The nom. sg. masc. ὁ . . . θερισμός (of θερισμός, -οῦ, ὁ, "The harvest") is the subj. of an implied ἐστίν (the adj. πολύς is the pred.). Θερισμός, used three times in this verse (though nowhere else in Luke-Acts), may refer to the salvation of God's people from judgment (F. Hauck, TDNT 3.133; Bock 995; Marshall 416; "eschatological salvation" Nolland 551). Δέ is contrastive ("but") to the previous μέν clause (ZG 217). The nom. pl. masc. οἱ . . . ἐργάται (of ἐργάτης, -ου, ὁ, "workers" HCSB, NIV) is the subj. of an implied εἰσίν (the adj. ὀλίγοι is the pred.). Οὖν introduces the deduction Jesus makes concerning what should be done about this great harvest: ask "the Lord" for workers. The "Lord" (κύριος) here could be:

1. the Lord Jesus (cf. κύριος in 10:1, 17; Green 411);
2. the Father (cf. κύριος in 10:21, 27; Bock 995; Bovon 2.26; Fitzmyer 846; Marshall 416); or
3. an ambiguous ref. that allows for both (Rowe 133–36).

In view of the use of κύριος in 10:1, 17, and Jesus' "sending" (ἀποστέλλω) of the disciples in 10:3 as "workers" (cf. 10:7), "the Lord of the harvest" here is the Lord Jesus (cf. also before and after this pericope, 9:54, 59, 61; 10:39, 40, 41). Δεήθητε 2nd pl. aor. pass. impv. of δέομαι "ask" (NIV), "pray" (HCSB, ESV; "ask for something pleadingly" BDAG 218a). For the use of ὅπως in place of an inf. see 7:3 (it introduces the content of the prayer; an obj. clause, Burton §200). Ἐκβάλῃ 3rd sg. 2nd aor. act. subjunc. of ἐκβάλλω.

10:3 Ὑπάγετε 2nd pl. pres. act. impv. of ὑπάγω. Ἰδού, see 1:20. Ἀποστέλλω, see 7:27.
Ὡς followed by the acc. pl. masc. ἄρνας (of ἀρήν, ἀρνός, ὁ, "lambs," only here in
the NT) assumes an implied form of ἀποστέλλω (BHGNT 344). Ἐν μέσῳ is locat.
("surrounded by wolves" NET; ἐν with a vb. of motion may mean "into" Z §99; ZG
218). The gen. (pl. masc.) λύκων (of λύκος, -ου, ὁ, "wolves") is partitive. The contrast
between lambs and wolves highlights the "perils, opposition, and hostility" which, like
Jesus, the disciples will experience (Fitzmyer 847). The saying may also point to Jesus
as the Shepherd who protects the flock of God (Marshall 417).

10:4 Βαστάζετε 2nd pl. pres. act. impv. of βαστάζω ("carry," prohibition with μή;
Wallace 487). The following three accs. are the obj. of the prohibition: βαλλάντιον
sg. neut. of βαλλάντιον, -ου, τό, "money bag" (ESV; "purse" NIV; only here, 12:33;
22:35, 36 in the NT); πήραν, "traveling bag" (HCSB; see 9:3); ὑποδήματα, "sandals"
(see 3:16; 15:22). The acc. μηδένα ("no one") is the obj. of the (hortatory) subjunc.
ἀσπάσησθε (2nd pl. aor. mid. subjunc. of dep. ἀσπάζομαι). The use of the subjunc.
may be due to the contingency of meeting someone along the way in order to obey
the command (BHGNT 345). The pres. impv. may view the prohibition as general (Z
§246; ZG 218), or it may focus on the process of traveling, whereas the aor. subjunc.
may take a summary view of the instructions regarding greeting (Huffman 115). The
prohibitions emphasize dependence (on the Lord of the harvest) and focused urgency
(the "greeting" may refer to an elaborate procedure, cf. H. Windisch, *TDNT* 1.499).

10:5 For εἰς ἣν δ' ἂν εἰσέλθητε οἰκίαν see 9:4 (cf. the sim. cstr. in 10:8, 10). The rel.
clause is referred to in the following clause with τῷ οἴκῳ τούτῳ. Λέγετε 2nd pl. pres.
act. impv. of λέγω. The adv. πρῶτον may modify εἰσέλθητε or λέγετε (all EVV). Εἰρήνη
could be a nom. abs. (Wallace 51) or the subj. of an implied vb. such as ἔστω (BHGNT
345). Although the greeting is normal practice, in this context εἰρήνη (see 1:79) is
related to God's salvation that comes through Jesus (Marshall 419; "the blessings of
the kingdom of God" Nolland 552). The "house" refers to the people in the house by
metonymy (Bock 998; Bovon 2.27–28; Marshall 419).

10:6 Ἐάν with the subjunc. ᾖ (3rd sg. pres. act. subjunc. of εἰμί) is the protasis of a
third-class cond. statement. Υἱὸς εἰρήνης (the subj. of the subjunc. ᾖ) is an idiom which
describes the person as characterized by (i.e., "in the likeness of") peace (MM 649a;
Z §42–43; cf. 1:79). Ἐπαναπαήσεται 3rd sg. fut. pass. indic. of dep. ἐπαναπαύομαι
"rest upon." For εἰ δὲ μή γε see 5:36 (here it is "but if not," sim. most EVV; "otherwise" BDAG 278d; this expression stands in for a [negated] repetition of the subjunc.
clause). Ἀνακάμψει 3rd sg. fut. act. indic. of ἀνακάμπτω (intrans.) "return" (i.e., it is
without effect, ZG 218; they should move on).

10:7 Αὐτῇ could be used as an intensive in the locat. phrase ἐν αὐτῇ δὲ τῇ οἰκίᾳ ("in
the same house" NRSV, HCSB, ESV; "in that very house" Robertson, *Pictures* 145)
or sim. to a demonstrative (NASB, R 686; Z §205; ZG 218; cf. the temp. cstr. 10:21).
Μένετε, see 9:4. The nom. pl. masc. of pres. act. ptcs. ἐσθίοντες (of ἐσθίω) and πίνοντες
(of πίνω) could be ptcs. of manner or attendant circumstance (BHGNT 346; cf. Wallace
627). The acc. pl. neut. art. τά with the prep. phrase παρ' αὐτῶν is the obj. of the ptcs.

The whole phrase is an idiom for what those in the house provide their guests (BDF §237[2]; ZG 218). Γάρ, causal (giving the reason for this command). The adj. ἄξιος is pred. (Wallace 308). The art. in ὁ ἐργάτης (see 10:2) is generic (Wallace 228). Μισθοῦ, "wages" (see 6:23; cf. 1 Tim 5:18). Μεταβαίνετε 2nd pl. pres. act. impv. of μεταβαίνω, "go," "move" (prohibition with μή). The pres. may be iter. ("keep moving" NASB; ZG 218; as a habit, Robertson, *Pictures* 146). Ἐξ οἰκίας εἰς οἰκίαν, "from house to house."

10:8 For εἰς ἣν ἂν πόλιν εἰσέρχησθε see 9:4 (sim. to 10:5). Εἰσέρχησθε 2nd pl. pres. mid. subjunc. of dep. εἰσέρχομαι. Δέχωνται, see 9:5. The rel. clause is picked up again with αὐτῇ in 10:9. Ἐσθίετε 2nd pl. pres. act. impv. of ἐσθίω. The art. ptc. τὰ παρατιθέμενα (acc. pl. neut. of pres. pass. ptc. of παρατίθημι, "set before") is subst.

10:9 Τοὺς . . . ἀσθενεῖς (acc. pl. masc. of ἀσθενής, -ές, "the sick") is the obj. of θεραπεύετε (2nd pl. pres. act. impv. of θεραπεύω). Λέγετε, see 10:5. Ἤγγικεν (3rd sg. pf. act. indic. of ἐγγίζω) could mean the kingdom has arrived ("has come upon you" NET; ZG 218) or that it is near and arriving soon ("near to you" NJB). The use of the pf. with ἐφ᾽ ὑμᾶς indicates that the disciples' announcement concerns the presence of an aspect of the (inaugurated) saving rule of God in their ministry as commissioned disciples of Jesus (Bock 1000; Marshall 422; Nolland 554) rather than an announcement of the soon arrival of the (future) kingdom (Fitzmyer 848–49).

10:10 For εἰς ἣν δ᾽ ἂν πόλιν εἰσέλθητε see 9:4 (sim. to 10:5, 8). Δέχωνται, see 9:5 (cf. 10:8; neg. with μή). The rel. clause is picked up again with αὐτῆς. Ἐξελθόντες (nom. pl. masc. of 2nd aor. act. ptc. of dep. ἐξέρχομαι) is an attendant circumstance ptc. and takes on the mood of the impv. εἴπατε (2nd pl. 2nd aor. act. impv. of λέγω; on the form see Z §489). Εἰς τὰς πλατείας αὐτῆς (acc. pl. fem. of πλατύς, -εῖα, ύ, "into its [broad] streets," cf. BDAG 823c; ZG 218) is locat. The disciples do not merely leave an unreceptive town shaking the dust from their feet, they proclaim (εἴπατε) the significance of these actions (Fitzmyer 849).

10:11 Κονιορτόν, "dust" (see 9:5), is the obj. of ἀπομασσόμεθα (1st pl. pres. mid. indic. of dep. ἀπομάσσομαι, "wipe off") and is modified by the attrib. ptc. κολληθέντα (acc. sg. masc. of aor. pass. ptc. of dep. κολλάομαι, "cling to"; intrans.) and ἐκ τῆς πόλεως ὑμῶν εἰς τοὺς πόδας. Ὑμῖν is a dat. of disadvantage ("against you"; ZG 219; Bock 1002; Marshall 423). For a similar expression (though with a different vb.) see 9:5. The strong adversative conj. πλήν introduces a statement that is true in spite of their rejection. The demonstrative pron. τοῦτο points forward ("cataphoric") to the statement introduced by ὅτι (R 401). Γινώσκετε 2nd pl. pres. act. impv. of γινώσκω. For ἤγγικεν see 10:9.

10:12 Ὅτι, recitative. Σοδόμοις is placed forward for emphasis and could be a dat. of ref. or advantage (BHGNT 350). The temp. expression ἐν τῇ ἡμέρᾳ ἐκείνῃ refers to the eschatological judgment (G. Delling, *TDNT* 2.952; Bock 1002; Fitzmyer 849; Nolland 555; cf. ἐν τῇ κρίσει in 10:14; 11:31, 32). The nom. sg. neut. comp. adj. ἀνεκτότερον (of ἀνεκτός, -όν, "bearable"; with the particle ἤ "than" BDAG 432d–33a; Robertson, *Pictures* 146) is the pred. of ἔσται (see 1:14). Τῇ πόλει ἐκείνῃ is a dat. of disadvantage.

The greater judgment that comes from rejecting the greater revelation in Christ is expanded upon in the following woes.

10:13 Οὐαί, see 6:24. Ὅτι, causal (giving the reason for this pronouncement of judgment). Εἰ introduces a second-class ("contrary to fact") cond. statement (Wallace 696; Z §313). The nom. αἱ δυνάμεις ("miracles") is modified by the attrib. γενόμεναι (nom. pl. fem. of 2nd aor. mid. ptc. of dep. γίνομαι) and is the subj. of ἐγενήθησαν (3rd pl. 2nd aor. pass. indic. of dep. γίνομαι). The adv. πάλαι ("long ago") is placed forward for emphasis (Fitzmyer 854). The particle ἄν introduces the apodosis of the cond. statement and relates to μετενόησαν (3rd pl. aor. act. indic. of μετανοέω). This is the first use of μετανοέω in Luke (cf. 11:32; 13:3, 5; 15:7, 10; 16:30; 17:3, 4; cf. μετάνοια in 3:3). Καθήμενοι (see 5:17) expresses manner and is modified by ἐν σάκκῳ [dat. sg. masc. of σάκκος, -ου, ὁ] καὶ σποδῷ ([dat. sg. fem. of σποδός, -οῦ, ἡ] "in sackcloth and ashes"). Σάκκος was made from animal (goat or camel) hair and in this context refers to humiliation and mourning for sin (BDAG 910d; G Stählin, *TDNT* 7.61–62). Jesus pronounces with authority the fact of judgment, the varying amounts of punishment that will be experienced, and what would have happened under different circumstances. The emphasis is on the great significance of what is now proclaimed about God's saving rule in Jesus (Nolland 560).

10:14 The strong adversative πλήν introduces the striking statement that despite the lack of repentance and opportunity for the notoriously wicked Tyre and Sidon, their day of judgment, though real, will be "more bearable" than these Galilean cities. Τύρῳ καὶ Σιδῶνι with the comp. ἀνεκτότερον, see 10:12. Ἐν τῇ κρίσει, see 10:12.

10:15 The pron. σύ emphasizes the shift in subj. to Capernaum. The separation of Capernaum from the ref. to Chorazin and Bethsaida may also emphasize this climactic focus on Capernaum. Ἕως with the gen. οὐρανοῦ is a marker of limit ("as far as" BDAG 423d). The fut. ὑψωθήσῃ (2nd sg. fut. pass. indic. of ὑψόω) with the neg. μή forms a rhetorical question which expects the answer "no" (ZG 219; Bock 1004). Καταβήσῃ 2nd sg. fut. mid. indic. of καταβαίνω (ᾅδου gen. sg. masc. of ᾅδης, -ου, ὁ, "Hades" most EVV; "hell" KJV, NJB; Bovon 2.30). The contrast between οὐρανοῦ and ᾅδου, together with ἐν τῇ ἡμέρᾳ ἐκείνῃ (10:12) and ἐν τῇ κρίσει (10:14), indicate that "Hades" here is a place of punishment (cf. 16:23).

10:16 Ἀκούων (see 6:47; "hears" [ESV] in this context is "listens" [most EVV]) is subst. (the gen. ὑμῶν is obj.). Ἀκούει 3rd sg. pres. act. indic. of ἀκούω. Ἀθετῶν nom. sg. masc. of pres. act. (subst.) ptc. of ἀθετέω, "reject." Ἀθετεῖ 3rd sg. pres. act. indic. of ἀθετέω. The fourfold use of ἀθετέω in this verse (elsewhere in Luke-Acts only in 7:30) indicates the emphasis in this section on the significance of rejecting the message about Jesus. To reject the people who bear this message is to reject Jesus. Furthermore, Jesus declares that to reject him is to reject "the one who sent" him (i.e., the Father). Ἀποστείλαντά, see 9:48 (subst.).

10:17 Ὑπέστρεψαν, see 2:20 (modified by μετὰ χαρᾶς). For the reading "72" see 10:1. Λέγοντες, see 1:66. Κύριε, voc. (cf. 10:1, 2). Καί is ascensive ("even"; ZG 219). The nom. pl. neut. τὰ δαιμόνια is the subj. of ὑποτάσσεται (3rd sg. pres. pass. indic. of ὑποτάσσω, "are subject to" ESV; "submit to" HCSB, NIV). The address κύριε and the (instr., Fitzmyer 861) prep. phrase ἐν τῷ ὀνόματί σου emphasizes Jesus' authority over the demonic realm (Nolland 562; cf. 10:19).

10:18 Ἐθεώρουν 1st sg. impf. act. indic. of θεωρέω. The impf. could be durative (ZG 219), though θεωρέω is most often found in the pres. and impf. (BDF §101; Fitzmyer 862; Nolland 564). This fall is linked in this context to the disciples' ministry of announcing the saving rule of God (Bock 1007; Marshall 429). Τὸν σατανᾶν (see 4:2) is the obj. and πεσόντα (acc. sg. masc. of 2nd aor. act. ptc. of πίπτω; the aor. may be "constative" Robertson, *Pictures* 148; Z §269; Marshall 428; ref. to a final fall, Nolland 563) is the complement (separated by ὡς, Wallace 184) in a double acc. cstr. (BDAG 454c). The placement of the ptc. at the end of the sentence could make it emphatic here (Bock 1006). Ἐκ τοῦ οὐρανοῦ could modify ἀστραπήν (acc. sg. fem. of ἀστραπή, -ῆς, ἡ; "like lightening from heaven" RSV, ESV, NIV) or πεσόντα ("fall from heaven" NRSV, NASB, HCSB).

10:19 Ἰδού, see 1:20. Δέδωκα 1st sg. pf. act. indic. of δίδωμι. The acc. τὴν ἐξουσίαν is the dir. obj. of δέδωκα. The art. pres. act. inf. τοῦ πατεῖν (of πατέω, "trample" HCSB; "tread" ESV; LN 15.226) is epex. (BHGNT 354; Wallace 607; cf. also Wallace 235). Ἐπάνω with the gen. functions as a prep. mng. "over," "on top of" (BDAG 359c; ZG 219) and also modifies ἐξουσίαν. Ὄφεων καὶ σκορπίων (gen. pl. masc. of ὄφις, -εως, ὁ, and σκορπίος, -ου, ὁ), "snakes and scorpions," in this context is likely symbolic of "the forces of the Evil One" (Nolland 565; cf. Fitzmyer 863). Ἐπί is a marker of "power, authority, control of or over someone" (BDAG 365d; here, πᾶσαν τὴν δύναμιν, "*all* the power"). "Satan" (10:18) is now described as "the enemy." Thus, the disciples success (10:17), and evidence of Satan's defeat (10:18), was because the disciples' ministered under the Lord Jesus' authority. The subjunc. ἀδικήσῃ (3rd sg. aor. act. subjunc. of ἀδικέω, "harm"; οὐδέν is the subj. [or an adv. acc. "harm you in nothing" Fitzmyer 863; cf. Marshall 429]) with οὐ μή is an emphatic negation (Z §444; ZG 219).

10:20 The conj. πλήν introduces a statement that will contrast their response to this significant gift from the Lord Jesus with a response to an even greater gift. The demonstrative pron. τοῦτο points forward ("cataphoric") to the statement introduced by ὅτι (see 10:11). Χαίρετε 2nd pl. pres. act. impv. of χαίρω (prohibition with μή). The contrast here, rather than an abs. prohibition, is more like "do not rejoice so much that . . . as that your names" (Sem., Z §445; ZG 219; Bock 1008; Marshall 430). The nom. pl. neut. τὰ πνεύματα is the subj. of ὑποτάσσεται (see 10:17; cf. Wallace 400). Since the first ὅτι is in appos. to ἐν τούτῳ (Wallace 459), the second ὅτι is unlikely to be causal (NKJV, NLT) but introduces the dir. obj. ("rejoice that" most EVV; Wallace 454; perhaps in appos. to an implied ἐν τούτῳ, BHGNT 355), giving the object of rejoicing (BDAG 1075a). The nom. pl. neut. τὰ ὀνόματα is the subj. of ἐγγέγραπται (3rd sg. pf. pass. indic. of ἐγγράφω). The pf. indicates a current state ("are written" most EVV; Bock 1008; Fitzmyer 863) and the pass. (together with ἐν τοῖς οὐρανοῖς) is ref. to divine action (Marshall 430). Unshakeable joy comes from the security of the disciple's relationship with God. Ἐν τοῖς οὐρανοῖς is locat.

10:21 For the pron. αὐτῇ (here in a temp. phrase, "in that same hour" HCSB; or "at that time" NIV; R 686) see 10:7. The expression closely links Jesus' words of rejoicing to the Father with his words about rejoicing to the disciples. Ἠγαλλιάσατο 3rd sg. aor. mid. indic. of ἀγαλλιάω, "exult," "rejoice" ("acknowledgement of divine beneficence and majesty," BDAG 351c). The absence of ἐν in 𝔓⁷⁵ A B C W (SBLGNT) is good evidence for its omission, though it does not affect the mng. (the presence of ἁγίῳ has solid ms. support). The phrase [ἐν] τῷ πνεύματι τῷ ἁγίῳ could be locat. "in a meta-phorical sense" (BHGNT 356) or instr. (Bock 1009; Nolland 571). Ἐξομολογοῦμαι 1st sg. pres. mid. indic. of ἐξομολογέω, "confess," "praise" (NASB, HCSB, NIV; with the dat., Fitzmyer 871), "thank" (NRSV, ESV; Nolland 571). The voc. κύριε is in appos. to the voc. πάτερ (cf. Wallace 70; note the use of κύριε for Jesus in 10:17, Rowe 137). The gen. τοῦ οὐρανοῦ καὶ τῆς γῆς is subord. Ὅτι could be causal ("because" NRSV, HCSB, NIV) or introduce indir. discourse ("that" RSV, NASB, ESV). Ἀπέκρυψας 2nd sg. aor. act. indic. of ἀποκρύπτω, "hide." The antecedent of ταῦτα is the promises of 10:20 (Fitzmyer 873). Σοφῶν gen. pl. masc. of σοφός, -ή, -όν, "wise." Συνετῶν gen. pl. masc. of συνετός, -ή, -όν, "understanding" (RSV, ESV), "intelligent" (NRSV, NASB), "learned" (HCSB, NIV). Σοφῶν καὶ συνετῶν are contrasted with νηπίοις (dat. pl. masc. subst. adj. of νήπιος, -α, -ον, "infants" NRSV, NASB, HCSB; "little children" ESV, NIV). In this context the contrast emphasizes the limitations of human endeavor and thus the need for divine revelation in coming to a saving knowledge of the Father. Καί may express a subord. link ("though you have hidden . . . you have revealed" Z §452; ZG 220; Marshall 434; though cf. Fitzmyer 873). Ἀπεκάλυψας 2nd sg. aor. act. indic. of ἀποκαλύπτω, "reveal" (note the assonance with ἀποκρύπτω, Marshall 434). The particle ναί and the nom. (for voc., BDF §147[3]; Z §34) πατήρ is an emphatic affirma-tion (BDAG 665c). Ὅτι, causal (giving the reason for the Father's [hiding and reveal-ing] actions). Οὕτως "this way" (NASB; "this was what" NIV) was "well-pleasing" (εὐδοκία, see 2:14) "before" him (ἔμπροσθέν σου; i.e., "well-pleasing in Your sight" NASB; "Your good pleasure" HCSB; "you were pleased to do" NIV; Z §83; ZG 220; cf. 5:19; 7:27). The verse emphasizes the initiative and sovereignty of God and thus the basis for the previously mentioned security of the disciples (10:20). The reason Jesus has such intimate knowledge of the Father's purposes is the subject of the following verse.

10:22 The nom. pl. neut. πάντα is the subj. of παρεδόθη (3rd sg. aor. pass. indic. of παραδίδωμι; cf. 4:6). Ὑπὸ τοῦ πατρός μου expresses ultimate agency. The nom. οὐδείς is the subj. of γινώσκει (3rd sg. pres. act. indic. of γινώσκω). The interr. pron. τίς is the pred. of ἐστίν and introduces "an indirect question that serves as the clausal comple-ment of γινώσκει" (BHGNT 357). The only exception (εἰ μή, cf. Z §§469–70; see 4:26) is the Father (ὁ πατήρ is the subj. of an implied γινώσκει). This exclusive knowledge concerning "who the Son is" is reciprocal with respect to the Father (the cstr. is iden-tical). However, there are others (καί) who can know who the Father is. The rel. pron. ᾧ (with the indef. ἐάν) introduces a clause which functions as the subj. of an implied γινώσκει τίς ἐστιν ὁ πατήρ (BHGNT 358; Marshall 435). The nom. ὁ υἱός is the subj. of βούληται (3rd sg. pres. mid. subjunc. of dep. βούλομαι, "will," "want"). The aor. act.

inf. ἀποκαλύψαι (of ἀποκαλύπτω) is complementary. On Jesus as υἱός (three times in this verse) see 1:32. The unique and exclusive relationship between the Son and the Father is stressed along with the distinction between the two in person and order. The Son is sovereign in election (10:22), but the Father has delegated "all things" to the Son (10:22a), things which in the context of Luke 10:21–22 include the authority to reveal a saving knowledge of the Father.

10:23 Στραφείς (see 7:9) is attendant circumstance (with εἶπεν). The opening clause shifts the focus from the revealing activity of the Father and Son (10:21–22) to the privileged position of the disciples as the recipients of this revelation (10:23–24; Nolland 576). Τούς functions here as a poss. pron. ("his disciples" HCSB, NIV; cf. Wallace 215). For the idiom κατ' ἰδίαν ("privately") see 9:10. The nom. adj. μακάριοι (see 6:20) is the pred. of an implied εἰσίν. The attrib. ptc. βλέποντες (see 8:10) modifies ὀφθαλμοί (the art. functions like a rel. pron., Wallace 215). Ὀφθαλμοί (a personification) signals "real, personal experience" (Marshall 438) though with the idea of "see with insight and response" (Nolland 576). The acc. pl. neut. rel. pron. ἅ with βλέπετε (see 8:18; "the things you see" HCSB) is a clause which is the obj. of βλέποντες.

10:24 Γάρ, causal (giving the reason the disciples are blessed). The focus here is on the salvation-historical privilege Jesus' disciples have with the arrival of the fullness of God's revelation in Jesus. Ὅτι introduces indir. discourse. Ἠθέλησαν 3rd pl. aor. act. indic. of θέλω. Ἰδεῖν, see 2:26 (complementary). The acc. pl. neut. rel. pron. ἅ introduces a rel. clause (ἃ ὑμεῖς βλέπετε; see 8:18; cf. 10:23; T 38) which is the obj. of ἰδεῖν (BHGNT 359). Εἶδαν 3rd pl. aor. act. indic. of ὁράω (neg. with οὐκ). Ἀκοῦσαι, see 6:18 (complementary, with ἰδεῖν). The acc. pl. neut. rel. pron. ἅ with ἀκούετε (see 8:18; "the things you hear" HCSB) is a clause which is the obj. of ἀκοῦσαι. Ἤκουσαν, see 1:58 (neg. with οὐκ).

FOR FURTHER STUDY

30. Mission (Israel and the Nations)

Bauckham, R. "The Restoration of Israel in Luke-Acts." Pages 325–70 in *The Jewish World around the New Testament*. Grand Rapids: Baker, 2010.

Bock, *Theology* 279–89, 291–302.

Larkin, W. J. "Mission in Luke." Pages 152–69 in *Mission in the New Testament: An Evangelical Approach*. Edited by W. J. Larkin and J. F. Williams. Maryknoll: Orbis, 1998.

Ravens, D. *Luke and the Restoration of Israel*. Sheffield: Sheffield Academic Press, 1995.

Schnabel, E. J. *DJG*[2] 604–10.

_____. *Early Christian Mission*. 2 vols. Downers Grove: InterVarsity, 2004.

Stenschke, C. W. *Luke's Portrait of Gentiles Prior to Their Coming to Faith*. WUNT 108. Tübingen: Mohr Siebeck, 1999.

Wilson, S. G. *The Gentiles and the Gentile Mission in Luke-Acts*. Cambridge: Cambridge University Press, 1973.

HOMILETICAL SUGGESTIONS

The Joy of Serving the Lord of the Harvest (10:1–24)
  1. Ministry depends on the Lord (10:1–4).
  2. Ministry re-presents the Lord's message (10:5–16).
  3. Ministry should find ultimate joy in knowing the Father through the Son (10:17–24).

4. Ministry Is Characterized by Compassion (10:25–37)

The structure of the discussion between Jesus and the "lawyer" follows a parallel question and answer pattern:

1. The lawyer's question (10:25)
2. Jesus' response with a question (10:26)
3. The lawyer's answer (10:27)
4. Jesus' response (10:28)

Then the pattern is repeated:

1. The lawyer's question (10:29)
2. Jesus' story (10:30–35), which introduces his response with a question (10:36)
3. The lawyer's answer (10:37a)
4. Jesus' response (10:37b)

10:25 Ἰδού, see 1:20. The nom. νομικός τις (see 7:30; the indef. pron. is adj., Wallace 347) is the subj. of ἀνέστη (see 4:16). Ἐκπειράζων (nom. sg. masc. of pres. act. ptc. of ἐκπειράζω, "test" most EVV; elsewhere in Luke, only 4:12) expresses purpose (Wallace 637; Bock 1023; "conative" Robertson, *Pictures* 151; Fitzmyer 880). Διδάσκαλε, voc. (see 7:40). The acc. interr. pron. τί introduces a dir. question and is the obj. of ποιήσας (see 6:49; the ptc. could be cond., Wallace 637; or express means [BHGNT 360]; i.e., with the acc. τί the question is lit. "by doing what will I inherit . . .?" Robertson, *Pictures* 151). Κληρονομήσω 1st sg. fut. act. indic. of κληρονομέω, "inherit" (the fut. is deliberative). To "inherit eternal life" is to receive the resurrection life of the age to come (Bock 1023; i.e., "life with God after death" Marshall 442; cf. the sim. question in 18:18).

10:26 The art. ὁ functions as the subj. of εἶπεν (see 1:29). The forward placement of ἐν τῷ νόμῳ focuses on the νόμος in this reply to the νομικός (BHGNT 361). The interr. τί and πῶς introduce dir. questions (BDAG 900d–901a). Γέγραπται, see 2:23. Ἀναγινώσκεις 2nd sg. pres. act. indic. of ἀναγινώσκω (the dir. obj. is implied). Although ἀναγινώσκεις means "understand" (NET; ZG 220; Nolland 583) here, the tr. "read" (most EVV) keeps the focus on "what is written" as that which is determinative (Marshall 442).

10:27 The art. ὁ functions as the subj. of εἶπεν. Ἀποκριθείς, see 1:19. The following is a quotation from Deut 6:5 and Lev 19:18. The fut. ἀγαπήσεις (2nd sg. fut. act. indic. of ἀγαπάω) functions as an impv. (Wallace 452, 569; Z §280; κύριον is the obj. with τὸν θεόν in appos.). Ἐξ may indicate source ("from") whereas ἐν (three times) is instr. ("with"; LXX only uses ἐξ [three times]). Ἰσχύϊ, "strength" (dat. sg. fem. of ἰσχύς, -ύος, ἡ; LXX has δύναμις). Διανοίᾳ, "mind" (see 1:51; not in LXX Deut 6:5; though it is frequently a variation for "heart" in the LXX, Nolland 584). Taken together, the four terms refer to the totality of a person's life committed to God's honor (as emphasized with the fourfold repetition of ὅλος, Edwards 319). The acc. πλησίον ("neighbor") is the obj. of an implied ἀγαπήσεις (cf. Lev 19:18). Πλησίον, "neighbor" (adv. "near" as a subst.; in form, the neut. of πλησίος, -α, -ον, BDAG 830b; the obj. of an implied impv.

ἀγαπήσεις). The acc. refl. pron. σεαυτόν, following ὡς, is the obj. of an implied (2nd sg. pres. act. indic.) ἀγαπᾷς (cf. BHGNT 362).

10:28 Ὀρθῶς, adv. (cf. 7:43) "correctly" (NASB, NIV), "right" (KJV, NRSV). Ἀπεκρίθης 2nd sg. aor. pass. indic. of dep. ἀποκρίνομαι. Jesus adds a command to his affirmation of a correct answer. Ποίει 2nd sg. pres. act. impv. of ποιέω (cf. τί ποιήσας, 10:25). Ζήσῃ 2nd sg. fut. mid. indic. of ζάω (cf. ζωὴν αἰώνιον, 10:25). The impv. is sim. to a cond., "if you do this, you will live" (cf. Lev 18:5; Marshall 444). Jesus' answer connects "doing" with "life" in response to the lawyer's question. The comprehensiveness of this correct answer (10:27), however, likely leads to the follow-up self-justifying question.

10:29 The art. ὁ functions as the subj. of εἶπεν (see 1:29; for πρός see 1:13). Θέλων nom. sg. masc. of pres. act. (causal) ptc. of θέλω. Δικαιῶσαι aor. act. (complementary) inf. of δικαιόω, "vindicate," "justify" (all EVV; cf. 16:15; 18:14; [18:9]; cf. also 7:29, 35; cf. the use of δίκαιος in contexts of "false righteousness" in 5:32; 15:7; [15:29]; 18:9; 20:20). The follow-up question is introduced as an attempt to vindicate his current conduct (Bock 1027). In light of his opening question (10:25), the following question, therefore, may further exemplify his antagonism toward Jesus. Καὶ τίς introduces a dir. question (BDAG 495b; BDF §442[8]; Z §459). Πλησίον, "neighbor" (see 10:27; on the anar. subst. cf. BDF §266; R 547, 765).

10:30 Ὑπολαβών nom. sg. masc. of 2nd aor. act. ptc. of ὑπολαμβάνω is attendant circumstance and has the mng. here of "took up the question" (HCSB; BDAG 1038c; LSJ 1886d; BHGNT 363; "replied" most EVV; this form and mng. is esp. prominent in LXX Job, Nolland 592). The nom. ἄνθρωπός τις (the subj. of κατέβαινεν 3rd sg. impf. act. indic. of καταβαίνω) is a common way Jesus' parables begin in Luke (12:16; [13:6]; 14:16; 15:11; 16:1, 19; [18:2]; 19:12; [20:9]). The dat. pl. masc. λῃσταῖς (of λῃστής, -οῦ, ὁ, "robber") is the complement to περιέπεσεν (3rd sg. 2nd aor. act. indic. of περιπίπτω, "fall in with" BDAG 804a). The masc. pl. rel. pron. ὅ (the antecedent is λῃσταῖς) is the subj. of ἀπῆλθον (see 2:15). Καὶ . . . καί, "both . . . and" (though for καί with the rel. pron. cf. Z §463; Bovon 2.57). The nom. pl. masc. of aor. act. ptcs. ἐκδύσαντες (of ἐκδύω, "take off," "stripped" all EVV; αὐτόν is the obj.) and ἐπιθέντες (2nd aor. of ἐπιτίθημι, "lay upon," "beat" most EVV; "wounded" NKJV) are temp. (πληγάς, acc. pl. fem. of πληγή, -ῆς, ἡ, "wounds," "blows" is the obj. of ἐπιθέντες; i.e., "lay blows upon"). Ἀφέντες (see 5:11) is attendant circumstance (with ἀπῆλθον). The acc. sg. masc. adj. ἡμιθανῆ (of ἡμιθανής, -ές, "half dead") modifies an implied αὐτόν. The man is helpless and in a desperate condition facing death.

10:31 Κατά with the acc. sg. fem. συγκυρίαν (of συγκυρία, -ας, ἡ) is "by chance" (most EVV; BDAG 513a; only here in the NT), "happened to be" (HCSB, NIV). The nom. ἱερεύς τις (see 1:5) is the subj. of κατέβαινεν (see 10:30). Ἰδών, see 1:12 (temp.; αὐτόν is the obj.). Ἀντιπαρῆλθεν 3rd sg. 2nd aor. act. indic. of dep. ἀντιπαρέρχομαι, "pass by on the opposite side." No reason is given for this sudden transfer except that it was when he saw the man.

10:32 Λευίτης is the subj. of ἀντιπαρῆλθεν (see 10:32). The Levite was a descendant of Levi, was involved with less important tasks at the temple, and was viewed as an assistant to the priests (BDAG 593a; LN 53.91). Γενόμενος (nom. sg. masc. of 2nd aor. mid. [attrib.] ptc. of dep. γίνομαι) is omitted in 𝔓⁷⁵ ℵᶜ B L. Its inclusion, however, in a wide range of mss. (inc. 𝔓⁴⁵ A C D), together with a sim. cstr. in Acts 27:7, may indicate its originality here (Metzger 128; Marshall 448). Together with κατὰ τὸν τόπον (cf. BDAG 511d), the expression emphasizes the Levite's close proximity ("arrived at the place" NKJV). Ἐλθών (see 7:3) and ἰδών (see 1:12; cf. 10:31) are temp. Ἀντιπαρῆλθεν, see 10:31. Again, no reason is given for the sudden move away from the man.

10:33 Σαμαρίτης . . . τις (placed forward to highlight the shift in focus, Bock 1031; Marshall 449; Nolland 594) is the subj. of ἦλθεν (see 2:27). Ὁδεύων (nom. sg. masc. of pres. act. ptc. of ὁδεύω, "go," "travel"; only here in the NT; cf. ὁδός in 9:57; 10:4, 31) could be attrib. (NASB) or temp. (NRSV, NIV). It may highlight more inconvenience for the Samaritan (BHGNT 365) or that this man who had compassion was on a journey (Fitzmyer 887). Κατ᾽ αὐτόν is spatial ("where the man was" NIV). Ἰδών (see 1:12; cf. 10:31, 32) is temp. In place of ἀντιπαρῆλθεν (10:31, 32), the vb. following ἰδών is ἐσπλαγχνίσθη (see 7:13; "had compassion"; cf. σπλάγχνα in 1:78). "Compassion" then is the turning point in the story (Nolland 594) as the following two verses elaborate on what this compassion looked like. In Luke's Gospel, σπλαγχνίζομαι only occurs here, in 7:13 (Jesus' compassion for the widow), and 15:20 (the father's compassion for the prodigal son as a description of Jesus' ministry of "welcoming" sinners); it is used in the other gospels for Jesus' ministry, e.g., in feeding the 5,000 and healing the sick.

10:34 Προσελθών (see 7:14) is attendant circumstance (with κατέδησεν 3rd sg. aor. act. indic. of καταδέω, "bind up," "bandaged" most EVV; only here in the NT; cf. LXX Ezek 34:16). Τραύματα (acc. pl. neut. of τραῦμα, -ατος, τό, "wounds"; only here in the NT) is the obj. of κατέδησεν. Ἐπιχέων (nom. sg. masc. of pres. act. ptc. of ἐπιχέω, "pour on"; only here in the NT) expresses manner (cf. BDF §73). The acc. ἔλαιον καὶ οἶνον ("oil [see 7:46] and wine") is the obj. of ἐπιχέω. Ἐπιβιβάσας (nom. sg. masc. of aor. act. ptc. of ἐπιβιβάζω, "put on"; only here, 19:35; Acts 23:24 in the NT; αὐτόν is the obj.) is attendant circumstance (with ἤγαγεν see 4:9). Κτῆνος acc. sg. neut. of κτῆνος, -ους, τό, "animal" (NKJV, HCSB, ESV), "donkey" (NIV), refers to a domesticated animal used for riding (BDAG 572c; LN 4.6; "horse or mule for riding" LSJ 1002c). Πανδοχεῖον acc. sg. neut. of πανδοχεῖον, -ου, τό, "inn" (only here in the NT). Ἐπεμελήθη 3rd sg. aor. pass. indic. of dep. ἐπιμελέομαι, "take care of" (the gen. αὐτοῦ is complementary, BDF §176[2]).

10:35 Ἐπί with the adv. αὔριον ("tomorrow") is temp. (BDAG 367a; "the next day" all EVV). Ἐκβαλών nom. sg. masc. of 2nd aor. act. (temp.) ptc. of ἐκβάλλω. The acc. δύο δηνάρια ("two denarii" HCSB, ESV, NIV; "two silver coins" NET; see 7:41) is the obj. of ἔδωκεν (see 6:4). Πανδοχεῖ dat. sg. masc. of πανδοχεύς, -έως, ὁ, "innkeeper." Ἐπιμελήθητι 2nd sg. aor. pass. impv. of dep. ἐπιμελέομαι, "take care of" (cf. 10:34; the gen. αὐτοῦ is complementary, Wallace 132). The rel. pron. ὅ with the indef. pron. τι and particle ἄν forms the subj. of the subjunc. προσδαπανήσῃς (2nd sg. aor. act. subjunc. of προσδαπανάω, "spend in addition"; only here in the NT; subjunc. with ἄν). The pres. mid. inf. ἐπανέρχεσθαι (dep. ἐπανέρχομαι, "return"; only here and 19:15 in the NT; the acc. με is the subj. of the inf.) with ἐν τῷ is temp. ("on my return journey" BDF §404[2]; Z §§387, 390). Ἀποδώσω 1st sg. fut. act. indic. of ἀποδίδωμι, "give back."

10:36 Τίς introduces a dir. question. The gen. τούτων τῶν τριῶν ("of these three") is partitive. Δοκεῖ, see 8:18. The adv. πλησίον ("neighbor"; see 10:27, 29) is the pred. of the (complementary) 2nd pf. act. inf. γεγονέναι (i.e., "which of these three does it seem to you became a neighbor"; γεγονέναι "proved to be," "turned out to be" BDAG 199b; cf. Z §289 for the pf.). Ἐμπεσόντος (gen. sg. masc. of 2nd aor. act. [subst.] ptc. of ἐμπίπτω, "fall into") modifies πλησίον (i.e., "a neighbor of the one who fell into"). Λῃστάς, "robbers" (acc. pl., see 10:30). The question recalls the beginning of this episode (10:25–27) when the lawyer correctly identified the need to love one's neighbor and then wanted further clarification on who his neighbor was.

10:37 The neighbor, said the lawyer, was "the one who showed" (ποιήσας, see 6:49) "mercy to him" (on μετά with ποιέω and ἔλεος see 1:72). This description may avoid saying "the Samaritan" (Bock 1034; Marshall 450), but it highlights the point of the story (Nolland 596; also noted by Bock and Marshall). "Compassion" (10:33) is now described as "showing mercy." In Luke's Gospel ἔλεος only occurs here and in chapter 1 where it refers to God's mercy to his people in the coming of Jesus (cf. 1:50, 54, 58, 72, 78 [with σπλάγχνα]). Πορεύου, see 5:24. Jesus' command ποίει repeats 10:28. Jesus has turned the lawyer's question around from a limiting "who is my neighbor?" to an open-ended "who can I be a neighbor to?" (Bock 1034; Fitzmyer 884; though cf. Nolland 597). Thus, the difficulty in "doing" this command comes not from the need for a precise definition of "neighbor" but from the need to have a heart of "compassion" (10:33). The inclusio with 10:25–28 in 10:36–37 may indicate that the "neighbor" the lawyer is to "love" is the despised one who stands before him "on the way" to Jerusalem showing divine compassion and mercy to the weak and needy (Just 454–55; cf. Bovon 2.60–65). To do "likewise" (ὁμοίως) is to follow the way of Jesus (cf. 6:31).

HOMILETICAL SUGGESTIONS

The Heart of Ministry (10:25–37)
1. Recognize the essence of God's will as love for God and people, and recognize our own inadequacy in this (10:25–28).
2. Recognize Jesus as the despised one who expresses compassion for us in going to the cross, and recognize our own need of his mercy (10:29–37a).
3. Recognize the pattern of compassion in Jesus' ministry as the way for us to follow (10:37b).

5. Ministry Prioritizes Undivided Attention to the Word of the Lord (10:38–42)

10:38 The inf. πορεύεσθαι (see 4:42) with ἐν . . . τῷ is temp. (the acc. pl. αὐτούς is the subj. of the inf.). Although the ref. to the journey to Jerusalem may indicate a new section in the narrative, the references to "entering" into a "village" and being "received" indicate a continuation of themes from 9:51–53; 10:1–10. Εἰσῆλθεν, see 1:40. Τινά is indef. (not interr. which would be τίνα, ZG 222). The nom. γυνὴ . . . τις (ὀνόματι is a dat. of ref. [Z §53] and Μάρθα is in appos. to γυνὴ . . . τις) is the subj. of ὑπεδέξατο (3rd sg. aor. mid. indic. of dep. ὑποδέχομαι, "receive," "welcome as a guest" NET; LN 34.53; only here and 19:6 in Luke; cf. δέχομαι in 9:48, 53; 10:8, 10). There is perhaps a parallel between ἄνθρωπός τις (10:30) and γυνὴ . . . τις (cf. 17:19–21). There are some vars. referring to "the house" or "her house." The omission of these in 𝔓⁴⁵⁻⁷⁵ B is likely original (Metzger 129; Marshall 452) so that the sentence ends with "received him."

10:39 The dat. (of poss.) sg. fem. demonstrative pron. τῇδε (of ὅδε, ἥδε, τόδε) refers to Martha (i.e., it is retrospective here, Wallace 328; used for ταύτῃ, BDF §§289, 290[1]; Z §213). The nom. sg. fem. ἀδελφή is the subj. of ἦν. Καλουμένη, see 8:2 (attrib.). Παρακαθεσθεῖσα (nom. sg. fem. of aor. pass. ptc. of dep. παρακαθέζομαι, "sit beside") could be temp. (if the rel. pron. ἥ as the subj. of ἤκουεν is included) or also attrib. (if ἥ is omitted; cf. BHGNT 369; cf. Z §463 for the use of καί with the rel. pron.). The external evidence is evenly divided for rdg. κυρίου (UBS⁵; most EVV), or Ἰησοῦ (SBLGNT; NKJV). Κύριος in 10:41 probably indicates that it should be read here (Fitzmyer 892; cf. Rowe 142–51 for the argument from internal evidence for the sequence κύριος, κύριε, κύριος in 10:39–41). Ἤκουεν 3rd sg. impf. act. indic. of ἀκούω. Mary thus epitomizes an appropriate response to Jesus; willingly submitting to him as Lord and listening to his word (cf. οἱ τὸν λόγον τοῦ θεοῦ ἀκούοντες, 8:21).

10:40 Περιεσπᾶτο 3rd sg. impf. pass. indic. of dep. περισπάομαι, "distracted" ("pulled away" LN 25.238). Περὶ πολλὴν διακονίαν is ref. ("with much serving" NKJV, ESV). Ἐπιστᾶσα (of ἐφίστημι, see 2:38) is attendant circumstance. The use of κύριε (voc.) here is ironic in light of the narrative use of κύριος in 10:19, 41, and Martha's demands (Rowe 150). Οὐ introduces a question that expects the answer "yes" (ZG 222; thus arguing that Jesus would either respond to her exhortation or show no concern). Μέλει 3rd sg. pres. act. indic. of μέλει, "it is a care" (impers.; with the dat. complement σοι, "do you not care"). Ὅτι introduces the content of the concern ("that"). Ἡ ἀδελφή μου is the subj. of κατέλιπεν (3rd sg. 2nd aor. act. indic. of καταλείπω, "leave"; με is the obj. and μόνην is the complement in a double acc. cstr.). The pres. act. inf. διακονεῖν (of διακονέω; cf. the positive uses of this vb. in 4:39; 8:3; 22:26–27, Nolland 604) could be epex. (BHGNT 370) or result (BDF §392[1f]; Bock 1041). Εἰπέ, see 4:3 (impv.). Ἵνα with the subjunc. συναντιλάβηται (3rd sg. 2nd aor. mid. subjunc. of dep. συναντιλαμβάνομαι, "help with"; μοι is complementary) may introduce a purpose clause (BHGNT 370; Bock 1041; or perhaps in place of a complementary inf., Z §407; Fitzmyer 894). In contrast to Mary's submissive attention to hearing Jesus' word, Martha demands Jesus do something for her and tells him what to say (Nolland 606).

10:41 Ἀποκριθείς, see 1:19. Κύριος (most EVV) is better attested than Ἰησοῦς (NKJV; see 10:39; cf. Rowe 142–51 on the internal evidence). The repetition of the voc. Μάρθα emphasizes Jesus' tenderness toward her (BDF §493[1]; cf. 6:46). Μεριμνᾷς 2nd sg. pres. act. indic. of μεριμνάω, "anxious" (ESV), "worried" (HCSB, NIV; cf. 12:11, 22, 25, 26 [12:29–31]; cf. μέριμνα 8:14). Θορυβάζῃ 2nd sg. pres. pass. indic. of θορυβάζω, "troubled" (ESV), "upset" (HCSB, NIV).

10:42 The gen. (sg. neut.) ἑνός (of εἷς, μία, ἕν, gen. ἑνός, μιᾶς, ἑνός; "one thing") is obj. (cf. 16:13). Γάρ is explanatory (Wallace 673; Nolland 605). Μαριάμ is the subj. of ἐξελέξατο (3rd sg. aor. mid. indic. of ἐκλέγω, "choose"). The acc. τὴν ἀγαθὴν μερίδα is the obj. of ἐξελέξατο. The positive adj. ἀγαθήν could be simply positive ("good" RSV, ESV; "made the right choice" HCSB) or used as a superl. ("best" NET; Wallace 298; Z §146; cf. BDF §245; Fitzmyer 894) or comp. ("better" NRSV; NIV; Marshall 454; listed as "possible" by Wallace 298). Μερίδα acc. sg. fem. of μερίς, -ίδος, ἡ, "part" (NRSV), "portion" (ESV). The "good portion" might be a figurative allusion to "the right meal," the word of the Lord (Bock 1042; cf. 4:4). The nom. sg. fem. rel. pron. ἥτις (cf. Z §218) refers back to this "good part" and is the subj. of ἀφαιρεθήσεται (3rd sg. fut. pass. indic. of ἀπαιρέω, "take away"; αὐτῆς is a gen. of separation; perhaps a ref. to the blessings of the kingdom to which Jesus' teaching testified [Marshall 454], or to the privilege of devoted attention to Jesus' word [Nolland 605]).

HOMILETICAL SUGGESTIONS

Priorities in Ministry (10:38–42)
1. Submit to Jesus as Lord and take heed to his word (10:38–39)
2. . . . rather than demand that Jesus take heed to our word (10:40).
3. Prioritize Jesus' word as the greatest blessing (10:42)
4. . . . rather than worry and fret over many distractions (10:41).

6. Prayerful Dependence on a Sovereign Father (11:1–13)

Prayer is the common theme of 11:1–13: (1) the disciples' prayer (11:1–4); (2) a parable (11:5–8) which is applied (11:9–10); and (3) a final illustration (11:11–13). The pericope is framed by references to God as "Father" (11:2, 13), and each section highlights aspects of God's character. The voc. Πάτερ is followed by five requests: two 2nd sg. requests (σου, 11:2) and three 1st pl. requests (ἡμῶν . . . ἡμῖν, ἡμῖν . . . ἡμῶν, ἡμᾶς, 11:3–4).

11:1 Ἐγένετο, see 1:5 (see 1:8 for the temp. cstr. with the inf. [εἶναι, see 2:4]). Αὐτόν is the subj. of the inf. (most EVV specify the subj. as Jesus for clarity). Προσευχόμενον is periph. (see 9:18 for the same cstr.; see 5:16 for refs. to Jesus and prayer). The location is general (ἐν τόπῳ τινί). Ὡς (temp., BDAG 1105d) and ἐπαύσατο (see 5:4) identify the timing of the request from one of his disciples ("when he stopped"). The gen. αὐτοῦ in τις τῶν μαθητῶν αὐτοῦ and τοὺς μαθητὰς αὐτοῦ is a gen. of relationship (for John's disciples and prayer cf. 5:33). Κύριε, voc. Δίδαξον 2nd sg. aor. act. impv. of διδάσκω (impv. as a request, Wallace 488). Προσεύχεσθαι, see 9:29. Ἐδίδαξεν 3rd sg. aor. act. indic. of διδάσκω.

11:2 Although the indef. temp. cstr. ὅταν ("when" most EVV; "whenever" HCSB) with the subjunc. προσεύχησθε (2nd pl. pres. mid. subjunc. of dep. προσεύχομαι) and the pres. impv. λέγετε (see 10:5) refers to general instructions rather than a prayer for all occasions, the general content of the prayer highlights what the fundamental concerns of any disciple of Jesus should be in prayer (cf. BDF §382[4]; Z §325). The additional "in heaven" (cf. NKJV) after the voc. Πάτερ in many mss. is likely an assimilation to Matt 6:9 (omitted in earlier mss. and most EVV; though cf. 11:13). The voc. Πάτερ sets the tone for the following requests (the context of family relationship as well as loving authority and dependence). Those who know Jesus can pray to God as their Father (cf. 10:21–22). The 3rd sg. aor. pass. impv. ἁγιασθήτω (from ἁγιάζω, "sanctify") shows a desire that the Father's name (i.e., reputation or character, Marshall 457) be "honored as holy" (HCSB; "hallowed" most EVV; "treated as holy" BDAG 10a). For the 3rd sg. impvs. ἁγιασθήτω and (2nd aor. act.) ἐλθέτω see NLT, NET; see Fantin 242–43. The ref. to the "kingdom" indicates that the Father is also the sovereign King. This is a request for the saving rule of God to be seen in fullness and is also a reminder that the arrival of the inaugurated saving rule of God is subject to the Father's purposes (see 4:43; cf. Acts 1:7). The disciples' proclamation of this kingdom must be accompanied with prayer (cf. refs. to the kingdom in 9:60, 62; 10:9, 11; 11:17–20). The additional clause in many mss. appears to be an assimilation to Matt 6:10 (Metzger 131–32).

11:3 Τὸν ἄρτον is synecdoche for "food" (cf. Luke 7:33; Marshall 458). The adj. ἐπιούσιον (acc. sg. masc. of ἐπιούσιος, "daily bread" most EVV) has been understood in three main ways (see BDAG 376d–77a; LN 67.183, 206):

1. "necessary for existence" (Fitzmyer 905; Marshall 460, though with a possible eschatological sense also included; Nolland 617, though combined with the next view)

2. "for the current day" (Bock 1054, though with a sense of necessity also included)
3. "for the coming day" (perhaps an eschatological sense of "for the age to come"; Bovon 2.90)

The pres. impv. δίδου along with the distributive prep. phrase τὸ καθ' ἡμέραν (the art. τό making the phrase subst., Wallace 236) makes the eschatological sense unlikely and a request for daily provision of necessities more likely (i.e., a combination of the first two views, Bock 1054; Nolland 617; pres. is iter. BDF §§335, 336[3], 337[4]; Robertson, *Pictures* 158; Z §242; ZG 222).

11:4 The dat. ἡμῖν following the aor. impv. ἄφες (see 6:42) is a dat. of advantage. Γάρ is causal. Rather than indicate a *quid pro quo* (Fitzmyer 899; Marshall 460), it indicates the experiential awareness of the reality of forgiveness in the lives of the disciples (καί "also"). The intensive pron. αὐτοί ("ourselves") is the subj. of ἀφίομεν (1st pl. pres. act. indic. of ἀφίημι, on the form cf. Z §493). Ὀφείλοντι dat. sg. masc. of pres. act. (attrib.) ptc. of ὀφείλω (modifying the dat. [of advantage] παντί; or subst., cf. BDF §413[2]) describes sinners as those "in debt" (HCSB, sim. NKJV, NRSV, NASB, ESV; see 7:41–43; 13:4; clearer than "everyone who sins" NIV). Εἰσενέγκῃς 2nd sg. 2nd aor. act. subjunc. of εἰσφέρω, "bring" (NRSV, HCSB; Robertson, *Pictures* 159), "lead" (ESV, NIV; Bovon 2.92; prohibition request with μή). The link with sin and forgiveness in this context indicates that εἰς πειρασμόν (see 4:13) is an acknowledgment of weakness and a request for help to avoid sin ("temptation"; a prayer for "spiritual protection" Bock 1055), rather than a request to be spared from trials (*pace* BHGNT 375; Nolland 618–19).

11:5 The interr. cstr. τίς ἐξ ὑμῶν is the subj. of ἕξει (3rd sg. fut. act. indic. of ἔχω; the fut. functions as a subjunc., BDF §366[1]; BHGNT 376; McKay 95; R 875) and πορεύσεται (3rd sg. fut. mid. indic. of dep. πορεύομαι). The cstr. τίς ἐξ ὑμῶν (tr. as "Suppose one of you" NRSV, NASB, HCSB; ἐξ is used for the partitive gen., Z §80) will occur regularly as an introduction to Jesus' parables (cf. 11:11; 12:25; 14:28; 15:4; 17:7; possibly a Sem., BDF §469; e.g., Hag 2:3). In this context it introduces a rhetorical question which runs through to the end of 11:7 (Bock 1058; 11:5–7 reflects Sem. coordinate style, with the protasis introduced by κἀκεῖνος in 11:7; BDF §442[3]; ZG 223; Marshall 464; Nolland 623–24). Πρὸς αὐτόν refers to the "friend" (i.e., the neighbor; thus, the 3rd sg. πορεύσεται is tr. as "you go [to him]" in NRSV, NIV; *pace* Fitzmyer [909] who tr. πορεύσεται as "he comes" with the "friend" as the subj.). Μεσονυκτίου gen. sg. neut. of μεσονύκτιον, -ου, τό, "midnight" (gen. of time, ZG 223). Εἴπῃ (3rd sg. 2nd aor. act. [deliberative] subjunc. of λέγω) parallels the previous two fut. indics. (Robertson, *Pictures* 159; Marshall 464; perhaps reflecting the implied cond. of the question ["if he goes"], Nolland 623–24). Φίλε, voc. Χρῆσόν 2nd sg. aor. act. impv. of κίχρημι, "lend."

11:6 Ἐπειδή is a marker of cause (BDAG 360d; BDF §455[1]; cf. 7:1), giving the reason for the request in 11:5. Παρεγένετο, see 8:19. The pronouns in the clause φίλος μου . . . πρός με refer to the subj. of 11:5 (τίς ἐξ ὑμῶν) so that this "friend" is the one who has come "on a journey" (HCSB), and this has prompted this subject's midnight visit to his neighbor friend (note that the arrival time of the traveler is not specified). The acc. rel. pron. ὅ introduces a rel. clause which is the obj. of ἔχω (see 7:40; Wallace 661; neg. with οὐκ). Παραθήσω 1st sg. fut. act. indic. of παρατίθημι, "set before" (the fut. may be used here in place of a subjunc. expressing consequence, BDF §379; Burton §318; ZG 223).

11:7 Κἀκεῖνος (nom. sg. masc., crasis of καὶ ἐκεῖνος, of ἐκεῖνος, -η, -ο) is the subj. of the (deliberative) subjunc. εἴπῃ (see 11:5; for ἀποκριθείς see 1:19) and refers to the neighbor who is being asked for bread. Ἔσωθεν, adv. "from inside." Κόπους acc. pl. masc. of κόπος, -ου, ὁ, "trouble." Πάρεχε, see 6:29 (the impv. is neg. with μή; "don't give me trouble," "do not bother me" most EVV; Huffman 142; in this context, "stop bothering me" cf. Robertson, *Pictures* 159; ZG 223; cf. the same idiom in 18:5). The "trouble" is then explained: the door is "already" (ἤδη) "closed" (κέκλεισται 3rd sg. pf. pass. indic. of κλείω, "locked" HCSB, NIV; "bolted" NJB), and everyone, including the children, are in bed (εἰς τὴν κοίτην [acc. sg. fem. of κοίτη, -ης, ἡ]; εἰς for ἐν, with a stative vb., BDF §205; Wallace 363; Z §§99–100). Παιδία, in this context is diminutive in mng. as well as form (of παῖς; BDAG 749d; ZG 223). Thus, he is "not able" (δύναμαι 1st sg. pres. mid. indic. of dep. δύναμαι; neg. with οὐ) to "get up and give" anything (ἀναστάς [see 4:38] is an attendant circumstance ptc. with the complementary inf. δοῦναί [see 1:73], ZG 223).

11:8 The point of the story in 11:5–7 is now given (λέγω ὑμῖν). Εἰ καί introduces the protasis of a (first-class) cond. sentence (completed with διά γε) and is concessive ("even though" NRSV, NASB, HCSB, NIV; BDAG 278d; BDF §372[3]; Burton §285; Robertson, *Pictures* 159; Wallace 663; see 18:4). The subj. of δώσει (see 1:32; neg. with οὐ, cf. BDF §428[1]) is the friend inside the house (specified in NET). Ἀναστάς (see 4:38) is attendant circumstance. Διά with the art. inf. εἶναι is causal (see 2:4; φίλον, adj., is a pred. acc., Wallace 192). Διά with the (emphatic) acc. (sg. fem.) τὴν ἀναίδειαν (of ἀναίδεια, -ας, ἡ) is also causal (the enclitic particle γέ serves to focus attention on a single idea and thus has a limiting function ["at least," NRSV; BDAG 190b–c; R 1148]; cf. 18:5). Ἀναίδεια is probably not merely "persistence" (NKJV, NJB, NRSV, NASB, HCSB; though cf. 11:9–10) but "shamelessness" ("shameless persistence" NLT; ZG 223; "impudence" ESV; "shameless audacity" NIV; "shameless asking" Cassirer; "lack of sensitivity to what is proper" BDAG 63d; LN 66.12; LSJ 105c; MM 33d). Although some view the pron. αὐτοῦ with ἀναίδειαν as a ref. to the person in the house (i.e., he acts [in a positive sense] "to avoid shame" NLT n.; "to preserve his good name" NIV n.; Marshall 465; Nolland 625–26), ἀναίδειαν αὐτοῦ should be understood as referring to the "shamelessness" of the one making the request (specified in NLT, NET, HCSB, NIV; cf. Bock 1059–60; Bovon 2.102–3; Fitzmyer 912) for the following reasons: (1) the original question refers to the one making the request (11:5); (2) the emphasis in 11:7 is on the *unwillingness* of the person in the house to get up to help; (3) the term ἀναίδεια is uniformly used in a thoroughly negative sense in Greek lit. outside the NT to refer to rude and offensive action (cf. Snodgrass's study of 258 occurrences); (4) the pron. αὐτῷ earlier in 11:8 refers to the one making the

request; (5) the immediately preceding αὐτοῦ refers to the petitioner; (6) the following application continues the point with an encouragement for the petitioner to keep
asking (11:9–10). Sim. to 18:1–8, the story provides a contrast to how God responds
to our requests (i.e., a "how much more" argument). God is not like the person in the
house (or the judge of 18:1–8); he is not unwilling to answer prayer. Ἐγερθείς nom. sg.
masc. of 2nd aor. pass. ptc. of ἐγείρω (attendant circumstance; intrans. "he will get up
and give" ZG 223). The gen. (complement) pl. neut. rel. pron. ὅσων with χρῄζει (3rd
sg. pres. act. indic. of χρῄζω, "have need of") is a rel. clause which is the obj. of δώσει
(BDAG 1089a; see 1:32, and above).

11:9 Κἀγώ (crasis of καὶ ἐγώ; the subj. of λέγω) links this conclusion to the preceding illustration ("So" NRSV, HCSB, NIV). Αἰτεῖτε 2nd pl. pres. act. impv. of αἰτέω.
Δοθήσεται, see 6:38. Ζητεῖτε 2nd pl. pres. act. impv. of ζητέω (cf. 12:29, 31). Εὑρήσετε,
see 2:12. Κρούετε 2nd pl. pres. act. impv. of κρούω, "knock." Ἀνοιγήσεται 3rd sg. 2nd
fut. pass. indic. of ἀνοίγω. The three pres. impvs. could be gnomic or iter. (HCSB; Z
§242; ZG 223; Bock 1060; Fitzmyer 914). The impvs. are an encouragement to keep
praying because of the willingness of God to answer prayer (i.e., not because of the
term ἀναίδεια). Δοθήσεται and ἀνοιγήσεται are divine passives (Z §236; Bock 1061;
Marshall 467; Fitzmyer 915).

11:10 Γάρ, causal (giving the reason for the encouragement to keep praying). Αἰτῶν,
nom. sg. masc. of pres. act. (subst.) ptc. of αἰτέω (see 1:66). Λαμβάνει, see 9:39 (here
"receives"). Ζητῶν nom. sg. masc. of pres. act. ptc. (subst.) of ζητέω. Εὑρίσκει 3rd sg.
pres. act. indic. of εὑρίσκω. Κρούοντι dat. sg. masc. of pres. act. ptc. (subst.) of κρούω,
"knock." Ἀνοιγήσεται (𝔓⁴⁵ ℵ C L; SBLGNT), see 11:9 (the pres. is found in 𝔓⁷⁵ B D).

11:11 The acc. τίνα . . . τὸν πατέρα (with the partitive ἐξ ὑμῶν, "from which father of
you," see 11:5) is the obj. of αἰτήσει (3rd sg. fut. act. indic. of αἰτέω; deliberative; the
acc. ἰχθύν [see 5:6] is perhaps the obj. of an implied inf. [of ἐπιδίδωμι], cf. BHGNT
380). The art. in ὁ υἱός (the subj. of αἰτέω) functions as a poss. pron. (Wallace 215).
Ὄφιν acc. sg. masc. "snake" (see 10:19; ἰχθύος, see 5:6). Ἐπιδώσει 3rd sg. fut. act.
indic. of ἐπιδίδωμι. The additional ref. to "bread" and a "stone" in many mss. may be
an assimilation to Matt 7:9 (Metzger 132).

11:12 Αἰτήσει, see 11:11. The acc. sg. neut. ᾠόν (of ᾠόν, -οῦ, τό) is "egg." Ἐπιδώσει, see
11:11. Σκορπίον acc. sg. masc. "scorpion." In Luke's Gospel the terms ὄφις ("snake")
and σκορπίος ("scorpion") are only found elsewhere in 10:19 where they are also found
together. In 10:19 they were symbolic of the forces of Satan that are overcome under
Jesus' authority in the disciples' proclamation of the kingdom.

11:13 Εἰ introduces the protasis of a first-class. cond. sentence. Οἴδατε 2nd pl. pf.
act. indic. of οἶδα (ὑμεῖς is the subj.). Ὑπάρχοντες (see 7:25) could be attrib. (NRSV,
NASB, HCSB, ESV) or *concessive (NIV). The acc. δόματα ἀγαθά ("good gifts") is
the obj. of the (complementary) pres. act. inf. διδόναι (of δίδωμι). The dat. neut. πόσῳ
(of πόσος) with the adv. μᾶλλον ("how much more") could be used as an interr. (KJV,
NASB, HCSB) or an exclamation (NKJV, NRSV, ESV, NIV; cf. BDAG 855d; BHGNT
381). The art. in the phrase ὁ ἐξ οὐρανοῦ is included (with other variations) in 𝔓⁴⁵ A B

C D (SBLGNT) and omitted in $\mathfrak{P}^{75}$ ℵ L Ψ (in brackets in UBS[5]). If included, the art. makes the prep. phrase attrib. and modifies ὁ πατήρ (all EVV; BDF §437; BHGNT 381; Fitzmyer 915; Marshall 469). If omitted, the prep. phrase modifies δώσει (see 1:32; "he will give the Holy Spirit from heaven," ZG 224; Nolland 631). Αἰτοῦσιν dat. pl. masc. of pres. act. (subst.) ptc. of αἰτέω (see 11:9–12). The concluding ref. to the Father and the Holy Spirit may form an inclusio with the opening ref. to the Father and the kingdom in 11:2. The outworking of the kingdom through Jesus' disciples will be by means of prayer and the empowering work of the Holy Spirit (cf. Acts 1:3–5, 6–8; cf. also the var. refs. to the Holy Spirit in mss. 162, 700, and Gregory of Nyssa for 11:2, Marshall 458).

FOR FURTHER STUDY

31. Prayer (11:1)

Crump, D. M. *DJG*[2] 684–91.

_____. *Jesus the Intercessor: Prayer and Christology in Luke-Acts.* WUNT 2/49. Tübingen: Mohr Siebeck, 1992.

*Marshall. I. H. "Jesus—Example and Teacher of Prayer in the Synoptic Gospels." Pages 113–31 in *Into God's Presence: Prayer in the New Testament.* Edited by R. N. Longenecker. Grand Rapids: Eerdmans, 2001.

*O'Brien, P. T. "Prayer in Luke-Acts." *TynBul* 24 (1973): 111–27.

*Snodgrass, K. "*Anaideia* and the Friend at Midnight." *JBL* 116 (1997): 505–13.

HOMILETICAL SUGGESTIONS

Knowing the Character of the Father Helps Us Pray to Him (11:1–13)

1. Recognize God's greatness (11:1–4).
2. Recognize God's generosity (11:5–10).
3. Recognize God's goodness (11:11–13).

7. The Lord Is Stronger Than Satan; the One Who Receives His Word Is Blessed (11:14–28)

11:14 Although no specific setting is given and a new topic is introduced here, the transition to this episode from the previous teaching on prayer is seamless (καί, "Now"; cf. βασιλεία 11:2, 17, 18, 20; ἐξ οὐρανοῦ 11:13 and 16). The impf. periph. cstr. ἐκβάλλων (nom. sg. masc. of pres. act. ptc. of ἐκβάλλω) with ἦν sets the scene for what follows (Marshall 472). The end of the verse indicates that the nom. sg. neut. adj. κωφόν ("mute"; see 1:22) does not refer to the demon as such but that the demon caused the person to be mute. Ἐγένετο, see 1:5. The gen. τοῦ δαιμονίου is the subj. of ἐξελθόντος (gen. sg. neut. of 2nd aor. act. ptc. of dep. ἐξέρχομαι) in a temp. gen. abs. cstr. (cf. Wallace 655). The nom. sg. masc. ὁ κωφός ("the mute man" ESV) is the subj. of ἐλάλησεν (see 1:55; in this context the vb. may be ingressive, NET; BDF §331; Fitzmyer 920). Ἐθαύμασαν, see 1:63.

11:15 The miracle is described succinctly in 11:14 in order to focus on Jesus' teaching (11:17–26) to the antagonistic responses by "some" (τινὲς δὲ ἐξ αὐτῶν, partitive, cf. 11:5) and "others" (ἕτεροι, 11:16). The response of τινὲς . . . ἕτεροι shows that ἐθαύμασαν (11:14) is not positive in this context. Ἐν Βεελζεβούλ is instr. (Z §119; Fitzmyer 920). The following appos. dat. (Wallace 153) explains that Βεελζεβούλ is a ref. to Satan (cf. σατανᾶς, 11:18; see 4:2) as "the ruler" (τῷ ἄρχοντι, dat. sg. masc. of ἄρχων, -οντος, ὁ; NRSV, HCSB; cf. 8:41) of demons (for Βεελζεβούλ cf. BDAG 173d; C. Brown, *NIDNTT* 3.472–73). Ἐκβάλλει 3rd sg. pres. act. indic. of ἐκβάλλω (note that the power to cast out demons is not denied).

11:16 Πειράζοντες (nom. pl. masc. of pres. act. ptc. of πειράζω; the obj. is an implied αὐτόν) expresses the purpose of the following request (ἐζήτουν, see 5:18; Wallace 636, 637). The impf. could be ingressive (NET) but is more likely to be iter. (NRSV, HCSB, ESV; Robertson, *Pictures* 161; though ζητέω is rarely aor.).

11:17 Εἰδώς, see 9:33 (causal, Wallace 631; for αὐτός see 1:17). Διανοήματα (acc. pl. neut. of διανόημα, -ατος, τό), "thoughts" (see 5:22, διαλογισμός). Ἐφ᾽ ἑαυτήν expresses opposition (BDAG 366a). Διαμερισθεῖσα nom. sg. fem. of aor. pass. (attrib.) ptc. of διαμερίζω, "divide" (cf. 11:18; 12:52–53). Ἐρημοῦται 3rd sg. pres. pass. indic. of dep. ἐρημόομαι, "desolate" (cf. BDAG 392a; LN 20.41), "destroyed" (ESV), "ruined" (NIV). Πίπτει 3rd sg. pres. act. indic. of πίπτω. In the final clause ἐπί could be "upon" (NRSV), but it probably again expresses opposition ("against" most EVV; BDAG 366a; Fitzmyer 921; Nolland 638). Thus, "house against house falls" reflects a similar image to the previous ref. to a kingdom ("divided" is supplied by most EVV).

11:18 Εἰ introduces the protasis of a first-class cond. sentence (i.e., "for the sake of argument" [cf. 11:19]; a sim. cstr. with εἰ is found in 11:19–20; the apodosis in this verse is completed with the question introduced by πῶς). The expression εἰ δὲ καί continues the point being made (cf. BDAG 278c). The last ref. to σατανᾶς was 10:18 where he was also described as "fallen" (πίπτω). Ἐφ᾽ ἑαυτόν, see 11:17. Διεμερίσθη 3rd sg. aor. pass. indic. of διαμερίζω, "divide." Σταθήσεται 3rd sg. fut. pass. indic. of ἵστημι

(intrans., "how can" ZG 224). Ὅτι, causal (giving the reason Jesus has given the preceding argument, "since" Z §420). Ἐν Βεελζεβούλ is instr. (Βεελζεβούλ is interchangeable here with σατανᾶς, cf. 11:15). Λέγετε, see 7:33. The (pres. act.) inf. ἐκβάλλειν (of
ἐκβάλλω) is used in indir. discourse (Robertson, *Pictures* 161).

11:19 For εἰ see 11:18. Ἐν Βεελζεβούλ is instr. (cf. 11:15). Ἐκβάλλω 1st sg. pres. act.
indic. of ἐκβάλλω. The nom. οἱ υἱοί (perhaps a ref. by metonymy to "followers," i.e.,
Jewish exorcists, LN 36.39; BHGNT 385; Bovon 2.120; Fitzmyer 921; Marshall 474;
Nolland 639; or a ref. to Jesus' disciples, Bock 1077–78; cf. 9:1; 10:17–19) is the subj.
of ἐκβάλλουσιν (3rd pl. pres. act. indic. of ἐκβάλλω). Ἐν τίνι (interr. pron.) is instr. Διὰ
τοῦτο, causal (referring back to the previous argument, Wallace 333). The pron. αὐτοί
(referring to the "sons") is the (emphatic, ZG 224) subj. of ἔσονται (3rd pl. fut. mid.
indic. of εἰμί). Κριταί nom. pl. masc. of κριτής, -οῦ, ὁ, "judge." The "judgment" could
be eschatological (whether with ref. to Jewish exorcists, Bovon 2.120; Fitzmyer 922;
Marshall 475; or to Jesus' disciples, Bock 1078) or simply "what will other Jewish
exorcists . . . make of such a view?" (Nolland 639).

11:20 For εἰ see 11:18. Ἐν δακτύλῳ (dat. sg. masc. of δάκτυλος, -ου, ὁ) is instr. and
refers by metonymy to the power of God (cf. LXX Exod 8:15; Marshall 475; Bovon
2.121 suggests "skillfulness"). Ἐκβάλλω, see 11:19. The particle ἄρα ("then") introduces the result of the protasis (BDAG 127c; BHGNT 386). Ἔφθασεν 3rd sg. aor.
act. indic. of φθάνω, "come" (most EVV), "arrived" (NLT; cf. NET; LN 13.123).
Although the aor. does not by itself refer to "realized eschatology" here, neither does
it just affirm the certainty or imminence of the kingdom (*pace* BHGNT 386; following
Caragounis). The arrival of the kingdom here is stated as a consequence (ἄρα) of Jesus'
ministry, in particular his display of divine power over demons. Ἐφ᾽ ὑμᾶς (locat.,
BDAG 366c) supports the idea of the arrival or presence of the eschatological kingdom
in a preliminary way (BDAG 169a, 1053d; Bock 1080; Fitzmyer 922; Marshall 476;
Nolland 640–41).

11:21 Ὅταν, perhaps "so long as" (NJB; ZG 224). Ὁ ἰσχυρός is the subj. of φυλάσσῃ
(3rd sg. pres. act. subjunc. of φυλάσσω, "guard") and continues the refs. to Satan in
these verses (cf. 11:15; though the art. here is generic, all EVV; ZG 224). The ptc.
of means καθωπλισμένος (nom. sg. masc. of pf. pass. ptc. of καθωπλίζω, "arm fully")
modifies φυλάσσῃ. Αὐλήν (acc. sg. fem. of αὐλή, -ῆς, ἡ), may refer to a walled enclo-
sure, such as a courtyard (MM 91d–92a), or to a dwelling complex which has a courtyard (LSJ 276c), such as a "palace" (RSV, NKJV, ESV; cf. LN 7.6), "castle" (NRSV;
Fitzmyer 922; Nolland 641), "estate" (HCSB), or more generally, "house" (NASB,
NIV; BDAG 150c also lists "palace" as probable; Bock 1083). The nom. pl. neut. of
pres. act. (subst.) ptc. ὑπάρχοντα (of ὑπάρχω, "be, exist," "possessions") is the subj. of
ἐστίν (a progressive present, Wallace 519). Ἐν εἰρήνῃ describes his "possessions" (in
the context of the language of "fully armed," "guard") as "safe" (ESV, NIV), i.e., from
danger (BDAG 287c; a Septuagintalism, Marshall 477).

11:22 The conj. ἐπάν ("when," "as soon as" ZG 224) is temp. The adj. ἰσχυρότερος is
comp. ("stronger"; αὐτοῦ is a gen. of comparison). Ἐπελθών (nom. sg. masc. of 2nd

aor. act. ptc. of dep. ἐπέρχομαι, "come upon," "attacks" most EVV) is attendant circumstance (with νικήσῃ 3rd sg. aor. act. subjunc. of νικάω, "overpower" NRSV, HCSB,
NIV). The acc. sg. fem. πανοπλίαν (of πανοπλία, -ας, ἡ, "full armor") is the obj. of αἴρει
(see 8:12). The "full armor" is that which he had trusted in (ἐπεποίθει 3rd sg. pluperfect
act. indic. of πείθω [intrans.]; ἐπί is used with the dat. rel. pron. ᾗ is used as a marker of
basis, BDAG 364d). Σκῦλα (acc. pl. neut. of σκῦλον, -ου, τό), "spoils" (NKJV), "plun-
der" (HCSB, NIV). Διαδίδωσιν 3rd sg. pres. act. indic. of διαδίδωμι, "divides" (most
EVV), "distribute" (NASB).

11:23 The ptc. ὤν (see 3:23; with the art. ὁ; neg. with μή) is attrib. Συνάγων nom. sg.
masc. of pres. act. (attrib.) ptc. of συνάγω (with the art. ὁ; neg. with μή). Σκορπίζει 3rd
sg. pres. act. indic. of σκορπίζω. This summary of the previous warfare imagery shows
there are only two alternatives (cf. 10:1–24).

11:24 The previous warning against neutrality seems to remain in view here. Experience
of an exorcism without an accompanying trust in the "stronger one" (11:22) still leaves
one weak and vulnerable to Satan's destructive designs (Fitzmyer 925). The subjunc.
ἐξέλθῃ (3rd sg. 2nd aor. act. subjunc. of dep. ἐξέρχομαι) with ὅταν is temp. The arts.
τό (with ἀκάθαρτον πνεῦμα) and τοῦ (with ἀνθρώπου) are generic. Διέρχεται 3rd sg.
pres. mid. indic. of dep. διέρχομαι. The gen. pl. masc. adj. ἀνύδρων, of ἄνυδρος, -ον,
"waterless" (most EVV; "arid" NIV), may refer to dry places such as a desert (NLT;
Bock 1091; Bovon 2.125; Fitzmyer 925) or to such places which are uninhabited with
people (Marshall 479). Ζητοῦν (nom. sg. neut. of pres. act. ptc. of ζητέω) may express
manner or purpose (BHGNT 389). Ἀνάπαυσιν acc. sg. fem. of ἀνάπαυσις, -εως, ἡ,
"rest." Εὑρίσκον (nom. sg. neut. of pres. act. ptc. of εὑρίσκω; neg. with μή) could be
temp. (NLT) or cond. (the following statement of the demon is not meant as inevitable, Bock 1093; Marshall 480; Nolland 645). Ὑποστρέψω 1st sg. fut. act. indic. of
ὑποστρέφω. Ἐξῆλθον 1st sg. 2nd aor. act. indic. of dep. ἐξέρχομαι.

11:25 Ἐλθόν nom. sg. neut. of 2nd aor. act. (temp.) ptc. of dep. ἔρχομαι. Εὑρίσκει, see
11:10 (the cond. force of 11:24b continues in paratactical style, with the apodosis
completed in 11:26, Marshall 480). The acc. sg. masc. of pf. pass. ptcs. σεσαρωμένον
(of σαρόω, "sweep") and κεκοσμημένον (of κοσμέω, "adorn," "in order" most EVV; cf.
BDAG 560c; Bovon 2.126) complement an implied τὸν οἶκον (cf. BDAG 411d; BDF
§416[2]; 15:8). The implication is that the house is clean and ordered but empty (clarified with an assimilation to Matt 12:44 in some mss.).

11:26 Πορεύεται, see 7:8. Παραλαμβάνει 3rd sg. pres. act. indic. of παραλαμβάνω.
The adj. πονηρότερα (of πονηρός) is comp. ("more evil"; ἑαυτοῦ is a gen. of comparison). Εἰσελθόντα nom. pl. neut. of 2nd aor. act. (temp. [BHGNT 390] or *attendant
circumstance [Wallace 643]) ptc. of dep. εἰσέρχομαι. Κατοικεῖ 3rd sg. pres. act. indic.
of κατοικέω, "dwell" (the subj. of the sg. vb. is neut. pl.). The nom. pl. neut. τὰ ἔσχατα,
of ἔσχατος, -η, -ον ("last things," "last state" ESV) is the subj. of γίνεται (3rd sg.
pres. mid. indic. of γίνομαι). The pred. adj. χείρονα (of κακός) is comp. ("worse"; τῶν
πρώτων is a gen. of comparison).

11:27 Ἐγένετο, see 1:5. The pres. act. inf. λέγειν with ἐν τῷ is temp. (see 1:8). The antecedent of ταῦτα is Jesus' teaching in 11:17–26 (BHGNT 390; Bovon 1.130). The subj. of the (attendant circumstance) ptc. ἐπάρασά (nom. sg. fem. of aor. act. ptc. of ἐπαίρω, "lift up"; φωνήν, "voice," is the obj.) is τις . . . γυνή (modified by the partitive ἐκ τοῦ ὄχλου; on the "unemphatic" order of τις φωνὴν γυνή cf. BDF §473[1]). Μακαρία is the pred. adj. of ἡ κοιλία (see 1:15) . . . καὶ μαστοί (nom. pl. masc. of μαστός, -οῦ, ὁ, "breasts"). Βαστάσασα nom. sg. fem. of aor. act. (attrib.) ptc. of βαστάζω, "bear." Ἐθήλασας 2nd sg. aor. act. indic. of θηλάζω ("suck," "nursed" most EVV). The saying, as an idiomatic reference to Jesus' mother (cf. NIV), is a way of complimenting Jesus (Bock 1094; Bovon 2.130; Fitzmyer 928), in this context, as the "stronger one" who overcomes such evil.

11:28 Αὐτὸς δέ (cf. 1:17; 3:23) and the particle μενοῦν ("rather," "on the contrary") emphasize Jesus' response to the woman's blessing. The particle μενοῦν, however, need not imply a rejection of the remark (*pace* Marshall 482; cf. BDAG 630d; BDF §450[4]; R 1151; Bock 1095; Bovon 2.131–32; Fitzmyer 927–29; a "correction" rather than a simple rejection or affirmation, Nolland 649; "even more" HCSB; cf. 1:45, 48). It may merely emphasize Jesus' point that a positive response to him must be accompanied with genuine adherence to his word (for τὸν λόγον τοῦ θεοῦ see 5:1; cf. also 6:46–49; 8:15, 21; 9:26, 35; 10:39). Μακάριοι is the pred. adj. of the (subst.) ptcs. ἀκούοντες (see 2:47) and φυλάσσοντες (see 2:8; "keep" HCSB, ESV; "obey" NIV).

HOMILETICAL SUGGESTIONS

Jesus or Satan (11:14–28)
1. The arrival of the kingdom leaves no room for neutrality (11:14–23).
2. Entrance into the kingdom requires a transforming trust in God's word (11:24–28).

8. Judgment Will Come for Rejecting Jesus' Word (11:29–32)

11:29 Ἐπαθροιζομένων gen. pl. masc. of pres. pass. ptc. of dep. ἐπαθροίζομαι, "gather together," "increasing" (most EVV; BDAG 357a; "pressed in" NLT; Nolland 651; temp. gen. abs. cstr.; τῶν . . . ὄχλων is the subj.). Ἤρξατο, see 4:21. The inf. λέγειν (see 3:8) is complementary. For γενεὰ αὕτη see 7:31. The acc. σημεῖον (cf. 11:16; three times in this verse) is the obj. of ζητεῖ (3rd sg. pres. act. indic. of ζητέω). Δοθήσεται, see 6:38 (neg. with οὐ). The gen. Ἰωνᾶ is epex. (Z §45; ZG 225; Marshall 484; Nolland 652; εἰ μή "except," see 4:26).

11:30 The ref. to Jonah in 11:29 is now explained (γάρ). Ἰωνᾶς is the subj. of ἐγένετο (σημεῖον is the pred.; Wallace 43). The ref. to Jonah being a sign "to the Ninevites" implies that the "sign" involves his warning of judgment which the Ninevites responded to with repentance (Nolland 653; cf. 11:32). Τῇ γενεᾷ ταύτῃ (see 7:31), is a dat. of advantage. The following verses (11:31–32) indicate that in this context the "sign" of the "Son of Man" involves the message of Jesus (the fut. ἔσται refers in this context to the earthly ministry of Jesus [Bock 1097; Fitzmyer 933, 936; Nolland 653] rather than his resurrection [Marshall 485] or second coming [Bovon 2.141]).

11:31 Βασίλισσα νότου, "queen of the south" (gen. sg. masc. of νότος, -ου, ὁ; on the anar. cstr. cf. Z §171). Ἐγερθήσεται 3rd sg. fut. pass. indic. of ἐγείρω (the parallel with ἀναστήσονται in 11:32 indicates that this refers to resurrection from the dead [BHGNT 393] rather than just "stand up with," "accuse" [*pace* Fitzmyer 936; Marshall 486]). For ἐν τῇ κρίσει see 10:12 (ἐν is temp. and refers to the final judgment [Nolland 650]; rather than just "rise up in judgment"). Τῆς γενεᾶς ταύτης, see 7:31. Κατακρινεῖ 3rd sg. fut. act. indic. of κατακρίνω, "condemn." Ὅτι, causal (giving the reason for this verdict). Ἦλθεν, see 2:27. Περάτων, gen. pl. neut. of πέρας, -ατος, τό, "end." The inf. ἀκοῦσαι (see 6:18) expresses purpose (ZG 225). The gen. Σολομῶνος is subj. For καὶ ἰδού see 1:20. The comp. neut. adj. πλεῖον is subst. ("something greater" ZG 225; with an implied ἐστίν). The neut. may refer to something about Jesus such as *his teaching (Bock 1098; Marshall 486; cf. 7:35; 10:21–22), or a quality or characteristic of Jesus (BHGNT 394; T 31). The use of ἀκοῦσαι here and κήρυγμα in 11:32 indicate that the point here is again the need to respond to the message of Jesus about his authority and right to bring God's promised saving rule. Not only is the teaching of Jesus greater than Solomon's wisdom, but the people have this message in their presence (ὧδε) and need not travel to "the ends of the earth" to hear it.

11:32 Ἀναστήσονται 3rd pl. fut. mid. indic. of ἀνίστημι. For ἐν τῇ κρίσει see 10:12. Τῆς γενεᾶς ταύτης, see 7:31. Κατακρινοῦσιν 3rd pl. fut. act. indic. of κατακρίνω, "condemn." Ὅτι, causal (giving the reason for this verdict). Μετενόησαν, see 10:13. Εἰς τὸ κήρυγμα ("at the proclamation" BDAG 291b; BDF §207[1]; Z §§98, 106; ZG 225) gives the occasion for this repentance (temp. NJB, NET; causal, BDAG 291c). For καὶ ἰδού see 1:20. Πλεῖον, see 11:31.

9. Jesus' Word Is a Shining Light (11:33–36)

11:33 The following sayings continue the emphasis on appropriate responses to Jesus' teaching (here described in terms of light; this saying is also given in 8:16). Jesus' word is light; it is wickedness to suggest further signs are required. Οὐδείς is the subj. of τίθησιν (see 8:16). Ἅψας, see 8:16 ("light," "kindle" with the acc., temp., Wallace 627). Μόδιον acc. sg. masc. of μόδιος, -ίου, ὁ, "basket" (LN 6.151). Εἰς κρύπτην is locat. (acc. sg. fem. of κρύπτη, -ης, ἡ, "in a cellar" NASB, HCSB, ESV; MM 361a; "hidden place" NET, sim. NIV; BDAG 570d; LN 28.78; ["crevice"] Fitzmyer 940; Marshall 488). The strong external evidence (Alexandrian and Western) favors the inclusion of οὐδὲ ὑπὸ τὸν μόδιον (SBLGNT; most EVV; brackets in UBS[5]; omitted by NRSV). There is an implied τίθησιν after ἀλλά. Λυχνίαν, "lampstand" (see 8:16). The purpose is then given (ἵνα with the subjunc. βλέπωσιν [see 8:10]). Εἰσπορευόμενοι, see 8:16 (subst.).

11:34 The art. and pron. with ὀφθαλμός indicate that this is the subj. of ἐστίν (NASB, HSCB, ESV, NIV; BHGNT 396; λύχνος, see 8:16; cf. 11:33, 36). "Your eye" refers by metonymy to that which perceives and receives, and "your whole body" to the person (for σῶμά see MM 621a; Bock 1100–01; Fitzmyer 940). Ὅταν with the subjunc. ᾖ (of εἰμί; see 10:6) is temp. (cf. 11:22). Ἁπλοῦς nom. sg. masc. of ἁπλοῦς, -ῆ, -οῦν, "single" (KJV; cf. BDAG 104c; MM 58b–c), "good" (NKJV, HCSB), "healthy" (NRSV, ESV, NIV; LN 23.132; "in good condition, sound" LSJ 191a; i.e., in the metaphorical sense of "whole-hearted, single-minded" Marshall 489; the contrast with πονηρός makes it unlikely that ἁπλοῦς is "generous," *pace* Fitzmyer 940). The nom. sg. neut. adj. φωτεινόν (of φωτεινός, -ή, -όν, "full of light") is pred. The conj. ἐπάν is temp. (see 11:22). Πονηρός, "bad" (NASB, HCSB, ESV; cf. 11:29, 39), "unhealthy" (NIV; cf. NRSV; BDAG 852a; "diseased" Nolland 656) is the pred. of an implied ὁ ὀφθαλμός σου. The nom. sg. neut. adj. σκοτεινόν (of σκοτεινός, -ή, -όν, "darkness") is pred. (the "second predicate position," Wallace 308).

11:35 Σκόπει 2nd sg. pres. act. impv. of σκοπέω, "consider" (NRSV), "watch out" (NASB), "take care" (HCSB). The pres. indicates continued care (Bock 1101). The neg. μή with the indic. ἐστίν adds a sense of apprehension to the statement ("lest" ESV; "whether . . . is not" NRSV; BDF §370; BHGNT 397; Robertson, *Pictures* 164; R 1045; Marshall 489). The art. τό turns the prep. phrase ἐν σοί into an attrib. adj. (BHGNT 397).

11:36 Εἰ introduces the protasis of a third-class cond. sentence as the conclusion to 11:33–36 (οὖν). Φωτεινόν, "full of light" (see 11:34) is pred. (τὸ σῶμά σου ὅλον is the subj. of an implied ἐστίν). The repetition of ὅλον and φωτεινόν is emphatic (Bock 1102). Ἔχον (nom. sg. neut. of pres. act. ptc. of ἔχω; neg. with μή) is in appos. to the neut. adj. φωτεινόν (BHGNT 398; ZG 226; see 11:34, the acc. μέρος τι σκοτεινόν ["any part darkened"] is the obj. of ἔχον). The adj. φωτεινόν is the pred. of ἔσται (the nom. adj. ὅλον is the subj., Marshall 490). The dat. τῇ ἀστραπῇ (see 10:18; "with its rays" NRSV, ESV) is instr. (Robertson, *Pictures* 164). Φωτίζῃ 3rd sg. pres. act. subjunc. of φωτίζω, "give light." The disciple of Jesus has received the light of the kingdom and anticipates the fullness of that kingdom (cf. Bock 1103; Marshall 487).

HOMILETICAL SUGGESTIONS

Why Is There Judgment for Rejecting Jesus? (11:29–36)

1. Jesus' message is greater than the greatest preachers of the past, and it is wickedness (πονηρά, 11:29) to seek for more (11:29–32).
2. Jesus' message is light in the midst of darkness, and it is wickedness (πονηρός, 11:34) to reject it (11:33–36).

10. Warnings to the Religious Leadership: Judgment Will Come (11:37–54)

11:37 The temp. inf. cstr. (ἐν τῷ and the inf. λαλῆσαι [see 1:19]) links the following episode closely with the preceding sayings: here is how the unresponsive react to the searching light of Jesus (cf. 11:53–54). The aor. inf. could refer to antecedent action ("When Jesus had finished speaking" NIV, sim. NJB, NASB; Z §390; ZG 226; Bock 1111; Fitzmyer 946; Marshall 493; Nolland 663), contemporaneous action ("While Jesus was speaking" ESV; cf. NRSV; "As He was speaking" HCSB; Edwards 353), or simply a marker of the general time of the event ("As he spoke" NET; Burton §109; Robertson, *Pictures* 165; Wallace 595). The context favors antecedent action here (see 1:8 for the temp. inf. cstr. and 3:21 for this cstr. with the aor. and examples in Luke). Ἐρωτᾷ 3rd sg. pres. act. indic. of ἐρωτάω (a historic pres., Robertson, *Pictures* 165; ZG 226). Pharisees (first mentioned, together with scribes, in 5:17) will be referred to repeatedly throughout the following discourse (11:38–39, 42–43, 53). Ὅπως is used with the subjunc. ἀριστήσῃ (3rd sg. aor. act. subjunc. of ἀριστάω, "eat a meal"; cf. ἄριστον, 11:38) to introduce indir. discourse (in place of ἵνα; BHGNT 400; McKay 116–17; Robertson, *Pictures* 165; ZG 226). Εἰσελθών (see 1:9) is attendant circumstance (with ἀνέπεσεν 3rd sg. 2nd aor. act. indic. of ἀναπίπτω, "recline"; cf. 14:10; 17:7; 22:14; cf. κατάκειμαι, 5:25, 29; 7:37).

11:38 Ἰδών, see 1:12 (temp.). Ἐθαύμασεν, see 7:9. Ὅτι could be causal or *introduce indir. discourse following the vb. of perception (BDAG 731d–32a; taking ἐθαύμασεν as trans., Wallace 553). Ἐβαπτίσθη 3rd sg. aor. pass. indic. of βαπτίζω (the pass. implies "his hands were not washed first" BHGNT 400; or the pass may be "permissive" ["did not allow himself to be washed"] Wallace 441; a ref. to "ritual washing" HCSB, sim. NASB; BDAG 164b; Robertson, *Pictures* 165; ZG 226; not prescribed in the Law, Bock 1111; Marshall 494). Πρὸ τοῦ ἀρίστου is temp. (πρό takes the gen; ἀρίστου gen. sg. neut. of ἄριστον, -ου, τό, "noon day meal" BDAG 131c; LSJ 241b; Bock 1111; Fitzmyer 947; Marshall 493–94).

11:39 For ὁ κύριος see 7:13. Jesus, the Lord, will follow this opening denunciation (11:39–41) with six woes: three regarding Pharisees (11:42–44) and three regarding scribes (11:46–52). The pron. ὑμεῖς with the adv. νῦν ("as it is" BDAG 681d; "as a matter of fact" ZG 226) is emphatic. The acc. neut. art. τό is subst. (cf. ZG 226) and makes the adv. ἔξωθεν ("outside") the obj. of καθαρίζετε (2nd pl. pres. act. indic. of καθαρίζω). The gen. τοῦ ποτηρίου καὶ τοῦ πίνακος (gen. sg. masc. of πίναξ, -ακος, ὁ, "of the cup and dish") is partitive. The nom. neut. art. τό is subst. and the adv. ἔσωθεν ("inside"; modified by the poss. ὑμῶν, Marshall 495) becomes the subj. of γέμει (3rd sg. pres. act. indic. of γέμω, "fill"; BHGNT 401). The gen. ἁρπαγῆς καὶ πονηρίας ("greed and wickedness" ESV, NIV; gen. sg. fem. of ἁρπαγή, -ῆς, ἡ; and of πονηρία, -ας, ἡ; cf. πονηρός, 11:34) is a gen. of content.

11:40 The masc. pl. adj. ἄφρονες (of ἄφρων, -ον, gen. –ονος; "fools") is voc. (cf. 12:20; D. Zeller, *EDNT* 1.184d–85b). Ποιήσας (see 6:49; subst.) is the subj. of ἐποίησεν (see 1:49). Καί, "also." The question with οὐχ expects the answer "yes" (BDF §427[2]; ZG 226). Thus, the division between the internal and external is impossible to maintain

(Bock 1114). For the acc. art. τό with ἔξωθεν and ἔσωθεν see 11:39 (here the obj. of ἐποίησεν; for the art. as subst., see Wallace 233).

11:41 Ἐνόντα (acc. pl. neut. of pres. act. [subst.] ptc. of ἔνειμι, "within," "from what is within" HCSB; "those things that are within" ESV; "inside you" NIV) could be adv. ("inwardly," T 247) but is likely the obj. of δότε (see 9:13) in a double acc. cstr. (or perhaps an acc. of respect, Bock 1114; Marshall 495; Nolland 664). The acc. sg. fem. ἐλεημοσύνην (of ἐλεημοσύνη, -ης, ἡ) is the complement in a double acc. cstr. (BHGNT 402; "as alms" ESV; δότε ἐλεημοσύνην, a Heb., Edwards 355). For καὶ ἰδού see 1:20. The adj. καθαρά ("clean") is pred.

11:42 The exclamation οὐαί (see 6:24) introduces a series of "woes" expressing the judgment that will come (cf. 11:50–51) because of what they do (ὅτι is causal) in contrast (ἀλλά) to what they ought to have done (11:41; Marshall 496). The dat. τοῖς Φαρισαίοις is in appos. to ὑμῖν. Ἀποδεκατοῦτε 2nd pl. pres. act. indic. of ἀποδεκατόω, "tithe." Ἡδύοσμον acc. sg. neut. of ἡδύοσμον, -ου, τό, "mint." Πήγανον acc. sg. neut. of πήγανον, -ου, τό, "rue." Λάχανον acc. sg. neut. of λάχανον, -ου, τό, "garden herb" (with anar. πᾶν "every kind of" Z §188; ZG 227). Καί, "yet" (NASB; "but" NIV). Παρέρχεσθε 2nd pl. pres. mid. indic. of dep. παρέρχομαι, "pass by," "neglect" (ESV, NIV; BDAG 776a). Κρίσιν, in this context is "justice" (cf. e.g., 20:47). The gen. τοῦ θεοῦ is obj. (Wallace 118; ZG 227; Marshall 498). The infs. ποιῆσαι (see 1:72; a "global" aor. Z §253; ZG 227) and παρεῖναι (2nd aor. act. inf. of παρίημι, "neglect"; neg. with μή) are complementary to ἔδει (3rd sg. impf. act. indic. of δεῖ, cf. 2:49; this vb. in the indic. is a "potential indic.," Wallace 452; cf. BDF §360[1]; Fitzmyer 948–49; "if you were to do . . ., it would be necessary to," Nolland 665–66). Κἀκεῖνα acc. pl. neut., see 11:7 ("and those things," "the others" HCSB, ESV) is the obj. of παρεῖναι.

11:43 For οὐαί and ὅτι see 11:42. Ἀγαπᾶτε, see 6:32. Πρωτοκαθεδρίαν acc. sg. fem. of πρωτοκαθεδρία, -ας, ἡ, "front seat" (HCSB), "best seat" (ESV), "most important seats" (NIV; cf. 14:7–11; 20:46 [pl. πρωτοκαθεδρίας]). Ἀσπασμούς, "greetings" (acc. pl. masc., see 1:29). Ἀγοραῖς, "marketplaces" (see 7:32).

11:44 For οὐαί and ὅτι see 11:42. Μνημεῖα, "tombs." Ἄδηλα nom. pl. neut. of ἄδηλος, -ον, "unmarked" (attrib. adj., Wallace 239). Καί is consecutive (Z §455γ; or equivalent to a rel. clause, Marshall 499). Περιπατοῦντες (nom. pl. masc. of pres. act. ptc. of περιπατέω) would be attrib. if the art. οἱ is included (א B C L). If it is omitted (𝔓75 A D K 𝔐), the ptc. could be temp. or concessive (BHGNT 404; ZG 227). Ἐπάνω, adv. "above," "over." Οἴδασιν 3rd pl. pf. act. indic. of οἶδα (neg. with οὐκ). The implication is that they are outwardly disguised containers of death and negatively influence others (perhaps by conveying uncleanness and defilement, Bock 1117).

11:45 Ἀποκριθείς, see 1:19. The Pharisees and "lawyers" are often grouped together (for νομικῶν see 7:30; cf. 5:17). Λέγει is a rare historic pres. in Luke (Wallace 529; Fitzmyer 949; Marshall 499; cf. φησίν 7:40). Διδάσκαλε, voc. (see 7:40). Λέγων could be temp. ("when you say" (HCSB, NIV) or express means ("in saying" ESV; ZG 227). Καί, "also." Ὑβρίζεις 2nd sg. pres. act. indic. of ὑβρίζω, "insult" (see 18:32).

11:46 For οὐαί and ὅτι see 11:42. Καί, "as well" (NASB), "also" (HCSB, ESV). Φορτίζετε 2nd pl. pres. act. indic. of φορτίζω, "load, burden." Φορτία (cognate) acc. pl. neut. of φορτίον, -ου, τό, "burden" (diminutive form of φόρτος without diminutive mng., Z §485; ZG 227; the double acc. cstr. is that of "person and thing" Wallace 182; i.e., "you load people with burdens" most EVV). Δυσβάστακτα acc. pl. neut. adj. of δυσβάστακτος, -ον, "hard to bear." The "burdens" in this context appear to be excessive rules that go beyond Scripture (Bock 1119). The intensive pron. αὐτοί is the subj. of προσψαύετε (2nd pl. pres. act. indic. of προσψαύω, "touch") and could be unstressed (Fitzmyer 949; see 1:17), but in this context it is likely emphatic (BDAG 152d; BHGNT 405; see 3:23). The dat. ἑνί is instr. (the gen. τῶν δακτύλων ὑμῶν ["one of your fingers"; see 11:20] is partitive). The dat. τοῖς φορτίοις ("these burdens" HCSB) is complementary (BDAG 887b).

11:47 For οὐαί and ὅτι see 11:42. Οἰκοδομεῖτε 2nd pl. pres. act. indic. of οἰκοδομέω. The gen. τῶν προφητῶν could be poss. or obj. ("to the prophets" HCSB; "for the prophets" NIV). Οἱ . . . πατέρες is the subj. of ἀπέκτειναν (3rd pl. aor. act. indic. of ἀποκτείνω).

11:48 The particle ἄρα ("therefore" HCSB) introduces the result of this activity (BDAG 127c). Συνευδοκεῖτε 2nd pl. pres. act. indic. of συνευδοκέω, "approve," "consent to." The dat. τοῖς ἔργοις is complementary (BDAG 970c). The gen. τῶν πατέρων ὑμῶν is subj. Ὅτι, causal. The intensive pron. αὐτοί is emphatic and contrasts with ὑμεῖς (Wallace 322; the contrast is marked by μὲν . . . δέ, Fitzmyer 950). For ἀπέκτειναν and οἰκοδομεῖτε see 11:47. The obj. τὰ μνημεῖα is implied (supplied in some mss.).

11:49 Διὰ τοῦτο is causal. Καί could be "also" (NRSV, ESV) or untranslated as part of a stereotyped expression διὰ τοῦτο καί (HCSB, NIV; Z §462; ZG 227). The phrase ἡ σοφία τοῦ θεοῦ could be a personification of God ("God in his wisdom" Robertson, *Pictures* 168; ZG 227; or "divine wisdom" Marshall 503–4; Nolland 671), a self-designation for Jesus (Fitzmyer 950; cf. 7:35; 11:31; cf. ναὶ λέγω ὑμῖν in 11:52), or a ref. to the totality of Scripture (Edwards 359; cf. Ezra 7:25). Ἀποστελῶ 1st sg. fut. act. indic. of ἀποστέλλω. For προφήτας καὶ ἀποστόλους ("emissaries" Nolland 668) cf. 13:34 (τοὺς προφήτας . . . τοὺς ἀπεσταλμένους); 20:10–12; Acts 7:52 (cf. πάντων τῶν προφητῶν, 11:50). The partitive ἐξ αὐτῶν ("some of them" BDAG 297d; Z §80; Marshall 505; cf. 11:5, 15) is the obj. of the 3rd pl. fut. act. indics. ἀποκτενοῦσιν (of ἀποκτείνω) and διώξουσιν (of διώκω).

11:50 Ἐκζητηθῇ 3rd sg. aor. pass. subjunc. of ἐκζητέω, "look for in the judicial sense" (BDAG 302d), "bring charges against" (LN 56.9; cf. NASB, ESV; "held responsible for" HCSB, NIV). Ἵνα with the subjunc. ἐκζητηθῇ expresses result (NLT, "therefore" NIV; BHGNT 407; Z §352; "purpose-result," Wallace 474; purpose, Marshall 505). Ἐκκεχυμένον nom. sg. neut. of pf. pass. (attrib.) ptc. of ἐκχέω, "shed," "pour out" (modifying τὸ αἷμα). Ἀπό with καταβολῆς (gen. sg. fem. of καταβολή, -ῆς, ἡ, "foundation"; the gen. κόσμου is obj.) is temp. Ἀπό with τῆς γενεᾶς ταύτης (see 7:31; in this context cf. 11:29–32) expresses source (lit. "required from this generation").

11:51 Ἀπὸ Ἄβελ . . . Ζαχαρίου (Gen 4:10; 2 Chron 24:22) is appos. to ἀπὸ καταβολῆς κόσμου (Marshall 506). The ref. to Abel indicates that the term "prophet" is being used in the broad sense of a person who speaks for God (Bock 1122). Ἀπολομένου gen. sg. masc. of 2nd aor. mid. (attrib.) ptc. of ἀπόλλυμι, "perished" (NRSV, HCSB, ESV; "was killed" NASB, NIV; modifying Ζαχαρίου). Μεταξύ, "between" (used as a prep. with the gen, BDAG 641b; ZG 228). Θυσιαστηρίου, "altar" (see 1:11). Οἴκου in this context refers to "the house of God" (NASB), i.e., "the temple" (NKJV, NJB; "sanctuary" NRSV, HCSB, ESV). With ναὶ λέγω ὑμῖν Jesus reaffirms what ἡ σοφία τοῦ θεοῦ said (11:49). Ἐκζητηθήσεται 3rd sg. fut. pass. indic. of ἐκζητέω, see 11:50.

11:52 For οὐαί and ὅτι see 11:42. For νομικῶν see 7:30 (cf. 5:17; above, 11:45–46). Ἤρατε 2nd pl. aor. act. indic. of αἴρω. Κλεῖδα acc. sg. fem. of κλείς, κλειδός, ἡ, "key." Γνώσεως, "knowledge" (the gen. could be appos. but is likely obj., "key to knowledge" NIV; ZG 228; Fitzmyer 951; Marshall 507; Nolland 669). The intensive pron. αὐτοί is the subj. of εἰσήλθατε (2nd pl. 2nd aor. act. indic. of dep. εἰσέρχομαι; cf. Z §489 for the form; neg. with οὐκ). Εἰσερχομένους (acc. pl. masc. of pres. mid. [subst.] ptc. of dep. εἰσέρχομαι) is the obj. of ἐκωλύσατε (2nd pl. aor. act. indic. of κωλύω; described as an "effective aorist" Z §252; ZG 228). Εἰσερχομένους is conative (NJB; Robertson, *Pictures* 169; Bock 1125). Thus, like the Pharisees (11:44), their unresponsiveness to Jesus is reflected in the effect they have on others.

11:53 Κἀκεῖθεν (only here, Mark 9:30, and eight times in Acts in the NT) is crasis of καὶ ἐκεῖθεν, "and from there." Ἐξελθόντος, see 11:14 (temp. gen. abs. cstr.; αὐτοῦ is the subj.). Ἤρξαντο, see 5:21. For οἱ γραμματεῖς καὶ οἱ Φαρισαῖοι cf. 11:37. Δεινῶς, adv. "vehemently," modifies the pres. act. inf. ἐνέχειν (of ἐνέχω, "bear ill will"). The combination has the mng. "act in a very hostile manner" (BDAG 215c; cf. NRSV, NASB), "to oppose . . . fiercely" (HCSB, NIV). Ἀποστοματίζειν pres. act. inf. of ἀποστοματίζω, "interrogate" (LSJ 220b), "question Him closely" (NASB; BDAG 122d; LN 33.183), "cross-examine" (HCSB), "besiege him with questions" (NIV). The "questions" may have the sense, however, of seeking to "make him repeat answers" (MM 70b; "force answers from him" NJB), "provoke him to speak" (RSV, ESV; ZG 228; "speak against" Nolland 669). Ἀποστοματίζω occurs only here in the NT. The infs. ἐνέχειν and ἀποστοματίζειν are complementary (following ἤρξαντο). Πλειόνων, adj., comp. for positive (Z §150; ZG 228; Marshall 508).

11:54 Ἐνεδρεύοντες (nom. pl. masc. of pres. act. ptc. of ἐνεδρεύω, "lie in wait," "plot to ambush," common in the LXX, only here and Acts 23:21 in the NT, though used figuratively here) expresses the manner in which the scribes and Pharisees went about the interrogations (cf. R 474; T 244). The aor. act. inf. θηρεῦσαι (of θηρεύω, "catch," "hunt," only here in the NT) expresses purpose. The expression θηρεῦσαί τι ἐκ τοῦ στόματος αὐτοῦ (lit. "to catch something from his mouth"; cf. BDF §217[3]; 22:71; ἀποστοματίζειν in 11:53) is "to trap Him in something He said" (HCSB).

HOMILETICAL SUGGESTIONS

How Could the Most Religious People Face the Most Severe Condemnation from Jesus? (11:37–54)

1. A concern for external appearances at the expense of internal realities (11:37–41)
2. A concern for peripheral minutia at the expense of essential matters (11:42)
3. A concern for personal prominence while conveying a deadly influence (11:43–44)
4. A concern to increase strict requirements for others and provide no help to maintain those requirements (11:45–46)
5. A consistent rejection of God's word that ultimately rejects Jesus (11:47–51)
6. A catastrophic distortion of the truth that hinders response to Jesus' word (11:52–54)

B. PRIORITIES AND ASSURANCES WITH THE
FINAL JUDGMENT IN VIEW (12:1–13:9)

An overall characteristic of this section is the constant reference to the final judgment and the significance of that for present priorities (indicated in the headings and exegetical notes below) that culminates with an exhortation to repent. A rationale for a section break is given in the introduction to 13:10.

1. Living with the Final Judgment in View Helps Disciples Remain Faithful in the Face of Persecution (12:1–12)

12:1 Ἐν with the dat. pl. rel. pron. οἷς is a temp. expression meaning "meanwhile" (NRSV, NIV; Wallace 342; ZG 228; "in these circumstances" HCSB, sim. NASB; BDAG 727c; in the context of the plots just mentioned, Fitzmyer 954). Ἐπισυναχθεισῶν gen. pl. fem. of aor. pass. ptc. of ἐπισυνάγω, "gather together" (temp. gen. abs. cstr.; μυριάδων [gen. pl. fem. of μυριάς, -άδος, ἡ, "ten thousand"; "many thousands" most EVV; with the partitive gen. τοῦ ὄχλου] is the subj., Marshall 511). Ὥστε with the pres. act. inf. καταπατεῖν (of καταπατέω, "trample on") gives the result of such large gathering crowds. Ἤρξατο, see 4:21. Λέγειν (see 3:8) is complementary. The adv. πρῶτον may emphasize the priority of the warning against the hypocrisy of the Pharisees (and modify προσέχετε; NIV mg.; Bovon 2.176), but in this context (cf. 12:4, 22, 32, 41; in contrast to τῶν μυριάδων τοῦ ὄχλου) it probably focuses Jesus' discussion on his disciples (modifying λέγειν; "he began to speak first to his disciples" NRSV, NIV; Bock 1133; Fitzmyer 954; Marshall 511; Nolland 677). Προσέχετε 2nd pl. pres. act. impv. of προσέχω, "give heed to" (an idiom with the refl. pron. ἑαυτοῖς which is found only here and 17:3; 21:34; Acts 5:35; 20:28 in the NT; ZG 228; Fitzmyer 954; for the form of the refl. pron. cf. Z §209). The pres. probably emphasizes constant vigilance (Bock 1133). Ἀπό with the gen. τῆς ζύμης (gen. sg. fem. of ζύμη, -ης, ἡ, "leaven"; modified by the gen. τῶν Φαρισαίων) expresses separation ("avoid" Robertson, *Pictures* 171). The rel. pron. ἥτις (for ἥ, Z §216) introduces a rel. clause which explains the "leaven of the Pharisees" as "hypocrisy" (ὑπόκρισις nom. sg. fem. of ὑπόκρισις, -εως, ἡ, "outward show" BDAG 1038b; "to give an impression of having certain purposes or motivations, while in reality having quite different ones" LN 88.227; cf. ὑποκριταί, 6:42; 12:56; 13:15; ὑποκρίνομαι, 20:20).

12:2 Συγκεκαλυμμένον (nom. sg. neut. of pf. pass. ptc. of συγκαλύπτω, "conceal," "cover up"; only here in the NT, though common in the LXX) with ἐστίν is a pf. periph. cstr. (with οὐδέν as the subj.). The rel. pron. ὅ is the subj. of ἀποκαλυφθήσεται (3rd sg. fut. pass. indic. of ἀποκαλύπτω, "reveal"; neg. with οὐκ; the double neg. is a strong affirmation, T 286; Marshall 512). The adj. κρυπτόν (see 8:17) is the pred. of an implied ἐστίν (with οὐδέν as implied the subj.). The rel. pron. ὅ is the subj. of γνωσθήσεται (3rd sg. fut. pass. indic. of γινώσκω; neg. with οὐ). Ἀποκαλυφθήσεται and γνωσθήσεται are divine passives (Fitzmyer 958).

12:3 Ἀντί with the gen. pl. rel. pron. ὧν could express cause ("For this reason" NJB; BHGNT 411; see 1:20) or result ("therefore" NRSV, HCSB, ESV; BDAG 88b; BDF

§208[1]; T 258; Wallace 343; Bock 1134; "accordingly" Fitzmyer 958; Marshall 512; Nolland 677). "Therefore" is more likely as the general rule of 12:2 is followed with specific ref. to the disciples (Marshall 512). The acc. pl. neut. rel. pron. ὅσα is the obj. of εἴπατε (2nd pl. 2nd aor. act. indic. of λέγω). Ἐν τῇ σκοτίᾳ (dat. sg. fem. of σκοτία, -ας, ἡ, "darkness") is locat. The rel. clause ὅσα . . . εἴπατε is the subj. of ἀκουσθήσεται (3rd sg. fut. pass. indic. of ἀκούω; modified by the locat. ἐν τῷ φωτί). The acc. sg. neut. rel. pron. ὅ is the obj. of ἐλαλήσατε (2nd pl. aor. act. indic. of λαλέω). The locat. πρὸς τὸ οὖς ("in an ear" HCSB; sim. NKJV, NIV) leads to the tr. of ἐλαλήσατε as "whispered" in most EVV. Ταμείοις dat. pl. neut. of ταμεῖον, -ου, τό, "inner rooms" (NASB, NIV; BDAG 988d; "store chamber" MM 624d), "private rooms" (HCSB, ESV), "behind closed doors" (NRSV). The rel. clause ὅ . . . ταμείοις is the obj. of κηρυχθήσεται (3rd sg. fut. pass. indic. of κηρύσσω). Δωμάτων, "housetops" (gen. pl. neut., see 5:19). Ἐπὶ τῶν δωμάτων in this context is idiomatic for "publicly" (LN 28.64).

12:4 The dat. τοῖς φίλοις (in appos. to ὑμῖν) in this context, as a further designation of Jesus' disciples, expresses the closeness of Jesus' relationship with his disciples in anticipation of the assurances of God's care for them (12:6–7; cf. τὸ μικρὸν ποίμνιον, 12:32). Φοβηθῆτε 2nd pl. aor. pass. subjunc. of dep. φοβέομαι (prohibition with μή; ingressive, Robertson, *Pictures* 172; regarding a future action, Z §246; or the aor. summarizes the action, "do not be afraid" NKJV, NIV; Huffman, 110, 186; see the pres. impv. in 12:7). Although ἀπό could be causal, it probably expresses separation here (BHGNT 413; cf. 12:1; a Heb. Robertson, *Pictures* 172; Marshall 513). Ἀποκτεινόντων (gen. pl. masc. of pres. act. ptc. of ἀποκτείνω) and ἐχόντων (see 7:42; neg. with μή; "have nothing" ESV; or perhaps "not able to" sim. HCSB, NIV; Fitzmyer 959) are subst. The acc. comp. adj. περισσότερόν (see 7:26; with the [enclitic] indef. pron. τι "anything more," ZG 229) is the obj. of the inf. ποιῆσαι (see 1:72). The fear of such people can lead to the insincerity mentioned in 12:1 (Nolland 681).

12:5 Ὑποδείξω, see 6:47 ("show" HCSB, NIV; "warn" NRSV, ESV). Φοβηθῆτε, see 12:4 (a deliberative subjunc.; trans. with the interr. pron. τίνα as the obj., Robertson, *Pictures* 172; ZG 229). Φοβήθητε 2nd pl. aor. mid. impv. of dep. φοβέομαι (the subst. ptc. τὸν . . . ἔχοντα [acc. sg. masc. of pres. act. ptc. of ἔχω] is the obj.). The art. aor. act. inf. ἀποκτεῖναι (of ἀποκτείνω) with μετά is temp. ("after he has killed" NRSV, ESV [i.e., referring to God]; Nolland 678; or, leaving the subject of the "killing" unexpressed, "after death" HCSB; sim. NIV; cf. Wallace 595; i.e., killed by human beings, Fitzmyer 959). Ἐξουσίαν, "authority" (NRSV, NIV, and most EVV; "power" RSV), is the obj. of τὸν . . . ἔχοντα. The 2nd aor. act. inf. ἐμβαλεῖν (of ἐμβάλλω, "throw"; only here in the NT, though common in the LXX) is epex. Γέενναν acc. sg. fem. of γέεννα, -ης, ἡ, "hell" (all EVV; "Gehenna" a transliteration of "Valley of Hinnom"). The combination of ναὶ λέγω ὑμῖν and the repetition of φοβήθητε (the third use of φοβέομαι in this verse to refer to fear of God) is an emphatic reaffirmation of this warning (Marshall 513).

12:6 Οὐχί, see 4:22. Just as fear of God helps overcome fear of persecutors (12:5), so also does trust in God's sovereign care (12:6–7; Marshall 514). Στρουθία nom. pl.

neut. of στρουθίον, -ου, τό, the diminutive of στρουθός "sparrow" (BDAG 949a). The ref. here is to "any small bird used for food" (Marshall 514; cf. MM 594a). Πωλοῦνται 3rd pl. pres. pass. indic. of πωλέω, "sell." Ἀσσαρίων gen. pl. neut. of ἀσσάριον, -ου, τό, a small Roman coin worth about one-sixteenth of a denarius (BDAG 144d–45a; a gen. of price, Wallace 122; ZG 229). BDAG also notes that two coins might equate to an hour's work and therefore "two pennies" (most EVV) is not accurate (though one sparrow is worth little). Ἐπιλελησμένον (nom. sg. neut. of pf. pass. ptc. of dep. ἐπιλανθάνομαι, "forget") with ἔστιν is periph. (cf. Wallace 649; ἕν with the partitive ἐξ αὐτῶν is the subj.).

12:7 Ἀλλά with καί is ascensive ("Indeed" HCSB, NIV; "[and not only this], but also" BDAG 45b). The fem. pl. αἱ τρίχες [see 7:38] . . . πᾶσαι is the subj. of ἠρίθμηνται (3rd pl. pf. pass. indic. of ἀριθμέω, "count," "number"). With φοβεῖσθε (see 2:10; prohibition with μή; the fifth use of φοβέομαι since 12:4), Jesus again exhorts his disciples not to be afraid. The impv. may imply the disciples are already afraid (ZG 229; see 12:4), ref. to a general attitude (Bock 1138), or view the action as a process (Huffman 114). Διαφέρετε (2nd pl. pres. act. indic. of διαφέρω, "differ"), with the gen. of comp. πολλῶν στρουθίων, has the mng. "more value than" (NRSV, ESV), "worth more than" (HCSB, NIV; BDAG 239b; Wallace 111; ZG 229).

12:8 Λέγω δὲ ὑμῖν, together with the subst. adj. πᾶς as a modifier of the indef. rel. cstr. ὃς ἄν, form an emphatic introduction to the following statement which is equivalent to an exhortation (Wallace 52–53 [with ref. to 12:10] and ZG 229 [cf. Z §§25, 31] describe πᾶς ὅς as a pendent nom. that is resumed by αὐτῷ; cf. Marshall 516). Ὁμολογήσῃ 3rd sg. aor. act. subjunc. of ὁμολογέω, "confess" (KJV, NASB), "acknowledges" (NRSV, HCSB, ESV, NIV), "openly declares himself for me" (NJB). Ἐν ἐμοί (and ἐν αὐτῷ) is used as a marker of close association (an Aram. BDAG 328c [ἐν], 708d [ὁμολογέω]; BDF §220[2]; R 475, 524, 588; ZG 229). For ὁ υἱὸς τοῦ ἀνθρώπου see 5:24 (used here in a play on words with ἔμπροσθεν τῶν ἀνθρώπων, Fitzmyer 960; Nolland 679; cf. 12:9). Ὁμολογήσει 3rd sg. fut. act. indic. of ὁμολογέω (with ἐν, BDF §220[2]).

12:9 Ἀρνησάμενος (nom. sg. masc. of aor. mid. [subst.] ptc. of dep. ἀρνέομαι, "deny," the aor. ptc. functions as a summary of complete denial, Bock 1140) is the subj. of ἀπαρνηθήσεται (3rd sg. fut. pass. indic. of dep. ἀπαρνέομαι, "deny"). Ἀρνέομαι is the antonym of ὁμολογέω ("acknowledge"). The compound ἀπαρνέομαι may be used for stylistic variation and have the same mng. as ἀρνέομαι (BHGNT 417), or it may emphasize the finality of the verdict ("reject" LN 34.49; Marshall 516). The subst. ptc. cstr. may have more rhetorical force than the rel. clause in 12:8 (BHGNT 416; or an equivalent cstr., R 1114). For ἐνώπιον τῶν ἀγγέλων τοῦ θεοῦ see 15:10.

12:10 For πᾶς (subst.) with the rel. pron. ὅς see 12:8. The fut. indic. ἐρεῖ (3rd sg. fut. act. indic. of λέγω) is probably sim. to an indef. aor. subjunc. cstr. (BDF §380[2]; R 957; see 19:40). Εἰς ("against") is used as "a marker of actions or feelings directed in someone's direction" in a hostile sense (BDAG 290a; βλασφημέω with εἰς is rare as the vb. usually takes an acc. as the obj., Fitzmyer 966; cf. 22:65). Ἀφεθήσεται 3rd sg. fut. pass. indic. of ἀφίημι (αὐτῷ is a dat. of advantage). Βλασφημήσαντι dat. sg. masc. of aor. act. (subst.) ptc. of βλασφημέω (a dat. of disadvantage). Just as "denying Jesus" results in being denied by God (12:9), so blaspheming the Holy Spirit results in receiving no forgiveness from God. The distinction in this verse, therefore, may be between "speaking a word" and "blaspheming" in the sense of either momentary versus permanent rejection (Bock 1143; Bovon 2.186) or acting in ignorance versus hardened opposition (Stein 348).

12:11 Εἰσφέρωσιν (3rd pl. pres. act. subjunc. of εἰσφέρω, "bring"; an impers. pl., Z §1) with ὅταν is temp. ("whenever" HCSB; Wallace 480; "frequentive" ZG 229; iter., Bovon 2.187). Ἐπί is locat. ("to" NKJV; "before" most EVV). Μεριμνήσητε 2nd pl. aor. act. subjunc. of μεριμνάω, "be anxious" (ESV), "worry" (most EVV; see 10:41; prohibition with μή). The adv. πῶς and interr. prons. τί . . . τί introduce indir. questions (BDAG 632b; referring to "both the general form of a speech and the actual content" Marshall 520). The subjuncs. ἀπολογήσησθε (2nd pl. aor. mid. subjunc. of dep. ἀπολογέομαι, "say in defense") and εἴπητε (2nd pl. 2nd aor. act. subjunc. of λέγω) are deliberative (retained in indir. questions, Robertson, *Pictures* 174; Z §348).

12:12 Γάρ, causal (giving the reason Jesus' disciples should not be anxious about what to say in these circumstances). Τὸ . . . ἅγιον πνεῦμα is the subj. of διδάξει (3rd sg. fut. act. indic. of διδάσκω; cf. 21:15, referring to Jesus). For αὐτῇ in the temp. ἐν αὐτῇ τῇ ὥρᾳ see 10:7 (cf. 10:21). The acc. pl. neut. rel. pron. ἅ (of ὅς, ἥ, ὅ) introduces a rel. clause which is the obj. of διδάξει (cf. BDF §298[4], BHGNT 418; T 49). Δεῖ, see 2:49. The inf. εἰπεῖν (see 5:14) is complementary. Whereas the one who blasphemes the Spirit receives no forgiveness, the disciple of Jesus is assured of the Spirit's help to testify allegiance to Jesus in the hour of trial.

HOMILETICAL SUGGESTIONS

Facing Persecution (12:1–12)

1. Don't be tempted into duplicity (12:1–3).
2. God is more powerful than the persecutor and he won't forget you (12:4–7).
3. Confess the Son and don't persistently reject the Spirit (12:8–10).
4. The Spirit will help you confess the Son (12:11–12).

2. Living with the Final Judgment in View Helps Clarify the Nature of True Wealth (12:13–21)

12:13 Ἐκ τοῦ ὄχλου is partitive (and connects this incident with the preceding; cf. 12:1). Διδάσκαλε, voc. (see 7:40). Εἰπέ, see 4:3. The aor. mid. inf. μερίσασθαι (of μερίζω, "divide"; τὴν κληρονομίαν [acc. sg. fem. of κληρονομία, -ας, ἡ, "inheritance"] is the obj.) is used for indir. discourse.

12:14 Ἄνθρωπε, voc. (possibly a more familiar tone, "friend" NRSV, HCSB; cf. 5:20; or "with a reproachful connotation" BDAG 82c; a rebuke, Bock 1149; Fitzmyer 969; forceful yet not necessarily insulting, Nolland 685). Κατέστησεν 3rd sg. aor. act. indic. of καθίστημι, "set" (NRSV), "appointed" (NASB, HCSB, NIV). The acc. με is the dir. obj., and the acc. κριτὴν ἢ μεριστήν ("judge [see 11:19] or arbitrator"; acc. sg. masc. of μεριστής, -οῦ, ὁ) is the complement in a double acc. cstr. (BDAG 492d cf. διαμερισμός in 12:51; διαμερίζω in 12:52–53). Ἐπί functions as a marker of "power, authority, control" over someone (BDAG 365d).

12:15 Ὁρᾶτε 2nd pl. pres. act. impv. of ὁράω. Φυλάσσεσθε 2nd pl. pres. mid. impv. of φυλάσσω (with the prep. of separation ἀπό, "look out for, avoid" BDAG 1068c; "guard against" BDF §149; ZG 230; the mid. could be refl., Wallace 417). Πλεονεξίας gen. sg. fem. of πλεονεξία, -ας, ἡ, "covetousness" (ESV), "greed" (NRSV, HCSB, NIV; "desiring to have more than one's due" BDAG 824d). Ὅτι, causal (giving the reason for this warning). The pres. act. inf. περισσεύειν (of περισσεύω, "increase," "abundance" most EVV) with ἐν τῷ is temp. (neg. with οὐκ; with the indef. pron. τινί [dat. of advantage], "not even when one has an abundance" NASB). The nom. ἡ ζωή is the subj. of ἐστίν. The antecedent of the poss. pron. αὐτοῦ is τινί (i.e., "not when one has . . . is his life" sim. NASB). Ἐκ with the subst. ptc. ὑπαρχόντων (see 8:3; αὐτῷ is a dat. of poss.) may be causal (BDAG 297a) or indicate source (BHGNT 420; R 598).

12:16 Παραβολή, see 8:4. The nom. ἡ χώρα ("land" in the sense of "cultivated land" "used for farming" BDAG 1094a) is the subj. (modified by the poss. gen. ἀνθρώπου τινὸς πλουσίου; the placement of this adnominal gen. is unemphatic, BDF §473[1]) of εὐφόρησεν (3rd sg. aor. act. indic. of εὐφορέω, "bear good crops," "very productive" NASB, HCSB; "produced plentifully" ESV; "yielded an abundant harvest" NIV).

12:17 Διελογίζετο, see 1:29. Ἐν with the refl. pron. ἑαυτῷ describes an inward process (BDAG 327a; "to himself" most EVV; cf. other soliloquies at 15:17–19; 16:3; 18:4; 20:13). The interr. τί introduces a dir. question. Ποιήσω 1st sg. aor. act. subjunc. of ποιέω (deliberative subjunc.; though it could also be a fut. act. indic., cf. BDF §366). Ὅτι, causal (giving the reason for his deliberation, Z §420). Ἔχω, see 7:40 (neg. with οὐκ). The adv. ποῦ introduces an indir. question. Συνάξω 1st sg. fut. act. indic. of συνάγω, "gather," "store" (most EVV; a deliberative fut., Robertson, *Pictures* 175). Καρπούς, "fruit," "crops" (most EVV).

12:18 The question τί ποιήσω (12:17) is answered with τοῦτο ποιήσω. Ποιήσω 1st sg. fut. act. indic. of ποιέω (although the same form as a subjunc. [see 12:17], it is a fut. indic. here as there is no deliberation; note also the following fut. indic. vbs.). The

acc. sg. neut. demonstrative pron. τοῦτο is the dir. obj. of ποιέω and points to the following clause (cataphoric, BHGNT 422). Καθελῶ 1st sg. fut. act. indic. of καθαιρέω,
"pull down" (NRSV), "tear down" (HCSB, ESV, NIV; the fut. is formed from the 2nd
aor. καθεῖλον, Robertson, *Pictures* 175; ZG 230). Ἀποθήκας, "storehouses," "barns"
(acc. pl. fem., see 3:17). The subst. comp. adj. μείζονας is the obj. of οἰκοδομήσω (1st
sg. fut. act. indic. of οἰκοδομέω). Συνάξω, see 12:17. Σῖτον, "wheat" (NLT; see 3:17),
"grain" (NRSV, HCSB, ESV). The double use of the pron. μου (cf. καρπούς μου, 12:17)
together with four 1st sg. vbs. highlights a focus on self (cf. 12:19; Bock 1152).

12:19 Ἐρῶ 1st sg. fut. act. indic. of λέγω. Τῇ ψυχῇ μου (dat. of indir. obj.; with the voc.
ψυχή), "to my soul" (NASB, NRSV, ESV) is synecdoche for "myself" (HCSB, NIV;
BHGNT 422; Bock 1152; Bovon 2.201; Fitzmyer 973; Marshall 523). The emphasis
on "self" continues the focus of 12:18. Ἔχεις 2nd sg. pres. act. indic. ἔχω. Κείμενα
acc. pl. neut. of pres. pass. (attrib.) ptc. of dep. κεῖμαι. Εἰς with ἔτη πολλά is temp.
("for many years"). The man then addresses himself with four (2nd sg.) impvs. (in
asyndeton). Ἀναπαύου pres. mid. of ἀναπαύω, "relax" (NRSV, ESV), "take life easy"
(NIV, sim. HCSB; BDAG 69d). Φάγε 2nd aor. act. of ἐσθίω. Πίε 2nd aor. act. of πίνω.
Εὐφραίνου pres. pass. of εὐφραίνω, "be merry" (NRSV, NASB, ESV, NIV), "have a
good time" (NJB), "enjoy yourself" (HCSB).

12:20 The masc. sg. adj. ἄφρων ("fool"; see 11:40) is voc. Ταύτῃ τῇ νυκτί, dat. of
time (denoting the point of time when the action of the vb. will be accomplished,
Wallace 157; emphatically placed, Marshall 524). The acc. τὴν ψυχήν (with the poss.
σου is the dir. obj. of ἀπαιτοῦσιν) is probably a ref. to the man's life (NRSV, HCSB,
NIV). As with 12:5, the assumption here is that judgment follows death (Nolland 687).
Ἀπαιτοῦσιν 3rd pl. pres. act. indic. of ἀπαιτέω, "demanded" (NRSV, HCSB, NIV),
"required" (NASB, ESV), "demanded back" (NET; BDAG 96a, with ref. to something
that is due such as a loan). The 3rd pl. form of ἀπαιτοῦσιν is an indef. pl. to avoid the
passive voice (McKay 19) or a circumlocution for God (BDF §130[2]; Robertson,
Pictures 176; Wallace 403; Z §2; ZG 230; Bock 1153; Fitzmyer 974; Nolland 687; see
6:38; it is unlikely to be a ref. to an angel of death in this context, *pace* Bovon 2.202;
Marshall 524). The acc. pl. neut. rel. pron. ἅ with ἡτοίμασας (see 2:31) is the subj. of
ἔσται (see 1:14; BHGNT 423; the subj. is the dat. [of poss.] sg. masc. interr. pron. τίνι).

12:21 Οὕτως introduces a concluding comparison. Θησαυρίζων (nom. sg. masc. of
pres. act. [subst.] ptc. of θησαυρίζω, "store up"; cf. θησαυρός in 12:33–34) is the subj.
of an implied ἐστίν (the refl. pron. ἑαυτῷ is either "with reference to himself" [Nolland
687] or a dat. of advantage [BHGNT 423]; cf. 12:18). Πλουτῶν (nom. sg. masc. of
pres. act. [subst.] ptc. of πλουτέω, "be rich"; neg. with μή) is the subj. of an implied
ἐστίν (εἰς is probably "with reference to" [cf. BDAG 291a], or advantage, in parallel
with the dat. ἑαυτῷ).

For Homiletical Suggestions see at the end of 12:34.

3. Living with the Final Judgment in View Helps Direct Attention away from Worry to Trust and Service Under God's Saving Rule with Treasure in Heaven (12:22–34)

12:22 The causal διὰ τοῦτο links Jesus' teaching here to the preceding warning (12:13–15) and parable (12:16–21), and it continues the focus on Jesus' disciples in this chapter (see 12:1; [δέ] "then" HCSB, NIV). Links to previous sections are also seen in the use of ψυχή (12:19–20, 22–23), μεριμνάω (12:11, 22, 25–26), and φοβέομαι (12:4–5, 7, 32). Whereas the previous section warned against storing up for self and not being rich toward God, this section will focus on the outcome of being rich toward God (cf. 12:21, 34): trust in God's provision and service in his kingdom. Μεριμνᾶτε 2nd pl. pres. act. impv. of μεριμνάω, see 10:41; in this context cf. 12:11, 25–26 ("anxious concern . . . apprehension about possible danger or misfortune," LN 25.225); prohibition with μή; the pres. may refer to a general rule (Z §§246, 248) or portray a constant attitude (Bock 1159). The dats. τῇ ψυχῇ and τῷ σώματι could be dats. of advantage (BDAG 632b; BDF §188[1]; ZG 231; cf. R 538–39) or ref. (BHGNT 425). As with 12:20, ψυχή refers to one's physical "life" (all EVV). The two acc. sg. neut. interr. prons. τί with φάγητε (2nd pl. 2nd aor. act. subjunc. of ἐσθίω) and ἐνδύσησθε (2nd pl. aor. mid. subjunc. of ἐνδύω, "put on" ESV, "wear" NRSV, HCSB, NIV; both deliberative subjuncs.) introduce indir. questions as the complement to μεριμνᾶτε τῇ ψυχῇ (cf. BDF §337[3]; BHGNT 425).

12:23 Γάρ, causal (giving the reason Jesus' disciples should not be anxious for these things; 12:23 provides reason #1 in a series). The adj. πλεῖόν is pred. (the neut. may be due to the subj. being abstract, BDF §131; BHGNT 425; Marshall 526). Τῆς τροφῆς (gen. sg. fem. of τροφή, -ῆς, ἡ, "food") and τοῦ ἐνδύματος (gen. sg. neut. of ἔνδυμα, -ατος, τό, "clothing") are gens. of comparison (ZG 231).

12:24 Κατανοήσατε 2nd pl. aor. act. impv. of κατανοέω, "consider." Κόρακας acc. pl. masc. of κόραξ, -ακος, ὁ, "ravens" (all EVV; or "crows" BDAG 559c). Ὅτι introduces an epex. clause ("for" NKJV, NASB; expressed with a colon in most EVV; Wallace 460; ZG 231). Σπείρουσιν 3rd pl. pres. act. indic. of σπείρω (neg. with οὐ). Θερίζουσιν 3rd pl. pres. act. indic. of θερίζω, "reap" (neg. with οὐδέ). The two negs. assume that though birds do not work, people do (Marshall 527). The antecedent of the masc. pl. rel. pron. οἷς is κόρακας (the dat. of the pron. is poss.). Ταμεῖον, "storeroom" (see 12:3). Ἀποθήκη, "barn" (nom. sg. fem., see 3:17; 12:18). Καί, "yet" (most EVV). Τρέφει 3rd sg. pres. act. indic. of τρέφω, "feed." Διαφέρετε, see 12:7 (followed by the gen. of comp., Wallace 111 [πετεινῶν, see 8:5]; thus, reason #2 is given).

12:25 For τίς . . . ἐξ ὑμῶν see 11:5 (12:25–26 adds reason #3). Μεριμνῶν (nom. sg. masc. of pres. act. ptc. of μεριμνάω, see 10:41; cf. 12:11, 22, 26) expresses means. Δύναται, see 3:8. Ἡλικίαν ("stature," see 2:52) and the unit of measurement πῆχυν (acc. sg. masc. of πῆχυς, -εως, ὁ, "cubit") could refer to:

1. height (RV, HCSB; BDAG 812b; BHGNT 427; cf. 19:3) or

2. age (NRSV, NASB, ESV, NIV [NJB appears to incorporate both]; MM 279a–
b; ZG 231; Bock 1161; Bovon 2.216; Fitzmyer 979; Marshall 528; Nolland
692).

The previous refs. to food (12:22–24) may mean that the point is the disciples did not
grow by worrying (i.e., hyperbolic irony, BDAG 812b [cf. 435d–36a]; BHGNT 427).
The following verse, however, refers to this as a "little thing" (12:26), something that
an additional eighteen inches in height is unlikely to be. It is also more likely that people would worry about extending their age than try to extend their height. The 2nd aor.
act. inf. προσθεῖναι (of προστίθημι) is complementary (with δύναται).

12:26 Εἰ introduces a first-class cond. (Z §303). The superl. acc. sg. neut. adj. ἐλάχιστον
(of ἐλάσσων, -ον, "least," "a very little thing" NIV; an elative superl., Robertson,
Pictures 177; Wallace 303) is the obj. of an implied complementary inf. "to do"
(NRSV, ESV). Δύνασθε, see 5:34. Μεριμνᾶτε, see 12:22.

12:27 Κατανοήσατε, see 12:24 (in 12:24 the illustration was from birds; in 12:25, flow-
ers; and in 12:28, grass). Κρίνα acc. pl. neut. of κρίνον, -ου, τό, "lilies" (NRSV, NASB,
ESV), "wildflowers" (HCSB, NIV; LN 3.32 due to uncertainty concerning the precise
referent of this term). The adv. πῶς is epex. and introduces an indir. question (BDAG
901b). Αὐξάνει 3rd sg. pres. act. indic. of αὐξάνω. The neut. pl. τὰ κρίνα is the subj.
of the 3rd sg. pres. act. indics. αὐξάνει, κοπιᾷ (of κοπιάω, "labor"; neg. with οὐ), and
νήθει (of νήθω, "spin"; neg. with οὐδέ). Περιεβάλετο 3rd sg. 2nd aor. mid. indic. of
περιβάλλω, "clothe" (intrans., Marshall 529; a constative aor., Z §253).

12:28 Εἰ introduces a first-class cond. The acc. sg. masc. τὸν χόρτον (of χόρτος, -ου, ὁ,
"grass") is the obj. of ἀμφιέζει (3rd sg. pres. act. indic. of ἀμφιέζω, "clothe"; only here
in the NT; the subj. is θεός). Χόρτον is described first with the locat. ἐν ἀγρῷ and ὄντα
(acc. sg. masc. of pres. act. [attrib.] ptc. of εἰμί; modified by the adv. σήμερον; " grass,
which is in the field today" HCSB), and then with βαλλόμενον (acc. sg. masc. of pres.
pass. [attrib.] ptc. of βάλλω; the attrib. ptcs. are in the second pred. position, Wallace
619) and the adv. αὔριον ("tomorrow") with the locat. εἰς κλίβανον (acc. sg. masc. of
κλίβανος, -ου, ὁ, "into the furnace" HCSB). The argument here is from the lesser to the
greater (πόσῳ μᾶλλον, "how much more"; see 11:13). Ὀλιγόπιστοι voc. pl. masc. adj.,
of ὀλιγόπιστος, -ον, "of little faith."

12:29 Καί introduces the conclusion to the illustrations ("So" NET; Marshall 529).
Ζητεῖτε, see 11:9 (cf. 12:31; neg. with μή; the pron. ὑμεῖς is emphatic, Robertson,
Pictures 177). The mng. of the pres. is "don't keep striving for" (HCSB, sim. NRSV),
or "do not have as your constant consideration" (Nolland 690; cf. NET, NIV; Bovon
2.219; *pace* Robertson, *Pictures* 177, the pres. impv. does not necessarily mean "stop
seeking"; cf. Huffman 43–44, 108). The acc. interr. prons. τί are the objs. of the (deliberative) subjuncs. φάγητε (see 12:22) and πίητε (2nd pl. 2nd aor. act. subjunc. of πίνω;
cf. 12:19) as the complement of ζητεῖτε. Μετεωρίζεσθε 2nd pl. pres. pass. impv. of
dep. μετεωρίζομαι, "keep worrying" (NASB, NRSV), "be anxious" (HCSB; cf. BDAG

642d ["be up in the air"]; MM 405b–c; prohibition with μή; again, the pres. does not necessarily mean "stop being anxious").

12:30 Γάρ, causal (giving the reason for the prohibition). The adj. πάντα could modify:

1. ταῦτα (acc. pl. neut. NKJV, NRSV, NASB, HCSB, sim. NIV; Fitzmyer 975; Marshall 529); or
2. τὰ ἔθνη (nom. pl. neut. RSV, ESV; BHGNT 429; Bock 1164; Bovon 2.220; Nolland 693; cf. 24:47; Acts 14:16; 15:17).

Since γάρ is postpositive and πάντα follows ταῦτα elsewhere in Luke (16:14; 18:21; 21:36; 24:9), it seems likely that "all these things" is meant here (cf. ταῦτα πάντα in some mss. of 12:31). Ἐπιζητοῦσιν 3rd pl. pres. act. indic. of ἐπιζητέω, "seek after" (the pl. vb. with the neut. pl. subj. may emphasize "the individuality of each subject" Wallace 400; cf. BDF §133[1]). Τὰ ἔθνη τοῦ κόσμου describes those who do not know God ("the pagan world" NIV; cf. BDAG 276d–277a), and therefore must worry about sustaining life (Marshall 529). The emphatic placement of ὑμῶν highlights the contrast between Jesus' disciples and "the nations" ("your Father"; BHGNT 430; Marshall 529). The disciples of Jesus, however, have God as their Father (and provider, cf. 11:2–3, 11–13; Nolland 693) who knows their needs. Οἶδεν 3rd sg. pf. act. indic. of οἶδα. Ὅτι introduces indir. discourse (following a vb. of perception, BDAG 732a). Χρῄζετε 2nd pl. pres. act. indic. of χρῄζω, "have need of" (τούτων, gen. complement).

12:31 The adversative πλήν introduces a contrast following the prohibition of 12:29. Ζητεῖτε, see 11:9 (in this context, see 12:29; "keep seeking" Bock 1164). For βασιλείαν see 4:43 (in light of 12:32, the ref. here is likely to the spiritual blessings of being under God's saving rule, cf. Marshall 530). The gen. pron. αὐτοῦ (the rdg. in ℵ B D*; τοῦ θεοῦ in some mss. is likely a scribal clarification) could be poss., subj., or both. The parataxis (καί) is essentially cond. (Marshall 530). The neut. pl. ταῦτα (i.e., the preceding ref. to life's material necessities) is the subj. of προστεθήσεται (3rd sg. fut. pass. indic. of προστίθημι; a "divine passive"). The prior assurances in the face of persecution and death (12:4–5) mean this is not a guarantee of material security. Life's uncertainty, however, "need not cause anxiety" (Marshall 530).

12:32 The impv. φοβοῦ (see 1:13) is a prohibition with μή (the pres. may refer to a general principle [Z §254] or to ongoing fear). The (nom. for voc., BDF §147[3]; R 465; Z §34) τὸ μικρὸν ποίμνιον ("little flock"; nom. sg. neut. of ποίμνιον, -ου, τό) identifies the disciples as vulnerable, yet under the Father's care (cf. φίλοις μου, 12:4). Robertson (*Pictures* 178) notes that ποίμνιον is not diminutive, thus μικρόν is not superfluous (ZG 232 thinks it is diminutive but that this has lost its force). Ὅτι, causal (giving the reason for the prohibition). Ὁ πατὴρ ὑμῶν (cf. 12:30) is the subj. of εὐδόκησεν (3rd sg. aor. act. indic. of εὐδοκέω, "take delight," "take pleasure"). The inf. δοῦναι (see 1:73) is complementary (ZG 232). To be given "the kingdom" means to be granted the blessings associated with being under God's saving rule (cf. 4:43; Bock 1165; Marshall 530).

12:33 Τὰ ὑπάρχοντα (see 11:21) is the obj. of πωλήσατε (2nd pl. aor. act. impv. of πωλέω). Ἐλεημοσύνην ("alms"; see 11:41) is the obj. of δότε (see 9:13; cf. the Father's "gift" [δοῦναι] in 12:32). The acc. βαλλάντια ("money bags"; see 10:4; here the container stands for the contents, Nolland 694) is the obj. of ποιήσατε (see 3:8; "make" HCSB; "provide" ESV, NIV) and is modified by παλαιούμενα (acc. pl. neut. of pres. pass. [attrib.] ptc. of παλαιόω, "become old," "wear out" NRSV, NASB, NIV; neg. with μή). The acc. θησαυρὸν [see 6:45] ἀνέκλειπτον ("unfailing treasure" NRSV, NASB; "inexhaustible treasure" HCSB; ἀνέκλειπτον acc. sg. masc. of ἀνέκλειπτος, -ον, "will not go out of existence" LN 13.99; "nonperishable" Bock 1166) is in appos. to βαλλάντια (Marshall 531; Nolland 694). Ἐν τοῖς οὐρανοῖς is locat. (cf. 10:20; 18:22). The adv. conj. ὅπου is locat. and introduces a clause which further explains the permanence and security of this treasure "in heaven" (cf. θησαυρίζω in 12:21). The nom. sg. masc. κλέπτης (of κλέπτης, -ου, ὁ, "thief") is the subj. of ἐγγίζει (3rd sg. pres. act. indic. of ἐγγίζω, "comes near" NRSV, HCSB, NIV; "approaches" RSV, ESV; neg. with οὐκ; cf. 10:9). The nom. sg. masc. σής (of σής, σητός, ὁ, "moth") is the subj. of διαφθείρει (3rd sg. pres. act. indic. of διαφθείρω, "destroy").

12:34 Γάρ, causal (giving the reason for the preceding exhortation). The adv. conj. ὅπου is locat. and introduces a clause which is the topic for the following clause (BHGNT 431). The ref. to ὁ θησαυρὸς ὑμῶν picks up on θησαυρὸν ἀνέκλειπτον in 12:33 (cf. 12:21). Θησαυρός [see 6:45] refers to "that which is valued" and καρδία to what one prioritizes (Bock 1167–68). The adv. ἐκεῖ is locat. and picks up on the previous locat. clause (καί, "also"). Ἔσται, see 1:14.

FOR FURTHER STUDY

See For Further Study § 34.

HOMILETICAL SUGGESTIONS

True Wealth (12:13–34)

1. Self-focused accumulation of possessions is judged at death (12:13–21).
2. The Father provides all we need for life (12:22–30).
3. True secure wealth, granted in God's kingdom, frees us to serve others (12:31–34).

4. Living with the Final Judgment in View Helps Focus on Faithful Service (12:35–48)

12:35 The following exhortations and parables are placed here without any explanatory or coordinating conj. (asyndeton, Marshall 532). Thus they appear to be a continuation of the preceding exhortations concerning "treasure in heaven" and encouragement for Jesus' disciples to live in light of the age to come (Marshall 535). Ἔστωσαν 3rd pl. pres. act. impv. of εἰμί. The impv. ἔστωσαν with αἱ ὀσφύες (nom. pl. fem. of ὀσφῦς, -ύος, ἡ, "loins," "waist") and περιεζωσμέναι (nom. pl. fem. of pf. pass. ptc. of περιζώννυμι, "gird about," "put a belt or sash around" BDAG 801a) is lit. "Let your loins be girded about" (KJV, sim. RSV); i.e., "See that you have your belts done up" (NJB). Most EVV paraphrase as "Be dressed ready for service" (NIV, sim. NRSV, NASB, ESV). The ref. to tucking in one's garment is idiomatic for being prepared for activity (BDAG 730c, 801a; "Be ready for service" HCSB; cf. Fitzmyer 987–88). Περιεζωσμέναι and καιόμενοι (nom. pl. masc. of pres. pass. ptc. of καίω, "burn"; λύχνοι, see 8:16) could be periph. (Robertson, *Pictures* 178–79) but are perhaps better viewed as pred. (following the impv. ἔστωσαν; BHGNT 433).

12:36 The following example illustrates the kind of readiness encouraged in the previous verse (cf. NIV which continues the sentence from 12:35). The nom. pl. masc. adj. ὅμοιοι (of ὅμοιος, -οία, -ον) is the pred. of an implied impv. (ἐστέ "be like," Marshall 535). Προσδεχομένοις, see 2:38 (attrib., modifying ἀνθρώποις). The adv. πότε with ἀναλύσῃ (3rd sg. aor. act. [deliberative] subjunc. of ἀναλύω, "return"; intrans. BDAG 67d; MM 36a) is an indef. temp. cstr. and introduces a clause in indir. discourse which modifies τὸν κύριον (tr. as an inf. in most EVV; e.g., "to return" NRSV, HCSB, NIV; BHGNT 434; Z §349; ZG 232). Within the parable (cf. οἱ δοῦλοι, 12:37), τὸν κύριον ἑαυτῶν refers to "their master" (most EVV; however, cf. 12:41). Γάμων gen. pl. masc. of γάμος, -ου, ὁ, "wedding feast" (NASB, ESV), "wedding banquet" (NRSV, HCSB, NIV). Ἵνα with the subjunc. ἀνοίξωσιν (3rd pl. aor. act. subjunc. of ἀνοίγω; modified by the adv. εὐθέως; the obj. "door" is implied) expresses purpose. The gen. sg. masc. of aor. act. ptcs. ἐλθόντος (2nd aor. act. of dep. ἔρχομαι) and κρούσαντος (of κρούω, "knock") are a temp. gen. abs. cstr. (without an explicit subject [i.e., κύριου] in the gen. BHGNT 434; BDF §423[1, 6]; Robertson, *Pictures* 179; Wallace 655; Z §§49–50; ZG 232).

12:37 Μακάριοι (see 6:20) is a pred. adj. and οἱ δοῦλοι ἐκεῖνοι is the nom. subj. of a verbless clause (with an implied εἰσίν; cf. 12:38). The acc. pl. masc. rel. pron. οὕς (the antecedent is οἱ δοῦλοι) is the obj. of εὑρήσει (3rd sg. fut. act. indic. of εὑρίσκω). Ἐλθών (see 7:3) could be attendant circumstance ("comes and finds") but is likely temp. ("when he comes" all EVV; ZG 232; paralleling the gen. abs. in 12:36). Γρηγοροῦντας (acc. pl. masc. of pres. act. ptc. of γρηγορέω, "watching" NIV; "alert" NRSV, HCSB; "awake" RSV, ESV) is the complement in a double acc. cstr. (BDAG 411d). For ἀμὴν λέγω ὑμῖν see 4:24. Ὅτι, recitative. Περιζώσεται 3rd sg. fut. mid. indic. of περιζώννυμι, see 12:35 (here "fasten his belt" NRSV; "get ready" HCSB; "dress himself to serve" NIV). Ἀνακλινεῖ 3rd sg. fut. act. indic. of ἀνακλίνω, with the acc. αὐτούς, "have them recline" (ESV, HCSB, NIV). Παρελθών (nom. sg. masc. of 2nd aor. act. ptc. of dep.

παρέρχομαι) is an attendant circumstance ptc. with διακονήσει (3rd sg. fut. act. indic. of διακονέω, "serve" HCSB, ESV; "wait [on them]" NASB, NIV; a "graphic" ptc., Z §363; the dat. αὐτοῖς is complementary).

12:38 Κἄν (crasis of καὶ ἐάν; "and if" NKJV; "Even if" NET; ZG 232; "whether" NASB) with the subjuncs. ἔλθῃ (see 1:43) and εὕρῃ (3rd sg. 2nd aor. act. subjunc. of εὑρίσκω) is cond. (introducing a third-class cond. cstr., Robertson, *Pictures* 179). Ἐν τῇ δευτέρᾳ and ἐν τῇ τρίτῃ φυλακῇ are temp. (the measurements may refer to four [Roman] watches [Bock 1175; Fitzmyer 988 tentatively] or three [Jewish] watches [Marshall 537; Nolland 702]; see BDAG 1067d; LN 67.196). The adv. οὕτως refers to γρηγοροῦντας in 12:37 ("finds them alert" HCSB; cf. BHGNT 435). For the cstr. with μακάριοι (see 6:20; cf. 12:37). Ἐκεῖνοι refers back to οἱ δοῦλοι (clarified in all EVV, and some mss.).

12:39 The acc. sg. neut. demonstrative pron. τοῦτο is the obj. of γινώσκετε (see 10:11; impv., Bovon 2.234) and points ahead ("cataphoric") to the statement introduced by ὅτι (cf. 10:11). Εἰ introduces a second-class cond. sentence ("contrary to fact" Z §313). The nom. sg. masc. ὁ οἰκοδεσπότης (of οἰκοδεσπότης, -ου, ὁ, "master of the house" ESV; "homeowner" HCSB, sim. NRSV, NIV) is the subj. of ᾔδει (see 6:8; a rare plu-perfect in the protasis of a second-class cond., perhaps functioning as an aor., Wallace 695; Marshall 538; cf. Z §317). Ποίᾳ ὥρᾳ dat. of time. Κλέπτης, "thief" (see 12:33; a generic ref. Marshall 538) is the subj. of ἔρχεται (see 3:16). The apodosis of the cond. sentence is introduced with ἄν (Robertson, *Pictures* 180). Ἀφῆκεν, see 4:39 (here "have let" NRSV, HCSB, NIV; "have allowed" NASB; ZG 233). The aor. pass. inf. διορυχθῆναι (of διορύσσω, "dig through" [the clay wall], "break through," "break into" BDAG 251b; ZG 233; Fitzmyer 989) is complementary.

12:40 The nom. pl. masc. adj. ἕτοιμοι (of ἕτοιμος, -η, -ον, "prepared") is the pred. of the impv. γίνεσθε (see 6:36). Ὅτι, causal (giving the reason they should be ready). The dat. sg. fem. rel. pron. ᾗ (of ὅς, ἥ, ὅ) and ὥρᾳ is a dat. of time ("at an hour" HCSB, ESV, NIV). Δοκεῖτε 2nd pl. pres. act. indic. of δοκέω (neg. with οὐ). Ἔρχεται, see 3:16 (the pres. tense may be fut. referring, Robertson, *Pictures* 180; Z §278; ZG 233). For ὁ υἱὸς τοῦ ἀνθρώπου see 5:24.

12:41 Following the parable about the return of ὁ κύριος (12:36–37), Peter's question to Jesus addresses him as κύριε (voc.; with ὁ κύριος in 12:42, the voc. here is more than "sir," Nolland 702). Πρός with ἡμᾶς and πάντας has the mng. "with reference/regard to" (BDAG 875a). Παραβολή, see 8:4. Λέγεις 2nd sg. pres. act. indic. of λέγω. The addition of καί indicates that Peter asks if the "Lord" is speaking only to "us" (ἡμᾶς), or to "everyone else *as well*" (NASB). However, πάντας may refer to the rest of the disciples (with ἡμᾶς referring to a smaller group such as the Twelve, Bovon 2.236–37) or to the crowd (Fitzmyer 989; Nolland 705; with ἡμᾶς referring to the disciples; cf. 12:1, 13, 22, 54). In light of 12:45–46, Jesus' reply indicates that he is speaking about all who are associated with him (12:46 indicates that some will be excluded), while focusing particularly on those with leadership responsibilities (12:42, 45 indicate that a distinction is made between servants; Bock 1178).

12:42 Following the voc. address to Jesus as κύριε, the reply comes from ὁ κύριος with a parable about a returning κύριος (cf. Rowe 151–54). The response to Peter's question is introduced with a question (τίς ἄρα, answered in 12:43) that invites the listener to identify with the following parable (Marshall 540). The attrib. adjs. ὁ πιστός and ὁ φρόνιμος ("faithful and wise"; nom. sg. masc. of φρόνιμος, -ον) both modify οἰκονόμος (nom. sg. masc. of οἰκονόμος, -ου, ὁ, "steward" RSV, NASB; "manager" NRSV, HCSB, ESV, NIV; cf. BDF §269; T 186–87; note the similar sounding οἰκονόμος ὁ φρόνιμος). This "manager" is then further described (the acc. rel. pron. ὅν). Ὁ κύριος is the subj. of καταστήσει (3rd sg. fut. act. indic. of καθίστημι, "put in charge"; cf. 12:14). Ἐπί is used as a marker of power or authority over someone (BDAG 365c–d). Θεραπείας, "household servants" (HCSB; [see 9:11]; LN 46.6; "servants" NIV; BDAG 453a; "household" ESV). The art. inf. τοῦ διδόναι (see 11:13) expresses purpose (BDF §§390[4], 400[5]; Z §383; the pres. is iter., ZG 233). Σιτομέτριον acc. sg. neut. of σιτομέτριον, -ου, τό, "allowance of food" (NRSV, sim. NIV; LN 5.3; MM 576a). Thus, the responsibility of the manager is to ensure timely (ἐν καιρῷ, "at the right time" BDAG 497d) care and provision for the servants.

12:43 For the cstr. with μακάριοι (see 6:20; cf. 12:37). Ἐκεῖνος here has the sense "that sort of servant" (Marshall 541). For the use of the pl. form of the rel. pron. ὅν in conjunction with ἐλθών (see 7:3) and εὑρήσει, see 12:37 (cf. 12:40). Ποιοῦντα (acc. sg. masc. of pres. act. ptc. of ποιέω) is the complement in a double acc. cstr. (BDAG 411d). The adv. οὕτως refers to τοῦ διδόναι . . . σιτομέτριον in 12:42 (see also οὕτως in 12:38).

12:44 For ἀληθῶς λέγω ὑμῖν see 9:27. Ὅτι, recitative. Ἐπί is used here as a marker of power, authority, or control over something (BDAG 365d; Robertson, *Pictures* 181; ZG 233). The faithful slave is appointed to a position of authority (Marshall 541). Ὑπάρχουσιν dat. pl. neut. of pres. act. (subst.) ptc. of ὑπάρχω. Καταστήσει, see 12:42.

12:45 Ἐάν introduces a third-class cond. sentence (Robertson, *Pictures* 181). Following the description of a faithful servant in 12:43–44, the cond. sentence here with the demonstrative pron. ἐκεῖνος introduces a description of how an unfaithful servant might act (12:45–48 will have three types of unfaithful servants). Εἴπη (see 11:5; the subj. is ὁ δοῦλος ἐκεῖνος) is subjunc. with ἐάν. Χρονίζει 3rd sg. pres. act. indic. of χρονίζω, "take time," "delay." The inf. ἔρχεσθαι (see 9:23) is complementary. Ἄρξηται (3rd sg. aor. mid. subjunc. of ἄρχω, "begin"; redundant, Marshall 542) is also subjunc. with ἐάν (also a third-class cond.). The pres. act. inf. τύπτειν (of τύπτω, "beat") is complementary. Τοὺς παῖδας [acc. pl. masc., see 1:54] καὶ τὰς παιδίσκας, "male and female slaves" (HCSB; acc. pl. fem. of παιδίσκη, -ης, ἡ). The particle τε with καί . . . καί is used as a marker connecting the following three infs. (BDAG 993d). The three pres. infs. ἐσθίειν (act. of ἐσθίω), πίνειν (act. of πίνω), and μεθύσκεσθαι (pass. of dep. μεθύσκομαι, "get drunk") are complementary (also following ἄρξηται).

12:46 Ἥξει 3rd sg. fut. act. indic. of ἥκω, "come." Ἐν followed by the dat. ἡμέρᾳ and dat. rel. pron. ᾗ (the rel. pron. could be dat. by attraction to the antecedent [Wallace 339; Z §16; ZG 233], or perhaps it follows another implied ἐν, BHGNT 439; McKay 147) is temp. ("on a day when" NRSV, ESV, NIV; sim. with ἐν ὥρᾳ ᾗ; Marshall 543 distinguishes between the first ἦ as a dat. of time, and the second ἦ as dat. by attraction). Προσδοκᾷ 3rd sg. pres. act. indic. of προσδοκάω, "look for," "expect" (neg. with οὐ). Γινώσκει, see 10:22 (neg. with οὐ). Διχοτομήσει 3rd sg. fut. act. indic. of διχοτομέω, "cut in two" (NKJV; BDAG 253a; LN 19.19; Bock 1182; Marshall 543; Nolland 705), "cut to pieces" (HCSB, NIV, sim. NRSV, NASB, ESV). BDAG states that there is no linguistic support for the figurative mng. "punish with utmost severity" (cf. RSV; cf. LN 38.12; LSJ 439c; Fitzmyer 990) or "cut him off" (cf. NJB, NRSV mg.; cf. MM 165d). The acc. sg. neut. τὸ μέρος (modified by the poss. αὐτοῦ, "his portion" NKJV; "him" most EVV) is the obj. of θήσει (3rd sg. fut. act. indic. of τίθημι). Ἀπίστων gen. pl. masc. (of ἄπιστος, -ον) "unbelievers" (NKJV, NASB, HCSB, NIV), "unfaithful" (NRSV, ESV; Robertson, *Pictures* 181; Fitzmyer 990). In this context ἀπίστων contrasts with πιστός (12:42). The image is that of the total rejection of a false teacher (Bock 1183).

12:47 The nom. ἐκεῖνος . . . ὁ δοῦλος is the subj. of δαρήσεται (3rd sg. 2nd fut. pass. indic. of δέρω, "beat"). The subj. ἐκεῖνος . . . ὁ δοῦλος is different to the previous slave as he is further described with the nom. sg. masc. of aor. act. (attrib.) ptcs. γνούς (2nd aor. of γινώσκω), ἑτοιμάσας (of ἑτοιμάζω), and ποιήσας (see 6:49; ἑτοιμάσας and ποιήσας are both neg. with μή). Πρός has the mng. "with reference to" or "in accordance with" (BDAG 875b). The acc. adj. πολλάς could mean "much" ("severely" HCSB) or "many" with an implied noun πληγάς ("blows") being supplied ("many blows" NIV; BDF §§154, 241[6]; Bock 1184; Fitzmyer 992; for the acc. following the pass. vb., cf. Robertson, *Pictures* 182; Z §72). The punishment, though "much," is not the total rejection of the previous slave. The distinction between the punishment of this slave and the following slave is based on the response of the slave to what he "knows."

12:48 The subst. ptc. ὁ . . . γνούς (see 12:47; neg. with μή; with the obj. "his master's will" implied, NET) is the subj. of δαρήσεται (see 12:47). The anar. ptc. ποιήσας (see 6:49; in this context, cf. 12:47) with δέ could be concessive ("but did," cf. NJB; BHGNT 441; Fitzmyer 991) or coordinate ("and did" HCSB, sim. most EVV). The anar. ptc. ποιήσας could modify δαρήσεται (BHGNT 441). The use of δὲ . . . δέ, however, indicates that the ptc. ποιήσας should be seen as subst. and parallel with γνούς. The neut. pl. ἄξια, modified by the complementary gen. πληγῶν (see 10:30), is "things deserving of blows" (HCSB; cf. Wallace 135). As with πολλάς in 12:47, the acc. adj. ὀλίγας could mean "little" ("lightly" HCSB) or "few" with an implied noun πληγάς ("blows") being supplied ("few blows" NIV). The adj. παντί could be a dat. of ref., or it could signify (with the dat. rel. pron. ᾧ) the topic that follows (cf. παρ' αὐτοῦ; the dat. παντί is by inverse attraction; BDF §§295, 466[3]; BHGNT 441; Z §19; ZG 233; Marshall 545; on the cstr. as replacing the nom., cf. R 767–68; Z §§25, 29; Fitzmyer 124–25). The parallel structure of the second half of the verse (with another dat. rel. pron. ᾧ) favors the latter. Ἐδόθη 3rd sg. aor. pass. indic. of δίδωμι (the subj. is the nom. adj. πολύ). Ζητηθήσεται 3rd sg. fut. pass. indic. of ζητέω, "seek," "required" (NRSV, HCSB, ESV), "demanded" (NIV). Παρέθεντο 3rd pl. 2nd aor. mid. indic. of παρατίθημι, "entrust." Αἰτήσουσιν 3rd pl. fut. act. indic. of αἰτέω (the acc. αὐτόν is the obj. and the acc. comp. adj. περισσότερον, "more" [see 7:26], may be the obj. of an implied inf.

δοῦναι, BHGNT 441). The 3rd pls. are indef. pls. (Robertson, *Pictures* 182; Wallace 403; Z §1; a ref. to the master, Bock 1186; to God, Marshall 545; since "the master" in the parable is "the Lord" Jesus, the indef. pl. refers to Jesus, Rowe 153–54).

HOMILETICAL SUGGESTIONS

Waiting for the Master to Return (12:35–48)

1. The servant who is always ready to serve will be served by the Lord (12:35–40).
2. The servant who faithfully cares for others will be rewarded with privileged responsibility by the Lord (12:41–44).
3. The supposed "servant" who abuses those under his care will be consigned to judgment with unbelievers by the Lord (12:45–46).
4. The servants who do not obey will be judged according to knowledge by the Lord (12:47–48).

5. Living with the Final Judgment in View Helps Understand the Significance of Jesus' Earthly Ministry (12:49–59)

12:49 As with 12:35, the following warnings are placed here without any explanatory or coordinating conj. (thus, again, appearing to be a continuation of the preceding exhortations concerning judgment). Ἦλθον 1st sg. aor. act. indic. of dep. ἔρχομαι. The 2nd aor. act. inf. βαλεῖν (of βάλλω) expresses purpose. The acc. πῦρ is emphatic (ZG 234). Ἐπὶ τὴν γῆν is locat. This purpose statement for Jesus "coming" with ref. to bringing divine judgment "on the earth" assumes he came from heaven (i.e., preexistence; Gathercole 161–63; cf. 5:32; 12:51). The neut. interr. pron. τί is used here as an "exclamatory expression of extent or degree" (BDAG 1007d; "how I wish . . .!" NRSV, NASB, HCSB, NIV; a Sem., BDF §§299[4], 360[4]; R 739, 917, 1193; Z §405). Ἀνήφθη 3rd sg. aor. pass. indic. of ἀνάπτω, "kindle" (most EVV), "set ablaze" (HCSB). Εἰ following θέλω expresses the content of the wish ("that [it were already kindled]" ESV; cf. BDAG 278a; LN 90.26; LSJ 480c; equal to ὅτι, Robertson, *Pictures* 182).

12:50 Ἔχω, see 7:40. The inf. βαπτισθῆναι (see 3:7) is epex. (with the cognate acc. βάπτισμα [see 3:3], which is likely a ref. to an inundation of divine judgment, Bock 1194; "immersed in disaster" Nolland 710, with ref. to the coming passion). Δέ may indicate that this "baptism" is the precondition for the judgment just mentioned (Marshall 547). Πῶς is used as an exclamation ("how . . .!" NASB, HCSB, ESV; BDAG 901c; BDF §436; Z §221; cf. 18:24). Συνέχομαι 1st sg. pres. pass. indic. of συνέχω, "oppress," "distress" (ESV; BDAG 971a), "constraint" (NIV). Ἕως followed by the gen. rel. pron. ὅτου with the subjunc. τελεσθῇ (3rd sg. aor. pass. subjunc. of τελέω) is a temp. cstr. (cf. "up to a point" LN 67.119; ZG 234; cf. BDAG 730b; Wallace 480).

12:51 Δοκεῖτε, see 12:40. Ὅτι introduces indir. discourse (replacing ἵνα after a vb. of perception, Z §380). Παρεγενόμην 1st sg. 2nd aor. mid. indic. of dep. παραγίνομαι, "come." The inf. δοῦναι (see 1:73) expresses purpose (cf. 12:49; perhaps replacing a fut. ptc., Z §282; ZG 234; a Sem. mng. "set," "put" Fitzmyer 997; Marshall 548). Ἐν τῇ γῇ is locat. The neg. οὐχί with λέγω ὑμῖν, and ἀλλ' with the disjunctive particle ἤ emphasizes the contrast (ἀλλ' ἤ, "but rather" NRSV, HCSB, ESV; "on the contrary" ZG 234). The acc. sg. masc. διαμερισμόν (of διαμερισμός, -οῦ, ὁ, "division"; cf. διαμερίζω in 12:52–53) is the obj. of an implied δοῦναι. This "division" is part of the judgment (12:49) which divides between the righteous and the wicked (Bock 1192; Marshall 547).

12:52 Γάρ is explanatory, confirming the previous general statement with more specific details (BDAG 189c). For ἀπὸ τοῦ νῦν see 1:48. Διαμεμερισμένοι (nom. pl. masc. of pf. pass. ptc. of διαμερίζω, "divide") with ἔσονται (see 11:19) is a fut. pf. periph. cstr. (cf. διαμερισμόν in 12:51; on the fut. pf. cf. T 89). The noms. τρεῖς and δύο are in appos. to πέντε. Ἐπί is a marker of "hostile opposition" (BDAG 366a; cf. LN 90.34).

12:53 The noms. πατήρ . . . καὶ υἱός are the subj. of διαμερισθήσονται (3rd pl. fut. pass. indic. of διαμερίζω, "divide"). For ἐπί in this context see 12:52 (the first dat. pair are followed by acc. arts. without any shift in mng.). The noms. μήτηρ . . . καὶ θυγάτηρ and πενθερὰ [see 4:38] . . . καὶ νύμφη ("mother-in-law . . . daughter-in-law" [nom. sg. fem. of νύμφη, -ης, ἡ]) are the subjs. of an implied διαμερισθήσονται. The three pairs are arranged chiastically to highlight the opposing factions (Marshall 549; cf. Mic 7:6).

12:54 The impf. ἔλεγεν may indicate the continuity of Jesus' illustration with the preceding statements (cf. 5:36). Καί "also" (omitted in NIV) indicates the continued inclusion of the disciples in the audience as Jesus now also addresses the crowds (12:1, 4, 22, 41). Ὅταν with the subjunc. ἴδητε (2nd pl. 2nd aor. act. subjunc. of ὁράω) is temp. Ἀνατέλλουσαν (acc. sg. fem. of pres. act. ptc. of ἀνατέλλω, "rise"; intrans.) could be attrib. (modifying νεφέλην, "cloud") or the complement in a double acc. cstr. (BDAG 279d; ZG 234). Ἐπὶ δυσμῶν is locat. (gen. pl. fem. of δυσμή, -ῆς, ἡ, "in the west"; referring to the setting sun, i.e., the west, BDAG 265c). Λέγετε, see 7:33. Ὅτι, recitative. The nom. sg. masc. ὄμβρος (of ὄμβρος, -ου, ὁ, "rainstorm," "thunderstorm" BDAG 705a; LN 14.12) is the subj. of ἔρχεται (see 3:16). Γίνεται, see 11:26 ("it happens").

12:55 Ὅταν introduces a temp. clause with an implied subjunc. ἴδητε (see 12:54). Πνέοντα (acc. sg. masc. of pres. act. ptc. of πνέω, "blow") could be attrib. (modifying νότον [see 11:31], "south wind") or the complement in a double acc. cstr. (see above, 12:54). Λέγετε ὅτι, see above (12:54). Καύσων nom. sg. masc. of καύσων, -ωνος, ὁ, "burning heat" (the subj. of ἔσται [see 1:14]). Γίνεται, see 11:26 (as above, 12:54).

12:56 Ὑποκριταί, voc. (see 6:42; cf. ὑπόκρισις, 12:1). The acc. τὸ πρόσωπον (here "appearance" most EVV; BDAG 888c; LN 24.24; modified by the poss. τῆς γῆς καὶ τοῦ οὐρανοῦ, "earth and sky") is the obj. of the (complementary) pres. act. inf. δοκιμάζειν (of δοκιμάζω, "test," "analyze" NASB; "interpret" most EVV). Οἴδατε, see 11:13. The placement of τὸ πρόσωπον . . . οὐρανοῦ and τὸν καιρὸν . . . τοῦτον (the obj. of the second δοκιμάζειν) emphasizes the contrast (BHGNT 446).

12:57 Δέ probably connects this rhetorical question (with the neut. interr. pron. τί) with the previous one ("And why"; omitted in NJB, HCSB, NIV). Ἀπό is a marker to indicate outcome from responsible agents (BDAG 107a; "for yourselves" most EVV; see Z §209 for the refl. pron.). The acc. sg. neut. adj. τὸ δίκαιον (of δίκαιος, -α, -ον, "what is right") is the obj. of κρίνετε (2nd pl. pres. act. indic. of κρίνω; neg. with οὐ).

12:58 Γάρ serves to reinforce the previous exhortation ("Thus" NRSV; or it may just have the force of δέ, Z §473; ZG 235). The importance of making a right judgment is now illustrated (Bock 1198). Ὡς with ὑπάγεις (2nd sg. pres. act. indic. of ὑπάγω) is temp. (HCSB). Ἀντιδίκου gen. sg. masc. of ἀντίδικος, -ου, ὁ, "adversary" (cf. 18:3). Ἐπ᾽ ἄρχοντα is locat. ("to the ruler" HCSB; "before the magistrate" NASB, ESV; "judge" BDAG 140d; LN 56.29). Ἐν τῇ ὁδῷ is temp. The combination of δός (2nd sg. 2nd aor. act. impv. of δίδωμι) with ἐργασίαν (acc. sg. fem. of ἐργασία, -ας, ἡ, "work," "effort") is an idiom for "take pains," "make an effort" (a Latinism, BDAG 243b; BDF §5[3b]; R 109; ZG 235). The pf. pass. inf. ἀπηλλάχθαι (of ἀπαλλάσσω, "be released," "settle" NASB, NRSV, HCSB, ESV; "get rid of" the accuser BDAG 96c; "dismissed as settled" LSJ 176c; Nolland 714) expresses purpose. Μήποτε with the subjunc. κατασύρῃ (3rd sg. pres. act. subjunc. of κατασύρω, "drag") expresses a negative purpose (see

14:8). Παραδώσει 3rd sg. fut. act. indic. of παραδίδωμι (κριτής, see 11:19). Πράκτορι dat. sg. masc. of πράκτωρ, -ορος, ὁ, "bailiff" (HCSB), "officer" (NRSV, ESV, NIV; someone under a judge's orders and in charge of a debtor's prison, BDAG 859d; LN 37.92; LSJ 1459a; MM 533b). Βαλεῖ 3rd sg. fut. act. indic. of βάλλω (the fut. indic. παραδώσει and βαλεῖ is used in place of the subjunc., BDF §369[3]; Z §342; ZG 235).

12:59 The subjunc. ἐξέλθῃς (2nd sg. 2nd aor. act. subjunc. of dep. ἐξέρχομαι) with οὐ μή is an emphatic neg. ("you will never get out" NRSV, HCSB, ESV; cf. Z §444). Ἕως with the subjunc. ἀποδῷς (2nd sg. 2nd aor. subjunc. of ἀποδίδωμι, "give back," "paid" all EVV; cf. 7:42) is an indef. temp. clause (without ἄν, Burton §323; R 976; with ref. to the fut., ZG 235). The λεπτός (adj. λεπτός, -ή, -όν; "small," neut. is subst. "small coin") was the smallest coin in circulation and worth about 1/128 of a denarius (cf. 21:2; with τὸ ἔσχατον, "the very last penny" ESV; cf. BDAG 592d; LN 6.79; MM 374a).

HOMILETICAL SUGGESTIONS

Jesus and Judgment (12:49–59)
1. Jesus came to bear judgment and bring judgment that will divide humanity (12:49–53).
2. Jesus' coming is a sign that warns of the impending judgment (12:54–56).
3. Impending judgment highlights the urgency of reconciling with God now (12:57–59).

6. Living with the Final Judgment in View Helps Underscore the Urgent Need to Repent (13:1–9)

13:1 Παρῆσαν 3rd pl. impf. act. indic. of πάρειμι, "be present" (NRSV, NASB, NIV; LN 85.23; ZG 235; Nolland 717). The mng. "arrived" (NJB; Bock 1204; Marshall 553) or "came" (HCSB; BDAG 773d; MM 492a; cf. BDF §322) is possible but may require an additional prep. such as εἰς or ἐκ (BHGNT 449; cf. LSJ 1333b). For αὐτῷ see 10:7 (here in a temp. phrase, "at that very time" ESV; or "at that time" NIV; R 686). The opening cstr. closely connects the following with the preceding discourses (Marshall 553; Nolland 717). Ἀπαγγέλλοντες (nom. pl. masc. of pres. act. ptc. of ἀπαγγέλλω) is probably attrib. ("there were some present . . . who told him" NRSV, ESV, sim. NIV) or attendant circumstance with παρῆσαν ("came and reported" HCSB). The gen. rel. pron. ὧν is poss. (modifying τῶν Γαλιλαίων). The "mix" (ἔμιξεν 3rd sg. aor. act. indic. of μίγνυμι, or μιγνύω, BDAG 650d) of the Galileans' blood "with their sacrifices" (θυσιῶν gen. pl. fem., see 2:24) is an idiom that means Pilate either had them killed while their animals were sacrificed or at least ordered their death at that time (BDAG 650d; LN 63.10; in the temple, Bovon 2.267; Marshall 553; or as they approached with their sacrifices, Bock 1204).

13:2 Ἀποκριθείς, see 1:19. Δοκεῖτε, see 12:40. Ὅτι introduces indir. discourse (following a vb. of perception). The demonstrative pron. οὗτοι in the pred. position modifies οἱ Γαλιλαῖοι as the subj. of ἐγένοντο (3rd pl. 2nd aor. mid. indic. of dep. γίνομαι). The nom. adj. ἁμαρτωλοί is pred. Παρά is used here as a "marker of comparative advantage" ("more than" BDAG 757d–58a; LN 78.29; BDF §236[3]; R 616; Z §145; "worse . . . than" most EVV). Jesus' assessment assumes sinfulness. The question is just whether they were more sinful (Nolland 719). Ὅτι, causal (giving the reason for their false evaluation). Πεπόνθασιν 3rd pl. 2nd pf. act. indic. of πάσχω (the pf. may indicate the state of affairs which led to this verdict, Marshall 554).

13:3 The adv. οὐχί is used here as a neg. reply (followed by ἀλλά, BDAG 742b; emphatic ZG 235; Marshall 554). Μετανοῆτε 2nd pl. pres. act. subjunc. of μετανοέω (neg. with μή). The subjunc. with ἐάν is a third-class cond. sentence (leaving open whether repentance will take place, Bock 1206). Πάντες could modify μετανοῆτε but likely modifies ἀπολεῖσθε (2nd pl. fut. mid. indic. of ἀπόλλυμι; all EVV) to complete the ref. to the other Galileans who were killed (Bock 1206; Fitzmyer 1008; Marshall 553). The adv. ὁμοίως is better tr. "as well" (HCSB, sim. NIV) rather than "likewise" (NASB, ESV) to avoid the misunderstanding that the point is about disaster by the same means (NET n.). The language of repentance (cf. μετάνοια in 3:3; μετανοέω in 10:13) in the context of the previous discussion about judgment indicates that the warning here concerns the greater consequences for the unrepentant before God after death (Bock 1206–7; Fitzmyer 1008; Marshall 554; cf. 12:20).

13:4 The nom. ἐκεῖνοι οἱ δεκαοκτώ ("those eighteen"; [indecl.]) is the subj. of the follow-up question, raised this time by Jesus (referred to again by αὐτοί, BHGNT 451; a pendent nom. Z §25–26; ZG 235). The eighteen are first described as those "upon whom" (ἐφ' οὕς) the tower (ὁ πύργος nom. sg. masc. of πύργος, -ου, ὁ) in Siloam "fell" (ἔπεσεν, see 8:5) and "killed" (ἀπέκτεινεν 3rd sg. aor. act. indic. of ἀποκτείνω). The question about these eigh-teen follows a similar pattern to 13:2 (for δοκεῖτε, ἐγένοντο, and παρά see 13:2) though the nom. pl. masc. ὀφειλέται ("debtors," of ὀφειλέτης, -ου, ὁ; cf. ὀφείλω, 7:41; 11:4) replaces ἁμαρτωλοί as the pred. ("worse culprits" NASB; "worse offenders" NRSV, ESV; "more guilty" NIV). Κατοικοῦντας acc. pl. masc. of pres. act. (attrib.) ptc. of κατοικέω (modifying πάντας τοὺς ἀνθρώπους, "all the others" ESV, NIV) may be followed with εἰς or ἐν, or take the acc. as here ("inhabit" BDAG 534d; BHGNT 451; "live in" most EVV).

13:5 The answer follows a sim. pattern to 13:3 except the adv. ὡσαύτως ("likewise" ESV) is used in place of ὁμοίως (probably for stylistic variation, BHGNT 452; Marshall 554; *pace* Bock 1207; the var. ὁμοίως may be to assimilate to 13:3). Whereas the pre-vious incident was perpetrated by Pilate, this accident may be interpreted as an act of God's judgment. Although these temporal incidents do not indicate a level of sinful-ness, they point to a greater disaster to come after death for the unrepentant.

13:6 For ἔλεγεν see 5:36 (cf. 3:7). Παραβολή see 8:4. Εἶχεν 3rd sg. impf. act. indic. of ἔχω (the subj. is the enclitic indef. pron. τις; sim. to ἄνθρωπός τις of other parables [10:30], Bovon 2.270). Συκῆν acc. sg. fem. of συκῆ, -ῆς, ἡ, "fig tree" (cf. 21:29) is modified by πεφυτευμένην (acc. sg. fem. of pf. pass. [attrib.] ptc. of φυτεύω, "plant"). Ἀμπελῶνι dat. sg. masc. of ἀμπελών, -ῶνος, ὁ, "vineyard" (cf. 20:9–16; Marshall 555). Ἦλθεν, see 2:27. Ζητῶν (see 11:10) could express manner or *purpose ("he went to look" NIV; R 1115; Wallace 637). Εὗρεν, see 4:17 (neg. with οὐχ).

13:7 The owner now speaks to the "vineyard worker" (HCSB; ἀμπελουργόν acc. sg. masc. of ἀμπελουργός, -οῦ, ὁ; BDAG 55a; MM 27d). Ἰδού, see 1:19. The neut. pl. τρία ἔτη ("three years") could be acc. expressing extent of time or nom. as an exclamation (BHGNT 453; cf. Wallace 59–60; or a parenthetical nom. BDF §144; Fitzmyer 1008; Marshall 555; cf. Wallace 53–54). Ἀπό with the rel. pron. οὗ is temp. with the pre-ceding time ref. ("since," see 7:45; "for" most EVV; ZG 235). The pres. ἔρχομαι (1st sg. pres. mid. indic. of dep. ἔρχομαι) and εὑρίσκω (1st sg. pres. act. indic. of εὑρίσκω; neg. with οὐχ) with the preceding past referring temp. expression portrays an action that continues into the present ("I have come . . . and find none" ESV; BDF §322; Wallace 520; Nolland 716 tr. ἔρχομαι as ingressive). For ζητῶν see 13:6 (for the form see 11:10). Ἔκκοψον 2nd sg. aor. act. impv. of ἐκκόπτω, "cut out" (i.e., of the vineyard, Robertson, *Pictures* 186; the antecedent of the dir. obj. fem. pron. αὐτήν is τῇ συκῇ, see 13:6). The interr. adv. ἱνατί is a shortened form (crasis) of ἵνα τί γένηται mng. "why" (BDAG 477b; R 739; ZG 235; καί, "even" NASB, HCSB; Bovon 2.271). Καταργεῖ 3rd sg. pres. act. indic. of καταργέω ("bring to nothing") may have the mng. here of caus-ing the ground to be unproductive (BDAG 525c; "no use" Robertson, *Pictures* 187) probably by "depleting the soil" of nutrients (NET; Bovon 2.271; Marshall 555) rather than simply "taking up space" (NLT).

13:8 Ἀποκριθείς, see 1:19 (the subj. is the gardener; on the redundant ἀποκριθείς with the historic pres. λέγει, see Wallace 625). Κύριε, voc. ("Sir" most EVV; ZG 236; "Lord" KJV, RV; referring to the owner). Ἄφες, see 6:42 ("leave"). Καί, "also" (HCSB, ESV). The acc. τοῦτο τὸ ἔτος expresses extent of time (cf. 13:7). For ἕως ὅτου ("until") see 12:50. The 1st sg. aor. act. subjuncs. σκάψω (of σκάπτω, "dig"; see 6:48) and βάλω (2nd aor. of βάλλω) are indef. temp. cstrs. with ἕως. Κόπρια, "manure" (ESV), "fertilizer" (NASB, sim. HCSB, NIV; acc. pl. neut. of κόπριον, -ου, τό [only here in the NT]; cf. fem. sg. in 14:35).

13:9 Κἄν (see 12:38) with the subjunc. ποιήσῃ (3rd sg. aor. act. subjunc. of ποιέω; with καρπόν a Sem. "bear fruit" ZG 236) introduces a third-class cond. sentence. Εἰς with μέλλον (acc. sg. neut. of pres. act. [subst.] ptc. of μέλλω) is temp. (lit. "in the coming [year]"; "next year" most EVV; BDAG 628b; R 594). The apodosis is omitted, but most EVV supply "fine" (NASB, NIV) or "well and good" (NRSV, ESV; cf. BDF §454[4]; "aposiopesis" R 1023; Bovon 2.273; Marshall 556). The omission, however, may serve to emphasize that this outcome is unlikely (NJB, HCSB). For εἰ δὲ μή γε see 5:36; 10:6 (the omission of the apodosis after an ἐάν clause and followed by εἰ δὲ μή γε occurs in the LXX, ZG 236). In this context, following an affirmative clause, it introduces a contrasting (μὲν . . . δέ) first-class. cond. ("otherwise" BDAG 278d; i.e., assuming this will be true). The first-class cond. indicates that the absence of fruit is more likely than fruit bearing (with the third-class cond., Bock 1210). Ἐκκόψεις 2nd sg. fut. act. indic. of ἐκκόπτω ("cut off"; see 13:7; a "volitive" fut., R 874).

HOMILETICAL SUGGESTIONS

The Necessity of Repentance (13:1–9)
1. There is greater suffering after death for all who do not repent (13:1–5).
2. There is mercy now so repent before time runs out (13:6–9).

C. BECAUSE OF JESUS THE HUMBLE JOYFULLY ANTICIPATE
THE CELEBRATION TO COME (13:10–15:32)

The previous episode culminates 12:1–13:9 with its emphasis on the final judgment. Although some suggest a narrative break with the travel note at 13:22, the following thematic connections throughout 13:10–35 and 14:1–35 tie this unit together (Nolland 722):

13:10–17 and 14:1–6	Sabbath healings
13:18–21 and 14:7–14	Parables about the kingdom (14:15 links kingdom and banquet)
13:22–30 and 14:15–24	Descriptions of who will be at the final kingdom banquet
13:31–35 and 14:25–35	Jesus travels to death in Jerusalem; disciples follow this pattern

References (in various ways) to the humble (13:11–12; 14:10–11, 13, 21, 23, 26–27, 33), the reversal to come (13:18–21, 30; 14:10–11, 21, 24), and celebration (13:13, 16–17, 29; 14:15–16) recur throughout this section. Luke 15 brings these themes together (15:6–7, 9–10, 21, 24, 32).

1. A Foretaste of Jesus' Saving Rule and Victory over Satan (13:10–21)

13:10 The impf. periph. cstr. of διδάσκων (see 4:31) with ἦν gives the setting for this incident. Ἐν μιᾷ τῶν συναγωγῶν is locat. (with a partitive gen.; on μιᾷ for τινί see Z §155). This is the last ref. to Jesus teaching in a synagogue in Luke. Ἐν τοῖς σάββασιν is temp. (for refs. to this term and Sabbath controversies see 4:16; for the periph. cstr. with the pl. see 4:31; the sg. is used in 13:14–16). The previous ref. to the Sabbath in Luke was 6:9 (in that context Jesus declared himself to be "Lord of the Sabbath" 6:5; see 13:15).

13:11 Ἰδού, see 1:19. The nom. γυνή, modified by ἔχουσα (nom. sg. fem. of pres. act. [attrib.] ptc. of ἔχω), is the subj. of an implied ἦν ἐκεῖ. The gen. ἀσθενείας (see 5:15) is likely a gen. of product ("sickness caused by a spirit" NASB, sim. NRSV, HCSB, NIV; BHGNT 456; Robertson, *Pictures* 187; Wallace 106; ZG 236; an Aram. Fitzmyer 1012; Marshall 557). The expression could be idiomatic for a "debilitating ailment" (Nolland 724); or an "evil influence" (Marshall 557; the cure is not described as an exorcism). The acc. ἔτη δεκαοκτώ ("eighteen years"; cf. 13:4) expresses extent of time. The nom. sg. fem. of pres. ptcs. συγκύπτουσα (act. of συγκύπτω, "bent over," "bent double" BDAG 953c; LN 17.32; LSJ 1668a; only here in the NT) and δυναμένη (mid. of dep. δύναμαι; neg. with μή) with ἦν are impf. periph. cstrs. The aor. act. inf. ἀνακύψαι (of ἀνακύπτω, "straighten up"; cf. Job 10:15) is complementary. Although εἰς τὸ παντελές (acc. sg. neut. of παντελής, -ές, as an adv. "fully," "completely"; only here and Heb 7:25 in the NT) could modify μὴ δυναμένη ("quite unable" NJB, NRSV, sim. "at all" HCSB, NIV; BDAG 754d [mng. 1b]; ZG 236; Bock 1215; Marshall 558;

Nolland 724 [due to the severity of the condition]), the word order favors ἀνακύψαι ("fully straighten" RSV, ESV; BDAG 754d [mng. 1a]; BHGNT 457; cf. Josephus refs. in Plummer 342).

13:12 Ἰδών, see 1:12 (temp.). Jesus is the one who takes the initiative. Προσεφώνησεν, "called out to" (HCSB, sim. RSV; BHGNT 457) or *"called her over" (ESV, sim. most EVV; see 6:13; 13:10 and 13a imply the second mng. here). Γύναι, voc. (a polite form of address, BDAG 209b). Ἀπολέλυσαι 2nd sg. pf. pass. indic. of ἀπολύω, "set free" (NRSV, NIV; BDAG 117d [often in contexts of debt or imprisonment]; LN 37.127; the pf. may emphasize the resulting state, Bock 1216; Fitzmyer 1013; Marshall 558; for the pass. see 13:13). Τῆς ἀσθενείας (see 5:15), gen. of separation.

13:13 Ἐπέθηκεν 3rd sg. aor. act. indic. of ἐπιτίθημι, "lay upon," "place upon." Τάς with χεῖρας functions as a poss. pron. (R 769–70). Παραχρῆμα, see 1:64 (in contrast to the eighteen years mentioned twice, 13:11, 16). Ἀνωρθώθη 3rd sg. aor. pass. indic. of ἀνορθόω, "was restored" (HCSB), "made straight" (RSV, ESV; BDAG 86b; LN 17.33 notes that ἀνακύπτω [13:11] may differ slightly in referring to a reversal of a process). The pass. may be a divine pass. (Bock 1216; Fitzmyer 1013); the emphasis in 13:12 is on the powerful word of Jesus. "Restoring" or "straightening" those who are "bowed down" is something for which the psalmists praise the Lord (cf. ἀνορθόω in LXX Pss 19:9; 144:14; 145:8). As happens regularly in Luke, God is glorified (ἐδόξαζεν 3rd sg. impf. act. indic. of δοξάζω; the impf. is probably ingressive, NRSV, NASB, HCSB; R 885; ZG 236; or durative, Fitzmyer 1013) because of Jesus' work (on δοξάζω in Luke see 2:20; 4:15).

13:14 Ἀρχισυνάγωγος refers to the ruler or leader of the synagogue (see 8:49; ἀποκριθείς, see 1:19; here indicating a response to the healing, Marshall 558) and is the subj. of ἔλεγεν (on ἔλεγεν with ἀποκριθείς see 3:11). Before being told what the synagogue ruler said, however, his attitude is described. Ἀγανακτῶν nom. sg. masc. of pres. act. (attrib.) ptc. of ἀγανακτέω, "be indignant." Ὅτι, causal (giving the reason for this anger, BDAG 5a; Bock 1217 suggests the possibility that ὅτι introduces indir. discourse, giving the ruler's thinking about Jesus). Τῷ σαββάτῳ is a dat. of time (Wallace 157). Ἐθεράπευσεν, see 7:21. Ὅτι (after ἔλεγεν τῷ ὄχλῳ), recitative (ZG 236; Marshall 558). The ruler ignores Jesus and directs his angry response to the crowd; perhaps in an attempt to marginalize the teaching and authority of Jesus. Ἕξ, "six" (indecl.). Ἐν with the rel. pron. αἷς (the antecedent is ἡμέραι) is temp. Δεῖ, see 2:49 (the ruler's use of δεῖ is contrasted with Jesus' use of ἔδει in 13:16, Fitzmyer 1011). The pres. mid. inf. ἐργάζεσθαι (of dep. ἐργάζομαι) is complementary. Ἐρχόμενοι (nom. pl. masc. of pres. mid. [attendant circumstance] ptc. of dep. ἔρχομαι) takes on the mood of θεραπεύεσθε (2nd pl. pres. pass. impv. of θεραπεύω). The neg. μή is used with an implied impv. θεραπεύεσθε. Although the ruler does not deny Jesus' ability to heal, he shows no compassion toward the woman's plight. In light of the instantaneous restoration at the word of Jesus (13:12–13), the ruler's strange complaint regarding work on the Sabbath (cf. above, 13:10) covers over fundamental antagonism toward Jesus.

13:15 Ἀπεκρίθη, see 4:4. The use of κύριος in this context of a Sabbath dispute recalls 6:5, the last Sabbath dispute in Luke (Fitzmyer 1011; Rowe 110; on the abs. use of κύριος see 7:13). Ὑποκριταί, voc. (see 6:42; cf. ὑπόκρισις, 12:1). The pl. in Jesus' reply suggests that the synagogue ruler's response is representative of others (perhaps those sitting in the front seats, 11:43!). The question with οὐ expects the answer "yes." Λύει 3rd sg. pres. act. indic. of λύω (note λύω in 13:16). Βοῦν acc. sg. masc. of βοῦς, βοός, ὁ, "ox." Ὄνον acc. sg. masc. of ὄνος, -ου, ὁ, "donkey." Φάτνης, "feeding trough" (HCSB; see 2:7; Fitzmyer 1013; possibly metonymy for "stall," NET n.). Ἀπαγαγών nom. sg. masc. of 2nd aor. act. (temp.) ptc. of ἀπάγω, "lead away." Ποτίζει 3rd sg. pres. act. indic. of ποτίζω (causative R 484; "to give drink to," "water"). See also 12:6–7 for a comparison between animals and human beings.

13:16 The acc. sg. fem. demonstrative pron. ταύτην is the emphatic subj. of the aor. pass. inf. λυθῆναι (of λύω; complementary inf. following ἔδει, see 11:42; ZG 236; note λύω in 13:15; on the pass. cf. 13:13). The acc. θυγατέρα is the pred. of οὖσαν (acc. sg. fem. of pres. act. [attrib.] ptc. of εἰμί; modifying the acc. ταύτην). The acc. sg. fem. rel. pron. ἥν (the antecedent is ταύτην) is the obj. of ἔδησεν (3rd sg. aor. act. indic. of dep. δέομαι, "bind"; the aor. is constative, BDF §332[1]; Marshall 559). For σατανᾶς see 4:2. Ἰδού, see 1:20 (an emphasis brought out by the tr. "eighteen long years" NRSV, NASB, NIV; cf. 13:11, 13). The question introduced by οὐκ expects the answer "yes." Δεσμοῦ, see 8:29, "bond" (NASB, ESV, sim. NIV), "imprisonment" (NET), "bondage" (HCSB). For the metaphorical use of δέομαι and δεσμός see BDAG 219c, 221d; MM 142c, 144a. Τῇ ἡμέρᾳ is a dat. of time (Wallace 157). Jesus' ref. to the Sabbath counters the ruler's complaint by declaring the Sabbath as the perfect day to provide release from the effect of Satan's work. Thus, in opposing Jesus, the synagogue ruler sides with Satan's destructive designs.

13:17 For ταῦτα and the gen. abs. cstr. see 9:34. Ἀντικείμενοι (nom. pl. masc. of pres. mid. [subst.] ptc. of dep. ἀντίκειμαι, "oppose"; modified by πάντες; on refs. for this cstr. see 1:66; for this vb. cf. 21:15) is the subj. of κατῃσχύνοντο (3rd pl. impf. pass. indic. of καταισχύνω, "put to shame," "humiliated"). Καί, "but" (HCSB, NIV). The second and third uses of πᾶς highlight the contrast between "all" those opposed to Jesus and "all" those who rejoice at "all" that he does (cf. 12:51–53; αἰσχύνη, δόξα, 14:9–10). Ἔχαιρεν 3rd sg. impf. act. indic. of χαίρω (cf. 1:14; 2:10). Ἐπί gives the basis for this joy (BDAG 365a). Ἐνδόξοις dat. pl. neut., see 7:25, "glorious things" (NASB, HCSB, ESV; cf. LXX Exod 34:10). Γινομένοις dat. pl. neut. of pres. mid. (attrib.) ptc. of dep. γίνομαι.

13:18 For ἔλεγεν here (with οὖν) see 5:36. The following teaching (still in the synagogue) on the kingdom of God (see 4:43) is an explanation (οὖν) of the preceding account of Jesus' power over Satan (Marshall 560). Jesus' cure of an unnamed woman with a bent-over back in an unnamed synagogue (cf. 13:10) in Israel is indicative of the presence of God's saving rule which will ultimately triumph. The dat. interr. pron. τίνι is the complement to the pred. adj. ὁμοία (see 6:47). For the interr. pron. τίνι with the fut. ὁμοιώσω see 7:31.

13:19 The dat. sg. masc. κόκκῳ (of κόκκος, -ου, ὁ, "grain") is the complement to the pred. adj. ὁμοία. The gen. sg. neut. σινάπεως (of σίναπι, -εως, τό, "of mustard") could be attrib. or a gen. of source (BHGNT 461; proverbial for something small, Marshall 561; Nolland 728; see C.–H. Hunzinger, *TDNT* 7.287–91). The acc. sg. masc. rel. pron. ὅν (the antecedent is κόκκῳ) is the obj. of ἔβαλεν (3rd sg. 2nd aor. act. indic. of βάλλω; here "sowed" HCSB, ESV; "planted" NIV). Λαβών (see 6:4) is an attendant circumstance ptc. with ἔβαλεν. In keeping with Luke's pairing of men and women, the use of γυνή in 13:21 indicates that ἄνθρωπος is "a man" here (most EVV; *pace* NRSV; see Fitzmyer 1017). Κῆπον acc. sg. masc. of κῆπος, -ου, ὁ, "garden" (with the refl. pron. ἑαυτοῦ as poss., Z §208). Ηὔξησεν 3rd sg. aor. act. indic. of αὐξάνω, "grow" (intrans.). Εἰς (following ἐγένετο) with the acc. δένδρον functions as a pred. nom. (a Sem. BDAG 291b; BDF §145[1]; R 458, 595–96; Wallace 47; Z §32; εἰς is used to express the goal or end, BDAG 288d). Τὰ πετεινὰ τοῦ οὐρανοῦ, see 8:5. Κατεσκήνωσεν 3rd sg. aor. act. indic. of κατασκηνόω, "dwell," "settle," "nested" (sim. most EVV; "perched" NIV). Κλάδοις dat. pl. masc. of κλάδος, -ου, ὁ, "branches." Although the size of the tree is not specified, the point is to contrast something small and seemingly insignificant (a seed) with the end result of something large enough (a tree) for birds to reside in safely (Bock 1225; Marshall 561).

13:20 Πάλιν (only 6:43; here; 23:20 in Luke) links the two comparisons. Τίνι ὁμοιώσω see 7:31 (cf. 13:18). The ref. to the kingdom of God (see 4:43) continues the discussion from the preceding episode (see 13:18).

13:21 See 13:19 for a sim. structure. The dat. ζύμῃ ("leaven"; see 12:1) is the complement to the pred. adj. ὁμοία. The acc. sg. fem. rel. pron. ἥν (the antecedent is ζύμη) is the obj. of ἐνέκρυψεν (3rd sg. aor. act. indic. of ἐγκρύπτω, "hide in" ESV; "mixed into" HCSB, NIV). Λαβοῦσα (nom. sg. fem. of 2nd aor. act. ptc. of λαμβάνω) is an attendant circumstance ptc. with ἐνέκρυψεν. Εἰς . . . σάτα τρία ("into three measures"; acc. pl. neut. of σάτον, -ου, τό) is locat. Gk. σάτον is the Heb. *seah*, a measure of about 16 lbs/7 kg (thus, three measures = approx. "50 pounds" HCSB; "about sixty pounds" NIV; cf. BDAG 917a). Ἀλεύρου (gen. sg. neut. of ἄλευρον, -ου, τό, "of flour") is a gen. of material (BHGNT 463). Ἕως with the rel. pron. οὗ is temp. ("until"; "extent of time up to a point" LN 67.119; cf. 12:50). Ἐζυμώθη 3rd sg. aor. pass. indic. of ζυμόω (with the subj. ὅλον, "all leavened" NRSV, ESV; "worked all through the dough" NIV, sim. HCSB). Again, something small is contrasted with something large (ὅλον). This comparison emphasizes the powerful influence of the kingdom (Marshall 562; Nolland 730–31).

HOMILETICAL SUGGESTIONS

Jesus Versus Satan (13:10–21)
1. Jesus' compassionate word frees us from Satan's cruelty (13:10–13).
2. Satanic opposition can arise from surprising places (13:14–16).
3. Jesus' liberating work now anticipates his final universal reign (13:17–21).

2. Surprise and Sadness for Many at Their Exclusion from the Banquet (13:22–30)

13:22 The impf. διεπορεύετο (3rd sg. impf. mid. indic. of dep. διαπορεύομαι, "journey through") may be used with the two pres. ptcs. of manner διδάσκων (see 4:31) and ποιούμενος (nom. sg. masc. of pres. mid. ptc. of ποιέω) to provide summary information as background to the following incident (BHGNT 463). The terms "journey" and "making way," however, indicate continuous action (Fitzmyer 1024; διαπορεύομαι is only either pres. [6:1; 18:36; Rom 15:24] or impf. [here; Acts 16:4] in the NT and in nearly all uses in the LXX). These vbs., together with the distributive κατὰ πόλεις καὶ κώμας (see the sg. cstr. in 8:1; cf. 9:6) and the ref. to Jesus "making his way" (πορείαν ποιούμενος; acc. sg. fem. of πορεία, -ας, ἡ, "journey," "trip"; on the noun having a verbal force in this cstr. cf. BDF §310[1]; Z §227) to Jerusalem, serve to keep the journey to Jerusalem (and specifically Jesus' death in Jerusalem; 13:22 prepares for 13:31–35) before the reader as the setting for Jesus' teaching (Nolland 733; on Ἱεροσόλυμα see 2:22; cf. 9:51–56).

13:23 Although the voc. κύριε could simply mean "sir" (NJB; Fitzmyer 1024), the question here concerning the final number of those who will be saved from the final judgment indicates a ref. to ultimate authority (see e.g., 5:8; 6:46; 7:6; 9:54; 10:2). As with 12:39, 41–42, after being addressed as "Lord," Jesus will go on to tell a parable about a "householder" who is "Lord" (13:25). The particle εἰ in this context introduces a dir. question (see refs. at 6:9; cf. also R 1024; T 333). Σῳζόμενοι (nom. pl. masc. of pres. pass. [subst.] ptc. of σῴζω) is the subj., and the adj. ὀλίγοι is the pred., of a verbless clause (BHGNT 464; with an implied fut. ἔσονται).

13:24 The pres. ἀγωνίζεσθε (2nd pl. pres. mid. impv. of dep. ἀγωνίζομαι, "struggle," "strive" NRSV, NASB, ESV; "make every effort" HCSB, NIV; cf. BDAG 17d; LN 68.74) may portray the progressive nature of the action (perhaps suggesting continuing effort, Bock 1234; Bovon 2.311; ZG 237) or simply the general nature of the command (BHGNT 464; cf. Fantin 97–98, 185; though the impv. with the inf. cstr. emphasizes "struggle" more than "enter"). Εἰσελθεῖν (see 6:6) is complementary (Wallace 599; twice in this verse). The cstr. refers to the effort required in responding to Jesus' message (i.e., repentance and giving attention to his message) so as to enter "through the narrow door" (διὰ τῆς στενῆς θύρας; gen. sg. fem. of στενός, -ή, -όν, "narrow"). Ὅτι, causal (giving the reason for this command to "make every effort"). Ζητήσουσιν 3rd pl. fut. act. indic. of ζητέω, "seek" ESV; "try" NRSV, HCSB, NIV). Ἰσχύσουσιν 3rd pl. fut. act. indic. of ἰσχύω, "be able" (neg. with οὐκ). The inability to enter is explained in the following verses as an attempt that comes too late.

13:25 For ἀφ᾿ οὗ see 7:45 ("from the time when"; ἄν with the following subjuncs. is temp.). The syntax of 13:25–26 is complicated. 13:25 is perhaps best understood as a two-part temp. clause in preparation for 13:26 (τότε . . .; BHGNT 465; ZG 237; Bovon 2.312–13; Nolland 734; though some see ἀφ᾿ οὗ ἄν as a continuation of 13:24, cf. ZG 237; Fitzmyer 1025; and some see the apodosis to ἀφ᾿ οὗ in the Lord's reply at the end of 13:25, Marshall 565–66). In addition to the marker τότε in 13:26, the following parallels between 13:25 and 13:26–27 reinforce this structure (Nolland 734):

13:25: (a) ἄρξησθε . . . λέγοντες, (b) καὶ . . . ἐρεῖ ὑμῖν, (c) οὐκ οἶδα . . .
13:26–27: (a) ἄρξεσθε λέγειν, (b) καὶ ἐρεῖ . . . ὑμῖν, (c) οὐκ οἶδα . . .

The sequence in 13:25 is as follows (a paratactic καὶ . . . καὶ . . . καί):

(1) The "master of the house" (οἰκοδεσπότης, see 12:39) "gets up" (ἐγερθῇ 3rd sg. 2nd aor. pass. subjunc. of ἐγείρω; intrans.) and "shuts" (ἀποκλείσῃ 3rd sg. aor. act. subjunc. of ἀποκλείω) the door.

(2) Then you begin (ἄρξησθε, see 3:8; followed by two complementary infs.) "to stand" (ἑστάναι 2nd pf. act. inf. of ἵστημι; intrans.) outside and "knock" (κρούειν pres. act. inf. of κρούω) on the door, saying (λέγοντες, see 1:66) "Lord, open up for us" (HCSB; κύριε, voc.; ἄνοιξον 2nd sg. aor. act. impv. of ἀνοίγω; ἡμῖν is a dat. of advantage).

(3) The master of the house (i.e., the Lord) will then say (ἀποκριθείς see 1:19; ἐρεῖ, see 12:10; the fut. highlights the expected response to the preceding events, BHGNT 466), "I don't know you or where you're from" (HCSB, sim. NKJV, NIV). The tr. accentuates the emphatic ὑμᾶς which is followed by the appos. πόθεν ἐστέ (BHGNT 466–67; Z §207; ἐστέ, see 6:22; οἶδα, see 4:34).

13:26 The adv. τότε ("then") completes the sequence begun in 13:25 with the temp. ἀφ᾽ οὗ. Ἄρξεσθε 2nd sg. fut. mid. indic. of ἄρχω. Λέγειν, see 3:8 (complementary inf.). Ἐφάγομεν 1st pl. 2nd aor. act. indic. of ἐσθίω. Ἐπίομεν 1st pl. 2nd aor. act. indic. of πίνω. Πλατείαις, see 10:10. Ἐδίδαξας 2nd sg. aor. act. indic. of διδάσκω.

13:27 Καί is contrastive. Ἐρεῖ, see 12:10. For the vars. λέγων, λέγω, and ἐρεῖ see Bock 1241–42. Οἶδα, see 4:34. If ὑμᾶς is included, then the statement is identical to 13:25 (see Metzger 137–38; Bock 1242). Ἀπόστητε 2nd pl. 2nd aor. act. impv. of ἀφίστημι, "depart" (intrans.). Πάντες ἐργάται, voc., "all workers" (see 10:2; cf. LXX Ps 6:9). The gen. (sg. fem.) ἀδικίας (of ἀδικία, -ας, ἡ) is obj. Physical proximity to Jesus' teaching (13:26) will be of no use when one meets him at the judgment as unrighteous and as one whom he does not know.

13:28 Ἔσται, see 1:14. Κλαυθμός nom. sg. masc. of κλαυθμός, -οῦ, ὁ, "weeping." Βρυγμός, nom. sg. masc. of βρυγμός, -οῦ, ὁ, "gnashing" (the gen. [pl. masc.] τῶν ὀδόντων [of ὀδούς, ὀδόντος, ὁ], "of teeth," is obj.). The combination suggests both sorrow and rage (cf. Acts 7:54); those who are shut outside the kingdom do not show remorse (cf. 16:19–31). Ὅταν with the subjunc. ὄψησθε (2nd pl. aor. mid. subjunc. of ὁράω) is temp. Τῇ βασιλείᾳ τοῦ θεοῦ (see 4:43; ἐν is locat.) is fut. here. Ἐκβαλλομένους (acc. pl. masc. of pres. pass. ptc. of ἐκβάλλω) is probably the complement with ὑμᾶς in a double acc. cstr. (perhaps following an implied ὄψησθε, BHGNT 469; cf. BDAG 719b; BDF §416[1]; here mng. "you yourselves" Z §208; ZG 238; an Aram., Marshall 567).

13:29 Ἥξουσιν 3rd pl. fut. act. indic. of ἥκω, "come." Ἀπό with ἀνατολῶν καὶ δυσμῶν (pl. "east and west" ["rising and setting"] BDAG 74b, 265c; ἀνατολή, see 1:78; δυσμή, see 12:54) and βορρᾶ καὶ νότου (gen. sg. masc. of βορρᾶς, -ᾶ, ὁ; for νότος see 11:31; "north and south" BDAG 181b, 679c) indicates source (the points of the compass are always anar., cf. BDF §253[5]; R 793–96). Ἀνακλιθήσονται 3rd pl. fut. pass. indic. of ἀνακλίνω, "recline" (intrans.; cf. 12:37).

13:30 Ἰδού, see 1:20. The nom. pl. masc. rel. pron. οἵ (the antecedent is ἔσχατοι which is the subj. of εἰσίν, see 7:25) is the subj. of ἔσονται (see 11:19; πρῶτοι is pred.). The second rel. pron. οἵ (the antecedent is πρῶτοι which is the subj. of εἰσίν) is the subj. of the following ἔσονται (ἔσχατοι is pred.). The anar. subjs. indicate that this is not an all encompassing ref. to "last" and "first" but that some who seem to be close will be far off and some who seem to be far off will be close (Bock 1240; Fitzmyer 1020, 1027).

For Homiletical Suggestions see the end of 13:35.

3. The Divine Plan for Jesus' Journey to Jerusalem (13:31–35)

13:31 Ἐν αὐτῇ τῇ ὥρᾳ, see 10:7, 21. The expression links 13:31–35 to the preceding exhortations and warnings; in particular, 13:30 (Nolland 740). Προσῆλθαν 3rd pl. 2nd aor. act. indic. of dep. προσέρχομαι (for the form see Z §489). Φαρισαῖοι, see 5:17. Λέγοντες, see 1:66. Ἔξελθε, see 4:35. Πορεύου, see 5:24. The repetitive "get out and go" is emphatic (cf. HCSB). Ἐντεῦθεν, adv. "from here." Ὅτι, causal (giving the reason for the departure). Ἡρῴδης (Antipas) see 3:19. Θέλει, see 5:39. The inf. ἀποκτεῖναι (see 12:5) is complementary. The encouragement to leave this region may be an attempt to help Jesus (Fitzmyer 1030) or an attempt to get Jesus out of their region (Marshall 571). The last mention of the Pharisees in 11:53–12:1 (and their consistent pattern, cf. refs. at 5:17) favors the latter (without diminishing the murderous intent of Herod; cf. 9:9, the last ref. to Herod). Jesus' reply shows that his ministry is determined by the outworking of God's saving plan rather than advice from the Pharisees (Bovon 2.324).

13:32 Πορευθέντες (see 7:22) is an attendant circumstance ptc. and takes on the mood of εἴπατε (see 10:10; impv.; Wallace 644). Τῇ ἀλώπεκι ταύτῃ ("that fox"; dat. indir. obj.; see 9:58) is metaphorical for craftiness (BDAG 49a; ZG 238), though in the wicked sense of "cunning and treacherous" (LN 88.120; cf. LSJ 75b) with destructive designs (Bock 1247). Ἰδού, see 1:20. Ἐκβάλλω, see 11:19. Ἀποτελῶ 1st sg. pres. act. indic. of ἀποτελέω, "bring to completion" (with ἰάσεις [acc. pl. fem. of ἴασις, -εως, ἡ], "perform cures" sim. most EVV; BDAG 123d; "completing cures" in the sense of completing a series of healings, LN 68.22). Τῇ τρίτῃ (dat. of time) following the advs. σήμερον καὶ αὔριον ("today and tomorrow") is a figurative ref. to a limited sequence of days (Bock 1247; a Sem., Marshall 571–72). Τελειοῦμαι 1st sg. pres. pass. indic. of τελειόω, "complete" ("I shall be perfected" NKJV; "I will complete My work" HCSB; "I will finish my course" ESV; "I reach my goal" NIV; "perfect, consummate" ZG 238; cf. 12:50; 22:37; the pres. may be fut. referring [BDF §323; Fitzmyer 1031; Marshall 571] or accentuate progress, Porter 231–32). The pass. may be a divine passive (i.e., completed by God, Fitzmyer 1031; Marshall 572). The mng. is accomplishment, not just cessation (Nolland 741).

13:33 Πλήν could be adversative ("nevertheless" NASB, ESV; BDAG 826c; BDF §449[1]; Fitzmyer 1031): despite the ref. to the completion of his work (13:32; or despite Herod's murderous intentions, Nolland 741), "nevertheless" Jesus must (δεῖ, see 2:49) continue along the way. Or, the conj. could function as an emphatic introduction to the following clause (Bock 1248; "moreover" Marshall 572; cf. NLT ["yes"]; BDAG 826c [mng. 1c]). Ἐχομένη (dat. [of time] sg. fem. of pres. mid. [subst.] ptc. of ἔχω) is used here for temp. proximity ("next," "immediately following" BDAG 422d; MM 270c) with an implied ἡμέρᾳ ("next day" most EVV; ZG 238; Fitzmyer 1031). The inf. πορεύεσθαι (see 4:42; with the acc. με as the subj.) is complementary (following δεῖ). Ὅτι, causal (giving the reason for this necessary journey). Ἐνδέχεται 3rd sg. pres. mid. indic. of dep. ἐνδέχομαι, "possible" (only here in the NT; impers. and neg. with οὐκ, "impossible" NRSV, sim. HCSB; BDAG 332b; MM 212a; ZG 238; "cannot be" NASB; ESV; "unthinkable" LN 71.4). The 2nd aor. mid. inf. ἀπολέσθαι (of ἀπόλλυμι) could be complementary or the subj. of ἐνδέχεται (cf. BHGNT 472). On Jesus as "prophet" see 4:24 (cf. also 7:16; 9:18–19). The point is that Herod brings no threat to Jesus' life as Jesus is accomplishing the divine plan that will bring death in Jerusalem.

13:34 Ἰερουσαλὴμ Ἰερουσαλήμ is an emphatic double voc. (see refs. at 6:46; cf. 10:41 for the double voc. in an emotional address). The (nom. sg. fem. of pres. act.) ptcs. ἀποκτείνουσα (of ἀποκτείνω) and λιθοβολοῦσα (of λιθοβολέω, "stone") could be attrib. or subst. in appos. to Ἰερουσαλήμ (BHGNT 472). Ἀπεσταλμένους acc. pl. masc. of pf. pass. (subst.) ptc. of ἀποστέλλω (the obj. of λιθοβολοῦσα). Τοὺς προφήτας καὶ . . . τοὺς ἀπεσταλμένους see 11:49. The antecedent of the fem. pron. αὐτήν is Ἰερουσαλήμ. The interr. adv. ποσάκις ("how often") may be used to introduce a question or an exclamation (BDAG 855c; MM 530a; Z §221 n. 6). Ἠθέλησα 1st sg. aor. act. indic. of θέλω. The aor. act. inf. ἐπισυνάξαι (of ἐπισυνάγω, "gather"; using the 1st aor. form, BDAG 382d; BDF §75) is complementary. The acc. sg. masc. rel. pron. ὅν and τρόπον (of τρόπος, -ου, ὁ; "which manner," "as" most EVV) functions as an adv. acc. and incorporates the previous ref. to the gathering of children into the following comparison (R 718–19; ZG 238; τρόπον being an acc. of respect, attracted to the rel. pron., Marshall 575). Ὄρνις (nom. sg. fem. of ὄρνις, -ιθος, ὁ and ἡ, "bird" LN 4.38; more specifically, "hen" all EVV; BDAG 724b; on the form cf. BDF §47[4]) is the subj. and νοσσιάν (acc. sg. fem. of νοσσιά, -ᾶς, ἡ; with the poss. ἑαυτῆς, "her brood" ESV; "her chicks" HCSB, NIV) the obj. of an implied ἐπισυνάγει. Τάς with πτέρυγας (acc. pl. fem. of πτέρυξ, -υγος, ἡ, "wing") functions as a poss. pron. God is often described in the OT as one who cares for the children of Israel under his "wings" (e.g., ὑπὸ τὰς πτέρυγας in LXX Ruth 2:12; Ps 90:4; cf. LXX Deut 32:11 also with νοσσιά). The refs. to sending prophets and often longing to gather the inhabitants of Jerusalem (though 13:33 has just highlighted his present journey to Jerusalem) identify Jesus with Yahweh (Gathercole 216–21). Καί, contrastive. Ἠθελήσατε (2nd pl. aor. act. indic. of θέλω; neg. with οὐκ) contrasts with ἠθέλησα earlier in this verse.

13:35 Ἰδού, see 1:20. Ἀφίεται (see 7:47 for the form; ὁ οἶκος is the subj.) with the dat. of disadvantage pron. ὑμῖν is "left to you" (NRSV); i.e., "abandoned to you" (HCSB; "forsaken" RSV, ESV; ἔρημος, "desolate" [NKJV, NASB, NIV] has strong early and diverse external mss. support for omission [perhaps added to assimilate to Matt 23:38 or Jer 22:5], Metzger 138). The divine pass. refers to the abandonment of Jerusalem by God (Marshall 576). The pres. may indicate a "fate already sealed" (Nolland 742). The reason the "house" (more likely a ref. to the people of Israel than the temple in this context, Bock 1250; Fitzmyer 1037; Marshall 576; Nolland 742; though cf. Bovon 2.329–30) is abandoned is immediately explained (λέγω δὲ ὑμῖν) with ref. to Jesus' departure (cf. 9:51). The subjunc. ἴδητε (see 12:54) with the double neg. οὐ μή is an emphatic neg. (fut. referring, BDF §365[2]; Z §444). Ἕως with the subjunc. εἴπητε (see 12:11) is temp. The temp. ἥξει [see 12:46] ὅτε is the rdg. with some vars. (NKJV, NJB, NRSV, NASB, HCSB). It is omitted in 𝔓⁴⁵, ⁷⁵ ℵ B (RSV, ESV, NIV) perhaps due to the unusual use of ὅτε with a subjunc. and the fut. indic. ἥξει after ἕως (Metzger 138; though cf. BDF §382[1, 2]; Z §336; ZG 239). Εὐλογημένος (see 1:42) is the pred. and ἐρχόμενος (see 6:47) the subj. of an implied ἐστίν (cf. LXX Ps 117:26). The ref. is likely to an eschatological welcome, though it is anticipated in 19:38 (Nolland 742).

HOMILETICAL SUGGESTIONS

How to Avoid a Surprising Rejection at the Banquet (13:22–35)

1. Take heed now rather than assume mere acquaintance with Jesus' teaching will ensure entrance (13:22–30).
2. Take shelter now under Jesus' divine care rather than assume Jesus' death was simply of human design (13:31–35).

4. A Sabbath Healing that Pictures the Restoration Jesus Brings in the Kingdom (14:1–14)

14:1 Καὶ ἐγένετο (see 1:5) with the temp. cstr. (inf. ἐλθεῖν [see 7:7] with ἐν τῷ) introduces a new pericope (see 3:21 and 11:37 for the aor. inf. with ἐν τῷ). Φαγεῖν (see 6:4) expresses the purpose for going to the house of this Pharisee (ἄρτον, "to eat bread" [NASB], idiomatic for "to eat a meal" [NRSV]; a Heb., ZG 239). The ref. to eating a meal at a Pharisee's house recalls earlier similar settings (for meal scenes at a Pharisee's house see 7:36–50; 11:37–54; cf. also 5:30; for Φαρισαίων see 5:17). The identification of the location (εἰς) as a house belonging to (τινος is poss.) "one of the rulers" of the Pharisees, and as taking place on a Sabbath (σαββάτῳ, dat. of time; this is the last of the Sabbath incidents in Luke, see refs. at 4:16), recalls the previous Sabbath incident (13:10–17) which involved a "ruler of the synagogue" (ἀρχισυνάγωγος, 13:14). In Luke-Acts ἄρχων mainly refers to leadership that is opposed to Jesus (cf. 8:41; 18:18; 23:13, 35; 24:20; and eleven times in Acts). Καὶ αὐτοί is unstressed and identifies a shift in subj. (Fitzmyer 1041; see 1:17; 3:23; 4:15; the pl. subj. will be identified in 14:3; καί is tr. as ὅτι in NKJV; Robertson, *Pictures* 194). Παρατηρούμενοι (nom. pl. masc. of pres. mid. ptc. of παρατηρέω, "watch closely"; periph. with ἦσαν) adds a specific note of hostility to these general indicators of a hostile setting (see the refs. in 6:7; cf. also 11:54).

14:2 Καὶ ἰδοὺ ἄνθρωπός (the apodosis to the introduction in 14:1, Fitzmyer 1040) balances καὶ ἰδοὺ γυνή in 13:11 (hence, "man," Nolland 746; all EVV; see 13:19). Following the description of the hostile setting in 14:1, the emphatic ἰδού (see 1:20), together with the specific location of the man as ἔμπροσθεν αὐτοῦ ("in front of him" HCSB, NIV; cf. 5:19; Z §83), may suggest a deliberate "plant" by the Pharisees (Bock 1256; Marshall 578). Since Jesus sends him away healed (14:4) and rebukes the host about his invitation practices (14:12–13), it is likely that the surprise here (καὶ ἰδού) concerns the presence of this uninvited, suffering guest (Fitzmyer 1041). The nom. sg. masc. pred. adj. ὑδρωπικός (of ὑδρωπικός, -ή, -όν, "suffering from dropsy" sim. most EVV) refers to the swelling of limbs with fluid and is symptomatic of serious disease (HCSB, sim. NIV; LN 23.164; Bock 1256; Nolland 746).

14:3 Ἀποκριθείς, see 1:19. Though tr. as "asked" in NRSV, NIV, due to the lack of a previous question, this may be Jesus' "response" (HCSB, sim. ESV) to their "watching" in 14:1 (i.e., to their thoughts, Robertson, *Pictures* 194; Bock 1257; Fitzmyer 1041 [or it is a stereotypical introduction]). The three vbs. of speech serve to emphasize what follows (BHGNT 476; citing Runge §7.3.1 [p. 154]). The pl. αὐτοί in 14:1 is now identified as τοὺς νομικοὺς καὶ Φαρισαίους (the two are often grouped together in Luke; for refs. see 5:17; 7:30; though here with one art. in which the first group is a subset of the second, Wallace 280; R 787). The aor. act. inf. θεραπεῦσαι (of θεραπεύω) with ἔξεστιν (see 6:2, 9) is complementary. Jesus is again presented as the "Lord of the Sabbath" (Fitzmyer 1040).

14:4 The nom. pl. masc. art. οἱ is the subj. of ἡσύχασαν (3rd pl. aor. act. indic. of ἡσυχάζω, "be silent"; "remained silent" sim. most EVV; BDAG 440c; LN 33.119;

four times in Luke-Acts out of five in the NT, though it is common in the LXX). The
reason for the silence is not given, though approval is unlikely (unintended agreement
is possible, Fitzmyer 1041). The 2nd aor. ptc. ἐπιλαβόμενος (see 9:47) is attendant
circumstance (and indicates some kind of physical contact, Bock 1258). Ἰάσατο, see
9:42. Ἀπέλυσεν, see 8:38 ("sent him away" NASB, HCSB, ESV; sim. NIV; "let him
go" RSV, NKJV; perhaps deliberately recalling last use of ἀπολύω [13:12]).

14:5 The nom. υἱὸς ἢ βοῦς ("son or ox" [see 13:15]; modified by τίνος ὑμῶν, "of which
of you"; for the cstr. τίνος ὑμῶν cf. 11:5; 14:28) is the subj. of πεσεῖται (3rd sg. fut.
mid. indic. of πίπτω; the fut. is used in a deliberative sense). Ὄνος ("donkey") is found
in place of υἱός in some mss. (NKJV), perhaps to assimilate to 13:15 and due to the
unusual combination of "son" with "donkey" (Metzger 138–39; though cf. Nolland
744). Φρέαρ acc. sg. neut. of φρέαρ, -ατος, τό, "a well." Ἀνασπάσει 3rd sg. fut. act.
indic. of ἀνασπάω, "pull up," "pull out" (with οὐκ the expected answer is "yes", of
course they would help their son or ox!). The comparison with care for the life of children and animals on the Sabbath also recalls the previous Sabbath incident (13:15–16).

14:6 Ἴσχυσαν 3rd pl. aor. act. indic. of ἰσχύω (neg. with οὐκ; cf. the similar sounding
ἡσύχασαν in 14:4). Ἀνταποκρίνομαι ("answer in return," "reply" NASB, NRSV, ESV;
here ἀνταποκριθῆναι is a complementary aor. pass. inf.) emphasizes an "implied opposition or contradiction" (LN 33.186; ZG 239). See also 14:4 (20:26).

14:7 Κεκλημένους (acc. pl. masc. of pf. pass. [subst.] ptc. of καλέω, "those who were
invited" HCSB, ESV) identifies the audience for the parable (see 8:4) and closely ties
the following parables (καλέω is used a further ten times in 14:8–24) with the preceding healing (for ἔλεγεν see 3:7; 5:36; Z §272). The description of this teaching as a
"parable" (see 8:4), together with the summary in 14:11 and the transitional question
in 14:15, link this teaching to the parables about the kingdom in 13:18–21 and how
to relate to God in his saving rule (Bovon 2.353; Marshall 582; Nolland 748; *pace*
Fitzmyer 1044 who calls this simply "secular, prudential wisdom"). The two units
here (14:7–11, 12–14) parallel the two parables in 13:18–19, 20–21 (Nolland 748; see
14:12 for the parallel structure of 14:8, 12). Ἐπέχων (nom. sg. masc. of pres. act. ptc.
of ἐπέχω, "hold toward," "aim at" [with the obj. τὸν νοῦν understood, R 477, 1202;
ZG 239; Fitzmyer 1046; Marshall 581]; "notice" BDAG 362c [with indir. question
following, "notice how"]; "watch" LN 24.33; "pay heed" MM 232a) could be temp. or
causal. In response to the Pharisees and lawyers "watching" Jesus closely, Jesus makes
an observation of his own concerning their choice (ἐξελέγοντο 3rd pl. impf. mid. indic.
of ἐκλέγω, "choose") of seating location (πρωτοκλισίας acc. pl. fem. of πρωτοκλισία,
-ας, ἡ, "best places" NKJV, HCSB; "places of honor" most EVV; i.e., close to the host,
BDAG 892d; see also πρωτοκαθεδρία, 11:43; πρωτοκαθεδρίας . . . καὶ πρωτοκλισίας,
20:46).

14:8 The parable consists of two parts that begin with ὅταν κληθῇς (14:8–9, and
14:10). Κληθῇς (2nd sg. aor. pass. subjunc. of καλέω; subjunc. with ὅταν) picks up
on καλέω in 14:7. Γάμους, "wedding" (see 12:36; the pl. could indicate a ref. to the
feast or banquet associated with Jewish weddings; all EVV; ZG 240; though the sg.

and pl. could be used interchangeably, BDAG 188d; MM 121b). Κατακλιθῇς 2nd sg. aor. pass. subjunc. of κατακλίνω, "recline" (HCSB; see refs. at 7:36; prohibition with μή). Πρωτοκλισίαν, see 14:7 (εἰς, locat.). Μήποτε is an emphatic "marker of negated purpose" and often expresses apprehension ("in case" NRSV; BDAG 648d; LN 89.62; BDF §370[2]; ZG 240; cf. 12:58; Fitzmyer 1046 argues for "result" here; "it may turn out that" Nolland 749). The nom. sg. masc. comp. adj. ἐντιμότερς ("more distinguished"; see 7:2; BDAG 340a; σου is a gen. of comparison) is the subj. of κεκλημένος (nom. sg. masc. of pf. pass. ptc. of καλέω; see 14:7). The ptc. is a pf. periph. cstr. with ᾖ (Wallace 649; for ᾖ see 10:6; subjunc. with μήποτε).

14:9 Ἐλθών (see 7:3) could be temp. (sim. to the more explicit temp. cstr. in 14:10b, ὅταν ἔλθῃ, BHGNT 479). The temp. cstr. in 14:10b may be influenced, however, by the temp. cstr. at the beginning of 14:10 (ὅταν κληθῇς). Thus, ἐλθών could be an attendant circumstance ptc. with ἐρεῖ (see 12:10; all EVV). Καλέσας (see 7:39; subst.) is the subj. of ἐρεῖ. Δός, see 12:58. The adv. τότε introduces the clause explaining the result of this command. The lengthy description conveys the drama of the shameful reversal (Bock 1264). Ἄρξῃ 2nd sg. fut. mid. indic. of dep. ἄρχομαι, "begin" (perhaps added to highlight the ongoing shame, BHGNT 480). Μετά is used as a marker of attendant circumstances (BDAG 637c; αἰσχύνης gen. sg. fem. of αἰσχύνη, -ης, ἡ; cf. δόξα in 14:10). The pres. act. inf. κατέχειν is complementary (of κατέχω, "to have a place as one's own, take into one's possession" BDAG 533b; "to occupy" NASB; ZG 240). The superl. adj. ἔσχατον could be elative (Wallace 303).

14:10 The contrastive conj. ἀλλά and temp. cstr. ὅταν κληθῇς (see 14:8) introduces the second part of the parable. Πορευθείς (nom. sg. masc. of aor. pass. ptc. of dep. πορεύομαι) is an attendant circumstance ptc. (with ἀνάπεσε 2nd sg. 2nd aor. act. impv. of ἀναπίπτω, "recline") and takes on the mood of the impv. (cf. Wallace 642–44; Z §363). Ἔσχατον in the locat. εἰς τὸν ἔσχατον τόπον contrasts with πρωτοκλισίαν in 14:8. Ἵνα introduces a purpose clause (BDF §369[2]; Z §340; or possibly result, Bock 1264; Marshall 582). Ἔλθη (see 1:43; subjunc.) is temp. with ὅταν. Κεκληκώς (nom. sg. masc. of pf. act. [subst.] ptc. of καλέω) is the subj. of ἐρεῖ (see 12:10; the fut. is used in place of the aor. subj., BDF §369[2]; R 984; Z §340). Φίλε, voc. Προσανάβηθι 2nd sg. 2nd aor. act. impv. of προσαναβαίνω, "move up." The comp. adj. ἀνώτερον (acc. sg. neut. of ἀνώτερος, -α, -ον), "higher" refers to "a better place" (NIV). The adv. τότε introduces a clause which contrasts with the parallel clause in 14:9. Ἔσται, see 1:14. Δόξα contrasts with αἰσχύνης in 14:9 (cf. καταισχύνω, ἔχαιρεν . . . ἐνδόξοις, 13:17). In contrast to "the last place," this "glory" (NKJV; "honor" sim. most EVV) will be "before all those reclining" (συνανακειμένων gen. pl. masc. of pres. mid. [subst.] ptc. of dep. συνανάκειμαι, "recline with").

14:11 Ὅτι could be causal or epex. as it introduces an explanatory clause (see the same statement in 18:14). Ὑψῶν (nom. sg. masc. of pres. act. [subst.] ptc. of ὑψόω; the pres. could be gnomic or customary, Wallace 523) is the subj. of ταπεινωθήσεται (see 3:5; cf. BDF §413[2]; R 772–73 for πᾶς with a subst. ptc.; for the generic arts. see Wallace 230). Ταπεινῶν (nom. sg. masc. of pres. act. [subst.] ptc. of ταπεινόω, "humble") is the subj. of ὑψωθήσεται (3rd sg. fut. pass. indic. of ὑψόω; a divine pass., Fitzmyer 1047; Nolland 749). This concluding summary points to an eschatological reversal. The proud who will not receive Jesus and therefore will not enter the kingdom are contrasted with the humble who do receive Jesus and enter the kingdom (cf. Bock 1265; Nolland 749 describes this as humbly recognizing one's own poverty before God; cf. 1:52; 13:30; 18:13–14).

14:12 Δὲ καί ("then also") and ἔλεγεν (see 5:36) serve to shift the focus to the second "parable" without changing the setting. The parallel structure with 14:8 includes the following (Nolland 748):

ὅταν κληθῇς . . . μὴ κατακλιθῇς . . . μήποτε . . . (14:8)
ὅταν ποιῇς . . . μὴ φώνει . . . μήποτε . . . (14:12)

Κεκληκότι (dat. sg. masc. of pf. act. [subst.] ptc. of καλέω) refers to the ruler of the Pharisees (14:1). Ποιῇς (2nd sg. pres. act. subjunc. of ποιέω; subjunc. with ὅταν) with the alternatives ἄριστον ἢ δεῖπνον ("a lunch or a dinner" HCSB; sim. NASB; NRSV, NIV) has the sense of doing "something that brings about an event" and is tr. as "give" (most EVV; BDAG 840b; ZG 240; "host" NET; see 5:29). See 11:38 for ἄριστον as a "noonday meal." Δεῖπνον (acc. sg. neut. of δεῖπνον, -ου, τό) is distinguished from ἄριστον (in this context with the disjunctive ἤ, "or") and refers to the main meal of the day ("dinner" BDAG 215c–d; Bock 1265; Bovon 2.356; Fitzmyer 1047; Marshall 583; cf. 14:16–17, 24; 20:46). Φώνει 2nd sg. pres. act. impv. of φωνέω ("call"; "invite" all EVV; prohibition with μή; the pres. with μή views the action as ongoing, Huffman 104, 144; cf. Z §246; ZG 240). The following four accs. identify the objs. of the prohibition (i.e., "the exclusive invitation of such guests" Robertson, *Pictures* 196; a Sem. idiom for "not so much . . . as rather" Marshall 583). Συγγενεῖς, "relatives" (see 1:58; 2:44; 21:16). Γείτονας πλουσίους, "rich neighbors" (acc. pl. masc. of γείτων, -ονος, ὁ and ἡ; cf. τοὺς φίλους καὶ τοὺς γείτονας, 15:6, 9). Μήποτε, see 14:8 ("in case" NRSV). Καί, "also." The pron. αὐτοί is the subj. of ἀντικαλέσωσιν (3rd pl. aor. act. subjunc. of ἀντικαλέω, "invite in return"). Ἀνταπόδομα nom. sg. neut. of ἀνταπόδομα, -ατος, τό, "repaid" (sim. most EVV; cf. ἀνταποδίδωμι, 14:14), is the subj. of γένηται (see 1:20; KJV; ἀντικαλέσωσίν and γένηται are subjunc. with μήποτε).

14:13 The acc. sg. fem. δοχήν (the obj. of ποιῇς, see 14:12) refers to "an elaborate meal" (see 5:29). Κάλει 2nd sg. pres. act. impv. of καλέω. The following four accs. identify the objs. of the impv. (cf. the corresponding four accs. in 14:12). Πτωχούς, "poor" (see 4:18; 14:21). Ἀναπείρους acc. pl. masc. "crippled" (of ἀνάπειρος, -ον; only here and 14:21 in the NT; the term may refer to those who have been maimed or mutilated and therefore crippled, LN 23.177; cf. ἀνάπηρος LSJ 116a). Χωλούς, "lame" (see 7:22; 14:21). Τυφλούς, "blind" (see 4:18; 14:21). The anar. masc. pl. adjs. are subst. ("poor people" Robertson, *Pictures* 197; the absence of καί [asyndeton] adds a staccato rhetorical effect here, BDF §460[3]; R 427; see 14:21; cf. also 7:22; Lev 21:17–23).

14:14 Ἔσῃ, see 1:20 (the adj. μακάριος is pred.). Ὅτι, causal (giving the reason for being blessed). Ἔχουσιν (see 5:31; neg. with οὐκ) with the 2nd aor. act. inf. (of indir. discourse) ἀνταποδοῦναί (of ἀνταποδίδωμι, "repay"; on the compound vb. see R 574; cf. ἀνταπόδομα, 14:12) is "they do not have (the means) to repay you" (NASB; ZG 240; ἔχω has the mng. "to be in a position to do something . . . be able" BDAG 421a). Γάρ, causal (again, giving the reason for being blessed). Ἀνταποδοθήσεται 3rd sg. fut. pass. indic. of ἀνταποδίδωμι (a divine pass., Bock 1267; Fitzmyer 1048). Ἀναστάσει in this context is "resurrection" (cf. 20:35; ἐν τῇ ἀναστάσει is temp.). Thus, as with 14:11, the picture here is of eschatological reward from God in contrast to self-promotion (other refs. to life beyond the grave may be found in e.g., 9:24; 10:14; 12:5; 13:28, Nolland 751).

HOMILETICAL SUGGESTIONS

We Belong to Jesus' Kingdom If . . . (14:1–14)

1. We are like the sick who are restored by Jesus' compassion (14:1–6).
2. We are like the lowly who are exalted by God's grace (14:7–11).
3. We are like the outsiders who require only God's approval (14:12–14).

5. The Surprising Participants in the Eschatological Banquet (14:15–24)

14:15 Συνανακειμένων (see 14:10; subst.; with the indef. pron. τις; the gen. is partitive, perhaps referring to the lawyers and Pharisees of 14:3) with ἀκούσας (see 6:49; temp.; the obj. is ταῦτα) places the following question and parable about a banquet in the same setting as the preceding meal scene. In the broader structure of this section, 14:15–24 corresponds to the question and parable about entrance to the eschatological banquet in 13:22–30 (Nolland 753). The nom. sg. masc. rel. pron. ὅστις (of ὅστις, ἥτις, ὅτι) introduces a clause which functions as the subj. of an implied ἐστίν (BHGNT 484, with the adj. μακάριος as the pred.; used here in light of 14:14). Φάγεται 3rd sg. fut. mid. indic. of ἐσθίω (ἄρτον refers to a meal, see 14:1). The ref. to eschatological reward (14:11, 14) in the context of this meal prompts a statement concerning potential participants in the eschatological banquet. Τῇ βασιλείᾳ τοῦ θεοῦ (locat.) see 4:43 (in this context see 13:18, 20, 28–29 [with ἀνακλίνω]).

14:16 For ἄνθρωπός τις see 10:30. Ἐποίει (see 9:43) in this context is "gave" (see 14:12; perhaps conative, "was planning to give" ZG 241; sim. Robertson, *Pictures* 197; Nolland 753). Δεῖπνον (see 14:12) with the adj. μέγα could be "a great dinner" (NRSV) or "a great banquet" (ESV, NIV). The adj. πολλούς (the obj. of ἐκάλεσεν 3rd sg. aor. act. indic. of καλέω; cf. 14:7) reinforces the image of a large banquet (cf. 14:22).

14:17 Ἀπέστειλεν, see 7:3. Τόν with δοῦλον may refer to the servant who customarily went to summon guests (Z §168; ZG 241; Fitzmyer 1055 suggests that evidence for this custom is late). Τῇ ὥρᾳ, dat. of time. The inf. εἰπεῖν (see 5:14) expresses purpose. Κεκλημένοις dat. pl. masc. of pf. pass. (subst.) ptc. of καλέω (dat. of indir. obj.). Ἔρχεσθε 2nd pl. pres. mid. impv. of dep. ἔρχομαι. Ὅτι, causal (giving the reason for coming). The adj. ἕτοιμα (see 12:40; "prepared," "ready") is pred. (R 656).

14:18 Ἤρξαντο, see 5:21. Ἀπὸ μιᾶς could mean "unanimously" ("with one accord" NKJV; "without exception" HCSB; the fem. μιᾶς may agree with an implied φωνῆς ["voice"], or γνώμης ["opinion"] BDAG 107b; R 653; ZG 241; Nolland 755; [the expression may be an Aram. for "at once" BDAG 107b; BDF §241[6]]) or "one after another" (NET; LN 61.2). Although there are three representative responses to follow, they are alike in "all" rejecting the invitation. The pres. mid. inf. παραιτεῖσθαι (of dep. παραιτέομαι, mng. "to avert something by request or entreaty" and thus, "excuse," "reject" BDAG 764b; MM 484a–b) is complementary. Ἠγόρασα 1st sg. aor. act. indic. of ἀγοράζω, "buy" (the acc. ἀγρόν is the obj.). The combination of ἔχω (see 7:40) with ἀνάγκην (acc. sg. fem. of ἀνάγκη, -ης, ἡ, "necessity") is "I must" ("I have need" BDAG 421d). Ἐξελθών (see 1:22) is an attendant circumstance ptc. with the complementary inf. ἰδεῖν (see 2:26): "I must go out and see it" (NRSV, HCSB, ESV; Z §363; ZG 241). Ἐρωτῶ 1st sg. pres. act. indic. of ἐρωτάω. The combination of ἔχε (2nd sg. pres. act. impv. of ἔχω) with παρῃτημένον (acc. sg. masc. of pf. pass. ptc. of dep. παραιτέομαι; the acc. ptc. is the complement of με, BDAG 421b; R 480, 1108 [or a ptc. of indir. discourse, R 1041, 1122; Wallace 646]) has the mng. "consider me excused" (NASB; i.e., "don't expect me to come" BDAG 421b, 764b).

14:19 The use of ἕτερος ("another one") indicates that a sample of the excuses is being given (Nolland 756). As with the first excuse, this one also concerns a purchase (ἠγόρασα, see 14:18). The acc. pl. neut. ζεύγη (of ζεῦγος, -ους, τό, "yoke," "pairs" NLT; ZG 241) modified by the gen. βοῶν ("oxen," see 13:15; 14:5) and the adj. πέντε is the obj. of the purchase. Πορεύομαι 1st sg. pres. mid. indic. of dep. πορεύομαι. The aor. act. inf. δοκιμάσαι (of δοκιμάζω, "examine" RSV, ESV; "try them out" NRSV, NASB, HCSB, NIV; "test for their usefulness" BDAG 255c) expresses purpose. The following request repeats 14:18.

14:20 The final example, "I married a wife" (ἔγημα 1st sg. aor. act. indic. of γαμέω; cf. BDF §101; cf. γυναῖκα in 14:26; 18:29), is followed with no further explanation or request to be excused. Διὰ τοῦτο, causal ("for that reason" NASB; the conceptual antecedent is the marriage, Wallace 333). Δύναμαι, see 11:7 (neg. with οὐ). The inf. ἐλθεῖν (see 7:7) is complementary.

14:21 Παραγενόμενος nom. sg. masc. of 2nd aor. mid. (temp.) ptc. of dep. παραγίνομαι. Ἀπήγγειλεν, see 8:47. Ὀργισθείς (nom. sg. masc. of aor. pass. ptc. of dep. ὀργίζομαι, "make angry") could express manner ("in anger said" RSV, sim. HCSB) or attendant circumstance with εἶπεν ("became angry and said" ESV; ingressive, Robertson, *Pictures* 199). Οἰκοδεσπότης, see 12:39 (cf. also the parallel parable, 13:25; both also with κύριος). Ἔξελθε, see 4:35 (modified here by the adv. ταχέως, "quickly"). Εἰς, locat. Τὰς πλατείας καὶ ῥύμας refers to "broad streets" (see 10:10) and "narrow streets" (acc. pl. fem. of ῥύμη, -ης, ἡ, "alleys" HCSB, NIV; "lanes" NRSV, NASB, ESV; though the art. treats the two groups as one, R 787; cf. Wallace 279; Bovon [2.372] suggests πλατεία refers to "town square"). The following four accs. are identical to 14:13 (though with a different order of the last two terms; here the one art. τούς identifies them as "overlapping groups" Wallace 280; the repetition of καί may add to the rhetorical effect [polysyndeton], R 427; though see BDF §460[3]). Εἰσάγαγε 2nd sg. 2nd aor. act. impv. of εἰσάγω, "lead," "bring in" (modified by the adv. ὧδε, "here").

14:22 The voc. κύριε ("Lord" RV, KJV) is the same κύριος referred to in 14:21 with the dat. and in 14:23 in the "absolute" sense as ὁ κύριος (cf. Rowe 146–47 for the significance of this for other uses of κύριος in Luke). The rel. pron. ὃ introduces a clause which is the subj. of γέγονεν (3rd sg. 2nd pf. act. indic. of dep. γίνομαι). Ἐπέταξας 2nd sg. aor. act. indic. of ἐπιτάσσω, "command." Τόπος, "place," "room" (all EVV; cf. 14:16).

14:23 For ὁ κύριος cf. 14:22. Ἔξελθε, see 4:35 (cf. above, 14:21). Ὁδούς acc. pl. fem. of ὁδός, -οῦ, ἡ; "roads" (NIV; ὁδός is a general term for a way for traveling, BDAG 691a; "highways" [most EVV] could be misunderstood). Φραγμούς acc. pl. masc. of φραγμός, -οῦ, ὁ, "hedges" (RSV, NKJV, NASB, ESV; "hedgerows" NJB; a fence or hedge that surrounds vineyards or houses, BDAG 1064d; where beggars are often found, Bock 1276; Marshall 590). The two terms together (the one fem. art. governs both terms, R 789) probably refer to the rural roads on the outskirts of a town (NLT; Nolland 757). Ἀνάγκασον εἰσελθεῖν parallels ἀνάγκην ἐξελθών in 14:18. In this context ἀνάγκασον (2nd sg. aor. act. impv. of ἀναγκάζω, "compel" NKJV, NRSV, NASB, ESV,

NIV; "urge" NET; cf. ἀνάγκη, 14:18) does not refer to physical violence but "strongly urge" (a "weakened sense" BDAG 60c; MM 31b; i.e., outcasts such as those of 14:13–14, 21, need strong persuasion to participate in such a feast, Bock 1277; Fitzmyer 1057). The inf. εἰσελθεῖν (see 6:6) is complementary. Ἵνα with the subjunc. γεμισθῇ (3rd sg. aor. pass. subjunc. of γεμίζω, "fill") is a purpose clause.

14:24 Γάρ is used here as a "marker of inference" providing a conclusion to the preceding account (BDAG 190a). Ὅτι, recitative. Κεκλημένων gen. pl. masc. of pf. pass. (attrib.) ptc. of καλέω (cf. 14:7; here referring back to 14:16–17; modifying τῶν ἀνδρῶν ἐκείνων). Γεύσεται 3rd sg. fut. mid. indic. of dep. γεύομαι, "taste." The gen. δείπνου (see 14:12, 16; modified by the poss. μου) is obj. Although the ref. to "my supper" might suggest the speaker here is the "master of the house" (14:21; i.e., "the Lord" 14:23), the shift to the 1st person and the pl. ὑμῖν at the beginning of this verse indicate that the speaker now is Jesus addressing again "those who were invited" (14:7; i.e., "the ones reclining" 14:15) to the meal at the Pharisee's house (Bock 1277 [cf. also 16:8b–13]; Marshall 590–91 sees the speaker as the host though the ref. to ὁ κύριος in 14:23 points to the application of the parable as one of response to Jesus' invitations). 14:24 parallels 13:29 (Nolland 758).

See Homiletical Suggestions after 14:35.

6. Leaving All to Follow Jesus (14:25–35)

14:25 Συνεπορεύοντο (see 7:11; αὐτῷ is the dat. complement) recalls the journey to Jerusalem mentioned in 13:22, 32–33 and anticipates the ref. to following Jesus and carrying one's cross in 14:26–27 (Nolland 762). Στραφείς (see 7:9 for the form and usage in Luke) is attendant circumstance. The acc. αὐτούς refers to the "large crowds" (ὄχλοι πολλοί) traveling with Jesus (cf. e.g., 5:15; 6:17; 7:11; 8:4; 9:37; 12:1).

14:26 Εἴ with the indef. pron. τις introduces a general first-class. cond. sentence (Wallace 706). Ἔρχεται, see 3:16 (cf. ὀπίσω μου, 14:27). Μισεῖ 3rd sg. pres. act. indic. of μισέω (neg. with οὐ, BDF §428[1]). The disjunctive here may be a vivid Heb. for expressing a greater and lesser degree (Z §445; ZG 241; cf. ἀγαπάω, 6:27, 35; 10:27–28; the use of ἀρνέομαι in 9:23 and ἀποτάσσομαι in 14:33 may suggest not psychological hate but renunciation, Marshall 592, citing O. Michel, *TDNT* 4.690–91). The following six acc. nouns τὸν πατέρα . . . τὰς ἀδελφάς are the obj. of μισεῖ (cf. γυναῖκα, 14:20; the arts. may be used due to the differing number and gender in the terms, R 789). The combination ἔτι τε καί is best tr. "yes, and even" (NASB, HCSB, ESV; external evidence favors reading δέ in place of τε [UBS⁵], Fitzmyer 1064). Τὴν ψυχὴν ἑαυτοῦ, see 9:24. Δύναται, see 3:8 (neg. with οὐ). The inf. εἶναί (see 2:4) is complementary (followed by the pred. nom. μαθητής, BHGNT 491; μου could be emphatic, Marshall 593; for μαθητής see 5:30).

14:27 The nom. sg. masc. rel. pron. ὅστις (generic, Wallace 344) is the subj. of βαστάζει (3rd sg. pres. act. indic. of βαστάζω, "bear," "carry"; neg. with οὐ) and introduces a rel.

clause which is the subj. of δύναται (cf. BHGNT 491; R 1159; the rest of the sentence reflects 14:26). The ref. to carrying one's "cross" (τὸν σταυρὸν ἑαυτοῦ, see 9:23) and coming "after" Jesus (ὀπίσω μου) parallels the ref. to hating one's own "life" (τὴν ψυχὴν ἑαυτοῦ) and coming "to" Jesus (πρός με) in 14:26 (see 9:23–24; some see a slight distinction between an initial coming "to" Jesus and an ongoing coming "after" Jesus, Bock 1284; Marshall 592). The ref. to "death to self" parallels the ref. to Jesus' journey to death in 13:31–33. The contrasts here emphasize the priority Jesus is to have. Ἔρχεται (see 3:16) with ὀπίσω is "follow" (NRSV, NIV; a Heb., ZG 241; see 9:23; see Marshall [593] for OT contrasts between "going after" false gods and the ways of Yahweh). The pres. βαστάζει . . . καὶ ἔρχεται portrays ongoing action (Bock 1286). The parallel structure is reinforced with the repetition of οὐ . . . μαθητής.

14:28 The following two illustrations support the previous statement (γάρ). Τίς . . . ἐξ ὑμῶν, see 11:5 (sim. 14:5). Θέλων (see 10:29; BHGNT 492) could be temp. (NASB), cond. ("if he wants"), or attrib. (modifying the interr. pron. τίς; for οὐχί see 4:22). The cstr. with the rhetorical question is sim. to 11:5 and favors a cond. mng. of the ptc. (Marshall 593). Πύργον, "tower" (see 13:4). The aor. act. inf. οἰκοδομῆσαι (of οἰκοδομέω) is complementary. Καθίσας (see 5:3) could be temp. or attendant circumstance (Z §363; Fitzmyer 1065). Ψηφίζει 3rd sg. pres. act. indic. of ψηφίζω, "count up," "calculate" (originally with pebbles, ψῆφος, BDAG 1098a; MM 698a; ZG 242). Δαπάνην acc. sg. fem. of δαπάνη, -ης, ἡ, "cost," "expense" (only here in the NT; cf. δαπανάω in 15:14). The particle εἰ could introduce an indir. (epex.) question (see refs. at 6:7; ZG 242; Marshall 594) or the protasis of a first-class cond. (BHGNT 492). Ἔχει, see 5:24 (the obj. "money" is implied; with the sense "to see if" R 1024). Εἰς expresses the goal (cf. BDAG 290d, BHGNT 492). Ἀπαρτισμόν acc. sg. masc. of ἀπαρτισμός, -οῦ, ὁ, "completion" (only here in the NT).

14:29 Μήποτε (with ἵνα and the subjunc. ἄρξωνται) is used as a "marker of negated purpose" and expresses apprehension (BDAG 648d; LN 89.62; Bovon 2.391; Marshall 594; "lest" NKJV; "otherwise" most EVV; see 14:8; BHGNT 490, 492 tr. as an adv. "never"). The gen. sg. masc. ptcs. θέντος (2nd aor. act. of τίθημι; the gen. αὐτοῦ is the subj. and the acc. θεμέλιον ["foundation," see 6:48] is the obj.) and ἰσχύοντος (pres. act. of ἰσχύω; neg. with μή) are a gen. abs. cstr. which could be temp. (NRSV, NASB, HCSB, ESV), cond. (NIV), or causal (BHGNT 490). The aor. act. inf. ἐκτελέσαι (of ἐκτελέω, "finish," "complete") is complementary (the term is used with ref. to bringing a job to completion, BDAG 310a; MM 198c; only in 14:29–30 in the NT). Θεωροῦντες nom. pl. masc. of pres. act. (subst.) ptc. of θεωρέω (cf. refs. at 4:11) is the subj. of ἄρξωνται (3rd pl. aor. mid. subjunc. of ἄρχω, "begin"; subjunc. following ἵνα). The pres. act. inf. ἐμπαίζειν (of ἐμπαίζω, "ridicule" NRSV, NIV; "mock" ESV; "make fun of" HCSB; the masc. obj. αὐτῷ is referred to in the earlier gen. abs. cstr., BDF §423[1]) is complementary (cf. ἄρξῃ μετὰ αἰσχύνης, 14:9).

14:30 Λέγοντες, see 1:66. Ὅτι, recitative (ZG 242). The nom. demonstrative pron. οὗτος (in the pred. position, modifying ἄνθρωπος as the subj. of ἤρξατο [see 4:21]) adds to the derisive tone in this response (Robertson, *Pictures* 202; Fitzmyer 1065; see refs.

at 15:30). The pres. act. inf. οἰκοδομεῖν (of οἰκοδομέω) is complementary. Ἴσχυσεν, see 6:48 (neg. with οὐκ; the ptc. is neg. with μή in 14:29). Ἐκτελέσαι, see 14:29. The imagery of "counting the cost" (14:28) is usually understood to mean that this illustration points to the high price involved in rejecting all other priorities to follow Jesus and encourages firm resolve in light of the consequences for lack of follow-through (Bock 1288; Fitzmyer 1062; Marshall 591; Nolland 766). The repetition of the negated ἰσχύω (14:29–30; following εἰ ἔχει εἰς ἀπαρτισμόν in 14:28) together with ἵνα μήποτε (14:29), however, highlights a lack of resources and discourages the building project. The illustration, therefore, may point to the foolishness of relying on one's own resources (Green 566).

14:31 Ἤ introduces a second illustration (cf. 14:28; the partitive ἐξ ὑμῶν is omitted since Jesus is not talking to kings, Marshall 594). As with θέλων in 14:28, πορευόμενος (nom. sg. masc. of pres. mid. ptc. of dep. πορεύομαι) could be temp. (NASB), cond., or attrib. (modifying τίς βασιλεύς). The 2nd aor. act. inf. συμβαλεῖν (of συμβάλλω, "meet with") expresses purpose (with the purpose phrase εἰς πόλεμον [acc. sg. masc. of πόλεμος, -ου, ὁ], "to wage war" NRSV; BDAG 956c). Οὐχί, see 4:22 (cf. 14:28). As in 14:28, καθίσας (see 5:3) could be temp. or attendant circumstance. Βουλεύσεται 3rd sg. fut. mid. indic. of dep. βουλεύομαι, "deliberate" (ESV; BDAG 181d [followed by an indir. question]; "think over carefully" LN 30.8), "consider" (NRSV, NASB, NIV). For εἰ see 14:28. Ἐν δέκα χιλιάσιν ("with 10,000"; dat. pl. fem. of χιλιάς, -άδος, ἡ) could be instr. (cf. NLT) or "sociative" ("concomitant circumstances," Z §116; ZG 242; cf. R 588–89). The aor. act. inf. ὑπαντῆσαι (of ὑπαντάω, "to meet") could be complementary or epex. (Burton §376). In this context ὑπαντῆσαι has a hostile mng. of "oppose" (HCSB; BDAG 1029c; Marshall 594; "meet in battle" LN 55.3). Ἐρχομένῳ dat. sg. masc. of pres. mid. (subst.) ptc. of dep. ἔρχομαι (the dat. is complementary following ὑπαντῆσαι). Μετά is used as a marker of association ("in company with" BDAG 636b; εἴκοσι χιλιάδων, "20,000"). Ἐπί, "against" (a marker of hostile opposition, BDAG 366a). Πορευόμενος and ἐρχομένῳ complement each other and picture an impending disaster.

14:32 Εἰ δὲ μή γε, see 5:36; 10:6 (here the "if not" cond. clause refers to being unable with 10,000 to oppose someone with 20,000; NIV). Αὐτοῦ is the subj. of ὄντος (gen. sg. masc. of pres. act. ptc. of εἰμί; modified by the advs. ἔτι and πόρρω ["far away"]) in a temp. gen. abs. cstr. Ἀποστείλας (nom. sg. masc. of aor. act. ptc. of ἀποστέλλω; the abstract acc. sg. fem. obj. πρεσβείαν of πρεσβεία, -ας, ἡ, "embassy" is used in the concrete sense of "ambassador" or "representative," BDAG 861c; ZG 242; only here and 19:14 in the NT) could express means (BHGNT 494–95) or attendant circumstance (Wallace 643) with ἐρωτᾷ (see 11:37). The neut. pl. art. τά is a nominalizer and makes the prep. phrase πρὸς εἰρήνην the obj. of ἐρωτᾷ (BHGNT 495). Πρός could express goal ("the things which lead to peace"; cf. BDAG 874c [mng. 3c]) or ref. ("the things which make for peace"; BDAG 875a–b; see 19:42). As noted in 14:30, the imagery of evaluating the battle situation is often understood as encouraging serious reflection on what is involved. Εἰ δυνατός ἐστιν (14:31; cf. ἰσχύω in 14:29–30) and εἰ δὲ μή γε (14:32; cf. ἵνα μήποτε in 14:29), however, again suggest an emphasis on a lack of resources (here explicitly stated in the contrasting size of the armies) along with a discouragement to undertake the project (made explicit in 14:32 in the second illustration; i.e., it would be foolish to commit one's meager army to this war). The illustration, therefore, may point again to the foolishness of relying on one's own resources (Green 566).

14:33 Ὑπάρχουσιν (see 12:44) may indicate a third "cost" of discipleship ("family," "cross," "possessions," Bock 1289; Fitzmyer 1062; Nolland 764). Οὕτως and οὖν, however, suggest that a summary conclusion is being given (restating the claims of 14:26–27 following the previous two illustrations, Marshall 591; cf. ἑαυτοῦ, 14:26–27, 33). Thus, "possessions" here may be an all-encompassing (modified by πᾶσιν τοῖς ἑαυτοῦ) ref. to one's own resources (which have just been shown to be inadequate). Πᾶς (modified by the partitive ἐξ ὑμῶν, cf. R 515; Wallace 85) is the subj. of δύναται (see 3:8; neg. with οὐ). The rel. pron. ὅς is the subj. of ἀποτάσσεται (3rd sg. pres. mid. indic. of dep. ἀποτάσσομαι, "renounce" RSV, ESV; "give up" NRSV, NIV; LN 57.70; "say good-bye" HCSB; Fitzmyer 1059; Marshall 594; cf. LN 33.23; 9:61; neg. with οὐκ). Οὐ . . . μαθητής repeats 14:26–27.

14:34 Οὖν indicates that the following is a further inference of the preceding teaching (cf. BDAG 736c; omitted in many later mss. and most EVV; included in 𝔓⁷⁵ ℵ B L; "Therefore" NASB; "Now" HCSB). The (first) nom. sg. neut. ἅλας (of ἅλας, -ατος, τό, "salt") is the subj., and the adj. καλόν ("useful" BDAG 504c–d) is the pred. in a verbless clause. Ἐάν introduces the protasis of a third-class cond. sentence. Καί, "even" (NASB; ZG 242; Marshall 595; the art. τό is generic). Μωρανθῇ 3rd sg. aor. pass. subjunc. of μωραίνω "make tasteless" (sim. NRSV, NASB, HCSB, ESV; "loses its saltiness" NIV; elsewhere "make foolish" BDAG 663b; LN 32.56; 79.44; the mng. "saltlessness" [as NIV] may derive from an Aram. play on words, Marshall 595). Ἐν is instr. (with τίνι; the pass. is impers. "by what means"; "how" most EVV; Wallace 435; Z §119). Ἀρτυθήσεται 3rd sg. fut. pass. indic. of ἀρτύω, "make salty" (HCSB, NIV; "saltiness be restored" NRSV, ESV; cf. ref. to salt from the Dead Sea in F. Hauck *TDNT* 1.229; Marshall 596). The deliberative fut. is rhetorical (R 889, 934; Wallace 468).

14:35 The nom. sg. neut. adj. εὔθετον (see 9:62; "fit," "suitable") is pred. Εἰς could express purpose (ZG 242; cf. BDAG 290a) or ref. (BDAG 291a). The mng. of οὔτε εἰς γῆν οὔτε εἰς κοπρίαν is disputed ("neither for soil nor for the manure pile" NRSV, sim. NASB, HCSB, ESV, NIV; the acc. κοπρίαν is fem. sg. [of κοπρία, -ας, ἡ; only here in the NT]; cf. the neut. pl. in 13:8). The following clause makes clear, however, that it is useless as the salt is "thrown out" (ἔξω βάλλουσιν 3rd pl. pres. act. indic. of βάλλω; the impers. pl. is a Sem. for the pass. Z §§1, 3). As with the two illustrations in 14:28–32, the point here may emphasize the uselessness of disciples who do not remain committed to Jesus (Bock 1292; Fitzmyer 1068; Marshall 596). Or these concluding statements may again indicate the inadequacy (here, uselessness) of relying on anything other than Jesus (Green 567–68). Ὁ ἔχων . . . ἀκουέτω, see 8:8. In the structure of this section, it is possible that salt that becomes useless parallels Jerusalem that has been abandoned (13:34–35).

HOMILETICAL SUGGESTIONS

The Surprising Attendees at Jesus' Kingdom Banquet (14:15–35)

1. Those who have no other priorities (14:15–24)
2. Those who give Jesus ultimate priority (14:25–27)
3. Those who know the inadequacy of their own resources (14:28–35)

or

3. Those who carefully consider the cost (14:28–35)

7. God's Celebration at the Return of the Lost (15:1–32)

These three parables mark off the whole chapter as a literary unit. After an introduction (15:1–3), the first two parables are a matching pair (reflecting other pairs in Luke, e.g., 13:18–21; 14:28–32; and male/female pairs, e.g., 13:19, 21). The third parable completes the picture with descriptions of the degradation of the lost, the decision to return, the delight of the father, and (returning to the introductory complaints of the Pharisees and scribes) the disdain of the older brother. Reference to the lowly and lost who lack resources, the response of the repentant, the exclusion from the banquet of those who reject the invitation, and the corresponding rejoicing for the undeserving who are graciously included in the kingdom's banquet summarize the themes of 13:10–14:35.

15:1 "Tax collectors" (see 3:12) and "sinners" are mentioned together as one subject (cf. 5:30; 7:34; πάντες is hyperbolic, Marshall 599; Nolland 768) though separated by the two arts. The following verse will again show that "sinners" is the broader term (see 5:8, 30, 32; 13:2). Ἐγγίζοντες (nom. pl. masc. of pres. act. ptc. of ἐγγίζω; cf. the similar sounding διαγογγύζω in 15:2) with ἦσαν (see 1:6) is an impf. periph. cstr. (Z §361). This cstr. is a common introductory cstr. in Luke (cf. e.g., 1:21; 4:31; Fitzmyer 1075–76). The inf. ἀκούειν (see 5:1; the gen. αὐτοῦ is obj.) expresses purpose (ZG 242) and recalls Jesus' exhortation "to hear" in 14:35 (Marshall 599).

15:2 The nom. pl. οἵ τε Φαρισαῖοι καὶ οἱ γραμματεῖς are also distinguished by the two arts. but combined together (τε . . . καί, "both . . . and," T 339) as the subj. of διεγόγγυζον (3rd pl. impf. act. indic. of διαγογγύζω, an onomatopoetic word; "murmur," "complain"; only here, 19:7 in the NT; see γογγύζω, 5:30). Διεγόγγυζον parallels the preceding periph. cstr. (with ἐγγίζοντες) and may be viewed as providing general background information (Marshall 599; Nolland 770), ingressive (NASB), or progressive (cf. NRSV, HCSB; Bovon 2.403; Fitzmyer 1076). Pharisees and scribes are often grouped together (see 5:17) in opposition to Jesus (e.g., 6:7; 11:53–54). Λέγοντες, see 1:66. Ὅτι, recitative (Wallace 455). The subj. (οὗτος, in a derisive sense, R 697; cf. 14:30; 15:30) and obj. (ἁμαρτωλούς) are placed forward for emphasis (BHGNT 498). Προσδέχεται 3rd sg. pres. mid. indic. of dep. προσδέχομαι, "receives" (NASB, ESV), "welcomes" (NRSV, HCSB, NIV), "have good will toward" (Nolland 770). Συνεσθίει 3rd sg. pres. act. indic. of συνεσθίω, "eat with" (αὐτοῖς is the dat. complement). Links with 5:30 include the following: the subj. (οἱ Φαρισαῖοι καὶ οἱ γραμματεῖς), the vb. (γογγύζω in 5:30), and the topic (association with οἱ τελῶναι καὶ οἱ ἁμαρτωλοί; including "eating" with them; ἐσθίω in 5:30).

15:3 The indir. obj. πρὸς αὐτούς could refer to the crowds (i.e., including "sinners") but is more likely a response to the objection of the Pharisees and scribes (Bock 1299). The sg. obj. τὴν παραβολὴν ταύτην introduces the following as a single three-part parable (cf. the sg. in 5:36; 14:7; Bock 1299; "a parabolic discourse" Marshall 600; 18:9 is sim., Nolland 770). Λέγων (see 1:63) serves here to introduce the following discourse (picking up again εἶπεν, BHGNT 498).

15:4 Τίς ἄνθρωπος (with the partitive ἐξ ὑμῶν, Z §80), see 11:5. Τίς γυνή in 15:8 indicates that ἄνθρωπος is "man" (NASB, HCSB, ESV; Nolland 770; see 13:19; 14:2; "one" in NRSV, NIV obscures this parallel). Ἔχων (see 3:11; the obj. ἑκατὸν πρόβατα is "100 sheep") and ἀπολέσας (see 9:25; the obj. is ἕν; ἐξ αὐτῶν is again partitive) could be attrib. (HCSB) or cond. (NASB; Wallace 633; Marshall 601; Nolland 768; cf. 14:28, 31). Καταλείπει 3rd sg. pres. act. indic. of καταλείπω, "leave" (neg. with οὐ; the art. τά makes the adj. ἐνενήκοντα ἐννέα the obj. ["the 99"]). Ἐν τῇ ἐρήμῳ (locat.) is better tr. "in the open country" (ESV, NIV; sim. NASB, HCSB; "pasture" BDAG 392a ["uninhabited area"]) rather than "in the desert" (NJB) or "in the wilderness" (NKJV, NRSV) as neglect of the ninety-nine is not the idea here. Ἐπί following πορεύεται (see 7:8; the pres. is durative, Robertson, *Pictures* 205) is used as a marker of movement, specifying direction or goal (BDAG 364a–b; "go after" most EVV; ZG 243). Ἀπολωλός acc. sg. neut. of 2nd pf. act. (subst.) ptc. of ἀπόλλυμι, "lost" (used eight times in this chapter and links the three parables together). Ἕως with εὕρη (see 12:38; subjunc.) is temp. and indicates the end of the time of searching (BDAG 422d–23a; LN 67.119; i.e., a persevering and successful search, Fitzmyer 1077; Marshall 601; Nolland 771).

15:5 Εὑρών nom. sg. masc. of 2nd aor. act. (temp.) ptc. of εὑρίσκω. Ἐπιτίθησιν 3rd sg. pres. act. indic. of ἐπιτίθημι. Ὤμους acc. pl. masc. of ὦμος, -ου, ὁ, "shoulder" (i.e., he brought the sheep back; αὐτοῦ is pleonastic, Z §197). Χαίρων (nom. sg. masc. of pres. act. ptc. of χαίρω) could be attendant circumstance, but it likely expresses manner here (HCSB, NIV; BHGNT 499). Terms for rejoicing occur repeatedly throughout this chapter (χαίρω, 15:5, 32; συγχαίρω, 15:6, 9; χαρά, 15:7, 10; εὐφραίνω 15:23, 24, 29, 32; see also the refs. in 2:10).

15:6 Ἐλθών, see 7:3 (temp.). Συγκαλεῖ 3rd sg. pres. act. indic. συγκαλέω, "call together" (seven times in Luke-Acts out of eight in the NT). The arts. in τοὺς φίλους καὶ τοὺς γείτονας function as poss. prons. ("his friends and neighbors," cf. Wallace 215; see 14:12). Λέγων could express manner, but it is probably attendant circumstance here (BHGNT 499). Συγχάρητε 2nd pl. 2nd aor. pass. impv. of συγχαίρω, "rejoice with" (cf. 1:58; 15:9; for the impv. as a request see Wallace 488). Ὅτι, causal (giving the reason for the joy). Εὗρον, see 7:9. Ἀπολωλός, see 15:4 (attrib., Wallace 618).

15:7 Ὅτι, recitative. Ἔσται, see 1:14 (the fut. may be customary [Bock 1302], "logical" [Nolland 773], or allude to the eschaton [Bock 1304; Fitzmyer 1077]). The locat. ἐν τῷ οὐρανῷ is a ref. to God (Bock 1302; see 15:10). Ἐπί with the dat. ἐνὶ ἁμαρτωλῷ (cf. 15:1–2) is a marker of basis for the joy ("because of" BDAG 365a; the ground for the emotion, Z §126). Μετανοοῦντι dat. sg. masc. of pres. act. (subst.) ptc. μετανοέω (see 3:3; 10:13). The repentance of the lost one is not part of the story when it involves a sheep or a coin. Repentance will, however, be included in the third parable when a person is involved. The particle ἤ functions as a comparative conj. ("more than"; though without a preceding comparative vb., BDAG 433a; BDF §245[3]; R 661; Z §145). Ἐνενήκοντα ἐννέα, "99" (with ἐπί, causal). The adj. δικαίοις is used subst. (see 5:32). The gen. μετανοίας (see 3:3) is obj. following χρείαν ἔχουσιν (see 5:31; for οἵτινες see 1:20). Although δίκαιος can refer to the "upright" in Luke (e.g., 1:6; 2:25; Nolland

774), the introduction (15:2) and the third parable (see 15:29) point to another use of
the "righteousness" language in Luke being employed here. Luke also regularly points
to a "self-justifying" attitude of the scribes and Pharisees (see δικαιόω in 10:29; 16:15;
δίκαιος in 18:9). Since all must repent (see 5:32), this is a rhetorical contrast and refers
to those who think they have no need to repent (Bock 1302).

15:8 Ἤ ("or") links these two parables together (cf. 14:31). Τίς γυνή see 11:5; 15:4
(here with οὐχί, "what woman . . . does she not" as a nom. abs., Fitzmyer 1081).
Ἔχουσα (see 13:11) could be attrib. (HCSB) or cond. (NASB; Nolland 774; in keeping
with following the cond. clause). The obj. of the ptc. δραχμὰς . . . δέκα, "ten drachmas,"
"ten silver coins" (most EVV; acc. pl. fem. of δραχμή, -ῆς, ἡ; only occurs in 15:8–9 in
the NT; cf. Matt 17:24) refers to a Greek silver coin which was about the same value
as a denarius (BDAG 261b; LN 6.76; MM 170d; cf. 7:41). Ἐάν with the subjunc.
ἀπολέσῃ (see 9:24; cf. ἀπόλλυμι in 15:4) is the protasis of a third-class cond. Οὐχί, see
4:22 (R 917; ZG 243). Ἅπτει 3rd sg. pres. act. indic. of ἅπτω ("light"; with the acc.
[λύχνον], see 8:16). Σαροῖ 3rd sg. pres. act. indic. of σαρόω, "sweep." Ζητεῖ, see 11:29.
Ἐπιμελῶς, adv. "carefully," "diligently" (only here in the NT). The extensive effort
(ἅπτει . . . σαροῖ . . . ζητεῖ) may add a slight difference to this parable (Bock 1303;
though the shepherd leaves the ninety-nine and "goes after" the lost one). For εὕρῃ (for
the form, see 12:38) with ἕως see 15:4 (a little more emphatic with the addition of the
rel. pron. οὗ, BHGNT 501).

15:9 Εὑροῦσα nom. sg. fem. of 2nd aor. act. (temp.) ptc. of εὑρίσκω (cf. εὑρών in 15:5).
The rest of the verse reflects 15:6 (though with the fem. gender, one [fem.] art. for
τὰς φίλας καὶ γείτονας [R 787; see 14:12], and a concluding rel. pron. and vb. in place
of the attrib. ptc. [the shepherd did not lose the sheep, Robertson, *Pictures* 207]).
Ἀπώλεσα 1st sg. aor. act. indic. of ἀπόλλυμι.

15:10 This verse reflects a shortened form of 15:7 (though with γίνεται [see 11:26] in
place of ἔσται, and ἐνώπιον τῶν ἀγγέλων τοῦ θεοῦ in place of the locat. ἐν τῷ οὐρανῷ).
The parallels favor taking the prep. ἐνώπιον as locat. ("in the presence of" BDAG
342c; "among" ZG 243; cf. 12:8–9) rather than as "in the opinion of" (*pace* BHGNT
502). The phrase may be a ref. to God rejoicing in the presence of, or along with,
the angels (Bock 1304; Fitzmyer 1081; Marshall 604), or a circumlocution for God
himself (Nolland 776). These locat. phrases in 15:7, 10, therefore, together with the
actions of the shepherd and woman in the stories, show that Jesus' actions referred to
in 15:2 are the outworking of God's salvific intentions (Nolland 771, 773).

15:11 Ἄνθρωπός τις (see 10:30) identifies the father as the main character of the following story. The ref. to the two sons anticipates the two-part nature of the story. The
impf. εἶχεν (see 13:6) may be used to provide background information (the rest of the
parable proceeds with aor. vbs. [BHGNT 503], until 15:16). Note ἔχων (15:4; a pres.
[masc.] ptc.), and ἔχουσα (15:8; a pres. [fem.] ptc.).

15:12 The nom. sg. masc. subst. comp. adj. νεώτερος (see 5:37; modified by the partitive gen. αὐτῶν) is the subj. of εἶπεν and the action up to 15:20b. Πάτερ, voc. (τῷ
probably functions as a poss. pron., cf. Wallace 215). Δός, see 12:58. Ἐπιβάλλον acc.

sg. neut. of pres. act. (attrib.) ptc. of ἐπιβάλλω (intrans.; modifying τὸ . . . μέρος, "the share . . . that falls to me" RSV, NASB; BDAG 368a; "the share . . . that belongs to me" LN 57.3; cf. the legal refs. in MM 235b–c; BDF §308). Οὐσίας gen. sg. fem. of οὐσία, -ας, ἡ, "property" (NRSV, ESV; "that which exists and therefore has substance" BDAG 740a), "estate" (NASB, HCSB, NIV; MM 467a; only here and 15:13 in the NT). The art. ὁ is the subj. of διεῖλεν (3rd sg. 2nd aor. act. indic. of διαιρέω, "divide," "distribute"). Αὐτοῖς is probably a dat. of indir. obj. Βίον (see 8:14), in this context refers to "resources needed to maintain life" (BDAG 177b; "his livelihood" NKJV; ZG 243; the art. [τόν] probably functions as a poss. pron. again here) and may allude to what would come to the son at the end of his father's life (Bock 1309).

15:13 The horror of the son's attitude toward his father is gradually unfolded as the request for the inheritance is followed by the son's departure (συναγαγὼν . . . ἀπεδήμησεν) and then squandering (διεσκόρπισεν) of the estate (Nolland 783). Μετά followed by the acc. πολλὰς ἡμέρας (neg. with οὐ) is temp. (litotes, "a few days later" NRSV; R 1163; cf. 7:6; Acts 1:5). Συναγαγών (nom. sg. masc. of 2nd aor. act. ptc. of συνάγω, perhaps with the idea of turning it into cash, BDAG 962c; MM 600b; "having sold off everything" ZG 243) is an attendant circumstance ptc. with ἀπεδήμησεν (3rd sg. aor. act. indic. of ἀποδημέω, "go on a journey"; in this context, with the locat. εἰς χώραν μακράν [acc. sg. fem. of μακρός, -ά, -όν] has the mng. "to leave home on a journey" LN 15.47; cf. 20:9; ingressive, Z §250). Διεσκόρπισεν (see 1:51), "scatter" (perhaps in contrast to συναγαγών, "gathered"), with ref. to the estate (οὐσίαν, see 15:12) here is "squandered" (most EVV), "wasted" (NKJV, NLT). Ζῶν (nom. sg. masc. of pres. act. ptc. of ζάω) expresses means (and is modified by the adv. ἀσώτως, "foolish" HCSB; "reckless" ESV ["senseless" LN 88.97]; "wastefully" ["prodigally"] BDAG 148a; cf. the noun ἀσωτία, "wastefulness" in contrast to σῴζω, BDAG 148a; ZG 243; or also ref. to "dissolute pleasures" Marshall 608).

15:14 Δαπανήσαντος gen. sg. masc. of aor. act. ptc. of δαπανάω, "spend freely" (cf. δαπάνη in 14:28; a temp. gen. abs. cstr.; αὐτοῦ is the subj.) highlights the timing of the great famine. The nom. fem. λιμός ("famine"; see masc. in 4:25, cf. MM 376b; BDF §2), modified by the fem. adj. ἰσχυρά, is the subj. of ἐγένετο. Κατά is distributive (BDAG 511c; the demonstrative pron. ἐκείνην notes that this is not the homeland, BHGNT 505). Καὶ αὐτός, see 1:17. Ἤρξατο, see 4:21. The pres. pass. inf. ὑστερεῖσθαι (of ὑστερέω, "lack," "need") is complementary.

15:15 Πορευθείς (see 14:10) is an attendant circumstance ptc. with ἐκολλήθη (3rd sg. aor. pass. indic. of dep. κολλάομαι, "join to," RSV, NKJV; "hired himself out to" NRSV, NASB, ESV; "associate with" having an economic connotation BDAG 556a; the pass. may be "causative/permissive," Wallace 441; the dat. ἑνί is complementary). The gen. pl. masc. πολιτῶν (of πολίτης, -ου, ὁ, "citizen"; cf. 19:14; Acts 21:39) is partitive (ἑνί is used for τινί, Z §155; Marshall 608). Ἔπεμψεν, see 7:6 (the change of subj. without an explicit signal may be Sem., Marshall 608; Nolland 783). The pres. act. inf. βόσκειν (of βόσκω, "to feed" [all EVV], "to tend to the needs of animals" [BDAG 181b]) expresses purpose. Χοίρους, "pigs" (see 8:32–33; the absence of the art. may draw attention to the [unclean and degrading] quality of the pigs, ZG 244).

15:16 Ἐπεθύμει 3rd sg. impf. act. indic. of ἐπιθυμέω, "desire," "longed" (HCSB, NIV). The impf. may be durative (Z §252; ZG 244) or emphasize an unfulfilled wish (BDF §359[2]; Fitzmyer 1088; Marshall 608). The aor. pass. inf. χορτασθῆναι (of χορτάζω, "eat to the full," "be filled with" sim. NRSV, HCSB) is complementary (this rdg. has early and wide [Alexandrian and Western] mss. support [UBS[5]]; the var. γεμίσαι τὴν κοιλίαν ἀπό ["to fill his stomach with"] is accepted by Bovon [2.422], Marshall [609], and Nolland [780] due to the unusual grammar [SBLGNT; NASB, NIV]). Κερατίων gen. pl. neut. of κεράτιον, -ου, τό, "carob pod" (in pl., the [bitter] fruit from a carob tree, BDAG 540d–41a; MM 341c; Nolland 783; used for fattening pigs, though eaten by poor people too, LN 3.46; only here in the NT; ἐκ may indicate means or source, ZG 244). The rel. pron. ὧν (partitive gen. [ZG 244] or gen. by attraction [BHGNT 506; Marshall 609]) is the obj. of ἤσθιον (3rd pl. impf. act. indic. of ἐσθίω). Καί, adversative. Ἐδίδου, see 9:16 (the impf. corresponds to ἐπεθύμει; the obj. could be these carob pods [NJB, HCSB] or other food ["anything" most EVV; Fitzmyer 1088]). His descent is complete: he is separated from the father, lives among the unclean, longs for the food of pigs, has no resources and no help.

15:17 Ἐλθών (see 7:3; temp.) with εἰς ἑαυτόν is idiomatic (BDAG 269b, 395a) for coming to a sensible conclusion ("when he came to his senses" NASB, HCSB, NIV; cf. 12:17). Ἔφη, see 7:44. The nom. pl. masc. πόσοι μίσθιοι ("how many hired [i.e., paid] workers"; πόσοι [of πόσος, -η, -ον] is used in an exclamatory sense, R 741; or like πῶς, Z §221; μίσθιος, -α, -ον, subst.; only here and 15:19 in the NT, refers to a day laborer, BDAG 653b) is the subj. of περισσεύονται (3rd pl. pres. mid. indic. of περισσεύω; when followed by the gen. "have an abundance of" BDAG 805c; BDF §172; R 510). Ἐγὼ δέ highlights the contrast between even a day laborer's abundance of food and his own deathly condition (cf. 15:24, 32). The dat. λιμῷ (see 4:25; "hunger" all EVV) with ἀπόλλυμαι (1st sg. pres. mid. indic. of ἀπόλλυμι) could be causal ("from hunger" NET; R 532; Wallace 168) or instr. (BHGNT 507). In this context ἀπόλλυμαι has the mng. "I perish" (ESV), "I am dying" (NRSV, NASB, HCSB, sim. NIV), though it prepares for the use of the vb. in 15:24, 32 (Nolland 784).

15:18 Ἀναστάς (see 4:38) is an attendant circumstance ptc. (cf. Z §363) with πορεύσομαι (1st sg. fut. mid. indic. of dep. πορεύσομαι; a volitive fut., R 874; on the combination of these two vbs. see 1:39). Ἐρῶ, see 12:19. Πάτερ, voc. Ἥμαρτον 1st sg. 2nd aor. act. indic. of ἁμαρτάνω. Εἰς is ref. to actions directed at someone in a hostile sense (BDAG 290b–c; "against"). Οὐρανόν is a circumlocution for God (cf. 15:7). The prep. ἐνώπιόν (the 2nd accent is from the enclitic σου) is used here in a sim. way to εἰς as "against" (NIV; BDAG 342d; a marker of "a participant whose viewpoint is relevant to an event . . ., in the sight of," LN 90.20; ZG 244; cf. LXX Exod 10:16; Nolland 784).

15:19 The aor. pass. inf. κληθῆναι (of καλέω; the nom. υἱός is the complement in a double nom. cstr.; cf. 1:32; BHGNT 508; R 1076) is epex. to the pred. adj. ἄξιος (for οὐκέτι . . . ἄξιος cf. 7:4 and 6 [ἄξιός . . . οὐ . . . ἱκανός]; 17:10 [δοῦλοι ἀχρεῖοι]). Ποίησόν, see 4:23. Μισθίων (partitive gen. pl. masc. "hired workers," see 15:17) is contrasted here with υἱός. The day laborer, being only hired a day at a time, was lower than a slave (δοῦλος, Bock 1313). Perhaps this response reflects one without resources seeking peace (cf. 14:32)?

15:20 Ἀναστάς (see 4:38) is attendant circumstance (with ἦλθεν see 2:27; the refl. pron. ἑαυτοῦ is used without emphasis, Z §§197, 208). The use of the advs. ἔτι ("still") and μακράν ("far away") together with ἀπέχοντος (of ἀπέχω, "be distant"; a temp. gen. abs. cstr. with the subj. αὐτοῦ; see 7:6 for the form and the opposite emphasis) emphasizes the distance (μακράν may be an adv. acc. or an acc. of extent of space [with ὁδόν implied], cf. BDAG 612a; Robertson, *Pictures* 210; Wallace 201; cf. the adv. πόρρω, 14:32). The father is the subj. of action now for the first time since 15:12b. Εἶδεν, see 5:2. Although the son is yet to express his confession, it is the sight of the returning son that leads to the father's compassionate initiative in restoration. Ἐσπλαγχνίσθη, see 7:13; 10:33 (cf. 1:78). Δραμών (nom. sg. masc. of 2nd aor. act. ptc. of τρέχω, "run") is an attendant circumstance ptc. with ἐπέπεσεν (see 1:12; with τὸν τράχηλον αὐτοῦ ["his neck"; acc. sg. masc. of τράχηλος, -ου, ὁ] is idiomatic for an affectionate embrace; "threw his arms around him" NIV; cf. Acts 20:37; common in the LXX). Κατεφίλησεν 3rd sg. aor. act. indic. of καταφιλέω, "kiss" (see 7:38).

15:21 Πάτερ . . . σου is as the son planned to say in 15:18b–19a. Some mss. add what was planned in 15:19b here too. The omission of these words has wide and early support so the addition here is likely due to scribal assimilation to 15:19b (Bock 1321; Fitzmyer 1090; Marshall 610; Nolland 780).

15:22 The conj. δέ together with the father's urgency (ταχύ neut. sg. [of ταχύς, -εῖα, -ύ] as an adv. "quickly") suggest that the Father's urgent response interrupted the son's words before he got to the request to be a hired worker (Bovon 2.427; Fitzmyer 1089; Marshall 610; these markers provide more evidence for this than the suggestion [by e.g., Bock 1314; Nolland 785] that the son now viewed the request to be a day laborer as an insult; furthermore [as Bock and Nolland rightly point out, *pace* Bailey 1976 183], there is no evidence in this context that the son leaves it out due to disappointment at not being able to earn his way back). Τοὺς δούλους αὐτοῦ highlights the father as the master of the household (Fitzmyer 1090). Ἐξενέγκατε 2nd pl. 2nd aor. act. impv. of ἐκφέρω, "bring out." The order of στολὴν τὴν πρώτην (acc. sg. fem. of στολή, -ῆς, ἡ; "the best robe" most EVV; "the special robe" BDAG 893d), noun-art.-adj., is the less common "third attributive position" in which the noun is often general and the adj. specifies (R 777; "a robe-the best one" Wallace 239, 307; Z §192). Ἐνδύσατε 2nd pl. aor. act. impv. of ἐνδύω. Δότε, see 9:13. Δακτύλιον acc. sg. masc. of δακτύλιος, -ου, ὁ, "ring" (only here in the NT; for the "finger," δάκτυλος, cf. 11:20). Thus, χεῖρα αὐτοῦ is used here with ref. to any part of the hand, including the finger (HCSB, NIV; BDAG 1082d; LN 8.30). Ὑποδήματα, "sandals" (acc. pl. neut., see 3:16; this implies he was barefoot and therefore highlights his restoration from destitution, Bock 1315). Εἰς (twice), locat. ("movement directed at a surface," "on" BDAG 289a; Sem., BDF §207[1]).

15:23 Φέρετε 2nd pl. pres. act. impv. of φέρω (the pres. may be used for the outset of the activity, Z §244; or it may add emphasis in contrast with the aor. impvs.
as indicated by the subsequent discussion concerning the fattened calf, BHGNT
510, citing Porter 355). Μόσχον acc. sg. masc. of μόσχος, -ου, ὁ, "calf" (modified by
the adj. σιτευτόν [of σιτευτός, -ή, -όν], "fattened" LN 44.2; therefore, perhaps mng.
"prized" LN 65.8). Θύσατε 2nd pl. aor. act. impv. of θύω, "sacrifice," "kill" (most
EVV), "slaughter" (HCSB). Φαγόντες (nom. pl. masc. of 2nd aor. act. ptc. of ἐσθίω) is
attendant circumstance (BDF §420[3]; Z §261; Bock 1315; Marshall 611; or possibly
a ptc. of means, cf. HCSB) with εὐφρανθῶμεν (1st pl. aor. pass. [hortatory] subjunc. of
εὐφραίνω, intrans.; cf. 15:5) and takes on the mood of the subjunc.

15:24 Ὅτι, causal (giving the reason for the celebration). Ἀνέζησεν 3rd sg. aor. act.
indic. of ἀναζάω, "come to life again." "Lost" and "found" highlight the link between
this parable and the preceding two (15:4, 6, 8–9), and they indicate that "dead"
and "alive" probably refer to the separation from and restoration to the relationship
(Nolland 786; though the link between "lost" and near physical "death" was alluded to
with ἀπόλλυμαι in 15:17). Ἀπολωλώς (nom. sg. masc. of 2nd pf. act. ptc. of ἀπόλλυμι;
intrans.; cf. 15:4) with ἦν is a pluperfect periph. cstr. (R 906; Wallace 649; or possibly
as a pred. adj., sim to νεκρὸς ἦν, Wallace 583). Εὑρέθη, see 9:36. The pres. pass. inf.
εὐφραίνεσθαι (of εὐφραίνω) is complementary (following ἤρξαντο, see 5:21).

15:25 Ὡς with ἐρχόμενος (see 6:47) is a temp. cstr. (with ἤγγισεν [see 7:12], "as he
came and approached" NET; Fitzmyer 1090; or attendant circumstance, Z §363; ZG
245). The dat. τῇ οἰκίᾳ may be complementary (BHGNT 511) or a dat. of destination
(Wallace 147). Ἤκουσεν, see 1:41. The gen. συμφωνίας (sg. fem. of συμφωνία, -ας, ἡ)
καὶ χορῶν is obj. ("music and dancing"; the pl. masc. χορῶν [of χορός, -οῦ, ὁ] is rhyth-
mic movements, BDAG 1087a–b; LN 15.244; or possibly singers, BDAG 1087a–b;
MM 690a).

15:26 Προσκαλεσάμενος, see 7:18 (temp.). Παίδων (partitive gen. pl. of παῖς [see 1:54];
ἕνα is used for τινά, Z §155; see 15:15) may refer to a special or young servant (Bock
1316; [though one of those is mentioned in 15:22] Bovon 2.428; Fitzmyer 1090) or
just to the slaves already mentioned (cf. δοῦλος, 15:22; Marshall 610; see 7:7; BDAG
750c; different from μίσθιος, 15:17, 19). Ἐπυνθάνετο (3rd sg. impf. mid. indic. of dep.
πυνθάνομαι, "inquire," "ask"; nine out of twelve refs. of this vb. in the NT are in Luke-
Acts; cf. 18:36) could be ingressive (NASB), iter. (Robertson, *Pictures* 212; Bock
1316), or due to the use of a vb. of asking (Z §272). The nom. sg. neut. interr. τί, with
the particle ἄν and the optative εἴη (see 1:29), introduces an indir. question (see refs. at
1:62 [cf. also 1:29]; here lit. "what these things might be"; sim. HCSB). The sg. τί, as
a pred., may be used with ταῦτα (BDF §299[1]; R 411, 736; ZG 245).

15:27 Ὅτι, recitative (Marshall 612; *pace* Bock 1316). Ἥκει 3rd sg. pres. act. indic.
of ἥκω, "have come," "be present" (BDAG 435c; MM 278d; stative, R 881; perfective,
Wallace 533). Ἔθυσεν 3rd sg. aor. act. indic. of θύω (with τὸν μόσχον τὸν σιτευτόν, see
15:23). Ὅτι (second), causal (giving the reason for the sacrifice/feast). Ὑγιαίνοντα (see

7:10) is the complement in a double acc. cstr. (BDAG 115b; the obj. of ἀπέλαβεν 3rd sg. 2nd aor. act. indic. of ἀπολαμβάνω, "receive back," NASB, ESV).

15:28 Ὠργίσθη 3rd sg. aor. pass. indic. of dep. ὀργίζομαι, "be angry" (in the pass. "became angry" NRSV, NASB, HCSB). Ὠργίσθη, with δέ, emphasizes the contrast with 15:27 (and the joy of 15:23–24; though cf. 2:4 on δὲ καί). The older son's anger is in response to the action of the father. Ἤθελεν 3rd sg. impf. act. indic. of θέλω (neg. with οὐκ; "refused" ESV, NIV; R 885; ZG 245). The inf. εἰσελθεῖν (see 6:6) is complementary. Ἐξελθών, see 1:22 (temp.). The contrast between εἰσελθεῖν and ἐξελθών highlights the "outsider" status of the older brother as well as the father's compassionate appeal to him. Παρεκάλει, see 8:41 (the impf. could be ingressive, NJB, NRSV, NASB; or iter., Robertson, *Pictures* 212; Bock 1317).

15:29 Ἀποκριθείς, see 1:19. Ἰδού see 1:20 (for ἰδού with an emphasis on the length of time, see 13:16). The acc. pl. neut. τοσαῦτα [of τοσοῦτος, -αύτη, -οῦτον] ἔτη ("so many years") expresses extent of time (R 470). The focus of ἰδού . . . παρῆλθον reflects the "self-justification" associated with the scribes and Pharisees in Luke (10:29; 16:15; 18:9), even as he refuses to obey the father's appeal to join the celebration. Δουλεύω (1st sg. pres. act. indic. of δουλεύω, "slaving" NIV; sim. BDAG 259c; pres. is durative, extending from past to present, R 879; Wallace 520) may refer to the elder son's obedient service (Nolland 787). The use of δοῦλος already in this context (15:22), however, indicates that the son mistakenly (and ironically) perceives his relationship with his father as one of slave to master and portrays the gracious father as unjust (Fitzmyer 1091; Marshall 612). Παρῆλθον 1st sg. 2nd aor. act. indic. of dep. παρέρχομαι, "pass by," "neglected" (NASB), "transgressed" (NKJV), "disobeyed" (most EVV; "to ignore something in the interest of other matters," BDAG 776a; see 11:42; here neg. with the adv. οὐδέποτε, "never"). Καί, contrastive (the preceding obedience ought to have been the basis for the following celebration; note the contrasting οὐδέποτε . . . οὐδέποτε). Ἔδωκας, see 7:44 (neg. with οὐδέποτε). Ἔριφον acc. sg. masc. of ἔριφος, -ου, ὁ, "he–goat," "young goat" (most EVV; BDAG 392d; LN 4.19; only here and pl. in Matt 25:32 in the NT; the goat is worth little and is intended as a contrast with the much more valuable fattened calf, Bock 1318; Fitzmyer 1091). Ἵνα with the subjunc. εὐφρανθῶ (1st sg. aor. pass. subjunc. of εὐφραίνω) expresses the purpose for receiving the goat.

15:30 The demonstrative pron. οὗτος together with the description of his brother as ὁ υἱός σου emphasizes the brother's derisive tone (BDF §290[6]; R 697; cf. e.g., 14:30; 18:11; 23:2, 35; and in this context, 15:2). The attrib. phrase that follows this nom. subj. and precedes ἦλθεν (see 2:27) further adds to this tone (BHGNT 514). Καταφαγών nom. sg. masc. of 2nd aor. act. (attrib.) ptc. of κατεσθίω, "devour" (see 8:5). Βίον, see 8:14; 15:12 (the elder son has not forgotten the distribution of 15:12, Nolland 787). Πορνῶν gen. pl. fem. of πόρνη, -ης, ἡ, "prostitute" (μετὰ πορνῶν may be a contrast to μετὰ τῶν φίλων μου, 15:29; it is possible that the older brother is exaggerating, or that this is implied in the ref. to ζῶν ἀσώτως [15:13]). Ἔθυσας 2nd sg. aor. act. indic. of θύω. Αὐτῷ, is a dat. of advantage. For θύω with σιτευτὸν μόσχον see 15:23, 27.

15:31 The father's tender (τέκνον, voc., perhaps idiomatically "my child," Fitzmyer 1091) response first reminds the elder son of his privileges before turning to the reasons for the celebration. The elder son is reminded (1) that he has always had access to the father (πάντοτε, adv., "always," contrasts with οὐδέποτε, 15:29; εἶ see 3:22; σύ may be emphatic, Robertson, *Pictures* 213), and (2) that he has had access to all the things of the father (the neut. pl. πάντα τὰ ἐμά is the subj. of ἐστίν; the neut. pl. poss. adj. σά is pred.). In the wider context of Luke's Gospel, this may refer to the privileged position of the leaders of Israel (cf. 20:9–19).

15:32 The forward placement and combination of the two aor. pass. infs. εὐφρανθῆναι (of εὐφραίνω) and χαρῆναι (2nd aor. of χαίρω) with ἔδει (see 11:42; the infs. are complementary) emphasizes the necessity for this joyful celebration (the heart of the three parables; see 15:5). Ὅτι, causal (giving the reason for the celebration). The father highlights the younger son's relationship to the older (ὁ ἀδελφός σου οὗτος contrasts with ὁ υἱός σου οὗτος, 15:30) and the transformation that has taken place (see the sim. structure in 15:24). Ἔζησεν 3rd sg. aor. act. indic. of ζάω, "is alive" (most EVV) or ingressive "come to life" (NJB, NRSV, sim. NASB; Burton §§41, 54; R 834; Wallace 559; Z §250). Ἀπολωλώς, see 15:24 (ἦν is implied; as with 15:24 this is probably a pluperfect periph. ptc. cstr.). Εὑρέθη, see 9:36 (cf. 15:24). These concluding words remind the reader that the father is the main character, and they reiterate the father's compassion and joy for the repentant son despite the complaints of the older brother.

FOR FURTHER STUDY

32. Joy (15:5)

Green, J. B. *DJG*² 448–49.

_____. "'We Had to Celebrate and Rejoice!': Happiness in the Topsy-Turvy World of Luke-Acts." Pages 169–85 in *The Bible and the Pursuit of Happiness: What the Old and New Testaments Teach Us About the Good Life*. Edited by B. A. Strawn. Oxford: Oxford University Press, 2012.

Morrice, W. G. *Joy in the New Testament*. Grand Rapids: Eerdmans, 1985.

Painter, J. *DJG*¹ 394–96.

HOMILETICAL SUGGESTIONS

A Joyful Celebration for the Repentant (15:1–32)

1. God's search-and-find operation is the reason for the celebration (15:1–10).
2. The desperate plight of the rescued magnifies the joy of the celebration (15:11–20a).
3. The compassion of God initiates the celebration (15:20b–24).
4. Those who refuse to embrace the ministry of Jesus will miss the celebration (15:25–32).

D. LIVING BY FAITH IN EXPECTATION OF THE FINAL KINGDOM
(16:1–18:8)

The relationship between this life and the age to come, whether at death (16:9, 22) or when the Son of Man returns (17:22–37; 18:8), continues to shape the priorities of this life. The focus in this section will move toward the need to live by faith in anticipation of that day (16:9–10; 17:5–6, 19; 18:8).

1. Our Master Determines Faithful Use of Possessions in This Age (16:1–31)

The overarching emphasis of this chapter is on the use of money in this age with a view to eternal realities beyond the grave (see 16:14 and the introduction to 16:19).

a. The Shrewd Manager: A Parable About Using the Money of This Age with the Age to Come in View (16:1–13)

16:1 Although the Pharisees are mentioned again in 16:14 (cf. 15:2), the audience is now widened to also (καί) include Jesus' disciples (Nolland 796; cf. 17:1, 22; 18:1). For ἔλεγεν see 3:7 (though see 6:20; BDF §329; Wallace 542 n. 6; Z §272). Δὲ καί see 2:4. Ἄνθρωπός τις (the subj. of ἦν) see 10:30. The nom. adj. πλούσιος could be pred. ("a certain man was rich who." Nolland 797) or attrib. ("There was a certain rich man who" sim. all EVV; Marshall 617). The nom. sg. masc. rel. pron. ὅς is the subj. of εἶχεν (see 13:6). Οἰκονόμον, "steward" (RSV, NKJV), "manager" (NRSV, HCSB, ESV; see 12:42; i.e., someone responsible to manage the estate, BDAG 698b; MM 442d–43a; Otto Michel, *TDNT* 5.149–50). The demonstrative pron. οὗτος refers to the manager (NASB; BDF §290; R 697) and is the subj. of διεβλήθη (3rd sg. 2nd aor. pass. indic. of διαβάλλω, "bring charges," "report"; not necessarily involving malice or falsehood on the part of those bringing the charges, MM 146d–47a; Fitzmyer 1099). The antecedent of the pron. αὐτῷ is the rich man. Διασκορπίζων (nom. sg. masc. of pres. act. ptc. of διασκορπίζω, "squandering" NRSV, NASB, HCSB; "wasting" ESV; see 1:51; 15:13) following ὡς is probably subst. (cf. BDAG 1105b; BDF §425[3] for ὡς; BHGNT 517). Ὑπάρχοντα (see 11:21; subst.) is the obj. of διασκορπίζων.

16:2 Φωνήσας (nom. sg. masc. of aor. act. ptc. of φωνέω) is attendant circumstance (with εἶπεν). The interr. pron. τί is probably the subj. and the demonstrative pron. τοῦτο the obj. of a verbless clause (with an implied ἐστίν; most EVV; though KJV tr. τοῦτο as the obj. of ἀκούω [see 9:9]; cf. BDF §299[1]; BHGNT 517; R 736, 916; Fitzmyer 1100; Marshall 617; Nolland 797). Ἀπόδος 2nd sg. 2nd aor. act. impv. of ἀποδίδωμι, "give," "turn in" (ESV; what is due, Z §132). Τὸν λόγον τῆς οἰκονομίας σου, "the account of your management" (ESV; for λογός as a formal accounting, see BDAG 600d; οἰκονομίας gen. sg. fem. of οἰκονομία, -ας, ἡ). Γάρ, causal (giving the reason for handing in the account). Δύνῃ 2nd sg. pres. mid. indic. of dep. δύναμαι (on the form see BDF §93; R 312; neg. with οὐ). The pres. act. inf. οἰκονομεῖν (of οἰκονομέω, "manage") is complementary (ἔτι, "still"; i.e., he cannot continue, ZG 246). The steward's dismissal implies that the records will confirm the charges (Bock 1328).

16:3 For ἐν ἑαυτῷ and soliloquies in Luke see 12:17. Ποιήσω with the interr. τί could be 1st sg. aor. act. subjunc. or fut. act. indic. of ποιέω. Ὅτι, causal (giving the reason for his uncertainty; Z §420; ZG 246). Ἀφαιρεῖται 3rd sg. pres. mid. indic. of ἀφαιρέω, "take away." The pres. indicates that his position (τὴν οἰκονομίαν, "the management" HCSB, ESV; see 16:2) is in the process of being taken away (i.e., the reports still need to come in; Marshall 618; Nolland 797; see the temp. cstr. in 16:4). The pres. act. inf. σκάπτειν (of σκάπτω, "dig"; see 6:48; associated with the hard labor of the uneducated, BDAG 926d) is complementary to ἰσχύω (1st sg. pres. act. indic. of ἰσχύω; cf. BDAG 484c; Burton §387). The pres. act. inf. ἐπαιτεῖν (of ἐπαιτέω, "beg") is complementary to αἰσχύνομαι (1st sg. pres. mid. indic. of dep. αἰσχύνομαι, "ashamed"; cf. BDAG 30b; BDF §392[1b]).

16:4 The interr. clause τί ποιήσω (see 16:3) is the obj. of ἔγνων (see 8:46; the aor. may be "dramatic" [Burton §45; R 842, 893; Wallace 565; Z §258; like "I've got it!" Bock 1328; Bovon 2.447; Fitzmyer 1100; *pace* T 74, gnomic is unlikely; cf. Marshall 618]). Ἵνα introduces a purpose clause. The subjunc. μετασταθῶ (1st sg. aor. pass. subjunc. of μεθίστημι, "remove," "depose" BDAG 625c; ἐκ expresses separation) with ὅταν is temp. Δέξωνται 3rd pl. aor. mid. subjunc. of dep. δέχομαι (the obj. is the enclitic με; the subj. "people" is supplied in most EVV; it is a ref. to the debtors; cf. 16:9). Εἰς τοὺς οἴκους αὐτῶν is locat. The play on the οἰκο– root in the prep. phrases ἐκ τῆς οἰκονομίας (see 16:2) and εἰς τοὺς οἴκους αὐτῶν may highlight the loss of his position as also a loss of house to live in (Nolland 798).

16:5 Προσκαλεσάμενος, see 7:18 (temp.; modifying ἔλεγεν [see 3:7; 6:20] which functions like an aor. here [see 3:11; Wallace 543]). The gen. (pl. masc.) τῶν χρεοφειλετῶν (see 7:41; "of the debtors"; only 7:41 and here in the NT) is partitive. The gen. τοῦ κυρίου is obj. ("who owed . . . his employer" NLT). The following two debtors are to be understood as samples (Fitzmyer 1100; Nolland 798). The interr. πόσον (a quantitative interr., Wallace 346) is the obj. of ὀφείλεις (2nd sg. pres. act. indic. of ὀφείλω).

16:6 Βάτος was a Heb. liquid measure of between eight and nine gallons (or about thirty-five liters, LN 81.20; βάτους acc. pl. masc. of βάτος, -ου, ὁ; only here in the NT; different to βάτος in 6:44). The amount of ἑκατὸν βάτους, "100 measures" (NASB, HCSB, ESV) or "nine hundred gallons" (NIV) is estimated to have been worth about 1,000 denarii (or three years' pay for a day laborer, Bock 1330–31; Marshall 619). Ἐλαίου, "olive oil" (see 7:46; gen. of content). Δέξαι 2nd sg. aor. mid. impv. of dep. δέχομαι. The acc. pl. neut. τὰ γράμματα (of γράμμα, -ατος, τό; "the things written") refers to the "bill" (most EVV; "invoice" HCSB; "promissory note" BDAG 205d; Bock 1331; Fitzmyer 1100; Marshall 619). Καθίσας (see 5:3; cf. 14:28, 31) is an attendant circumstance ptc. (with γράψον 2nd sg. aor. act. impv. of γράφω) and takes on the mood of the impv. (Wallace 643; Z §363). The adv. ταχέως may modify καθίσας (most EVV), γράψον (NJB), or both (NLT; BHGNT 521). The reduction to πεντήκοντα ("50 [measures]") halves the amount owed. No explanation is given for how the steward reduced the amounts in 16:6–7 (e.g., whether by lowering the price [falsifying the accounts, Bovon 2.448; Nolland 800], removing the interest rate [Marshall 614–15], or removing the steward's own commission; the master's praise in 16:8 suggests the last option as likely, see Bock 1329–30; Fitzmyer 1101).

16:7 Ἔπειτα, adv. "then." For πόσον ὀφείλεις see 16:5 (the pron. σύ identifies a specific shift in addressee, BHGNT 521). Κόρους acc. pl. masc. of κόρος, -ου, ὁ, "measure" (a Heb. dry measure for wheat or grain of between ten and twelve bushels, or about 390 liters, BDAG 560b; LN 81.21; the noun occurs only here in the NT, though fourteen times in the LXX). With the change from oil to wheat (σίτου; gen. of content; see 3:17), the amount of ἑκατὸν κόρους "100 measures" (NASB, HCSB, ESV) is about "1,000 bushels" (NLT, NIV; or 40,000 liters) and is estimated to have been worth about 2,500–3,000 denarii (or eight to ten years of wages for a day laborer, Bock 1331; though cf. the smaller figures in Fitzmyer 1101). For δέξαι σου τὰ γράμματα and γράψον see 16:6. The reduction to ὀγδοήκοντα ("80 [measures]" or "800 bushels" NLT) takes twenty measures of wheat off the debt (i.e., about twenty percent; though the amount is worth about 500–600 denarii and sim. to the previous debtor's, Marshall 619; Nolland 799).

16:8 Ἐπήνεσεν 3rd sg. aor. act. indic. of ἐπαινέω, "praise." Ὁ κύριος (the subj. of ἐπήνεσεν) is likely the "master" (κύριος) of 16:3, 5 (i.e., the "rich man," 16:1; cf. 12:37; 14:21–23 for sim. parabolic uses of κύριος) so that 16:8a is still part of the parable. Since the manager is praised for acting "shrewdly," the attrib. gen. ἀδικίας (BDF §165; R 496, 651; Z §40; "unrighteousness"; see 13:27; 16:9; 18:6) may refer to his prior conduct of squandering that led to the rich man's decision to take his position away (16:1–3; Bock 1332, 1343; Fitzmyer 1101) rather than to the activity just mentioned in reducing the debts of the rich man's debtors (16:5–7; see the various views in Bock 1339–43). In view of 16:8b, 9, ἀδικίας describes the steward as characteristically of this world and acting in a "this–worldly" way (Bovon 2.448; Marshall 620; Nolland 801; though Bovon and Nolland view the steward as acting unrighteously throughout). Ὅτι, causal (giving the reason for the praise). The adv. φρονίμως "shrewdly" (NRSV, NIV; "astutely" HCSB; "wisely" KJV; only here in the NT) modifies ἐποίησεν (see 1:49). It is possible that the first ὅτι introduces indir. discourse and the second dir. discourse (cf. BDF §470[2]; Marshall 619). The ref. to οἱ υἱοὶ τοῦ αἰῶνος τούτου (in this context, those "whose outlook is entirely conditioned by this world," ZG 246; cf. Z §42; elsewhere in the NT only in 20:34) likely indicates that Jesus is introducing his first short application of the parable's point (Bock 1332; though 16:9 [καὶ ἐγὼ ὑμῖν λέγω] may serve as a more explicit shift to Jesus' application from the parable, Rowe 156). Thus, the second ὅτι is likely causal, giving the reason for the shrewd action, and likening the manager to "the sons of this age" (Fitzmyer 1108; Nolland 801). The nom. pl. masc. comp. adj. φρονιμώτεροι ("more shrewd" NRSV, NIV; "more astute" HCSB; "wiser" KJV; of φρόνιμος [see 12:42]; with ὑπέρ instead of a gen. of comp., BDF §185[3]; R 633; ZG 246) is pred. of εἰσίν. Τοὺς υἱοὺς τοῦ φωτός is a common description of God's people in Judaism and the NT (see refs. in Bock 1332; Marshall 621). Εἰς is "with reference to" (BDAG 291a; Fitzmyer 1108). Εἰς τὴν γενεὰν τὴν ἑαυτῶν ("in dealing with their own generation" NRSV, ESV; "in dealing with their own kind" NIV, sim. NASB) modifies φρονιμώτεροι (cf. γενεά in 7:31).

16:9 Καὶ ἐγὼ ὑμῖν λέγω introduces an explicit concluding application from the parable that recalls 16:4 (ἵνα ὅταν . . . δέξωνται . . . εἰς . . .). Ποιήσατε, see 3:8 ("make" most EVV; "gain" NIV; ἑαυτοῖς is a dat. of advantage; cf. Z §209 for the form). Ἐκ expresses means (R 598; Bock 1333; cf. Fitzmyer 1109 who summarizes other options such as separation ["apart from"] and comparison ["rather than"]). Μαμωνᾶ gen. sg. masc. of μαμωνᾶς, -ᾶ, ὁ, "mammon" (used by Luke three out of the four occurrences in the NT; 16:9, 11, 13; and Matt 6:24) is a Heb. or Aram. term for wealth or property (BDAG 614d; "wealth" ESV, NIV; "money" HCSB). The gen. τῆς ἀδικίας is attrib. (Wallace 88; see 16:8). In light of the following temp. clause (ὅταν ἐκλίπῃ), "unrighteous" seems to refer to wealth or money as associated with this world and its tendency to ensnare people in the limited horizon of this world and in ungodly pursuits (i.e., not wealth gained dishonestly; Bock 1334; Fitzmyer 1109; Marshall 621). Ἵνα with the subjunc. δέξωνται (see 16:4) expresses purpose (the acc. ὑμᾶς is the obj.). Ὅταν with the subjunc. ἐκλίπῃ (3rd sg. 2nd aor. act. subjunc. of ἐκλείπω, "fail" HCSB, ESV; "runs out" NET; "gone" NRSV) is temp. The var. 2nd pl. ἐκλίπητε (NKJV) is weakly attested and likely a later scribal clarification (Fitzmyer 1110; Marshall 621). Ἐκλείπω highlights the "this-worldly" limitation of money. The 3rd pl. δέξωνται may be an Aram. in place of the passive ("you will be welcomed" NIV; Z §1; Fitzmyer 1110; perhaps as an indir. ref. to God, Z §2; ZG 247; Bock 1334), a ref. to angels as a circumlocution for God (Marshall 621–22), or (more likely in this context) to the "friends" as a circumlocution for God (cf. 16:4; Nolland 808). Σκηνάς acc. pl. fem., see 9:33, "dwellings" (HCSB, ESV, NIV).

16:10 The subst. adj. πιστός (modified by ἐν ἐλαχίστῳ; superl. "least" NKJV [see 12:26; 19:17]; possibly for the elative, Wallace 303; Bovon 2.461; "very little" most EVV; Marshall 623) is the subj. of ἐστίν and begins a more general application from the parable which is applied in 16:11–12 (cf. 12:42; 19:17). "Faithful with very little" is living with the future in mind and being faithful in "making friends" for the age to come with "worldly wealth." Καί, "also." The adj. πιστός (modified by ἐν πολλῷ) is pred. The subst. adj. ὁ . . . ἄδικος (nom. sg. masc. of ἄδικος, -ον, "unrighteous" NASB, HCSB; "untrustworthy" when in contrast with πιστός, BDAG 21a; "dishonest" ESV, NIV; modified by ἐν ἐλαχίστῳ) is the subj. of ἐστίν. Καί, "also." The adj. ἄδικός (modified by ἐν πολλῷ) is pred.

16:11 Εἰ introduces a first-class cond. (Z §303) which begins a specific development of 16:10 (οὖν). For ἀδίκῳ μαμωνᾷ see μαμωνᾶ τῆς ἀδικίας in 16:9 (though here with the adj. ἄδικος in place of the gen. noun). Ἐγένεσθε 2nd pl. 2nd aor. mid. indic. of dep. γίνομαι (neg. with οὐκ; the adj. πιστοί is pred.). The subst. acc. sg. neut. adj. ἀληθινόν (of ἀληθινός, -ή, -όν, "true [riches]" most EVV; "what is genuine" HCSB; "something of real value" ZG 247) is the obj. of πιστεύσει (3rd sg. fut. act. indic. of πιστεύω; "trust" HCSB, NIV; "entrust" NASB, ESV; BDAG 818a; the interr. τίς is the subj.). In this context, ἀληθινόν refers to that which is characteristic of the new age and may refer to reward in the age to come for faithful service (Marshall 623). Note the parallels throughout 16:10–12 which pick up on the statements of 16:9. These verses continue the future-oriented perspective of the parable (cf. 12:33–34; 19:15–19).

16:9	ἐκ τοῦ μαμωνᾶ τῆς ἀδικίας	εἰς τὰς αἰωνίους σκηνάς
16:10	ἐν ἐλαχίστῳ	ἐν πολλῷ
16:11	ἐν τῷ ἀδίκῳ μαμωνᾷ	τὸ ἀληθινὸν
16:12	ἐν τῷ ἀλλοτρίῳ	τὸ ὑμέτερον

16:12 Εἰ introduces a first-class cond. which introduces another (καί) illustration of 16:10. Ἀλλοτρίῳ dat. sg. neut. of ἀλλότριος, -α, -ον, "what belongs to another" (BDAG 47d). For πιστοὶ οὐκ ἐγένεσθε see 16:11. The subst. acc. sg. neut. adj. ὑμέτερον (of ὑμέτερος, -α, -ον, "that which is your own" ESV) is the obj. of δώσει (see 1:32; the interr. τίς is the subj.). This seems to be another contrast between that which is associated with this world though given by God and that which belongs to the "sons of the light" as those who are of the age to come.

16:13 This verse summarizes all of 16:1–12. Οἰκέτης nom. sg. masc. of οἰκέτης, -ου, ὁ, "household slave" (HCSB; BDAG 694c; MM 440c; "a servant in a household" LN 46.5; omitted in NIV ["servant" most EVV]; a more generic ref. than οἰκονόμος in 16:1, 3, 8 [Fitzmyer 1110]; modified by the adj. οὐδείς). Δύναται, see 3:8. The pres. act. inf. δουλεύειν (of δουλεύω) is complementary (BDAG 259c). Δουλεύω in this context refers to "exclusive loyalty and service" (Marshall 624). The dat. δυσὶ κυρίοις is complementary (BDAG 259c). The conjs. ἤ . . . ἤ are "either . . . or." Γάρ, causal (giving the reason no house servant can serve two masters). Μισήσει 3rd sg. fut. act. indic. of μισέω. Ἀγαπήσει, see 7:42 (for μισέω and ἀγαπάω see refs. at 14:26). Ἀνθέξεται 3rd sg. fut. mid. indic. of dep. ἀντέχομαι, "be devoted to" (the gen. ἑνός is complementary, BDAG 87c–d). Καταφρονήσει 3rd sg. fut. act. indic. of καταφρονέω, "despise" (the gen. τοῦ ἑτέρου is complementary, BDAG 529c). The terms "hate," "love," "devoted," and "despise" parallel one another in a chiastic pattern (Nolland 807; cf. BDF §§489–92). Δύνασθε, see 5:34 (neg. with οὐ). The inf. δουλεύειν is complementary. Μαμωνᾷ (see 16:9; a complementary dat.) is personified as an idol in opposition to God (Bock 1336).

FOR FURTHER STUDY

33. Slavery (16:13)

Beavis, M. A. "Ancient Slavery as an Interpretive Context for the New Testament Servant Parables with Special Reference to the Unjust Steward (Luke 16:1–8)." *JBL* 111 (1992): 37–54.

Bradley, K. *Slaves and Masters in the Roman Empire.* Oxford: Oxford University Press, 1987.

Clarke, A. D. *DJG²* 869–74.

Harrill, J. A. *Slaves in the New Testament: Literary, Social, and Moral Dimensions.* Minneapolis: Fortress Press, 2006.

*Harris, M. J. *Slave of Christ: A New Testament Metaphor for Total Devotion to Christ.* Downers Grove: InterVarsity, 1999.

Matthewson, D. "The Parable of the Unjust Steward (Luke 16:1–13): A Reexamination of the Traditional View in Light of Recent Challenges." *JETS* 38 (1995): 29–40.

Udoh, F. "The Tale of an Unrighteous Slave (Luke 16:1–8[13])." *JBL* 128 (2009): 311–35.

HOMILETICAL SUGGESTIONS

Wisdom with Wealth (16:1–13)

1. Our use of money is temporary, but it can be used for eternal good (16:1–9).
2. Our faithfulness with money is a little thing that can lead to eternal reward (16:10–12).
3. Our exclusive service belongs to God not money (16:13).

*b. Responses to the Pharisees: Jesus' Authority in Relation to Judgment and Law
(16:14–18)*

16:14 Ἤκουον (3rd pl. impf. act. indic. of ἀκούω; the impf. is durative, Robertson, *Pictures* 219) links 16:14–15 to the preceding discussion on money. The ref. to God's evaluation in 16:14–15 may also anticipate 16:19–26 (just as 16:16–18 may anticipate 16:27–31; Nolland 809). The nom. pl. masc. οἱ Φαρισαῖοι (see 5:17) is modified by the pred. adj. φιλάργυροι (of φιλάργυρος, -ον, "lovers of money"; only here and 2 Tim 3:2 in the NT; perhaps in contrast to those who ποιήσατε φίλους, 16:9) and the attrib. ptc. ὑπάρχοντες (see 7:25; Wallace 619; sim. 11:13; 23:50; and common in Acts, Fitzmyer 1113). Ἐξεμυκτήριζον 3rd pl. impf. act. indic. of ἐκμυκτηρίζω, "ridiculed" (ESV), "scoffing" (NASB, HCSB), "sneering" (NIV; fig. "to turn up the nose at" LN 33.409; cf. BDAG 307a; only here and 23:35 in the NT; cf. LXX Pss. 21:8; 34:16).

16:15 Δικαιοῦντες (nom. pl. masc. of pres. act. [subst.] ptc. of δικαιόω, "justify"; see refs. at 10:29; cf. 15:29) is pred. (Burton §433; R 1108; the art. is subst. rather than anaphoric; cf. Z §166). The first use of the prep. ἐνώπιον could mean "in the opinion of" (see below) or locat. "in the sight of" (NRSV, HCSB), "in the presence of" (BDAG 342c, mng. 2b; "before" ESV; BHGNT 526). Their "self–justifying" presentation of themselves to impress others is an outworking of their love for money and antagonism toward God (cf. Fitzmyer 1113; Nolland 810). The contrasting (δέ) ref. to God's knowledge (γινώσκει, see 10:22) of their hearts highlights again the hypocritical actions of the Pharisees (see 12:1; cf. 11:43–44; τὰς καρδίας ὑμῶν contrasts with ἐνώπιον τῶν ἀνθρώπων). Ὅτι, causal (giving a reason why their "self-justification" is rejected, Marshall 626). The subst. nom. sg. neut. adj. τὸ . . . ὑψηλόν (of ὑψηλός, -ή, -όν, "high"; "highly admired" HCSB; "exalted" ESV) is the subj. of an implied ἐστίν (for sim. refs. to human pride cf. also 13:30; 14:11; 18:13–14). Ἐν ἀνθρώποις parallels ἐνώπιον with the mng. "in the opinion of" (see below). Βδέλυγμα, (pred.) nom. sg. neut. of βδέλυγμα, -ατος, τό, "abomination" (NKJV, NRSV, ESV), "detestable" (NASB, NIV), "revolting" (HCSB; "something disgusting that arouses wrath" BDAG 172a). The second use of ἐνώπιον (τοῦ θεοῦ) has the mng. "in the opinion/ judgment of" (BDAG 342d; mng. 3; LN 90.20). The description here of one "exalted" or "admired by people" (HCSB) yet under the judgment of God anticipates the rich man in 16:19–26.

16:16 The nom. ὁ νόμος καὶ οἱ προφῆται is the subj. of a verbless clause. The phrase is a way of summarizing the whole of the OT (cf. 9:30; 16:29, 31; therefore οἱ προφῆται refers to books, Marshall 628). The omitted vb. could be εὐαγγελίζω, from the parallel in the second half of the verse ("proclaimed" NASB, NIV), or a form of ἐστίν ("were" NKJV, HCSB, ESV) which may have the mng. "were in effect" (NRSV), "were in force" (NET). The prep. μέχρι followed by the gen. is a "marker of continuance in time up to a point" (BDAG 644b–c; ZG 247). Ἀπὸ τότε ("from then on") is temp. It is debated as to whether μέχρι Ἰωάννου and ἀπὸ τότε place John in the era of ὁ νόμος καὶ οἱ προφῆται. Although Acts 1:22 and the use of εὐαγγελίζω in Luke 3:18 indicate that John may be placed in the new era (Marshall 628–29; Nolland 822), descriptions of

John in 3:1–6 and 7:28 seem to view him as the greatest and last of the prophets of the old era (cf. Bock 1351). He is the greatest, however, because he introduces Jesus (Luke 1–2). Εὐαγγελίζεται 3rd sg. pres. pass. indic. of εὐαγγελίζω (the subj. is ἡ βασιλεία τοῦ θεοῦ, see 4:43). Βιάζεται (3rd sg. pres. mid. or pass. indic. of dep. βιάζομαι, "force") has been understood in the following four ways (Bock 1352–53):

1. mid. negatively ("using violence against it" BHGNT 525, 527; εἰς is used with ref. to opposition);
2. mid. positively ("tries to enter it by force" NRSV; "forcing their way into it" NIV; sim. NKJV, NASB, ESV; BDAG 175d; i.e., requires decisive action, cf. 13:24; Bovon 2.466; Marshall 630; Nolland 821);
3. pass. negatively ("is forced into it"; the least likely lexically and contextually); or
*4. pass. positively ("is strongly urged" HCSB, sim. NET; BDAG 176a; MM 109d; cf. 14:23; Bock 1353; Fitzmyer 1117).

The last mng. is found in the mid. in LXX Gen 33:11; Judg 19:7; 2 Sam 13:25, 27. The sim. παραβιάζομαι is also used with this mng. in Luke 24:29; Acts 16:15 (the only uses of this vb. in the NT).

16:17 The temporal nature of "the law and the prophets" until John and the proclamation of the kingdom in Jesus' ministry (16:16) is now balanced with a reaffirmation of the eternal authority of the law as that which points to Jesus (Marshall 630; see the views summarized in Bock 1355–56). The comp. adj. εὐκοπώτερον (see 5:23) is pred. (followed by the comp. conj. ἤ). The 2nd aor. act. inf. παρελθεῖν (of παρέρχομαι) and the acc. subj. of the inf. τὸν οὐρανὸν καὶ τὴν γῆν (a ref. to the created order; cf. 21:33; Isa 51:6; note also the temporal nature of money in 16:9) is the subj. of ἐστίν (Burton §384). Κεραίαν acc. sg. fem. of κεραία, -ας, ἡ, "stroke" (projection or hook as part of a letter, BDAG 540b; LN 33.37; modified by the adj. μίαν "one"). The acc. μίαν κεραίαν is the subj. of the 2nd aor. act. inf. πεσεῖν (of πίπτω, "drop out" HCSB, NIV; "fail" NKJV, NASB; BDAG 815d).

16:18 The nom. sg. masc. of pres. act. ptcs. ἀπολύων (of ἀπολύω, "release," "divorce" most EVV; BDAG 118a; LN 34.78) and γαμῶν (of γαμέω) are attrib. (modifying πᾶς; on the cstr. art.-ptc.-καί-ptc. see Wallace 275; Nolland [822] understands ἀπολύων . . . καί as "divorces . . . in order to"). The pres. is gnomic (Burton §124; Wallace 523). Μοιχεύει 3rd sg. pres. act. indic. of μοιχεύω ("commit adultery"; cf. Lev 20:10). The subst. nom. ptc. ὁ . . . γαμῶν is the subj. of the second μοιχεύει. Ἀπολελυμένην (acc. sg. fem. of pf. pass. [subst.] ptc. of ἀπολύω, "a woman divorced") is the obj. of ὁ . . . γαμῶν. This saying on divorce may be given as an example of the continuing validity of the law as taken up and elaborated upon authoritatively by Jesus in the new era of the kingdom (Marshall 631). The permanency of marriage between a man and woman is assumed in both cases (cf. Matt 5:32; 19:9, Bock 1357–58).

HOMILETICAL SUGGESTIONS

Jesus' Teaching on God's Knowledge and God's Word (16:14–18)

1. External appearances may impress people, but God knows and judges the heart (16:14–15).
2. God reveals his standard in his word, as interpreted and proclaimed by Jesus (16:16–18).

c. Lazarus and the Rich Man: A Warning About Using Money in this Age Without Regard for the Age to Come (16:19–31)

This pericope illustrates Jesus' warnings about loving money rather than God, his teaching on God's knowledge of the heart, and God's judgment of that which is outwardly impressive (16:13–15). The pericope also illustrates Jesus' teaching on the sufficiency of the law and the prophets to warn of judgment to come even as he authoritatively portrays the permanence and pain of that judgment (16:16–18).

16:19 Ἄνθρωπος . . . τις see 10:30 (though cf. also 14:2). Ἄνθρωπος . . . τις ἦν πλούσιος repeats the introduction to 16:1. For πλούσιος see 6:24; 12:16 ($\mathfrak{P}^{75}$ adds the name Νευης, but this is too poorly attested to be original; Fitzmyer 1130). Ἐνεδιδύσκετο 3rd sg. impf. mid. indic. of ἐνδιδύσκω, "dress" (the impf. may be used to provide background information [BHGNT 530], or is a "customary" impf. [NASB, HCSB]; Robertson, *Pictures* 220; Marshall 635). Πορφύραν καὶ βύσσον acc. sg. fem. of πορφύρα, -ας, ἡ; of βύσσος, -ου, ἡ; "purple [cloth] and fine linen." Πορφύρα may refer to outer garments and βύσσος to undergarments (Bock 1365; Fitzmyer 1130–31). Εὐφραινόμενος (nom. sg. masc. of pres. pass. ptc. of εὐφραίνω) is modified by the adv. λαμπρῶς ("luxuriously," "living in ostentatious luxury" LN 88.255; only here in the NT) and together may refer to "feasting lavishly" (HCSB, sim. NRSV, ESV; MM 267a; Bock 1365; Fitzmyer 1131; Marshall 635) or more generally to living "in luxury" (NIV, sim. NASB). Εὐφραίνω is used in 15:23–24, 29, 32 for a special celebration. Here, however, the celebration is "every day" (καθ᾽ ἡμέραν).

16:20 The adj. πτωχός (modified by the appos. Λάζαρος and the dat. of ref. ὀνόματι; Z §53) functions as a subst. and with τις is the subj. of ἐβέβλητο (3rd sg. pluperfect pass. indic. of βάλλω). Πρὸς τὸν πυλῶνα "at the gate" (locat.), acc. sg. masc. of πυλών, -ῶνος, ὁ (πυλών often refers to the gateways of cities, temples, and palaces, BDAG 897c–d). In the context of 16:19, πυλῶν ("gate") may indicate a mansion or luxurious residence. This is the only time a person is named in a parable of Jesus. The mng. of Λάζαρος, "God helps," may be significant. It was, however, a common Heb. name (from Eleazer; Fitzmyer 1131). In this literary context the use of his name by the rich man in 16:24 shows that he knew who Lazarus was (Bock 1366; Fitzmyer 1133; Nolland 828). The pass. may suggest that Lazarus was placed at the gate (NASB, HCSB, ESV, NIV; perhaps indicating that he was crippled, Bock 1366; Nolland 828), or it may refer more generally to his state ("at his gate lay a poor man" NRSV; BDAG 163c; the pass. being intrans., "lie ill," BDF §347[1]; ZG 247; Marshall 635). Εἱλκωμένος nom. sg. masc. of pf. pass. (attrib.) ptc. (of dep. ἑλκόομαι, "cause sores/ulcers," pf. pass. "covered with sores"; BDAG 318a; on the form see BDF §68; R 364; in contrast to the "clothing" of the rich man).

16:21 Ἐπιθυμῶν nom. sg. masc. of pres. act. (attrib.) ptc. of ἐπιθυμέω, "desire" (the pres. may express an unfulfilled wish, Marshall 635; cf. 15:16). The inf. χορτασθῆναι (see 15:16) is complementary. Πιπτόντων gen. pl. neut. of pres. act. (subst.) ptc. of πίπτω (gen. following ἀπό). In contrast (ἀλλά) to this possibility of even a little nourishment of bits (neut. pl.) from the table (τραπέζης gen. sg. fem. of τράπεζα, -ης, ἡ), "even" (καί; "not only so but" ZG 248; cf. R 1186) unclean dogs (κύνες nom. pl. masc. of κύων, κυνός, ὁ, BDAG 579d; either wild street dogs or perhaps watch dogs owned by the rich man, LN 4.34; Nolland 828–29) came (ἐρχόμενοι, see 13:14) and licked (ἐπέλειχον 3rd pl. impf. act. indic. of ἐπιλείχω; only here in the NT) his sores (τὰ ἕλκη acc. pl. neut. of ἕλκος, -ους, τό; cf. ἑλκόομαι in 16:20). Outwardly, it appears that the rich man is blessed and Lazarus abandoned.

16:22 With ἐγένετο δέ (see 1:5; here signaling a development in this account), the 2nd aor. act. inf. ἀποθανεῖν (of ἀποθνῄσκω; the subj. is the acc. τὸν πτωχόν) and the aor. pass. inf. ἀπενεχθῆναι (of ἀποφέρω, "carry off"; the acc. αὐτόν is the subj.; ὑπὸ τῶν ἀγγέλων indicates ultimate agency) provide background information for the following events (cf. ZG 248). The scene shifts from the contrasting earthly circumstances during life, to contrasting circumstances after life on earth. Εἰς τὸν κόλπον Ἀβραάμ, locat. (idiomatic for "to Abraham's side" HCSB, ESV, NIV; see 6:38). Being with Abraham indicates he is welcomed into heaven (cf. 13:28; 23:43; Abraham's wealth would also be assumed knowledge). The phrase is sim. to OT refs. to going to the "fathers" (Gen 15:15; 47:30; Deut 31:16; Bock 1368; Fitzmyer 1132). The rich man "also" (δὲ καί; see 2:4) died (ἀπέθανεν; see 8:52) and was buried (ἐτάφη 3rd sg. 2nd aor. pass. indic. of θάπτω). The ref. to the rich man's burial may add to the contrast in how the two men were treated by others on earth.

16:23 The locat. ἐν τῷ ᾅδῃ ("in Hades" most EVV; "in hell" KJV, NET; see 10:15) is contrasted with where Abraham and Lazarus are. Ἐπάρας, see 6:20 (is temp.). Ὑπάρχων (see 9:48; temp. or manner, BHGNT 532 ; the act. voice is stative, Wallace 413) with ἐν βασάνοις ("in torment"; dat. pl. fem. of βάσανος, -ου, ἡ; ἐν is a marker of state or condition, BDAG 327b; cf. R 586) indicates that in this context ᾅδης is a place of punishment (as 10:15 [in other contexts it may ref. more generally to the place of the dead, Acts 2:27, 31]). Βάσανος, "severe pain occasioned by punitive torture" BDAG 168c ("being tormented" NRSV; cf. LN 24.90; MM 104c; ZG 248). Ὁρᾷ 3rd sg. pres. act. indic. of ὁράω (a historical pres. giving emphasis to what follows, Bock 1369; cf. 13:28). Ἀπὸ μακρόθεν emphasizes the separation between the rich man and Abraham and Lazarus ("a long way off" HCSB). Ἐν τοῖς κόλποις αὐτοῦ, locat. (see 6:38; 16:22; for the pl. see BDF §141[5]; R 408; T 27).

16:24 Καὶ αὐτός, see 1:17. Φωνήσας (see 16:2) is an attendant circumstance ptc. with εἶπεν (Z §262). Πάτερ is voc. and Ἀβραάμ is voc. in appos. (cf. 3:8). The rich man addresses Abraham with two 2nd sg. aor. act. impvs: ἐλέησον (of ἐλεέω, "have mercy" [cf. 17:13; 18:38–39]; the obj. is the enclitic με) and πέμψον (of πέμπω, "send"; the obj. is Λάζαρον. Ἵνα followed by the two subjuncs. expresses the purpose of these commands. Βάψῃ 3rd sg. aor. act. subjunc. of βάπτω, "dip" (the acc. sg. neut. τὸ ἄκρον [of ἄκρον, -ου, τό, "the tip"] is the obj.; the gen. τοῦ δακτύλου ["finger"; see 11:20] is partitive, Wallace 86). The gen. ὕδατος could be a gen. of place (R 495; Wallace 124; Marshall 637), content (BDF §172), or separation (BHGNT 533; partitive, "some water" ZG 248). Καταψύξῃ 3rd sg. aor. act. subjunc. of καταψύχω, "refresh," "cool" (all EVV; the acc. τὴν γλῶσσάν is the obj.). Τὴν γλῶσσάν μου is hyperbole to stress how severe the torment is (Fitzmyer 1133). Ὅτι, causal (giving the reason for these commands). Ὀδυνῶμαι 1st sg. pres. pass. indic. of dep. ὀδυνάομαι, "suffer torment" (BDAG 692b; "in agony" most EVV; "in anguish" ESV; see refs. at 2:48). Ἐν τῇ φλογὶ ταύτῃ (dat. sg. fem. of φλόξ, φλογός, ἡ, "in this flame" HCSB, ESV) is locat. The request to send Lazarus to bring relief to him shows that the rich man knew Lazarus when he was alive on earth (see 16:20) and that the change in circumstances after life brings no change in attitude.

16:25 Τέκνον, voc. Μνήσθητι 2nd sg. aor. pass. impv. of dep. μιμνῄσκομαι. Ὅτι introduces the discourse content ("that," following vbs. of mental or sense perception, BDAG 732a). Ἀπέλαβες 2nd sg. 2nd aor. act. indic. of ἀπολαμβάνω, "receive" (perhaps with ἀπό "in full," R 1379; Z §132). Ἐν τῇ ζωῇ σου is temp. ("in your lifetime" ESV, NIV). The acc. τὰ κακά is the obj. of an implied ἀπέλαβεν (BHGNT 534; the art. with τὰ ἀγαθά . . . τὰ κακά is subst., Wallace 233). Παρακαλεῖται 3rd sg. pres. pass. indic. of παρακαλέω, "comfort" (modified by the adv. ὧδε; a divine pass., Fitzmyer 1133). Ὀδυνᾶσαι 2nd sg. pres. pass. indic. of dep. ὀδυνάομαι (see 2:48; 16:24). The condemnation illustrates the outcome of 16:13–15.

16:26 Ἐν πᾶσι τούτοις is an idiom expressing addition ("besides all this" most EVV; BDAG 783c; "as if all this is not enough" ZG 248; Fitzmyer 1133). The locat. μεταξὺ ἡμῶν καὶ ὑμῶν ("between us and you") with the nom. χάσμα μέγα ("a great chasm") confirms the emphasis in 16:23 on the separation between the rich man and Abraham and Lazarus. Χάσμα (nom. sg. neut. of χάσμα, -ατος, τό, "chasm"; only here in the NT) refers to the "unbridgeable space between Abraham and the place of torture" (BDAG 1081c; cf. LN 1.54). The unchangeable nature of that separation is confirmed with the pf. ἐστήρικται (3rd sg. pf. pass. indic. στηρίζω, "establish," "fixed" most EVV; a divine pass., Bock 1373; Fitzmyer 1133–34). Ὅπως may introduce a purpose (ZG 248) or result clause (with the following two subjuncs., Marshall 638). Θέλοντες (see 8:20; subst.) is the subj. of δύνωνται (3rd pl. pres. mid. subjunc. of dep. δύναμαι; neg. with μή). The 2nd aor. act. inf. διαβῆναι (of διαβαίνω, "cross over"; modified by the adv. ἔνθεν, "from here") is complementary. Διαπερῶσιν 3rd pl. pres. act. subjunc. of διαπεράω, "cross over" (modified by the adv. ἐκεῖθεν, "from there").

16:27 In light of the preceding emphasis on the impossibility of any relief for the rich man, he therefore (οὖν) redirects his requests (still expecting Lazarus to be his messenger, Marshall 638). Ἐρωτῶ, see 14:18. Πάτερ, voc. (perhaps a play on "father" for Abraham here and in 16:24; Fitzmyer 1134). Ἵνα introduces indir. discourse (ἐρωτῶ . . . ἵνα "I ask . . . that"; used for the inf., Z §407). Πέμψῃς 2nd sg. aor. act. subjunc. of πέμπω.

16:28 Γάρ is a marker of clarification regarding the "father's house" and forms part of a parenthetical clause (Marshall 638; ἔχω, see 7:40). Ὅπως with the subjunc. διαμαρτύρηται (3rd sg. pres. mid. subjunc. of dep. διαμαρτύρομαι, "testify," NKJV; "warn" most EVV; "solemnly urge, exhort, warn" BDAG 233b) is a purpose clause which continues from the request in 16:27. Ἵνα also introduces a purpose clause (R 1046). Καί, "also." Ἔλθωσιν 3rd pl. 2nd aor. act. subjunc. of dep. ἔρχομαι (neg. with μή). The gen. βασάνου (see 16:23) is attrib. The rich man's request implies that he should have had such special warning too.

16:29 Ἔχουσι 3rd pl. pres. act. indic. of ἔχω. For Μωϋσῆς in Luke see 9:30 (here an alternative form of the acc., R 268; ZG 248). The ref. here is to the writings of Moses and the prophets as a summary for the entire OT. Ἀκουσάτωσαν 3rd pl. aor. act. impv. of ἀκούω (with the obj. gen. αὐτῶν, "they should listen to them" NRSV, HCSB; cf. Wallace 486; see 11:28; 16:17).

16:30 The neg. οὐχί is the rich man's emphatic reply to Abraham (for πάτερ Ἀβραάμ see 16:24) concerning the sufficiency of the OT to warn his family about the prospect of judgment after death. He moves from sending orders to arguing with Abraham and denying the sufficiency of Scripture. In contrast (ἀλλά) to Scripture ("Moses and the prophets"), the rich man suggests that something else, a visit from the afterlife, is required (cf. 11:16, 29–32). Ἐάν introduces the protasis of a third-class cond. (fut. referring, Z §320; a suggestion that is presented as possible, though not yet occurring, Bock 1376). Πορευθῇ 3rd sg. aor. pass. subjunc. of dep. πορεύομαι (the indef. pron. τις is the subj.; ἀπὸ νεκρῶν indicates source; the prep. phrase is def. without the art., R 791). Μετανοήσουσιν 3rd pl. fut. act. indic. of μετανοέω.

16:31 Εἰ introduces the protasis of a first-class cond. (Z §306; assumed as true in this context, i.e., "and they don't," Bock 1376; Marshall 639). For "Moses and the prophets" see 16:29. Ἀκούουσιν, see 7:22 (neg. with οὐκ). Ἐάν introduces a third-class cond. (R 1382; presented as a possibility, Marshall 639). Ἀναστῇ 3rd sg. 2nd aor. act. subjunc. of ἀνίστημι (intrans.; the subj. is the indef. pron. τις). A resurrection "from the dead" (ἐκ νεκρῶν indicates source) moves beyond the rich man's original request for a visit from the afterlife. Πεισθήσονται 3rd pl. fut. pass. indic. of πείθω. Interestingly, Jesus' resurrection appearances in Luke-Acts are to disciples, and the resurrection is not presented in isolation but as the fulfillment of Scripture and Jesus' word (24:6–8, 25–27, 44–46; cf. Bock 1377).

FOR FURTHER STUDY

34. Heaven and Hell (16:22–23)

Dixon, L. *The Other Side of the Good News: Contemporary Challenges to Jesus' Teaching on Hell*. Ross-Shire: Christian Focus, 2003.

Green. J. B. *DJG*[2] 370–75.

Lehtipuu, O. "The Rich, the Poor, and the Promise of an Eschatological Reward in the Gospel of Luke." Pages 229–46 in *Other Worlds and Their Relation to This World: Early Jewish and Ancient Christian Traditions*. Edited by T. Nicklas, J. Verheyden, E. M. M. Eynikel, and F. G. Martinez. Leiden: Brill, 2010.

Lunde, J. *DJG*[1] 307–11.

Olmstead, W. G. *DJG*[2] 458–62.

*Yarbrough, R. W. "Jesus on Hell." Pages 67–90 in *Hell Under Fire: Modern Scholarship Reinvents Eternal Punishment*. Edited by C. Morgan and R. Peterson. Grand Rapids: Zondervan, 2004.

HOMILETICAL SUGGESTIONS

Jesus' Teaching on the Other Side of the Good News (16:19–31)

1. Outward appearances in this life are temporary and may be deceiving (16:19–21).
2. The verdict in the next life is permanent and determined by God (16:22–26).
3. The condition of those encountering judgment in the next life is never-ending torment (16:22–28).
4. The character of those encountering judgment in the next life remains proud and unrepentant (16:22–28).
5. Scripture is sufficient to teach and warn about the nature of judgment in the next life (for loving money rather than responding to God in this life) (16:29–31).

2. Caring for and Forgiving Fellow Believers by Faith (17:1–6)

The sayings in 17:1–6 are perhaps grouped together by refs. to "into/in the sea" (17:2, 6; Nolland 835). Final judgment is still in view (17:1–2), though the focus now is on caring for fellow believers (i.e., not causing them to stumble, 17:1–2) and forgiving repentant believers (17:3–4). Despite the apparent difficulty in these requirements, it is the presence of even mustard-seed-sized faith (17:5–6) that is important, not the amount of faith.

17:1 The nom. sg. neut. adj. ἀνένδεκτον (of ἀνένδεκτος, -ον, "impossible") is pred. (only here in the NT). The art. inf. τοῦ . . . ἐλθεῖν is epex. (see 7:7; BHGNT 538–39; R 996; neg. with μή; on τοῦ . . . μή with vbs. of hindering/ceasing, see BDF §400[4]; on Luke's use of τοῦ see Burton §§404–5; R 1002; Z §386). The acc. pl. neut. τὰ σκάνδαλα (of σκάνδαλον, -ου, τό, "stumbling block"; as an enticement to apostasy, or more broadly, a temptation to sin, BDAG 926b; Fitzmyer 1138; Marshall 640; cf. 17:2) is the subj. of the inf. The double neg. has the mng. "stumbling blocks are sure to come" (NET; cf. R 1171). Despite (πλήν, adversative) the inevitability (NASB) of occasions for stumbling (NRSV), those "through whom" (διά with the gen. rel. pron. expresses intermediate agency) they come (ἔρχεται, see 3:16; the neut. pl. takes a sg. vb. here) are held accountable (for οὐαί see 6:24; αὐτῷ is implied, ZG 249).

17:2 Εἰ introduces a first-class cond. clause (BHGNT 540; T 92; Z §311; ZG 249; though BDF §§360[4]; 372[3]; Marshall 641 see this as an "unreal" cond.). The protasis εἰ . . . θάλασσαν in the structure of the sentence is the subj. of λυσιτελεῖ (3rd sg. pres. act. indic. of λυσιτελέω, "it is better"; impers.; [only here in the NT]; implying a comp. with ἤ, BDF §245[3]; Robertson, *Pictures* 226; Z §145; ZG 249). The nom. sg. masc. λίθος ("stone") modified by μυλικός (of μυλικός, -ή, -όν, "belonging to a mill"; "millstone"; referring to the heavy upper stone for grinding grain, LN 7.70) is the subj. of περίκειται (3rd sg. pres. pass. indic. of dep. περίκειμαι, "place around," "hung around" most EVV; τράχηλον, "neck"; see 15:20). Ἔρριπται 3rd sg. pf. pass. indic. of ῥίπτω, "throw." The point is to highlight the severity of the judgment. It would be better to die by such violent means before acting as a stumbling block (Marshall 641). Ἤ introduces the second part of the comparison. Ἵνα introduces the content (lit. "it is better if . . . than that . . ."; Burton §214; R 992; in place of an inf., Z §§406–7) and functions sim. to εἰ in the first part (BHGNT 540; R 997). Σκανδαλίσῃ 3rd sg. aor. act. subjunc. of σκανδαλίζω, "cause to stumble" (NRSV, HCSB, NIV [cf. 7:23; the cognate σκάνδαλα, 17:1]; "cause to sin" RSV, ESV). Τῶν μικρῶν τούτων (partitive gen.) highlights the vulnerability of Jesus' disciples (cf. 10:21; 12:32). The demonstrative pron. τούτων may even refer to people present (Marshall 641).

17:3 Προσέχετε ἑαυτοῖς see 12:1. This exhortation could go with 17:3b–4 (KJV, RSV). Its function as a warning may fit better with 17:1–2 (NA²⁸; NIV; Bock 1386; Bovon 2.495; cf. Fitzmyer 1139). It is possibly transitional and combines 17:1–2 and 3–4 (Marshall 642; Nolland 837). Ἐάν introduces a third-class cond. (in this context as a hypothetical situation, Wallace 696). Ἁμάρτῃ 3rd sg. 2nd aor. act. subjunc. of ἁμαρτάνω. The nom. ἀδελφός emphasizes the familial relationship among fellow disciples of Jesus. Ἐπιτίμησον 2nd sg. aor. act. impv. of ἐπιτιμάω ("rebuke"; "warn in order to prevent an action or bring one to an end" BDAG 384d; "express strong disapproval" LN 33.419; the dat. αὐτῷ is complementary). Ἐάν introduces another third-class cond. Μετανοήσῃ 3rd sg. aor. act. subjunc. of μετανοέω (see 10:13; cf. μετάνοια in 3:3). Ἄφες, see 6:42 (here the impv. is "forgive"; αὐτῷ is a dat. of advantage).

17:4 Ἐάν introduces a third-class cond. The adv. ἑπτάκις ("seven times"; τῆς ἡμέρας is a gen. of time; the art. is distributive, "in the day" ESV; R 769; ZG 249) modifies ἁμαρτήσῃ (3rd sg. aor. act. subjunc. of ἁμαρτάνω; on the form see Z §491). Εἰς σέ specifies that the sin is directed "against" the disciple (implied in 17:3 and added there for clarity in some later mss.). Ἐπιστρέψῃ 3rd sg. aor. act. subjunc. of ἐπιστρέφω ("return"; modified by ἑπτάκις). Λέγων (see 1:63) does not imply that the repentance is merely outward (Marshall 643). Μετανοῶ 1st sg. pres. act. indic. of μετανοέω (cf. 17:3). Ἀφήσεις 2nd sg. fut. act. indic. of ἀφίημι (the fut. is impv. and seems to be parallel with ἄφες [17:3], Wallace 570; Z §280; Fitzmyer 1141; Marshall 643; αὐτῷ is a dat. of advantage).

17:5 Πρόσθες 2nd sg. 2nd aor. act. impv. of προστίθημι, "add to," "increase" (an impv. to express a request, R 948; Wallace 488; ἡμῖν is a dat. of advantage). Πρόσθες has the mng. "add to" their faith (BDAG 885c, mng. 1a; Bock 1389; Bovon 2.496; Fitzmyer 1143; Marshall 644; Nolland 838) rather than "grant" a gift of faith (BDAG 885d, mng. 2). The use of κύριος reflects the understanding of the apostles that Jesus has the authority and ability to provide faith. The use of οἱ ἀπόστολοι may highlight that all of Jesus' disciples, even the apostles, depend on him for help to respond in this way.

17:6 Εἰ with ἔχετε (2nd pl. pres. act. indic. of ἔχω) is a first-class cond. protasis (assumed as true for the sake of argument, BDF §372[1a]; T 92; i.e., the issue is not the quantity but the presence of faith, Bock 1390). The apodosis with ἄν is a second-class cond. (contrary to fact; i.e., not true for the sake of the argument, Wallace 694; without denying that the apostles had faith, Nolland 838–39; i.e., a "mixed cond." R 921, 1015, 1022; T 92; Z §§310, 329; ZG 249). Κόκκον σινάπεως (here κόκκον is acc.; σινάπεως is an attrib. gen.), see 13:19. Ἐλέγετε 2nd pl. impf. act. indic. of λέγω (here, "you can say" HCSB, NIV; "you could say" NRSV, ESV; Z §310). Τῇ συκαμίνῳ dat. sg. fem. of συκάμινος, -ου, ἡ, "mulberry tree" (which grew to about twenty feet; distinguished from συκομορέα ["sycamore tree"] in 19:4; cf. BDAG 955a; MM 595d–96a; LN 3.6; dat. of indir. obj). The demonstrative pron. ταύτῃ is omitted in early and diverse mss. (though if present it may ref. to a specific tree in their presence, Marshall 644; if absent, the art. is "deictic" anyway, Wallace 221). Ἐκριζώθητι 2nd sg. aor. pass. impv. of ἐκριζόω, "uproot." Φυτεύθητι 2nd sg. aor. pass. impv. of φυτεύω, "plant" (perhaps divine passives; ἐν may be used for εἰς, here after a vb. of motion, Z §99). Ὑπήκουσεν 3rd sg. aor. act. indic. of ὑπακούω, "obey" (the apodosis of a second-class cond. with ἄν). The saying is obviously a rhetorical ref. to seemingly impossible things that could be done if one trusts in God. In this context the "spectacular" activity carried out by faith is that of forgiving a repentant believer.

HOMILETICAL SUGGESTIONS

See also at the end of 17:19.

How Do We Care for Fellow Believers? (17:1–6)

1. We watch ourselves that we don't cause them to sin (17:1–3a).
2. We warn them when they sin (17:3).
3. We forgive them when they sin against us and repent (17:3–4).
4. We rely in faith on the Lord's help to do this (17:5–6).

3. Serving by Grace Does Not Obligate the Master to Reward the Slave (17:7–10)

There is no explicit connection in 17:7, though it is possible that the demands of 17:1–6 are now viewed as an expected part of serving God. Obeying them does not form the basis of a "claim upon God" (Nolland 841).

17:7 Τίς . . . ἐξ ὑμῶν (see 11:5) is completed with two rhetorical questions in 17:8–9 (though 17:7 functions as the first of three rhetorical questions, most EVV; the assumed answer to this first question would be "no" or "no one," Marshall 646–47; Nolland 841). Ἔχων (see 3:11) could be attrib. (cf. 14:28), cond. (Bock 1392), or a subst. pred. of a verbless clause (BHGNT 543; with ἐστίν to be supplied, Marshall 646; Nolland 841). The acc. sg. masc. of pres. act. ptcs. ἀροτριῶντα (of ἀροτριάω, "plow") and ποιμαίνοντα (of ποιμαίνω, "shepherd") are attrib. and modify δοῦλον. The rel. pron. ὅς (the antecedent is τίς) is the subj. of ἐρεῖ (see 12:10; αὐτῷ is a dat. of indir. obj.). Εἰσελθόντι dat. sg. masc. of 2nd aor. act. (attrib) ptc. of dep. εἰσέρχομαι (modifying αὐτῷ, ZG 250). Ἐκ τοῦ ἀγροῦ indicates source. Παρελθών (see 12:37; modified by the adv. εὐθέως) is an attendant circumstance ptc. and takes on the mood of the impv. ἀνάπεσε (see 14:10; Wallace 644; ZG 250).

17:8 Ἀλλά continues the ὅς clause and introduces a contrast to the preceding (with οὐχί [see 4:22] "and not rather" BDF §448[4]). Ἐρεῖ, see 12:10 (cf. 17:7). Ἑτοίμασον 2nd sg. aor. act. impv. of ἑτοιμάζω. The interr. τί with δειπνήσω (1st sg. aor. act. subjunc. or fut. act. indic. of δειπνέω, "eat") forms the dir. obj. of ἑτοίμασον (τί may be used for the rel. ὅ, BDF §298[4]; Z §221). Περιζωσάμενος (nom. sg. masc. of aor. mid. ptc. of περιζώννυμι, "get ready" HCSB; see περιζώννυμι in 12:35) could be temp. or attendant circumstance with διακόνει (2nd sg. pres. act. impv. of διακονέω; the pres. may highlight ongoing service, Moule 20, 135; Marshall 647). Ἕως is temp. and expresses contemporaneous time here ("while"; BDAG 423c; R 976; ZG 250). Φάγω (of ἐσθίω) and πίω (of πίνω) both 1st sg. 2nd aor. act. subjunc. (with ἕως). Μετὰ ταῦτα is temp. Φάγεσαι (of ἐσθίω; on the form, see BDF §87; Z §488) and πίεσαι (of πίνω) both 2nd sg. fut. mid. indic. (the subj. is σύ).

17:9 The rhetorical question introduced by μή expects the answer "no" (expressed with "I think not" NKJV; "He does not . . . does he?" NASB; sim. NET; cf. BDF §427[2]). The expression ἔχει [see 5:24] χάριν followed by the dat. of advantage τῷ δούλῳ is "be grateful" (NJB; ZG 250; "thank the slave" NET, sim. most EVV). Ὅτι, causal (giving the reason for the supposed expression of thanks). Ἐποίησεν, see 1:49. Διαταχθέντα acc. pl. neut. of aor. pass. (subst.) ptc. of διατάσσω, "command," NASB). The point assumes a context of ancient slavery; the slave's obedience to the master's commands does not put the master under obligation to the slave (Marshall 647).

17:10 Οὕτως introduces Jesus' application of the parable (cf. 12:21; 14:33; 15:7, 10; 21:31). Ὑμεῖς is the subj. of λέγετε (see 10:5; impv.). Καί, "also." Ὅταν with the subjunc. ποιήσητε (2nd pl. aor. act. subjunc. of ποιέω) is temp. The adj. πάντα alludes to the comprehensiveness of 17:7–8 (Nolland 842). Διαταχθέντα, see 17:9 (perhaps a divine pass., Fitzmyer 1146). Ὅτι, recitative. Δοῦλοι (and adj. ἀχρεῖοι) is the pred. of ἐσμέν (δοῦλοι ἀχρεῖοι [nom. pl. masc. of ἀχρεῖος, -ον], "unprofitable servants" NKJV;

"slaves undeserving of special praise" NET; LN 33.361; ZG 250; "unworthy" NASB, ESV, NIV; Bock 1394; Marshall 647; BDAG 160b suggests there is a play on the cognate noun χρεῖος ["debt"] with the mng. obligation-free, or "owed nothing" Nolland 842). The rel. clause ὃ ὠφείλομεν ποιῆσαι is the obj. of πεποιήκαμεν (1st pl. pf. act. indic. of ποιέω). Ὠφείλομεν 1st pl. impf. act. indic. of ὀφείλω (with an inf. "ought," ZG 250; highlights the obligation to serve God, Marshall 648). The inf. ποιῆσαι (see 1:72) is complementary.

HOMILETICAL SUGGESTIONS

See the end of 17:19.

4. Saving Faith Is Expressed in Thankfulness to Jesus (17:11–19)

The topic of faith continues from the emphasis in 17:5–6. The nature of genuine faith is now identified in the unlikely person of the thankful Samaritan (17:19).

17:11 Καὶ ἐγένετο, see 1:5. The inf. πορεύεσθαι (see 4:42) with ἐν τῷ is temp. expressing contemporaneous time ("while traveling" HCSB; Wallace 595). This is the third travel note that specifically mentions Jerusalem (cf. 9:51–56; 13:22, 33; the last ref. to travel was 14:25). The next and final ref. to travel to Jerusalem will be 18:31–34). Apart from 9:51 there is no obvious reason to view these travel notes as structure markers (Nolland 845). Καὶ αὐτός see 1:17 (cf. also 3:23; paratactic here with καὶ ἐγένετο, Fitzmyer 1152). Διήρχετο, see 5:15. Διά followed by the acc. μέσον with διήρχετο is "through the midst of" (NKJV; BDF §222 suggests "through" and a corrupt text [cf. BDAG 635a]; though cf. R 581). This unusual combination of διὰ μέσον probably gave rise to the gen. var. rdg. μέσου. The following ref. to both Σαμαρείας καὶ Γαλιλαίας, however, may indicate the mng. "passing along between" (RSV, ESV, sim. most EVV; i.e., "along the border between" NIV, sim. NJB, NLT; BDAG 635a; Bock 1401; Marshall 650; Nolland 845). The ref. to "Samaria and Galilee" helps to explain the combination of Samaritan and Jewish responses in this episode (Nolland 846).

17:12 Εἰσερχομένου gen. sg. masc. of pres. mid. ptc. of dep. εἰσέρχομαι (temp. gen. abs. cstr.; αὐτοῦ is the subj. cf. Z §49). Εἴς τινα κώμην is locat. Ἀπήντησαν 3rd pl. aor. act. indic. of ἀπαντάω, "meet" (the subj. is δέκα λεπροὶ ἄνδρες "ten leprous men" NASB; for "leprosy" see 4:27; 5:12). Ἔστησαν, see 7:14 (the subj. is the rel. pron. οἵ). Πόρρωθεν, adv. "at a distance" (only here and Heb 11:13 in the NT).

17:13 Ἦραν 3rd pl. aor. act. indic. of αἴρω (the nom. αὐτοί is the subj.). Λέγοντες, see 1:66. Ἰησοῦ, voc. Ἐπιστάτα, see 5:5 (voc. in appos., Wallace 71; though elsewhere in Luke it is used by disciples). Ἐλέησον, see 16:24 (the obj. is ἡμᾶς).

17:14 Ἰδών, see 1:12 (is temp.). Πορευθέντες (see 7:22) is an attendant circumstance ptc. and takes on the mood of the impv. ἐπιδείξατε (2nd pl. aor. act. impv. of ἐπιδείκνυμι, "show"; Wallace 644; for the compound form see Z §484; for the form of the refl. pron. see Z §209). For a sim. command to demonstrate cleansing from leprosy to the priests, see 5:14 (where "priest" is sg.; see 1:5). Ἐγένετο, see 1:5. The inf. ὑπάγειν (see 8:42; the acc. αὐτούς is the subj.) with ἐν τῷ is temp. and expresses contemporaneous time ("while they were going" HCSB; cf. 17:11; Nolland [846] suggests healing took place "as [they] set off"). Ἐκαθαρίσθησαν 3rd pl. aor. pass. indic. of καθαρίζω. Thus, Jesus heals from a distance (as in 7:1–10).

17:15 The nom. εἷς (ἐξ αὐτῶν is partitive, see Z §80) is the subj. of ὑπέστρεψεν (see 1:56). Ἰδών (see 1:12) could be causal (Nolland 846), but is probably temp. here (most EVV; Bovon 2.505; Fitzmyer 1155). Ὅτι is a marker of content (following vbs. denoting mental or sense perception, BDAG 731d–732a; Wallace 458). Ἰάθη, see 8:47 (in place of ἐκαθαρίσθησαν in 17:14). Δοξάζων (see 5:25) with μετὰ φωνῆς μεγάλης expresses manner. On δοξάζω in Luke, see 2:20. Interestingly, the man "returned" (see

1:56) to Jesus, giving glory to God. Why not give glory to God along the way to the priests or temple (Nolland 847)?

17:16 Ἔπεσεν, see 8:5. For a sim. ref. to ἔπεσεν ἐπὶ πρόσωπον, see 5:12. Παρὰ τοὺς πόδας αὐτοῦ see refs. at 8:35. Εὐχαριστῶν (nom. sg. masc. of pres. act. ptc. of εὐχαριστέω) expresses manner. As is common in Luke, praising God is paralleled with praising Jesus (see refs. at 9:43; this is the only ref. to giving thanks to Jesus in the NT; elsewhere thanks is addressed to God, Fitzmyer 1155). Καὶ αὐτός may be emphatic as this detail is dramatically held back until this point (see 3:23; cf. 1:17; Robertson, *Pictures* 228; Bock 1403; Marshall 651; Plummer 404). Σαμαρίτης is pred. (Samaritans are mentioned in 9:52; 10:33; 17:16; Samaria is mentioned in 17:11).

17:17 Ἀποκριθείς, see 1:19. Jesus' response in 17:17–18 consists of three rhetorical questions. For οὐχί see 4:22 (R 917). Ἐκαθαρίσθησαν, see 17:14. The nom. οἱ . . . ἐννέα ("the nine") is the subj. of an implied equative vb. (cf. ZG 251). The interr. ποῦ, placed at the end in the second rhetorical question, is emphatic (Bock 1404; Fitzmyer 1155; Plummer 404; ἐννέα, "nine"; indecl.).

17:18 The final rhetorical question introduced with οὐχ expects the answer "yes" (most EVV; though NJB; Nolland 844, 847, tr. this verse as a statement). Εὑρέθησαν 3rd pl. aor. pass. indic. of εὑρίσκω (with the mng. "found, appear, prove, be shown [to be]" BDAG 412b). The nom. ptc. ὑποστρέψαντες (see 7:10) is the complement in a double nom. cstr. (with the subj. identified in the vb., BHGNT 549). The inf. δοῦναι (see 1:73) expresses purpose. On δοξάζω in Luke, see 2:20 (see 2:14 for δόξα). For εἰ μή see 4:26. Ἀλλογενής nom. sg. masc. of ἀλλογενής, -ές, "foreigner" (only here in the NT, though common in the LXX [cf. Isa 56:3, 6]; and notably on the inscription of the temple barrier, BDAG 46c; MM 23a; Marshall 652). The ref. to the Samaritan as ἀλλογενής implies the other nine were Jews. The nom. ὁ ἀλλογενὴς οὗτος is the subj. of an implied repetition of the first half of the verse (in the sg.).

17:19 Ἀναστάς (see 4:38) is an attendant circumstance ptc. (with πορεύου see 5:24) and takes on the mood of the impv. (Wallace 644). For ἡ πίστις σου σέσωκέν σε see 7:50 (cf. 8:48; "saved you" NJB; "made you well" most EVV). The distinction between the Samaritan, who gave glory to God, and the other nine indicates that "saved" here is more than "cleansed" from leprosy (17:14, 17) or "healed" (17:15; Bock 1405; *pace* Plummer 405). It also seems likely, therefore, that the other nine did not have the faith that saves as the Samaritan did (*pace* Marshall 652). As with 7:50, the phrase relates to faith in Jesus as the means by which one's relationship with God is restored.

HOMILETICAL SUGGESTIONS

The Outworking of Faith (17:1–19)

1. Watches out for other believers with concern (17:1–6)
2. Obeys God with gratitude (17:7–10)
3. Glorifies God with thankfulness (17:11–19)

5. The Kingdom Has Arrived in Jesus and Will Come in Fullness with His Return (17:20–37)

a. Exhortation to Pharisees: Recognize the Presence of the Kingdom in Jesus (17:20–21)

17:20 Ἐπερωτηθείς nom. sg. masc. of aor. pass. (temp.) ptc. of ἐπερωτάω. The connection with the preceding pericope is general (hence, "once" is added by NRSV, NIV, sim. NET). There may be a link with the Pharisees not seeing the presence of the kingdom in Jesus as sim. to the nine in 17:11–19 (sim. to 13:10–17 and 18–21; Marshall 652). For "Pharisees" see 5:17 (last mentioned in 16:14). Πότε, adv., "when?" (as an indir. interr., ZG 251). For ἡ βασιλεία τοῦ θεοῦ (the subj. of ἔρχεται [see 3:16]) see 4:43. The pres. ἔρχεται (see 3:16) in the question and in Jesus' answer (the second ἔρχεται is neg. with οὐκ) perhaps highlights the process of the kingdom's arrival (Bock 1412; "would come . . . is not coming" ESV; on a fut. use of ἔρχεται see BDF §323[1]; Moule 7; Marshall 654). Ἀπεκρίθη, see 4:4. Μετὰ παρατηρήσεως expresses manner. Παρατηρήσεως gen. sg. fem. of παρατήρησις, -εως, ἡ, "observation" (NKJV; MM 490b), "something observable" (HCSB, sim. NIV); "in such a way that its rise can be observed" (BDAG 772a; LSJ 1327c); "in such a way that it can be closely watched" (LN 24.48; the noun occurs only here in the NT; παρατηρέω occurs four times in Luke-Acts out of six in the NT [see 6:7]). This may refer to signs that were expected to accompany the arrival of the kingdom (cf. RSV, NASB; Ernst H. Riesenfeld *TDNT* 8.150; Bock 1413–14; Fitzmyer 1160; Marshall 654; Nolland [852] broadens the ref. to prognostication in general).

17:21 Ἐροῦσιν 3rd pl. fut. act. indic. of λέγω (neg. with οὐδέ; the pl. is indef., "no one will say" HCSB; Fitzmyer 1160). Ἰδού, see 1:20. The advs. ὧδε and ἐκεῖ, separated by the conj. ἤ ("or"), stand alone (BHGNT 551–52). Γάρ, causal (giving the reason the previous declarations will not be made). For ἡ βασιλεία τοῦ θεοῦ see 4:43. Ἐντὸς ὑμῶν ἐστιν contrasts with μετὰ παρατηρήσεως (17:20). Ἐντός (an adv. functioning as a prep. with the gen., BDAG 340d) only occurs here and Matt 23:26 in the NT (with eight LXX refs., all followed by a sg. noun or pron.). Ἐντὸς ὑμῶν could be understood as:

1. "within you" (NKJV) in an internal sense (with ὑμῶν being understood as a ref. to people in general rather than the Pharisees, BHGNT 552; R 641; Robertson, *Pictures* 229);
2. within "your power of choice" (ZG 251–52; Fitzmyer 1161–62; though this does not seem to answer the question); or
*3. "in your midst" (NASB, NIV, sim. RSV, ESV; "among you" NRSV, HCSB).

The pl. ὑμῶν, the explicit shift in audience to disciples in 17:22, and the use of ἐντὸς ἡμῶν in place of ἐν ἡμῖν in Exod 17:7 (Aquila), all favor understanding this phrase as "in your midst" (see Bock 1415–17; Marshall 655–56; cf. Bovon 2.516–17; Harris 261). This, together with ἐστίν (perhaps emphatically placed, Bock 1417), suggests a ref. to the arrival already of God's saving rule in the person of Jesus (see 4:43; 7:28;

9:2 [9:6]; 10:9, 11; 11:20; 16:16; Nolland [853–54] views this as a fut. ref., see Bock 1417).

b. Encouragement to Suffering Disciples: The Justice of the Kingdom Will Come with the Son of Man's Return (17:22–37)

17:22 Εἶπεν δὲ πρὸς τοὺς μαθητάς identifies a shift in audience and, as will become evident, a shift in focus from the presence of the kingdom to the future return of Jesus. Ἐλεύσονται ἡμέραι (see 5:35) alludes to a common OT phrase used for approaching judgment (Bock 1426; Fitzmyer 1168; Marshall 657; cf. 19:43; 21:6; 23:29). Ὅτε ("when"), temp. Ἐπιθυμήσετε 2nd pl. fut. act. indic. of ἐπιθυμέω, "desire" (ESV), "long" (NRSV, HCSB, NIV). The inf. ἰδεῖν (see 2:26) is complementary (BDAG 371d–72a). The acc. sg. fem. μίαν (of εἷς, μία, ἕν) is the obj. of ἰδεῖν ("one"; some suggest this is a [Heb.] synonym for "first," Plummer 407; cf. BDAG 293a [though this verse is not listed there; BDAG 291c lists this verse for "one" quantitatively]). The gen. τῶν ἡμερῶν is partitive (on the numeral εἷς with the partitive gen. in Luke, see Fitzmyer 121–22; see 5:17; 8:22; 20:1). The gen. τοῦ υἱοῦ τοῦ ἀνθρώπου (see 5:24) expresses the characteristic of these days though the relationship is not made explicit (perhaps a ref. to his return [NLT] or the days characterized by his rule in fullness when he returns; cf. 17:26; the sg. "day" is used in 17:24, 30; cf. Bock 1427–28; Fitzmyer 1168–69; Marshall 659). Ὄψεσθε 2nd pl. fut. mid. indic. of ὁράω (neg. with οὐκ).

17:23 Ἐροῦσιν, see 17:21. The structure of a statement followed by the prohibitions is essentially a cond. (Marshall 659). Ἰδού, see 1:20. For ἐκεῖ ἤ . . . ὧδε see 17:21 (though in this context the ref. appears to be to the Son of Man; "he is" NIV; of the numerous vars. this reading, supported by Alexandrian mss., is the most likely [UBS⁵; SBLGNT omits ἤ]; the vars. do not affect the sense). Ἀπέλθητε 2nd pl. 2nd aor. act. subjunc. of dep. ἀπέρχομαι ("go"; on the compound form, see Z §133). Διώξητε 2nd pl. aor. act. subjunc. of διώκω, "run after" (NASB, HCSB, sim. NIV; BDAG 254a), "follow" (NKJV, ESV), "set off in pursuit" (NJB, NRSV). Both subjuncs. are prohibitions with μή and μηδέ (regarding future action, ZG 252; after a neg. vb, μηδέ is "or").

17:24 Ὥσπερ introduces a comparison that is completed with οὕτως. Γάρ, causal (giving the reason there is no need to go out looking for the Son of Man after the claims made by some [17:23]). The nom. ἡ ἀστραπή ("lightning," see 10:18) is the subj. of λάμπει (3rd sg. pres. act. indic. of λάμπω, "shine"). The cognate ptc. ἀστράπτουσα (nom. sg. fem. of pres. act. ptc. of ἀστράπτω, "flash") is probably attrib. (BHGNT 553; though it could be temp. [NASB]; only here and 24:4 in the NT; cf. 9:29). Ἐκ expresses source and εἰς goal ("from . . . to"). The arts. τῆς and τήν are subst. and a fem. noun such as γῆς ("earth"), μερίδος ("part" NKJV, NASB; BDF §241[1]), or χώρας ("region") is implied (and acc. forms with τήν; cf. R 1202; ZG 252; Bock 1429–30; Marshall 660; Fitzmyer 1169–70). The combination of ἀστραπὴ ἀστράπτουσα . . . λάμπει with the prep. phrase emphasizes the visibility of the Son of Man's coming (Bock 1429; Fitzmyer 1169–70; Marshall 661). The temp. ἐν τῇ ἡμέρᾳ αὐτοῦ is omitted in 𝔓⁷⁵ B D and thus has good Alexandrian and Western support for the shorter rdg.

The longer rdg. is included in all EVV and in brackets in UBS⁵. Since the expression is not found elsewhere in the NT, the longer rdg. may be the more difficult and therefore original (the similar ending of ἀνθρώπου and αὐτοῦ may have led to the omission [homoeoteleuton, Metzger 142]). The sg. "day" of the Son of Man here and 17:30 alludes to "the day of Yahweh" (Marshall 661).

17:25 Δεῖ, see 2:49. The acc. pron. αὐτόν is the subj. of the (complementary) inf. παθεῖν (see 9:22; the acc. πολλά is the obj.). The inf. ἀποδοκιμασθῆναι (see 9:22) is also complementary. Ἀπό expresses agency and is used for ὑπό (see 6:18). Τῆς γενεᾶς ταύτης, see 7:31. For the Son of Man suffering must precede glory (cf. 9:22, 26; the implication is that this is also the case for his disciples, Marshall 661).

17:26 Καθώς introduces a comparison that is completed with οὕτως (paralleled in 17:28–30 with ref. to Lot; καθὼς ἐγένετο "just as it was" most EVV). The temp. ἐν ταῖς ἡμέραις Νῶε refers to the time "when Noah lived" (see 1:5; "in Noah's day" NJB, NLT). Ἔσται, see 1:14. Καί, "also." For "the days of the Son of Man" see 17:22 (the pl. parallels ἐν ταῖς ἡμέραις Νῶε). In this context the phrase seems to refer to a period of time immediately preceding the return of the Son of Man (Bock 1431; Marshall 663). The comparisons with Noah and Lot are framed with ἐν ταῖς ἡμέραις τοῦ υἱοῦ τοῦ ἀνθρώπου (17:26) and ᾗ ἡμέρᾳ ὁ υἱὸς τοῦ ἀνθρώπου ἀποκαλύπτεται (17:30). The likeness to "the day(s) of the Son of Man" is then developed in 17:31–35.

17:27 The following four impfs. (in asyndeton) describe how "it was" in the days of Noah (i.e., "customary" impfs., Wallace 548; iter. Bock 1432). Ἤσθιον, see 6:1. Ἔπινον 3rd pl. impf. act. indic. of πίνω. Ἐγάμουν 3rd pl. impf. act. indic. of γαμέω. Ἐγαμίζοντο 3rd pl. impf. pass. indic. of γαμίζω, "give in marriage." In the context of the flood story, these seemingly neutral activities may be associated with moral corruption (Bock 1432; Fitzmyer 1170), or simply unpreparedness (Marshall 663–64) and complacency (Nolland 860). Ἄχρι ἧς ἡμέρας is temp. (ἄχρι is a marker of continuous time up to a point, BDAG 160d; ZG 252; on rel. pron. see Z §17). Εἰσῆλθεν, see 1:40 (the nom. Νῶε is the subj.). Κιβωτόν acc. sg. fem. of κιβωτός, -οῦ, ἡ, "ark." i.e. Ἦλθεν, see 2:27 (the nom. sg. masc. κατακλυσμός [of κατακλυσμός, -οῦ, ὁ, "flood"] is the subj.). Ἀπώλεσεν 3rd sg. aor. act. indic. of ἀπόλλυμι (the acc. πάντας is the obj.).

17:28 Καθώς introduces a comparison that is completed with an implied οὕτως . . . τοῦ υἱοῦ τοῦ ἀνθρώπου (as in 17:26). Ἐγένετο ἐν ταῖς ἡμέραις see 17:26. The first two impfs. repeat 17:27 (ἤσθιον, ἔπινον). The following four vbs. are all 3rd pl. impf. act indic.: ἠγόραζον (of ἀγοράζω, "buy"), ἐπώλουν (of πωλέω, "sell"), ἐφύτευον (of φυτεύω, "plant"), ᾠκοδόμουν (of οἰκοδομέω, "build"). As with 17:27, there may be an implicit criticism of such activities, or they may simply refer to "the normal rhythms of life" (Nolland 860).

17:29 The dat. rel. phrase ᾗ . . . ἡμέρᾳ is temp. (R 522; Wallace 155; for the rel. pron. see R 718; Z §18; Marshall 664). Ἐξῆλθεν, see 2:1 (the nom. Λώτ is the subj.). Ἔβρεξεν, see 7:44 ("rain"). The sg. neut. nouns πῦρ and θεῖον ([of πῦρ, -ός, τό; of θεῖον, -ου, τό]; "fire and sulfur"; perhaps a hendiadys, "burning sulfur" Nolland 861) could be the nom. subj. of ἔβρεξεν ("fire and sulfur rained" RSV, HCSB, ESV, NIV) or the acc. obj. (either "it rained fire and sulfur" NRSV, sim. NKJV, NASB; or "He rained fire and sulfur"; BDAG 184a; BDF §129; Bock 1434; Marshall 664; LXX Gen 19:24 has κύριος ἔβρεξεν . . . θεῖον καὶ πῦρ). Ἀπ᾽ οὐρανοῦ shows the source of the judgment as from God (the prep. phrase is def. without the art., R 791). For ἀπώλεσεν πάντας see 17:27.

17:30 Κατά is a marker of a "norm of similarity" (BDAG 512c–13a; with τὰ αὐτὰ ἔσται "it will be the same"; ZG 252; i.e., following this same pattern, Bock 1434). For ᾗ ἡμέρᾳ see 17:29 (cf. the pl. refs. in 17:22). The phrase here forms an inclusio with 17:26. Ἀποκαλύπτεται (3rd sg. pres. pass. indic. of ἀποκαλύπτω) indicates that the earlier refs. to "the days of the Son of Man" were referring to the time of his return (Fitzmyer 1171).

17:31 The implications of 17:26–30 are now brought out in a series of warnings. Ἐν ἐκείνῃ τῇ ἡμέρᾳ is temp. The rel. pron. ὅς is the subj. of ἔσται (see 1:14) and introduces a rel. clause (ὅς ἔσται . . . ἐν τῇ οἰκίᾳ; cf. BDF §380[2]; Marshall 665) which is the subj. of καταβάτω (3rd sg. 2nd aor. act. impv. of καταβαίνω; prohibition with μή; the clause functions as a cond., BDF §380[2]; cf. R 440, 959). Ἐπὶ τοῦ δώματος, locat. (gen. sg. neut., see 5:19; "on the housetop" HCSB, ESV, NIV; with ref. to "the level surface of a flat roof" BDAG 266b). The nom. pl. τὰ σκεύη ("goods," see 8:16) is the subj. of an implied equative vb. (cf. BDF §269; T 325). The aor. act. inf. ἆραι (of αἴρω) expresses purpose (ZG 252). The art. ὁ turns the prep. phrase ἐν ἀγρῷ into the subj. of ἐπιστρεψάτω (3rd sg. aor. act. impv. of ἐπιστρέφω; prohibition with μή). Εἰς τὰ ὀπίσω is locat. ("to the things behind"; "back" sim. most EVV; see 9:62).

17:32 Μνημονεύετε 2nd pl. pres. act. impv. of μνημονεύω, "remember" (followed by the gen. complement τῆς γυναικός; BDAG 655b). This is the only ref. to Lot's wife in the NT (cf. Gen 19:26). The idea is to take heed and learn not to look back with attachment to the things of this world (cf. Marshall 665; cf. 9:23–25, 62; 14:26–27). This idea is then summarized in 17:33.

17:33 The nom. sg. masc. rel. pron. ὅς with ἐάν is the subj. of ζητήσῃ (3rd sg. aor. act. subjunc. of ζητέω) and introduces an indef. rel. clause (ὅς ἐάν . . . περιποιήσασθαι) which is the subj. of ἀπολέσει (see 9:24; R 957; Z §335). The aor. mid. inf. περιποιήσασθαι (of dep. περιποιέομαι, "preserve" ESV; "keep" NASB, NIV; only here, Acts 20:28; 1 Tim 3:13 in the NT) is complementary (for this rdg. over σῶσαι see Metzger 142). The rel. pron. ὅς with ἄν is the subj. of ἀπολέσῃ (see 9:24; BDF §380[3]; Z §§336, 341). The rel. clause functions as the subj. of ζῳογονήσει (3rd sg. fut. act. indic. of ζῳογονέω, "preserve alive," "preserve" most EVV; only here, Acts 7:19; 1 Tim 6:13 in the NT).

17:34 The introductory λέγω ὑμῖν may signal a concluding application concerning the suddenness of this judgment (Marshall 667; the phrase often introduces a concluding application or summary, cf. 14:24; 15:7, 10; 16:9; 18:8, 14). Ταύτῃ τῇ νυκτί is a dat. of time (ZG 252; the ref. to "night" is for the purposes of the illustration only). Ἔσονται, see 11:19 (the subj. is δύο). Ἐπὶ κλίνης μιᾶς ("in one bed"; see 5:18; 8:16) is locat. Παραλημφθήσεται 3rd sg. fut. pass. indic. of παραλαμβάνω (the subj. is ὁ εἷς; perhaps a divine pass., Fitzmyer 1172; Marshall 668). Ἀφεθήσεται, see 12:10 (here, "left"; the subj. is ὁ ἕτερος; also pass.). In 17:34 ὁ εἷς . . . ὁ ἕτερος is masc. whereas in 17:35 ἡ μία . . . ἡ . . . ἑτέρα is fem. (the masc. may allow for either the man or his wife to be taken/left, Marshall 668). The emphasis here is on the separation that will occur at the judgment. The ref. to Noah and Lot in the immediately preceding context suggests being left to face judgment (Bock 1437; Bovon 2.523; Fitzmyer 1172; Marshall 668; Nolland 862).

17:35 Ἀλήθουσαι (nom. pl. fem. of pres. act. ptc. of ἀλήθω, "grind"; only here, Matt 24:41 in the NT) with ἔσονται (see 11:19; cf. 17:34) is a fut. periph. ptc. cstr. (R 889). The locat. prep. phrase ἐπὶ τὸ αὐτό means "together" (BDAG 153d; MM 94a; cf. Acts 1:15; 2:1, 44, 47; 4:26). Ἀλήθουσαι seems to refer to a hand mill for grinding grain which was normally operated by two women (BDAG 43d–44a; LN 46.16; all EVV). Παραλημφθήσεται, see 17:34 (the fem. ἡ μία is the subj.). Ἀφεθήσεται, see 12:10 (as with 17:34, "left"; the fem. ἡ . . . ἑτέρα is the subj.; on the addition of 17:36 see Metzger 142–43).

17:37 Ἀποκριθέντες, see 9:19 (see also 1:19). Λέγουσιν, see 9:18 (a historical pres., Wallace 625; the subj. is the disciples [cf. 17:22]). In the context of allusions to judgment in 17:26–35 and in Jesus' answer in 17:37b, the question "where, Lord?" (ποῦ, κύριε;) may be a ref. to where the judgment will take place (Bock 1438). The nom. τὸ σῶμα ("body" NASB; "corpse" NRSV, HCSB, ESV; BDAG 983c; MM 620d) is the subj. of an implied ἐστίν (T 305). The verbless clause ὅπου τὸ σῶμα is then picked up with the adv. ἐκεῖ (R 969). Καί, "also." Ἀετοί (nom. pl. masc. of ἀετός, -οῦ, ὁ) could refer to "eagles," but the ref. to being "gathered" (ἐπισυναχθήσονται 3rd pl. fut. pass. indic. of ἐπισυνάγω, "gather") over dead bodies indicates that "vultures" are meant (most EVV; BDAG 22d; LN 4.42). The ref. here seems to be to the visibility (Fitzmyer 1173; Marshall 669; cf. 17:24), certainty, and finality (Bock 1440) of judgment for those who are not prepared at the Son of Man's return.

FOR FURTHER STUDY

35. The Son of Man

Bock, D. L. *DJG*² 894–900.
_____. 1.924–30.
Caragounis, C. C. *The Son of Man: Vision and Interpretation*. WUNT 38. Tübingen: Mohr Siebeck, 1986.
Hurtado, L. W. and P. L. Owen, eds. *"Who Is This Son of Man?" The Latest Scholarship on a Puzzling Expression of the Historical Jesus*. London: T&T Clark, 2011.
Kim, S. *The Son of Man as the Son of God*. Grand Rapids: Eerdmans, 1983.
*Marshall, I. H. *DJG*¹ 775–81.
*Michel, O. and I. H. Marshall. *NIDNTT* 3.613–34.
Nickelsburg, G. W. E. *ABD* 6.137–50.

36. The Second Coming and Eschatology in Luke

Bock, *Theology* 389–406.

Carroll, J. T. *Response to the End of History: Eschatology and Situation in Luke-Acts.* Atlanta: Scholars Press, 1988.

Gaventa, B. R. "The Eschatology of Luke-Acts Revisited." *Encounter* 43 (1982): 27–41.

Schellenberg, R. S. *DJG*[2] 232–39.

Stein, R. H. "Jesus, the Destruction of Jerusalem, and the Coming of the Son of Man in Luke 21:5–38." *SBJT* 16 (2012): 18–27.

Witherington, B., III. *Jesus, Paul, and the End of the World.* Downers Grove: InterVarsity, 1992.

HOMILETICAL SUGGESTIONS

The Certainties Concerning God's Saving Rule (17:20–37)

1. The kingdom of God has come already in Jesus (17:20–21).
2. The kingdom of God will come in fullness when Jesus returns visibly (17:22–24).
3. The kingdom of God will come only because of Jesus' suffering and death (17:25).
4. The kingdom of God will come with certain judgment upon those unprepared (17:26–30).
5. The kingdom of God will come with sudden judgment upon those attached to this world (17:31–36).

6. While Waiting for the Son of Man's Return, Faith Is Evidenced in Persistent Prayer (18:1–8)

Although prayer is prominent in 18:1–8 and 18:9–14, references to the Son of Man's return and longing for vindication link this parable to the preceding eschatological discourse. The ref. to faith also picks up on 17:5–6, 19.

18:1 Ἔλεγεν, see 6:20 (cf. 5:36). For παραβολήν see 8:4. The antecedent of the indir. obj. αὐτοῖς is τοὺς μαθητάς (17:22; cf. 6:39; 21:29). Πρός with the art. pres. act. inf. δεῖν (of δεῖ, see 2:49) may reflect a Heb. prep. cstr. for ref. ("about" NJB, NRSV, sim. HCSB; BDF §402[5]; Burton §§107, 414; R 1003, 1075; "with regard to" T 144; Fitzmyer 1178; Marshall 671; Nolland 867). The cstr. here, however, fits with its more common function to express purpose ("to this end" KJV; sim. RV; "to the effect that they ought" RSV, ESV; "to show them that they should" NIV, sim. NASB; BHGNT 561; ZG 253; Bock 1447). The two phrases πάντοτε προσεύχεσθαι and μὴ ἐγκακεῖν are parallel with each clarifying the meaning of the other (Nolland 867). The inf. προσεύχεσθαι (see 9:29) is complementary (with δεῖν; the acc. αὐτούς is the subj.). The pres. act. inf. ἐγκακεῖν (of ἐγκακέω) is complementary (with δεῖν, functioning as a prohibition, Huffman 224). The pres. infs. are in keeping with πάντοτε (ZG 253; in the sense of continual rather than continuous prayer, Bock 1447; Marshall 671). Ἐγκακέω, "lose heart" (NKJV, NRSV, NASB, ESV), "become discouraged" (HCSB), "give up" (NIV; Fitzmyer 1178), "grow tired" (Bock 1447) is always negated in the NT (here with μή; it only occurs here and five times in the Pauline Epistles).

18:2 Λέγων (see 1:63) introduces the parable. The indef. nom. sg. masc. κριτής τις (κριτής, see 11:19) is the subj. of ἦν (on the indef. pron. with parables, see 10:30). The indef. ἔν τινι πόλει is locat. Φοβούμενος nom. sg. masc. of pres. mid. ptc. of dep. φοβέομαι (neg. with μή; the obj. is τὸν θεόν; cf. 2 Chron 19:7). Ἐντρεπόμενος nom. sg. masc. of pres. pass. ptc. of ἐντρέπω ("regard" NKJV; "respect" NASB, HCSB; "show deference" BDAG 341a; see 18:4; 20:13; neg. with μή; the anar. obj. ἄνθρωπον is used generically in this comparison with God, Wallace 253). The ptcs. could be periph. with ἦν but are more likely both attrib. (modifying κριτής τις; cf. the use of ἦν in 18:3). Thus, they focus more on the judge's character than his actions (BHGNT 561).

18:3 As with 18:2 (following the attrib. understanding of the ptcs. there), the nom. χήρα (see 2:37; 7:12) is the subj. of ἦν, and ἐν τῇ πόλει ἐκείνῃ is locat. The impf. ἤρχετο (3rd sg. impf. mid. indic. of dep. ἔρχομαι) is iter. ("kept coming" most EVV; ZG 253; Bock 1448; Bovon 2.529; Fitzmyer 1179; Marshall 672; Nolland [867] views it as customary, "used to come"). The pres. ptc. λέγουσα (see 1:24) is attendant circumstance with the impf. ἤρχετο (to emphasize the continuous requests). Ἐκδίκησόν 2nd sg. aor. act. impv. of ἐκδικέω, "avenge" (KJV, RV; LSJ 504c; MM 193a), "vindicate" (RSV; Bock 1446), "give me legal protection" (NASB), "give me justice" (ESV, HCSB, sim. NKJV, NRSV, NIV; BDAG 300d; LN 56.35; Fitzmyer 1179; Marshall 672; Nolland 868). Ἀπό with τοῦ ἀντιδίκου μου ("my adversary" NKJV, RSV, HCSB, ESV, NIV; "my opponent" NASB, NRSV; "my enemy" NJB, NLT; "accuser" BDAG 88c [or "enemy/opponent"]; see 12:58) could reflect opposition ("against" most EVV) or separation ("from" NASB; i.e., "from the adversary's attacks" BHGNT 562).

18:4 For ἤθελεν see 15:28 (neg. with οὐκ; the impf. probably matches ἤρχετο in 18:3). Ἐπί with the acc. sg. masc. χρόνον is a temp. marker (though indef.; "for a while" most EVV; "for some time" NIV; answering the question "how long?" BDAG 367b; an acc. of duration, BDF §§233[3], 455[3]; ZG 253). Μετὰ . . . ταῦτα is temp. For ἐν ἑαυτῷ and soliloquies in Luke see 12:17. Εἰ introduces a first-class cond. (Z §303; ZG 253). With καί, the protasis in this context is concessive ("even though" sim. most EVV; BDAG 278d; Burton §284; Robertson, *Pictures* 231; Bock 1449; see sim. cstr. in 11:8). Φοβοῦμαι 1st sg. pres. mid. indic. of dep. φοβέομαι (cf. 18:2; neg. with οὐ [for οὐ in cond. clauses cf. Burton §469; R 1012]; οὐ . . . οὐδέ "neither . . . nor" ESV). Ἐντρέπομαι 1st sg. pres. pass. indic. of ἐντρέπω (see 18:2).

18:5 Διά with the art. pres. act. inf. παρέχειν (of παρέχω, "give," "grant"; the acc. τὴν χήραν [see 2:37] ταύτην is the subj.) is causal (on διὰ τό and inf. cf. R 966; for γέ see 11:8). Παρέχειν with κόπον is "cause trouble" (BDAG 776d; acc. sg. masc., see the cstr. in 11:7; pres. "keeps bothering" ESV, NIV [sim. HCSB]). Ἐκδικήσω 1st sg. fut. act. indic. of ἐκδικέω (see 18:3). Ἵνα with the subjunc. ὑπωπιάζῃ (3rd sg. pres. act. subjunc. of ὑπωπιάζω) expresses purpose (neg. with μή). Ὑπωπιάζω occurs only here and 1 Cor 9:27 in the NT. In this context it could mean:

1. lit. "strike under the eye" or "give a black eye" (BDAG 1043b, mng. 1; "slap me in the face" NJB; "attack me" NIV);
2. fig. "slander" or "besmirch" (i.e., "shame") from the idiom "to blacken the face" (BDAG 1043b, listed under mng. 2; Bovon 2.534 [possible]; Marshall 673 [possible]; Nolland 868); or
*3. fig. "wear out" (NRSV, NASB, HCSB, sim. NKJV; "beat down" ESV; BDAG 1043b, mng. 2; "gradually wear me out" [pres.] BDF §207[3]; "annoy and wear out" LN 25.245; MM 661c; LSJ 1904b; Bock 1449; Fitzmyer 1179 [possible]; Marshall 673).

The judge does not appear to be worried about the first two options (18:2, 4), so the third view is more likely. Ἐρχομένη (nom. sg. fem. of pres. mid. ptc. of dep. ἔρχομαι) expresses means. The temp. εἰς τέλος could modify ὑπωπιάζῃ ("in the end wear me out" Cassirer; cf. BDAG 998c; "completely" BDF §207[3]; "utterly shame me" Nolland 865) or ἐρχομένη ("continually coming" NRSV, NASB, sim. NKJV, ESV; "persistent coming" HCSB [though the tr. "continually" or "persistent" may just reflect the pres. tense]; Z §249; ZG 253; Bock 1450; Marshall 673).

18:6 For ὁ κύριος see 7:13 (i.e., Jesus is the speaker here). Ἀκούσατε 2nd pl. aor. act. impv. of ἀκούω. The indir. question introduced with τί (which is the obj. of λέγει) functions as the complement of ἀκούσατε (BHGNT 564). The gen. τῆς ἀδικίας is attrib. (R 496; Wallace 87; Z §40; see 13:27; 16:8–9; κριτής, see 11:19).

18:7 The double neg. οὐ μή with the subjunc. ποιήσῃ (see 13:9) is an emphatic rhetorical question (with ref. to the fut. expecting the answer "yes, God most certainly will bring justice," BDF §365[4]; Burton §172; R 930, 1158; Wallace 468–69; Z §444). Ποιήσῃ with ἐκδίκησιν is equivalent to ἐκδικέω in 18:3, 5 (acc. sg. fem. of ἐκδίκησις, -εως, ἡ, here "avenge" NKJV; "vindicate" RSV; "bring about justice" NASB, NIV; sim. HCSB, ESV). The gen. τῶν ἐκλεκτῶν is obj. ("for his chosen ones" NIV, sim. most EVV; the only time the pl. of ἐκλεκτός is used in Luke-Acts [cf. the sg. in 23:35]; the gen. αὐτοῦ could be subj. or poss., Wallace 127). The use of τῶν ἐκλεκτῶν αὐτοῦ emphasizes God's commitment to his people in contrast to the picture of an unjust judge and an unknown widow (cf. Nolland 869). Βοώντων gen. pl. masc. of pres. act. (attrib.) ptc. of βοάω, "cry out" (cf. 9:38; 18:38; the pres. is iter., Bock 1451; continuous action, Fitzmyer 1180), describing "the standing characteristic of God's people" (Marshall 674). Ἡμέρας καὶ νυκτός is a gen. of time (BDF §186[2]; noting the kind of time [i.e., daytime and nighttime] rather than extent, R 495; Wallace 123–24; ZG 253). Μακροθυμεῖ 3rd sg. pres. act. indic. of μακροθυμέω. The antecedent of the pl. masc. pron. αὐτοῖς (dat. following ἐπί, see below) is τῶν ἐκλεκτῶν (gen. pl. masc. of ἐκλεκτός, -ή, -όν, i.e., not their enemies, who are not mentioned here). The syntax of οὐ μὴ ποιήσῃ . . . καὶ μακροθυμεῖ (with a change from subjunc. to indic.) could be understood in one of the following ways (see Bock 1451–54 [Marshall 674–75] for other interpretations [12!] including some where ἐπ' αὐτοῖς is a ref. to the enemies of the elect):

1. as just one rhetorical question (in which μακροθυμεῖ may refer to God's patience and forbearing; "though he bears long with them" NKJV; BDAG 612d [mng. 2]; Robertson, *Pictures* 232; where καί is concessive [ZG 253]; ἐπί is "for" or "with"; Marshall 675 [or, μακροθυμεῖ is linked to βοώντων and refers to God's apparent delay]);

2. one rhetorical question up to νυκτός with καὶ μακροθυμεῖ beginning a statement (perhaps referring to God's patience [BHGNT 565]; or his delay [Bovon 2.536]; or his generous long-suffering nature with his people [Nolland 865, 869–70]); or

3. two rhetorical questions where μακροθυμεῖ begins the second question or the second part of a compound question (and perhaps refers to God's "delay"; most EVV; BDAG 612d [mng. 3]; LN 67.126; "slow to help" LSJ 1074d; i.e., will he "keep putting them off?" NLT, NIV; where ἐπί is "over"; Bock 1453–54; Fitzmyer 1180).

18:8 Λέγω ὑμῖν see 17:34. Ὅτι, recitative. For ποιήσει (3rd sg. fut. act. indic. of ποιέω) with ἐκδίκησιν see 18:7. The gen. αὐτῶν is obj. Ἐν τάχει (dat. sg. neut. of τάχος, -ους, τό, used adv.) expresses manner (BDF §219[4]; R 589; ZG 254 describes this as "sociative," cf. Z §116). Although the phrase may mean "suddenly" (J. Horst, *TDNT* 4.381; cf. refs. in Bock 1455), the context and the other uses of the phrase in the NT (e.g., Acts 12:7; 22:18; 25:4) favor the mng. "quickly/speedily" (all EVV; i.e., "soon"; BDAG 993a; MM 627b–c; Bock 1455; Fitzmyer 1180–81; Marshall 676; Nolland 870). For ὁ υἱὸς τοῦ ἀνθρώπου see 5:24. Ἐλθών, see 7:3 (temp., Fitzmyer [1181] sees this as a nom. abs.). The particle ἆρα is used as a "marker of a tone of suspense or impatience in interrogation" (BDAG 127d; LN 69.14; LSJ 233a; ZG 254; cf. R 1176).

Εὑρήσει, see 12:37, 43 (in a sim. eschatological context, Marshall 676). The art. in the obj. τὴν πίστιν may be anaphoric and point to the faith that leads to the persistent prayer mentioned in 18:1 (Fitzmyer 1181; or an Aram. signifying faithfulness [in prayer], Marshall 676). Thus, (1) God most certainly will bring justice for his people; (2) unlike the unjust judge, he will answer their prayers for justice "soon" (viewed from the perspective of eternity, Marshall 676; or in stages, Nolland 871); and (3) God's people are exhorted to continue to evidence their trust in him through prayer.

HOMILETICAL SUGGESTIONS

Why Should We Keep Praying and Not Give Up in the Face of Adversity? (18:1–8)
1. God does care about the cries of his people (18:1–6).
2. God will most certainly answer with justice for his chosen ones (18:7).
3. The wait will not have seemed long when he answers (18:8a).
4. Continued prayer expresses our faith while we wait for Jesus to return (18:8b).

E. HOW TO ENTER THE KINGDOM: PART 1 (18:9–30)

The focus shifts now from how to wait for the consummation of the kingdom to how one gains entry to the kingdom. Entry is described in a variety of ways: justification (18:9–14), receiving and entering the kingdom (18:15–17), and inheriting eternal life/entering the kingdom/being saved/receiving eternal life (18:18–30). Those who enter are variously described in terms of their lack of self-reliance (see the headings below).

1. Those Who Humbly Confess Their Sins and Cry for Mercy Are Justified (18:9–14)

18:9 The obj. of εἶπεν is the acc. τὴν παραβολὴν ταύτην at the end of the verse. Καί, "also." For δὲ καί see 2:4. Although πρός could be "against" (cf. BDAG 874d), Luke uses the prep. to indicate the addressees of the following parable (see e.g., 1:13; Bock 1461; Marshall 678). Πεποιθότας (acc. pl. masc. of 2nd pf. act. ptc. of πείθω; intrans.) could be attrib. (BDF §412[4]) or subst. (R 1107; cf. refs. for the ptc. ἀκούσαντες at 1:66). Ἐπί with the dat. ἑαυτοῖς is a "marker of basis for a state of being, action, or result" (BDAG 364d; "trusted in themselves" HCSB, ESV). Although ὅτι could be causal (BDAG 732c, mng. 4a; Marshall 678; Nolland 875), in this context (after a vb. of "thinking, judging, believing, hoping," BDAG 732a) it is better understood as a marker of content ("that" sim. all EVV; i.e., explaining what it was about themselves that they were trusting in; the tense of dir. speech is retained, Z §347; ZG 254; Bock 1460). The adj. δίκαιοι is pred. (cf. 10:29). Ἐξουθενοῦντας (acc. pl. masc. of pres. act. ptc. of ἐξουθενέω, "despise" RSV, NKJV; "treated . . . with contempt" ESV, sim. NRSV, NASB; "looked down on" HCSB, NIV; cf. 23:11) is linked with πεποιθότας with the one art. τούς and καί. Τοὺς λοιπούς (subst. "everyone else" HCSB, NIV; BDAG 602c) is the obj. of ἐξουθενοῦντας.

18:10 The nom. pl. masc. ἄνθρωποι δύο is the subj. of ἀνέβησαν (3rd pl. 2nd aor. act. indic. of ἀναβαίνω; i.e., up the hill to the temple; cf. κατέβη in 18:14; also used with ref. to Jerusalem, cf. 2:42). Εἰς τὸ ἱερόν ("the temple complex" HCSB; see 2:27) is locat. The inf. προσεύξασθαι (see 6:12) expresses purpose (Burton §366; R 990; ZG 254). The "two men" are then identified with two verbless clauses with a nom. subj. (ὁ εἷς and ὁ ἕτερος, see 7:41) and pred. (Φαρισαῖος [see 5:17] and τελώνης [see 3:12; cf. 5:30; 7:34; 15:1]).

18:11 Σταθείς (nom. sg. masc. of aor. pass. ptc. of ἵστημι; intrans.; see Z §§231, 365) could be temp. or *attendant circumstance (Bock 1462; Fitzmyer 1186) with προσηύχετο (3rd sg. impf. mid. indic. of dep. προσεύχομαι). The aor. ptc. σταθείς is found only in Luke-Acts in the NT (cf. also 18:40; 19:8; Acts 2:14; 17:22; 27:21). Πρὸς ἑαυτόν could modify σταθείς ("standing by himself" NRSV, ESV, sim. NIV; or an Aram. adding emphasis to the ptc. "took his stand" HCSB; Marshall 679). This would, however, be a rare use of this phrase as καθ᾽ ἑαυτόν would be more likely (e.g., mss. D; BHGNT 568; cf. Bovon 2.546–47 who nevertheless suggests both options). Thus, πρὸς ἑαυτόν is more likely the indir. obj. of προσηύχετο and is either "to himself" (NJB, NASB; BDAG 269b ["in silence"], 875c; Bock 1462) or (perhaps more likely, given the content of the prayer that follows) "about himself" (NET; Fitzmyer 1186; Nolland 876). For the mss. order of ταῦτα πρὸς ἑαυτόν see Metzger 143; Fitzmyer 1186. Ὁ θεός is nom. for voc. (with the art., Z §§33, 34). Εὐχαριστῶ 1st sg. pres. act. indic. of εὐχαριστέω (the dat. σοι is complementary). Ὅτι, following εὐχαριστῶ, is a marker of content ("that"; BDAG 415d; R 1035). His thankfulness might be directed to God (perhaps indicating his understanding that God has enabled him to be confident of his own righteousness [18:9]), but the Pharisee is the subj. of his prayer (εἰμί) in contrast to others (οὐκ . . . ὥσπερ οἱ λοιποί; Robertson, *Pictures* 233). For οἱ λοιποί see 18:9 (the gen. τῶν ἀνθρώπων [used generically] is partitive, R 502; Wallace 86; εἰσίν is assumed). The following three nom. masc. pls. ἅρπαγες (of ἅρπαξ, -αγος; "thieves" NRSV; "swindlers" NASB; "extortioners" ESV; cf. BDAG 134c), ἄδικοι ("unrighteous" HCSB; see 16:10), and μοιχοί (of μοιχός, -οῦ, ὁ, "adulterers") are in appos. to οἱ λοιποί. Καί, "even" (ZG 254). The demonstrative pron. οὗτος has a derogatory emphasis (R 697; Bock 1462–63; Fitzmyer 1187; cf. 15:2; see οὗτος in 18:14).

18:12 The Pharisee's focus on himself continues with three 1st sg. vbs. Νηστεύω 1st sg. pres. act. indic. of νηστεύω, "fast" (a customary pres., R 880; Wallace 522; cf. 5:33–34). Τοῦ σαββάτου, following the adv. δίς ("twice"), is a gen. of time (R 505; indicting the kind of time rather than extent; "during the week," Wallace 123, 202; Bock [1463] describes it as a distributive gen.). Ἀποδεκατῶ 1st sg. pres. act. indic. of ἀποδεκατόω, "tithe" (with πάντα as the obj.; cf. 11:42; an acc. of ref., Bock 1463). Κτῶμαι 1st sg. pres. mid. indic. of dep. κτάομαι, "acquire," "get" (i.e., his income, Robertson, *Pictures* 233; with ὅσα as the obj.).

18:13 The humility of the tax collector is now contrasted (δέ) with the Pharisee as he displays the opposite of self-confidence before God. The pf. ptc. ἑστώς (see 1:11; intrans.; see Z §365; modified by μακρόθεν, "from far off") could be attrib. or temp. (BHGNT 569; "graphic" Z §365). The nom. ὁ . . . τελώνης (cf. 18:10) is the subj. of ἤθελεν (see 15:28; neg. with οὐκ; the impf. parallels the impf. προσηύχετο). The compound neg. adv. οὐδέ ("not even") strengthens rather than cancels the previous neg. οὐκ (BHGNT 569; citing McKay 72). The aor. act. inf. ἐπᾶραι (of ἐπαίρω) is complementary (the acc. τοὺς ὀφθαλμούς is the obj.). Ἔτυπτεν 3rd sg. impf. act. indic. of τύπτω, "beat" (τὸ στῆθος acc. sg. neut. of στῆθος, -ους, τό, "breast" [ESV], "chest" [HCSB] is the obj.; the impf. is probably iter., HCSB; Robertson, *Pictures* 233; the action is "a sign of contrition or sorrow," BDAG 1020c; Bock 1464; Fitzmyer 1188; Marshall 680 [referring to the heart as the seat of sin]; cf. 23:48). Λέγων is probably attendant circumstance (BHGNT 569). The tax collector's prayer is also addressed to God (for ὁ θεός see 18:11), but it is actually a request that highlights the reason for his humility before God. Ἱλάσθητί (the second accent is from the enclitic μοι [a dat. of advantage]), 2nd sg. aor. pass. impv. of dep. ἱλάσκομαι, "be propitious" (MM 303b; ZG 254; "cause to be favorably inclined or disposed, propitiate, conciliate" BDAG 473d–74a; "turn Your wrath from me" HCSB; cf. Marshall 680), "be merciful" (sim. most EVV; cf. BDAG 474a; LSJ 828b; the pass. is "causative/permissive," Wallace 441). The dat. τῷ ἁμαρτωλῷ is in appos. to μοι. The art. is omitted in most EVV (except e.g., NASB; cf. R 756). It may be *par excellence* or simple identification (Wallace 223). The tax collector views himself as the sinner (or the worst of sinners; T 173) whereas the Pharisee thought of others as sinners (Robertson, *Pictures* 234).

18:14 Λέγω ὑμῖν see 17:34. Κατέβη, see 2:51 (corresponding to ἀναβαίνω in 18:10). The two demonstrative pronouns οὗτος . . . ἐκεῖνον emphasize the contrast between the two men (BDAG 301d; R 702–3; οὗτος refers to the last mentioned [R 703] and may also contrast with the derisive use of οὗτος in 18:11). Δεδικαιωμένος (nom. sg. masc. of pf. pass. ptc. of δικαιόω; see refs. at 10:29; cf. 15:29; in this context cf. 18:9) expresses manner. In the context of the tax collector's description of himself as "the sinner" before God who appeals for God's favor in place of wrath, the ptc. shows that his request has been answered. The verdict has been rendered (the pf. tense) and God has declared (the pass. is a divine pass.) the tax collector "right" before him (Fitzmyer 1188; "acquitted by God" Marshall 680; *pace* Bock [1465] who says there are no soteriological issues raised here other than a general request for mercy). That this favorable verdict comes by grace is seen in the intended contrast with those who were confident of their own righteousness in the opening statement (18:9). Εἰς τὸν οἶκον is locat. (modifying κατέβη). Παρά in the phrase παρ᾽ ἐκεῖνον is a marker of comparison in the sense of "to the exclusion of" (BDAG 301d, 758a; "rather than the other" sim. all EVV; cf. LN 89.132; Wallace 297; Z §145; ZG 254; cf. BDF §185[3]; Bovon 2.551; different to 13:2, 4). Ὅτι, causal (giving the reason for the tax collector's justification). See 14:11 for the rest of the verse. In this context the last statement refers to the self-confidence of those in 18:9 and the Pharisee in 18:11–12.

HOMILETICAL SUGGESTIONS

Contrasting Approaches to God (18:9–14)

1. Contrasting confidence (ἐφ᾽ ἑαυτοῖς ὅτι εἰσὶν δίκαιοι, 18:9; οὐκ ἤθελεν οὐδὲ τοὺς ὀφθαλμοὺς ἐπᾶραι, 18:13)
2. Contrasting comparisons (ἐξουθενοῦντας τοὺς λοιπούς, 18:9; μοι τῷ ἁμαρτωλῷ, 18:13)
3. Contrasting content (πρὸς ἑαυτὸν . . . εὐχαριστῶ σοι ὅτι οὐκ εἰμί . . ., 18:11; ἱλάσθητι, 18:13)
4. Contrasting conclusion (οὗτος δεδικαιωμένος . . . παρ᾽ ἐκεῖνον, 18:14a)
5. Contrasting condition (ὅτι πᾶς ὁ ὑψῶν ἑαυτὸν . . . ὁ δὲ ταπεινῶν ἑαυτόν, 18:14b)

2. Those Who Come to Jesus with the Dependent Trust of a Child Will Enter the Kingdom (18:15–17)

18:15 Προσέφερον 3rd pl. impf. act. indic. of προσφέρω (the pl. is indef., "people" NRSV, NIV; Z §1). The impf. may be conative (ZG 254), customary ("used to bring" Fitzmyer 1193), or *progressive ("were bringing" sim. most EVV; Bock 1469). For δὲ . . . καί see 2:4 ("even" HCSB, ESV; Marshall 682; "also" NIV). Τὰ βρέφη (acc. pl. neut.), see 1:41 (the art. is probably generic [as a class], Marshall 682). In view of 18:16–17 (cf. 2 Tim 3:15), τὰ βρέφη may be "infants" (NKJV, NRSV, HCSB, ESV) or "little children" (NLT; Bock 1469) rather than "babies" (NASB, NET, NIV). Ἵνα with the subjunc. ἅπτηται expresses purpose (BDF §369[1]). Ἅπτηται 3rd sg. pres. mid. subjunc. of ἅπτω, "touch" most EVV (perhaps to convey a blessing or for healing; perhaps "hold" BDAG 126d; MM 72d; the gen. αὐτῶν is complementary). Ἰδόντες, see 2:17 (temp.). The impf. ἐπετίμων (3rd pl. impf. act. indic. of ἐπιτιμάω) could be ingressive (NASB, NET), iter. (Robertson, *Pictures* 234), or conative (Bock 1469; Fitzmyer 1194; Marshall 682; cf. BDF §326). The antecedent of the dat. pl. masc. pron. is the subj. of προσέφερον (i.e., not the neut. τὰ βρέφη but those who brought the infants [specified in NET]).

18:16 Προσεκαλέσατο 3rd sg. aor. mid. indic. of dep. προσκαλέομαι ("called for" NRSV, NASB; "called . . . to him" RSV, ESV, NIV; "invited" HCSB; the antecedent of the acc. pl. neut. αὐτά is τὰ βρέφη [18:15]; now specified as "children" in NET, NIV). The following two impvs. are both directed to the disciples and express the same idea positively and negatively (joined by καί, Bock 1470). Ἄφετε 2nd pl. 2nd aor. act. impv. of ἀφίημι (here, "let" most EVV). The acc. pl. neut. παιδία ("children" RSV, NASB, ESV; "little children" NRSV, HCSB, NIV; now in place of τὰ βρέφη) is the subj. of the (complementary) inf. ἔρχεσθαι (see 9:23; Wallace 194). Κωλύετε, see 9:50 (prohibition with μή; perhaps forbidding continuing an action [Z §246; ZG 255; as 18:15 supports in this context] or viewing the action as an ongoing process [Huffman, 144]). The antecedent of αὐτά (the obj. of μὴ κωλύετε) is now τὰ παιδία. Γάρ, causal (giving the reason for allowing children to come to Jesus). For ἡ βασιλεία τοῦ θεοῦ see 4:43 (the subj. of ἐστίν). The gen. τῶν . . . τοιούτων is probably poss. ("belongs to such as these" NASB, HCSB, NIV, sim. most EVV; "belongs to those who are like these children" NLT). Thus, those who "belong to the kingdom of God" are those who have "come to (Jesus)" (ἔρχεσθαι πρός με).

18:17 For ἀμὴν λέγω ὑμῖν see 4:24. Λέγω ὑμῖν see also 17:34. The rel. pron. ὅς is the subj. of δέξηται ("receive" most EVV; "welcome" NJB, HCSB; see 9:48; the particle ἄν with the subjunc. is indef., "whoever"; neg. with μή). The rel. clause ὃς . . . παιδίον functions as the subj. of εἰσέλθη (3rd sg. 2nd. aor. act. subjunc. of dep. εἰσέρχομαι; with οὐ μή the subjunc. is an emphatic neg.). Although δέξηται may well include the idea of "receive the message/messenger of the kingdom" (Marshall 683), the parallel δέξηται . . . εἰσέλθη indicates that εἰσέλθη need not refer exclusively to the future (*pace* Marshall 683. Bock [1471] and Fitzmyer [1194] see a broad ref. to all periods of the kingdom; Nolland [882] suggests a ref. to both present and ultimate entrance into the kingdom). The nom. sg. παιδίον ("child") is the subj. of an implied δέχεται τὴν βασιλείαν τοῦ θεοῦ (BHGNT 573). The comp. conj. ὡς in this context refers to "coming to Jesus" (ἔρχεσθαι πρός με, 18:16) with the trust or dependence of a child (Bock 1470; cf. προσέφερον, 18:15).

HOMILETICAL SUGGESTIONS

Entering the Kingdom as a Child (18:15–17)
1. We are dependent, like children (προσέφερον, 18:15).
2. We are invited, like children (προσεκαλέσατο, 18:16).
3. We are to come to Jesus, like children (ἔρχεσθαι πρός με, 18:16).

3. Those Who Abandon Self-Reliance to Follow Jesus Will Inherit Eternal Life (18:18–30)

18:18 The close connection of this pericope with the preceding (καί, "now" NKJV, NET; cf. refs. to "entering" "the kingdom of God" in 18:24–25, 29) serves to highlight the contrast in the two approaches to Jesus. Ἐπηρώτησέν, see 8:30 (τις . . . ἄρχων is the subj.; see 14:1 for ἄρχων in Luke; the type of "ruler" is not specified here). Διδάσκαλε ἀγαθέ, voc. (for διδάσκαλε see 7:40). For this question see 10:25.

18:19 The neut. interr. τί here is asking "why?" Λέγεις, see 12:41 (here "call"). The acc. ἀγαθόν is the complement in a double acc. cstr. The nom. ἀγαθός is the pred. adj. of an implied ἐστίν. For εἰ μή see 4:26 (cf. 5:21). The nom. εἷς is the subj. of an implied ἐστὶν ἀγαθός (BHGNT 574). The nom. ὁ θεός is in appos. to εἷς ("but One—God" HCSB, sim. NKJV; "except God alone" NIV, sim. most EVV; BDAG 292d; ZG 255). For various interpretations of Jesus' response see Bock 1477–78; Fitzmyer 1199. Jesus may be challenging the man's flattery and the integrity of his interest in doing what Jesus teaches about God's will.

18:20 Οἶδας 2nd sg. pf. act. indic. of οἶδα (the acc. pl. fem. τὰς ἐντολάς is the obj.). The following four 2nd sg. aor. act. subjuncs. are prohibitions with μή (perhaps forbidding specific actions [Z §246; ZG 255], though more likely the aor. prohibition views the action as a whole [Huffman, 188]; cf. Exod 20:12–16 and Deut 5:16–20 where οὐ with fut. indics. are used). Μοιχεύσῃς, of μοιχεύω ("commit adultery"). Φονεύσῃς, of φονεύω ("murder"). Κλέψῃς, of κλέπτω ("steal"). Ψευδομαρτυρήσῃς, of ψευδομαρτυρέω ("bear false witness"). Τίμα 2nd sg. pres. act. impv. of τιμάω ("honor").

18:21 The acc. ταῦτα πάντα is the obj. of ἐφύλαξα (1st sg. aor. act. indic. of φυλάσσω, "kept" HCSB, ESV, NIV; "observed" RSV; "to keep a law . . . from being broken" BDAG 1068d; "obey" LN 36.19 [NLT]). Ἐκ in ἐκ νεότητος (gen. sg. fem. of νεότης, -ητος, ἡ) is a "marker denoting temporal sequence" (BDAG 297d–98a; "from" or "since" all EVV; "from my youth up" KJV; cf. MM 424d–25a).

18:22 Ἀκούσας, see 6:49 (temp.; 18:22–24 open with a link that shows each response as directly linked to the preceding statement or action, cf. BHGNT 575). The nom. ἕν is the subj. of λείπει (3rd sg. pres. act. indic. of λείπω, "lack"; impers.; σοι could be a dat. of ref. or disadvantage, R 541; "still one thing is left/lacking for you"; cf. BDF §189[3]; BHGNT 576). Jesus' instructions include two aor. impvs. with a promise and a final pres. impv. (the impvs. function conditionally with the fut. indic., Fantin 362). Πώλησον 2nd sg. aor. act. impv. of πωλέω (with πάντα as the obj.). Ἔχεις, see 12:19 (with ὅσα as the obj.; cf. a sim. cstr. in 18:12). Διάδος 2nd sg. 2nd aor. act. impv. of διαδίδωμι, "distribute" (NKJV, NRSV, HCSB, ESV; "give" NIV; the proceeds from the sale ["the money" NRSV] is the implied obj.; the pl. indir. obj. πτωχοῖς is abs. "the poor," ZG 255). Ἕξεις 2nd sg. fut. act. indic. of ἔχω (with the obj. θησαυρόν ["treasure," see 6:45] either parallel to "eternal life" [Marshall 685; see 12:33] or gifts/rewards that accompany eternal life [Bock 1481; Fitzmyer 1200]). The adv. δεῦρο ("come") functions as an interjection (BDAG 220b) with the following impv. ἀκολούθει (see 5:27;

see refs. at 5:11). The impv. ἀκολούθει shows that the point here is dependent trust in Jesus who is to have priority over everything (cf. 5:11, 28; 14:26–27, 33; 18:28–30).

18:23 Ἀκούσας, see 6:49 (temp.; cf. 18:22). The nom. sg. masc. adj. περίλυπος (of περίλυπος, -ον, "very sad") is pred. Ἐγενήθη 3rd sg. 2nd aor. pass. indic. of dep. γίνομαι. The reason he became very sad is because (γάρ, causal) he was "extremely rich" (ESV; the adj. πλούσιος is pred.; the adv. σφόδρα ["extremely"] is often used with adjs., BDAG 980a).

18:24 The temp. ptc. ἰδών (see 1:12) links the following as a comment on the preceding incident (cf. 18:22). For the probable inclusion of περίλυπον γενόμενον (acc. sg. masc. of aor. mid. ptc. of γίνομαι; the complement in a double acc. cstr., NKJV, HCSB, ESV) see Metzger 143. The interr. πῶς with δυσκόλως is used as an exclamation ("with what difficulty!" ZG 255; see refs. at 12:50). The adv. δυσκόλως ("with difficulty") modifies εἰσπορεύονται (3rd pl. pres. mid. indic. of dep. εἰσπορεύομαι). The pres. may be fut. referring (Robertson, *Pictures* 235; the fut. form of this vb. is not found in the NT, Marshall 687), gnomic (Bock 1485), or highlight the present possibility (Nolland 890). The subst. ptc. οἱ . . . ἔχοντες (see 5:31; with τὰ χρήματα [acc. pl. neut. of χρῆμα, -ατος, τό, "wealth"; cf. Acts 4:37; 8:18, 20; 24:26] as the obj.) is the subj. of εἰσπορεύονται. For τὴν βασιλείαν τοῦ θεοῦ see 4:43 (in this context cf. 18:16–17, and 18:18, 22 [i.e., associated with "eternal life" and "treasure in heaven"]).

18:25 Γάρ is used here as a marker of clarification (BDAG 189d; "Indeed" NRSV, NIV; "In fact" NLT). The comparison introduced by the pred. adj. εὐκοπώτερον (see 5:23) is completed with ἤ ("easier . . . than," BDAG 432d–33a). The acc. sg. masc. κάμηλον (of κάμηλος, -ου, ὁ, "camel"; not a mistaken ref. to "rope," R 192) is the subj. of the inf. εἰσελθεῖν (see 6:6; the inf. clause is the subj. of ἐστίν, BHGNT 577; Burton §§374, 384; R 1058). Τρήματος βελόνης, "eye of a needle" ([τρήματος gen. sg. neut. of τρῆμα, -τος, τό, "opening"]; βελόνης gen. sg. fem. of βελόνη, -ης, ἡ, possibly a sewing needle, LN 6.215; Nolland 892). The saying refers to something very large (the largest animal around; O. Michel, *TDNT* 3.593) and something miniscule (the smallest opening that was used; Bock 1485; Fitzmyer 1204). It is hyperbole for something impossible (see 18:26–27). The acc. sg. masc. (subst.) adj. πλούσιον (of πλούσιος, -α, -ον) is the subj. of the second εἰσελθεῖν.

18:26 The subst. ptc. ἀκούσαντες (see 1:66) is the subj. of εἶπαν. Καί, "then" (NRSV, NASB, HCSB, ESV; "in that case" [NJB] when introducing a question, Z §459; ZG 255). The interr. τίς is the subj. of δύναται (see 3:8). The aor. pass. inf. σωθῆναι (of σῴζω) is complementary (here, in parallel with inheriting "eternal life," having "treasure in heaven," and entering "the kingdom of God"; 18:18, 22, 24–25; cf. 13:23, 29). The question is essentially: "if the rich (who seem to be obviously blessed by God) can not enter, then who can?"

18:27 The subst. nom. pl. neut. adj. ἀδύνατα (of ἀδύνατος, -ον, "the things that are impossible" NASB) is the emphatic subj. of ἐστίν and is balanced with the nom. pl. neut. pred. adj. δυνατά. Παρά may be used as a "marker of one whose viewpoint is relevant, in the sight or judgment of someone" (cf. BHGNT 578, citing BDAG 757b, mng. 2; LN 90.20) or as a marker of personal reference as almost equivalent to the dat. (BDAG 757c, mng. 3; "for" NRSV; as a marker of potential agent, LN 90.3; ZG 255). In the contrast between ἀνθρώποις and τῷ θεῷ, ἀνθρώποις is generic ("people" NASB).

18:28 Ἰδού, see 1:20. Ἀφέντες (see 5:11) is attendant circumstance with ἠκολουθήσαμέν (1st pl. aor. act. indic. of ἀκολουθέω [see 5:11]; the enclitic σοι is the complement), though as a necessary prerequisite to the vb. (i.e., "left . . . to follow" NJB, NIV). The statement parallels the requirement given in 18:22. The acc. pl. neut. obj. (of ἀφέντες) τὰ ἴδια (of ἴδιος, -α, -ον, "our own things") may refer to their homes (NRSV, NASB, ESV) or to their possessions and what belongs to them more generally (cf. HCSB, NIV; BDAG 467c; MM 298c–d; ZG 256).

18:29 For ἀμὴν λέγω ὑμῖν see 4:24. Λέγω ὑμῖν see also 17:34. Ὅτι, recitative. The rel. clause ὅς . . . θεοῦ could be understood as the pred. of ἐστίν (with οὐδείς as the subj.; BHGNT 579). Ἐστίν, however, is probably impers. here and the rel. clause modifies οὐδείς ("there is no one who." NRSV, NASB, HCSB, ESV; BDAG 283b, R 726). Ἀφῆκεν, see 4:39 (ὅς is the subj.; the following accs. οἰκίαν . . . τέκνα are the obj.). In the context of this list of personal relationships, οἰκίαν may refer to "household" or "family" (Marshall 688). The refs. to "wife" and "children" may assume the consequences if one chose to give up the possibility of marriage (Bock 1489; Marshall 688; γονεῖς, see 2:27). Ἕνεκεν (followed by the gen.) is causal (giving the reason for leaving; BDAG 334d).

18:30 The rel. pron. ὅς (paralleling 18:29) is the subj. of ἀπολάβῃ (3rd sg. 2nd aor. act. subjunc. of ἀπολαμβάνω, "get back" NRSV [see refs. at 6:34]; for the compound vb. see Z §132; the acc. pl. neut. adj. πολλαπλασίονα [of πολλαπλασίων, -ον, "many times as much"] is the obj.). The subjunc. with the double neg. οὐχὶ μή is an emphatic negation (with ref. to the fut., Z §444). The temp. ἐν τῷ καιρῷ τούτῳ (perhaps equivalent to ἐν τῷ αἰῶνι τούτῳ, ZG 256; Fitzmyer 1206) modifies πολλαπλασίονα. The temp. ἐν τῷ αἰῶνι τῷ ἐρχομένῳ (the ptc. [see 14:31] is attrib.) modifies (the acc.) ζωὴν αἰώνιον (which is also the obj. of ἀπολάβῃ; more clearly seen in HCSB).
ἀπολάβῃ
    πολλαπλασίονα
        ἐν τῷ καιρῷ τούτῳ
        καὶ ἐν τῷ αἰῶνι τῷ ἐρχομένῳ
    ζωὴν αἰώνιον

Thus, the reward is described in terms of a two-age framework in the center of the chiasm: this age ("many times as much") and the age to come ("eternal life," an inclusio with 18:18).

HOMILETICAL SUGGESTIONS

The Promise of Eternal Life (18:18–30)

1. Is only for those who abandon all self-reliance and follow Jesus (πώλησον καὶ διάδος . . . ἀκολούθει μοι, 18:18–23).

2. Is only received because of God's doing, not ours (δυνατὰ παρὰ τῷ θεῷ, 18:24–27).

3. Is a secure reward that more than compensates for losses in this life (οὐ μὴ ἀπολάβῃ, 18:28–30).

F. HOW TO ENTER THE KINGDOM: PART 2 (18:31–19:44)

This final section of the journey to Jerusalem is characterized by numerous geographical references that conclude this journey (Nolland 898; though he begins this section at 18:35):

ἀναβαίνομεν εἰς Ἰερουσαλήμ (18:31)
ἐγγίζειν . . . εἰς Ἰεριχώ (18:35)
διήρχετο τὴν Ἰεριχώ (19:1)
ἐγγὺς εἶναι Ἰερουσαλήμ (19:11)
ἀναβαίνων εἰς Ἰεροσόλυμα (19:28)
ἤγγισεν εἰς Βηθφαγὴ καὶ Βηθανίαν (19:29)
ἐγγίζοντος . . . πρὸς τῇ καταβάσει τοῦ ὄρους τῶν ἐλαιῶν (19:37)
ὡς ἤγγισεν ἰδὼν τὴν πόλιν (19:41)

Many of the themes from 18:9–30 continue in this section: receiving mercy (18:38–39), being saved (18:42; 19:10), and entry to or exclusion from the kingdom as related to one's response to the king (19:11–27 and 28–44). The emphasis, however, is now more on who Jesus is (suffering Son of Man, Son of David, saving Son of Man, king and Lord) and what he does (mercifully grants spiritual sight, seeks and saves the lost, rewards his servants and judges his enemies). The section begins with Jesus' final and most detailed prediction of the suffering that is ahead for him in Jerusalem (18:31–34; the meaning of which is hidden from the disciples), and it concludes with Jesus' grief over the judgment that lies ahead for Jerusalem (19:41–44; "what would bring peace" is also hidden). The dramatic final statement of this long journey to Jerusalem is that Jerusalem failed to recognize "the time of God's coming."

1. God's Saving Plan Is Accomplished Through the Suffering Son of Man (18:31–34)

18:31 Παραλαβών (see 9:10; for τοὺς δώδεκα see 9:1) is attendant circumstance (with εἶπεν). Ἰδού, see 1:20. Ἀναβαίνομεν 1st pl. pres. act. indic. of ἀναβαίνω (cf. 2:42; 18:10; 19:28). The nom. πάντα γεγραμμένα (nom. pl. neut. of pf. pass. ptc. of γράφω [see 2:23 for the pf.]; the ptc. is subst., cf. refs. at 1:66 for ἀκούσαντες) is the subj. of τελεσθήσεται (3rd sg. fut. pass. indic. of τελέω, "accomplished" NRSV, NASB, HCSB, ESV; "fulfilled" NIV). The pass. γεγραμμένα is a divine pass. followed by διὰ τῶν προφητῶν that expresses intermediate agency (Wallace 434). The pass. τελεσθήσεται is also a divine pass. (Fitzmyer 1209). The pass. vbs. highlight God's plan as well as his carrying out of that plan in and through Jesus' death. Τῷ υἱῷ could modify γεγραμμένα as a dat. of ref. (as the semantic obj., Wallace 146; Bock 1496; as equivalent to περί with the gen., Marshall 690; Nolland 895; cf. 24:44, 46), or τελεσθήσεται perhaps as a dat. of disadvantage (R 539; Robertson, *Pictures* 237; ZG 256; Fitzmyer 1209; cf. 5:24).

18:32 Γάρ is used here as a marker of clarification (BDAG 189d; R 1190). The following four vbs. are all 3rd sg. fut. pass. indic. Παραδοθήσεται, of παραδίδωμι (the agents of this pass. vb. are identified elsewhere in Luke as the Jewish leadership, cf. 9:22, 44; 20:20 [22:4, 6, 21–22, 48]; 23:25; 24:7, 20). The dat. τοῖς ἔθνεσιν identifies the indir. obj. (and the agents of the following actions, Marshall 690). Ἐμπαιχθήσεται, of ἐμπαίζω, "mock" (see 22:63; 23:11, 36; cf. 14:29). Ὑβρισθήσεται, of ὑβρίζω, "insult" (NKJV, NRSV, HCSB, NIV; LN 33.390; or "shamefully treated" RSV, ESV, sim. NASB; LN 88.130; "to treat in an insolent or spiteful manner . . . scoff at, insult" BDAG 1022c). Ἐμπτυσθήσεται, of ἐμπτύω, "spit upon" (onomatopoeic, Bock 1497).

18:33 Μαστιγώσαντες (nom. pl. masc. of aor. act. ptc. of μαστιγόω, "flog"; in this context, "to beat with a whip or lash" as punishment administered to those condemned to death, BDAG 620c; cf. LN 19:9; MM 390c–d) is temp. (HCSB, ESV). Ἀποκτενοῦσιν, see 11:49 (the subj. is "the Gentiles" from 18:32 [Bock 1498; Fitzmyer 1210]; though cf. 20:14–15; Acts 3:15). For τῇ ἡμέρᾳ τῇ τρίτῃ see 9:22. Ἀναστήσεται 3rd sg. fut. mid. indic. of ἀνίστημι (intrans.; cf. 24:7, 46; cf. ἐγείρω in 9:22; 24:6, 34).

18:34 The Twelve's (αὐτοί, see 18:31; unstressed, see 1:17) lack of understanding is emphasized with three statements, each joined with καί (see also 9:45). Συνῆκαν, see 2:50 (the acc. οὐδέν is the obj.; the gen. τούτων is partitive, cf. R 751). Κεκρυμμένον (nom. sg. neut. of pf. pass. ptc. of κρύπτω, "hide"; a divine pass., Bock 1499; cf. 19:42; see παρακαλύπτομαι in 9:45) could be pred. (Wallace 618) or, with ἦν, a pluperfect periph. cstr. (BHGNT 582). Ἐγίνωσκον 3rd pl. impf. act. indic. of γινώσκω (neg. with οὐκ; the impf. may be durative, Robertson, *Pictures* 237). Λεγόμενα acc. pl. neut. of pres. pass. (subst.) ptc. of λέγω ("the things that were said" NASB; "what Jesus meant" NET).

HOMILETICAL SUGGESTIONS

The Death and Resurrection of Christ (18:31–34)

1. Fulfills the sovereign plan of God in Scripture (18:31).
2. Overcomes the worst of human sin (18:32–33).
3. Requires divine enabling to understand its significance (18:34).

2. Spiritual Sight Is Granted by Jesus Through Faith (18:35–43)

18:35 This account describes the fourth and last miracle of the journey to Jerusalem (cf. 13:10–17; 14:1–6; 17:11–19). Ἐγένετο, see 1:5. The pres. act. inf. ἐγγίζειν (of ἐγγίζω; the acc. pron. αὐτόν is the subj.) with ἐν τῷ is temp. Εἰς Ἰεριχώ is locat. (if ἐγγίζειν is understood in a spatial/locational sense, the prep. and vb. may mean "in the vicinity of, near" BDAG 288d–89a; "in the neighborhood of" Z §97; thus, leaving the direction unspecified, cf. 19:29; 24:28; esp. 18:40; Stanley E. Porter, "'In the Vicinity of Jericho': Luke 18:35 in the Light of its Synoptic Parallels," *BBR* 2 [1992]: 91–104). Jericho and Jerusalem have already been linked in Luke's narrative (10:30; see introduction to 18:31 for the increasing geographical refs. as the journey nears Jerusalem). Ἐκάθητο 3rd sg. impf. mid. indic. of dep. κάθημαι (τυφλός τις is the subj.; the adj. is abs. "blind man"). Παρά with the acc. τὴν ὁδόν is "beside the road" (BDAG 757d [mng. C1bα]; ZG 256; see 8:5). Ἐπαιτῶν (nom. sg. masc. of pres. act. ptc. of ἐπαιτέω, "beg") probably expresses manner.

18:36 Ἀκούσας, see 6:49 (temp.). Διαπορευομένου (gen. sg. masc. of pres. mid. ptc. of dep. διαπορεύομαι, "go by") could be attrib. (modifying the obj. gen. ὄχλου), the complement in a double gen. cstr. (BHGNT 583), or a temp. gen. abs. cstr. (Wallace 655). Ἐπυνθάνετο, see form and refs. at 15:26. The nom. sg. neut. interr. τί with the optative εἴη (see 1:29) introduces an indir. question (see refs. at 1:29; 8:9; "what this was" NASB; "what this meant" HCSB, ESV).

18:37 Ἀπήγγειλαν, see 7:18 (an indef. pl., Z §1). Ὅτι could be recitative (most EVV) or introduce indir. discourse ("that"; NKJV, NASB; R 1035). The nom. ὁ Ναζωραῖος is in appos. to Ἰησοῦς. The term is probably a ref. to Jesus' (obscure) place of origin (cf. Acts 2:22; 3:6; 4:10; 6:14; 22:8; [24:5]; 26:9; cf. the adj. in Luke 4:34; 24:19; see refs. to Ναζαρέθ in 1:26; cf. Bock 1506–7; Fitzmyer 1215; Marshall 693; Nolland 899). Παρέρχεται 3rd sg. pres. mid. indic. of παρέρχομαι (the pres. may be retained in indir. discourse, Robertson, *Pictures* 238).

18:38 Ἐβόησεν, see 9:38 (in the near context see 18:7). Υἱέ is voc. in appos. to the voc. Ἰησοῦ (R 464; Wallace 71). For refs. to Δαυίδ see 1:27; 2:4. Ἐλέησόν με, see 16:24 (and the refs. there).

18:39 The subst. ptc. προάγοντες (nom. pl. masc. of pres. act. ptc. of προάγω, "go before," "in front" [i.e., of the crowd] most EVV [as intrans. R 800]; "led the way" NASB, NIV) is the subj. of ἐπετίμων (see 18:15). Ἵνα with the subjunc. σιγήσῃ (3rd sg. aor. act. subjunc. of σιγάω, "be silent"; the aor. may be understood in an ingressive sense here, "become silent"; Robertson, *Pictures* 238; Z §250; ZG 256) could be tr. as introducing indir. discourse ("telling him to be quiet" sim. most EVV; BDAG 476b–c) or as a purpose clause ("to get him to be quiet," NET; BHGNT 584). The cstr. functions as a prohibition ("Stop speaking!" Huffman, 304). The pron. αὐτός is emphatic (see 3:23; cf. 1:17; Nolland 900). The dat. πολλῷ expresses the degree of difference (R 532; Wallace 166–67; with μᾶλλον, "much more"). Ἔκραζεν 3rd sg. impf. act. indic. of κράζω. The shift to ἔκραζεν from ἐβόησεν may reflect a more specific cry (Bock 1509, citing Plummer 431), or it may be a stylistic change (cf. 9:38–39). Ἐλέησόν με, see 16:24 (and the refs. there).

18:40 Σταθείς (see 18:11; "stopped" most EVV) is attendant circumstance with ἐκέλευσεν (3rd sg. aor. act. indic. of κελεύω, "order"). The aor. pass. inf. ἀχθῆναι (of ἄγω) in an inf. of indir. discourse ("ordered . . . to be brought"; with αὐτόν [i.e., "the beggar" NET] as the subj.; "that he be brought" HCSB; an inf. in indir. command, Robertson, *Pictures* 238; Wallace 605). Ἐγγίσαντος (gen. sg. masc. of aor. act. ptc. of ἐγγίζω) with the gen. αὐτοῦ as the subj. is a temp. gen. abs. cstr. (Wallace 655; Z §49). Ἐπηρώτησεν, see 8:30.

18:41 The interr. τί σοι . . . ποιήσω (see 12:17 [deliberative, Burton §171; R 935]; σοι is a dat. of advantage) is the clausal complement of θέλεις (see 9:54; BHGNT 585; with ἵνα implied, Marshall 694; though BDF §465[2] views θέλεις as parenthetical). Κύριε, voc. (see 5:8; 7:6). Ἵνα may be used in an impv. sense ("Let [me see again]" NJB, NRSV, ESV; Z §415), or it may introduce the complement to an implied θέλω ("I want [to see]" HCSB, NIV; Bock 1510; Marshall 694; in place of an inf., Z §406; cf. ZG 257). Ἀναβλέψω 1st sg. aor. act. subjunc. of ἀναβλέπω, "see" (HCSB, NIV), or "see again" (NRSV, sim. NASB, ESV; ZG 257; i.e., implying that he once could see; cf. 4:18; 7:22; used three times in this context, here, 18:42, 43).

18:42 Ἀνάβλεψον 2nd sg. aor. act. impv. of ἀναβλέπω (see 18:41). For ἡ πίστις σου σέσωκέν σε see 7:50.

18:43 Παραχρῆμα, see 1:64. Ἀνέβλεψεν 3rd sg. aor. act. indic. of ἀναβλέπω (see 18:41). For ἠκολούθει αὐτῷ see 5:28 (the impf. is probably ingressive, NASB, HCSB [progressive, Fitzmyer 1217]; see refs. at 5:11; in this context cf. 18:22, 28). Δοξάζων (see 5:25) expresses manner. On δοξάζω in Luke, see 2:20. Refs. to the "people" (λαός, last used in 9:13) will occur repeatedly in the last chapters of Luke (eighteen times between 19:47 and 24:19; cf. "all the people" at 19:48 and 21:38, Nolland 901). Ἰδών, see 1:12 (temp.). Ἔδωκεν, see 6:4 (the sg. πᾶς ὁ λαός is the subj.; αἶνον [acc. sg. masc. of αἶνος, -ου, ὁ, "praise"] is the obj.).

HOMILETICAL SUGGESTIONS

Why We Praise God for Jesus (18:35–43)

1. We praise God for the mercy Jesus provides for us in our desperate plight (τυφλός τις . . . ἐλέησόν με, 18:35–39).
2. We praise God for the sight Jesus provides for us in our blindness (ἀναβλέψω, 18:40–42).
3. We praise God for the powerful saving transformation Jesus works in us through our cries of faith (παραχρῆμα ἀνέβλεψεν . . . ἠκολούθει αὐτῷ, 18:42–43).

3. Jesus Came to Seek and Save the Lost (19:1–10)

Jesus' encounter with Zacchaeus comes at the conclusion of the long journey to Jerusalem (the following parable is transitional) and culminates a series of episodes from 18:9 that highlight entry into the kingdom. Zacchaeus' conversion illustrates the fruit of repentance and faith when someone who is both wealthy (cf. 3:10–12; 19:2; e.g., in contrast to 12:13–21; 16:19–31; esp. 18:18–23) and an outsider (cf. 5:27–32; 19:7) responds to Jesus and enters the kingdom. This is the second event associated with Jericho (18:35; 19:1); both use the terminology of "seeing" (ἀναβλέπω 18:41–43; 19:5; ὁράω 19:3–4, 7) and present the crowd as an obstacle (Fitzmyer 1222; Green 667). Jesus again overcomes someone's inability to "see." The emphasis in this account is that Jesus does what is "impossible with men" but "possible with God" (18:27 HCSB)—he enables a rich man to enter the kingdom of God and "be saved" (cf. 18:25–26; 19:9–10). The initiative of Jesus in finding Zacchaeus and bringing salvation to him illustrates the mission of Jesus and the reason for the journey to Jerusalem (19:10).

19:1 Εἰσελθών (see 1:9) is temp. (modifying διήρχετο [see 5:15]). The impfs. in the first three verses (διήρχετο, 19:1; ἦν, 19:2; ἐζήτει, ἠδύνατο, 19:3) may be to provide background information for the following events (BHGNT 587, though cf. 19:3; ZG 257).

19:2 Καὶ ἰδού, see 1:20. The dat. ὀνόματι is a dat. of ref. (i.e., "by name" ZG 257; see BDF §§160, 197; Z §53). Καλούμενος (nom. sg. masc. of pres. pass. ptc. of καλέω) is attrib. modifying ὀνόματι (i.e., "called by name Zacchaeus" RV, sim. NASB) but is pleonastic (ZG 257; i.e., "named Zacchaeus" most EVV). For καὶ αὐτός, twice in this verse, see 1:17. The first καὶ αὐτός functions as a relative pronoun (R 723–24; Z §455e; "who was a chief tax collector" HCSB). "Tax collectors" and "sinners" are often mentioned together (cf. τελώνης in 5:30; 7:34; 15:1; 18:13). Ἀρχιτελώνης (pred.) nom. sg. masc. of ἀρχιτελώνης, -ου, ὁ, "chief tax collector," perhaps indicates that Zacchaeus was "head of a group of tax-collectors who were responsible for customs dues in the area on goods passing from Peraea into Judaea" (Marshall 696). The term is not found in Greek literature earlier than Luke (BDAG 139b; Fitzmyer 1223) and may simply emphasize that Zacchaeus is "a *chief, rich* tax collector, the sinner supreme" (Nolland [904] citing O'Hanlon). The repetition of καὶ αὐτός (οὗτος in place of αὐτός in some mss. may be to avoid repetition, BHGNT 587) adds to the dramatic effect (ἦν is implied).

19:3 The impf. ἐζήτει (see 9:9) is probably conative ("he was trying to see" NASB, HCSB; Robertson, *Pictures* 239; Wallace, 553). The inf. ἰδεῖν (see 2:26) is complementary. The nom. interr. pron. τίς as the subj. of the subord. clause has become the obj. of the previous vb. ("to see who Jesus was," most EVV; R 423 [on τίς functioning as a rel. pron. see R 738]; cf. also 23:8). The pres. ἐστίν is an example of the pres. being retained in indir. discourse (here, after a vb. of perception, Wallace 537–39; Z §347). Καί ("but") together with the neg. οὐκ and impf. ἠδύνατο (3rd sg. impf. mid. indic. of dep. δύναμαι) contrasts with the impf. of ἐζήτει ("but he was not able," HCSB). Ἀπό is causal ("because of the crowd" NASB, HCSB; "on account of the crowd" NRSV,

ESV; cf. BDAG 106a; R 580; ZG 257; Bock 1517; Fitzmyer 1223; cf. 21:26; 22:45) rather than simply expressing the vantage point (i.e., "from the crowd") from which Zacchaeus was trying to see Jesus (BHGNT 588; though cf. the same phrase in 19:39). Ὅτι introduces an explanatory clause. Ἡλικίᾳ ("in stature," see 2:52) is a dat. of ref. ("small in stature" NASB, ESV; see Z §53). Together with the adj. μικρός the term may refer to age (Green 669–70; see 12:25) or height (i.e., "short" HCSB, NIV; see 2:52). The following actions of climbing up a tree in order to see suggest that height is primarily in view here (BDAG 436a; MM 279a; Robertson, *Pictures* 239; Bock 1517; Bovon 2.597; Fitzmyer 1223; Marshall 696).

19:4 Προδραμών (nom. sg. masc. of 2nd aor. act. ptc. of προτρέχω, "run ahead") is attendant circumstance with ἀνέβη (see 2:4; "he ran ahead and climbed," NRSV, ESV, NIV). Εἰς τὸ ἔμπροσθεν ("to the front"; the adv. with the art. is subst. cf. R 547) is a pleonastic expansion of προδραμών (BDF §484; R 1205; for the vars. see Bock 1524; Nolland 903). Ἐπί is locat. Συκομορέα acc. sg. fem. of συκομορέα, -ας, ἡ, refers to a "sycamore fig tree" (BDAG 955b; LN 3.7; C.–H. Hunzinger, *TDNT* 7.758; cf. 17:6). The purpose of Zacchaeus' run and ascent up the tree is in order that (ἵνα with the subjunc.) he might see (ἴδῃ, see 2:26; cf. 19:3) Jesus (αὐτόν). Ὅτι introduces a causal clause. The demonstrative pron. ἐκείνης may be gen. due to the preposition διά in the verb διέρχεσθαι (R 472, 476), or it could be a gen. of place ("through that way" NASB; see BDF §186[1]; ZG 257; Wallace 124). Robertson (*Pictures* 239; also R 652, 709; T 16) suggests that the fem. is because the fem. noun ὁδός ("way") is understood. The pres. mid. inf. διέρχεσθαι (of dep. διέρχομαι, "pass through") is complementary with ἤμελλεν (which has an irregular augment, ZG 257). The impf. of ἤμελλεν following a causal ὅτι is probably progressive (Wallace 553; "since Jesus was coming that way" NIV).

19:5 Ὡς is temp. ("when"). Ἦλθεν, see 2:27. Ἐπί is locat. Ἀναβλέψας (see 9:16) is attendant circumstance (with εἶπεν). The additional εἶδεν αὐτόν, καί in many mss. (cf. 𝔐; KJV) may be due to scribal expansion (cf. Marshall 697). Ζακχαῖε is voc. of Ζακχαῖος. Σπεύσας (nom. sg. masc. of aor. act. ptc. of σπεύδω, "make haste," "hurry") could be an attendant circumstance ptc. and take on the mood of the 2nd sg. 2nd aor. impv. κατάβηθι (from καταβαίνω, "come/go down") and be tr. "hurry and come down" (NRSV, NASB, HCSB, ESV, sim. NKJV; see Wallace 640–44; Z §262; ZG 257; Nolland 903). It is more likely, however (together with 19:6), to be an adv. ptc. of manner ("come down immediately" NIV, sim. NET; R 1127; Bock 1518). Γάρ introduces the explanation for Jesus' command. The aor. inf. μεῖναι (of μένω, "remain"; "stay" most EVV) is complementary with δεῖ (see 2:49; the acc. με is the subj. of the inf.). The use of σήμερον ("today") and δεῖ accentuates the urgency and the divine plan in Jesus' initiative, deliberate actions, and command to Zacchaeus.

19:6 As with 19:5, σπεύσας is more likely an adv. ptc. of manner ("he came down quickly" [NET, sim. HCSB], rather than "he hurried and came down" [NASB, ESV, sim. NKJV]). The repetition of both σπεύσας and καταβαίνω from 19:5 (κατέβη, see 2:51) highlights the obedient response of Zacchaeus to Jesus' summons. Χαίρων (see

15:5) is also an adv. ptc. of manner modifying ὑπεδέξατο (see 10:38; "welcome," "receive as a guest") so most EVV translate as variations of "he received/welcomed him gladly."

19:7 Ἰδόντες (see 2:17; cf. 19:3–4) is temp. Πάντες is the nom. subj. of διεγόγγυζον (see 15:2), "murmur" (KJV, RSV); "complain" (HCSB); "grumble" (NRSV, NASB, ESV); "mutter" (NIV). The impf. διεγόγγυζον is ingressive (NASB, sim. NRSV, HCSB, NIV). Λέγοντες, see 1:66. Ὅτι, recitative. Παρά with the dat. ἁμαρτωλῷ expresses the idea of "in the presence of" or proximity ("with" KJV, HCSB; BDF §238; R 614; ZG 257; Harris 171). The aor. act. inf. καταλῦσαι (of καταλύω "rest," "find lodging" BDAG 522a) expresses purpose (following εἰσῆλθεν [see 1:40], "he has gone in to be the guest" NRSV, ESV; LN 34.61).

19:8 Σταθείς (see 18:11) is attendant circumstance (with εἶπεν). Although the timing of Zacchaeus' statement is not stated explicitly (e.g., at a meal inside the house or outside before the people, Marshall 697), the account implies that it takes place publicly at about this time at the tree (Robertson, *Pictures* 240; Bock 1519; Fitzmyer 1225). The acc. pl. neut. τά nominalizes the adj. ἡμίσιά (of ἥμισυς, -εια, -υ, "half") and thus the adj. (together with the subst. ptc. ὑπαρχόντων "possessions"; see 8:3) is the dir. obj. of δίδωμι (BHGNT 590; the gender and number of τὰ ἡμίσιά have assimilated to τῶν ὑπαρχόντων; see BDF §164[5]; T 210). The enclitic personal pron. μου (modifying τῶν ὑπαρχόντων) has its accent on the previous word (ἡμίσιά, "half"). The gen. τῶν ὑπαρχόντων is partitive (R 502; Wallace 84–85). Some distinguish between the first use of κύριος by Luke as "the Lord" and the voc. use by Zacchaeus as "sir" (cf. ZG 258; Fitzmyer 202–3, 574, 659). Rowe [150–51], however, notes the frequent juxtaposition of nonvocative and vocative uses of κύριος in Luke as part of the high Christology of Luke (see 5:8 [voc.]; 7:13 [abs.]; cf. 10:39–41). The first-class cond. statement (εἴ plus the indicative; R 1008; Wallace 690–94) in this context likely indicates that the subj. is real (i.e., "if, and I have") and refers to the extent of the extortion rather than cast doubt on the reality of it (Marshall 698). Ἐσυκοφάντησα 1st sg. aor. act. indic. of συκοφαντέω, "extort," "to secure someth. through intimidation" (BDAG 955b; cf. a different use in Luke 3:14). The gen. (of separation) masc. (τινός) and the acc. (direct object) neut. (τι) indefinite prons. together here mean "anything from anyone" (see R 742). The pres. δίδωμι ("I give"; see 4:6) and ἀποδίδωμι (1st sg. pres. act. indic. of ἀποδίδωμι, "I give back"; on the use of ἀπό see Z §132; Harris 67) have been understood as:

1. iter. or customary presents in which Zacchaeus is defending himself against false accusations by referring to his customary conduct (R 880; Fitzmyer 1220–21, 1225; Green 671–72); or
*2. futuristic presents expressing intention or determination ("I will give . . . I will give back" NASB; NLT; sim. HCSB; i.e., "I am determined to give," R 870; T 63; ZG 258; Bovon 2.598–99; Marshall 697–98; Nolland 906; the pres. may highlight the commitment; "here and now I give" NIV).

The following words of Jesus that salvation has come "today" (19:9) and that he has come to save the "lost" (19:10), together with the first-class cond. statement in this verse, indicate that the pres. tenses here more likely show a determination to repay past wrongs (Bock 1520) as evidence of repentance (cf. 3:12–14) than an account of Zacchaeus' customary conduct. Τετραπλοῦν acc. sg. neut. of τετραπλοῦς, -ῆ, -οῦν, "four times," "fourfold," expresses a generosity beyond legal requirements (Lev 6:5; Num 5:6–7 required repayment plus an additional fifth; the fourfold payment required in Exod 22:1 [cf. 2 Sam 12:6] related to stealing livestock).

19:9 Although πρὸς αὐτόν is most likely simply "to him" (most EVV), it is possible that it could be "with regard to him" or "about him" (cf. 20:19; ZG 258; Fitzmyer 1225; Marshall 698; e.g., "Jesus responded, 'Salvation has come'" NLT; ὅτι, recitative). The use of the third person at the end of the verse suggests that although Jesus is responding to Zacchaeus (πρὸς αὐτόν), he intends his remarks for everyone (Bock 1522). The absence of the art. before the nom. subj. σωτηρία (see 1:69; cf. 1:47) is common before abstract nouns (Wallace 249–50). In light of the reference to σώζω in the near context of 18:26 (cf. also 18:14) and Jesus' statement in 19:10 in the immediate context, σωτηρία here refers to Zacchaeus' new status before God rather than his vindication before the crowd (*pace* Green 672). Καθότι is a causal conj. ("because," "for"; R 963; see 1:7) giving the reason for the previous statement concerning the arrival of salvation. Αὐτός is the nom. subj. (υἱός is the pred. nom.), and καί here is "adjunctive" ("he too" or "he also"; "even this tax-collector" Marshall 698; though the use of αὐτός here is probably emphatic, "this man too" NIV). Υἱὸς Ἀβραάμ (gen. of relationship) in this context could be a statement that Zacchaeus is an Israelite despite his occupation (e.g., Bock 1522 ["a purely racial designation"]; Fitzmyer 1226; Marshall 698). It could, however, be a ref. to Zacchaeus as one who has responded in faith to the word of Jesus—a "true" son of Abraham (cf. Luke 3:8; perhaps in parallel with 18:42; cf. also Rom 4:11, 12, 16; Gal 3:7; Ellis 220–21).

19:10 Γάρ introduces the following as a summarizing explanation (BDAG 189d). Placed here at the climactic point in the Lukan narrative (before the transitional parable leading to the entrance into Jerusalem), the statement probably functions as a summarizing explanation not only of the preceding episode but also of the ministry of Jesus in Luke's Gospel. The aor. act. infs. ζητῆσαι (of ζητέω) and σῶσαι (of σώζω) express purpose; this is the mission (ἦλθεν, see 2:27; cf. 1:78; 5:32; 12:51) of "the Son of Man" (the art. probably referring to the "well known" Son of Man of Dan 7:13 [Wallace 225, 240]; see 5:24). Ἀπολωλός (see 15:4) is subst. (on ἀπολωλός as a collective sg. see R 411, 764, 1109). The pf. highlights the state ("that which is lost"). The combination of ζητέω and τὸ ἀπολωλός reflects the description of the divine mission to seek the lost in LXX Ezek 34:16 (τὸ ἀπολωλὸς ζητήσω, cf. also Ezek 34:4, 11, 22; Luke 15:4, 6).

FOR FURTHER STUDY

37. Tax Collectors and Zacchaeus (19:2)

Donahue, J. R. *ABD* 6.337–38.

Hagner, D. A. *ISBE* 742–43.

*Hamm, D. "Luke 19,8 Once Again: Does Zacchaeus Defend or Resolve?" *JBL* 107 (1988): 431–37.

*_____. "Zacchaeus Revisited Once More: A Story of Vindication or Conversion?" *Bib* 72 (1991): 249–52.

Hillyer, N. *NIDNTT* 3.755–59.

Mitchell, A. C. "The Use of συκοφανεῖν in Luke 19,8: Further Evidence for Zacchaeus' Defense." *Bib* 72 (1991): 546–47.

_____. "Zacchaeus Revisited: Luke 19,8 as a Defense." *Bib* 71 (1990): 153–76.

Okorie, A. M. "The Characterization of the Tax Collectors in the Gospel of Luke." *CurTM* 22 (1995): 27–32.

*Schmidt, T. E. *DJG*¹ 804–6.

HOMILETICAL SUGGESTIONS

The Mission of the Son of Man Illustrated (19:1–10)

1. The plight of Zacchaeus (19:1–4)
2. The initiative of Jesus (19:5)
3. The response of Zacchaeus (19:6–8)
4. Jesus' explanation (19:9–10)

4. Jesus Will Reward His Servants and Judge His Enemies at the Consummation of the Kingdom (19:11–27)

This parable is the concluding parable of the preceding journey narrative and also a transition to the coming rejection in Jerusalem. An interim period between Jesus' resurrection and his return is assumed (12:35–48; 17:20–37; 18:1–8), in which faithful service in light of the future is encouraged. The emphasis here, however, lies on the unfaithful "other" (19:20) slave and the judgment of those who refuse the king (for comparison with Matt 25:14–30 see Bock 1527). The parable culminates a series of contrasts (from 18:9) between those who enter the kingdom and those who do not (e.g., 18:14, 17, 23–24, 32, 38–39, 19:6–7). The description of final judgment for the enemies of the kingdom is in keeping with temporal judgment described in 19:43–44 and 21:20–24 as an anticipation of the final judgment (21:25–28, 34–36; cf. 20:43). Although Jesus is about to enter Jerusalem, this does not mean the consummation of the kingdom is about to occur. Furthermore, Jesus' rejection and crucifixion are not a denial of the inauguration of his kingdom (or of final judgment); it is the very means by which this saving rule is established.

19:11 Ἀκουόντων (gen. pl. masc. of pres. act. ptc. of ἀκούω) with the gen. pron. is a temp. gen. abs. cstr. that links the following parable with the preceding teaching of Jesus about his saving purposes (the pres. suggesting that "the preceding sayings are still ringing in their ears" Marshall 703; the antecedent of αὐτῶν is the group in 19:7). Προσθείς (nom. sg. masc. of 2nd aor. act. ptc. of προστίθημι, "add") is attendant circumstance with εἶπεν (with the sense of "he said *further*"; "he went on to tell" NRSV, HCSB, NIV, sim. RSV, ESV; cf. Luke 20:1; Acts 12:3; a Septuagintalism, BDF §§419[4], 435b; R 551, 1127; T 227; Fitzmyer 1234). Two reasons are given for the addition of this parable at this time: (1) "because" (διὰ τό and the inf.; cf. R 1071; Wallace 597) he was (the acc. αὐτόν is the subj. of εἶναι [see 2:4]; on αὐτόν cf. T 148) near Jerusalem (ἐγγύς, adv.; see the introduction to 18:31 and ἐγγίζω in 18:35), and (2) because they thought (i.e., the listening crowd; the acc. αὐτούς is the subj. of the pres. act. inf. δοκεῖν, of δοκέω; ὅτι introduces indir. discourse) the kingdom of God would appear with this imminent arrival in Jerusalem. Παραχρῆμα (see 1:64) together with μέλλει and the complementary pres. pass. inf. ἀναφαίνεσθαι (from ἀναφαίνω act. "bring to light"; pass. "appear" Marshall 703), highlight the heightened expectation at this point (for associations of God's rule with Jerusalem cf. Pss 2:1–7; 110:1–2; Isa 52:7–10).

19:12 The introductory εἶπεν οὖν (the conj. is omitted by NIV) again ties the following parable to the reason just given. The nom. sg. masc. (subst.) adj. εὐγενής, "noble" (of εὐγενής, -ές; cf. Acts 17:11 though in a different sense, Marshall 703; *pace* Garland 759, the term is not from "the perverted standards of this world") modifies ἄνθρωπός τις ("a certain nobleman" NKJV; "a man of noble birth" NIV). For ἄνθρωπός τις see 10:30. The two infs. indicate the purpose (ZG 258) for his departure (ἐπορεύθη, see 1:39) to a far country (εἰς χώραν μακράν, see 15:13). He went in order to receive (λαβεῖν, see 6:34) for himself (refl. pron. dat. of advantage ἑαυτῷ) a kingdom and then to return (aor. act. inf. of ὑποστρέφω, "turn," intrans. "return" ZG 258; though Marshall 703, describes the inf. as "rather loosely added"). The point here is that there will be a gap of some time (in contrast to the "immediately" of 19:11, Fitzmyer 1234; Nolland 914). The combination of λαβεῖν and βασιλείαν ("to receive a kingdom" RSV, NASB) means to be "appointed king" (NIV) and does not necessarily imply a negative acquisition ("take") of royal power (*pace* Garland 760). Jesus' rule comes about "by the path of suffering and death" (Marshall 704).

19:13 Καλέσας (see 7:39) is probably an attendant circumstance ptc. with ἔδωκεν (see 6:4) and εἶπεν ("He called . . . gave . . . and told them" HCSB; or temp. cf. ESV). The king gives to ten of his slaves (δέκα δούλους ἑαυτοῦ) ten minas (δέκα μνᾶς, acc. pl. fem. of μνᾶ, μνᾶς, ἡ)—i.e., one per slave (one mina = 100 drachmas = approximately four months wages if Sabbaths are not included). The 2nd pl. aor. mid. impv. πραγματεύσασθε (of dep. πραγματεύομαι) "do business" (NRSV, NASB), "engage in business" (HCSB, ESV), "trade" (RSV), here means "make a profit" (hence "put this money to work" NIV). Ἐν ᾧ ἔρχομαι, temp., "while I am gone" (NLT; Fitzmyer 1235; Nolland 914; though most EVV "until I come [back]"; Z §99; ZG 258; Bovon 2.613) identifies the period of time for the use of their minas.

19:14 Δέ introduces a contrast between the slaves of 19:13 and the "citizens" of the king ("subjects" HCSB, NIV; οἱ πολῖται [see 15:15] from πολίτης; Nolland 914 suggests therefore that the ref. here is to "some" of his citizens). His citizens are described as hating him (3rd pl. impf. act. indic. of μισέω, "hate"; the impf. may indicate ongoing hatred), and they will be described as the king's enemies in 19:27 (see also 1:71 for μισέω and ἐχθρός). This hatred is expressed in the "delegation" (πρεσβείαν; ZG 258; see 14:32) which they send (3rd pl. 2nd aor. act. indic. of ἀποστέλλω) after him (cf. similarities in Josephus, *Antiquities* 17.299–314). The improper prep. ὀπίσω takes the gen. (hence ὀπίσω αὐτοῦ). Λέγοντες (see 1:66) following ἀποστέλλω expresses purpose (BHGNT 595; "to say" NIV). The delegation is sent in order to state that they do not want (θέλομεν 1st pl. pres. act. indic. of θέλω; the pres. is also progressive, R 879; neg. with οὐ) "this man to rule over us." The aor. act. infin. βασιλεῦσαι (of βασιλεύω, "reign," "rule") is complementary (the acc. τοῦτον is the subj. of the inf.; perhaps ingressive "become king" Z §250; ZG 258). Ἐπί in the context of a vb. denoting rule or power means "over" (BDAG 365d; ZG 258–59).

19:15 Καί ἐγένετο (see 1:5, 23) introduces the events which follow the return of the king. Ἐν τῷ with the 2nd aor. act. inf. ἐπανελθεῖν (of dep. ἐπανέρχομαι, "return") is temp. ("at his return" HCSB; T 145; Z §387–88; ZG 259; see the pres. form of this inf. in 10:35; see 1:8 for the temp. inf. cstr. and 3:21; 11:37 for options for this cstr. with the aor. and other examples in Luke; the acc. pron. αὐτόν is the subj.). Λαβόντα acc. sg. masc. of 2nd aor. act. (temp.) ptc. of λαμβάνω. The acc. case of λαβόντα is to agree with the acc. subj. of the inf. (BHGNT 595). As with 19:12, the combination of λαβεῖν and βασιλείαν means to be "made king" (NIV; "crowned king" NLT). Εἶπεν has the force of "commanded" (RSV) or "ordered" (NRSV, NASB, ESV; ZG 259). He ordered that "these slaves" (the acc. τοὺς δούλους τούτους is the subj. of the pass. inf.)

be "called" (RSV, NASB, ESV) or "summoned" (NRSV, HCSB) to him. The aor. pass. inf. φωνηθῆναι (of φωνέω) is an inf. used in indir. discourse (R 1048). The rel. pron. further defines "these slaves" as those "to whom he had given the money." Δεδώκει 3rd sg. pluperfect act. indic. of δίδωμι. The minas are now described more generally as τὸ ἀργύριον "money" (all EVV; see 9:3). The purpose of this summons (ἵνα with the 3rd sg. 2nd aor. act. subjunc. γνοῖ, of γινώσκω; on the form see R 308) is that the king would know how much they had earned (3rd pl. aor. mid. indic. of dep. διαπραγματεύομαι, "gain by trading," "earn"; see 19:13). Τί could be indef. ("who had gained something") or interr. ("who had gained what," Marshall 705; BDF §95[2]).

19:16 The first (ὁ πρῶτος) slave arrived (παρεγένετο, see 8:19; a "consummative aorist" Wallace 560) and gave his report. Λέγων (see 1:63) is probably a ptc. of manner ("came . . . saying" RSV, NKJV, ESV; cf. 19:18, 20; BHGNT 596–97; though *pace* BHGNT, the use of the ptc. in 19:20 makes it unlikely that the ptc. here is portraying "the slave eagerly announcing his success as he is coming in") than simply attendant circumstance (HCSB, NIV; cf. Wallace 640–45). The slave addresses the king as Lord (voc. κύριε "Lord" KJV, NRSV, ESV; "Master" NKJV, NASB, HCSB; "Sir" NIV). His report is that the Lord's mina (ἡ μνᾶ σου) had made (προσηργάσατο 3rd sg. aor. mid. indic. of dep. προσεργάζομαι, "make more") ten more minas (see 19:13).

19:17 The Lord then praises the slave with an adverb in exclamation (εὖγε, adv. "well done!" "excellent!" [only here in the NT]; cf. εὐγενής in 19:12) and the attrib. voc. adj. ἀγαθὲ δοῦλε (in the anar. first attrib. position, Wallace 310). The reason given for this praise is because (on the location of the causal ὅτι cf. T 345) the slave has been (ἐγένου 2nd sg. 2nd aor. mid. indic. of dep. γίνομαι) faithful (πιστός) with "very little" (ἐλαχίστῳ, superl. adj. of ἐλάσσων, "lesser" [see 12:26; 16:10]; T 31; for the elative, Wallace 303; ἐν is ref.). Then the slave is rewarded with a promotion to share in the kingly authority (cf. 22:30). The 2nd sg. pres. act. impv. ἴσθι from εἰμί "be" is part of a periph. cstr. with ἔχων (see 3:11; Burton §97; R 330, 890; T 89; Wallace 648; Z §360; ZG 259)—with ἐξουσίαν, "have authority" (HCSB; ZG 259 suggests an ingressive mng. here "take authority"). Ἐπάνω here is an improper prep. with the gen. (i.e., "over ten cities" NASB, ESV; BDAG 359c [cf. 10:19]; for ἐπί Z §84; ZG 259).

19:18 Likewise the second slave came (ἦλθεν, see 2:27) and gave his report (λέγων, see 19:16). This time the Lord's mina (ἡ μνᾶ σου, κύριε) has made (ἐποίησέν, see 1:49, here "made") five minas (see 19:13, 16).

19:19 The king's instruction to this slave (dat. τούτῳ) is, "You will be over five cities" (sim. HCSB). Γίνου 2nd sg. pres. mid. impv. of dep. γίνομαι, "be." Ἐπάνω, see 19:17. The account of the second slave is described briefly, in order to move quickly to the last slave, the focus of the parable (the praise and explanation given in 19:17 is likely understood here, Nolland 915).

19:20 The rest of the slaves are skipped over to focus on this final slave (*pace* Nolland [915] who suggests that Luke has forgotten the number is ten; and Marshall [706] who suggests the story must have originally had only three servants). This slave is "the other" (NRSV) or simply "another" (most EVV; on this use of ἕτερος see R 749; Z §153; ZG 259; not necessarily simply "third" *pace* NLT; BDF §306[2]; T 197). This slave came (ἦλθεν, see 2:27) and presented (ἰδού, see 1:20) the Lord's mina (see 19:13) as the one which he has kept hidden away (ἀποκειμένην acc. sg. fem. of pres. pass. ptc. of dep. ἀπόκειμαι, "put away for safe keeping" BDAG 113a; LN 85.53). The combination of εἶχον (1st sg. impf. act. indic. of ἔχω) with the pres. ptc. ἀποκειμένην could be equivalent to an impf. periph. cstr. (R 375; Wallace 647 [possible]). Or, with the acc. rel. pron. ἥν as the direct obj. of εἶχον, the acc. ptc. ἀποκειμένην could be the complement in a double acc. cstr. (BHGNT 598; R 906, 1389; cf. Robertson, *Pictures* 242). The mina was hidden in a σουδάριον (dat. sg. neut. of σουδάριον, -ου, τό, either a facecloth or "handkerchief" NASB, ESV; "piece of cloth" NRSV, NIV; BDAG 934b–c).

19:21 The reason the slave gives for his actions (γάρ) is that he was afraid (ἐφοβούμην 1st sg. impf. mid. indic. of dep. φοβέομαι) of the king. The impf. perhaps indicates continued fear (Robertson, *Pictures* 242). The reason for the slave's fear is because (ὅτι, causal, R 997) the king is (εἶ, see 3:22) a "severe man" (pred. nom). Αὐστηρός nom. sg. masc. of αὐστηρός, -ά, -όν, "austere" (NKJV), "harsh" (NRSV), "exacting" (NASB), "severe" (RSV, ESV), "hard" (NIV), "tough" (HCSB; cf. BDAG 151d). The slave then illustrates this severity by describing the king as one who "takes" (αἴρεις 2nd sg. pres. act. indic. of αἴρω) what he did not place down (ἔθηκας 2nd sg. aor. act. indic. of τίθημι). Money might be in view here too (hence for αἴρω "withdraw" NET; "collect" HCSB; and for τίθημι "deposit" NRSV, HCSB, ESV; "lay down" RSV, NASB; "put in" NIV; "what isn't yours" NLT). Furthermore, the king is described as one who "reaps" (θερίζεις 2nd sg. pres. act. indic. of θερίζω; neg. with οὐκ) what he did not sow (ἔσπειρας 2nd sg. aor. act. indic. σπείρω; neg. with οὐκ). Each rel. clause introduced by the rel. pron. ὅ serves as the obj. of αἴρεις and θερίζεις respectively (cf. BHGNT 599). The slave paints a picture of the king as one who takes from others what he does not work for. Some see this as an accurate picture of a wicked ruler (Garland 761). In light of 19:17 and 19, however, the slave appears to have a wrong understanding of the king (Nolland 916; cf. also 15:29–30).

19:22 In contrast to the commendations and rewards given to the previous slaves, the king's extended response (λέγει is a historical pres. Fitzmyer 1237; Nolland 916) to this slave highlights the judgment the slave will face from the king (κρινῶ 1st sg. fut. act. indic. of κρίνω, "condemn" RSV, NJB, ESV; BDAG 568b–c) on the basis of the slave's own words (ἐκ τοῦ στόματός). The slave is first addressed (voc.) as a "wicked" slave (πονηρὲ δοῦλε, the attrib. adj. contrasts with ἀγαθὲ δοῦλε in 19:17; on the voc. see Wallace 68). The king then repeats the slave's description (ᾔδεις 2nd sg. plupf. act. indic. of οἶδα, with impf. force, ZG 259) of the king (from 19:21) with a change in the first word of each pair from pres. act. indic. to nom. sg. masc. of pres. act. (attrib.) ptcs. (the 2nd sg. aor. ἔθηκας and ἔσπειρας become 1st sg.).

19:23 Καί when introducing a question here has the sense of "then" (most EVV; Z §459; ZG 259). Διὰ τί ("why") introduces the dir. question on the basis of the previous argument of the slave (BDAG 225d). Ἐδωκάς (see 7:44) here has the idea of "deposit"

(NLT; most EVV "put"). As in 19:15, the king's mina is described here as "money" (ἀργύριον, see 9:3). Τράπεζα, "table" (see 16:21), is used here as "banker's table" ("in the bank" most EVV; "put . . . on deposit" NIV; BDAG 1013c; ZG 259). Κἀγώ here uses καί in a "consecutive" or "final" sense "so that" (NIV; Z §455γ; ZG 259). The temp. ἐλθών (see 7:3) is part of a second class ("contrary to fact") cond. clause with ἄν ("when I returned I would have" HCSB; BDF §360[2]; R 922, 1023; Z §313–14; ZG 259). Τόκῳ dat. sg. masc. of τόκος (of τόκος, -ου, ὁ, "interest," ZG 259). The antecedent of the sg. neut. pers. pron. αὐτό is τὸ ἀργύριον. Ἔπραξα 1st sg. aor. act. indic. of πράσσω ("do," "perform") when used in contexts of collecting taxes, duties, and interest is "collect" (most EVV; BDAG 860d). The point is not that the king affirms the servant's characterization (*pace* Garland 762) but that even if the slave thought this he should have at least exerted some effort—even his mistaken view of the king is no excuse (Bock 1539).

19:24 The king then (καί) speaks to those standing nearby (τοῖς παρεστῶσιν is a subst. use of the dat. pl. masc. of 2nd pf. [intrans.] act. ptc. of παρίστημι, "present," "stand by"; i.e., "bystanders" NRSV, NASB). It is possible that these are the other slaves (of 19:13 and 15; Bock 1540) or other lesser servants (Marshall 707), but the designation here suggests perhaps guards or people of the king's court ("attendants" NET; Fitzmyer 1238; Nolland 916). The order is given to "take" (ἄρατε 2nd pl. aor. act. impv. of αἴρω) the mina from him (ἀπ᾽ αὐτοῦ, expressing separation) and give it (δότε, see 9:13) to the one who has ten minas (see 19:13; τῷ . . . ἔχοντι is a subst. ptc. [see 3:11]).

19:25 Those standing by (in the parable, not the audience of Jesus) protest in response to what the king has just said (hence καί is "but" NKJV, HCSB): this slave already has (ἔχει, see 5:24) ten minas.

19:26 Λέγω ὑμῖν, see 17:34 (in the context of the next verse, it is the king in the parable speaking, rather than Jesus offering a concluding summary; though cf. 14:24). Ὅτι, recitative. The king then states the principle behind his actions. As with 19:24, ἔχοντι is subst. (see 3:11; see refs. at 1:66 for ἀκούσαντες). Δοθήσεται (see 6:38) implies that "[more] will be given" (most EVV). But (δέ) from "the one who does not have" (τοῦ μὴ ἔχοντος, gen. sg. masc. of pres. act. ptc. of ἔχω; also subst.) even (καί) what he has (ἔχει, see 5:24) "will be taken away" (ἀρθήσεται, see 8:18 for an explanation of this clause). The acc. sg. neut. rel. pron. ὅ is the direct obj. of ἔχει and the rel. clause serves as the subject of ἀρθήσεται (BHGNT 602). Thus the "other" slave is left with nothing. He has been described as "wicked" and gave evidence of never really knowing the king. Rather than seeing his gift as gracious, he viewed him as hard and unjust. Thus, although this last slave is associated with the king's servants, he is ultimately like those who do not want the king to rule over them (perhaps, with the events in Jerusalem immediately ahead, like Judas).

19:27 With πλήν ("but," "however"; for ἀλλά, ZG 259) the focus shifts back to the king's enemies of 19:14 who do not want him to rule over them (cf. also 20:43). The attrib. adj. ἐχθρός in τοὺς ἐχθρούς μου τούτους is "these enemies of mine" (most EVV).

The attrib. ptc. τοὺς . . . θελήσαντάς (acc. pl. masc. of aor. act. ptc. of θέλω; neg. with μή) further describes these enemies. The inf. βασιλεῦσαι (see 19:14) is complementary. The acc. τοὺς ἐχθρούς μου τούτους is the obj. of the impv. ἀγάγετε (2nd pl. 2nd aor. act. impv. of ἄγω, "lead"; here "bring" all EVV). Κατασφάξατε 2nd pl. aor. act. impv. of κατασφάζω, "slaughter" (NRSV, HCSB, ESV), "kill" (NIV), "execute" (NLT). The judgment of these enemies is to take place in the presence of the king himself (ὧδε . . . ἔμπροσθέν μου; cf. 5:19; 12:8–9; 14:2). In the context of the events about to take place in Jerusalem, this group probably reflects the Jewish leadership. Such judgment from God is not foreign to Luke's Gospel (cf. e.g., 10:12–15; 12:5, 9, 20, 47; 13:28; 16:23–28; 17:26–37; 19:43–44; 20:43; 21:20–24, 34–36; 23:28–31; *pace* Garland 762–63).

HOMILETICAL SUGGESTIONS

As King, Jesus Will Reward His Servants and Judge His Enemies (19:11–27)
1. Jesus became king and he will return (19:11–15).
2. Jesus will reward faithful servants generously (19:13, 15–19).
3. Jesus will judge false servants fairly (19:20–26).
4. Jesus will judge enemies finally (19:27).

5. The Final Approach of the King to Jerusalem and the Announcement of Judgment on Jerusalem (19:28–40, 41–44)

These two accounts are closely connected in describing both the final approach to Jerusalem (19:28–40) and what happens when Jesus sees Jerusalem (19:41–44). Jesus' grief at the judgment to fall on Jerusalem is the climactic end to the journey narrative. The arrival of the king and the judgment on those who do not want this king to rule over them links this approach to Jerusalem to the previous parable (Nolland 910, 921).

19:28 Though some see 19:28 as a conclusion to the previous parable (perhaps as an inclusio with 19:11; Garland 758; Nolland 917), it is probably better seen as a resumption of the travel theme as 19:29 shows (though, as with 19:11, the opening καὶ εἰπὼν ταῦτα maintains the close connection to the previous pericope, Bovon 3.7; Marshall 711). Εἰπών (see 9:22) is temp. (with ἐπορεύετο [see 4:30]; HCSB). The impf. ἐπορεύετο highlights the continuation of the journey (Fitzmyer 1247). The adv. ἔμπροσθεν might mean "ahead" (i.e., continuing the journey, "went on ahead" most EVV; "toward" NLT; BDAG 324b; ZG 260; "forward" Bock 1552) or "in front of" in the sense of "leading the way" (cf. Mark 10:32; Bovon 3.7; Fitzmyer 1247; Marshall 711; Nolland 917). Ἀναβαίνων (nom. sg. masc. of pres. act. ptc. of ἀναβαίνω) is perhaps a ptc. of manner or epex. explaining how he continued his journey (going "up" here refers to the higher elevation of Jerusalem [cf. 2:4, 42]; for the form Ἱεροσόλυμα see 2:22; εἰς is locat.).

19:29 On καὶ ἐγένετο see 1:5, 23. Ὡς is temp. "when" (see 1:23). The vb. ἐγγίζω (here ἤγγισεν, see 7:12; "when he was near" NJB; cstr. with dat. or πρός or εἰς, Z §§51, 97; ZG 260; see 18:35) for the approach to Jerusalem was used in 18:35 and 19:11, and it will be used three times in this final approach (19:29, 37, 41) to heighten the anticipation. Εἰς Βηθφαγὴ καὶ Βηθανία is locat. Καλούμενον (see 6:15) is attrib. ("the mount called [the mount] 'of Olives;'" cf. Zech 14:4–5; Acts 1:12; on the options for accenting Ἐλαιῶν [gen. pl. fem. of ἐλαία, -ας, ἡ] cf. BDAG 313c; BDF §143; R 154, 267, 458–59; Marshall 712). Ἀπέστειλεν, see 7:3.

19:30 Λέγων modifies ἀπέστειλεν in 19:29 ("he sent . . . saying"; a ptc. of means, BHGNT 605). Ὑπάγετε, see 10:3. The adv. κατέναντι (cf. R 644) "opposite" (NKJV; BDAG 530d; LN 83.42) is used here in the sense of the village "ahead of you" (NRSV, HCSB, NIV); "in front of you" (ESV); "that village over there" (NLT). The prep. and rel. pron. ἐν ᾗ are locat. ("in which"). Εἰσπορευόμενοι (see 8:16) is temp. (HCSB, NIV). Εὑρήσετε, see 2:12. Πῶλον acc. sg. masc. of πῶλος, -ου, ὁ, "colt" (i.e., of a donkey; cf. Gen 49:11; Zech 9:9; i.e., not a horse; cf. O. Michel, TDNT 6.959–61; Marshall 712; Nolland 924). Δεδεμένον (acc. sg. masc. of pf. pass. ptc. of dep. δέομαι) could be attrib. or the complement in a double acc. cstr. ("a colt tied" most EVV; BDAG 411d). Ἐκάθισεν, see 4:20 (perhaps the "new colt" [πῶλον νέον] of Zech 9:9 is in view here; cf. also 23:53; Nolland 924–25). Πώποτε adv. "ever," "at any time" (following a neg. ZG 260). The nom. pl. masc. of aor. act. ptc. λύσαντες (of λύω) is an attendant circumstance ptc. (with the impv. ἀγάγετε see 19:27) and takes on the mood of the verb it modifies ("untie it and bring it" most EVV; cf. Wallace 644).

19:31 The following instructions about what to say to anyone who asks them why they are doing this continue the emphasis on Jesus' knowledge of the events to follow and make it less likely that this is a result of a prearrangement Jesus has made (Bock 1555; Fitzmyer 1249; Nolland 924; *pace* Marshall 710, 713). It is also possible that the donkey owners are known to the disciples. Ἐάν and the 3rd. sg. pres. act. subjunc. ἐρωτᾷ of ἐρωτάω is the protasis of a third-class cond. sentence. Λύετε (2nd pl. pres. act. indic. of λύω) with διὰ τί asks "why are you untying it?" The fut. ἐρεῖτε (see 4:23) functions as an impv. (Z §280; ZG 260; Marshall 713 a "polite imperative"). Ὅτι could be causal (NKJV; Marshall 713; Nolland 921), recitative (most EVV; BDF §470[1]; Bovon 3.8; Fitzmyer 1249), or introduce indir. discourse (i.e., "say that"; ZG 260). Ὁ κύριος could be referring to Jesus as "the Master," or, with the wider Lukan usage in mind, "the Lord" (see 7:13). The gen. αὐτοῦ could be:

1. obj. gen. of χρείαν ("The Lord has need of it" most EVV; Fitzmyer 1249; Nolland 925); or
*2. a gen. of poss. of ὁ κύριος ("its Lord"; see οἱ κύριοι αὐτοῦ in 19:33, confirming a poss. gen. here, BHGNT 606; "its (real) owner" Marshall 713; Rowe 161).

Ἔχει, see 5:24. On the possible custom see Bock 1549–50, 1554; Bovon 3.8. The emphasis here, however, is on the authority of Jesus (Nolland 925).

19:32 The nom. pl. masc. of 2nd aor. act. ptc. ἀπελθόντες (of ἀπέρχομαι "depart," "go away") is attendant circumstance (with εὗρον see 2:46; "left and found it" HCSB, sim. ESV). The subj. of this action is the subst. ptc. ἀπεσταλμένοι (nom. pl. masc. of pf. pass. ptc. of ἀποστέλλω, "send," "those who were sent"; Wallace 621). Εἶπεν could be used as a pluperfect here ("had said," Z §290; ZG 260). The emphasis with καθὼς εἶπεν αὐτοῖς is on the development of events according to Jesus' word (and not yet on the disciples' answer according to Jesus' instructions; cf. Matt 21:6; Mark 11:6).

19:33 The gen. abs. cstr. of λυόντων (gen. pl. masc. of pres. act. ptc. of λύω) together with the gen. pron. αὐτῶν is temp. ("As they were untying"). Although οἱ κύριοι refers to the colt's "owners" (all EVV; ZG 260; perhaps a husband and wife, T 22; Bock 1555; Fitzmyer 1250), the term here enables a deliberate play on words.

ὁ κύριος αὐτοῦ (19:31)
οἱ κύριοι αὐτοῦ (19:33)
ὁ κύριος αὐτοῦ (19:34)

As anticipated by Jesus in 19:31, the disciples are asked why they are untying the colt.

19:34 The disciples reply as they were instructed in 19:31. On ὅτι and the gen. pron. αὐτοῦ see 19:31. The parallel with οἱ κύριοι αὐτοῦ in 19:33 suggests that αὐτοῦ here and in 19:31 is poss.

19:35 The two disciples bring (ἤγαγον, see 4:29; trans., R 799) the colt to Jesus. Ἐπιρίψαντες nom. pl. masc. of aor. act. (temp.) ptc. of ἐπιρίπτω, "throw on" (NRSV, HCSB; on the form cf. R 212) with ἐπεβίβασαν (3rd pl. aor. act. indic. of ἐπιβιβάζω, "cause to mount" [i.e., on an animal; BDAG 368b; LN 15.98; Robertson, *Pictures*

244]; "had Jesus get on it"; cf. 1 Kings 1:33). Τὰ ἱμάτια is likely their outer garments ("cloaks" NRSV, ESV, NIV; Bock 1556; see 6:29).

19:36 Πορευομένου (gen. sg. masc. of pres. mid. ptc. of dep. πορεύομαι) with the gen. pron. αὐτοῦ is a temp. gen. abs. cstr. The impf. ὑπεστρώννυον (3rd pl. impf. act. indic. of ὑποστρωννύω, "spread out underneath") highlights the continuous action ("people kept spreading" NRSV; sim. NASB, HCSB; Robertson, *Pictures* 244; Nolland 926; on the form cf. R 318; Z §493; ZG 260). The ref. to disciples in 19:37 indicates that the disciples are involved here too (Bock 1557; Marshall 714). The emphasis here (with royal motifs sim. to 1 Kings 1:33; 2 Kings 9:13; and language reflecting Zech 9:9) is on the royal treatment of Jesus (Pao and Schnabel 354d–55a).

19:37 Ἐγγίζοντος (gen. sg. masc. of pres. act. ptc. of ἐγγίζω; modified by the adv. ἤδη) with the gen. pron. αὐτοῦ is a temp. gen. abs. cstr. ("when he came near" NIV). The dat. sg. fem. καταβάσει (of κατάβασις, -εως, ἡ, "descent") could refer to the slope of the hillside ("near the descent" NKJV, NASB; "at the descent" KJV, RSV; πρός with the dat. is locat. "at" R 623–24; T 274; ZG 260) or the path down the mount (NRSV, HCSB; "the place where the road goes down" NIV). Ἤρξαντο (see 5:21; pl. with the collective nom. ἅπαν τό πλῆθος as the subj.) is followed by the complementary pres. act. inf. αἰνεῖν (of αἰνέω, "praise"; cf. 2:13). Χαίροντες (nom. pl. masc. of pres. act. ptc. of χαίρω, "rejoice"; cf. 2:10) expresses manner ("began to praise God joyfully" NRSV, HCSB). The dat. φωνῇ μεγάλῃ is instr. syntactically but functions as a dat. of manner (cf. 1:42; 4:33; 8:28; 23:46; Acts 7:57, 60; 8:7; BHGNT 608). The disciples were praising God about (περί with gen.) "all the miracles they had seen" (a retrospective look back at Jesus' ministry, Nolland 926; cf. Luke 7:22). The gen. pl. fem. rel. pron. ὧν (of ὅς, ἥ, ὅ) is gen. "by attraction" (Robertson, *Pictures* 245; R 719; Z §16; ZG 260, attracting its gen. from πασῶν . . . δυνάμεων).

19:38 Λέγοντες, see 1:66 (showing how the praising of God in 19:37 is carried out; it is specifically praise for Jesus, Bock 1558; Marshall 715; cf. Ps 118:26 [LXX 117]). Although cited in Luke 13:35, the context of 19:44 and the praise of the disciples rather than the nation show that 19:38 is not the fulfillment of 13:35. Εὐλογημένος (see 1:42) is used as a pred. adj. ("blessed is the one who comes"). The nom. ὁ βασιλεύς is unique to Luke's use of Ps 118 (not found in 13:35; though cf. John 12:13) and is in appos. to ὁ ἐρχόμενος "blessed is the king who comes" (most EVV; Nolland 926; on ὁ ἐρχόμενος see 6:47; cf. also 3:16; 7:19–20; 13:35; Mal 3:1). The reference to ὁ βασιλεύς emphasizes the royal theme here (cf. 1:32; 18:38, 40; Zech 9:9). Ἐν ὀνόματι κυρίου modifies ὁ ἐρχόμενος. Thus, ὁ κύριος (19:31, 34) comes ἐν ὀνόματι κυρίου (cf. 19:44; Rowe 165). The adj. ὑψίστοις is superl. ("in the highest" ESV, NIV; see 1:32; the neut. pl. is "heaven" ZG 260; "highest heaven" NRSV, HCSB). The nom. nouns εἰρήνη and δόξα recall 2:14 and are the subjects of their respective nom. clauses. Peace ἐν οὐρανῷ seems unusual (in contrast to ἐπὶ γῆς in 2:14), and could be:

1. what will be achieved in heaven through Jesus' exaltation (Bovon 3.9; Nolland 927);

2. the gift of peace which is in heaven but which Jesus is now bringing (Fitzmyer 1251); or

*3. together with δόξα they are both ways of ascribing praise to God here; he is the God of peace and glory (cf. Rev 7:10; Bock 1558; Marshall 716).

19:39 Καί introduces a contrast with 19:38 ("but" NLT, NET). In this context ἀπὸ τοῦ ὄχλου may indicate the vantage point from which some of the Pharisees speak (cf. 19:3), or it may be partitive indicating that they are "some in the crowd" (most EVV; see BHGNT 609 citing BDAG 105b). The Pharisees address Jesus, the one whom the disciples have praised as "the king" (19:38), as "teacher" (voc., see 7:40), and instruct him to "rebuke" (ἐπιτίμησον, see 17:3; with dat., LSJ 667a) his disciples. The last interaction between Jesus and the Pharisees was in 17:20 in a discussion about the arrival of the kingdom (cf. 5:17; with dat, LSJ 6672). This is the last reference to the Pharisees in Luke's Gospel; the previous parable should be kept in view (esp. 19:14).

19:40 Although ἀποκριθείς (see 1:19) is pleonastic with εἶπεν (Wallace 625, 650; Z §366) the three vbs. of speaking ("He answered and said, 'I tell you'" RV) accentuate the speech which follows. Ἐάν and the 3rd. pl. fut. act. indic. σιωπήσουσιν (of σιωπάω, "keep silent"; BDAG 925d; on the form cf. R 333) is the protasis of a third-class cond. sentence (i.e., a hypothetical cond. cl.). Although a fut. indic. is sometimes used (Burton §§250, 254; R 1010), a third-class cond. clause is usually followed by a subjunc. (BDF §373[2]; Z §341; hence the less difficult aor. subjunc. in some later mss.). Κράξουσιν 3rd pl. fut. act. indic. of κράζω. On οἱ λίθοι cf. 3:8. The occasion is so momentous that creation would cry out if praise was silenced (Nolland 927).

19:41 Ὡς is temp. with ἤγγισεν (see 7:12; cf. 19:29; "when he drew near" ESV; BDAG 1105d). Ἰδών (see 1:12) could be temp. with ἔκλαυσεν (3rd sg. aor. act. indic. of κλαίω, "weep," BDAG 545d; "when he drew near and saw the city, he wept" ESV, sim. HCSB, NIV) or attendant circumstance (NASB; R 834, T 71–72 call this an ingressive aor. "burst into tears"; on κλαίω cf. 7:13, 38; 8:52; Bovon 3.17). Ἐπί functions here as a "marker of feelings directed toward someone" (BDAG 366c; "over" most EVV; ZG 260). These verses bring a dramatic conclusion to the journey narrative (cf. 2 Kings 8:11–12; Jer 9:1 [8:23 MT], 13:17; Bock 1560; Fitzmyer 1258; Nolland 931). Jesus' grief here must be kept in view for the announcement of judgment that follows (and for 19:27).

19:42 Λέγων, see 1:63 (here with ref. to 19:41, indicating the expression of grief). Ὅτι, recitative. Εἰ introduces a "contrary to fact" second-class cond. (BDF §454[4]; Wallace 695–96; though without ἄν and the apodosis, indicating an unfulfilled cond. "if you had known in this day"; cf. BDF §§359[1], 482; R 1023, 1203; Z §313; ZG 260–61; Bock 1561; Fitzmyer 1258; cf. Isa 48:18). Ἔγνως 2nd sg. 2nd aor. act. indic. of γινώσκω. Although ἐν τῇ ἡμέρᾳ ταύτῃ might refer to the approach to Jerusalem specifically (i.e., contrasting with the praise of the disciples, Nolland 931), the parallel with τὸν καιρὸν τῆς ἐπισκοπῆς σου indicates that response to Jesus' ministry in general is in view (though culminating with the imminent events in Jerusalem; on ἐν with ταύτῃ cf. R 522–23). Καί is ascensive and with σύ here adds emphasis (repeating the subject from ἔγνως "you, even you" NRSV, ESV, NIV; note also the concentration of 2nd pers. prons. in 19:42–44, Bovon 3.16, 17; on the additional particle and pron. in some mss. see Metzger 145). The acc. pl. neut. art. τά is subst. ("the things") and πρός is a "marker of movement or orientation toward someone/something" (BDAG 874a; i.e., "the things that would lead to/bring about peace"; "the way to peace" NLT). Peace, in the wider context of Luke's Gospel, is peace with God (see refs. at 1:79; Bock 1561; Bovon 3.17; Marshall 718; *pace* Garland [773] who sees it as "external concord" with Rome, citing 14:32). The shorter Alexandrian rdg. in ℵ B L Θ which omits σου after εἰρήνην is perhaps the more difficult and thus most likely rdg. in this context with so many 2nd pers. prons. The tr. of νῦν δέ "but now" (all EVV) could be "but as it is" (ZG 261; Marshall 718). The 3rd sg. 2nd aor. pass. indic. ἐκρύβη, of κρύπτω, "hide," refers back to the neut. pl. art. τά (i.e., "what would bring you peace—but now it is hidden from your eyes" HCSB, NIV, sim. NRSV, ESV; cf. ZG 261; on ἐκρύβη ἀπό cf. R 483; on ἐκρύβη as an "effective" or "resultant" aor. cf. R 835). The blindness here is likely due to God's judicial action (Bock 1561; a divine pass. Fitzmyer 1258; i.e., rather than Satan, *pace* Nolland 931; cf. 8:10; 23:34; Acts 3:17; 13:27; Acts 28:26–27; similarly with Jesus' disciples, Luke 9:45; 18:34; 24:16, 31, 45).

19:43 Ὅτι, causal (giving a further explanation for why Jesus weeps over the city), is to be taken with εἰ ἔγνως ("if only you knew . . ., for the consequences . . . are fearful" Marshall 718). Ἥξουσιν, see 13:29 (of ἥκω; on this common phrase of the prophets cf. e.g., Isa 39:6; Jer 7:32; 9:25; on ἥξουσιν as a practical fut. pf. cf. R 907). Καί in this context of the fut. vbs. is "when" (BDF §442[4]; R 1183; Z §455δ; ZG 261; Marshall 718). Παρεμβαλοῦσιν 3rd pl. fut. act. indic. of παρεμβάλλω "set up," "throw up" (BDAG 775a) together with the acc. sg. masc. χάρακά, "stake" (of χάραξ, -ακος, ὁ; the sg. is collective for a wall of stakes, "barricade" ESV; "embankment" HCSB, NIV; BDAG 1078b) and the dat. σοι (a dat. of disadvantage, "against you") is "throw up a barricade against you" (NASB) or "build an embankment against you" (HCSB, NIV). Περικυκλώσουσιν 3rd pl. fut. act. indic. of περικυκλόω, "surround," "encircle" (BDAG 802b–c; R 617). Συνέξουσίν 3rd pl. fut. act. indic. συνέχω, "hem in" (BDAG 971a). The adv. πάντοθεν is "from all sides." The description is of a siege in which the city is entirely surrounded and the enemy is pressing in on the city (Bock 1561–62; reflecting Israel's earlier judgment that led to exile, Garland 774).

19:44 Ἐδαφιοῦσίν 3rd pl. fut. act. indic. of ἐδαφίζω, "dash to the ground" (RSV, NIV); "level to the ground" (NASB); "tear down to the ground" (ESV); "crush" (HCSB). The term (found only here in the NT) in this context refers to the dashing of people to the ground and therefore refers to dead bodies (cf. refs. in Bock 1563; Nolland 932). The ref. to τὰ τέκνα σου probably refers to the city and her citizens (Bock 1563; Bovon 3.18) though such a destruction would include children (cf. refs. in Marshall 719; Nolland 932). Ἐν σοί is locat. ("within your walls" NIV; "within you" most EVV). Ἀφήσουσιν 3rd pl. fut. act. indic. of ἀφίημι, "leave" (the phrase "they will not leave one stone upon another within you" is a ref. to total destruction, cf. 21:6). Ἀντί with the gen. pl. neut. rel. pron. ὧν is a causal expression (lit. "in return for which things"; "because"; T 258;

Wallace 342–43; ZG 261). Jerusalem will face this destruction "because" the people did not "recognize" (NRSV, NASB, HCSB, NIV; Marshall 719; "know" RSV, ESV; with the ethical connotation of commitment, ZG 261; for ἔγνως see 19:42; cf. Acts 13:27) "the time of your visitation" (i.e., Jesus' visitation "is the presence of God," Rowe 166). Ἐπισκοπῆς gen. sg. fem. of ἐπισκοπή, -ῆς, ἡ ("a visitation," "overseeing") might be a "visitation" in judgment (cf. Isa 10:3; LXX Jer 6:15 ἐν καιρῷ ἐπισκοπῆς αὐτῶν). The parallel with 19:42, however, indicates a positive sense of God's saving action (cf. Exod 3:16; 4:31; 13:19; BDAG 379d; H. Beyer, *TDNT* 2.607 §2a; Bock 1563; Marshall 719; Nolland 932; Pao and Schnabel 357a; see ἐπισκέπτομαι and refs. in 1:68), which, if rejected, becomes the basis for judgment (Garland 774). As with 19:42, this is a reference to God's "visitation" in Jesus' ministry generally (culminating with the imminent events in Jerusalem). The gen. with καιρός is "the time when [God] visited you" in which σου is an obj. gen. (BHGNT 613).

FOR FURTHER STUDY

38. The Triumphal Entry

Huffman, D. S. "Receiving Jesus as Messiah King: A Synoptic Study on the Way to Luke's Triumphal Entry Account." *SBJT* 17 (2012): 4–17.
Kinman, B. *Jesus' Entry into Jerusalem: In the Context of Lukan Theology and the Politics of His Day.* Leiden: E. J. Brill, 1995.
_____. "The 'A-Triumphal' Entry (Luke 19:28–48): Historical Backgrounds, Theological Motifs and the Purpose of Luke." *TynBul* 45 (1994): 189–93.
Watts, R. E. *DJG*² 980–85.

HOMILETICAL SUGGESTIONS

The Coming King (19:28–44)

1. Jesus comes in accordance with his authoritative word (19:28–34).
2. Jesus comes in the midst of joyful praise from those who receive him (19:35–40).
3. Jesus comes in anticipation of fearful judgment for those who reject him (19:41–44).

VI. The Lord Accomplishes the Salvation of the Kingdom (19:45–24:53)

A. TESTING AND TEACHING IN THE TEMPLE INCLUDING JUDGMENT ON THE TEMPLE HIERARCHY AND SYSTEM (19:45–21:38)

Following the long journey, this is the first event that happens once Jesus arrives in Jerusalem. The focus on the temple hierarchy and system will remain until 21:38. In Luke's narrative the last time Jesus was in the temple was in Luke 2:46–47 (at the age of twelve). Thus, Luke frames his Gospel narrative with references to the temple. The oracle of judgment against the city in 19:44 indicates that this action in the temple is a pointer to the end of the temple system. It is also an act of purification before Jesus demonstrates that he is the Lord of the temple in his teaching and his conflicts with the temple hierarchy.

1. Judgment and Cleansing of the Temple (19:45–46)

19:45 Καί may be translated "then" to indicate the close connection with the previous verses (NRSV). Εἰσελθών (see 1:9) is temp. Ἱερόν is a ref. to the "temple courts" (NIV; "temple complex" HCSB; i.e., the court of the Gentiles, Bock 1578; Fitzmyer 1267; cf. 2:27). Ἤρξατο, see 4:21. The inf. ἐκβάλλειν (see 11:18) is complementary ("throw out" HCSB; "drive out" NRSV, ESV, NIV). Πωλοῦντας (acc. pl. masc. of pres. act. [subst.] ptc. of πωλέω, "sell") is the obj. of the inf. ("began to throw out those who were selling" HCSB). The only action described is that of Jesus driving people out of the temple.

19:46 Λέγων accompanies the actions of the previous verse and provides an explanation (see 19:42; "manner," BHGNT 614). Γέγραπται, see 2:23. The first part of Jesus' statement cites Isa 56:7. The fut. ἔσται (see 1:14) is probably used here with impv. force (Z §280; ZG 261). The omission of "for all nations" may serve to focus more specifically on the legitimate ("house of prayer") versus the illegitimate ("den of robbers") use of the temple. The nom. pron. ὑμεῖς is placed forward for emphasis ("but you"). The second part of Jesus' statement cites Jer 7:11 from Jeremiah's temple sermon. Ἐποιήσατε 2nd pl. aor. act. indic. of ποιέω. The acc. sg. neut. σπήλαιον (of σπήλαιον, -ου, τό, "cave," "den" all EVV; i.e., "hideout" BDAG 938a) is the complement in the double acc. cstr. (BDAG 840c; R 480; T 246). Λῃστῶν gen. pl. masc. (see 10:30) "robbers" (ESV, NIV), "thieves" (HCSB). In the context of the following temple section (cf. 20:1, 47), this refers to the corrupt temple hierarchy who find a home in the temple system (cf. Jer 7; 2 Chron 7:19–22).

2. Conflict with the Temple Hierarchy and Teaching from the Lord of the Temple (19:47–21:38)

References to Jesus' daily teaching activity in the temple frame this scene in Luke 19:47–21:38 (cf. Acts 2:46–47 and 5:42). The twin themes of Jesus teaching and the plot to kill Jesus orient readers to the nature of the following questions. The conflicts with the Jerusalem hierarchy in Luke 20 focus on the issue of Jesus' authority. The chapter progresses from failed attempts to undermine Jesus' authority to a statement of Jesus' ultimate authority and a condemnation of the authority of the temple leadership.

a. Introductory Frame: Jesus Teaching in the Midst of Murderous Intentions (19:47–48)

19:47 The impf. periph. cstr. (cf. Z §361) of ἦν and διδάσκων (see 4:31) may "summarize subsequent events and draw this scene to a close" (BHGNT 615). However, together with the idiom τὸ καθ᾽ ἡμέραν ("every day"; the acc. art. τό makes the distributive καθ᾽ ἡμέραν an adv. acc.; R 487, 550; ZG 261 calls the art. redundant), the impf. emphasizes repeated activity here (Burton §34; R 888; Wallace 648; Fitzmyer 1270; Marshall 722). The impf. ἐζήτουν (see 5:18) could be progressive (perhaps in parallel to the impf. periph. cstr. "he was teaching . . . [they] were seeking" ESV, sim. HCSB, NIV), ingressive ("began planning" NLT), conative ("trying to seek," Robertson, *Pictures* 247), or *iter. ("kept looking" NRSV; Wallace 547; Fitzmyer 1270). The inf. ἀπολέσαι (see 4:34; "destroy" HCSB, ESV; "kill" NRSV, NIV; "assassinate" NET) is complementary (Wallace 599). The nom. pl. οἱ πρῶτοι ("the leaders" NRSV, NIV; "prominent leaders" NET; "principal men" RSV, ESV; "leading men" NASB) forms part of the subj. of ἐζήτουν (on πρῶτοι cf. Acts 13:50; 17:4; 25:2; 28:7, 17; the καί could be epex., Bovon 3.21).

19:48 Καί is contrastive. The impf. εὕρισκον (3rd pl. imperf. act. indic. of εὑρίσκω) probably emphasizes repeated but unsuccessful attempts ("could not find" HCSB, NIV; cf. Robertson, *Pictures* 247; Bock 1580). The art. τό makes the interr. τί ποιήσωσιν subst. and the obj. of εὕρισκον (ZG 261; an indir. question, R 766; T 182; Marshall 89; see 1:62). The subjunc. ποιήσωσιν (3rd pl. aor. act. subjunc. of ποιέω) is deliberative and highlights the uncertainty of completing the action here ("could not find anything that they might do" NASB; Z §348; ZG 261). The reason for this is "because" (γάρ) all the people "were hanging on" (ἐξεκρέματο 3rd sg. imperf. mid. indic. of ἐκκρεμάννυμι, "hang on," "to pay close attention to someone or something." BDAG 305b; on the form cf. R 317) or "were captivated by" (HCSB) what they were hearing. The gen.

αὐτοῦ is probably an obj. gen. either of the previous verb ("hung upon him" RV) or the following ptc. ("to hear him" KJV). Ἀκούων (see 6:47) could be temp. ("as they were listening to him" BHGNT 616) or manner ("hung upon him, listening" RV; i.e., "hung on his words" NIV, sim. ESV; Burton §444; R 1127; ZG 261). This distinction between the leaders and the people is maintained throughout the following chapters (e.g., 22:2) until 23:13.

b. Jesus Is Questioned About the Source of His Authority (20:1–8)

20:1 Ἐγένετο, see 1:5. Μιᾷ is followed by a partitive gen. (Fitzmyer 121–22; see 5:12, 17). Διδάσκοντος (gen. sg. masc. of pres. act. ptc. of διδάσκω) and εὐαγγελιζομένου (gen. sg. masc. of pres. mid. ptc. of εὐαγγελίζω), with the gen. subj. αὐτοῦ is a temp. gen. abs. cstr. ("as He was teaching . . . and proclaiming the good news" HCSB; on Jesus preaching "the gospel" cf. [2:10]; 4:18, 43; 7:22; 8:1; 16:16; Bock 1584; Nolland 943; *pace* Fitzmyer 148 and Marshall 722 [though cf. 724] who see no preaching of the gospel in this section; Bovon [3.25] suggests that the καί before εὐαγγελιζομένου is epex.). Ἐπέστησαν 3rd pl. 2nd aor. act. indic. of ἐφίστημι, intrans. "stand over," "come upon" ("came up" HCSB, ESV; "confronted" NASB). The subjs. here are the same as 9:22 and, in this context, the same group as 19:47 (Nolland 943).

20:2 Λέγοντες, see 1:66 (with πρός + acc, cf. Fitzmyer 116). Εἰπόν 2nd sg. 2nd aor. act. impv. of λέγω (here, "Tell us," most EVV). Ἐν ποίᾳ ἐξουσίᾳ is instr. ("by what authority"; Z §119; ZG 261). The pres. ποιεῖς (2nd sg. pres. act. indic. of ποιέω) indicates ongoing activity. The antecedent of ταῦτα ("these things") is probably the temple cleansing as well as the ongoing teaching and preaching activity referred to in 20:1 (Marshall 724–25). The subst. ptc. δούς (nom. sg. masc. of 2nd aor. act. ptc. of δίδωμι) is the subj. of ἐστίν (the interr. pron. τίς is pred.). The two questions focus on the issue of "authority" (Fitzmyer 1275) though the first (ἐν ποίᾳ) alludes to the sphere or nature of Jesus' authority (e.g., rabbinic, prophetic, etc, Marshall 724) and the second (τίς) focuses more specifically on the source or person who authorizes Jesus (Bock 1585; Nolland 943; BDAG 844a identifies ποῖος with τίς; cf. 4:6).

20:3 Ἀποκριθείς, see 1:19. Ἐρωτήσω 1st sg. fut. act. indic. of ἐρωτάω. Κἀγώ, "I also" (R 1180; crasis of καὶ ἐγώ). Λόγον here has the sense of "something" ("one thing" NKJV; "a question" most EVV; BDAG 599b; ZG 261; on counter questions cf. Marshall 725). Εἴπατέ μοι (see 10:10, "you tell me") counters εἰπὸν ἡμῖν of 20:2.

20:4 Τὸ βάπτισμα (see 3:3) is the nom. subj. of ἦν (the gen. Ἰωάννου is subj.; cf. 1:76; 3:22; 7:29–30). Ἐξ οὐρανοῦ ("from heaven") is a circumlocution for "from God" (ZG 261; Fitzmyer 1275; referring to the source; in this contrast, ἀνθρώπων is used generically; "people" NET; "human origin" NRSV, NIV; cf. 16:15; 18:27).

20:5 Συνελογίσαντο 3rd pl. aor. mid. indic. of dep. συλλογίζομαι "reasoned" (NKJV, NASB; BDAG 956a; Marshall 725); "discussed" (most EVV; the aor. may be ingressive, BDF §331; Fitzmyer 1275). Πρὸς ἑαυτούς is "with one another" (ESV), "among themselves" (HCSB, NIV; ZG 261) in which the refl. pron. is functioning as a reciprocal pron. (BHGNT 618; Wallace 418). Λέγοντες, see 1:66. Ὅτι, recitative. The following subjuncs. εἴπωμεν (see 9:54) with ἐάν in 20:5b and 20:6a are two third-class cond. clauses that express their dilemma and confirm their unwillingness to state the truth (Z §320; Robertson, *Pictures* 249; thus with no indication of preference, Bock 1587). On the fut. ἐρεῖ see 12:10. Διὰ τί is causal ("because of what"; "why"). Ἐπιστεύσατε 2nd pl. aor. act. indic. of πιστεύω (neg. with οὐκ; the dat. αὐτῷ is complementary, BDAG 816d).

20:6 On ἐάν εἴπωμεν see 20:5. Καταλιθάσει 3rd sg. fut. act. indic. of καταλιθάζω (with ἡμᾶς) "stone us" (most EVV; "stone us to death" NASB; BDAG 521b). Πεπεισμένος nom. sg. masc. of pf. pass. ptc. of πείθω ("persuaded" NIV; "convinced" most EVV; ZG 262) with ἐστίν is periph. with the pf. indicating a settled state or conviction (Burton §84; Robertson, *Pictures* 250; Wallace 649). The inf. εἶναι (see 2:4) is used in indir. speech (Robertson, *Pictures* 250). The acc. Ἰωάννην is the subj. and προφήτην the pred. of the equative inf. (Wallace 192, 195; cf. also 1:76; 7:26–30; cf. below, 20:10–12).

20:7 Ἀπεκρίθησαν 3rd pl. aor. pass. indic. of dep. ἀποκρίνομαι, "answer" (i.e., the deliberation is over). The pf. act. inf. εἰδέναι (of οἶδα; neg. with μή) is used in indir. speech ("they answered that they did not know" HCSB, ESV; R 1036; Nolland 944). Πόθεν, "whence"; "where it came from" (ESV; an interr. adv.).

20:8 For the prep. phrase after the neg. adv. οὐδέ see 20:2 (λέγω, may be fut. referring [see δίδωμι and ἀποδίδωμι in 19:8]). Ποιῶ 1st sg. pres. act. indic. of ποιέω.

HOMILETICAL SUGGESTIONS

How Jesus Faced Hostile Questioners (19:47–20:8)
1. He continued to present the gospel (19:47–20:1).
2. He raised further questions for self-evaluation (20:2–7).
3. He withheld answers to allow for the evidence already given to be considered (20:8).

c. The Source of Jesus' Authority Illustrated (20:9–19)

This parable covers the whole history of Israel and focuses on the issue of who has the legitimate authority over God's people (20:2). Although the parable is told to the people (20:9), it is directed against the leaders (20:19) who are the tenant farmers and are distinguished from the people (20:16, 19; cf. 11:52; their responsibility will be taken away, cf. 22:28–30; Acts 1:1–11). Jesus, as "the Son," is distinguished from the servants sent by the owner of the vineyard (20:13–14).

20:9 The inf. λέγειν (see 3:8) is complementary with ἤρξατο (see 4:21; a "formula of transition" ZG 262). Πρὸς τὸν λαόν connects the parable to 19:48; 20:1 (Nolland 950). For ἄνθρωπός τις see 10:30. Ἐφύτευσεν 3rd sg. aor. act. indic. of φυτεύω "plant" (ἀμπελῶνα, "vineyard," is the obj.; the term occurs six times in 20:9–16; see 13:6). Ἐξέδετο 3rd sg. 2nd aor. mid. indic. of ἐκδίδωμι "leased" (HCSB) "rented it out" (NASB; cf. BDAG 300c–d; MM 192; Bovon 3.38–39; on the form cf. BDF §94[1]; R 308). The mid. voice may emphasize the subj. of the action (i.e., "for himself"; ZG 262; Marshall 728). The acc. sg. masc. pron. αὐτόν (of αὐτός, -ή, -ό, the antecedent is ἀμπελῶνα [see 13:6; cf. 20:10–16]) is the obj. of ἐξέδετο. The dat. pl. masc. γεωργοῖς (of γεωργός, -οῦ, ὁ, "tenant farmers" HCSB; BDAG 196a; cf. 20:10, 14, 16) is the indir. obj. of ἐξέδετο. Ἀπεδήμησεν (see 15:13) "went away" (HCSB; an ingressive aor. Z §250; ZG 262). The acc. χρόνους ἱκανούς ("a long time" most EVV) is an acc. for the extent of time (R 470; ZG 262).

20:10 The dat. of time καιρῷ means "at the appropriate time" (BDAG 497d; i.e., "at harvest time" HCSB; cf. BDF §200; R 522; Wallace 157; ZG 262; Bovon 3.39; Fitzmyer 1283; see καιρός in 19:44). For ἀπέστειλεν (of ἀποστέλλω) see 7:3. The fut. indic. δώσουσιν (see 6:38) with ἵνα indicates the purpose for sending the slave (δοῦλον is the obj.) to the farmers (BDF §369[2]; Burton §§198–99; R 872, 984; Bock 1597). On the pattern of God sending servants to Israel see 11:47–51 (in this context cf. 20:4–7). The fut. indicates expectation (Z §340). The prep. phrase ἀπὸ τοῦ καρποῦ τοῦ ἀμπελῶνος either (BHGNT 621):

1. leaves implicit the dir. object (e.g., "*his share* of the produce of the vineyard" NRSV); or
*2. is partitive (e.g., "some fruit from the vineyard" HCSB; R 519; Fitzmyer 1283).

Instead, the farmers "sent him away" (ἐξαπέστειλαν 3rd pl. aor. act. indic. of ἐξαποστέλλω) "empty" (i.e., "empty-handed" most EVV; Bovon 3.36; the acc. sg. adj. κενόν [see 1:53] is the complement with αὐτόν in a double acc. cstr.; BDAG 346a; cf. Wallace 186). The aor. ptc. δείραντες (nom. pl. masc. of aor. act. ptc. of δέρω, "beat"), following the aor. ἐξαπέστειλαν, is probably temp. ("after beating him they sent him"; the variation in word order in some mss. does not affect the mng.).

20:11 Προσέθετο 3rd sg. aor. mid. indic. of προστίθημι, "add," is used with the sense of "again" or "in addition" (BDAG 885d; BDF §435; R 551, 1078 [a Heb.]; ZG 262; Bovon 3.39; Fitzmyer 1284; see 19:11). On ἕτερον see refs. in 19:20 (here used for the second slave, R 748). The aor. act. infin. πέμψαι (of πέμπω) is complementary to προσέθετο ("he proceeded to send" NASB). The acc. κἀκεῖνον ("that one also"; see 11:7) is the dir. obj. of ἐξαπέστειλαν (see 20:10). The two aor. ptcs. δείραντες (see 20:10) and ἀτιμάσαντες (nom. pl. masc. of aor. act. ptc. of ἀτιμάζω, "insulted" NRSV; "treated . . . shamefully" NASB, HCSB, ESV, NIV; cf. BDAG 148d; LN 88.127) are temp.

20:12 On προσέθετο and πέμψαι see 20:11. They "wounded" (τραυματίσαντες nom. pl. masc. of aor. act. ptc. of τραυματίζω; also temp.; Fitzmyer 1284) this slave, and then "threw him out" (ἐξέβαλον, see 4:29). Καί, "also" (cf. κἀκεῖνον in 20:11), may downplay any sense of escalation until the sending of the son in 20:13 (Nolland 951). The addition of ἀτιμάσαντες in 20:11 (from 20:10), however, does indicate an intensification in opposition (Bock 1599).

20:13 Ὁ κύριος here is "owner" (most EVV; cf. LXX Isa 5:7). For soliloquies in Luke see 12:17 (cf. Fitzmyer 1284; Nolland 951). Ποιήσω could be either 1st sg. fut. act. indic. or 1st. sg. aor. act. subjunc. (of ποιέω). Both forms could be used in deliberative questions (see 12:17 and 20:15 below; Robertson, *Pictures* 250; Z §341; ZG 262). The emphasis is on the owner's patience, planning, and deliberation. Πέμψω 1st sg. fut. act. indic. of πέμπω. The acc. phrase τὸν υἱόν μου τὸν ἀγαπητόν (attrib. adj.) is the dir. obj. of πέμψω (on the second art. cf. BDF §270[1]; Bovon 3.40; on Jesus' unique relationship with God as Son, see refs. at 1:32; cf. 3:22; 9:35). The adv. ἴσως is "perhaps" (most EVV; expressing the hope for a different outcome, BDAG 484d). Ἐντραπήσονται 3rd pl. 2nd fut. pass. of ἐντρέπω, "respect" (most EVV; see 18:2; here, on the basis of status, LN 87.11).

20:14 Ἰδόντες, see 2:17 (temp., HCSB; αὐτόν is the obj.). The impf. διελογίζοντο (3rd pl. impf. mid. indic. of dep. διαλογίζομαι, "reasoned" NASB; "discussed" HCSB) may be impf. to introduce the following dir. speech (Z §272) or ingressive ("began to discuss"). Λέγοντες, see 1:66. Κληρονόμος nom. sg. masc. of κληρονόμος, -ου, ὁ, "heir" (pred. of ἐστίν). Ἀποκτείνωμεν (1st pl. aor. act. subjunc. of ἀποκτείνω) is a hortatory subjunc. ("let us kill"; ZG 262). The subjunc. γένηται (see 1:20) with ἵνα expresses purpose. Κληρονομία, "inheritance" [see 12:13], is the subj. of γένηται (perhaps assuming that the owner's absence is permanent, Nolland 954). The pron. ἡμῶν is a pred. gen. of poss. (R 497; Bock 1600).

20:15 Ἐκβαλόντες (nom. pl. masc. of 2nd aor. act. ptc. of ἐκβάλλω) could be temp. or attendant circumstance with ἀπέκτειναν ("they threw him out . . . and killed him"; see 11:47). On ἔξω with gen. for ἐκ cf. Z §84. The interr. τί introduces a rhetorical question that is answered in 20:16. Ὁ κύριος τοῦ ἀμπελῶνος is the subj. of the (deliberative, R 875) fut. ποιήσει (see 18:18).

20:16 Ἐλεύσεται 3rd sg. fut. mid. indic. of dep. ἔρχομαι. Ἀπολέσει, see 9:24 (here, "destroy" most EVV). Γεωργούς, see 20:9. Δώσει, see 1:32. Ἀκούσαντες, see 1:66 (temp.; HCSB, ESV). The subjs. are "the people" (20:9) who are listening to the parable and react to the sequence of events. This is the only occurrence of μὴ γένοιτο in the

NT outside of Paul's letters (for γένοιτο see 1:38; "may it never be" NASB; an optative of wishing, Burton §§175–77; R 939; Wallace 482).

20:17 Ἐμβλέψας (nom. sg. masc. of aor. act. ptc. of ἐμβλέπω, "look at") is probably attendant circumstance (with εἶπεν). Γεγραμμένον (see 4:17) is attrib. modifying τοῦτο (i.e., "what, then, is [the meaning of] this that is written"; ἐστίν has the sense of "mean" ZG 262; a citation from Ps 118:22 [LXX 117:22]; cf. also Luke 19:38). The acc. λίθον is the topic of what follows but is acc. by "inverse relative attraction" where an antecedent is put into the case of the following rel. pron. (BDF §295; BHGNT 625; R 718; Z §19; Marshall 732). Ἀπεδοκίμασαν 3rd pl. aor. act. indic. of ἀποδοκιμάζω "reject" (cf. 9:22; 17:25). The subst. ptc. οἰκοδομοῦντες (nom. pl. masc. of pres. act. ptc. of οἰκοδομέω "build") is the subj. of ἀποδοκιμάζω. For ἐγενήθη see 18:23. Εἰς with the acc. (κεφαλήν; with the gen. sg. fem. γωνίας of γωνία, -ας, ἡ, ["corner"], lit. "head of the corner" RSV) is used in place of a predicate nom. (following γίνομαι, Wallace 47; Z §32). The whole prep. phrase means "has become the cornerstone" (HCSB, ESV, NIV; not capstone, cf. BDAG 209d, 542b; Bock 1603; Fitzmyer 1282; Pao and Schnabel 364c).

20:18 Πεσών (see 5:12; subst.; the art. aor. ptc. is used generically, Wallace 230, 615) is the subj. of συνθλασθήσεται (3rd sg. fut. pass. indic. of συνθλάω, "broken to pieces" most EVV; "crush" BDAG 972a; of divine punishment MM 607d; cf. Isa 8:14–15). The whole phrase ἐφ' ὃν δ' ἂν "on whomever" (NASB) is resumed with the pron. αὐτόν (BHGNT 626). Πέσῃ 3rd sg. 2nd aor. act. subjunc. (with ἂν) of πίπτω. Λικμήσει 3rd sg. fut. act. indic. of λικμάω "crush" ("it will grind him to powder!" HCSB; BDAG 596b; LSJ 1050a; MM 376a–b; cf. Dan 2:34–35, 40; 44–45).

20:19 Ἐζήτησαν 3rd pl. aor. act. indic. of ζητέω. The 2nd aor. act. inf. ἐπιβαλεῖν (of ἐπιβάλλω, "lay on") is complementary with ἐζήτησαν (cf. 22:53). Καί (before ἐφοβήθησαν [see 2:9]) is adversative (R 1183; Z §455β). Γάρ, causal (giving the reason for their anger, Robertson, *Pictures* 251; i.e., qualifying ἐζήτησαν not ἐφοβήθησαν, Marshall 732). On ἔγνωσαν see 2:43. Πρὸς αὐτούς means "with respect to them" (i.e., "against them" all EVV; BDAG 875a; BDF §239[6]; R 626; ZG 263; Bovon 3.44; Fitzmyer 1287; εἶπεν is used here in indir. speech; Z §346).

HOMILETICAL SUGGESTIONS
The Murder of God's Son (20:9–19)
1. The patience of the Father illustrated: finally the Son is sent (20:9–13)
2. The judgment of the Father illustrated: fitting punishment for rejecting the Son (20:14–16)
3. The significance of the Son applied: facing the consequences (20:17–19)

d. Jesus Is Questioned About the Authority of Caesar (20:20–26)

In their attempts to trap Jesus, this time the leaders send spies to trick Jesus into either siding with the Roman emperor (and implicitly pitting him against the Jewish people) or opposing the Roman emperor (and implicitly putting himself at risk).

20:20 Παρατηρήσαντες nom. pl. masc. of aor. act. ptc. of παρατηρέω "watch closely" (in a pejorative sense "lie in wait for"; BDAG 771d; Fitzmyer 1294; the subj. of the clause continues from 20:19) may imply the obj. "him" ("they watched him" NRSV, NASB, ESV, NIV) or the implied obj. might be "watching for their opportunity" (NLT, sim. NJB; Robertson, *Pictures* 252; ZG 263). It is perhaps best left unexpressed as "they watched closely" (HCSB). The ptc. is attendant circumstance (with ἀπέστειλαν see 19:14; ZG 263). The acc. pl. masc. adj. ἐγκαθέτους, of ἐγκάθετος, -ον, "hired to lie in wait," is the obj. of ἀπέστειλαν and is subst. ("spies" all EVV; BDAG 272c; cf. LXX Job 19:12; 31:9). Ὑποκρινομένους (acc. pl. masc. of pres. mid. ptc. of dep. ὑποκρίνομαι, "pretend") is attrib. with ἐγκαθέτους "spies who pretended." Ἑαυτούς is the acc. subj. of the complementary inf. εἶναι (see 2:4; or an inf. of indir. discourse, R 481, 1036). Δικαίους is the pred. acc. of εἶναι (BDF §157[2]; 397[2]; on the refl. pron. cf. BDF §406[1]; on false righteousness in Luke see refs. at 10:29). The subjunc. ἐπιλάβωνται, 3rd pl. 2nd aor. mid. subjunc. of dep. ἐπιλαμβάνομαι, "take hold of" (RSV); "catch" (HCSB, ESV); "take advantage of" (NET; cf. BDAG 374b; BDF §170[2]) with ἵνα expresses purpose. The subj. gen. αὐτοῦ modifies the obj. gen. λόγου ("his word"; i.e., "him in something he said" ESV; cf. BDAG 599b; R 508; ZG 263; see 20:26). The 2nd aor. act. inf. παραδοῦναι (of παραδίδωμι, "hand over") with ὥστε may express result (BHGNT 629; Fitzmyer 1295) or purpose (R 990, 1089; Wallace 591; Bovon 3.52; Marshall 734; Nolland 956; "intended result" BDF §391[3]; Burton §371; cf. Z §352). The dat. τῇ ἀρχῇ καὶ τῇ ἐξουσίᾳ is the indir. obj. of παραδοῦναι ("to the rule and the authority" NASB; a hendiadys "authoritative jurisdiction" Garland 800; cf. LN 37.36; Bovon 3.53 connects the use of ἐξουσία here to 22:53). The gen. (sg. masc.) τοῦ ἡγεμόνος (of ἡγεμών, -όνος, ὁ) is subj. ("the governor's rule and authority" HCSB).

20:21 Ἐπηρώτησαν 3rd pl. aor. act. indic. of ἐπερωτάω, "asked" (ESV; "questioned" HCSB, NIV). Λέγοντες, see 1:66. Διδάσκαλε, voc. (see 7:40). Οἴδαμεν 1st pl. pf. act. indic. of οἶδα. The adv. ὀρθῶς ("correctly" HCSB; "rightly" ESV) modifies λέγεις (see 12:41) and διδάσκεις (2nd sg. pres. act. indic. of διδάσκω). Λαμβάνεις (2nd sg. pres. act. indic. of λαμβάνω; neg. with οὐ) with πρόσωπον (lit. "receive a face") is an idiom mng. "show partiality" (HCSB, NIV; ZG 263; Fitzmyer 115, 1295; Nolland 958). On τὴν ὁδόν τοῦ θεοῦ cf. Deut 8:6; 10:12–13; Pss 27:11; 119:15; Acts 18:25–26; 19:9; 22:4; 24:14. Ἐπ' ἀληθείας is "on the basis of truth" or "in accordance with the truth" (NIV; "truthfully" HCSB; BDAG 365c). The reference to Jesus' teaching as accurate, uncompromising, and truthful is meant by the spies to be disarming (Nolland 958).

20:22 For ἔξεστιν see 6:2 (here, "loyal to God" Nolland 958; for ἔξεστιν with an inf. and acc. cf. BDF §409[3]; ZG 263). The dat. Καίσαρι "Caesar" ("the emperor" NRSV; also 20:24) and the acc. φόρον is the dir. obj. of the complementary inf. δοῦναι (see 1:73; the inf. could also be viewed as the subj., Burton §384; Wallace 601). Φόρον acc.

sg. masc. of φόρος, -ου, ὁ, "taxes" (NRSV, HCSB, NIV; "tribute" ESV; "tribute tax" NET) refers to a land or poll tax paid to a foreign ruler (BDAG 1064a; LN 57.182; K Weiss, *TDNT* 9.81; Bovon 3.53; cf. also 2:1–7; 23:2).

20:23 Κατανοήσας (nom. sg. masc. of aor. act. ptc. of κατανοέω, "detected" NASB; "perceived" ESV; "saw through" NIV; BDAG 522d) could be attendant circumstance with εἶπεν ("he perceived . . . and said" ESV), temp. ("after perceiving . . . he said"), or *causal (cf. "detecting . . . He said" HCSB). The obj. of κατανοήσας is πανουργίαν (acc. sg. fem. of πανουργία, -ας, ἡ, "craftiness" HCSB, ESV; BDAG 754b; "deceit" NET).

20:24 Δείξατέ 2nd pl. aor. act. imp. of δείκνυμι, "show" (followed by the enclitic μοι as the indir. obj.). Δηνάριον, see 7:41. The gen. interr. pron. τίνος is poss. ("whose"). Ἔχει, see 5:24. Εἰκόνα is "image" (HCSB, NIV; cf. LXX Gen 1:26; "likeness" NASB; ESV). Ἐπιγραφήν acc. sg. fem. of ἐπιγραφή, -ῆς, ἡ, "inscription" (HCSB, ESV, NIV; "title" NRSV). On the image of Tiberius and the inscription on a denarius cf. Bock 1612; Fitzmyer 1296; Marshall 735–36.

20:25 The conj. τοίνυν, "accordingly" ("then" most EVV), is stronger than οὖν (BDF §451[3]; ZG 263; an "emphatic marker of result, often associated with exhortation" LN 89.51; LSJ 1801d). The impv. ἀπόδοτε (2nd pl. 2nd aor. act. impv. of ἀποδίδωμι) could be tr. "give" (NRSV; cf. "render" NKJV, NASB, ESV; "pay" NJB; Marshall 736) or *"give back" (HCSB, NIV; Z §132; Bock 1613; Bovon 3.54; cf. e.g., 4:20; 7:42; 9:42; 19:8). The poss. gen. Καίσαρος with the acc. pl. neut. art. τά ("the things that are Caesar's"; ZG 263) is the dir. obj. of ἀπόδοτε (the dat. Καίσαρι is the indir. obj.; so also with τὰ τοῦ θεοῦ τῷ θεῷ). Jesus' answer is essentially "give back to Caesar what belongs to him." The implication, however, is that (as bearers of God's image, Fitzmyer 1293) we owe our ultimate allegiance to God (for a brief summary of views see Fitzmyer 1291–94; Nolland 959–61).

20:26 For ἴσχυσαν (neg. with οὐκ) see 14:6. The 2nd aor. mid. inf. ἐπιλαβέσθαι (of dep. ἐπιλαμβάνομαι, "to catch"; cf. 20:20) is complementary with ἴσχυσαν. The subj. gen. αὐτοῦ modifies ῥήματος (see 20:20). The prep. ἐναντίον "before," "in the sight of" takes the gen. ("in the presence of the people" ESV; "in public" HCSB, NIV). Θαυμάσαντες (nom. pl. masc. of aor. act. ptc. of θαυμάζω) is probably causal here with the (ingressive) ἐσίγησαν (see 9:36; "being amazed . . . they became silent" NRSV, HCSB; ZG 264; Robertson, *Pictures* 253). Ἐπὶ τῇ ἀποκρίσει is also causal (dat. sg. fem., see 2:47; "stunned by his answer" NET; cf. BDAG 365a).

FOR FURTHER STUDY

39. Rome and Caesar in Luke's Gospel (20:22–25)

Ball, D. T. "What Jesus Really Meant by 'Render unto Caesar.'" *BibRev* 19.2 (2003): 14–17, 52.

Bryan, C. *Render to Caesar: Jesus, the Early Church, and the Roman Superpower.* Oxford: Oxford University Press, 2005.

Cassidy, R. J. *Jesus, Politics, and Society: A Study of Luke's Gospel.* Maryknoll: Orbis, 1978.

Giblin, C. H. "'The Things of God' in the Question concerning Tribute to Caesar (Lk 20:25; Mk 12:17; Mt 22:21)." *CBQ* 33 (1971): 510–27.

Kim, S. *Christ and Caesar: The Gospel and the Roman Empire in the Writings of Paul and Luke.* Grand Rapids: Brazos, 2009.

Oakes, P. *DJG*[2] 810–19.

Pinter, D. "The Gospel of Luke and the Roman Empire." Pages 101–15 in *Jesus is Lord, Caesar Is Not: Evaluating Empire in New Testament Studies.* Edited by S. McKnight and J. Modica. Downers Grove: InterVarsity, 2013.

*Walton, S. "The State They Were In: Luke's View of the Roman Empire." Pages 1–41 in *Rome in the Bible and the Early Church.* Edited by P. Oakes. Carlisle: Paternoster, 2002.

HOMILETICAL SUGGESTIONS

Religion and Politics! (20:20–26)
1. A false dilemma? God or Caesar? (20:20–22)
2. A faithful response (20:23–26)
   a. The (limited) things of Caesar
   b. The (all-encompassing) things of God

e. Jesus Is Questioned About the Resurrection and Moses' Authority (20:27–40)

20:27 The nom. pl. masc. indef. pron. τινες (with the partitive gen. τῶν Σαδδουκαίων, who are mentioned only here in Luke; cf. Acts 4:1; 5:17; 23:6–8) is the subj. of ἐπηρώτησαν (see 20:21). Προσελθόντες (see 8:24) is attendant circumstance with ἐπηρώτησαν ("Some . . . came up and questioned Him" HCSB). Οἱ ἀντιλέγοντες (nom. pl. masc. of pres. act. ptc. of ἀντιλέγω, "speak against," "oppose"; see Metzger 145–46 for this rdg. instead of λέγοντες) is attrib. with the nom. subj. τινες. (though in sense it refers to the gen pl. Σαδδουκαίων, R 458 [the nom. sometimes being left unaltered]; Z §14; Bock 1628; Fitzmyer 1303). The neg. μή with the inf. εἶναι (see 2:4; used for indir. speech here) is redundant (if ἀντιλέγοντες is the rdg.; R 1171; common with vbs. of denial, ZG 264).

20:28 Λέγοντες, see 1:66. The ref. to Moses (the subj. of ἔγραψεν 3rd sg. aor. act. indic. of γράφω) refers to the custom of "levirate marriage" (Gen 38:8; Deut 25:5–10; Ruth 3–4), though the point of the question is to make belief in the resurrection look foolish. The pron. ἡμῖν is a dat. of adv. ("for us"). The layout is explained below.

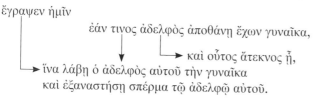

ἔγραψεν ἡμῖν

    ἐάν τινος ἀδελφὸς ἀποθάνῃ ἔχων γυναῖκα,

        καὶ οὗτος ἄτεκνος ᾖ,

ἵνα λάβῃ ὁ ἀδελφὸς αὐτοῦ τὴν γυναῖκα

καὶ ἐξαναστήσῃ σπέρμα τῷ ἀδελφῷ αὐτοῦ.

Ἐάν with the subjunc. ἀποθάνῃ (3rd sg. 2nd aor. act. subjunc. of ἀποθνήσκω, "die") is a third-class cond. clause (with a temp. idea, Bock 1628). The indef. masc. pron. τινος is a gen. of relationship with ἀδελφός ("a man's brother"). Ἔχων (see 3:11) could be temp. with ἀποθάνῃ ("while having"; "dies, having a wife." NKJV, NASB, ESV; ZG 264) or attrib. with ἀδελφός ("a man's brother has a wife" HCSB). The antecedent of the demonstrative pron. οὗτος (the subj. of the subjunc. ᾖ [see 10:6]) is ἀδελφός. Ἄτεκνος (pred.) nom. sg. masc. of ἄτεκνος, -ον, "childless." Ἵνα is the complement of ἔγραψεν ("Moses wrote for us that"; BDF §392[1d]; Z §§406–8; Fitzmyer 1304). The subjunc. λάβῃ (3rd sg. 2nd aor. act. subjunc. of λαμβάνω, "take" HCSB, ESV; "marry" NRSV, NIV) has an impv. force here ("his brother should" NASB, HCSB; "the man must" ESV, NIV; BDF §470[1]; Z §415; Bock 1628; Marshall 739). The subj. of λάβῃ is ὁ ἀδελφός αὐτοῦ and points back to the indef. pron. τινος ("that man" [NET, sim. NRSV, ESV, NIV] helps with clarity in tr.). The subjunc. ἐξαναστήσῃ (3rd sg. aor. act. subjunc. of ἐξανίστημι, "raise up") is subjunc. following ἵνα and also complements ἔγραψεν. Σπέρμα, "seed" (KJV); "offspring" (HCSB, ESV, NIV); "children" (NRSV). Τῷ ἀδελφῷ is a dat. of adv. "for his brother."

20:29 Οὖν marks a transition from the background provided in 20:28 ("now" most EVV). The subj. of ἦσαν (see 1:6) is ἑπτὰ . . . ἀδελφοί ("seven brothers"). Λαβών (see 6:4) is temp. (NJB, NLT; or attendant circumstance) with ἀπέθανεν (see 8:52).

20:30 Along with ὁ τρίτος ("third") in 20:31, ὁ δεύτερος ("second") is the nom. subj. of ἔλαβεν in 20:31 (Bock 1621; Marshall 740).

20:31 Ὁ τρίτος (with ὁ δεύτερος) is the subj. of ἔλαβεν (see 5:26). As with 20:28, 29, ἔλαβεν ("took" HCSB), means "married" (NRSV, NIV). Ὡσαύτως "likewise." Κατέλιπον (3rd pl. 2nd aor. act. indic. of καταλείπω, "leave") with the neg. οὐ and τέκνα is "left no children" (HCSB, ESV). Ἀπέθανον 3rd pl. 2nd aor. act. indic. of ἀποθνήσκω.

20:32 Ὕστερον of ὕστερος, -α, -ον, neut. as an adv. "finally" (most EVV; "Afterward" ESV; comp. for superl. Z §147). On ἀπέθανεν see 8:52 (cf. 20:29).

20:33 The nom. ἡ γυνή (the subj. of γίνεται [see 11:26]), the gen. τίνος αὐτῶν ("of which of them"; "whose" most EVV), and the pred. nom. γυνή is lit. "the woman . . . is the wife of which of them?" (BHGNT 635; "whose wife will the woman be?" NRSV, HCSB, ESV; ZG 264). Ἐν τῇ ἀναστάσει is temp. ("at the resurrection" NIV). Γάρ, causal (giving the reason for the supposed dilemma). Οἱ . . . ἑπτά is the nom. subj. of ἔσχον (3rd pl. 2nd aor. act. indic. of ἔχω; a "constative" aor. Robertson, *Pictures* 253). The acc. sg. fem. γυναῖκα is the complement in a double acc. cstr. with αὐτήν ("had her as wife" ESV; ZG 264; appos. Robertson, *Pictures* 254).

20:34 Jesus distinguishes between "this age" and "the age to come" ("that age") and highlights their mistaken idea that the age to come is simply an extension of this age (on οἱ υἱοὶ τοῦ αἰῶνος see 16:8, though with a different mng.; on this distinction between the two ages, cf. also 18:30). Οἱ υἱοί here is "those who belong to" (NRSV; a Heb., cf. BDAG 1025a–b; Z §§42–43). The pres. γαμοῦσιν (3rd pl. pres. act. indic. of γαμέω, "marry") is probably "gnomic." Γαμίσκονται (3rd pl. pres. pass. indic. of γαμίσκω, "to give in marriage"; pass. "are given" all EVV).

20:35 Καταξιωθέντες (nom. pl. masc. of aor. pass. ptc. of καταξιόω, "consider worthy"; BDAG 523c; a divine pass. Fitzmyer 1305) is subst. ("those who are counted worthy" HCSB). The first difference therefore is that not all will participate in the blessings of the age to come. The aor. act. inf. τυχεῖν (of τυγχάνω, "to take part" HCSB; "to attain" ESV) is probably epex. of καταξιωθέντες (BDAG 523c; BDF §392[1c]). The gen. phrases τοῦ αἰῶνος ἐκείνου and τῆς ἀναστάσεως τῆς ἐκ νεκρῶν are gen. complements of τυχεῖν (R 509, T 232). Οὔτε . . . οὔτε is "neither . . . nor" (R 1189). The second difference is that marriage is not a feature of that age. Γαμοῦσιν, see 20:34. Γαμίζονται 3rd pl. pres. pass. indic. of γαμίζω, "give in marriage."

20:36 Γάρ, causal (explaining why marriage will not be present in the age to come, Bock 1623). The inf. ἀποθανεῖν (see 16:22) is complementary to δύνανται (3rd pl. pres. mid. indic. of dep. δύναμαι; neg. with οὐδέ). The adv. ἔτι in neg. statements (with οὐδέ) is "no longer" (NET; BDAG 400b; "anymore" in most EVV). The nom. pl. masc. adj. ἰσάγγελοι (of ἰσάγγελος, -ον), "like angels" (NRSV, HCSB; "equal to angels" ESV), is the pred. adj. of εἰσίν. The causal conj. γάρ shows that "equal to angels" is with respect to "not able to die" (Nolland 966). The idiom τῆς ἀναστάσεως υἱοί means "sharers of the resurrection" (Fitzmyer 1306; Nolland 966; for υἱοί cf. 20:34). Ὄντες, see 6:3 (causal, "since they are" HCSB, NIV).

20:37 Jesus then argues from Scripture (also from Moses). The conjs. ὅτι δέ ("but that") introduce the clausal complement of ἐμήνυσεν (Wallace 454; Fitzmyer 1306; placed forward for emphasis, BHGNT 636). Ἐγείρονται, see 7:22 (a divine pass. Fitzmyer 1306; intrans. ZG 264). Καί is ascensive ("even Moses"). Ἐμήνυσεν 3rd sg. aor. act. indic. of μηνύω "make known" ("revealed" NET; BDAG 648c; "indicated" HCSB; "showed" ESV). Ἐπὶ τῆς βάτου ("at the bush," locat.) refers to the "passage about the bush" (BDAG 171d; ZG 264; Marshall 742; see 6:44; on the fem. of τῆς βάτου cf. BDF §49[1]). Ὡς could be causal ("for" NIV; ZG 264), temp. ("when" KJV) or locat. ("where" HCSB, ESV). The subj. of λέγει (here, "calls") could be impers. "it says" (Nolland 966) or Μωϋσῆς (Bock 1625; Fitzmyer 1306). The acc. κύριον is the obj. where τὸν θεόν . . . καὶ θεόν . . . καὶ θεόν is the complement in a double acc. cstr. (BHGNT 637; ZG 264; cf. Acts 3:13; on the Granville Sharp cstr. of one art. with nouns joined with καί see Wallace 274). Ἀβραάμ . . . Ἰσαάκ . . . Ἰακώβ are indecl. but gen. here (ZG 264).

20:38 θεός is the pred. nom. of ἔστιν ("He is not the God" all EVV; BDF §273; ZG 264; Fitzmyer 1306; Marshall 743). Ζώντων gen. pl. masc. of pres. act. (subst.) ptc. of ζάω ("the living"). The absence of the art. before the adj. νεκρῶν and ζώντων is probably qualitative (Z §179). Γάρ, causal. The dat. αὐτῷ is a dat. of ref. ("to him" or "before him"; cf. BDF §192; Z §56; Bovon 3.73 suggests either "from him" or "for him"). Ζῶσιν 3rd pl. pres. act. indic. of ζάω. The point appears to be that the present existence of the patriarchs means God is able to call himself their God, and his future promise for them still stands (Bock 1629; Fitzmyer 1306–7; Marshall 743; Nolland 967; Pao and Schnabel 370b; on Abraham cf. Luke 16:22).

20:39 Ἀποκριθέντες, see 9:19 (cf. 1:19). The adv. καλῶς "well" modifies εἶπας (2nd sg. 2nd aor. act. indic. of λέγω, "you have spoken"). This is perhaps spoken by some Pharisees who, though opposed to Jesus, were happy to see the position of the Sadducees refuted (Robertson, *Pictures* 254) and unwittingly acknowledge the teaching authority of Jesus. For διδάσκαλε see 7:40.

20:40 Γάρ strengthens the force of 20:39 (BHGNT 638). The impf. ἐτόλμων (3rd pl. impf. act. indic. of τολμάω, "dare"; the pl. being "intentionally broad," Bock 1626) could be used to summarize subsequent events (BHGNT 638). The pres. act. inf. ἐπερωτᾶν (of ἐπερωτάω, "ask," "question") is complementary with ἐτόλμων. The use of οὐδέν after an inf. neg. with οὐ (here, the temp. οὐκέτι) is common (Burton §482; R 1162).

HOMILETICAL SUGGESTIONS

The Resurrection (20:27–40)
1. The realities of life and marriage and belief in the resurrection (20:27–33)
2. The differences between this age and the age to come (20:34–36)
3. Scriptural confirmation: God is the God of the living (20:37–40)

f. Jesus Questions His Accusers About His Own Authority: He Is Lord! (20:41–44)

Jesus has left each group with nothing more to say. The issue of Jesus' authority has been the dominant topic throughout this series of exchanges. Therefore Jesus' question here concludes this section by highlighting that as Lord he (not the temple hierarchy) is the one with ultimate authority.

20:41 The audience (αὐτούς) for Jesus' question is not specified at this point (the scribes in 20:39 are likely in view; a change of audience is specified in 20:45). Following their acknowledgement of the teaching authority of Jesus, Jesus has a question about Scripture of his own for them. Πῶς could have the force of "why" (Bock 1634; "how is it possible that" Marshall 747) or "how" in the sense of how is this title interpreted (Bovon 3.82; λέγουσιν, see 9:18). Τὸν χριστόν is the acc. subj. of the inf. εἶναι (see 2:4; on the art. subj. see Wallace 195; the inf. is used in indir. discourse, Burton §112; Robertson, *Pictures* 254). Υἱόν is a pred. acc. with the inf. (Wallace 190–92). The question begins with the assumption that the Messiah will be a descendant of David (on David in Luke-Acts see 1:27).

20:42 Αὐτός is intensive ("David himself"; R 686; see 3:23). Ἐν βίβλῳ [see 3:4] ψαλμῶν (gen. pl. masc. of ψαλμός, -οῦ, ὁ; "in the book of the Psalms"; referring to Ps 110 [LXX Ps 109]) is locat. Jesus' argument is based on the Davidic authorship of the psalm (as seen in the superscription of the psalm; cf. Bock 1635; Nolland 973). Κύριος (i.e., Yahweh) is the nom. subj. of εἶπεν. The dat. τῷ κυρίῳ is the indir. obj. The pron. μου shows that the person being addressed is David's Lord (Bock 1636; cf. 1:43). Κάθου 2nd sg. pres. mid. impv. of dep. κάθημαι, "sit." Ἐκ is used with the plural of δεξιός in a locat. sense ("at the right side" BHGNT 639; see 1:11). The "right hand" of God is a common image in the OT for the power of God to rule and deliver (see 22:69; cf. Exod 15:6; Pss 18:35; 44:3; 60:5; 98:1). This kind of extravagant language is found throughout this psalm (cf. 110:4, 6).

20:43 Ἕως ἄν with θῶ (1st sg. 2nd aor. act. subjunc. of τίθημι) is a temp. clause. The acc. sg. neut. ὑποπόδιον (of ὑποπόδιον, -ου, τό, "footstool") is the complement in a double acc. cstr. (with the acc. τοὺς ἐχθρούς, ZG 265). This indicates a period of time in which, although the Lord will rule, this rule will be contested by enemies before a final consummation of that rule (see ἐχθρούς in 19:27).

20:44 Οὖν introduces an inference from 20:43. Δαυίδ is the subj. of καλεῖ (see 14:13). Κύριον is the complement in a double acc. cstr. (with the acc. αὐτόν, BDAG 502d). Καὶ πῶς ("how then"; Z §459; ZG 265; "in what sense" Bock 1640) introduces a dir. question (ἐστίν here, "is he"; υἱός is the pred. nom.; "so how is he his son?" ESV). The statement contains an implicit cond. "If David then calls him 'Lord,' how can he be his son?" (NET; Marshall 749). This does not deny the Messiah's Davidic descent (Bock 1639; see 1:27; cf. 20:41). It does show, however, that "son of David" does not encapsulate all there is to say about the Messiah: he is Lord (for the use of κύριος to ref. to both θεός and Ἰησοῦς in Luke see Rowe 175–76).

HOMILETICAL SUGGESTIONS

The Authority of Jesus (20:41–44)
1. David's son anticipated by all (21:41)
2. David's Lord announced by David himself (21:42–44)

g. Jesus' Condemnation of the Scribes (20:45–21:4)

After declaring his own authority as Lord, Jesus now turns to the condemnation await-
ing the scribes and the temple system as a whole (21:5–36). In this section his condemnation of the scribes comes in two parts which are linked with references to widows
(χήρα, 20:47; 21:2–3) and the livelihood of widows (οἰκία, 20:47; πάντα τὸν βίον,
21:4). The self-focus of these leaders is matched by their ill-treatment of the most
vulnerable. The account of the destitute widow who hands over her last remaining
coins to a corrupt temple system (cf. 20:46) is "exhibit A" of the destruction of widow's livelihood. The rest of chapter 21 will elaborate on the judgment to come on this
temple system.

(1) Beware of the Scribes (20:45–47)

20:45 Ἀκούοντος (gen. sg. masc. of pres. act. ptc. of ἀκούω) with παντὸς τοῦ λαοῦ (the
subj. of the ptc.) is a temp. gen. abs. cstr. The specific ref. to Jesus' disciples highlights
the shift in audience from the previous section. The disciples remain the audience for
the following lament in 21:1–4 and subsequent warning concerning the temple.

20:46 Προσέχετε (see 12:1) with ἀπό (here, "a marker to indicate separation," BDAG
105a; BDF §149) is "beware of" (all EVV; ZG 265; a Heb. Marshall 749; the pres. may
emphasize constant vigilance, Bock 1642). The "scribes" are then described with two
gen. pl. masc. of pres. act. (attrib.) ptcs. (1) θελόντων (of θέλω; "the scribes, who want
to" HCSB; or "like to" ESV; BDAG 448b; ZG 265; i.e., it is a ref. to scribes in general
[Bock 1644], rather than a subgroup of "those scribes who like to" *pace* Nolland 976;
cf. 5:17). The pres. act. inf. περιπατεῖν (of περιπατέω) is complementary. The prep.
ἐν with στολαῖς ("long robes," see 15:22) is often used with descriptions of clothing
(cf. BDAG 327b, 946d; priestly robes, Fitzmyer 1318). (2) φιλούντων (of φιλέω). The
three accs. ἀσπασμούς ("greetings," see 1:29; 11:43), πρωτοκαθεδρίας ("best seats";
BDAG 892c–d; see 11:43), and πρωτοκλισίας ("places of honor"; BDAG 892d; see
14:7–8) are the dir. obj. of φιλούντων. The overall emphasis is on self-importance and
prominence. Ἐν ταῖς ἀγοραῖς ("in the marketplaces," see 7:32), ἐν ταῖς συναγωγαῖς ("in
the synagogues"), and ἐν τοῖς δείπνοις ("banquets" HCSB; "feasts" ESV; see 14:12)
are locat.

20:47 The nom. pl. masc. rel. pron. οἵ is the subj. of κατεσθίουσιν (3rd pl. pres. act.
indic. of κατεσθίω, "devour"; cf. BDAG 532a; LN 57.247). Οἰκίας "houses" (most
EVV) could also have ref. to contents ("property" NET; cf. BDAG 695b; LN 57.21;
ZG 265; χηρῶν gen. pl. fem., see 2:37; 7:12). This may have been done by taking
advantage of widows in managing their property (cf. Bock 1643; Fitzmyer 1318;
Marshall 750; Nolland 976). Προφάσει dat. sg. fem. of πρόφασις, -εως, ἡ, "for a pre-
tense" (ESV; "for appearance's sake" NASB; "for a show" NIV). Μακρά acc. neut.
pl. "long" (see 15:13; neut. as an adv.; acc. extent of time) modifies προσεύχονται (3rd
pl. pres. mid. indic. of dep. προσεύχομαι; ZG 265). They cover up their treatment of
widows with "the façade of religious piety" (Fitzmyer 1317). The demonstrative pron.
οὗτοι is the subj. of λήμψονται (3rd pl. fut. mid. indic. of λαμβάνω). Περισσότερον is

a comp. adj. "greater" [see 7:26] modifying κρίμα (acc. sg. neut. of κρίμα, -ατος, τό, "condemnation" NRSV, NASB, ESV; cf. also 12:47–48; Fitzmyer 1319; Nolland 977; "punishment" HCSB; i.e., an eschatological judgment, Bovon 3.87).

(2) Exhibit A: A Destitute Widow (21:1–4)

In light of the immediate context, in this account Jesus probably laments the effect of the temple system on this poor widow (Fitzmyer 1321; Green 728–29) rather than praise her generosity (Bock 1644–47; Bovon 3.95–96; Nolland 979). See A. G. Wright, "The Widow's Mites: Praise or Lament? A Matter of Context," *CBQ* 44 (1982): 256–65.

21:1 Ἀναβλέψας (see 9:16) could be temp. or attendant circumstance with εἶδεν (see 5:2; BHGNT 641; Z §363; ZG 265). With ἀναβλέψας δὲ εἶδεν a clear link is made with the preceding verses (Fitzmyer 1321). Τοὺς . . . πλουσίους (continuing the focus on the leadership, Nolland 978) is the dir. obj. of εἶδεν. Βάλλοντας (acc. pl. masc. of pres. act. [attrib.] ptc. of βάλλω) modifies τούς . . . πλουσίους (ZG 265). Εἰς τὸ γαζοφυλάκιον is locat. (acc. sg. neut. of γαζοφυλάκιον, -ου, τό, "treasury"; "offering box" ESV; cf. BDAG 186c; LN 6.141; perhaps a ref. to receptacles in a room by the Court of Women, Marshall 751). The acc. pl. neut. τὰ δῶρα (of δῶρον, -ου, τό) is the dir. obj. of βάλλοντας.

21:2 The repetition of εἶδεν (see 5:2) may reflect a measure of parallelism between 21:1 and 2, Nolland 979). The acc. sg. fem. τινα χήραν [see 2:37; 7:12] πενιχράν ("a certain poor widow"; πενιχράν acc. sg. fem. of πενιχρός, -ά, -όν, "in need of things relating to livelihood" BDAG 795d; LN 57.49) is the obj. of εἶδεν. Βάλλουσαν (acc. sg. fem. of pres. act. ptc. of βάλλω) is the complement in a double acc. cstr. (BHGNT 642; or attrib. modifying τινα χήραν πενιχράν). Λεπτά, "small copper coins" (most EVV; see 12:59).

21:3 For ἀληθῶς λέγω ὑμῖν see 9:27. Ὅτι, recitative. The nom. ἡ χήρα αὕτη ἡ πτωχή "this poor widow" is the subj. of ἔβαλεν (see 13:19; the acc. adj. πλεῖον is the dir. obj.). Thus, the situation of the woman as a widow in poverty is again highlighted (cf. 21:2). The gen. πάντων is comp. (ZG 265; i.e., proportionately more, Marshall 752).

21:4 The reason (γάρ) the poor widow gave more than anyone else is now given. Πάντες . . . οὗτοι ("all these" HCSB) is the (emphatic, Nolland 979) subj. of ἔβαλον (3rd pl. 2nd aor. act. indic. of βάλλω). The ptc. in ἐκ τοῦ περισσεύοντος αὐτοῖς (gen. sg. neut. of pres. act. ptc. of περισσεύω "abound") is subst. (i.e., "out of that which abounds to them"; the prep. phrase is partitive). The dat. αὐτοῖς is poss. ("their abundance" ESV). The locat. prep. phrase εἰς τὰ δῶρα (see 21:1) could mean *"put in gifts" (HCSB), "put into the offering" (NASB; Marshall 752; Nolland 979; metonymy for the "offering-chest" Garland 818), or "threw in among the [other] gifts" (ZG 265). The contrastive αὕτη δέ is probably emphatic (see 3:23). Ὑστερήματος (gen. sg. neut. of ὑστέρημα, -ατος, τό, "that which is lacking"; "poverty" most EVV; BDAG 1044a) is a gen. of source. The acc. πάντα τὸν βίον ("all she had to live on" most EVV; see βίος 8:14; 15:12) is the dir. obj. of ἔβαλεν (see 13:19; for εἶχεν see 13:6). This final phrase both reinforces the earlier statements about the poverty of the widow and adds to this a picture of destitution in the setting of a temple complex with scribes who devour the livelihood of widows (19:47; 20:47). The fate of the temple system is the topic of the next section.

HOMILETICAL SUGGESTIONS

The Character of Corrupt Authority (20:45–21:4)
1. Corrupt authority is to be warned of (20:45–46a).
2. Corrupt authority is obsessed with self-importance (20:46).
3. Corrupt authority is callous toward the vulnerable (20:47a; 21:2–4).
4. Corrupt authority can appear impressively devoted to God (20:47b; 21:1).
5. Corrupt authority will face the reality of severe judgment from God (20:47c).

h. The Destruction of Jerusalem and the Return of the Son of Man at the End (21:5–36)
This section focuses on the judgment that will come upon the temple system of the Jerusalem leadership. The event on the near horizon (the destruction of Jerusalem) is an anticipation of the end (the return of the Son of Man and the final judgment; see 21:25). There are also numerous refs. that anticipate events to follow in Luke-Acts (see refs. in Green 732). The message is to remain faithful (21:8–9, 13, 19, 34, 36), trusting in God's sovereign purposes (21:9, 15, 18, 22, 24, 27–28, 31, 33).

(1) Opening Observations Concerning the Temple and Its Destruction (21:5–6)

21:5 The gen. indef. pron. τινων and gen. ptc. λεγόντων (see 2:13) is a temp. gen. abs. cstr. (ESV) and provides the setting and introduction to εἶπεν (i.e., to the judgment Jesus will announce in 21:6). Although the introduction is general (i.e., not necessarily still in the temple courts, Bock 1661; *pace* Fitzmyer 1330), the ref. to ἱερόν (the "temple complex" HCSB) indicates a continuation of topic from the previous section (cf. ἱερόν in 19:45–20:1). Ὅτι introduces indir. speech. The dat. λίθοις καλοῖς καὶ ἀναθήμασιν is instr. (BHGNT 644; Robertson, *Pictures* 256; "with beautiful stones and gifts dedicated to God" HCSB; ἀναθήμασιν dat. pl. neut. of ἀνάθημα, -ατος, τό, "offering," see BDAG 63a; LN 53.18). Κεκόσμηται 3rd sg. pf. pass. indic. of κοσμέω, "adorned" (most EVV; the pf. tense is retained in indir. discourse, Robertson, *Pictures* 256).

21:6 Jesus' reply highlights the danger of thinking that what appears outwardly impressive is a sign of God's favor. The acc. pl. neut. rel. pron. ἅ is the obj. of θεωρεῖτε (2nd pl. pres. act. indic. of θεωρέω) and introduces the topic that follows (BHGNT 644; the acc. pl. neut. demonstrative pron. ταῦτα agrees with the rel. pron. BDF §466[1]; acc. of respect, ZG 265; a pendent cstr. R 416; Wallace, 52; Nolland 988; Marshall 759). "These things" are referred to again in the ref. to "stone upon stone." For ἐλεύσονται ἡμέραι see 5:35 (and 17:22). Ἐν αἷς is temp. (the antecedent of the rel. pron. is the fem. ἡμέραι). Ἀφεθήσεται (see 12:10, here "left") with λίθος ἐπὶ λίθῳ is a general ref. to total destruction (Bock 1662; c.f. 19:44). The rel. pron. ὅς (agreeing with λίθος) is the subj. of καταλυθήσεται (3rd sg. fut. pass. indic. of καταλύω, here "thrown down").

(2) General Events that Are Not Directly Connected to the End (21:7–11)

The ref. to "the end" (21:9) indicates that these verses describe general events that characterize life in this world through to the "final" end (Bock 1666; Marshall 764; not only events prior to the destruction of Jerusalem, *pace* Fitzmyer 1334–35; Nolland 993). These events are *not* signs of the destruction of Jerusalem or the end of the world.

21:7 Ἐπηρώτησαν, see 20:21. Λέγοντες, see 1:66. For διδάσκαλε see 7:40. Πότε "when?" Ἔσται, see 1:14. The interr. pron. τί is the pred. nom. of a verbless clause (with the nom. τὸ σημεῖον; cf. T 305). Ὅταν with the subjunc. μέλλῃ (3rd sg. pres. act. subjunc. of μέλλω) is temp. (the vb. adds a sense of imminency, BHGNT 645). The pres. mid. inf. γίνεσθαι (of γίνομαι) is complementary. The two questions are synonymous. Although the context of 21:6 indicates that the destruction of the temple is the focus of the disciples' question (Fitzmyer 1331), for some this event was not easily separated from the events of the end (e.g., 19:11; cf. Bock 1663; Marshall 761). Jesus' answer will distinguish between the fall of Jerusalem and the end as well as allude to the similarities.

21:8 The pres. impv. βλέπετε (see 8:18) followed by the subjunc. πλανηθῆτε (2nd pl. aor. pass. subjunc. of πλανάω, "deceive") emphasizes constant vigilance. The subjunc. with μή often accompanies vbs. of warning (Wallace 477; on the use of βλέπω followed by a prohibitory subjunc. cf. Burton §209; R 932–33, 996; Huffman 245–47). The reason (γάρ) for this vigilance is because many will come (ἐλεύσονται, see 5:35) claiming to have the authority of Christ (on ἐπὶ τῷ ὀνόματί μου see BDAG 366d; Nolland 991), and therefore to be the Messiah (for λέγοντες ἐγώ εἰμί the NLT has "claiming, 'I am the Messiah;'" Marshall 763). Associated with this claim is the claim that the (eschatological) end time is "at hand" (ἤγγικεν, see 10:9; Bock 1664). The prohibition "do not go after them" (πορευθῆτε 2nd pl. aor. pass. subjunc. of dep. πορεύομαι; the aor. prohibition [with μή] could be ingressive but likely views the action as a whole [Huffman 188]) is an idiom referring to association (BHGNT 646; "don't believe them" NLT; "follow" ZG 266; Bock 1664; Bovon 3.110; cf. Acts 5:36–37; 21:38).

21:9 Ὅταν with the subjunc. ἀκούσητε (2nd pl. aor. act. subjunc. of ἀκούω) is an indef. temp. clause (the following accs. of ref. mean "about wars," Wallace 133). Πολέμους, "wars" (see 14:31). Ἀκαταστασίας acc. pl. fem. (of ἀκαταστασία, -ας, ἡ) "disturbances" (NASB), "insurrections" (NRSV; BDAG 35c), "rebellions" (HCSB), "uprisings" (NIV). Πτοηθῆτε (2nd pl. aor. pass. subjunc. of dep. πτοέομαι, "terrify"; the aor. prohibition [with μή] views the action as a whole, Huffman 110; cf. Fantin 164; Wallace 469) refers to a sense of terror and distress (BDAG 895b; Bovon 3.110; Fitzmyer 1336; only here and 24:37 in the NT). The basis for assurance (γάρ, causal) is the sovereign timetable of God: these things "must happen first" (δεῖ, see 2:49; the inf. γενέσθαι [see 3:22] is complementary). The pron. ταῦτα refers to the things just listed in 21:8–9 rather than the earlier ref. to the destruction of Jerusalem in 21:6–7 (Fitzmyer 1336). The term πρῶτον highlights the time sequence; they are not an indication that the end is about to come (the adv. εὐθέως modifies an implied vb. such as ἐλεύσεται, BHGNT 646; cf. HCSB, NIV). Τὸ τέλος introduces the distinction that Jesus is going to make between the destruction of Jerusalem and the eschatological end (Bock 1666; Marshall 764; though it may refer to the destruction of the temple, Bovon 3.111; Fitzmyer 1336; Nolland 992).

21:10 The impf. ἔλεγεν may express a continuation of speech ("he continued" NASB; cf. 5:36; refs. at 6:20; i.e., not necessarily a significant transition, Fitzmyer 1337). The sense of the fut. pass. ἐγερθήσεται (see 11:31; intrans. ZG 266) here is "rise up in arms" (NET; cf. LN 55.2). Ἐπί is a marker of opposition ("against"; BDAG 366a; ZG 266).

21:11 The use of τε . . . τε "groups the two kinds of woes" (Robertson, *Pictures* 258; Marshall 765). The first set are grouped as the subj. of ἔσονται (see 11:19): the nom. pl. masc. σεισμοί [of σεισμός, -οῦ, ὁ] μεγάλοι ("great earthquakes"), and λιμοὶ [see 4:25] καὶ λοιμοί ([of λοιμός, -οῦ, ὁ] "famines and plagues"; cf. Acts 11:28; a similar sounding "literary pair" [parechesis] R 1201; Fitzmyer 1337; Nolland 992), modified by the distributive κατὰ τόπους ("in various places" most EVV; ZG 266; "in place after place" Marshall 765; cf. Acts 16:26). The second set are grouped as the subj. of ἔσται (see 1:14): the nom. pl. neut. φόβητρα (of φόβητρον, -ου, τό, "something. unusual that causes fear" BDAG 1062a; LN 25.258; "terrifying sights" HCSB; "terrors" NASB, ESV; "fearful events" NIV), and σημεῖα μεγάλα ("great signs"), modified by ἀπ᾽ οὐρανοῦ.

(3) Persecution Is in the Immediate Future for the Disciples (21:12–19)

21:12 Although the events of 21:8–11 do not indicate the nearness of the end, the immediate future (the temp. prep. πρό "before" takes the gen., BDAG 864b; Wallace 379 [though possibly expressing superiority, R 622]) for the disciples is one characterized by persecution (Bock 1668). The laying on (ἐπιβαλοῦσιν 3rd pl. fut. act. indic. of ἐπιβάλλω, "lay on/put on") of hands here has the idea of "seize" (NET) or "arrest" (NRSV). Διώξουσιν, "persecute," see 11:49. The following ptcs. elaborate on the "arrest" and persecution. Παραδιδόντες (nom. pl. masc. of pres. act. ptc. of παραδίδωμι, "hand over") probably expresses result (BHGNT 647; or means). The art. in τὰς συναγωγὰς καὶ φυλακάς unites the two distinct entities due to their common opposition to Jesus' disciples (Wallace 286). Ἀπαγομένους (acc. pl. masc. of pres. pass. ptc. of ἀπάγω, "lead away"; here "you will be brought") modifies the acc. ὑμᾶς and so is attrib. (focusing on the referent rather than the action, BHGNT 647–48; Robertson, *Pictures* 258; Nolland 996; here "led" or "brought" in the sense of being a prisoner or one condemned; thus, "stand trial" NLT). Ἡγεμόνας acc. pl. masc. "governors" (see 20:20. For the refs. to synagogues and prisons followed by kings and governors see Bock 1668–69; Fitzmyer 1340; Nolland 996). The causal prep. ἕνεκεν ("on account of"; takes the gen.; R 641; cf. διά in 21:17) gives the reason for the persecution (ἕνεκεν τοῦ ὀνόματός μου is association with Jesus; "because you are my followers" NLT).

21:13 Ἀποβήσεται 3rd sg. fut. mid. indic. of ἀποβαίνω, "go away"; used fig. for result, "lead to," "turn out" (BDAG 107c; indicating the result of the persecution). The dat. ὑμῖν is either a dat. of advantage ("lead to an opportunity for you" HCSB; Robertson, *Pictures* 258; Bock 1669) or a dat. of ref. (perhaps NIV "And so you will"). In the context of 21:12, εἰς μαρτύριον is "to witness" (HCSB; "bear testimony to me" NIV; Bock 1670; Bovon 3.112; Nolland 996; cf. 24:48; Acts 1:8; 4:33) rather than provide "evidence" against the persecutors (Marshall 767–68).

21:14 Θέτε (2nd pl. 2nd aor. act. impv. of τίθημι) with ἐν ταῖς καρδίαις ὑμῶν is an idiom mng. "determine" or "resolve" (NET; "make up your minds" HCSB; Bock 1670; Nolland 996; see 1:66; 9:44). The pres. act. inf. προμελετᾶν (of προμελετάω, "practice beforehand," or "prepare" [neg. with μή]; like rehearsing a speech, BDAG 872c; Bock 1670; Fitzmyer 1340; Marshall 768) is the obj. of θέτε. The aor. pass. inf. ἀπολογηθῆναι (of ἀπολογέομαι "to defend oneself") is the complementary obj. of the previous inf. προμελετᾶν ("prepare," i.e., "not to prepare your defense" HCSB; rather than "worry," *pace* Bovon 3.112; on this use of the complementary inf. cf. BDF §392[2]; R 1094).

21:15 Γάρ, causal (giving the reason the disciples need not prepare a defense). The Lord Jesus himself (ἐγώ is emphatic, Fitzmyer 1340; Marshall 768; see 12:11–12) will give (δώσω, see 4:6) them (1) words to say (στόμα "mouth" ESV; by metonymy "words" HCSB), and (2) "wisdom" (σοφίαν; cf. Acts 6:10). The dat. fem. rel. pron. ᾗ (agreeing with the fem. antecedent σοφίαν) is the dat. complement of the inf. ἀντιστῆναι (BHGNT 649; dat. as indir. obj. ZG 266; i.e., the wisdom is "that which" they will not be able to withstand). The two 2nd aor. act. infs. ἀντιστῆναι (intrans. ZG 266; of ἀνθίστημι "resist" HCSB; "to withstand" ESV; cf. Acts 6:10) and ἀντειπεῖν (of ἀντιλέγω "refute" NASB; "to contradict" HCSB; cf. Acts 4:14) are both complementary with δυνήσονται (3rd pl. fut. mid. indic. of dep. δύναμαι). The subst. ptc. ἀντικείμενοι (see 13:17; "opponents" NASB; "adversaries" HCSB, ESV, NIV; on the repeated ἀντί cf. R 573) is the subj. of δυνήσονται (οὐ δυνήσονται . . . ἅπαντες is Sem. for "none . . . will be able" ZG 267; as most EVV).

21:16 Παραδοθήσεσθε 2nd pl. fut. pass. indic. of παραδίδωμι, "betrayed" (HCSB), "delivered up" (ESV; ὑπό with the pass. expresses ultimate agency, Wallace 433). Καί here is "even." Γονέων, "parents" (see 2:27; cf. 12:52–53; 18:29). Συγγενῶν, "relatives" (most EVV; "kinsmen" RSV; see 1:58; cf. 14:12, 26). Θανατώσουσιν 3rd pl. fut. act. indic. of θανατόω, "put to death" (or causative, "have you put to death" NET, sim. KJV; Robertson, *Pictures* 259; ZG 267; cf. Acts 7:60; 12:2; 26:10). Ἐξ ὑμῶν is partitive ("some of you"; with τινες implied; BDAG 443d; BDF §164[2]; R 599; ZG 267).

21:17 The fut. ἔσεσθε (of εἰμί, see 6:35) with μισούμενοι (nom. pl. masc. of pres. pass. ptc. of μισέω) is a fut. pass. periph. cstr. ("you will be hated") in which the pres. ptc. is progressive (cf. Burton §71; R 878, 889; T 89; Wallace 649; ZG 267; the fut. periph. cstr. is rare but found in 1:20; 5:10; 21:17, 24; 22:69). Πάντων is either a rhetorical ref. to "many" or to all those outside the Christian community (Bock 1672; cf. Acts 28:22). Again the reason (διά followed by the acc. τὸ ὄνομά μου) for this hatred is association with Christ (see 21:12).

21:18 Θρίξ, "hair" (see 7:38). The subjunc. ἀπόληται (3rd sg. 2nd aor. mid. subjunc. of ἀπόλλυμι) with the double neg. οὐ μή is emphatic ("you will certainly not perish"; Wallace 469; Z §444; ZG 267; "there is 'no way' such destruction will occur" Bock 1673). Some think that since 21:16 only refers to some who will be put to death, this verse must refer to others who will be physically protected (Nolland 997–98; cf. Acts 27:34). In light of the following verse, however, this is better understood as fig. language for ultimate spiritual protection (Robertson, *Pictures* 259; Bock 1673; Bovon 3.113; Marshall 769; cf. 12:4–7).

21:19 Ἐν τῇ ὑπομονῇ ὑμῶν, "by your endurance" (HCSB, ESV; BDAG 1039d; "by standing firm" NLT), is instr. (cf. 8:15; 9:24). Most EVV tr. the aor. impv. κτήσασθε (2nd pl. aor. mid. impv. of dep. κτάομαι, "acquire," "gain") with a fut. indic. ("you will gain"; Fitzmyer 1341; some mss. have a fut. indic. [A B ƒ¹³; NA²⁵], perhaps in conformity to earlier fut. indics., Metzger 147; the impv. has better external support and is the harder rdg.). The NIV places the impv. force of the verse on the prep. phrase ("Stand firm, and you will win life"). The HCSB follows the syntax of the Greek by tr. κτήσασθε as an impv. ("By your endurance gain your lives"; sim. NKJV; see Fantin 175–77; the repetition of the pron. ὑμῶν is not emphatic, R 681, 683). As with 21:18, this verse is not a ref. to physical preservation (*pace* Nolland 998), but rather that saving faith is persevering faith. To trust in Jesus is to have (eternal) life even in the face of death.

(4) The Destruction of Jerusalem as a Picture of Final Judgment (21:20–24)

In light of the time notes in 21:9, 12, it is only at this point that Jesus specifically refers to the question about Jerusalem which began this section (21:5–7).

21:20 Ὅταν with the subjunc. ἴδητε is temp. (see 12:54). Κυκλουμένην (acc. sg. fem. of pres. pass. ptc. of κυκλόω, "surround") could be attrib. modifying the acc. Ἰερουσαλήμ, or the complement in a double acc. cstr. (BDAG 279c–d; BHGNT 651). Στρατοπέδων gen. pl. neut. (of στρατόπεδον, -ου, τό, "camps," "armies." The impv. γνῶτε (2nd pl. 2nd aor. act. impv. of γινώσκω) with the temp. τότε is "then know" (NRSV, ESV, sim. HCSB; Robertson, *Pictures* 259; "then you will know" NIV). Ὅτι is a marker of content (following vbs. of perception, BDAG 731d; ἤγγικεν, see 10:9). Ἐρήμωσις, "desolation." The gen. αὐτῆς is obj. (the antecedent is Ἰερουσαλήμ; see 19:43–44).

21:21 Τότε ("then") parallels τότε in 21:20 (both following ὅταν "when" in 21:20; see the questions in 21:7, πότε ["when"] . . . καὶ . . . ὅταν). The three arts. οἱ are nominalizers making ἐν τῇ Ἰουδαίᾳ . . . ἐν μέσῳ αὐτῆς . . . ἐν ταῖς χώραις the subjs. of the 3rd pl. pres. impvs. that follow them (BHGNT 651–52). Thus, (1) those in Judea should "flee" φευγέτωσαν (act. of φεύγω) "to the mountains" (most EVV; εἰς τὰ ὄρη is locat.); (2) those inside the city of Jerusalem (οἱ ἐν μέσῳ αὐτῆς, ZG 267; Bock 1677; Bovon 3.115) should "leave" ἐκχωρείτωσαν (act. of ἐκχωρέω); and (3) those out in the country" should "not enter" εἰσερχέσθωσαν (mid. of dep. εἰσέρχομαι; prohibition with μή) "the city" (αὐτήν probably picks up on the fem. αὐτῆς). The point is to avoid the city of Jerusalem at all costs.

21:22 Ὅτι, causal (giving the reason for such avoidance of Jerusalem). These are (the demonstrative pron. αὗται is the subj. of εἰσίν) the days (ἡμέραι is the pred. nom.) of "vengeance" (most EVV; "punishment" NIV; BDAG 301a [mng. 3]; LN 38.8; common OT language for God's judgment, e.g., Jer 46:10 [LXX 26:10]; 51:6 [LXX 28:6]). Following ἡμέραι, the gen. ἐκδικήσεως (see 18:7–8) has the mng aor. pass. "characterized by punishment" or "when punishment comes" (Wallace 80–81). The aor. pass. inf. τοῦ πλησθῆναι of πίμπλημι may be epex. modifying ἐκδικήσεως (BHGNT 652; Burton §400; R 1061) or express purpose (R 1088; Robertson, *Pictures* 259; Fitzmyer 1345 [cf. BDF §400]; either purpose or result, ZG 267 [cf. Z §§351, 383]). The acc. πάντα τὰ γεγραμμένα is the subj. of the inf. (cf. NASB; for γεγραμμένα see 18:31).

21:23 The interjection οὐαί "woe" (HCSB; "alas" ESV) in this context is an expression of how terrible the judgment will be for the following groups (cf. NLT; NIV; Marshall 773; see 6:24). Two groups are indicated with two dat. (of disadvantage) pl. fem. of pres. act. (subst.) ptcs. (1) ταῖς . . . ἐχούσαις (of ἔχω) with ἐν γαστρί (see 1:31) is an idiom referring to pregnant women (Fitzmyer 1346). (2) ταῖς θηλαζούσαις (of θηλάζω, "those nursing," Fitzmyer 1346). Γάρ, causal (giving the reason it will be so horrible). There will be (ἔσται, see 1:14) "great distress" (nom. sg. fem., ἀνάγκη [see 14:18, here, "distress"] μεγάλη) on the land (HCSB, ἐπὶ τῆς γῆς, i.e., in this context, of Judea, Bock 1679; Marshall 773; Nolland 1002; the art. τῆς may have demonstrative force here in light of the following τούτῳ, Fitzmyer 1346; though most EVV have "on the earth") and (divine) wrath (ὀργή) against "this people" (τῷ λαῷ τούτῳ, dat. of disadvantage).

21:24 Πεσοῦνται 3rd pl. fut. mid. indic. of πίπτω, "fall." The dat. στόματι ("by the mouth [idiom for "edge"] of the sword"; ZG 267; "sharpness" Bovon 3.114) is instr. (BDF §195[1]; R 534; μαχαίρης gen. sg. fem. of μάχαιρα, -ης, ἡ). Αἰχμαλωτισθήσονται 3rd pl. fut. pass. indic. of αἰχμαλωτίζω, "lead captive." Πατουμένη (nom. sg. fem. of pres. pass. ptc. πατέω "tread," "trample") with the fut. ἔσται is a fut. periph. cstr. ("will be trampled"; see 21:17 for this cstr.). The conj. and rel. pron. ἄχρι οὗ with the subjunc. πληρωθῶσιν (3rd pl. aor. pass. subjunc. of πληρόω) is temp. ("until [the time when]" R 974; Wallace 677). The gen. ἐθνῶν in the phrase καιροὶ ἐθνῶν has the sense of "the time period when the Gentiles exercise power" (BHGNT 653 with ref. also to Ἡρῴδου in 1:5; Bovon 3.116; Marshall 773; cf. 21:22), rather than a time of judgment for the nations (Nolland 1002–3; on the anar. ἐθνῶν cf. Z §182; ZG 267). It is with this end point in view (καιροὶ ἐθνῶν) that Jesus then turns to events of a more universal nature that are associated with the return of the Son of Man at the end (cf. συνοχὴ ἐθνῶν, 21:25).

(5) The Return of the Son of Man at the End (21:25–28)

Although some see this section as still referring to the destruction of Jerusalem, the ref. to redemption (21:28), the universal language ("the earth" 21:25; "nations" 21:25; "the inhabited word" 21:26; "all those" on "all the earth" 21:35), and the way the "coming of the Son of Man" is used elsewhere in Luke (cf. 9:26; 12:40; 17:22–24, 30; 18:8), indicate that Jesus is here speaking about his future return and the final day of the Lord's judgment.

21:25 There will be (ἔσονται, see 11:19) signs in the sun (ἡλίῳ dat. sg. masc. of ἥλιος, -ου, ὁ), moon (σελήνη dat. sg. fem. of σελήνη, -ης, ἡ; the first two nouns are monadic and def., R 794; Wallace 249), and stars (ἄστροις dat. pl. neut. of ἄστρον, -ου, τό). Likewise, on the earth nations will be (ἔσται is implied) in distress (συνοχὴ ἐθνῶν, a subj. gen.; συνοχή [nom. sg. fem. of συνοχή, -ῆς, ἡ] refers to a "high degree of anxiety" BDAG 974b; perhaps with a sense of feeling "trapped" Bock 1682). Ἐν ἀπορίᾳ (dat. sg. fem. of ἀπορία, -ας, ἡ, "anxiety" or "perplexity") may now indicate the cause of the distress or the circumstance of the distress (BHGNT 654; "helpless" Bovon 3.116). The gen. ἤχους [gen. sg. neut., see 4:37] θαλάσσης καὶ σάλου [gen. sg. masc. of σάλος, -ου, ὁ, "surging waves"] "roaring of the sea and waves" gives the cause of the perplexity (ESV; ZG 268; Marshall 775).

21:26 The gen. ptc. ἀποψυχόντων (gen. pl. masc. of pres. act. ptc. of ἀποψύχω, "faint") and the gen. ἀνθρώπων is a gen. abs. cstr. expressing the result from the previous events

("People will faint" HCSB; NIV; BHGNT 654; Bovon 3.117; the term may refer to physical fainting [LN 23.184] or in a psychological sense to total discouragement [LN 25.293]; BHGNT 654). Ἀπό, causal ("People will faint from fear" NRSV, HCSB; ZG 268; Bovon 3.117; it governs the following two nouns, R 566). Ἐπερχομένων (gen. pl. neut. of pres. mid. [subst.] ptc. of dep. ἐπέρχομαι, "things coming upon") is the obj. of προσδοκίας (gen. sg. fem. of προσδοκία, -ας, ἡ, "expectation" NASB, HCSB; "foreboding" NRSV, ESV). Οἰκουμένη (dat. sg. fem., see 2:1), "the (inhabited) world," is one of the indicators that more universal events are in view here. The reason for such "fear and expectation of what is coming on the world" is because (γάρ) "the powers of the heavens" (ESV) will be shaken σαλευθήσονται (3rd pl. fut. pass. indic. of σαλεύω, "shake"). This may refer again to *"the heavenly bodies" (NIV; Bock 1683; Marshall 775) or to spiritual powers ("celestial powers" HCSB; as a ref. to God's enemies, Fitzmyer 1350). The refs. in 21:25 favor the former.

21:27 Τότε is temp. ("then"). Ὄψονται 3rd pl. fut. mid. indic. of ὁράω. Ἐρχόμενον (acc. sg. masc. of pres. mid. ptc. of dep. ἔρχομαι) is either attrib. (modifying τὸν υἱόν) or the complement in a double acc. cstr. (BDAG 719b–c). Νεφέλῃ dat. sg. fem. of νεφέλη, -ης, ἡ, "cloud" (locat.; see Acts 1:11; Dan 7:13–14). Μετὰ δυνάμεως καὶ δόξης πολλῆς indicates manner (BHGNT 655). The combination of a cloud with power and glory is a reference to divine authority and presence (cf. Exod 16:10; 34:5; Num 11:25; [LXX 14:10]; cf. also Luke 9:26; Marshall 776). On this as coming to earth rather than an ascent to God or the events of AD 70, see Marshall 776 (and the refs. in the introduction to 21:25).

21:28 Ἀρχομένων (gen. pl. neut. of pres. mid. ptc. of ἄρχω, "begin") with the gen. demonstrative pron. τούτων is a temp. gen. abs. cstr. ("when these things begin"; R 1396). "These things" in this context probably refers to the dramatic cosmic signs causing fear among the nations (21:25–26; Marshall 777). The inf. γίνεσθαι (see 21:7) is complementary. Ἀνακύψατε 2nd pl. aor. act. impv. of ἀνακύπτω, "straighten up" (NASB, ESV); "stand up" (HCSB, NIV). Ἐπάρατε 2nd pl. aor. act. impv. of ἐπαίρω, "lift up." The reason for this confidence (in contrast to the fear in 21:26, Fitzmyer 1350) is because (διότι, causal) "redemption" (ἀπολύτρωσις nom. sg. fem. of ἀπολύτρωσις, -εως, ἡ; see 1:68) is near (ἐγγίζει, see 12:33). In this context the term refers to redemption in its fullness (cf. "kingdom of God" 21:31).

(6) Encouragements to Persevere (21:29–36)

21:29 For this use of παραβολή see 4:23; 5:36; 6:39 (cf. 8:4). Ἴδετε 2nd pl. 2nd aor. act. impv. of ὁράω, "look." Συκῆν, "fig tree" (see 13:6–7).

21:30 Ὅταν with the subjunc. προβάλωσιν is temp. (3rd pl. 2nd aor. act. subjunc. of προβάλλω, "put forth"; i.e., "they put out [leaves]"; Fitzmyer 1352; Marshall 778). With the adv. ἤδη the sense is "as soon as" (NASB, HCSB, ESV; ZG 268; "after" Marshall 778; the double use of ἤδη in this verse emphasizes "the presence of the signs in the end-time" Bovon 3.120). Βλέποντες (see 8:10) is attendant circumstance (or a ptc. of means, cf. Wallace 628) with the indic. γινώσκετε (cf. 10:11). Ὅτι is a marker

of content (following vbs. of perception, BDAG 731d). Ἀφ᾽ ἑαυτῶν "from yourselves"
with βλέποντες is "you can see for yourselves" (HCSB, NIV). Θέρος nom. sg. neut. of
θέρος, -ους, τό, "summer." For ἐγγύς see 19:11.

21:31 Ὅταν with the subjunc. ἴδητε (see 12:54; in this context cf. 21:20, 29) is temp.
Γινόμενα (see 9:7) could be attrib. with ταῦτα or a complement in a double acc. cstr.
(BDAG 279c–d; BDF §157[1]). Γινώσκετε could be 2nd pl. pres. act. indic. ("you
know" NRSV, ESV, NIV; Bovon 3.121) or impv. ("recognize" NASB, HCSB; "know"
NET; Fitzmyer 1351); the context indicates that an impv. is in view here (i.e., as you
know about leaves and summer, so also know this). For ὅτι see 21:30. The adv. ἐγγύς
is the predicate of ἐστίν. Ἡ βασιλεία τοῦ θεοῦ here is a ref. to the consummation of the
kingdom in fullness (as with the "Son of Man coming" in 21:27 and "redemption" in
21:28).

21:32 For ἀμὴν λέγω ὑμῖν see 4:24. Οὐ μή with the subjunc. παρέλθῃ (3rd sg. 2nd aor.
act. subjunc. of dep. παρέρχομαι, "pass away") is an emphatic neg. The nom. ἡ γενεὰ
αὕτη is the subj. of παρέλθῃ. Ἕως ἄν with the subjunc. γένηται (see 1:20) is an indef.
temp. clause ("until all things take place" NASB; HCSB). See Bock 1688–92 for six
main views of the reference to "this generation" and to "all things." The destruction of
Jerusalem might be in view "as a type of the end of the world" (Robertson, *Pictures*
262). The refs. to "this generation" elsewhere in Luke (see 7:31; cf. Acts 2:40; LXX
Ps. 11:8) slightly favor the view that Jesus is referring to a continuation of wicked
opposition to his people right to the end when there will be both final vindication for
his people and judgment of the wicked (cf. Green 742).

21:33 Παρελεύσονται 3rd pl. fut. mid. indic. of dep. παρέρχομαι (cf. 21:32). Οὐ μή
with παρελεύσονται is again an emphatic neg. (the fut. and subjunc. could be used
interchangeably, R 873; Z §341; ZG 268; some mss. read an aor. subjunc.). Jesus both
affirms the temp. nature of creation and the everlasting permanence of his own words
(οἱ δὲ λόγοι μου), placing his words in the same eternal category as Scripture, the word
of God (see 9:26; 16:17; Ps 119:89; Isa 40:8).

21:34 For προσέχετε with ἑαυτοῖς ("watch out for yourselves" LN 27.59), see 12:1.
Μήποτε with the subjunc. βαρηθῶσιν (3rd pl. aor. pass. subjunc. of βαρέω, "burden,"
"weigh down"; see 9:32) expresses a neg. purpose clause ("Be on your guard so that"
HCSB). The nom. αἱ καρδίαι is the subj. of βαρηθῶσιν. Ἐν κραιπάλῃ καὶ μέθῃ καὶ
μερίμναις βιωτικαῖς is instr. Κραιπάλη dat. sg. fem. of κραιπάλη, -ης, ἡ, "drunken
behavior which is completely without moral restraint" (LN 88.286; cf. BDAG 564a).
Μέθη dat. sg. fem. of μέθη, -ης, ἡ, "drunkenness." Μερίμναις, "worries" (dat. pl. fem.,
see 8:14; modified by the adj. βιωτικαῖς [of βιωτικός, -ή, -όν] "of daily life"). The
subjunc. ἐπιστῇ (3rd sg. 2nd aor. act. subjunc. of ἐφίστημι, "come upon"; for ἐπί see
BDAG 366c; LN 90.57; R 542) with the earlier μήποτε also expresses a neg. purpose
clause (the aor. prohibition may be ingressive [Robertson, *Pictures* 262] or summarize
the action [Huffman 248]). The adj. αἰφνίδιος (nom. sg. fem. of αἰφνίδιος, -ον, "sudden") functions as an adv. (BDAG 31c; BDF §243; R 550; the image is completed in
21:35). The nom. ἡ ἡμέρα ἐκείνη (see 12:12; 17:31) is the subj. of ἐπιστῇ.

21:35 The conj. ὡς and παγίς (nom. sg. fem. of παγίς, -ίδος, ἡ, "trap") could either:

*1. complete the metaphor of 21:34 ("suddenly like a trap" NASB, ESV, NIV, sim. RV, NRSV, HCSB; SBLGNT; UBS⁵; in which the postpositive γάρ begins a new explanation following ἐπεισελεύσεται; א B D); or

2. introduce the reason given in 21:35 ("For as a snare it shall come" KJV, sim. NKJV; with the postpositive γάρ placed after ὡς παγίς; A C N W *f*¹·¹³ 𝔐).

The combination of early Alexandrian and Western mss. favor the first option (the second option may also be an assimilation to Isa 24:17; Metzger 147). Γάρ, causal (giving the reason for the warning in 21:34). There will be no escape because that day will be sudden (21:34) and universal (21:35). Ἐπεισελεύσεται 3rd sg. fut. mid. indic. of dep. ἐπεισέρχομαι, "overtake" (NET), "come upon" (ESV). Καθημένους acc. pl. masc. of pres. mid. (subst.) ptc. of dep. κάθημαι, "sit," "live" (most EVV).

21:36 The impv. ἀγρυπνεῖτε (2nd pl. pres. act. impv. of ἀγρυπνέω, "be alert") here means to remain faithful ("constant watch" Bock 1694; Fitzmyer 1356). Δεόμενοι (nom. pl. masc. of pres. mid. ptc. of dep. δέομαι, "pray") could be an attendant circumstance ptc. with the impv. ("Be always on the watch, and pray" NIV; BHGNT 660; cf. Nolland 1013) or instr. indicating the means ("Be alert . . . praying" NRSV, HCSB; Stein 530). Ἵνα may introduce indir. discourse ("that"; Z §407), or a purpose clause (Robertson, *Pictures* 262; ZG 268; Stein 530; cf. 18:1) with the aor. subjunc. κατισχύσητε (2nd pl. aor. act. subjunc. of κατισχύω, "have strength," "be able"). The 2nd aor. act. inf. ἐκφυγεῖν (of ἐκφεύγω, "to flee away," "escape") is complementary. Μέλλοντα acc. pl. neut. of pres. act. (subst.) ptc. of μέλλω ("the things which are about to"). The inf. γίνεσθαι (see 21:7) is complementary (with μέλλοντα). The aor. pass. inf. σταθῆναι (of ἵστημι, intrans.) is complementary (with κατισχύσητε). The phrase σταθῆναι ἔμπροσθεν τοῦ υἱοῦ τοῦ ἀνθρώπου (see 5:24) is idiomatic for "standing with approval in deliverance" (Bock 1695; with a "favorable verdict" Marshall 783; cf. Nolland 1013; see 21:27–28).

i. Concluding Summary: Jesus Teaches the People in the Temple (21:37–38)

These verses frame the entire unit from 19:47–48 (cf. 20:1). The emphasis on the favor that Jesus is enjoying from the people (λαός) has run throughout this section (cf. 19:48 [ὁ λαὸς . . . ἅπας]; 20:1, 6, 19, 26, 45; 21:38 [πᾶς ὁ λαός]).

21:37 The impf. periph. ptc. cstr. ἦν . . . διδάσκων summarizes subsequent events (BHGNT 660) but also emphasizes Jesus' continual activity of teaching in this context (Fitzmyer 1358). The acc. τὰς ἡμέρας . . . τὰς δὲ νύκτας also highlights duration of time (BDF §161[2]; R 470; ZG 269; Bock 1695; Bovon 3.124; Fitzmyer 1358; Marshall 784). Ηὐλίζετο 3rd sg. impf. mid. indic. of dep. αὐλίζομαι, "spend the night" (HCSB), "lodged" (ESV). Εἰς in place of ἐν is common in Luke (BDF §205; Fitzmyer 1358). For τὸ ὄρος τὸ καλούμενον see 19:29.

21:38 For πᾶς ὁ λαός see 18:43 (19:48). Ὤρθριζεν 3rd sg. impf. act. indic. of ὀρθρίζω "rise early in the morning" (cf. Nolland 1015; the sg. vb. is used with a collective sg.

subj., Wallace 400). The impf. indicates customary action. The inf. ἀκούειν (see 5:1) expresses purpose ("to listen," with the obj. gen. αὐτοῦ BDF §390; ZG 269; Fitzmyer 1358). Some mss. in *f*¹³ place John 7:53–8:11 here after 21:38.

HOMILETICAL SUGGESTIONS

Preparing for the End (21:5–38)

1. Don't be easily taken in by events that aren't signs of the end (21:5–11).
2. Don't worry beforehand about how you will bear witness to persecutors (21:12–19).
3. Be assured, although the end will be worse than the judgment on Jerusalem, Jesus will return to deliver his people (21:20–28).
4. Trust in Jesus' sure word in the midst of temptations to give up (21:29–38).

B. PREPARING FOR AND EXPLAINING THE
MEANING OF JESUS' DEATH (22:1–38)

The focus now turns to events directly leading to Jesus' death and resurrection. Luke 22–24 completes the predictions Jesus has made since 9:22.

1. Betrayal: The Satanic Conspiracy that Led to Jesus' Death (22:1–6)

22:1 The impf. ἤγγιζεν (3rd sg. impf. act. indic. of ἐγγίζω) indicates that the "festival" (HCSB, NIV; "feast" ESV; see 2:41–42) "was drawing near" (HCSB). The gen. (pl. neut.) τῶν ἀζύμων (of ἄζυμος, -ον, "unleavened") is appos. (R 416, 498; Wallace 98; for the pl. cf. BDF §141[3]). The festival is then further described with the attrib. ptc. λεγομένη (nom. sg. fem. of pres. pass. ptc. of λέγω) as that festival "which is called" Passover. Since the festival went for a week and followed the day of Passover, the one name was sometimes used for both feasts (cf. Deut 16:1–8).

22:2 The impf. ἐζήτουν (see 5:18) could be conative (NET; Robertson, *Pictures* 264) or portray the continued planning of the chief priests and scribes in the lead up to the festival (Bock 1703; Bovon 3.133; Marshall 787). The art. τό nominalizes the interr. clause πῶς ἀνέλωσιν αὐτόν as the dir. obj. of ἐζήτουν (BHGNT 662; R 427; an indir. question, BDF §267[2]; R 766; ZG 269; see 1:62; cf. 22:4, 23, 24). Ἀνέλωσιν 3rd pl. 2nd aor. act. (deliberative) subjunc. of ἀναιρέω, "take away," "destroy," "kill" (R 1031; Z §347; ἀναιρέω is common in the LXX and occurs here, 23:32, and nineteen times in Acts out of twenty-four in the NT). The reason (γάρ) for their action is their fear (ἐφοβοῦντο, see 9:45) of the people (see 18:43; in this context, 21:38).

22:3 The murderous intentions of the chief priests and scribes provide the context for Satan's (see 4:2) entry into Judas (εἰσῆλθεν, see 1:40; an ingressive aor. Robertson, *Pictures* 264; cf. John 13:2; Acts 5:3). Καλούμενον (see 6:15) is attrib. (for Ἰσκαριώτην see 6:16 where the Sem. form Ἰσκαριώθ is used). The acc. ptc. ὄντα (of εἰμί, see 12:28) is also attrib. modifying Ἰούδαν so that Judas is also described as being "numbered among the Twelve" (HCSB; ἀριθμοῦ gen. sg. masc. of ἀριθμός, -οῦ, ὁ, "number").

22:4 Ἀπελθών (see 5:14) is an attendant circumstance ptc. with συνελάλησεν (3rd sg. aor. act. indic. of συλλαλέω, "talk with," "discuss"). Στρατηγοῖς (dat. pl. masc. of στρατηγός, -οῦ, ὁ, "officers" NASB, ESV) is probably a shortened form of the full title στρατηγὸς τοῦ ἱεροῦ (hence "officers of the temple guard" NIV; cf. LN 37.91; cf. 22:52; Acts 4:1; 5:24, 26; the ten NT occurrences of στρατηγός are all in Luke-Acts). The cstr. τὸ . . . αὐτόν deliberately parallels 22:2 (Nolland 1030). Παραδῷ 3rd sg. 2nd aor. act. (deliberative, R 1031) subjunc. of παραδίδωμι, "hand over," "betray."

22:5 The response of delight from the Jewish leaders (ἐχάρησαν 3rd pl. 2nd aor. pass. indic. of χαίρω; an ingressive aor. Robertson, *Pictures* 265) is because Judas has solved their dilemma and will give them the opportunity they have been looking for. So they agreed with one another (as indicated by συν in συνέθεντο 3rd pl. 2nd aor. mid. indic. of συντίθημι, "agree"; intrans.; cf. BDAG 975d; ZG 269) to give (the inf. δοῦναι [see

1:73] is complementary) money (ἀργύριον, see 9:3) to him (note παραδῷ . . . δοῦναι . . . παραδοῦναι, 22:4–6).

22:6 Καί and the compound ἐξωμολόγησεν (3rd sg. aor. act. indic. of ἐξομολογέω, mid. "confess"; here "consent") complete 22:5 and indicate Judas' agreement with their offer. The impf. ἐζήτει (see 9:9) again indicates Judas' continued efforts following the agreement (BDF §325; Bock 1706; iter. Fitzmyer 1375). Εὐκαιρίαν acc. sg. fem. of εὐκαιρία, -ας, ἡ, "good opportunity" (NASB, HCSB). The art. inf. τοῦ παραδοῦναι (see 20:20; the acc. αὐτόν is the dir. obj.; the dat. αὐτοῖς is the indir. obj.) may indicate the purpose of seeking for this opportunity (Z §386; ZG 269), or it is *epex., further explaining εὐκαιρίαν (a common Lukan cstr.; BHGNT 664; Burton §400; R 1067–68, 1076; Wallace 607). The prep. ἄτερ ("without," "apart from"; only here, 22:35 in the NT) is followed by the gen. (i.e., "when the crowd was not present" HCSB).

HOMILETICAL SUGGESTIONS

Surprising Participants in the Wicked Plan for Jesus' Death (22:1–6)

1. The religious leaders pursued the way (22:1–2).
2. One of Jesus' own followers presented the means (22:4–6).
3. Satan provided the inspiration (22:3).

2. Passover: Jesus' Death Is a Willing Sacrifice that Inaugurates the New Covenant (22:7–20)

22:7 Whereas the festival was drawing near in 22:1, now the "day of unleavened bread" (ἡ ἑορτή is probably assumed and includes the Passover) has "arrived" (NLT; ἦλθεν, see 2:27; cf. 22:14). The antecedent of the (temp.) dat. rel. pron. ᾗ is ἡ ἡμέρα. Ἔδει, see 11:42; 2:49. The pres. pass. inf. θύεσθαι (of θύω, "sacrifice") is complementary. Πάσχα is metonymy for "Passover lamb" (Bock 1710).

22:8 Ἀπέστειλεν, see 7:3 (for Πέτρον καὶ Ἰωάννην see refs. at 8:51). Εἰπών (see 9:22) could express means (BHGNT 665) or attendant circumstance (Z §262; ZG 269). Πορευθέντες (see 7:22) is an attendant circumstance ptc. (with ἑτοιμάσατε see 3:4; cf. 22:9, 12–13) and takes on the mood of the impv. ("go and prepare"; cf. Wallace 644). The pron. ἡμῖν is a dat. of advantage. Τὸ πάσχα here is "the Passover meal" (NRSV, HCSB; ZG 269; Bock 1710). The purpose (ἵνα followed by the subjunc.) of the preparations is that they may eat it together (φάγωμεν 1st pl. 2nd aor. act. subjunc. of ἐσθίω).

22:9 Εἶπαν, in this context, "asked." Ποῦ introduces a dir. question. Θέλεις, see 9:54. The subjunc. ἑτοιμάσωμεν (1st pl. aor. act. subjunc. of ἑτοιμάζω) is deliberative (without ἵνα, Burton §171; Robertson, *Pictures* 266; cf. 9:54; 18:41).

22:10 Ἰδού is "listen" (NRSV, HCSB; "behold" ESV; omitted in NASB, NIV; see 1:20). Εἰσελθόντων (gen. pl. masc. of 2nd aor. act. ptc. of dep. εἰσέρχομαι) and pron. ὑμῶν is a temp. gen. abs. cstr. of concordant action ("As you enter" NIV; Z §49; ZG 270; Fitzmyer 1383). Συναντήσει 3rd sg. fut. act. indic. of συναντάω "meet" (ὑμῖν is the dat. complement, BDAG 965b; ἄνθρωπος is the subj.). Κεράμιον acc. sg. neut. of κεράμιον, -ου, τό, "jar" (ὕδατος [see 3:16], a gen. of content), is the acc. obj. of βαστάζων (nom. sg. masc. of pres. act. ptc. of βαστάζω, "carry"; attrib. modifying ἄνθρωπος). Ἀκολουθήσατε 2nd pl. aor. act. impv. of ἀκολουθέω, "follow" (αὐτῷ is the dat. complement, BDAG 36d). Εἰσπορεύεται 3rd sg. pres. mid. indic. of dep. εἰσπορεύομαι.

22:11 The fut. indic. ἐρεῖτε (see 4:23) is used as an impv. (Z §280; ZG 270). Οἰκοδεσπότη τῆς οἰκίας, "owner of the house" (NRSV, NASB, NIV), "master of the house" (ESV) in which τῆς οἰκίας is pleonastic (see 12:39; BDF §484; R 1205). Λέγει σοι ὁ διδάσκαλος when followed by ποῦ is probably "the Teacher asks" (HCSB, NIV). Κατάλυμα, "lodging place," "guest room" (see 2:7). The subjunc. φάγω (see 17:8) may be deliberative, following ὅπου (BHGNT 667; R 955), or complementary, expressing purpose (BDF §378; Burton §318; Z §343; ZG 270; Marshall 792).

22:12 Κἀκεῖνος ("Then he" HCSB; see 11:7; the paratactic cstr. is Sem., Marshall 792) is the subj. of δείξει (3rd sg. fut. act. indic. of δείκνυμι, "show"). Ἀνάγαιον μέγα ("large upper room"; acc. sg. neut. of ἀνάγαιον, -ου, τό) is the dir. obj. of δείξει. Ἐστρωμένον acc. sg. neut. of pf. pass. (attrib.) ptc. of στρωννύω, "furnished" (Bock 1713; Fitzmyer 1383) modifies the acc. ἀνάγαιον μέγα. Ἑτοιμάσατε, see 3:4 (22:8).

22:13 Ἀπελθόντες (see 19:32) is probably attendant circumstance with εὗρον (see 2:46; "they went and found"; the obj. ["it" HCSB, ESV; "things" NIV] is implied). Καθώς emphasizes the exact fulfilment of what Jesus "had said" (εἰρήκει 3rd sg. pluperfect act. indic. of λέγω, cf. Wallace 585; Z §290; cf. 19:32). Ἡτοίμασαν 3rd pl. aor. act. indic. of ἑτοιμάζω.

22:14 The temp. ὅτε ἐγένετο ἡ ὥρα (see 1:5) completes the temp. refs. in 22:1, 7. Ἀνέπεσεν, see 11:37 (the implied subj. is Jesus). The addition of καὶ οἱ ἀπόστολοι σὺν αὐτῷ (ἀναπίπτω needs to be supplied, Fitzmyer 1384) keeps the focus on Jesus (BHGNT 668; the use of ἀπόστολοι in this setting may anticipate their role in 22:29–30). This verse provides the setting for the Passover meal (Bock 1718; [transitional] Bovon 3.145; Marshall 794; though Fitzmyer 1376 places the verse as the conclusion to 22:7–13).

22:15 The cognate dat. (of manner) ἐπιθυμίᾳ ("with desire") with ἐπεθύμησα (1st sg. aor. act. indic. of ἐπιθυμέω, "desire") reflects a Heb. inf. abs. cstr. (from the LXX) emphasizing the action of the vb. ("I have earnestly desired" NASB, ESV; BDF §198[6]; R 531; Wallace 169; Z §60; Bock 1719; Bovon 3.156; Fitzmyer 1395; Marshall 795). The inf. φαγεῖν (see 6:4) is complementary. Τοῦτο τὸ πάσχα "this Passover" ("lamb" [22:7] or "meal" [22:8]) is the dir. obj. The inf. παθεῖν (see 9:22) with πρὸ τοῦ is temp. (see refs. at 2:21). The acc. με is the subj. of παθεῖν ("before I suffer"; see 9:22).

22:16 Γάρ, causal (giving the reason for his desire to eat this Passover meal). Ὅτι, recitative. The double neg. οὐ μή with the 2nd aor. subjunc. φάγω (see 17:8) is emphatic and future referring (BDF §365; Z §444; ZG 270; αὐτό [the antecedent is τὸ πάσχα] is the obj.). For ἕως ὅτου see 12:50 (neut. sg. in agreement with αὐτό; πληρωθῇ 3rd sg. aor. pass. subjunc.). The pass. is probably a divine pass. The implied subj. is τὸ πάσχα. However, the ref. to πληρωθῇ ἐν τῇ βασιλείᾳ τοῦ θεοῦ together with the following reinterpretation of this meal (to remember Jesus) and inauguration of the *new* covenant, indicate that Jesus refers to an ultimate fulfillment in an eschatological sense (rather than a future reinstitution of some sacrifices, *pace* Bock 1721). Ἐν τῇ βασιλείᾳ τοῦ θεοῦ could be locat. or temp. (rather than instr., *pace* Fitzmyer 1397).

22:17 The sequence begins with this first cup (of four in a Passover meal, Bock 1723; Nolland 1051). The two nom. sg. masc. of aor. ptcs. δεξάμενος (mid. of dep. δέχομαι) and εὐχαριστήσας (act. of εὐχαριστέω) are probably temp. (NASB). Λάβετε 2nd pl. 2nd aor. act. impv. of λαμβάνω. Διαμερίσατε 2nd pl. aor. act. impv. of διαμερίζω ("divide" ESV, NIV; "share" NASB, HCSB; i.e., pass the cup to each person BHGNT 669; LN 22.17). Εἰς ἑαυτούς is locat. ("among yourselves"; Z §209; ZG 270).

22:18 Jesus reaffirms (γάρ) the reason for his desire to have this Passover meal (22:16). As with 22:16, the double neg. οὐ μή with the subjunc. πίω (see 17:8) is emphatic. For ἀπὸ τοῦ νῦν see 1:48. Γενήματος gen. sg. neut. of γένημα, -ατος, τό, "fruit," "produce." Ἀπὸ τοῦ γενήματος τῆς ἀμπέλου ("from the fruit of the vine"; gen. sg. fem. of ἄμπελος, -ου, ἡ) is a ref. to the wine of the Passover meal (NLT; Bock 1724; Fitzmyer 1398). Ἕως (cf. 22:16) with the gen. rel. pron. οὗ is a temp. rel. phrase with the subjunc. ἔλθῃ (see 1:43; i.e., "until the time when" BHGNT 670).

22:19 The two aor. ptcs. λαβών (see 6:4) and εὐχαριστήσας (see 22:17) are probably temp. with the following ἔκλασεν (3rd sg. aor. act. indic. of κλάω, "break") and ἔδωκεν (see 6:4; "when He had taken some bread and given thanks, He broke it and gave it" NASB; cf. 22:17). In the NT κλάω is always used for breaking bread (cf. 24:30; Acts 2:46; 20:7, 11; 27:35). The neut. τοῦτο has assimilated to the pred. (neut.) σῶμα (BDF §132[1]). Ἐστίν has the mng. "represents" since Jesus is present as he gives them the bread (BDAG 284a; Bock 1724–25). The external evidence (early, Alexandrian and Western) is overwhelmingly in favor of the inclusion of 22:19b–20 (τὸ ὑπὲρ ὑμῶν . . . ἐκχυννόμενον). It is only omitted in some Western mss. (D), probably due to the unusual sequence of cup-bread-cup (Metzger 148–49, 164–66 [on so-called "Western non-interpolations"]; Bock 1721–22; Bovon 3.155). In the setting of a Passover meal, ὑπὲρ ὑμῶν, with the attrib. ptc. τὸ . . . διδόμενον (nom. sg. neut. of pres. pass. ptc. of δίδωμι; modifying τὸ σῶμά) has a vicarious sense (Bock 1725; the pres. ptc. is probably fut. referring [see refs. at 1:35] and is used as a rel. clause, BDF §412; Fitzmyer 1400). Τοῦτο is the dir. obj. of the impv. ποιεῖτε (see 3:4) and points forward to breaking and sharing bread after Jesus' ascension. The purpose (εἰς, ZG 271; Harris 97) of taking this bread will be to remember (not the deliverance from Egypt, but) Jesus (τὴν ἐμὴν ἀνάμνησιν [acc. sg. fem. of ἀνάμνησις, -εως, ἡ]; i.e., Jesus and his sacrificial death for them; cf. 1 Cor 11:24). The acc. adj. ἐμήν [of ἐμός, -ή, -όν] is obj. (R 685; Harris 97).

22:20 The use of the adv. ὡσαύτως ("likewise") here with ref. to the cup implies the same action of taking (with λαβών understood) the cup as the previous verse (HCSB, NIV; now the third of the four cups, Bock 1727). The art. aor. act. inf. τὸ δειπνῆσαι (of δειπνέω, "eat"; i.e., the Passover meal, Marshall 805) with μετά is temp. (the action of the inf. occurs before the controlling vb.; tr. with "after"; R 1074; Wallace 595). The nom. τοῦτο τὸ ποτήριον is the subj. of a clause in which ἐστίν must be supplied (cf. 22:19). Ἡ καινὴ διαθήκη is the pred. nom. (cf. Jer 31:31 διαθήκην καινήν). Ἐν τῷ αἵματί μου is instr. indicating the means by which the new covenant is established ("established by My blood" HCSB; ZG 271; Nolland 1054; [causative] Marshall 807; Nolland 1054; cf. Exod 24:8 τὸ αἷμα τῆς διαθήκης). The nom. sg. neut. of pres. pass. ptc. ἐκχυννόμενον (of ἐκχέω, "pour out") could be attrib. modifying the nom. sg. neut. τοῦτο τὸ ποτήριον ("this cup that is poured out for you" NRSV, ESV; the cup by meton-ymy refers to its contents, Marshall 806). It is possible that the ptc. agrees "in sense, but not in case" (Fitzmyer 1403; cf. Bovon 3.159; Nolland 1054) with the dat. τῷ αἵματί μου (NIV). Note the parallel between τὸ ὑπὲρ ὑμῶν διδόμενον (22:19) and τὸ ὑπὲρ ὑμῶν ἐκχυννόμενον (22:20). As with 22:19, Jesus' death is both vicarious and sacrificial.

HOMILETICAL SUGGESTIONS

Redemption Pictured (22:7–20)

1. The lamb of the Passover pointed to our ultimate redemption through Jesus' death (22:7–18).
2. The bread of the Lord's Supper points us to Jesus' sacrificial death for us (22:19).
3. The cup of the Lord's Supper points us to the blessings of the new covenant through Jesus' death (22:20).

3. Final Teaching: Jesus Knows His Death Will Fulfill God's Plan and What the Future Holds for His Disciples (22:21–38)

This section is Jesus' final block of teaching to his disciples before the events surrounding his crucifixion. Jesus' knowledge and power are again highlighted.

a. Jesus Knows the Betrayer and God's Plan (22:21–23)

22:21 The emphatic adversative πλήν together with ἰδού (see 1:20) mark a sharp contrast from the preceding to shift the focus to the following statement (Fitzmyer 1409; Marshall 808). "The hand" (ἡ χείρ) of the one betraying Jesus could be synecdoche for the person (Fitzmyer 1409). The pres. (subst.) ptc. παραδιδόντος (gen. sg. masc. of pres. act. ptc. of παραδίδωμι; cf. 22:4) could be fut. referring (Marshall 809) or highlight the current process of the betrayal (Bock 1733). Τραπέζης, "table" (see 16:21). The phrase μετ' ἐμοῦ ἐπὶ τῆς τραπέζης does not specifically identify Judas as the betrayer (cf. 22:23) but emphasizes the closeness of the betrayer to Jesus. Ἐπί is locat. (either "at" [HCSB] or "on" [most EVV]; the art. may have demonstrative force, Fitzmyer 1410; cf. 22:30).

22:22 Ὅτι, causal ("for"; omitted in NIV; explaining why there is a betrayer present, BHGNT 672). Μὲν . . . πλήν highlights the contrast more than μὲν . . . δὲ (R 1152, 1153). Κατά followed by ὡρισμένον (acc. sg. neut. of pf. pass. [subst.] ptc. of ὁρίζω, "determine"; a divine pass.) specifies that the "going" (the pres. πορεύεται [see 7:8] perhaps indicates that this is already in progress) of the Son of Man is "in accordance with" (Cassirer) God's determination (cf. Acts 2:23; 4:28). The pf. probably highlights the settled state. Οὐαί, see 6:24. Τῷ ἀνθρώπῳ (dat. of disadvantage) could be a play on τοῦ ἀνθρώπου (see 9:44). Δι' οὗ expresses intermediate agency (cf. Wallace 433–34). Παραδίδοται 3rd sg. pres. pass. indic. of παραδίδωμι (see 18:32 [22:4–6, 21]).

22:23 Ἤρξαντο, see 5:21. The pres. act. inf. συζητεῖν (of συζητέω, "discuss" NASB; "argue" HCSB; "question" ESV, NIV) is complementary. For the art. τό and the interr. clause τίς . . . πράσσειν (here, the dir. obj. of συζητεῖν; R 430) see 22:2. The optative (εἴη, of εἰμί, see 1:29) could be a "potential optative" ("who it could be"; without ἄν, Z §356; ZG 271) or an "oblique optative" used in indir. speech ("who it was"; Wallace 483; Z §346; ZG 271; a cstr. found only in Luke's writings in the NT). Μέλλων (nom. sg. masc. of pres. act. [subst.] ptc. of μέλλω) with the complementary pres. act. inf. πράσσειν (of πράσσω) expresses future action ("which of them it could be who was going to do this" ESV, sim. HCSB).

b. Jesus Determines the Character of the Apostles' Leadership in His Kingdom (22:24–30)

22:24 Ἐγένετο δὲ καί (see 1:5; 2:4) links this "dispute" (φιλονεικία nom. sg. fem. of φιλονεικία, -ας, ἡ; only here in the NT; it is the subj. of ἐγένετο) closely with the preceding argument (cf. 9:44–46). For the art. τό and the interr. clause τίς . . . μείζων (here, in appos. to φιλονεικία) see 22:2 (cf. 9:46). Δοκεῖ, see 8:18 (of δοκέω, intrans.

"regarded" NASB, ESV; "considered" HCSB, NIV; the indic. is retained for the indir. question, R 1031). The complementary inf. εἶναι (see 2:4) is used in indir. discourse (after vbs. of perception, Wallace 605). The comp. adj. μείζων is used as a superl. (BDF §244; Robertson, *Pictures* 269; Z §§147–50; ZG 271; cf. 22:26–27).

22:25 The gen. τῶν ἐθνῶν may be obj. or a gen. of subordination (Wallace 119). Κυριεύουσιν (3rd pl. pres. act. indic. of κυριεύω, "lord over") takes the gen. (hence αὐτῶν, R 510; Wallace 134; the pres. is probably gnomic). Ἐξουσιάζοντες nom. pl. masc. of pres. act. (subst.) ptc. of ἐξουσιάζω ("those who have authority over" HCSB). Εὐεργέται nom. pl. masc. of εὐεργέτης, -ου, ὁ, "benefactor" (see BDAG 405b–c; MM 261a–b; G. Bertram, *TDNT* 2.654–55). Καλοῦνται 3rd pl. pres. pass. indic. of καλέω (pass. "are called" most EVV; mid. "call themselves" NIV; or perhaps, "let/have themselves [be] called" Fitzmyer 1416–17; Nolland 1064).

22:26 The nom. ὑμεῖς is the subj. of an implied vb. (ἐστέ, NIV; BHGNT 675; or ποιήσετε, BDF §480[5]; Marshall 812) and introduces an emphatic contrast (with ἀλλά, Fitzmyer 1417). The subst. adjs. μείζων (the subj.) and νεώτερος (see 5:37; 15:12) could be comp. (Bock 1736) or comp. in form but superl. in mng. (BHGNT 675; Marshall 813). Γινέσθω 3rd sg. pres. mid. impv. of dep. γίνομαι. The nom. sg. masc. of pres. ptcs. ἡγούμενος (mid. of dep. ἡγέομαι, "leader" NRSV, NASB, ESV, sim. HCSB; "one who rules" NIV; cf. Acts 15:22) and διακονῶν (act. of διακονέω; cf. 8:3; 12:37; following ὡς expresses manner, Burton §446) are subst.

22:27 Γάρ is explanatory. On μείζων see 22:26 (comp. here). The pres. ptcs. ἀνακείμενος (nom. sg. masc. of pres. mid. ptc. of dep. ἀνάκειμαι, "recline [at a table]") and διακονῶν (see 22:26) are subst. The rhetorical question is answered with another question (οὐχί, see 4:22, in terms of customary estimation). The pron. ἐγώ is emphatic. For ὡς ὁ διακονῶν see 22:26 (though Jesus is ὁ μείζων).

22:28 Διαμεμενηκότες (nom. pl. masc. of pf. act. [subst.] ptc. of διαμένω, "remain"; "stood by Me" NASB, HCSB; "stayed with me" ESV; cf. Acts 1:21–22) is a pred. nom. (Burton §433; R 1108). The pf. and prep. may emphasize persistence and loyalty over the course of Jesus' ministry (Bock 1739; Fitzmyer 1418). Πειρασμοῖς, "trials" (dat. pl. masc., see 4:13).

22:29 Διατίθεμαι (1st sg. pres. mid. indic. of διατίθημι, "confer" NRSV, NIV; "assign" RSV, ESV; "grant" NASB; "bestow" HCSB) with βασιλείαν means to grant the "role of ruling" (LN 37.105; cf. also BDAG 238c; cf. Deut 29:13; Acts 3:25; though NASB has the ἵνα clause of 22:30 as the obj.). The pres. emphasizes the imminence of the conferral in light of the Son's return to the Father (note the Father's conferral in 12:32; note also the unique relationship implied in ὁ πατήρ μου; see 1:32). This conferral is in keeping with the pattern (καθώς) of what the Father has done for Jesus (Marshall 816). Διέθετο 3rd sg. 2nd aor. mid. indic. of διατίθημι.

22:30 Ἵνα followed by the two 2nd pl. pres. act. subjuncs. ἔσθητε (of ἐσθίω, "eat") and πίνητε (of πίνω, "drink") indicates that the purpose of the conferral of this rule is fellowship with the Lord Jesus in his kingdom (ZG 271 suggests that the subjunc.

could indicate result; cf. Z §352; the cstr. may also be explanatory, Nolland 1066; note τραπέζης μου . . . βασιλείᾳ μου here and ἡ βασιλεία τοῦ θεοῦ in 22:16, 18). Τραπέζης, "table" (see 16:21; 22:21). The fut. καθήσεσθε (2nd pl. fut. mid. indic. of dep. κάθημαι, "sit") may be part of the ἵνα clause (as with ESV, NIV; Z §340; ZG 271) or a new statement coordinate with 22:29 (BHGNT 678; cf. NRSV, HCSB). Κρίνοντες (nom. pl. masc. of pres. act. ptc. of κρίνω) expresses manner. Jesus' (twelve) apostles are the new leaders of God's people (cf. Acts 1:8, 21–26).

c. Jesus Predicts Peter's Temporary Failure and Preserves Peter's Faith from Satan's Destructive Designs (22:31–34)

22:31 On double vocs. see 6:46 (for εἶπεν δὲ ὁ κύριος [A D 𝔐] see Rowe 177). The interjection ἰδού (see 1:20) intensifies the following warning ("listen!" NRSV; "look out!" HCSB; omitted NIV). Ἐξητήσατο 3rd sg. aor. mid. indic. of dep. ἐξαιτέομαι, "asked" (HCSB, NIV), "demanded" (NRSV, NASB, ESV). The pl. ὑμᾶς (acc. obj. of σινιάσαι) indicates that Satan (see 4:2; 22:3) has all the apostles in view including Peter. The art. aor. act. inf. τοῦ σινιάσαι (of σινιάζω, "sift") could express purpose (Robertson, *Pictures* 270; Wallace 592; ZG 272; Bock 1742) or indir. discourse (BHGNT 678). The phrase "sift you like wheat" (σῖτον, see 3:17) is an idiom mng. "pick you apart" or "leave you in pieces" (Bock 1742). The image suggests destruction, as the following contrast indicates (cf. Bovon 3.177).

22:32 Ἐγώ is emphatic (Stein 552). Ἐδεήθην, see 9:40 (here, "prayed" most EVV; "pleaded" NLT). The use of ἵνα with the subjunc. ἐκλίπῃ (see 16:9; neg. with μή) may express purpose (Robertson, *Pictures* 270) or introduce indir. discourse (BHGNT 679; both purpose and the content of the prayer, Marshall 821). The gen. σου is subj. ("your faith"). The point is not that Peter will never fail but that his faith will not "disappear" (Marshall 821) or drain "away to nothing" (Nolland 1072). His failure will be tempo- rary (Bock 1742). The nom. σύ is emphatic (Fitzmyer 1425). Ἐπιστρέψας (nom. sg. masc. of aor. act. ptc. of ἐπιστρέφω, intrans. "turned back" HCSB, NIV; "turned again" NASB, ESV; "repented and turned to me again" NLT; BDAG 382b) is temp. together with the adv. ποτέ ("once"; cf. Wallace 642; in keeping with Lukan usage this is the likely mng. rather than viewing the ptc. as trans. and attendant circumstance ["turn . . . and strengthen"; cf. Fitzmyer 1425; Marshall 822). Στήρισον 2nd sg. aor. act. impv. of στηρίζω, "strengthen."

22:33 Κύριε, voc. (see 5:8). The pred. adj. ἕτοιμος (see 12:40) with εἰμί is "I am ready." Καὶ . . . καί is "both . . . and" The inf. πορεύεσθαι (see 4:42) is epex. to ἕτοιμος (cf. BDAG 401b; R 659). Φυλακήν, "prison" (cf. Acts 5:19; 12:4).

22:34 The fut. φωνήσει (3rd sg. fut. act. indic. of φωνέω, intrans.) in this context with the subj. ἀλέκτωρ (nom. sg. masc. of ἀλέκτωρ, -ορος, ὁ, "rooster") and neg. οὐ is "will not crow" (most EVV). Ἕως with the subjunc. ἀπαρνήσῃ (2nd sg. aor. mid. subjunc. of dep. ἀπαρνέομαι, "deny") is temp. (without ἄν, Burton §323; R 976; cf. 22:57–61). The acc. pron. με is the dir. obj. of the inf. εἰδέναι (see 20:7; used in indir. discourse;

"that you know me"; Burton §§112, 390; R 908; ZG 272). Jesus knows that Peter will not only deny knowing him, but he will do it soon and multiple times.

d. Jesus Prepares His Disciples for Opposition Following His Own Suffering (22:35–38)

22:35 Ἀπέστειλα 1st sg. aor. act. indic. of ἀποστέλλω. Ἄτερ, see 22:6. Βαλλαντίου, "money bag" (see 10:4). Πήρας, "traveling bag" (HCSB; see 9:3; 10:4). Ὑποδημάτων, "sandals" (see 3:16). The neg. μή expects the answer "no." Ὑστερήσατε 2nd pl. aor. act. indic. of ὑστερέω, "lack." Οὐθενός gen. sg. neut. of οὐδείς, "nothing." The ref. here could be back to 9:3 or 10:4.

22:36 The contrastive ἀλλὰ νῦν signals the change. The obj. of ἔχων (see 3:11; subst.) is βαλλάντιον (see 10:4; 22:35). The impv. ἀράτω (of αἴρω, see 9:23) has the implied objs. βαλλάντιον and πήραν. The implied obj. of ὁ μὴ ἔχων is μάχαιραν ([see 21:24] Nolland 1076; see options in Bock 1746–47; Fitzmyer 1431–32; Marshall 825). Πωλησάτω 3rd sg. aor. act. impv. of πωλέω, "sell." Ἀγορασάτω 3rd sg. aor. act. impv. of ἀγοράζω, "buy." In the context of the disciples' apparent misunderstanding in 22:38, this is likely to be a metaphorical ref. to preparedness for future opposition (Bock 1747; Fitzmyer 1432; Marshall 825; Nolland 1076).

22:37 Γάρ, causal (giving the reason for the change that is coming). It is because ("for"; omitted in NIV) of the suffering and rejection that Jesus himself is soon to face. The acc. demonstrative pron. τοῦτο is the subj. of the aor. pass. inf. τελεσθῆναι (of τελέω, "fulfilled"). Γεγραμμένον (see 4:17) is attrib., modifying τοῦτο (and points forward to the quotation from Isa 53:12). The inf. τελεσθῆναι is complementary with δεῖ (see 2:49). In this context (with δεῖ) the pass. τελεσθῆναι is a "divine passive." The art. τό (as an introduction to the citation, cf. Marshall 826; Nolland 1076) functions as a nominalizer (see 22:2) so that the following clause καὶ μετὰ ἀνόμων ἐλογίσθη is epex. to τοῦτο τὸ γεγραμμένον (BHGNT 683; appos., R 401; n., LXX ἐν τοῖς ἀνόμοις). Ἀνόμων gen. pl. masc. (of ἄνομος, -ον), "lawless" (NRSV), "transgressors" (NASB, ESV, NIV), "outlaws" (HCSB). Ἐλογίσθη 3rd sg. aor. pass. indic. of dep. λογίζομαι, "counted" (NRSV, HCSB), "numbered" (NASB, ESV, NIV). The art. τό nominalizes the prep. phrase as the subj. of τέλος ἔχει (see 5:24; "has its fulfillment" ESV; i.e., ref. to Scripture and reemphasizing fulfillment, ZG 272; or "reaches its goal," Fitzmyer 1433; though Marshall [826] sees a ref. to Jesus' life drawing to an end [BDAG 998b]). Isa 53:12 culminates the suffering servant song of 52:13–53:12 and, in this context, introduces the events of Jesus' suffering and death (Pao and Schnabel 388a–d).

22:38 Μάχαιραι [nom. pl. fem., see 21:24] . . . δύο is the subj. of a verbless clause (with εἰσίν implied). The neut. pred. adj. ἱκανόν ("sufficient," "enough") in this context is unlikely to mean "two swords are enough" (cf. 22:50–51). It is more likely that this is idiomatic for "it is enough [of the matter]," or "That's enough!" (NIV; "Enough of that!" HCSB; ZG 272; Bovon 3.183; Marshall 827; cf. Deut 3:26).

HOMILETICAL SUGGESTIONS

Our Suffering Savior Prepares Us to Follow Him (22:21–38)
1. Jesus shows that even the betrayal of a close follower is under the purposes of God (22:21–22).
2. Jesus models the pattern of service as the way to lead among the people of God (22:23–30).
3. Jesus knows the weakness of his followers yet preserves them from Satan to keep them in the service of God (22:31–34).
4. Jesus warns of the reality of opposition in keeping with his own suffering as the servant of God (22:35–38).

C. EVENTS THAT SHOW JESUS' INNOCENCE AND GOD'S JUDGMENT IN THE DEATH OF JESUS (22:39–23:49)

A major turning point occurs here with Jesus' departure to the Mount of Olives. Jesus is alone with his disciples but apart from the crowd. This provides the opportunity for Judas to lead the Jerusalem leaders to Jesus, and with his arrest the trials and crucifixion follow.

1. Prayer in the Face of Trial (22:39–46)

This account is framed by Jesus' exhortations to pray (προσεύχεσθε, 22:40, 46), and it centers on his own prayer (προσηύχετο, 22:41, 44) and answer to prayer (22:43). The larger section also concludes with Jesus in prayer to his Father (23:46).

22:39 Ἐξελθών (see 1:22) could be temp. or attendant circumstance with ἐπορεύθη (see 1:39; the 3rd sg., with καὶ οἱ μαθηταί at the end of the verse, focuses on the action of Jesus). Ἔθος, see 1:9. Τὸ ὄρος τῶν ἐλαιῶν, see 19:29, 37; 21:37. Ἠκολούθησαν, see 5:11 (the dat. αὐτῷ is complementary, BDAG 36d).

22:40 Γενόμενος, see 10:32 (temp., ESV). Ἐπὶ τοῦ τόπου is locat. (i.e., Gethsemane; for γίνομαι with ἐπί in this sense cf. 3:2; 24:22). The pres. impv. προσεύχεσθε (see 6:28) may highlight continual action (Bock 1757). The inf. εἰσελθεῖν (see 6:6; neg. with μή) with εἰς πειρασμόν (acc. sg. masc., see 4:13; cf. 11:4; 22:46) may express the content of the prayer (an obj. clause, Burton §200), or that the purpose of the prayer is for strength in the face of temptation ("that you will not give in to temptation" NLT; Robertson, *Pictures* 272).

22:41 Καὶ αὐτός (see 1:17; 3:23). Ἀπεσπάσθη 3rd sg. aor. pass. indic. "withdraw." Λίθου, an obj. gen. Βολήν acc. sg. fem. of βολή, -ῆς, ἡ, "throw" (acc. of extent of space, R 469; Wallace 202; ZG 272). Θείς nom. sg. masc. of 2nd aor. act. (temp.) ptc. of τίθημι. Γόνατα, "knees" (acc. pl. neut., see 5:8; on this posture in intense prayer cf. Acts 7:60; 9:40; 20:36; 21:5). The impf. προσηύχετο (see 18:11) could be ingressive (NASB, HCSB) or iter. (Robertson, *Pictures* 272; the aor. is read in 𝔓⁷⁵ א).

22:42 Εἰ with βούλει (2nd sg. pres. mid. indic. of βούλομαι, "wish," "want"; on the form cf. R 193, 339) is the protasis of a first-class cond. (or it may introduce a dir. question, Marshall 831). Παρένεγκε 2nd sg. 2nd aor. act. impv. of παραφέρω "take away," "remove" (introduces the apodosis, R 1023; though if the inf. is read [παρενέγκαι, א K L], then it breaks off without apodosis [aposiopesis, BDF §482], perhaps emphasizing strong emotion). The acc. τοῦτο τὸ ποτήριον ("this cup"; the obj. of the impv.) in the context of a ref. to the will of the Father refers to the cup of God's wrath (cf. Isa 51:17, 22; Jer 25:15 [32:15 LXX]; 49:12 [30:6 LXX]). This helps explain both why Jesus is in agony in this context and why his death is that of the suffering servant. The contrastive conj. πλήν shows that despite the horrific prospect of wrath ahead of him, Jesus agrees with the Father's will. The nom. τὸ θέλημά . . . τὸ σόν (neg. with μή) is the subj. of the impv. γινέσθω (see 22:26).

22:43 Although the external evidence for the omission of 22:43–44 is strong ($\mathfrak{P}^{75}$ A B; RSV), their inclusion ($\aleph^{*,2}$ D K L 𝔐) is likely since there are no Synoptic parallels to these verses, and there appears no reason for a scribe to add them here (see Bock 1763–64 for responses to Fitzmyer [1444] and Nolland [1080–81]). Most versions include the verses (though with brackets in UBS⁵; NET, NRSV, HCSB). Ὤφθη, see 1:11 ("appeared"; αὐτῷ is the dat. complement). Ἐνισχύων (nom. sg. masc. of pres. act. ptc. of ἐνισχύω, "strengthen"; trans. (elsewhere only Acts 9:19 [intrans.] in the NT) expresses purpose.

22:44 Γενόμενος (see 10:32) could be *temp. (as with 22:40), manner, or causal. Ἀγωνίᾳ dat. sg. fem. of ἀγωνία, -ας, ἡ, "agony," "anguish." Ἐκτενέστερον (acc. sg. neut. of ἐκτενής, -ές) is a comp. adj. used as an adv. (when neut.; "more earnestly" ESV, NIV; "more fervently" HCSB; BDAG 310c; ZG 273). The impf. προσηύχετο (see 18:11) is progressive. Ἱδρώς nom. sg. masc. of ἱδρώς, -ῶτος, ὁ, "sweat." Θρόμβοι nom. pl. masc. of θρόμβος, -ου, ὁ, "drop," "clot." The gen. αἵματος is attrib. (but note the comp. ὡσεί). The attrib. ptc. καταβαίνοντες (nom. pl. masc. of pres. act. ptc. of καταβαίνω, "go down"; modifying the nom. pl. masc. θρόμβοι) indicates an emphasis on the "falling" (i.e., the metaphorical ref. is to the amount of sweat, Bock 1762).

22:45 Ἀναστάς (see 4:38; intrans.) and ἐλθών (see 7:3) could be temp. (HCSB), or ἐλθών could be attendant circumstance with εὗρεν (see 4:17; ESV). Κοιμωμένους (acc. pl. masc. of pres. mid. ptc. of dep. κοιμάομαι, "sleep") is the complement with αὐτούς in a double acc. cstr. (cf. BDAG 411d). Ἀπὸ τῆς λύπης is causal (gen. sg. fem. of λύπη, -ης, ἡ; "because of grief" NRSV, sim. HCSB, NIV; R 580; ZG 273; Harris 66; "emotional exhaustion," Bock 1762; Bovon 3.203–4; Nolland 1084; cf. 19:3). The art. τῆς is used with an abstract noun (λύπης; Wallace 227).

22:46 Καθεύδετε 2nd pl. pres. act. indic. of καθεύδω, "sleep." Ἀναστάντες (see 4:29) could be temp. (BHGNT 688) or *attendant circumstance with the following impv. προσεύχεσθε (see 6:28; cf. 22:40) in which it takes on the mood of the impv. ("get up and pray" most EVV). Ἵνα with the subjunc. εἰσέλθητε (see 9:4; neg. with μή) may express *purpose (as indicated by the punctuation of a comma in UBS⁵; HCSB, NIV; i.e., "pray, so that"), or it may introduce a content clause ("pray that" NRSV, NASB, ESV; an obj. clause, Burton §200; cf. Wallace 475; εἰς πειρασμόν, see 4:13; 22:40).

HOMILETICAL SUGGESTIONS

Prayer in the Face of Trial (22:39–46)

1. Jesus models prayerful dependence before the trial comes (22:39–41, 45–46).
2. Jesus combines earnest prayer and submission to the Father's will (22:42, 44).
3. Jesus knows answered prayer even in the midst of an unimaginable ordeal (22:43).

2. Betrayal and Arrest (22:47–53)

Judas reappears on the scene for the betrayal and arrest of Jesus. Nevertheless, Jesus is compassionate and commanding in the face of evil.

22:47 For ἔτι αὐτοῦ λαλοῦντος see 8:49. The temp. gen. abs. cstr. closely links these events to the preceding account. The interjection ἰδού (see 1:20) highlights the new situation ("suddenly" NRSV, HCSB). Judas (last mentioned by name in 22:3 with ref. to Satan) is identified (λεγόμενος nom. sg. masc. of pres. pass. [subst.] ptc. of λέγω) not only as "one of the Twelve" (the nom. εἷς is appos.), but as "leading" (προήρχετο 3rd sg. impf. mid. indic. of dep. προέρχομαι, "go before," "lead") the crowd to Jesus. Ἤγγισεν, see 7:12. The aor. act. inf. φιλῆσαι (of φιλέω, "kiss"; as a [supposed] "concrete expression of love" Bock 1767; Fitzmyer 1450; BDAG 1056d–57a) expresses purpose (ZG 273).

22:48 Ἰούδα, voc. The instr. dat. φιλήματι (of φίλημα, "with a kiss"; R 533; see 7:45) is placed forward for emphasis (Bock 1768; Fitzmyer 1450; Marshall 836). Παραδίδως 2nd sg. pres. act. indic. of παραδίδωμι, "betray" (see refs. at 18:32).

22:49 Ἰδόντες, see 2:17 (is temp.). The art. οἱ nominalizes the prep. phrase περὶ αὐτόν ("when those who were around him saw"; "Jesus' followers" NIV). Ἐσόμενον acc. sg. neut. of fut. mid. (subst.) ptc. of εἰμί, "what was going to happen" NASB, HCSB, NIV (one of only thirteen fut. ptcs. in the NT; cf. R 1118). Εἰ begins a dir. question (i.e., "tell us if we should"; or "should we" NRSV, HCSB, NIV; cf. BDAG 278b; BDF §440[3]; R 916, 934; Z §401; ZG 273). The fut. πατάξομεν (1st pl. fut. act. indic. of πατάσσω, "strike") is deliberative (BDF §366[2]; Burton §§70, 169; R 876; Z §341; ZG 273). Ἐν μαχαίρῃ is instr. ("with a sword"; see 21:24; BDF §195[1a]; Robertson, *Pictures* 273; ZG 273; Harris 36, 119; cf. 22:36–38).

22:50 Ἐπάταξεν 3rd sg. aor. act. indic. of πατάσσω (cf. 22:49). The apostle who struck with his sword is unidentified here (εἷς τις ἐξ αὐτῶν, "a certain one of them"; Peter in John 18:10). The gen. τοῦ ἀρχιερέως is poss. of the acc. dir. obj. τὸν δοῦλον ("the slave of the high priest"). Ἀφεῖλεν 3rd sg. 2nd aor. act. indic. of ἀφαιρέω, "take away," "cut off." Τὸ οὖς αὐτοῦ τὸ δεξιόν, "his right ear" (οὖς acc. sg. neut. of οὖς, ὠτός, τό).

22:51 Ἀποκριθείς, see 1:19. Ἐᾶτε (2nd pl. pres. act. impv. of ἐάω, "permit," "allow") with ἕως τούτου ("leave off until this") is an idiom mng. "to cease from what one is doing" ("No more of this" NRSV, HCSB, NIV; BDAG 269c; BHGNT 691; LN 68.35; ZG 273) rather than "let them have their way" (NEB; Nolland 1088). Ἁψάμενος (see 8:45; of ἅπτω, "touch"; the gen. [sg. neut.] τοῦ ὠτίου [of ὠτίον, -ου, τό, "ear"] is obj.; diminutive of οὖς [22:50] so perhaps "outer ear," or equivalent to οὖς, BDAG 1107c; BDF §111[3]) is an attendant circumstance ptc. with ἰάσατο (see 9:42; ἰάομαι occurs eleven times in Luke).

22:52 Παραγενομένους acc. pl. masc. of 2nd aor. mid. (attrib.) ptc. of dep. παραγίνομαι, "come," "arrive," modifies ἀρχιερεῖς καὶ στρατηγοὺς τοῦ ἱεροῦ καὶ πρεσβυτέρους ("the . . . who had come" NASB). Παραγενομένους with ἐπί is "come against" (NASB; BDAG 364b) or "come for" (HCSB). Στρατηγούς acc. pl. masc., see 22:4. Λῃστήν (of

λῃστής, see 10:30) has been tr. as "robber" (NASB, ESV), "outlaw" (NET), *"criminal" (HCSB), "dangerous revolutionary" (NLT), and "leading a rebellion" (NIV).
Although "revolutionary" is a possible mng. (BDAG 594a–b [mng. 2]; LN 39.37),
Luke's usage in 10:30, 36; 19:46 indicates that "criminal" (BDAG 594a–b [mng. 1]
or "violent robber" (LN 57.240) is more likely in view (placed forward for emphasis,
Bock 1772). Ἐξήλθατε, see 7:24. Μετὰ μαχαιρῶν καὶ ξύλων, "with swords and clubs"
(μετά in the sense of "having," Harris 163; μαχαιρῶν gen. pl. fem., see 21:24; ξύλων
gen. pl. neut. of ξύλον, -ου, τό, "wood").

22:53 Καθ' ἡμέραν is distributive ("day after day" ESV; cf. 11:3). Ὄντος (see 14:32;
of εἰμί) with μου (the subj. of the ptc.) is a temp. gen. abs. cstr. ("while I was with
you" HCSB). Ἐξετείνατε (2nd pl. aor. act. indic. of ἐκτείνω, "stretch out"; neg. with
οὐκ) with τὰς χεῖρας ἐπ' ἐμέ is "lay hands on me" (NRSV, ESV, sim. HCSB, NIV) or
"arrest" (NLT; cf. 20:19). The phrase ἡ ἐξουσία τοῦ σκότους may be pred. along with
ἡ ὥρα ("and the power of darkness" ESV, sim. HCSB) or the subj. of an implied vb.
("when the power of darkness reigns" NLT, sim. NIV; the gen. τοῦ σκότους could be
subj. or attrib.; cf. 22:3, 31–32).

HOMILETICAL SUGGESTIONS

The Actions of Jesus in the Face of an Evil Arrest (22:47–53)
1. Jesus takes command and highlights the hypocrisy of the betrayer (22:47–48).
2. Jesus provides compassionate healing and demonstrates the injustice of the
   arrest (22:49–52).
3. Jesus permits the rule of evil in his arrest and points out the cowardly timing
   (22:53).

3. Peter's Denials and Jesus' Trials (22:54–23:25)

a. Peter's Denials Fulfill the "Word of the Lord" (22:54–62)

22:54 Συλλαβόντες (nom. pl. masc. of 2nd aor. act. ptc. of συλλαμβάνω, "take," in this context "seize" HCSB, ESV, NIV; "arrest" NASB) could be temp. (NASB) or attendant circumstance with ἤγαγον (see 4:29) and εἰσήγαγον (3rd pl. aor. act. indic. of εἰσάγω; HCSB; on the repetition of εἰς with certain vbs. see R 559). Ἠκολούθει, see 5:28 (the impf. may provide background information for the following events or is perhaps conative or iter., Marshall 841). Μακρόθεν, adv. "from afar" (i.e., "at a distance").

22:55 The two gen. pl. masc. of aor. act. ptcs. περιαψάντων (of περιάπτω, "kindle"; perhaps for those who were there to sit "around" it, LN 14.65; LSJ 1368c) and συγκαθισάντων (of συγκαθίζω, intrans. "sit down together") are either *part of a temp. gen. abs. cstr. with the subj. not specified ("when they" ESV; Fitzmyer 1464), or perhaps attrib. modifying αὐτῶν ("Peter was sitting among those who had" BHGNT 694; Bock 1782). Αὐλῆς, "courtyard" (see 11:21). Ἐκάθητο, see 18:35. The nom. adj. μέσος could be pred. (modifying Πέτρος, Robertson, Pictures 274) but functions here as an adv. (with the partitive αὐτῶν, BHGNT 694).

22:56 Παιδίσκη τις ("a servant girl"; see 12:45) is the subj. of εἶπεν. Ἰδοῦσα (of ὁράω, see 8:47) and ἀτενίσασα (nom. sg. fem. of aor. act. ptc. of ἀτενίζω, "gaze," "stare," followed by dat.) are probably temp. (HCSB). The gaze of the servant girl leads to the first denial, and the gaze of the Lord concludes the scene (ἐνέβλεψεν, 22:61; Nolland 1094). Καθήμενον, see 5:27. Πρὸς τὸ φῶς is spatial ("facing the light," Robertson, Pictures 274). Καὶ οὗτος "this man too" (probably a derogatory οὗτος, R 697; Fitzmyer 1464).

22:57 Ἠρνήσατο 3rd sg. aor. mid. indic. of dep. ἀρνέομαι, "deny" (cf. ἀπαρνέομαι 22:34, 61). Οἶδα, see 4:34 (neg. with οὐκ; 22:34). Γύναι, voc. (here with a tone of disrespect, BDAG 209a; cf. 5:8; BDF §474[6] for the position of the voc.).

22:58 Μετά with the acc. sg. neut. adj. βραχύ (of βραχύς, -εῖα, -ύ, "little") is temp. ("After a little while" HCSB; R 612). The ref. to someone else (ἕτερος, "another," masc.) indicates that the accusations of the slave girl have been joined by others (Bock 1784). Ἰδών (see 1:12) could be temp. (NRSV) or attendant circumstance with ἔφη (see 7:44; "saw him and said" most EVV). Καὶ σύ is placed forward for emphasis ("you also" ESV; R 678; Fitzmyer 1464; εἶ, see 3:22). Ἄνθρωπε, voc. (with a reproachful connotation, BDAG 82c; cf. γύναι, 22:57).

22:59 Διαστάσης (gen. sg. fem. of 2nd aor. act. ptc. of διΐστημι, "pass," "go away"; intrans. LN 67.84) is in a temp. gen. abs. cstr. in which the gen. ὥρας μιᾶς is the subj. ("After about an hour had passed" NASB). Διϊσχυρίζετο 3rd sg. impf. mid. indic. of dep. διϊσχυρίζομαι, "insist" (the impf. is iter. HCSB; Robertson, Pictures 275). Ἐπ' ἀληθείας ("on the basis of truth") is synonymous with the adv. ἀληθῶς, strengthening the accusation (BDAG 43a; BHGNT 696). For μετ' αὐτοῦ note μετὰ σοῦ in 22:33. Γάρ, causal. Καί is "also" (R 697–98; omitted in NIV). The anar. pred. nom. Γαλιλαῖος is probably qualitative (Wallace 265).

22:60 Ἄνθρωπε, see 22:58. The acc. rel. pron. ὅ with λέγεις (see 12:41) is the obj. of οἶδα (see 4:34). Παραχρῆμα, see 1:64. The temp. gen. abs. cstr. (λαλοῦντος [see 8:49] αὐτοῦ) emphasizes the link between the denial and rooster crow. For ἐφώνησεν (see 8:54) with ἀλέκτωρ see 22:34 (i.e., the fulfillment is explicitly noted).

22:61 Στραφείς (see 7:9) is an attendant circumstance ptc. with ἐνέβλεψεν (3rd sg. aor. act. indic. of ἐμβλέπω, "look at"; τῷ Πέτρῳ is the dat. complement; note that the subj. is ὁ κύριος, see 7:13). Ὑπεμνήσθη 3rd sg. aor. pass. indic. of ὑπομιμνήσκω, "remember." The gen. τοῦ ῥήματος τοῦ κυρίου is the gen. complement of ὑπεμνήσθη (BDAG 1039d; R 509). This terminology is reminiscent of refs. to divine speech in the OT (e.g., ῥῆμα κυρίου in Gen 15:1). The content (ὅτι, recitative) of what the Lord had said reflects 22:34. Πρίν with the aor. act. inf. φωνῆσαι (of φωνέω) is temp. ("solemnly predictive" Burton §65; R 873). Ἀπαρνήσῃ, see 22:34.

22:62 Ἐξελθών (see 1:22) is attendant circumstance with ἔκλαυσεν (see 19:41; ἔκλαυσεν could be described as an ingressive aor. "burst into tears," Robertson, *Pictures* 276). Πικρῶς, adv. "bitterly."

b. Jesus' Testimony Before the Council (22:63–71)

The treatment Jesus faces also fulfills his earlier predictions. Jesus' sovereign authority is emphasized as he claims to be the one with ultimate judging authority as the Son of Man, Lord, and Son of God. Jesus' own words convince the temple leaders they have all the evidence they need.

22:63 Συνέχοντες nom. pl. masc. of pres. act. (attrib.) ptc. of συνέχω, "hold" ("guarding" NIV) modifies οἱ ἄνδρες (most EVV supply "Jesus" for αὐτόν to indicate the shift from Peter in 22:62). The impf. ἐνέπαιζον (3rd pl. impf. act. indic. of ἐμπαίζω, "mock") could be ingressive (NRSV, HCSB, NIV; Robertson, *Pictures* 276; Bock 1789) or progressive (perhaps to parallel Peter's denials, Marshall 846). To "mock" is to "make fun of someone by pretending that he is not what he is or by imitating him in a distorted manner" (LN 33.406; see 18:32). Δέροντες (nom. pl. masc. of pres. act. ptc. of δέρω, "beat") could be temp. (ESV) or attendant circumstance (NRSV, HCSB, NIV).

22:64 Περικαλύψαντες nom. pl. masc. of aor. act. (temp.) ptc. of περικαλύπτω, "cover" ("After blindfolding" HCSB). The impf. ἐπηρώτων (see 3:10) could be ingressive (BHGNT 698) but is more likely iter. (HCSB, ESV). Λέγοντες, see 1:66. Προφήτευσον 2nd sg. aor. act. impv. of προφήτευω, "prophesy." Παίσας (nom. sg. masc. of aor. act. [subst.] ptc. of παίω, "strike") is the subj. of ἐστίν ("who is the one who hit You?" NASB).

22:65 The acc. pl. neut. ἕτερα πολλά is the obj. of ἔλεγον (see 4:22; described as adv. accs. to βλασφημοῦντες by Fitzmyer 1466). Βλασφημοῦντες (nom. pl. masc. of pres. act. ptc. of βλασφημέω, "blaspheme") probably expresses manner (BHGNT 698; cf. Burton §121). Although the term may be tr. as "insulting" (NRSV, NIV), the descriptions of Jesus in this context (22:69–70) suggest the stronger sense of "blaspheming" (ESV, sim. HCSB; LN 33.400; Marshall 846; εἰς, see 12:10).

22:66 Ὡς with ἐγένετο ἡμέρα is temp. ("when day came"; i.e., "daylight" HCSB). Πρεσβυτέριον, "assembly of elders" (nom. sg. neut. of πρεσβυτέριον, -ου, τό; cf. BDAG 861d; Acts 22:5), is the subj. of συνήχθη (3rd sg. aor. pass. indic. of συνάγω, "gather together"). The elders are specified with the appos. nom. ἀρχιερεῖς τε καὶ γραμματεῖς (τε καί combines the two, BDF §444[4]; R 1179). Ἀπήγαγον 3rd pl. 2nd aor. act. indic. of ἀπάγω, "lead away" (or causative, "had him brought," Nolland 1109). Τὸ συνέδριον αὐτῶν (acc. sg. neut. of συνέδριον, -ου, τό), could refer to "their council chamber" (NASB; "meeting room" BDAG 967c–d [mng. 3]), or, "their council" (NRSV, ESV; MM 604c), which is the Sanhedrin (HCSB; BDAG 967c [mng. 1c]; on the sequence of trials see Bock 1793).

22:67 Λέγοντες, see 1:66. Εἰ could introduce a first-class cond. clause (i.e., "if [for the sake of argument], you are . . . tell us"; BDF §372[1]; Robertson, *Pictures* 277; Z §303; ZG 275) or an interr. ("tell us whether"). Εἶ (of εἰμί), see 3:22. Εἰπόν (impv.), see 20:2. Jesus' response (ἐάν with the subjunc. εἴπω 1st sg. 2nd aor. act. subjunc. of λέγω) is a third-class cond. clause (i.e., hypothetical; cf. Burton §285b) which does not provide them with an answer. Οὐ μή with the subjunc. πιστεύσητε (2nd pl. aor. act. subjunc. of πιστεύω) is emphatic (Robertson, *Pictures* 277).

22:68 As with 22:67, ἐάν with the subjunc. ἐρωτήσω (1st sg. aor. act. subjunc. of ἐρωτάω, "ask") is a third-class cond. clause. Again, οὐ μή with the subjunc. ἀποκριθῆτε (2nd pl. aor. pass. subjunc. of dep. ἀποκρίνομαι, "answer") is emphatic (see 20:1–8).

22:69 Ἀπὸ τοῦ νῦν, see 1:48. Ἔσται (see 1:14) with καθήμενος (nom. sg. masc. of pres. mid. ptc. of dep. κάθημαι, "sit") is a fut. periph. cstr. (see 21:17 for this cstr.; see 5:24 for ὁ υἱὸς τοῦ ἀνθρώπου). The locat. ἐκ δεξιῶν τῆς δυνάμεως τοῦ θεοῦ ("at the right hand of the power of God"; see NLT; Harris 106–7) is a circumlocution for the sovereign rule of God in which Jesus is both identified with God the Father and yet is distinct from him (see 20:42). The allusion to Ps 110:1 (and Dan 7:13) together with the use of the term δύναμις in the context of a trial before the ruling council (22:66) emphasizes where the true locus of divine authority resides. Jesus is actually the Judge over them (Pao and Schnabel 391c).

22:70 The pron. σύ is emphatic. Εἶ (of εἰμί), see 3:22. In this context (22:69), Jesus as "Son" refers to an exalted claim of a unique relationship with God the Father (Bock 1801–2; Fitzmyer 1468; Marshall 851; see 10:21–22; refs. at 1:32) rather than a mere synonym for Messiah (*pace* Nolland 111). Ἔφη, see 7:44. Jesus' reply, ὑμεῖς λέγετε [see 7:33] ὅτι ἐγώ εἰμι, "you say that I am" (HCSB, ESV, NIV; note σὺ οὖν . . . ὑμεῖς) with the emphatic pron. ὑμεῖς provides qualified agreement to their claim (BDF §441[3]; [perhaps ironic] Bock 1802; Bovon 3.246; Fitzmyer 1468; Marshall 851; *pace* Nolland 1111).

22:71 Τί, interr. pron. "why?" Ἔχομεν, see 3:8. The gen. μαρτυρίας ("testimony"; the sg. highlights Jesus' own testimony as that which secures the verdict) is obj. following the dir. obj. χρείαν ("need of testimony"; ZG 275). Γάρ, causal. The pron. αὐτοί is intensive ("ourselves"). Ἠκούσαμεν, see 4:23 (ἀπὸ τοῦ στόματος αὐτοῦ, cf. 11:54).

HOMILETICAL SUGGESTIONS

Trust the Truth of Jesus' Word Even in Trying Times (22:54–71)
1. Jesus' word is fulfilled even in words of weak denial (22:54–62).
2. Jesus' word is fulfilled even in words of mocking blasphemy (22:63–64).
3. Jesus' word is fulfilled even in words of blind accusation (22:66–71).

c. A Trial Before Pilate (23:1-5)

The involvement of Pilate and his interactions with the Jewish leadership link the sequence of events in 23:1-25. The widespread culpability in the death of Jesus is evident in the range of participants. The overall emphasis, however, is on the innocence of Jesus.

23:1 Ἀναστάν (nom. sg. neut. of 2nd aor. act. ptc. of ἀνίστημι, "rise"; intrans.) is attendant circumstance with ἤγαγον (see 4:29; pleonastic, Fitzmyer 1474; on the pl. vb. as "according to sense" cf. R 404, 1390). The nom. ἅπαν τὸ πλῆθος is the subj. (on πλῆθος for the Sanhedrin cf. Acts 23:7). Ἐπὶ τὸν Πιλᾶτον is locat. (BDAG 366a; ZG 275).

23:2 The inf. κατηγορεῖν (see 6:7; 23:10, 14; the gen. αὐτοῦ is obj.) is complementary following ἤρξαντο (see 5:21; Wallace 599). Λέγοντες, see 1:66. The fronting of τοῦτον probably emphasizes the derogatory tone (Bock 1810; Fitzmyer 1474; Marshall 852; Nolland 1117). Εὕραμεν 1st pl. 2nd aor. act. indic. of εὑρίσκω, "find" (cf. Z §489 for the form). The following three acc. sg. masc. of pres. act. ptcs. are together the complement in a double acc. cstr. (with the acc. τοῦτον; BDAG 412a; BHGNT 703):

διαστρέφοντα, of διαστρέφω, "perverting" (NRSV), "subverting" (HCSB, NIV), "misleading" (NASB, ESV; Bock 1810; Marshall 852; cf. LN 31.71; 88.264; cf. 9:41)

κωλύοντα, of κωλύω, "forbidding"

λέγοντα, of λέγω, "saying" (NRSV, HCSB, ESV; "claiming" NLT, NET)

The three ptcs. could introduce three charges (Bock 1810; Bovon 3.253; Marshall 852):

1. leading the nation astray (διαστρέφοντα τὸ ἔθνος, cf. NLT) perhaps (from their perspective) as a false prophet, disturbing the peace (Bock 1810; cf. 23:5), or, if it is a general introduction, the following charges clarify that this is leading astray from loyalty to Rome (Nolland 1117);
2. forbidding the payment of taxes to Caesar (φόρους acc. pl. masc., see 20:22; "tribute tax" NET; "tribute" ESV; "taxes" HCSB, NIV; LN 57.182; the inf. διδόναι [see 11:13] is for indir. discourse; a false charge in light of 20:20–26); or
3. claiming to be the Messiah, a king (the acc. refl. pron. ἑαυτόν is the subj. of the inf. εἶναι [see 2:4] which is used in indir. discourse [Wallace 194–195]; χριστόν is the pred. acc. and βασιλέα is in appos. to χριστόν, Wallace 190–92; "Christ, a king" Marshall 853; Nolland 1118; cf. Fitzmyer 1475 "an anointed king"); true, though not as a political threat (again see 20:20–26).

Or it is possible that the first καί is explicative ("that is") and introduces the two ptcs. καὶ κωλύοντα . . . καὶ λέγοντα as two examples of the first, more general, charge (cf. BDF §444[3]; Fitzmyer 1473–74; Nolland 1117).

23:3 Pilate's question here specifically picks up on the third charge. Ἡρώτησεν, see 5:3. The nom. pron. σύ is the subj. of εἶ (see 3:22; in a question here "Are you . . .?"; ZG 275). Ὁ βασιλεύς is the pred. nom. (on the art. in the pred. cf. Z §§172–75). Jesus' answer (ἀποκριθείς, see 1:19; ἔφη, see 7:44; Z §366), σὺ λέγεις (see 12:41) is not a denial of this claim but rather a qualified endorsement of it (see 22:70; ZG 275; Bock 1811; Bovon 3.255; perhaps with an emphatic σύ, Fitzmyer 1475).

23:4 Τοὺς ὄχλους may refer to the rest of the Sanhedrin (see 22:66; 23:1), to a gathering of others (Bock 1812), or to the people in anticipation of 23:13, 18 (Fitzmyer 1476). Εὑρίσκω, see 13:7 (in contrast to εὕραμεν in 23:2; neg. with the emphatic οὐδέν; cf. 23:14; BHGNT 704; Bock 1812). The subst. use of αἴτιον (acc. sg. neut. of αἴτιος, -ία, -ον, "responsible," "guilty") has the mng. "ground for legal action" (BDAG 31c; "basis for a charge" NIV, sim. NRSV, HCSB; cf. αἴτιον in 23:14, 22). Ἐν is ref. This is the first of many refs. to Jesus' innocence (cf. 23:14–15, 20, 22, 41, 47).

23:5 Ἐπίσχυον (3rd pl. impf. act. indic. of ἐπισχύω, "insist"; only here in the NT) implies "both continuity and strong effort" (LN 68.71; the subj. οἱ is likely the chief priests, Fitzmyer 1476; Marshall 853). The impf. therefore may be iter. (NASB, HCSB; or ingressive, NLT). Ὅτι, recitative. Ἀνασείει 3rd sg. pres. act. indic. of ἀνασείω, "stirs up" (most EVV), "incites" (NET; Nolland 1118). Ἀνασείει τὸν λαόν repeats the idea of διαστρέφοντα τὸ ἔθνος in 23:2 (cf. also ἀποστρέφοντα τὸν λαόν in 23:14; Marshall 853). Διδάσκων (see 4:31) expresses means ("by teaching" ZG 275; explaining how Jesus was inciting the people). Καθ' ὅλης τῆς Ἰουδαίας is distributive ("throughout all Judea" HCSB, ESV). "Judea" here includes Galilee and refers to the Roman province of Judea (Bovon 3.256; Nolland 1119). Ἀρξάμενος nom. sg. masc. of aor. mid. ptc. of ἄρχω, "beginning" (epex. ptc. of manner, modifying an implied vb., BHGNT 705; R 413, 1203; cf. Acts 1:22; 10:37).

d. A Trial Before Herod (23:6–12)

Pilate's decision to send Jesus to Herod may further highlight his weakness in seeking to pass the responsibility off to someone else. Jesus' appearance before Herod serves to add to the number of those antagonistic to Jesus and add another official testimony to Jesus' innocence (cf. 23:15).

23:6 The temp. ἀκούσας (see 6:49) links the following incident with the preceding. Ἐπηρώτησεν, see 8:30. Εἰ is used as an indir. interr. ("he asked whether the man was" ESV; R 916; Z §402; ZG 275). Γαλιλαῖος pred. nom. adj. (cf. Wallace 264–65; cf. 13:1–2; 22:59).

23:7 Ἐπιγνούς, see 5:22 (temp.). Ἐκ τῆς ἐξουσίας Ἡρῴδου refers to the region of Herod's jurisdiction (so most EVV; ZG 275; Bock 1818; Fitzmyer 1481; Nolland 1123; for Herod Antipas see 3:19). Ἀνέπεμψεν 3rd sg. aor. act. indic. of ἀναπέμπω "send back" (due to the use of the vb. in 23:11, 15 [back to Pilate], this is unlikely to be the technical sense of sending someone "up" to a higher authority, Bock 1818; Marshall 855; pace BDAG 70a [mng. 2]; [cf. MM 37a]; Fitzmyer 1481). Ὄντα (see 12:28) is attrib. modifying Ἡρῴδην ("to Herod, who was"). The pron. αὐτόν is intensive ("himself").

On the form of Ἱεροσολύμα see 2:22. The temp. ἐν ταύταις ταῖς ἡμέραις refers to the time of the feast.

23:8 Ἰδών, see 1:12 (temp.). Ἐχάρη (3rd sg. 2nd aor. pass. indic. of χαίρω), together with the adv. λίαν, is "he rejoiced greatly." Ἐξ ἱκανῶν χρόνων is temp. ("a long time" NRSV, HCSB, NIV; on the temp. use of ἐκ cf. R 597). Θέλων (see 10:29) together with ἦν is an impf. periph. cstr. that also highlights the ongoing desire of Herod to see Jesus (R 884; rendered as a pluperfect in English, "he had wanted" HCSB; ZG 275). The inf. ἀκούειν (see 5:1) with διὰ τό is causal (BDF §402[1]; Wallace 597 [2:4; 8:6]; with the force of impf. though pluperfect in English, cf. ZG 275–76). Ἤλπιζεν 3rd sg. impf. act. indic. of ἐλπίζω. The inf. ἰδεῖν (see 2:26) is complementary (following ἤλπιζεν). The indef. τι σημεῖον ("some sign"; see 11:16, 29; but see also 9:9; 13:31) is the dir. obj. of the inf. Γινόμενον (acc. sg. neut. of pres. mid. ptc. of γίνομαι) is the complement in a double acc. cstr. (with τι σημεῖον, BDAG 197a–b; BHGNT 707).

23:9 The impf. of ἐπηρώτα (3rd sg. impf. act. indic. of ἐπερωτάω) could be iter. (HCSB; Marshall 856) or perhaps conative (Bock 1819; Fitzmyer 1481). Ἐν λόγοις ἱκανοῖς is instr. ("with many questions" NIV; ZG 276). The mid. ἀπεκρίνατο (see 3:16) in this context may emphasize the subj. (i.e., "he answered nothing [in his own defense]," Wallace 421; the dat. αὐτῷ is the indir. obj.).

23:10 The pluperfect εἱστήκεισαν (3rd pl. pluperfect act. indic. of ἵστημι, "stand," intrans.) here emphasizes more the result than the completed action ("stood by" NRSV, HCSB, ESV) and may be tr. as impf. (NASB, NIV; ZG 276). Εὐτόνως ("vehemently") is an adv. of manner modifying the ptc. of manner κατηγοροῦντες (nom. pl. masc. of pres. act. ptc. of κατηγορέω, "accuse"; cf. 23:2). The gen. αὐτοῦ is obj.

23:11 The three nom. sg. masc. of aor. act. ptcs.:

> ἐξουθενήσας (of ἐξουθενέω, "despise," "treat with contempt," BDAG 352c),
> ἐμπαίξας (of ἐμπαίζω, "mock"; see 18:32; 22:63; 23:36),
> περιβαλών (2nd aor. of περιβάλλω, "clothe")
> and the aor. indic. ἀνέπεμψεν (see 23:7) could be tr. as follows (cf. BHGNT 708–9):

1. all three ptcs. are temp. before ἀνέπεμψεν; "after treating him with contempt, mocking him, and dressing him . . . they sent him";
*2. the two ptcs. ἐξουθενήσας and ἐμπαίξας are temp., and the ptc. περιβαλών is attendant circumstance with ἀνέπεμψεν; "after treating him with contempt and mocking him, [they] dressed him . . . and sent him" (NASB); sim. NRSV, ESV; BHGNT 708; Bock 1820 n. 9; Bovon 3.269; Fitzmyer 1478);
3. the three ptcs. and ἀνέπεμψεν are attendant circumstance; "treated him with contempt, mocked him, dressed him . . ., and sent Him back" (HCSB; sim. KJV)

4. the ptc. περιβαλών could express means; "after treating him with contempt and mocking him by putting elegant clothes on him" (cf. Marshall 857, "epex. of the preceding ptcs."); or

5. the ptc. περιβαλών refers to the beginning point of the contempt and ridicule (Nolland 1124)

There is not much difference in mng. between the first three, and the clothing is meant to be derogatory anyway (options 4 and 5). If καί is present before ὁ Ἡρώδης, then the sense could be "even" or "also," emphasizing Herod's inclusion (on this longer rdg. see Metzger 152). Στρατεύμασιν dat. pl. neut. of στράτευμα, -ατος, τό, "army," pl. "soldiers." The acc. sg. fem. ἐσθῆτα [of ἐσθής, -ῆτος, ἡ, "clothing"] λαμπράν [of λαμπρός, -ά, -όν, "shining"; regal, Bock 1821] is the dir. obj. of περιβαλών (i.e., "dressed Him in a brilliant robe" HCSB).

23:12 Ὅ τε Ἡρώδης καὶ ὁ Πιλᾶτος is the subj. of ἐγένοντο (see 13:2; on the pl. vb. cf. R 405). The dat. sg. fem. pron. αὐτῇ (of αὐτός, αὐτή, αὐτό) is used here in a demonstrative sense ("that very day" HCSB, ESV; BHGNT 709; R 686). Γάρ is explanatory. The impf. προϋπῆρχον (3rd pl. impf. act. indic. of προϋπάρχω, "be before," "exist before") together with ὄντες (see 6:3) is an unusual use of the periph. ptc. in an impf. cstr. ("before this they had been" ESV; BDF §414[1]; R 888, 1121; Z §360). Ἐν ἔχθρᾳ is "at enmity" (ESV; "hostile" HCSB; "enemies" NRSV, NRSV). An ironic reconciliation (Bock 1822).

e. Sentencing by Pilate and Release of Barabbas (23:13–25)

The sequence of trials comes to a climax here with Pilate's repeated statements of Jesus' innocence. The Jewish leader, now with the support of the people, oppose Pilate's requests. It is the will of the people, rather than justice, that Pilate ultimately submits to.

23:13 Συγκαλεσάμενος (see 9:1) could be temp. with εἶπεν (22:14; KJV) or attendant circumstance ("Pilate called . . . and said" most EVV). For ἄρχων see refs. in 14:1. The reference to τὸν λαόν here introduces a shift from the previous attitudes of the people in 21:38; 22:2 (see 18:43; 19:48).

23:14 Προσηνέγκατε 2nd pl. aor. act. indic. of προσφέρω, "bring." Ἀποστρέφοντα acc. sg. masc. of pres. act. (subst.) ptc. of ἀποστρέφω, "turn away," "perverting" NRSV; "subverts" HCSB; "inciting the people to rebellion" NIV (see διαστρέφοντα in 23:2; ἀνασείει in 23:5; with ὡς, "as one who was misleading" ESV; on ὡς cf. BDF §425[3]). Ἀνακρίνας (nom. sg. masc. of aor. act. ptc. of ἀνακρίνω, "examine") could be temp. with εὗρον (see 7:9 [23:2, 4]; NASB, HCSB, ESV) or attendant circumstance (NRSV, NIV). The acc. οὐθὲν . . . αἴτιον is the dir. obj. of εὗρον in which οὐθέν is placed forward for emphasis (BHGNT 711; αἴτιον, see 23:4). The gen. rel. pron. ὧν introduces the rel. clause and could be a gen. of ref. (BHGNT 711; "regarding the things you are charging against him"; or by attraction to an implied τούτων, R 511; cf. R 1141; Marshall 859). Κατηγορεῖτε 2nd pl. pres. act. indic. of κατηγορέω, "accuse" (cf. 23:2).

23:15 The adversative ἀλλά with οὐδὲ Ἡρώδης is "But not even Herod" (Fitzmyer 1485; Marshall 859; "Neither has Herod" most EVV). Γάρ is explanatory. Ἀνέπεμψεν, see 23:7. Θανάτου is the gen. complement of ἄξιον ("worthy of death"; Wallace 134–35). Πεπραγμένον (nom. sg. neut. of pf. pass. ptc. of πράσσω, "do") with ἐστίν is a pf. periph. cstr. ("has been done" NASB, ESV; for completed action, Burton §84; R 903; Wallace 649; rendered in the active voice in NRSV, HCSB, NIV). Αὐτῷ ("by him" i.e., Jesus) is a rare dat. of agency (cf. BDF §191; R 534, 542; Wallace 165, 373; Z §59; Bock 1828; Marshall 859) rather than a dat. of indir. obj. ("to him"; i.e., by Herod in further support of Jesus' innocence, *pace* Fitzmyer 1485).

23:16 Παιδεύσας (nom. sg. masc. of aor. act. ptc. of παιδεύω, "punish") is temp. with the fut. ἀπολύσω (1st sg. fut. act. indic. of ἀπολύω; "I will punish him and then release him" NIV). Παιδεύω refers here to punishment by whipping (BDAG 749c; MM 474b) which would be carried out under Pilate's orders ("I will have Him whipped" HCSB, sim. NRSV; to appease the crowd, and perhaps to avoid crucifixion, Marshall 859; cf. ἀπολύω in 23:18, 20, 22, 25). The wide discrepancies in the mss. for 23:17 indicate a late scribal addition to assimilate to Mark 15:6/Matt 27:15 (omitted in UBS[5] and most EVV; brackets in NKJV, NASB, HCSB).

23:18 Ἀνέκραγον 3rd pl. 2nd aor. act. indic. of ἀνακράζω, "cry out" (on the form see BDF §75). Παμπληθεί, adv. "all together" (BDAG 753b; LN 59.28; only here in the NT). Λέγοντες, see 1:66. Αἶρε 2nd sg. pres. act. impv. of αἴρω, "take away" (here with the sense "to do away with," "to kill," Fitzmyer 1490, Marshall 860; cf. Acts 21:36; 22:22). Ἀπόλυσον, see 9:12; 23:16. The dat. ἡμῖν could be indir. obj. ("to us" HCSB) or advantage ("for us" NRSV; cf. BHGNT 713). Βαραββᾶς, ironically from Aram. "son of the Father" (Bock 1829; Fitzmyer 1490).

23:19 The nom. sg. masc. rel. pron. ὅστις introduces a parenthesis which explains who Barabbas was (used for ὅς cf. Z §§215–16). Βληθείς (nom. sg. masc. of aor. pass. ptc. of βάλλω) with ἦν is a rare aor. periph. cstr. (BDF §355[1]; R 375, 860; Wallace 746; Z §360). Διά, causal. Two reasons are given for why Barabbas was thrown into prison: (1) An "insurrection" (most EVV; "rebellion" HCSB; BDAG 940c; στάσιν acc. sg. fem. of στάσις, -εως, ἡ; note the irony with 23:2, 5) that had happened in the city (γενομένην acc. sg. fem. of 2nd aor. mid. [attrib.] ptc. of dep. γίνομαι, modifying στάσιν); and (2) murder (φόνον acc. sg. masc. of φόνος, -ου, ὁ).

23:20 Πάλιν, see 23:16 (cf. 23:4). Προσεφώνησεν, see 6:13 (here, "addressed"). Αὐτοῖς is dat. complement (BDAG 887b; BDF §202). Θέλων, see 10:29 (causal; NLT, NET). The aor. act. inf. ἀπολῦσαι (of ἀπολύω; see 23:16) is complementary.

23:21 The impf. ἐπεφώνουν (3rd pl. impf. act. indic. of ἐπιφωνέω, "cry out against," "shout") is iter. (Marshall 860; the art. οἱ refers to αὐτοῖς in 23:10, R 695). Λέγοντες, see 1:66. The double 2nd sg. pres. act. impv. σταύρου (of σταυρόω) is emphatic (on σταυρόω cf. BDAG 941c; Bock 1830–31; Fitzmyer 1491; the pres. may view the crucifixion events as a process, that the crowd insists should get underway [cf. Huffman 102–04]; Bovon [3.283] suggests the pres. views the shouting as persistent).

23:22 With τρίτον the repeated attempts of Pilate to release Jesus on the basis of Jesus' innocence is again emphasized (within 23:13–25 see 23:16, 20, 22; cf. 23:4). Jesus' innocence is highlighted, first with a question (γάρ, often untranslated in questions, BDAG 189c [mng. 1f]; ἐποίησεν, see 1:49), then with a restatement of Pilate's findings (combining the wording of 23:14 and 15). Also, παιδεύσας . . . ἀπολύσω repeats 23:16.

23:23 The impf. ἐπέκειντο (3rd pl. impf. pass. indic. of dep. ἐπίκειμαι, "be urgent," "press upon"; cf. BDAG 373d; LN 68.16) emphasizes their relentless insistence (Fitzmyer 1492; see ἐπισχύω 23:5). The dat. φωναῖς μεγάλαις is instr. Αἰτούμενοι (nom. pl. masc. of pres. mid. ptc. of αἰτέω) expresses means (modifying ἐπέκειντο). In this context αἰτέω has the mng. "demand" (most EVV; cf. BDAG 30b; Bock 1831; Fitzmyer 1492) rather than "ask" (NASB). The acc. αὐτόν is the subj. of the aor. pass. inf. σταυρωθῆναι (of σταυρόω [cf. 23:21]; the inf. is used in indir. discourse). The impf. κατίσχυον (3rd pl. impf. act. indic. of κατισχύω, "prevailed"; BDAG 534b; only here, 21:36; and Matt 16:18 in the NT) could be ingressive (NASB; or that their voices "grew stronger/louder" ZG 277).

23:24 Ἐπέκρινεν 3rd sg. aor. act. indic. of ἐπικρίνω, "decided" (HCSB, ESV, NIV; "come to a conclusion," LN 30.75; perhaps "pronounced sentence" NASB; Fitzmyer 1492). Pilate has given in to the crowd's demands (τὸ αἴτημα αὐτῶν; acc. sg. neut. of αἴτημα, -τος, τό). The inf. γενέσθαι (cf. 3:22) is used in indir. discourse (ἐπικρίνω is often followed by an inf., BDAG 374b).

23:25 Ἀπέλυσεν, see 8:38 (the last use of ἀπολύω in this section [and Luke], see 23:16). Τὸν . . . βεβλημένον is subst. (acc. sg. masc. of pf. pass. ptc. of βάλλω, "the one who had been thrown"). The repetition from 23:19 emphasizes the ironic contrast with the one who is to be punished in his place. The acc. sg. masc. rel. pron. ὅν is the obj. of ᾐτοῦντο (3rd pl. impf. mid. indic. of αἰτέω). The impf. reflects again their continued insistence (see 23:5, 23). Pilate delivered (παρέδωκεν 3rd sg. aor. act. indic. of παραδίδωμι, cf. refs. in 18:32) Jesus over to their will. The ref. to ὅν ᾐτοῦντο (regarding Barabbas) and τῷ θελήματι αὐτῶν (regarding Jesus) emphasizes the will of the people and the weakness of Pilate.

FOR FURTHER STUDY

40. The Trials of Jesus

Bock, D. L. "Jesus as Blasphemer." Pages 76–94 in *Who Do My Opponents Say That I Am? An Investigation of the Accusations Against Jesus.* Edited by S. McKnight and J. B. Modica. London: T&T Clark, 2008.

*Bock, D. L. *Luke 9:51–24:53.* See pages 1775–82, 1791–94.

Brown, R. E. *The Death of the Messiah: From Gethsemane to the Grave: A Commentary on the Passion Narratives in the Four Gospels.* 2 vols. New York: Doubleday, 1994.

Bruce, F. F. "The Trial of Jesus." Pages 7–20 in *Studies of History and Tradition in the Four Gospels.* Edited by R. T. France and D. Wenham. Sheffield: JSOT Press, 1980.

*Cohick, L. H. *DJG*[2] 972–79.

*Köstenberger, A. J., and J. Taylor. *The Final Days of Jesus.* Wheaton: Crossway, 2014.

Skinner, M. L. *The Trial Narratives: Conflict, Power, and Identity in the New Testament.* Louisville: Westminster John Knox, 2010.

See also For Further Study §41

4. The Crucifixion (23:26–49)

a. On the Way to the Crucifixion (23:26–31)

23:26 Ὡς with the aor. ἀπήγαγον (see 22:66) could imply that it was while Jesus was being led away from the preceding scene that they saw Simon ("as they led him away" NRSV, HCSB, ESV, sim. NIV; ZG 277; Marshall 863), or that the leading away has already happened and Simon was spotted at a point further along ("when they led Him away" RV, NASB; "when/after" BDAG 1105d; cf. BDF §455[2, 3]; see BHGNT 717; the pl. may refer to those mentioned in 23:13 or to the soldiers in anticipation of 23:32, 36). Ἐπιλαβόμενοι (nom. pl. masc. of 2nd aor. mid. ptc. of dep. ἐπιλαμβάνομαι, "take hold of," "seized") is attendant circumstance with ἐπέθηκαν (3rd pl. aor. act. indic. of ἐπιτίθημι, "lay upon," "place upon"). Τινα Κυρηναῖον is acc. in appos. to Σίμωνα (HCSB; on the gen. rdg. in some mss. see BDF §170[2]). Ἐρχόμενον (see 21:27) is attrib. modifying Σίμωνα. Ἀπ᾽ ἀγροῦ could refer to a piece of land ("field," "farm") or the "country" (all EVV; BDAG 15d–16a; ZG 277). The pres. act. inf. φέρειν (of φέρω, "to carry") expresses the purpose for placing the cross upon Simon (cf. 9:23; 14:27; epex., Marshall 863). The prep. ὄπισθεν ("behind") takes the gen.

23:27 The impfs. ἠκολούθει (see 5:28), ἐκόπτοντο ("mourning"; see 8:52), and ἐθρήνουν (3rd pl. impf. act. indic. of θρηνέω, "lament," "wail") are all progressive. Πολὺ πλῆθος τοῦ λαοῦ καὶ γυναικῶν (HCSB, NIV; cf. 23:48–49) is the subj. of ἠκολούθει. The nom. pl. fem. rel. pron. αἵ is the subj. of ἐκόπτοντο καὶ ἐθρήνουν (the antecedent is γυναικῶν, "women who were").

23:28 Στραφείς (see 7:9) is attendant circumstance (with εἶπεν). The phrase θυγατέρες Ἰερουσαλήμ and the reference to τὰ τέκνα ὑμῶν indicate that the women are referred to as representatives of the city (and nation; Bock 1845). The pres. prohibition not to weep (κλαίετε 2nd pl. pres. act. impv. of κλαίω; note the chiasm: μὴ κλαίετε . . . κλαίετε) for Jesus but for themselves and their children could highlight the prohibition of a continuous activity (Huffman 144) or, in this context (23:27), an action already in progress that should be stopped ("stop weeping for Me" NASB; BDAG 646a; Z §246; ZG 277). Ἐπί (three times in this verse) is used here as a "marker of feelings directed toward someone" (BDAG 366c; BHGNT 718). Both Jesus' entry into Jerusalem (19:41–44) and his departure from it are characterized by weeping over the future judgment of the city.

23:29 The reason (ὅτι) for the weeping is now given as the judgment that is coming on the city. As he goes to his crucifixion, Jesus is the judge. Ἔρχονται ἡμέραι (3rd pl. pres. mid. indic. of dep. ἔρχομαι) is a common phrase in the OT prophets. Ἐροῦσιν, see 17:21. The adj. μακάριαι is pred. The nom. pl. fem. αἱ στεῖραι [see 1:7] καὶ αἱ κοιλίαι [see 1:15] . . . καὶ [masc.] μαστοί [see 11:27] are the subj. of the verbless equative clause (BHGNT 719). The rel. clause αἵ οὐκ ἐγέννησαν (3rd pl. aor. act. indic. of γεννάω) modifies αἱ κοιλίαι ("wombs"). The rel. clause οἵ οὐκ ἔθρεψαν (3rd pl. aor. act. indic. of τρέφω, "nourish," "feed"; "nursed" most EVV) modifies μαστοί (cf. 1:25; 11:27).

23:30 Ἄρξονται 3rd pl. fut. mid. indic. of ἄρχω. Λέγειν (see 3:8) is complementary (the dat. τοῖς ὄρεσιν ["to the mountains"] is the indir. obj.). Πέσετε 2nd pl. 2nd aor. act. impv. of πίπτω, "fall." Τοῖς βουνοῖς (dat. pl. masc., see 3:5; "to the hills") is the indir. obj. of an implied λέγειν (BHGNT 719). Καλύψατε 2nd pl. aor. act. impv. of καλύπτω, "cover."

23:31 The reason (ὅτι) for this cry to the mountains and hills is because (in a lesser-to-greater argument) of the horror that is to come. Εἰ introduces a first-class cond. (Z §303; ZG 277). Ἐν τῷ ὑγρῷ ξύλῳ (dat. sg. neut. of ὑγρός, -ά, -όν ["green"]; of ξύλον, see 22:52; "when the tree is green" NASB, NIV; "when the wood is green" NRSV, HCSB, ESV) is "in the case of" (referring to the general context in which this takes place, BHGNT 720; R 587; Nolland 1138). The acc. ταῦτα is the dir. obj. of ποιοῦσιν (see 6:33; cf. 23:34). The pl. of ποιοῦσιν is indef. (Wallace 402–3; for [divine] pass., Z §§1–2; ZG 277; Nolland 1138; "if such things are done" NET, sim. NJB, NLT). Ἐν τῷ ξηρῷ "when it is dry" (HCSB, ESV; dat. sg. neut., see 6:6). The interr. τί, with the subjunc. γένηται (see 1:20), asks a question of future possibility (BDF §366[1]; T 99; a "deliberative *real* subjunctive" Wallace 467; ZG 277; a "rhetorical question of fact" Burton §169) which could refer to (see Bock [1847] for more options):

1. God's judgment on the Son (the innocent one), and the much more severe judgment for the sinful nation (deserving of judgment; cf. Bock 1847; Fitzmyer 1498; Marshall 865); or
2. more generally "the inevitability and the scale of the judgment to fall" (Nolland 1138).

b. Jesus Crucified and Mocked (23:32–43)

23:32 Ἤγοντο (3rd pl. impf. pass. indic. of ἄγω, "lead"). Καί "also." Ἕτεροι κακοῦργοι δύο is the subj. of ἤγοντο (nom. pl. masc. [subst.] adj. of κακοῦργος, -ον). "Two others, who were criminals" (ESV) makes clear that Jesus is not a criminal too (cf. ἕτερος in R 748; ZG 277; see 23:33; cf. 22:37). The aor. pass. inf. ἀναιρεθῆναι (of ἀναιρέω, "put to death" NRSV, ESV; "executed" HCSB, NIV) is an inf. of purpose.

23:33 Ἦλθον, see 1:59. Καλούμενον (see 6:15) is attrib. modifying τὸν τόπον. Κρανίον, "Skull" (Golgotha in Aramaic, cf. John 19:17; *calvaria* in Latin, from which the English word *Calvary* is derived; cf. NKJV; a pred. acc., Wallace 191). Ἐσταύρωσαν 3rd pl. aor. act. indic. of σταυρόω (cf. 23:21). The acc. αὐτὸν καὶ τοὺς κακούργους distinguishes between Jesus and "the criminals." The rel. prons. ὃν μὲν . . . ὃν δέ ("one . . . the other") are in appos. to τοὺς κακούργους (a demonstrative use of the prons., R 695–96; ZG 278). Ἐκ with the gen. pl. neut. δεξιῶν (and here with ἀριστερῶν, of ἀριστερός, -ά, -όν, "left"; an example of a def. anar. prep. phrase, R 792) is locat. (see 1:11).

23:34 Ὁ . . . ποιοῦσιν is omitted in many mss. (Alexandrian and Western), though included by many too (SBLGNT; brackets in UBS[5]). The prayer is not found in the other Gospels so that may be the reason for its omission by some scribes (and it may have been viewed as contrary to 23:28–31). Internal evidence, such as the sim. prayer by Stephen (Acts 7:60) and the Lukan theme of forgiveness, supports the original inclusion of the prayer (see Bock 1867–68; Bovon 3.307; Marshall 867–68; cf. 6:28). Ἄφες, see 6:42 (here, "forgive"). The dat. αὐτοῖς may be a dat. of advantage or complement (BHGNT 721). Οἴδασιν, see 11:44. Ποιοῦσιν, see 6:33 (cf. 23:31). Διαμεριζόμενοι (nom. pl. masc. of pres. mid. ptc. of διαμερίζω, "divide") may be temp. (Nolland 1141), or express purpose ("cast lots to divide" NRSV, ESV; Bock 1841). Ἔβαλον, see 21:4. Κλήρους acc. pl. masc. of κλῆρος, -ου, ὁ, "lots" (most EVV; BDAG 548b; "dice" NLT, NET).

23:35 Εἱστήκει 3rd sg. plupf. act. indic. of ἵστημι "stand" (with ὁ λαός as a collective sg. subj., Wallace 400). Θεωρῶν (nom. sg. masc. of pres. act. ptc. of θεωρέω) expresses manner ("stood by watching"). The impf. ἐξεμυκτήριζον (see 16:14) is probably iter. (HCSB). Δὲ καὶ οἱ ἄρχοντες ("even the leaders" HCSB, sim. NASB; or "also the leaders") may indicate the participation of both the people and the leaders in the mocking (Marshall 869). Or καί could anticipate a parallel use of καί in 23:36 ("the leaders sneered . . . and the soldiers mocked"), thus separating the people from the leaders in this verse (Nolland 1147; perhaps continuing a more positive portrait of the people from 23:27; cf. 23:48). Λέγοντες, see 1:66. The aor. ἔσωσεν (3rd sg. aor. act. indic. of σῴζω) is constative (looking at Jesus' ministry as a whole, Z §253; ZG 278). Σωσάτω 3rd sg. aor. act. impv. "Let him save" (see σῴζω 23:37, 39; Jesus is crucified as "Savior," Fitzmyer 1501; cf. 1:47; 2:11; 9:24). Εἰ introduces the protasis of a first-class cond. (assumed true for the sake of argument, Burton §245; R 1009; ZG 278). Οὗτος is probably derogative (cf. 23:2). Ὁ χριστός is the pred. nom. and ὁ ἐκλεκτός (see 18:7) is in appos. (cf. 9:20, 35).

23:36 Ἐνέπαιξαν 3rd pl. aor. act. indic. of ἐμπαίζω "mock" (see 18:32; 22:63; 23:11). Οἱ στρατιῶται nom. pl. masc. of στρατιώτης, -ου, ὁ, "soldier." The two nom. pl. masc. of pres. ptcs. προσερχόμενοι (mid. of dep. προσέρχομαι) and προσφέροντες (act. of προσφέρω, "offer") express means (i.e., the mocking was done by "coming up and offering"). Ὄξος acc. sg. neut. of ὄξος, -ους, τό, "sour wine" (BDAG 715d; MM 452d–53a).

23:37 Λέγοντες, see 1:66. Εἰ introduces another first-class cond. (see 23:35). Σύ may be emphatic here. Σῶσον 2nd sg. aor. act. impv. of σῴζω (cf. 23:35, 39).

23:38 Ἐπιγραφή, "inscription" (see 20:24; BDAG 369d; cf. BDF §5[1]; "written notice" NIV; the subj. of ἦν). Ἐπί is locat. ("above/over," R 604). Ὁ βασιλεύς is the pred. nom. of the verbless clause (οὗτος is the subj.). The omission of the ref. to the three languages in some early mss. (and the variation in other mss.) indicates a later scribal assimilation to John 19:20 (Metzger 154; cf. NKJV).

23:39 Εἷς, i.e., "one of two" (ZG 278). Κρεμασθέντων gen. pl. masc. of aor. pass. (attrib.) ptc. of κρεμάννυμι, "hang" (modifying the gen. pl. κακούργων [see 23:32]; NASB, ESV). Ἐβλασφήμει 3rd sg. impf. act. indic. of βλασφημέω (see 22:65), "blasphemed" (NRSV; Marshall 871) or "hurled insults" (NIV; sim. most EVV). The impf. could be iter. (NRSV) or ingressive (HCSB). For οὐχί see 4:22 (used sarcastically here; equivalent to a cond., Marshall 871). Σῶσον σεαυτόν repeats the taunt of 23:37.

23:40 Ἀποκριθείς, see 1:19. Ἐπιτιμῶν (see 4:41) expresses manner. Ἔφη, see 7:44. The neg. οὐχί in the question expects a positive answer but is used as a rebuke here. Φοβῇ 2nd sg. pres. mid. indic. of dep. φοβέομαι. Οὐδέ "not even" (i.e., "Don't you even fear God?" HCSB, sim. NASB; the adv. may modify "fear" Fitzmyer [1509], "you" Marshall [871–72], "God" Nolland [1151]; cf. 12:4–5; 18:2, 4; to mock Jesus is failing to fear God, Marshall 872). Ὅτι gives the reason for such fear. Ἐν τῷ αὐτῷ κρίματι ("under the same sentence of condemnation" ESV; see 20:47) expresses the context that the criminal is in (BHGNT 724; with αὐτός as an identifying adj., Wallace 349).

23:41 Ἡμεῖς is the subj. of an implied vb. (probably a cognate of κρίμα, 23:40; BHGNT 724). Δικαίως, adv. "justly." Γάρ introduces further support for the justness of the criminals' condemnation (emphasized with the forward placement of ἄξια; see 23:15). Together with the rel. pron. ὧν and ἐπράξαμεν (1st pl. aor. act. indic. of πράσσω), ἄξια . . . ὧν ἐπράξαμεν has the mng. "what our deeds deserve" (NIV). The rel. pron. ὧν is used for ἐκείνων ἅ and has attracted the case of its antecedent (R 720; Z §16; ZG 278; ἄξιος takes the gen., see 23:15). Ἀπολαμβάνομεν 1st pl. pres. act. indic. of ἀπολαμβάνω, "getting back" (HCSB; "what is due" Z §132; ZG 278; see refs. at 6:34). Ἄτοπον acc. sg. neut. of ἄτοπος, -ον, "out of place," "wrong" (most EVV). Ἔπραξεν 3rd sg. aor. act. indic. of πράσσω. Pilate, Herod, and now this criminal have all declared Jesus' innocence.

23:42 Ἔλεγεν, see 5:36; 6:5 (a "dramatic impf." that introduces a vivid statement, Wallace 543; though Bovon [3.311] sees persistence here). Μνήσθητί, see 16:25 (the second accent is from the enclitic μου). Ὅταν with ἔλθῃς (2nd sg. 2nd aor. act. subjunc. of dep. ἔρχομαι) is temp. Εἰς τὴν βασιλείαν σου is locat. (perhaps referring to the final consummation, or at least an undefined future [Harris 169]; he confesses Jesus' kingship on the cross [cf. 23:2, 3, 37–38] and entrusts his future fate into Jesus' hands; on the var. ἐν see Metzger 154; Bock 1869; Marshall 872).

23:43 For ἀμήν σοι λέγω see 4:24 ("I assure you" HCSB). Ἐμοῦ is the emphatic form of ἐγώ. Ἔσῃ, see 1:20. Jesus gives assurance that matches the criminal's request. The general temp. "when you come" is matched with an emphatic and specific "today" (i.e., following death; cf. 12:20; 16:22–23; Acts 7:59). The locat. "into your kingdom" becomes the personal "with me in paradise" (Harris 169). Παραδείσῳ dat. sg. masc. of παράδεισος, -ου, ὁ, "paradise," a term used for the place of God's presence in the garden of Eden (e.g., Gen 2:9–10; Ezek 31:8) and the restoration of Eden (Isa 51:3; cf. Rev 2:7; 2 Cor 12:4). Jesus exercises his saving rule by his word from the cross (cf. 23:35–38).

c. The Death of Jesus (23:44–49)

23:44 Ὡσεί with numbers is a marker of approximation (BDAG 1106d). Ὥρα ἕκτη, "sixth hour" (nom. sg. fem., see 1:26; i.e., "about noon," HCSB, NIV; ἤδη, "now," "by this time"). Ἐπί with ἐγένετο refers to motion (BDAG 364b; cf. Fitzmyer 1517). Ὥρας ἐνάτης, "ninth hour" (i.e., "three in the afternoon," NRSV, NIV). The darkness may be Satanic (Nolland 1156, 1160; 22:53), though 22:42 (cf. 23:31, 40–41) suggests it is more likely an indicator of God's judgment (alluding to the "day of the Lord"; cf. Bock 1858; Fitzmyer 1517).

23:45 The gen. τοῦ ἡλίου is the subj. of the gen. ptc. ἐκλιπόντος (gen. sg. masc. of 2nd aor. act. ptc. of ἐκλείπω, "fail" NRSV, HCSB, ESV; "stopped shining" NIV; BDAG 306a "cease to shine"; MM 195 "fail"; i.e., not necessarily "eclipse" as ZG 279; cf. all other NT uses in Luke 16:9; 22:32; Heb 1:12). The gen. abs. cstr. is causal (giving the reason for the darkness mentioned in 23:44). Ἐσχίσθη 3rd sg. aor. pass. indic. of σχίζω, "to split," "tear." Καταπέτασμα nom. sg. neut. of καταπέτασμα, -ατος, τό, "curtain," is the subj. of ἐσχίσθη. Μέσον pred. adj. as an adv. acc. ("down the middle" HCSB; "in two" ESV, NIV). For views regarding which curtain and the significance of the tearing see Bock 1860–61; Nolland 1157. In Luke, ναός is only found elsewhere in 1:9, 21, 22 (Zechariah went in; the people waited outside).

23:46 Φωνήσας (see 16:2) is in attendant circumstance (with εἶπεν). The dat. φωνῇ μεγάλῃ is syntactically instr. though semantically the phrase expresses manner (BHGNT 727). Πάτερ, voc. (cf. 10:21; here, an inclusio with 22:42). Παρατίθεμαι 1st sg. pres. mid. indic. of παρατίθημι, "put," "place"; mid. "entrust" (BDAG 772b). Εἰπών (see 9:22) is temp. The locat. εἰς χεῖράς σου is synecdoche for "to you" (BHGNT 727; idiomatic for the Father's powerful care, BDAG 1083a). Ἐξέπνευσεν 3rd sg. aor. act. indic. of ἐκπνέω, "breathe out," "breathed his last" (most EVV).

23:47 Γενόμενον (acc. sg. neut. of 2nd aor. mid. (subst.) ptc. of dep. γίνομαι; "what happened" HCSB; perhaps referring to 23:43, 46) is the obj. of ἰδών (see 1:12; temp.; ὁ ἑκατοντάρχης "the centurion" [see 7:2] is the subj.). Ἐδόξαζεν, see 13:13 (cf. 2:20; 4:14 for δοξάζω in Luke). The impf. is probably ingressive (NASB, HCSB). Ὄντως, "truly," "really" (HCSB), "certainly" (NRSV, ESV), is an adv. from the ptc. of εἰμί ("in reality" ZG 279). Δίκαιος, is a pred. adj. "righteous" (NKJV, HCSB, NIV; Bovon 3.328; Nolland 1159, i.e., in a "right relationship to God" [cf. 1:6; 2:25; 23:50; cf. δικαίως 23:41]; incorporating, but more than just "innocent" NRSV, NASB, ESV; Bock 1863; Marshall 876).

23:48 Συμπαραγενόμενοι nom. pl. masc. of 2nd aor. mid. (attrib.) ptc. of dep. συμπαραγίνομαι, "come together," "gather"; (perhaps continuing the distinction between the people and the rulers, cf. 23:35). Ἐπὶ τὴν θεωρίαν ταύτην indicates purpose ("for this spectacle" NRSV, HCSB, ESV; BDAG 366a; acc. sg. fem. of θεωρία, -ας, ἡ). Γενόμενα (see 4:23; subst.; pl.; cf. the sg. in 23:47) is the obj. of θεωρήσαντες (nom. pl. masc. of aor. act. [temp.] ptc. of θεωρέω). Τύπτοντες (nom. pl. masc. of pres. act. ptc. of τύπτω, "strike," "beat"; with στήθη "breasts" a sign of lament; perhaps guilt and contrition, see 18:13 [Bock 1865; Fitzmyer 1520]) probably expresses manner with ὑπέστρεφον (3rd pl. impf. act. indic. of ὑποστρέφω, "return"; intrans.). The impf. of ὑπέστρεφον could be ingressive (NASB; Marshall 877). The refs. to the grieving crowd and women in 23:48–49 serve as an inclusio with 23:27 (Nolland 1135, 1159; with links in 23:48–49 also to 23:35).

23:49 The nom. pl. πάντες οἱ γνωστοί . . . καὶ γυναῖκες is the subj. of εἱστήκεισαν (see 23:10; "all who knew him, including the women" HCSB; sim. NIV; γνωστοί [see

2:44] is subst., Wallace 233). Συνακολουθοῦσαι nom. pl. fem. of pres. act. (attrib.) ptc. of συνακολουθέω, "follow," "accompany" (modifying γυναῖκες; "the women who had followed him"; R 778; Wallace 307; the pres. is progressive [ἀπὸ τῆς Γαλιλαίας]). Ὁρῶσαι (nom. pl. fem. of pres. act. ptc. of ὁράω) syntactically refers to the women as those who were watching (cf. NJB, NET; BHGNT 729). The anar. ptc. is probably adv. rather than attrib. and may be tr. as a ptc. of manner either modifying εἱστήκεισαν (such that both groups "stood at a distance, watching these things" NRSV, HCSB, ESV, NIV; Nolland 1160), another implied εἱστήκεισαν (BHGNT 729–30), or a ptc. expressing purpose ("to see"; Bock 1866). Μακρόθεν (adv.) may reflect merely a practical precaution (Nolland 1160; though note 22:54b which may indicate more of a criticism here). The ref. to the women who were watching these things anticipates 24:1.

FOR FURTHER STUDY

41. The Crucifixion and Death of Jesus

*Bauckham, R. J. God Crucified: Monotheism and Christology in the New Testament. Grand Rapids: Eerdmans, 1998.

Chapman, D. W. Ancient Jewish and Christian Perceptions of Crucifixion. Grand Rapids: Baker, 2010.

*Chapman, D. W., and E. J. Schnabel. The Trial and Crucifixion of Jesus. WUNT 344. Tubingen: Mohr Siebeck, 2015.

Dennis, J. DJG² 172–92.

Evans, C. A. "Jewish Burial Traditions and the Resurrection of Jesus." JSHJ 3 (2005): 233–48.

Green, J. B. The Death of Jesus: Tradition and Interpretation in the Passion Narrative. WUNT 2/33. Tübingen: Mohr Siebeck, 1988.

_____. "'Was It Not Necessary for the Messiah to Suffer These Things and Enter into His Glory?' The Significance of Jesus' Death for Lukan Soteriology." Pages 71–85 in The Spirit and Christ in the New Testament and Christian Theology. Edited by I. H. Marshall, V. Rabens, and C. Bennema. Grand Rapids: Eerdmans, 2012.

*Hengel, M. Crucifixion in the Ancient World and the Folly of the Message of the Cross. Tr. by J. Bowden. Philadelphia: Fortress, 1977.

*Larkin, W. "Luke's Use of the Old Testament as a Key to His Soteriology." JETS 20 (1977): 325–35.

HOMILETICAL SUGGESTIONS

Salvation Accomplished (23:1–49)

1. Jesus, the innocent one, goes to the cross in place of the guilty (23:1–25).
2. Jesus, the compassionate one, warns of consequences on the way to the cross (23:26–31).
3. Jesus, the reigning one, saves on the cross (23:32–43).
4. Jesus, the righteous one, accomplishes the Father's will (22:42; 23:44–49).

or

1. Jesus, though innocent and righteous, experienced . . .

   a. False accusations and injustice (23:1–25).
   b. Mockery and humiliation (23:1–25, 32–39).
   c. Flogging and crucifixion (23:16, 22, 33).
   d. Day of the Lord; judgment (22:42; 23:31, 44–45).
2. So we, though sinful, may experience . . . .
   a. Forgiveness from the Father (23:34).
   b. Eternal presence with Jesus (23:43).
   c. The reign of Jesus in paradise (23:43).

How to Receive the Greatest Promise Ever (23:40–43)

1. Confess the justness of the punishment we deserve (23:40–41a).
2. Acknowledge the purity of Jesus (23:41b).
3. Turn to Jesus as King and Savior (23:42).
4. Receive the gracious promise of Jesus' eternal presence in paradise (23:43).

D. THE REALITY AND SIGNIFICANCE OF JESUS' RESURRECTION (23:50–24:53)

1. The Evidence of an Empty Tomb (23:50–24:12)

a. Witnesses to the Placement of Jesus' Body in the Tomb (23:50–56)

23:50 The nom. ἀνήρ (ὀνόματι is a dat. of ref.) is the subj. of the following verses and is picked up with οὗτος in 23:52 (BDF §290[1]; T 45). Ὑπάρχων (see 9:48) is attrib. modifying ἀνήρ (βουλευτής, nom. sg. masc. of βουλευτής, -οῦ, ὁ, "council member" [i.e., of the Sanhedrin, LN 11.85] is pred.). The nom. ἀνὴρ ἀγαθὸς καὶ δίκαιος is in appos. (NASB; cf. 1:6; 2:25; 23:47; Acts 11:24).

23:51 Οὗτος introduces a parenthetical clarification (οὗτος . . . αὐτῶν, R 434). The impf. ἦν with συγκατατεθειμένος (nom. sg. masc. of pf. pass. ptc. of dep. συγκατατίθεμαι, "agree with," "consent to"; neg. with οὐκ) is a pluperfect periph. cstr. (Wallace 583, 649). Βουλῇ (dat. sg. fem., see 7:30), "purpose," "plan" (NRSV, NASB, HCSB; "decision" ESV, NIV; dat. complement expressing association, R 529). Πράξει dat. sg. fem. of πρᾶξις, -εως, ἡ, "deed," "action" (αὐτῶν refers to the antecedent βουλευτής according to sense, BDF §282[3]). Ἀπὸ Ἀριμαθαίας (the gen. πόλεως τῶν Ἰουδαίων is appos.) continues the description of Joseph from 23:50. Joseph was "waiting" (προσεδέχετο 3rd sg. impf. mid. indic. of dep. προσεδέχομαι, "wait for," "waiting expectantly for" NRSV; "looking forward to" HCSB) the kingdom of God (see 2:25, 38; cf. 4:43).

23:52 Οὗτος (see 1:17) is the subj. of ᾐτήσατο (3rd sg. aor. mid. indic. of αἰτέω) and resumes the introduction of Joseph from 23:50. Προσελθών (see 7:14) is attendant circumstance (with ᾐτήσατο). The dat. τῷ Πιλάτῳ is called a "dative of destination" by Wallace (147–48; a dat. complement of προσελθών, BDAG 878b; BHGNT 731). Τὸ σῶμα is used here, 23:55 and 24:3 (cf. 24:23) to specify both that Jesus was physically dead and that the body that went into the tomb also came out of the tomb.

23:53 Καθελών (nom. sg. masc. of aor. act. ptc. of καθαιρέω, "take down") could be temp. or attendant circumstance with ἐνετύλιξεν (3rd sg. aor. act. indic. ἐντυλίσσω, "wrap up") and ἔθηκεν (see 6:48). The acc. sg. neut. pron. αὐτό is the obj. of ἐνετύλιξεν (agreeing with σῶμα). The dat. (sg. fem.) σινδόνι (of σινδών, -όνος, ἡ, "fine linen cloth") is instr. The acc. sg. masc. pron. αὐτόν (or neut. αὐτό, see Fitzmyer 1529) is the dir. obj. of ἔθηκεν. Ἐν μνήματι "in a tomb" is locat. (see 8:27; 24:1). Λαξευτῷ dat. sg. neut. of λαξευτός, -ή, -όν, "cut into the rock" (NASB, HCSB; LN 19.26). The gen. rel. pron. οὗ functions as an adv. "where." The impf. ἦν with κείμενος (nom. sg. masc. of pres. pass. ptc. of dep. κεῖμαι) is an impf. periph. cstr. (BHGNT 732; ZG 279; "where no one had ever been placed"; R [906] and Wallace [649] describe this as a pluperfect periph. cstr.; the negs. οὐκ . . . οὐδεὶς οὔπω strengthen the negation, Burton §489; R 1165).

23:54 Ἡμέρα [pred. nom.] . . . παρασκευῆς "day of preparation" (gen. sg. fem. of παρασκευή, -ῆς, ἡ, i.e., the day associated with preparation [for the Sabbath], BHGNT 732; R 493). Ἐπέφωσκεν 3rd sg. impf. act. indic. of ἐπιφώσκω, not "dawn," but "begin" (most EVV; Fitzmyer 1529). The impf. may be ingressive "beginning to approach" (cf. NJB; R 885).

23:55 Κατακολουθήσασαι (nom. pl. fem. of aor. act. ptc. κατακολουθέω, "follow") is attendant circumstance (with ἐθεάσαντο 3rd pl. aor. mid. indic. of dep. θεάομαι, "see"). The women (αἱ γυναῖκες) are further described with the indef. rel. pron. αἵτινες (for ὅς, Z §216) and the pluperfect periph. cstr. of the impf. ἦσαν and συνεληλυθυῖαι (nom. pl. fem. of pf. act. ptc. of dep. συνέρχομαι; "who had come with him"; see Wallace 583, 649). The use of ὡς refers to the manner (BHGNT 733; R 1032). Ἐτέθη 3rd sg. aor. pass. indic. of τίθημι.

23:56 Ὑποστρέψασαι (nom. pl. fem. of aor. act. ptc. of ὑποστρέφω, "return") is attendant circumstance (with ἡτοίμασαν see 22:13). Ἀρώματα acc. pl. neut. of ἄρωμα, -ατος, τό, "spice" (BDAG 140d). Μύρα, acc. pl. neut., see 7:37. The perfumes and spices would be to lower the stench and perhaps slow decomposition (Bock 1877; they do not appear to be expecting a resurrection in the near future). Τὸ . . . σάββατον is an acc. of time. Μέν anticipates δέ in 24:1 and links the two verses together. Ἡσύχασαν, see 14:4 (here, "rested").

b. Witnesses to the Absence of Jesus' Body in the Tomb (24:1–12)

24:1 On δέ see 23:56. Τῇ . . . μιᾷ is a dat. of time (with the fem. ἡμέρα implied). Σαββάτων (a partitive gen.) with τῇ . . . μιᾷ means "first [day] of the week" (BDF §247[1]). Time notes throughout the chapter explicitly link events to this same day (cf. 24:13, 33, 36). The gen. sg. masc. ὄρθρου βαθέως (of ὄρθρος, -ου, ὁ, "dawn"; of βαθύς, -εῖα, ύ, "deep") together mean "very early in the morning" (a gen. of time; cf. BDAG 162d, 723a; BDF §186[2]; R 495). Ἐπὶ τὸ μνῆμα is locat. ("to the tomb"; see 8:27). Φέρουσαι (nom. pl. fem. of pres. act. ptc. of φέρω; for ἀρώματα see 23:56) expresses manner, modifying ἦλθον (see 1:59). The acc. rel. pron. ἅ is the dir. obj. of ἡτοίμασαν (see 22:13; cf. R 718).

24:2 Εὗρον, see 2:46. Ἀποκεκυλισμένον (acc. sg. masc. of pf. pass. ptc. of ἀποκυλίω, "roll away") is the complement of λίθον in a double acc. cstr. (BDAG 411d; BHGNT 734). Μνημείου, "tomb" (see μνῆμα in 23:53; 24:1).

24:3 Εἰσελθοῦσαι nom. pl. fem. of aor. act. (temp.) ptc. of dep. εἰσέρχομαι. Εὗρον (see 2:46) is repeated from 24:2, now with οὐχ for "the body of the Lord Jesus" ("Lord Jesus" is used only here in Luke, but fifteen times in Acts). On the so-called "Western noninterpolations" of 24:3, 6, 12, 36, 40, 51–52, see 22:19b.

24:4 Καὶ ἐγένετο, see 1:5. The acc. αὐτάς is the subj. of the temp. inf. cstr. ἐν τῷ ἀπορεῖσθαι (pres. mid. inf. of ἀπορέω; "while they were perplexed"). For ἄνδρες δύο as a ref. to angels, cf. 24:23; Acts 1:10. Ἐπέστησαν, see 20:1 (here, "stood by"; the dat. αὐταῖς is complementary). Ἐν ἐσθῆτι ("in clothing"; see 23:11) indicates the "condition" (i.e., what they were wearing, BDAG 327b). Ἀστραπτούσῃ dat. sg. fem. of pres. act. (attrib.) ptc. of ἀστράπτω, "flash," "dazzling" (most EVV; cf. 17:24) modifies ἐσθῆτι.

24:5 The gen. (pl. fem.) adj. ἐμφόβων (of ἔμφοβος, -ον, "terrified") and γενομένων (gen. pl. fem. of 2nd aor. mid. ptc. of dep. γίνομαι) form a gen. abs. cstr. along with κλινουσῶν (gen. pl. fem. of pres. act. ptc. of κλίνω "bow"; "as they were frightened and bowed" ESV; the acc. τὰ πρόσωπα is the dir. obj. of κλινουσῶν). The gen. abs. cstr. could be temp. or causal (BHGNT 735–36). Εἶπαν, i.e., "the men." Ζητεῖτε, see 11:9. Ζῶντα acc. sg. masc. of pres. act. (subst.) ptc. of ζάω (perhaps "the living One" NASB; Bovon 3.358 [citing Bengel]; cf. 24:23; Acts 1:3).

24:6 Ἠγέρθη (see 7:16; 9:7), could be pass. (HCSB; a divine pass., Bock 1891; Bovon 3.351; Fitzmyer 1545; Nolland 1190; e.g., Acts 3:15) or intrans. ("he has risen" most other EVV; cf. 11:8; 13:25 [24:7]). Μνήσθητε 2nd pl. aor. pass. impv. of dep. μιμνῄσκομαι, "remember." Ὡς functions as ὅτι though perhaps with more of a focus on manner (BHGNT 736; R 1032). Ἐλάλησεν, see 1:55. The ptc. ὤν (see 3:23, of εἰμί) is temp. (with ἔτι, "while he was still").

24:7 Λέγων with ὅτι may introduce dir. discourse (HCSB, NIV) or indir. discourse ("that the Son of Man" NRSV, NASB, ESV). The acc. τὸν υἱόν (τοῦ ἀνθρώπου) could be the subj. of the following infs., or perhaps an acc. of respect as the conceptual subj. (given prominence as the obj. of the leading verb, BDF §476[3]; BHGNT 737; Bock 1893; "proleptic" Fitzmyer 1545; "anticipatory" Marshall 886). The infs. παραδοθῆναι (aor. pass. inf. of παραδίδωμι; cf. 9:44; 18:32; 22:4, 6) . . . σταυρωθῆναι (see 23:23) . . . ἀναστῆναι (2nd aor. act. inf. of ἀνίστημι; cf. 18:33) are complementary with δεῖ (see 2:49). The shift to the act. voice of the last inf. ("and rise") is reflected in most EVV (pass. in NIV; cf. 9:22). Τῇ τρίτῃ ἡμέρᾳ, see 9:22.

24:8 Ἐμνήσθησαν 3rd pl. aor. pass. indic. of dep. μιμνῄσκομαι, "remember." Τῶν ῥημάτων, obj. gen. Αὐτοῦ, subj. gen.

24:9 Ὑποστρέψασαι, see 23:56 (temp.). Ἀπήγγειλαν, see 7:18. Ἕνδεκα, "eleven" (indecl.).

24:10 Three of those who were called αἱ γυναῖκες in 23:55 are now identified. Ἦσαν (see 1:6) could be "they were" or perhaps "the [women] were" if this is viewed as explaining the masc. πᾶσιν τοῖς λοιποῖς of 24:9, Fitzmyer 1546; cf. 8:2–3). The art. ἡ should be read with an implied μήτηρ and the gen. Ἰακώβου is a gen. of relationship (R 501; Wallace 83–84). These three, and others (καὶ αἱ λοιπαὶ σὺν αὐταῖς) are probably all the subj. of ἔλεγον (see 4:22; BHGNT 738; not just αἱ λοιπαί, Bock 1897; [iter., Fitzmyer 1547]; Marshall 887; the acc. ταῦτα is the dir. obj.). On ἀπόστολος in Luke see 6:13.

24:11 Ἐφάνησαν 3rd pl. aor. pass. indic. of φαίνω, in mid/pass "appear" (τὰ ῥήματα ταῦτα is the subj.). The prep. ἐνώπιον ("before," takes the gen.) has the sense of "in the sight of, in the opinion of" (BDAG 342d; LN 90.20). Λῆρος nom. sg. masc. of λῆρος, -ου, ὁ, "complete and utter nonsense" (LN 33.380; cf. NET; BDAG 594a). The impf. ἠπίστουν (3rd pl. impf. act. indic. of ἀπιστέω, "disbelieve") perhaps parallels the impf. ἔλεγον of 24:10. Αὐταῖς is fem. pl. in agreement with 24:10 and the dat. complement of ἠπίστουν (R 540).

24:12 Ἀναστάς (see 4:38) could be an attendant circumstance ptc. with ἔδραμεν (3rd sg. aor. act. indic. of τρέχω, "run"; a "graphic" ptc. used as a Sem. idiom in movement, Z §363). Παρακύψας nom. sg. masc. of aor. act. (temp.) ptc. of παρακύπτω, "stoop to look" BDAG 767c; "peer into" Robertson, *Pictures* 292; Bock 1899; Fitzmyer 1547; cf. MM 486d; not necessarily "stoop down," Marshall 889. Βλέπει 3rd sg. pres. act. indic. of βλέπω, a historical pres. Τὰ ὀθόνια acc. pl. neut. of ὀθόνιον, "linen cloth" (used in the NT only for burial cloths; diminutive form of ὀθόνη though not necessarily with diminutive force, BDAG 693a; LN 6.154; BDF §111[3–4]). The acc. pl. neut. adj. μόνα (of μόνος, -η, -ον, "alone") is a complement in a double acc. cstr. (BDAG 179a; BHGNT 739). Ἀπῆλθεν, see 1:23. Θαυμάζων (nom. sg. masc. of pres. act. ptc. of θαυμάζω, "wonder") describes the manner in which Peter "departed." Πρὸς ἑαυτόν could modify θαυμάζων ("wondering to himself" NIV, sim. NKJV) or ἀπῆλθεν in the sense of "to his home" (RV, NASB; sim. NRSV, HCSB, ESV; Fitzmyer 1548; Marshall 889). Γεγονός acc. sg. neut. of pf. act. (subst.) ptc. of dep. γίνομαι.

FOR FURTHER STUDY

42. The Resurrection of Jesus in Luke's Gospel

*Anderson, K. L. *"But God Raised Him from the Dead": The Theology of Jesus' Resurrection in Luke-Acts.* Bletchley: Paternoster, 2006.

*_____. *DJG²* 774–89.

Bayer, H. F. *DJG²* 692–95.

Dillon, R. J. *From Eye-Witnesses to Ministers of the Word: Tradition and Composition in Luke 24.* Rome: Biblical Institute Press, 1978.

Marshall, I. H. "The Resurrection of Jesus in Luke." *TynBul* 24 (1974): 55–98.

O'Toole, R. F. "Luke's Understanding of Jesus' Resurrection-Ascension-Exultation." *BTB* 9 (1979): 106–14.

Peterson, D. "Resurrection, Apologetics and the Theology of Luke-Acts." Pages 29–57 in *Proclaiming the Resurrection.* Edited by P. M. Head. Carlisle: Paternoster, 1998.

Talbert, C. H. "The Place of the Resurrection in the Theology of Luke." *Int* 46 (1992): 19–30.

Thompson, A. J. *The Acts of the Risen Lord Jesus: Luke's Account of God's Unfolding Plan.* Downers Grove: InterVarsity Press, 2011. See pages 71–101.

Wright, N. T. *The Resurrection of the Son of God.* Minneapolis: Fortress, 2003.

2. The Evidence of Jesus' Physical Appearances and the Testimony of Scripture as Taught by Jesus and Grasped by Divine Illumination (24:13–35)

On the broad chiastic structure of this account, centering in the statement that Jesus is alive (24:23b), see Green 842; Nolland 1177–78.

24:13 Καὶ ἰδού, see 1:20. Ἐξ may be redundant here (reflecting the greater use of prepositions in Hellenistic Greek, Z §80; the antecedent of αὐτῶν is τοῖς λοιποῖς of 24:9). The temp. ἐν αὐτῇ τῇ ἡμέρᾳ explicitly links the following appearance of Jesus with the preceding discovery of the empty tomb (Fitzmyer 1560; cf. 24:1). The impf. ἦσαν (see 1:6) with πορευόμενοι (see 1:6) is an impf. periph. cstr. Ἀπέχουσαν acc. sg. fem. of pres. act. (attrib.) ptc. of ἀπέχω, "be distant" (intrans., LN 85.16), modifies κώμην, "village." Σταδίους ἑξήκοντα ἀπὸ Ἰερουσαλήμ, "60 stadia from Jerusalem" (about seven miles [eleven km]; acc. pl. masc. of στάδιος, -ου, ὁ; see BDAG 940a for Greek/Roman/ English measurements; on the pl. form cf. BDF §49[3]). The description dat. + ὄνομα + name (ᾗ ὄνομα Ἐμμαοῦς) is a cstr. only found in Luke in the NT (cf. 1:26–27; 2:25; 8:41; common in the LXX, Fitzmyer 1555; on the possible location see Bock 1909–8; Fitzmyer 1561–62).

24:14 For καὶ αὐτοί see 1:17; 4:15 (on καὶ αὐτός). Ὡμίλουν 3rd pl. impf. act. indic. of ὁμιλέω, "talk." Συμβεβηκότων gen. pl. neut. of pf. act. (attrib.) ptc. of συμβαίνω, "come to pass" ("all these things that had happened" ESV).

24:15 Καὶ ἐγένετο, see 1:5. The pres. act. infs. ὁμιλεῖν (from ὁμιλέω, cf. 24:14) and συζητεῖν (from συζητέω, "discuss") with ἐν τῷ are temp. (the acc. αὐτούς is the subj.). The pron. αὐτός is intensive. Ἐγγίσας nom. sg. masc. of aor. act. (temp.) ptc. of ἐγγίζω. Συνεπορεύετο (3rd sg. impf. mid. indic. of dep. συμπορεύομαι, "go with") could be ingressive (NASB, HCSB; Marshall 893).

24:16 Δέ introduces a parenthetical remark so the reader will understand the account. Ἐκρατοῦντο 3rd pl. impf. pass. indic. of κρατέω, "hold back," "prevent" (a divine pass., Bock 1910; Fitzmyer 1563; Marshall 893; pace Nolland 1201, there is no ref. to Satan here; cf. 9:45; 18:34; 24:31, 45). The cstr. τοῦ with the aor. act. inf. ἐπιγνῶναι could indicate purpose (Marshall 893), result (Burton §403; Wallace 592; Z §352), or be epex. (BHGNT 743; Bock 1909; expressing the obj. of restraint, Fitzmyer 1563).

24:17 The interr. pron. τίνες is the pred. nom. in a clause with an implied εἰσίν. The acc. pl. masc. rel. pron. οὕς is the dir. obj. of ἀντιβάλλετε (2nd pl. pres. act. indic. of ἀντιβάλλω, "exchange"; "to discuss, implying conflicting opinions" LN 33.160; on the compound vb. cf. R 573). Περιπατοῦντες, see 11:44 (temp.). Ἐστάθησαν 3rd pl. aor. pass. indic. of ἵστημι (intrans. "stood still" most EVV). Σκυθρωποί nom. pl. masc. of σκυθρωπός, -ή, -όν, a sad or sullen appearance (BDAG 933a).

24:18 Ἀποκριθείς, see 1:19. The nom. εἷς is the subj. of εἶπεν. Ὀνόματι is a dat. of ref. (the Gk. Κλεοπᾶς is abbreviated from Κλεόπατρος and may be an equivalent of the Sem. Κλωπᾶς, BDAG 547b; BDF §125[2]; Marshall 894; cf. John 19:25; though Bock 1911; Bovon 3.373; Fitzmyer 1563 are against this connection). The nom. σὺ μόνος is the subj. of παροικεῖς (2nd sg. pres. act. indic. of παροικέω, "live as stranger," "visit";

thus, *"the only one visiting" NASB, NIV; "the only visitor" HCSB, ESV; not "only a stranger" KJV; the pron. is emphatic, Wallace 322; "Are you alone so much of a stranger . . .?" Marshall 894). The indecl. Ἰερουσαλήμ could be a dat. of location (cf. BDAG 779b [under παροικέω mng. 1]) or an acc. complement of παροικεῖς (cf. LXX Gen 17:8; BDAG 779b [mng. 2a]; BHGNT 744). Καί could be used here as a rel. pron. ("who" most EVV; though see NASB; Z §455e). Ἔγνως, see 19:42. Γενόμενα, see 4:23 (subst.). The antecedent for the fem. αὐτῇ is Ἰερουσαλήμ.

24:19 The acc. pl. neut. interr. pron. ποῖα agrees with τὰ γενόμενα from 24:18 (BDF §298[2]; perhaps implying ἔγνων [BHGNT 744] and γενόμενα [BDAG 844a]). The acc. pl. neut. art. τά nominalizes the prep. phrase (Wallace 236; cf. 24:27). The gen. τοῦ Ναζαρηνοῦ (cf. 18:37) is in appos. to Ἰησοῦ. The rel. pron. ὅς is the subj. of ἐγένετο. The nom. προφήτης is in appos. to the pred. nom. ἀνήρ (the word in appos. carries the main idea, R 399). The nom. adj. δυνατός could be modifying προφήτης (e.g., "a prophet mighty in deed and word" ESV) or subst. in appos. (e.g., "a prophet, one who was powerful" BHGNT 745). On Jesus as a prophet in Luke, see 4:24–27; 7:16; 9:8, 18–19, 35; 13:31–35. On ἐναντίον ("in the judgment of") see 1:6; 20:26 (see ἐνώπιον in 24:11).

24:20 Ὅπως introduces an indir. question ("indicating how something took place" LN 89.86, BDAG 718a; BDF §300[1]; R 731, 985; further developing τὰ περὶ Ἰησοῦ). Τε . . . καί, "both betrayed . . . and crucified" (Wallace 672). Οἱ ἀρχιερεῖς καὶ οἱ ἄρχοντες ἡμῶν (with perhaps an inclusive "our" Wallace 399) is the nom. subj. of παρέδωκαν (3rd pl. aor. act. indic. of παραδίδωμι). Κρίμα, see 20:47. Ἐσταύρωσαν, see 23:33.

24:21 Ἠλπίζομεν 1st pl. impf. act. indic. of ἐλπίζω. Μέλλων (see 22:23) is subst. The pres. mid. inf. λυτροῦσθαι (of λυτρόομαι, "redeem"; see λύτρωσις in 1:68; 2:38) is complementary. Ἀλλά γε καί introduces an emphatic contrast ("Indeed" NASB; BDF §439[2]). Σὺν πᾶσιν τούτοις links to a new factor (BDAG 962b; "besides all this" most EVV; BDF §221; "what is more" NIV). The anar. ταύτην is "this is the third day" (BDAG 741c; "this, a third day" R 701). The subj. of ἄγει (3rd sg. pres. act. indic. of ἄγω; with the acc. τρίτην ταύτην ἡμέραν) may be Jesus ("He is spending the third day," BDAG 16d, BDF §129), another implied subj. ("the sun[rise] brings the third day," as idiomatic for "this is now the third day," BHGNT 747), or an impers. subj. ("it is 'leading/bringing' the third day"; or "it is now the third day," most EVV; BDAG 16d; Moule 27; Fitzmyer 1565). For ἀφ' οὗ see 7:45. Ταῦτα refers to τὰ γενόμενα (24:18).

24:22 Ἐξ ἡμῶν is partitive. Ἐξέστησαν, see 8:56 (trans.; ἡμᾶς is the dir. obj.). Γενόμεναι, see 10:13 (temp., along with εὑροῦσαι in 24:23). The nom. pl. fem. adj. ὀρθριναί (of ὀρθρινός, -ή, -όν), "early in the morning," is used adv. (BDF §243; R 657; ZG 282). Ἐπὶ τὸ μνημεῖον is locat.

24:23 Εὑροῦσαι nom. pl. fem. of aor. act. (temp.) ptc. of εὑρίσκω (with γενόμεναι in 24:22; "when they were at the tomb . . . and did not find" NASB). With ἦλθον (see 1:59) λέγουσαι (nom. pl. fem. of pres. act. ptc. of λέγω) expresses manner. Καί could be ascensive ("even" ESV; ZG 282) or additional ("also" NASB; Marshall 896). Ὀπτασίαν ἀγγέλων, "vision of angels." The pf. act. inf. ἑωρακέναι (of ὁράω) is used for indir. discourse ("that they had seen"; cf. Wallace 605; ὀπτασίαν [see 1:22] is the obj., R 1038). The antecedent of the rel. pron. οἵ is ἀγγέλων. Λέγουσιν, see 9:18 (the pres. is retained for indir. discourse). The pres. act. inf. ζῆν (of ζάω) is also used in indir. discourse ("that he was alive"; though the pres. may highlight the force of the message, NLT; Bock 1915; Marshall 896).

24:24 Ἀπῆλθον, see 2:15. The art. τῶν nominalizes the prep. phrase σὺν ἡμῖν ("some of those who were with us"). Εὗρον, see 2:46 (for οὕτως καθώς, cf. R 968). The pron. αὐτόν is placed forward for emphasis (NASB, ESV; Bock 1915; Fitzmyer 1565; Marshall 896). Εἶδον, see 2:20.

24:25 Καὶ αὐτός, see 1:17; 3:23. The interjection ὦ with the voc. pl. masc. ἀνόητοι (of ἀνόητος, -ον, subst. "foolish") καὶ βραδεῖς (of βραδύς, -εῖα, -ύ, subst. "slow") emphasizes deep emotion (Wallace 68–69; Z §35). Τῇ καρδίᾳ is a dat. of ref. (Z §53; ZG 282). The art. inf. τοῦ πιστεύειν is epex. (R 1076; Wallace 607; Fitzmyer 1565; τοῦ is pleonastic, ZG 282). Ἐπί with πιστεύειν here is "believe in" (functioning as a complementary dat., BDAG 364d). The rel. pron. οἷς is dat. by attraction to its antecedent πᾶσιν (Robertson, *Pictures* 293–94; Z §16). Ἐλάλησαν 3rd pl. aor. act. indic. of λαλέω.

24:26 Οὐχί, see 4:22. The infs. παθεῖν (see 9:22) and εἰσελθεῖν (see 6:6; 9:26) are complementary following ἔδει (see 11:42; 24:7). Καί could be used in a "final" or "consecutive" sense (Z §455γ).

24:27 Ἀρξάμενος (see 23:5) expresses manner. Διερμήνευσεν 3rd sg. aor. act. indic. of διερμηνεύω, "interpret" (NRSV, HCSB, ESV), "explain" (NASB, NIV; cf. LN 33.148). The art. τά nominalizes the prep. phrase περὶ ἑαυτοῦ (Wallace 236; cf. 24:19). The ref. to the starting point (ἀρξάμενος) and the repetition of πᾶς for the (former and latter) prophets and "all the Scriptures" emphasize comprehensiveness (cf. 24:44).

24:28 Ἤγγισαν 3rd pl. aor. act. indic. of ἐγγίζω. Οὗ, adv. "where." Ἐπορεύοντο, see 2:3. Προσεποιήσατο 3rd sg. aor. mid. indic. of προσποιέω, "acted as though" (NASB, sim. ESV); "gave the impression that" (HCSB; BDAG 884c); "continued on as if" (NIV, sim. NRSV; "pretend" is too strong in this context, Marshall 897). Πορρώτερον, comp. adv. (R 298) of πόρρω, "far away," "farther." The inf. πορεύεσθαι (see 4:42) is complementary (BHGNT 750).

24:29 Παρεβιάσαντο 3rd pl. aor. mid. indic. of dep. παραβιάζομαι, "urge strongly" (cf. Acts 16:15; cf. also βιάζομαι in Luke 16:16). Λέγοντες, see 1:66. Μεῖνον 2nd sg. aor. act. impv. of μένω. The reason for their insistence that Jesus remain with them is because (ὅτι) it is "toward evening" (πρὸς ἑσπέραν, acc. sg. fem. of ἑσπέρα, -ας, ἡ; R 625) and the day is now "almost over" (HCSB, κέκλικεν 3rd sg. pf. act. indic. of κλίνω, "decline," "come to an end" LN 68.51; intrans.). Εἰσῆλθεν, see 1:40. The art. inf. τοῦ μεῖναι (see 19:5) expresses purpose (R 1088; Fitzmyer 1567).

24:30 Καὶ ἐγένετο, see 1:5. Ἐν τῷ with the aor. pass. inf. κατακλιθῆναι is temp. (of κατακλίνω, "recline" NASB, HCSB; "when he had taken his place" ZG 282; see 3:21 for this cstr.). Λαβών (see 6:4) is probably attendant circumstance with εὐλόγησεν (see 2:28; "blessed" most EVV; "gave thanks" NIV; "ask God to bestow favor upon" LN

33.470). Κλάσας nom. sg. masc. of aor. act. (temp.) ptc. of κλάω, "break," modifies ἐπεδίδου (3rd sg. impf. act. indic. of ἐπιδίδωμι, "give to"; ingressive, NIV, NASB; Robertson, *Pictures* 294).

24:31 The gen. pron. αὐτῶν is poss. with the nom. subj. οἱ ὀφθαλμοί. Διηνοίχθησαν 3rd pl. aor. pass. indic. of διανοίγω, "open" (a divine pass.; cf. 24:32, 45; cf. 24:16). Ἐπέγνωσαν, see 1:22. Ἄφαντος (nom. sg. masc. of ἄφαντος, -ον) with ἐγένετο is "became invisible," "vanished" (NRSV, NASB, ESV); "disappeared" (HCSB, NIV).

24:32 Οὐχί, see 4:22. Καιομένη (nom. sg. fem. of pres. pass. ptc. of καίω, "burn") is an impf. periph. cstr. with ἦν (R 888; the sg. καρδία is distributive, BDF §140). Ὡς is temp. (R 974). The impfs. ἐλάλει (see 1:64) and διήνοιγεν (3rd sg. impf. act. indic. of διανοίγω, "open"; see 24:31; here in the sense of "explain" NASB, HCSB; LN 33.142) highlight the ongoing activity along the way. The second temp. clause (with ὡς) is in appos. to the first.

24:33 Ἀναστάντες (see 4:29) is probably attendant circumstance (with ὑπέστρεψαν see 2:20; pleonastic, Fitzmyer 1568). Αὐτῇ τῇ ὥρᾳ "that same hour" (NRSV, ESV); "at once" (NIV); "there and then" (ZG 283; cf. 24:1). Ἠθροισμένους (acc. pl. masc. of pf. pass. ptc. of ἀθροίζω, "gather," cf. LN 15.129) is the acc. complement of τοὺς ἕνδεκα (BDAG 411d; BHGNT 753; 24:9). The second τούς nominalizes the prep. phrase σὺν αὐτοῖς ("the Eleven and those with them gathered together" HCSB, sim. ESV).

24:34 The acc. pl. masc. of pres. act. ptc. λέγοντας (of λέγω) looks back to the gathered group of 24:33. Ὅτι, recitative. For ὁ κύριος see 7:13. Ὄντως, see 23:47. Ἠγέρθη, see 7:16; 9:7; 24:6. Ὤφθη, see 1:11.

24:35 The impf. ἐξηγοῦντο (3rd pl. impf. mid. indic. of dep. ἐξηγέομαι, "relate" NASB, "describe" HCSB; αὐτοί is the subj.) could be ingressive (NASB, HCSB) or progressive (most EVV). The acc. art. τά nominalizes the prep. phrase ἐν τῇ ὁδῷ (see also 24:19, 27; Wallace 236). The use of ὡς may emphasize manner (BHGNT 754). Ἐγνώσθη 3rd sg. aor. pass. indic. of γινώσκω (cf. 24:18, 31) with the dat. αὐτοῖς may be "recognized by them" (NIV, NASB) or "made known to them" (NRSV, HCSB, sim. ESV; R 534). Κλάσει, dat. sg. fem. of κλάσις, -εως, ἡ, "breaking." Ἐν τῇ κλάσει τοῦ ἄρτου could be temp. (NIV) or more generally the context for the action ("in the breaking of the bread" NRSV, HCSB, ESV; BHGNT 754; "in the case of" R 587; i.e., "at the meal").

3. The Evidence of Jesus' Physical Presence with His (Wary) Disciples (24:36–43)

24:36 The temp. gen. abs. cstr. (λαλούντων gen. pl. masc. of pres. act. ptc. of λαλέω; αὐτῶν is the subj.; ταῦτα is the dir. obj.) links this appearance to the preceding events (see 24:1). Αὐτός is the nom. subj. of ἔστη (see 6:8; intrans.) and adds emphasis ("He himself" HCSB; Robertson, *Pictures* 295; Fitzmyer 1575). Λέγει, a historical pres. In this context "the conventional greeting is transformed" (Marshall 901; εἰρήνη, see 1:79.).

24:37 Πτοηθέντες (nom. pl. masc. of aor. pass. ptc. of dep. πτοέομαι, "terrify"; "were startled" most EVV; only here and 21:9 in the NT) with γενόμενοι (see 1:2; here with the adj. ἔμφοβοι, "became terrified"; see 24:5) may be causal (BHGNT 756) or temp. Ἐδόκουν 3rd pl. impf. act. indic. of δοκέω, "think." Πνεῦμα here has the sense of "ghost" (NRSV, HCSB, NIV) or "noncorporeal being" (BDAG 833d; i.e., a "bodiless Jesus" Stein 617). The pres. act. inf. θεωρεῖν (of θεωρέω) is for indir. discourse ("thought that they were seeing" NRSV, NASB; Wallace 605; ZG 283).

24:38 The two questions address (1) their mood, and (2) their lack of perception (Bock 1932). Τεταραγμένοι (nom. pl. masc. of pf. pass. ptc. of ταράσσω, "disturb," "trouble") with the pres. ἐστέ is a pf. periph. cstr. ("why are you troubled" HCSB, ESV, NIV; Robertson, *Pictures* 296; cf. 1:12). Διὰ τί is causal (sim. to τί, R 739). Διαλογισμοί, "doubts" (see 2:35), is the subj. of ἀναβαίνουσιν (3rd pl. pres. act. indic. of ἀναβαίνω; on the idiom see BDAG 58d; ZG 283). Ἐν τῇ καρδίᾳ ὑμῶν is locat. (a collective sg.). On "the heart" cf. 2:35; 24:25. In light of 24:37 (ἐδόκουν πνεῦμα θεωρεῖν) and the following verses, the doubts may relate to whether this was Jesus in the flesh.

24:39–40 The rebuke concerning doubts is then followed by an invitation to see the evidence. Ἴδετε, see 21:29 (here 2x). Ὅτι, appos. (BHGNT 757) or epex. (Fitzmyer 1576). Αὐτός is pred. nom. ("it is I myself" most EVV; Robertson, *Pictures* 296; ZG 283). Ψηλαφήσατε 2nd pl. aor. act. impv. of ψηλαφάω, "touch" (most EVV). The second ἴδετε has the sense of "understand" (ZG 283; cf. NLT "make sure"). The second ὅτι could be a marker of content ("see that"), introduce dir. discourse (NIV; Fitzmyer 1576), or *causal (HCSB, ESV) in which πνεῦμα (cf. 24:37) and ἐμέ are emphatic (explaining why they should touch Jesus; Bock [1933] prefers "explanatory" to causal). Ὀστέα acc. pl. neut. (of ὀστέον, -ου contracted ὀστοῦν, -οῦ, τό; on the form see R 203, 260), "bones." Ἔχει, see 5:24. Θεωρεῖτε, see 21:6. Ἔχοντα (see 12:5) is the complement in a double acc. cstr. (with ἐμέ, ZG 283). Εἰπών, see 9:22 (temp.; τοῦτο is the dir. obj.). Ἔδειξεν, see 4:5.

24:41 Ἀπιστούντων (gen. pl. masc. of pres. act. ptc. of ἀπιστέω, cf. 24:11) and αὐτῶν (the subj. of the ptc.) is a temp. gen. abs. cstr. (with ἔτι, cf. 8:49). This may be a statement of unbelief or (with the following prep. phrase) a rhetorical expression of amazement (Bock 1934). Ἀπό, causal (see 19:3; 22:45). Χαρᾶς, "joy" (something like "too good to be true" Robertson, *Pictures* 296, ZG 283; Marshall 902). Θαυμαζόντων (see 9:43) is also part of the temp. gen. abs. cstr. (for concordant participles see Z §§48–49). Ἔχετε, see 17:6. The adj. βρώσιμον (acc. sg. neut. of βρώσιμος, -ον, "eatable") with the indef. pron. τί is "anything to eat" (BDAG 184d). Ἐνθάδε, adv. "here" (elsewhere, only John 4:15–16, five times in Acts).

24:42–43 The nom. pl. art. οἱ is the subj. of ἐπέδωκαν (3rd pl. aor. act. indic. of ἐπιδίδωμι, "give to"; the acc. μέρος ["piece"] is the dir. obj.). The gen. ἰχθύος (see 5:6; ὀπτοῦ gen. sg. masc. of ὀπτός, -ή, -όν, "broiled") is partitive. Λαβών (cf. 6:4) could be temp. or attendant circumstance with ἔφαγεν (see 4:2). The prep. ἐνώπιον ("before"; takes the gen.; note, not σύν, Bovon 3.393) emphasizes the physical reality of the resurrected Jesus in the disciples' presence (anticipating 24:48). The meal scene is the setting in which Jesus is made known through Scripture and his teaching (correctly

Nolland 1215; though not "eucharistic theology" [*pace* Nolland 1215] as Jesus is the only one eating [fish]).

4. The Significance of Jesus' Resurrection (24:44–53)

a. The Outworking of God's Saving Plan for the Nations (24:44–49)

24:44 Εἶπεν δὲ πρὸς αὐτούς is a general introduction and not an explicit temp. link as elsewhere in the chapter (cf. 24:1; while αὐτούς suggests continuity, the temp. ἔτι ὢν [see 3:23] σὺν ὑμῖν suggests a later setting). The demonstrative pron. οὗτοι is the pred. nom. of a verbless clause (implying εἰμί) and points forward to the ὅτι clause. Οἱ λόγοι is the subj. (i.e., "My words that I spoke were these," BHGNT 758; ZG 283). Ἐλάλησα 1st sg. aor. act. indic. of λαλέω. Ὅτι introduces the clause epex. to οὗτοι (Marshall 904). The aor. pass. inf. πληρωθῆναι (of πληρόω) is complementary. The acc. pl. πάντα τὰ γεγραμμένα (see 18:31) is the subj. of the inf. (cf. 24:25). The art. τοῖς with προφήταις καὶ ψαλμοῖς indicates that the two nouns are united but distinct entities (Wallace 286–87; ψαλμοῖς [see 20:42] is probably a ref. to the "Writings" more broadly, Marshall 905).

24:45 Διήνοιξεν 3rd sg. aor. act. indic. of διανοίγω, "open" (cf. 24:31, 32). Νοῦν acc. sg. masc. of νοῦς, νοός, ὁ, "mind." The pres. act. art. inf. τοῦ συνιέναι (of συνίημι, "understand") is likely to express purpose (cf. 24:16) given the subsequent explanation from the Scriptures (BHGNT 759) rather than result (Wallace 592; cf. also Z §§352, 383; ZG 283; cf. 24:31).

24:46 Ὅτι, recitative. The adv. οὕτως may point forward to the (epex.) infs. (HCSB, NIV; BHGNT 760) or refer back to 24:44 (NJB; Marshall 905). Γέγραπται, see 2:23. The infs. παθεῖν (see 9:22) and ἀναστῆναι (see 24:7; for ἐκ νεκρῶν cf. Wallace 363; for τῇ τρίτῃ ἡμέρᾳ see 9:22), and κηρυχθῆναι in 24:47 (aor. pass. inf. of κηρύσσω) are infs. of indir. discourse though they all explain what is written in the Scriptures.

24:47–48 For κηρυχθῆναι see 24:46. Ἐπὶ τῷ ὀνόματι is an idiom which gives the ground of authority (cf. NLT; BDAG 366d; ZG 284). The acc. μετάνοιαν ("repentance"; see 3:3) is the subj. of κηρυχθῆναι. Εἰς ἄφεσιν, see 1:77; 3:3. Εἰς πάντα τὰ ἔθνη is locat. (cf. BDAG 289c). Ἀρξάμενοι (nom. pl. masc. of aor. mid. ptc. of ἄρχω) probably modifies κηρυχθῆναι (in manner) giving the starting point (all EVV, against UBS⁵; cf. BDF §§137[3], 419[3]; BHGNT 760). The pl. may have no syntactical connection ("anacoluthon," Robertson, *Pictures* 297) or may be influenced by the following ὑμεῖς (ZG 284). Ὑμεῖς is the subj. of a verbless clause (implying εἰμί). The gen. τούτων may be obj. (or gen. of ref., BHGNT 761).

24:49 Ἀποστέλλω, see 7:27 (a "futuristic present" Marshall 907; cf. 6:13). The gen. τοῦ πατρός is subj. ("what my Father promised" NRSV, HCSB). Ἐφ᾿ ὑμᾶς is locat. The pron. ὑμεῖς adds emphasis to the command to "stay" (καθίσατε 2nd pl. aor. act. impv. of καθίζω, intrans.; Fitzmyer 1585). Ἕως and rel. pron. οὗ with the pass. subjunc. ἐνδύσησθε (see 12:22; here metaphorical) is temp. (see 13:21). Ἐξ ὕψους ("from on high" most EVV; "from heaven" NLT; see 1:78) indicates source (i.e., God, LN 1.13). The acc. δύναμιν is the dir. obj. of ἐνδύσησθε.

b. Jesus Now Reigns and Is Rightfully Worshipped (24:50–53)

24:50 Δέ is general, unlike the explicit temp. links elsewhere in the chapter (see 24:1, 44). Luke has compressed what will be developed in more detail in Acts 1:1–11. Ἐξήγαγεν 3rd sg. 2nd aor. act. indic. of ἐξάγω, "lead out." Ἕως with πρός is a marker of limit (BDAG 423d; BHGNT 762; "pleonastic" ZG 284). Βηθανίαν, Bethany is on the Mount of Olives (cf. 19:29; Acts 1:12). Ἐπάρας (see 6:20) is attendant circumstance with εὐλόγησεν (see 2:28; LN 33.470; cf. 1:21–22; the temp. cstr. in 24:51 may indicate that this is ingressive, Fitzmyer 1590; the aor. is more likely just looking at the action as a whole).

24:51 Καὶ ἐγένετο, see 1:5. The temp. inf. cstr. ἐν τῷ εὐλογεῖν (pres. act. inf. of εὐλογέω; the acc. αὐτόν is the subj. and αὐτούς the obj.) highlights simultaneous action with διέστη (3rd sg. 2nd aor. act. indic. of διΐστημι, "part," "go away"; intrans.; LN 15.50; Wallace 595). Ἀνεφέρετο, 3rd sg. impf. pass. indic. of ἀναφέρω, "bring up," "was carried up" (NRSV, NASB, HCSB, ESV), "was taken up" (NIV; BDAG 75a; cf. 9:51; Acts 1:2, 9, 11, 22).

24:52–53 Προσκυνήσαντες nom. pl. masc. of aor. act. (temp.) ptc. of προσκυνέω. The only other uses of προσκυνέω in Luke's Gospel are in 4:7–8 where Jesus quotes from Deut 6:13 that it is only "the Lord your God" who is to receive worship (cf. Acts 10:25–26). Note also another close association between Jesus and God (see 9:43) in the chiastic structure of 24:52–53.

Καὶ αὐτοὶ προσκυνήσαντες αὐτὸν
        ὑπέστρεψαν εἰς Ἰερουσαλὴμ μετὰ χαρᾶς μεγάλης
        καὶ ἦσαν διὰ παντὸς ἐν τῷ ἱερῷ
εὐλογοῦντες τὸν θεόν

Ὑπέστρεψαν, see 2:20 (with εἰς Ἰερουσαλήμ, see 24:33). Ἦσαν, see 1:6. Διὰ παντός is idiomatic for "always" ("continually" most EVV; ZG 284; cf. 2:37). Εὐλογοῦντες (nom. pl. masc. of pres. act. ptc. of εὐλογέω, "bless," "praise") could be periph. with ἦσαν (R 887–88), or since ἦσαν may be modified by ἐν τῷ ἱερῷ, the ptc. could express manner (BHGNT 763).

With references to Jerusalem (see 1:5; 2:22, 25, 38), the temple (see 1:9, 21–22; 2:27, 37, 46), and praising God (see 1:64; 2:28), Luke concludes his Gospel where he began. Hopes for the fulfillment of God's promises (Luke 1–2) are realized in the risen Lord Jesus. God has come to his people, and so Jesus is to be worshipped.

FOR FURTHER STUDY

43. The Ascension

Bryan, D. K., and D. W. Pao, eds. *Ascent Into Heaven in Luke-Acts: New Explorations of Luke's Narrative Hinge*. Minneapolis: Fortress, 2016.

Donne, B. K. *Christ Ascended: A Study in the Significance of the Ascension of Jesus Christ in the New Testament*. Exeter: Paternoster, 1983.

Maile, J. F. "The Ascension in Luke-Acts." *TynBul* 37 (1986): 29–59.

Parsons, M. C. *The Departure of Jesus in Luke-Acts: The Ascension Narratives in Context*. Sheffield: JSOT Press, 1987.

*Walton, S. *DJG*[2] 59–61.

Zwiep, A. W. *The Ascension of the Messiah in Lukan Christology*. Leiden: Brill, 1997.

HOMILETICAL SUGGESTIONS

Jesus Is Alive! (23:50–24:53)

1. Assurances that Jesus is alive (23:50–24:43)
   a. The testimony of the empty tomb (23:50–24:12)
   b. The testimony of Jesus' physical appearances (24:13–43)
   c. The testimony of Jesus' word (24:6–8, 25–27 [44])
   d. The testimony of Scripture (24:27 [44–46])
   e. The "inner" testimony of illumination (24:16, 31–32 [45])

2. Since Jesus is alive . . . (24:44–53)
   a. we know Jesus accomplished God's saving plan (24:44–46).
   b. we know Jesus will be proclaimed to the nations by his people empowered by the Spirit (24:47–49).
   c. we know Jesus continues to reign (24:50–51).
   d. we know Jesus is worthy of worship (24:52–53).

Exegetical Outline

2. The Authority of Jesus' Teaching Demonstrated in Capernaum
   (4:31–44)
   a. The Authority of Jesus' Word Demonstrated over Demons in the
      Synagogue (4:31–37)
   b. The Authority of Jesus over Sickness and Jesus' Continued
      Preaching (4:38–44)
3. The Lord's Power Provides Promise for Peter's Proclamation (5:1–11)
4. Jesus Heals a Man with Leprosy by His Powerful Word (5:12–16)
5. Jesus Forgives Sins and Demonstrates His Authority by Healing a
   Paralytic with His Powerful Word (5:17–26)
6. Levi Follows Jesus (5:27–32)
7. The Presence of the Bridegroom and the Newness that Jesus Brings
   (5:33–39)
8. Jesus Is Lord of the Sabbath (6:1–11)
   a. Jesus Determines What Is Legitimate to Do on the Sabbath (6:1–5)
   b. Jesus Demonstrates His Authority as Lord and Does What Is
      Good on the Sabbath (6:6–11)
9. Jesus Chooses and Designates Twelve Disciples as Apostles (6:12–16)
10. Jesus the Lord Requires Hearing and Obeying His Words (6:17–49)
    a. The Setting (6:17–19)
    b. Jesus Pronounces Blessing and Woe (6:20–26)
    c. Jesus Defines How His Disciples Should Respond in Love to
       Their Enemies (6:27–38)
    d. Responding to Jesus' Teaching (6:39–49)
B. The Nature of Jesus' Salvation and the Response of Faith (7:1–8:56)
   1. Two Miracles that Demonstrate Jesus' Power (7:1–17)
      a. Faith in the Power of Jesus' Word (7:1–10)
      b. Jesus' Mercy for the Grieving and Power over Death (7:11–17)
   2. Jesus' Saving Rule Explained with Reference to John the Baptist
      (7:18–35)
      a. Jesus Is Defined in Response to John's Expectations (7:18–23)
      b. John Is Defined in Relation to the Arrival of the Kingdom
         Through Jesus (7:24–28)
      c. John and Jesus Are Both Defined in Relation to Reactions to
         God's Plan (7:29–35)
   3. Jesus' Saving Rule Demonstrated in the Forgiveness of Sins Received
      by Faith (7:36–50)
   4. Jesus' Saving Rule Explained with Reference to the Varying
      Responses (8:1–21)
      a. A Transitional Summary: Jesus Preaches the Kingdom Far and
         Wide (8:1–3)
      b. Jesus Explains the Varied Responses to His Proclamation of the
         Kingdom (8:4–15)

      c. Jesus Insists on the Importance of Careful Listening to His Teaching (8:16–18)

      d. Jesus Defines His Family as Those Who Hear and Obey God's Word (8:19–21)

    5. Four Miracles that Demonstrate Jesus' Power (8:22–56)

      a. Jesus' Power over a Life-Threatening Storm (8:22–25)

      b. Jesus' Power over Life-Threatening Demons (8:26–39)

      c. Jesus' Power over Debilitating Disease and Death (8:40–56)

  C. The Nature of Following a Suffering Savior: Training the Twelve (9:1–50)

    1. The Twelve Are Sent Out to Preach the Kingdom with Nothing for the Journey (9:1–9)

    2. The Twelve Are Taught that Jesus Provides (9:10–17)

    3. Who Is Jesus? (9:18–36)

      a. The Suffering Messiah (9:18–27)

        i. Jesus Is the Messiah (9:18–20)

        ii. Jesus Is the Messiah Who Will Suffer, Die, and Rise (9:21–22)

        iii. Because Jesus Is the Suffering Messiah, His Followers Must Also Be Prepared to Suffer to the Point of Death in Order to Gain Life (9:23–27)

      b. The Glorious Son of the Father (9:28–36)

    4. Jesus Has the Power of God over Demons, Yet He Is Going to Suffer (9:37–45)

    5. A Lesson on Greatness (9:46–50)

V. Teaching that Explains the Saving Rule of the Lord (9:51–19:44)

  A. Ministry Under the Lord to Those Who Welcome and Those Who Reject His Word (9:51–11:54)

    1. The Lord Shows How to Respond to Opposition in Samaria on the Way to Jerusalem (9:51–56)

    2. The Lord Must Have Priority in the Kingdom (9:57–62)

    3. Ministry Is Initiated by the Lord of the Harvest (10:1–24)

    4. Ministry Is Characterized by Compassion (10:25–37)

    5. Ministry Prioritizes Undivided Attention to the Word of the Lord (10:38–42)

    6. Prayerful Dependence on a Sovereign Father (11:1–13)

    7. The Lord Is Stronger Than Satan; the One Who Receives His Word Is Blessed (11:14–28)

    8. Judgment Will Come for Rejecting Jesus' Word (11:29–32)

    9. Jesus' Word Is a Shining Light (11:33–36)

    10. Warnings to the Religious Leadership: Judgment Will Come (11:37–54)

  B. Priorities and Assurances with the Final Judgment in View (12:1–13:9)

    1. Living with the Final Judgment in View Helps Disciples Remain Faithful in the Face of Persecution (12:1–12)

2. Living with the Final Judgment in View Helps Clarify the Nature of True Wealth (12:13–21)

3. Living with the Final Judgment in View Helps Direct Attention away from Worry to Trust and Service Under God's Saving Rule with Treasure in Heaven (12:22–34)

4. Living with the Final Judgment in View Helps Focus on Faithful Service (12:35–48)

5. Living with the Final Judgment in View Helps Understand the Significance of Jesus' Earthly Ministry (12:49–59)

6. Living with the Final Judgment in View Helps Underscore the Urgent Need to Repent (13:1–9)

C. Because of Jesus the Humble Joyfully Anticipate the Celebration to Come (13:10–15:32)

1. A Foretaste of Jesus' Saving Rule and Victory over Satan (13:10–21)

2. Surprise and Sadness for Many at Their Exclusion from the Banquet (13:22–30)

3. The Divine Plan for Jesus' Journey to Jerusalem (13:31–35)

4. A Sabbath Healing that Pictures the Restoration Jesus Brings in the Kingdom (14:1–14)

5. The Surprising Participants in the Eschatological Banquet (14:15–24)

6. Leaving All to Follow Jesus (14:25–35)

7. God's Celebration at the Return of the Lost (15:1–32)

D. Living by Faith in Expectation of the Final Kingdom (16:1–18:8)

1. Our Master Determines Faithful Use of Possessions in this Age (16:1–31)

    a. The Shrewd Manager: A Parable About Using the Money of This Age with the Age to Come in View (16:1–13)

    b. Responses to the Pharisees: Jesus' Authority in Relation to Judgment and Law (16:14–18)

    c. Lazarus and the Rich Man: A Warning About Using Money in this Age Without Regard for the Age to Come (16:19–31)

2. Caring for and Forgiving Fellow Believers by Faith (17:1–6)

3. Serving by Grace Does Not Obligate the Master to Reward the Slave (17:7–10)

4. Saving Faith Is Expressed in Thankfulness to Jesus (17:11–19)

5. The Kingdom Has Arrived in Jesus and Will Come in Fullness with His Return (17:20–37)

    a. Exhortation to Pharisees: Recognize the Presence of the Kingdom in Jesus (17:20–21)

    b. Encouragement to Suffering Disciples: The Justice of the Kingdom Will Come with the Son of Man's Return (17:22–37)

6. While Waiting for the Son of Man's Return, Faith is Evidenced in Persistent Prayer (18:1–8)

E. How to Enter the Kingdom: Part 1 (18:9–30)
   1. Those Who Humbly Confess their Sins and Cry for Mercy Are Justified (18:9–14)
   2. Those Who Come to Jesus with the Dependent Trust of a Child will Enter the Kingdom (18:15–17)
   3. Those Who Abandon Self-Reliance to Follow Jesus Will Inherit Eternal Life (18:18–30)
F. How to Enter the Kingdom: Part 2 (18:31–19:44)
   1. God's Saving Plan Is Accomplished Through the Suffering Son of Man (18:31–34)
   2. Spiritual Sight Is Granted by Jesus Through Faith (18:35–43)
   3. Jesus Came to Seek and Save the Lost (19:1–10)
   4. Jesus Will Reward His Servants and Judge His Enemies at the Consummation of the Kingdom (19:11–27)
   5. The Final Approach of the King to Jerusalem and the Announcement of Judgment on Jerusalem (19:28–44)
VI. The Lord Accomplishes the Salvation of the Kingdom (19:45–24:53)
   A. Testing and Teaching in the Temple Including Judgment on the Temple Hierarchy and System (19:45–21:38)
      1. Judgment and Cleansing of the Temple (19:45–46)
      2. Conflict with the Temple Hierarchy and Teaching from the Lord of the Temple (19:47–21:38)
         a. Introductory Frame: Jesus Teaching in the Midst of Murderous Intentions (19:47–48)
         b. Jesus Is Questioned About the Source of His Authority (20:1–8)
         c. The Source of Jesus' Authority Illustrated (20:9–19)
         d. Jesus Is Questioned About the Authority of Caesar (20:20–26)
         e. Jesus Is Questioned About the Resurrection and Moses' Authority (20:27–40)
         f. Jesus Questions His Accusers About His Own Authority: He Is Lord! (20:41–44)
         g. Jesus' Condemnation of the Scribes (20:45–21:4)
            (1) Beware of the Scribes (20:45–47)
            (2) Exhibit A: A Destitute Widow (21:1–4)
         h. The Destruction of Jerusalem and the Return of the Son of Man at the End (21:5–36)
            (1) Opening Observations Concerning the Temple and Its Destruction (21:5–6)
            (2) General Events that Are Not Directly Connected to the End (21:7–11)
            (3) Persecution Is in the Immediate Future for the Disciples (21:12–19)
            (4) The Destruction of Jerusalem as a Picture of Final Judgment (21:20–24)

Appendix

Common, simple verb forms not parsed in the *Guide*.

ἐγένετο, 3rd sg. 2nd aor. mid. indic. of γινόμαι

εἰμί, 1st sg. pres. act. indic. of εἰμί

ἐστίν, 3rd sg. pres. act. indic. of εἰμί

ἦν, 3rd sg. impf. act. indic. of εἰμί

λέγω, 1st sg. pres. act. indic. of λέγω

λέγει, 3rd sg. pres. act. indic. of λέγω

ἔλεγεν, 3rd sg. impf. act. indic. of λέγω

εἶπεν, 3rd sg. 2nd aor. act. indic. of λέγω

εἶπαν, 3rd pl. 2nd aor. act. indic. of λέγω (cf. Z §489)

λέγων, nom. sg. masc. pres. act. ptc. of λέγω (see refs. at 1:63).

Grammar Index

Scripture Index

Genesis

1:26 *319*
2:9–10 *366*
4:10 *196*
15:1 *354*
15:8 *18*
15:15 *260*
17:8 *375*
18:14 *25*
19:24 *274*
19:26 *274*
22:1 *68*
30:23 *21*
33:11 *257*
38:8 *321*
47:30 *260*
49:11 *305*

Exodus

2:24 *37*
3:12 *37*
3:16 *310*
4:31 *310*
8:15 *188*
10:16 *245*
13:2 *49*
13:12 *49*
13:19 *310*
15:6 *324*
16:10 *335*
17:7 *271*
20:12–16 *286*
22:1 *297*
23:20 *121*
24:8 *343*
34:5 *335*
34:10 *222*
40:35 *24*

Leviticus

5:11 *50*
6:5 *297*

12:3–4 *49*
12:4 *49*
12:8 *50*
13–14 *87*
18:5 *177*
19:18 *176*
20:10 *257*
21:17–23 *232*

Numbers

5:6–7 *297*
6:3 *17*
6:10 *50*
11:16 *168*
11:24–25 *168*
11:25 *335*
11:26 *168*
15:38–39 *144*

Deuteronomy

3:26 *347*
5:16–20 *286*
6:5 *176*
6:13 *69, 380*
6:16 *70*
8:2 *68*
8:3 *69*
8:6 *318*
10:12–13 *318*
10:22 *168*
13:4 *68*
16:1–8 *339*
18:15 *158*
22:12 *144*
23:25 *97*
25:5–10 *321*
29:13 *345*
31:16 *260*
32:11 *227*

Judges

3:25 *116*

19:7 *257*

Ruth

2:12 *227*
3–4 *321*

1 Samuel

1–2 *50*
17:12 *42*
17:58 *42*
24:7 *50*
26:9 *50*
26:11 *50*
26:16 *50*
26:23 *50*

2 Samuel

7:16 *42*
12:6 *297*
13:25 *257*
13:27 *257*

1 Kings

1:33 *307*

2 Kings

2:9–11 *164*
8:11–12 *308*
9:13 *307*

2 Chronicles

6:30 *90*
7:19–22 *312*
19:7 *277*
24:22 *196*

Ezra

7:25 *196*

Esther

7:9 *57*

20:36	*349*
20:37	*124, 246*
20:38	*56*
21:1	*116*
21:5	*349*
21:20	*73*
21:24	*12*
21:26	*166*
21:34	*12*
21:36	*361*
21:37–39	*107*
21:38	*330*
21:39	*244*
22:3	*141*
22:4	*318*
22:5	*355*
22:8	*292*
22:10	*27*
22:11	*152*
22:12	*50*
22:18	*279*
22:22	*361*
22:25	*107*
22:30	*12*
23:3	*107*
23:6–8	*321*
23:7	*357*
23:21	*197*
23:24	*178*
23:26	*12*
24:3	*12*
24:14	*318*
24:26	*287*
25:2	*312*
25:4	*279*
25:11	*107*
25:17	*116*
25:26	*12*
26:4	*11*
26:5	*11*
26:7	*53*
26:9	*292*
26:10	*332*
26:16	*11*
26:18	*68, 74*
26:25	*12*
26:25–29	*107*
27:7	*178*
27:15	*140*

27:18	*116*
27:21	*281*
27:34	*332*
27:35	*343*
28:7	*312*
28:14–15	*4*
28:17	*312*
28:22	*332*
28:26–27	*309*
28:30	*4*

Romans

4:11	*297*
4:12	*297*
4:16	*297*
4:19	*49*
9:17	*166*
10:7	*140*
15:24	*224*

1 Corinthians

9:27	*278*
11:2	*10*
11:23	*10*
11:24	*343*
15:3	*10*

2 Corinthians

7:11	*28*
12:4	*366*

Galatians

3:7	*297*

Philippians

2:15	*159*

Colossians

4:6	*75*
4:14	*4, 75*

2 Thessalonians

2:15	*10*

1 Timothy

1:7	*89*

3:13	*274*
5:18	*170*
6:13	*274*

2 Timothy

2:15	*xxvi*
3:2	*256*
3:15	*284*
3:16	*xxvi*
4:11	*4*

Philemon

24	*4*

Hebrews

1:1	*9*
1:12	*367*
7:25	*220*
11:13	*269*
11:32	*10*
12:15	*102*

James

1:13	*68*

1 Peter

2:4	*113*
2:6	*113*
3:20	*113*

2 Peter

1:15	*156*
1:16	*160*

1 John

1:1	*11*

Jude

3	*10*

Revelation

1:17	*85*
2:7	*366*
7:10	*308*